THE LOEB CLASSICAL LIBRARY

FOUNDED BY JAMES LOEB 1911

EDITED BY

JEFFREY HENDERSON

PHILOSTRATUS AND EUNAPIUS

LCL 134

PHILOSTRATUS
LIVES OF THE SOPHISTS

EUNAPIUS
LIVES OF PHILOSOPHERS

WITH AN ENGLISH TRANSLATION BY

WILMER CAVE WRIGHT

HARVARD UNIVERSITY PRESS
CAMBRIDGE, MASSACHUSETTS
LONDON, ENGLAND

First published 1921
Reprinted 1952, 1961, 1968, 1989, 1998, 2005

LOEB CLASSICAL LIBRARY® is a registered trademark
of the President and Fellows of Harvard College

ISBN 0-674-99149-4

Printed on acid-free paper and bound by
Edwards Brothers, Ann Arbor, Michigan

CONTENTS

CONTENTS

PHILOSTRATUS

INTRODUCTION

THE island Lemnos was the ancestral home of the Philostrati, a family in which the profession of sophist was hereditary in the second and third Christian centuries. Of the works that make up the Philostratean corpus the greater part belong to the author of these *Lives*. But he almost certainly did not write the *Nero*, a dialogue attributed by Suidas the lexicographer to an earlier Philostratus; the first series of the *Imagines* and the *Heroicus* are generally assigned to a younger Philostratus[1] whose premature death is implied by our author who survived him and was probably his father-in-law; and the second series of the *Imagines* was by a Philostratus who flourished in the third century, the last of this literary family.

There are extant, by our Philostratus, the *Gymnasticus*, the *Life of Apollonius of Tyana*, the *Lives of the Sophists*, the *Erotic Epistles*, and a brief discourse (διάλεξις) *On Nature and Law*, a favourite commonplace of sophistic. In the *Lives* he quotes the *Life of Apollonius* as his own work, so that his authorship of the two most important works in the corpus is undisputed.

Flavius Philostratus was born about 170, perhaps

[1] For Philostratus "the Lemnian" see marginal pp. 627–628.

ix

in Lemnos, and studied at Athens with Proclus, Hippodromus, and Antipater, and at Ephesus with the aged Damianus from whom he learned much of the gossip that he retails about the second-century sophists. Philostratus wrote the *Lives* of his teachers. Some time after 202, perhaps through the influence of the Syrian sophist Antipater, who was a court favourite, he entered the circle of the philosophic Syrian Empress, Julia Domna. Julia spent much of her time in travelling about the Empire, and Philostratus may have gone with her and the Emperor Septimius Severus to Britain[1] in 208, and to Gaul in 212; and we may picture him at Pergamon, Nicomedia, and especially at Antioch,[2] where Julia preferred to reside. All three towns were centres of sophistic activity. The husband of Julia, the Emperor Septimius Severus, was himself a generous patron of letters, and, as Philostratus says, loved to gather about him the talented from all parts. But it was Julia who, first as his consort, and later as virtual regent in the reign of her son Caracalla, gave the court that intellectual or pseudo-intellectual tone which has reminded all the commentators of the princely Italian courts of the Renaissance. I say pseudo-intellectual, because, when Philostratus speaks of her circle of mathematicians and philosophers, it must be remembered that the former were certainly astrologers—the Syrian Empress was deeply dyed

[1] This is Münscher's conclusion from a remark in the *Life of Apollonius* v. 2, where Philostratus says that he has himself observed the ebb and flow of the Atlantic tides in "the country of the Celts." But this may have been Gaul, not Britain.

[2] In the dedication to Gordian Philostratus refers to their intercourse at Antioch.

with Oriental superstition—and that the latter were nearly all sophists. However, to converse with sophists on equal terms, as Julia did, she must have been well read in the Greek classics, and so we find Philostratus, in his extant letter[1] to her, reminding her of a discussion they had had on Aeschines, and defending Gorgias of Leontini from his detractors. We do not meet with such another court of literary men until, in the fourth century, the Emperor Julian hastily collected about him the sophists and philosophers who were so soon to be dispersed on his death. Cassius Dio[2] tells us that Julia was driven by the brutality of her husband to seek the society of sophists. However that may be, it was during her son's reign that she showed especial favour to Philostratus. After her downfall and death he left Antioch and went to Tyre, where he published the work called generally the *Life of Apollonius*, though the more precise translation of its title would be *In Honour of Apollonius*. His wife, as we learn from an inscription[3] from Erythrae, was named Aurelia Melitine. From the same source we may conclude that the family had senatorial rank, which was no doubt bestowed on Philostratus during his connexion with the court. We have no detailed knowledge of the latter part of his life, but he evidently settled at Athens, where he wrote the *Lives of the Sophists*. He survived as late as the reign of Philip the Arab.[4] Like other Lemnians he had the privilege of Athenian citizenship, and he is

---

[1] *Letter* 63.   [2] lxxv. 15.
[3] Dittenberger, *Sylloge* i. 413.
[4] A.D. 244–249; the Emperor Philip was elected by the army after the murder of Gordian III.

variously called in antiquity "Tyrian," from his stay in Tyre, "Lemnian," and "Athenian." That he himself preferred the last of these epithets may be gathered from the fact that he calls the younger Philostratus "the Lemnian," evidently to avoid confusion with himself.

Philostratus dedicates the *Lives* to Gordian, and on this we depend for the approximate date of their composition. Gordian was consul for the second time in 229–230, and, since Philostratus suddenly changes his form of address, first calling him consul and then proconsul, he seems to have written the dedication when Gordian was proconsul of Africa, immediately after his consulship. Gordian at the age of eighty assumed the purple in 238, and shortly after committed suicide. The *Lives* were therefore ready to publish between the years 230 and 238, but there is no certain evidence for a more precise date.

Philostratus in writing the *Lives* evidently avoided the conventional style and alphabetical sequence used by grammarians for biographies; for he had no desire to be classed with grammarians. He wrote like a well-bred sophist who wished to preserve for all time a picture of the triumphs of his tribe, when sophists were at the height of their glory. His *Lives*, therefore, are not in the strict sense biographies. They are not continuous or orderly in any respect, but rather a collection of anecdotes and personal characteristics. He seldom gives a list of the works of a sophist, and when he does, it is incomplete, so far as we are able to check it, as we can for Dio or Aristeides. He was, like all his class, deeply interested in questions of style and the

various types in vogue, but he must not be supposed to be writing a handbook, and hence his discussions of style are capricious and superficial. He had collected a mass of information as to the personal appearance, manners and dress, temperament and fortune of the more successful sophists, and the great occasions when they triumphantly met some public test, and he shows us only the *splendeurs,* not the *misères* of the profession. He has no pity for the failures, or for those who lost their power to hold an audience, like Hermogenes, who " moulted " too early, and from a youthful prodigy fell into such insignificance that his boyish successes were forgotten. But to those who attained a ripe old age and made great fortunes Philostratus applies every possible superlative. They are the darlings of the gods, they have the power of Orpheus to charm, they make the reputation of their native towns, or of those in which they condescend to dwell. In fact, he did not observe that he made out nearly every one of these gifted beings to be the greatest and most eloquent of them all. Polemo and Herodes are his favourites, and for them he gives most details, while for Favorinus he is unusually consecutive. But no two *Lives* show the same method of treatment, a variety that may have been designed. He succeeded in founding a type of sophistic biography, and in the fourth century, in Eunapius, we have a direct imitation of the exasperating manner and method of Philostratus. To pronounce a moral judgement was alien to this type of biography. Philostratus does so occasionally and notably in the *Life* of Critias, whom he weighs in the balance. This is, perhaps, because, as a tyrant,

INTRODUCTION

Critias was often the theme of historical declamations, and Philostratus takes the occasion to use some of the commonplaces of the accusation and defence.

After his hurried and perfunctory review of the philosophers who were so eloquent that they were entitled to a place among the sophists, of whom the most important are Dio Chrysostom and Favorinus, he treats of the genuine sophists; first, the older type from Gorgias to Isocrates; then, with Aeschines, he makes the transition to the New Sophistic. Next comes a gap of four centuries, and he dismisses this period with the bare mention of three insignificant names which have no interest for him or for us, and passes on to Nicetes of Smyrna in the first century A.D. This break in the continuity of the *Lives* is variously explained. Kayser thinks that there is a lacuna in the MSS., and that Philostratus could not have omitted all mention of Demetrius of Phaleron, Charisius, Hegesias, who is regarded as having founded Asianism, not long after the death of Alexander the Great; or of Fronto, the "archaist," that is to say Atticist, the friend and correspondent of Herodes Atticus, not to speak of others. In ignoring the sophistic works of Lucian in the second century, Philostratus observes the sophistic convention of silence as to one who so excelled and satirized them all. He was a renegade not to be named. In accounting for the other omissions, a theory at least as likely as Kayser's is that there lay before Philostratus other biographies of these men, and that he had nothing picturesque to add to them. Hesychius evidently used some such source, and Philostratus seems to refer to it when he remarks with complete vagueness that on this or that question, usually the

place of birth or the death of a sophist, "some say" this and "others" that. In the *Life* of Herodes he says that he has given some details that were unknown "to others"; these were probably other biographers. Thus he arrives at what is his real aim, to celebrate the apotheosis of the New Sophistic in the persons of such men as Polemo, Scopelian, and, above all, Herodes Atticus, with whom he begins his Second Book.

Without Philostratus we should have a very incomplete idea of the predominant influence of Sophistic in the educational, social, and political life of the Empire in the second and third Christian centuries. For the only time in history professors were generally acknowledged as social leaders, went on important embassies, made large fortunes, had their marriages arranged and their quarrels settled by Emperors, held Imperial Secretaryships, were Food Controllers,[1] and high priests; and swayed the fate of whole cities by gaining for them immunities and grants of money and visits from the Emperor, by expending their own wealth in restoring Greek cities that were falling into decay, and not least by attracting thither crowds of students from the remotest parts of the Empire. No other type of intellectual could compete with them in popularity, no creative artists existed to challenge their prestige at the courts of phil-Hellenic Emperors, and though the sophists often show jealousy of the philosophers, philosophy without eloquence was nowhere. But besides all this, they kept alive an interest in the

[1] Lollianus in the second, and Prohaeresius in the fourth century, were appointed to the office of στρατοπεδάρχης, for which Food Controller is the nearest equivalent.

INTRODUCTION

Greek classics, the ἀρχαῖοι or standard authors; and a thorough knowledge of the Greek poets, orators, and historians such as we should hardly find equalled among professors of Greek to-day was taken for granted in Syrian, Egyptian, Arab, and Bithynian humanists, who must be able to illustrate their lectures with echoes of Homer, Plato, Thucydides, and Demosthenes. In their declamations historical allusions drawn from the classics played much the same part and were as essential as the heroic myths had been to the *Odes* of Pindar or Bacchylides. Not only were they well read, but their technical training in rhetoric was severe, and they would have thought any claim of ours to understand the art of rhetoric, or to teach it, superficial and amateurish. We do not even know the rules of the game. Moreover, they had audiences who did know those rules, and could appreciate every artistic device. But to be thus equipped was not enough. A successful sophist must have the nerve and equipment of a great actor, since he must act character parts, and the terminology of the actor's as well as the singer's art is frequently used for the sophistic profession; he must have unusual charm of appearance, manner, and voice, and a ready wit to retort on his rivals. All his training leads up to that highest achievement of the sophist, improvisation on some theme which was an echo of the past, stereotyped, but to be handled with some pretence to novelty. The theme was voted by the audience or propounded by some distinguished visitor, often because it was known to be in the declaimer's *répertoire*. He must have a good memory, since he must never repeat himself except by special request, and then he must do so with

perfect accuracy, and, if called on, must reverse all his arguments and take the other side. These themes were often not only fictitiously but falsely conceived, as when Demosthenes is represented pleading for Aeschines in exile, a heart-breaking waste of ingenuity and learning; or paradoxical, such as an encomium on the house-fly. Lucian from his point of view ridiculed the sophists, as Plato had satirized their intellectual and moral weakness in his day, but the former could not undermine their popularity, and the latter might well have despaired if he could have foreseen the recurring triumphs of the most sensational and theatrical forms of rhetoric in the second, third, and fourth Christian centuries. For now not only the middle-class parent, like Strepsiades in the *Clouds*, encourages his son to enter the sophistic profession; noble families are proud to claim kinship with a celebrated sophist; sophists preside at the Games and religious festivals, and, when a brilliant sophist dies, cities compete for the honour of burying him in the finest of their temples.

The official salaries were a small part of their earnings. Vespasian founded a chair of rhetoric at Rome,[1] and Hadrian (the Emperor) and Antoninus endowed Regius Professorships of rhetoric and philosophy in several provincial cities. At Athens and, later, Constantinople, there were salaried imperial chairs for which the normal pay was equivalent to about £350, and professors enjoyed certain immunities and exemptions that were later to be reserved for the clergy. The profession was definitely organized by Marcus Aurelius, who assigned an official chair to

[1] A.D. 67–79.

rhetoric and another to political oratory, and as a rule himself made the appointment from a list of candidates. Many municipalities maintained salaried professors. But, once appointed, a professor must rely on his powers of attraction ; there was complete liberty in education ; anyone who wished could open a school of rhetoric ; and sometimes a free lance would empty the lecture theatre of the Regius Professor, as Libanius did in the fourth century. Nor did the Christian Emperors before Julian interfere with the freedom of speech of famous sophists, though these were usually pagans without disguise who ignored Christianity. In order to reserve for pagan sophists the teaching of the classics Julian tampered with this freedom and, as is described in the *Lives* of Eunapius, extended the powers of the crown over such appointments.

Political oratory, which was a relatively severe type and must avoid emotional effects and poetical allusions, was reduced to school exercises and the arguing of historical or pseudo-historical themes, and was not so fashionable or so sought after by sophists as the chair of pure rhetoric. Though officially distinct in the second century, the " political " chair was gradually absorbed by its more brilliant rival, and in the third and fourth centuries no talented sophist would have been content to be merely a professor of political oratory, a πολιτικός. The study of law and forensic oratory was on a still lower plane and is referred to with some contempt by Philostratus. The writing of history was an inferior branch of literature. In short every form of literary composition was subservient to rhetoric, and the sophists whom Plato perhaps hoped to discountenance with a

xviii

definition were now the representatives of Hellenic culture. " Hellene " had become a technical term for a student of rhetoric in the schools.

Philostratus had no foreboding that this supremacy was doomed. For him, as for Herodes, Sophistic was a national movement. The sophist was to revive the antique purer form of religion and to encourage the cults of the heroes and Homeric gods. This was their theoretical aim, but in fact they followed after newer cults—Aristeides for instance is devoted to the cult of Asclepius whose priest he was, and there were probably few like Herodes Atticus, that ideal sophist, who was an apostle of a more genuinely Hellenic culture and religion. By the time of Eunapius the futility of Philostratus' dream of a revival of Greek religion and culture is apparent, Sophistic is giving way to the study of Roman law at such famous schools as that of Berytus, and the best a sophist can hope for is, like the sober Libanius, to make a living from his pupils and not to become obnoxious to the all-powerful prefects and pro-consuls of the Christian Emperors who now bestow their favours on bishops.

There are two rival tendencies in the oratory of the second and third centuries, Asianism and Atticism. The Asiatic style is flowery, bombastic, full of startling metaphors, too metrical, too dependent on the tricks of rhetoric, too emotional. In short, the Asianic declaimer aims at but never achieves the grand style. The Atticist usually imitates some classical author, aims at simplicity of style, and is a purist, carefully avoiding any allusion or word that does not occur in a writer of the classical period. In Aristeides, we have the works of an

Atticist, and we know that he had not the knack of
"improvisation" and was unpopular as a teacher.
He was thought to be arid, that is, not enough of an
Asianist to please an audience that was ready to go
into ecstasies over a display of "bombast and im-
portunate epigram." Philostratus never uses the
word Asianism, but he criticizes the "Ionian" and
"Ephesian" type of rhetoric, and it was this type
which then represented the "theatrical shameless-
ness" that in the first century Dionysius of Halicarnassus deplored.

Philostratus was one of those who desired to
achieve simplicity of style, ἀφέλεια, but when a
sophist attempts this the result is always a spurious
naïveté such as is seen at its worst in the *Imagines*,
the work of his kinsman. Above all the classical
writers he admires for his style Critias, who was
the ideal of Herodes Atticus also, and the fluent
eloquence of Aeschines. He was an Atticist, but not
of the stricter type, for he held that it was tasteless
and barbarous to overdo one's Atticism. He writes
the reminiscence Greek of the cultured sophist,
full of echoes of the poets, Herodotus, Plato, and
Xenophon. His sentences are short and co-ordinated,
his allusions are often so brief that he is obscure, and
in general he displays the carelessness of the gentle-
manly sophist, condescending to write narrative. If
we may judge from his scornful dismissal of Varus as
one who abused rhythmical effects in declamation, he
himself avoided such excess in his sophistic exercises,
μελέται, which are no longer extant. He was a devoted
admirer of Gorgias, and in one passage [1] at least he

---

[1] *Life of Hadrian*, p. 589, where he carefully distinguishes
between δωρεαί and δῶρα.

INTRODUCTION

imitates the careful distinction of synonyms that was characteristic of Prodicus. In fact he regarded the Atticizing sophists of his day as the true descendants of the Platonic sophists, and scolds Plutarch[1] for having attacked, in a work that has perished, the stylistic mannerisms of Gorgias. Like all his Greek contemporaries he lacked a sense of proportion, so that his literary criticisms are for the most part worthless, and the quotations that he asks us to admire are puerile. He longed for a revival of the glories of Hellenism, but it was to be a literary, not a political revival, and he shows no bitterness at the political insignificance of Greece. The Hellenes must impress their Roman masters with a sense of the inferiority of Roman culture and he will then have nothing to complain of. In the opinion of the public, improvisation was the highest achievement of Sophistic, and so thought Philostratus. He believed that the scorn of Aristeides for this fashionable form of display, ἐπίδειξις, masked chagrin at his failure, and dismisses with contempt[2] the later career of Hermogenes the technical writer; whereas Norden[3] praises Hermogenes for giving up declamation and devoting himself to more sober and scientific studies. Philostratus has preserved the renown of a number of these improvisators who, but for him, would have perished as completely as have the actors and dancers of those centuries. More than half the sophists described by him are ignored even by Suidas. Yet they were names to conjure with in the schools of rhetoric all through the Roman world, until the Christian Fathers and the rhetoric of the pulpit took

[1] *Letter* 63.   [2] See p. 577 for Hermogenes.
[3] *Antike Kunst-Prosa* i. 382.

INTRODUCTION

the place of the declaimers. Christianity was fatal
to Sophistic, which seems to wither, like a Garden
of Adonis, never deeply rooted in the lives of the
common people. But sophists for centuries had
educated Christians and pagans alike, and it was from
their hands, unintelligent and sterile as they often
were in their devotion to Hellenic culture, that the
Church received, though without acknowledgement,
the learning of which she boasted, and which she in
her turn preserved for us.

The following notices of the sophists of whom we
know more than is to be found in Philostratus are
intended to supplement him with dates and facts
that he ignored, or to correct his errors. They are
in the order of the *Lives*.

EUDOXUS of Cnidus (408–352 B.C.), famous for his
researches in geometry, astronomy, and physics, was
for a short time a pupil of Plato. He went to
Magna Graecia to study with Archytas the Pythagorean, and to Egypt in the reign of Nectanebus.
Strabo [1] describes his observatories at Heliopolis and
Cnidus. He opened a school at Cyzicus and made
laws for Cnidus. [2] Plutarch [3] praises the elegance of
his style.

LEON of Byzantium was a rhetorician and historian
about whom we have confused and contradictory
accounts in Suidas and Hesychius, especially as to
the precise part that he played when Philip of
Macedon tried to take Byzantium in 340 B.C. The
story is partly told by Plutarch, *Phocion* 14, where

[1] xvii. 806.   [2] Diogenes Laertius viii. 88.
[3] *Marcellus* 4.

Leon probably played the part there assigned to one Cleon.

DIAS may be, as Natorp suggests, a mistake for Delios. Others read Bias. Delios of Ephesus is mentioned by Plutarch as a contemporary of Alexander the Great. In any case we know nothing more of this philosopher than is related here.

CARNEADES (213–129 B.C.) is reckoned as an Athenian, though he was born at Cyrene. He founded the New Academy at Athens, and in 155 was sent to Rome on an embassy for the Athenians. He is so celebrated as a philosopher that Philostratus, whose interest is in the genuine sophists, can dismiss him in a sentence, but no doubt Cato, who disapproved of his influence at Rome, would have called him a sophist.

PHILOSTRATUS the Egyptian was not connected with the Lemnian family. But for the facts of his life something may be added to the scant notice by his biographer. In his *Life of Antony* 80 Plutarch relates that after the defeat of Antony by Octavian, the latter pardoned the members of Cleopatra's circle, among them Areius[1] the Stoic, who was then in Alexandria. "Areius craved pardon for himself and many others, and especially for Philostratus the most eloquent man of all the sophists and of orators of his time for present and sudden speech; howbeit he falsely named himself an Academic philosopher. Therefore Caesar, who hated his nature and conditions, would not hear his suit. Thereupon Philostratus let his grey beard grow long, and followed Areius step by step in a long mourning gown, still buzzing in his ears this Greek verse:

[1] See Julian, *The Caesars* 326 B ; Cassius Dio lvi. 43.

A wise man if that he be wise indeed
May by a wise man have the better speed.

Caesar understanding this, not for the desire he had
to deliver Philostratus of his fear, as to rid Areius of
malice and envy that might have fallen out against
him, pardoned him." We have also an epigram
by Crinagoras of Mytilene, a contemporary, a lament
over the downfall of this favourite of princes:—
" O Philostratus, unhappy for all thy wealth, where
are those sceptres and constant intercourse with
princes? . . . Foreigners have shared among them
the fruit of thy toils, and thy corpse shall lie in
sandy Ostrakine." [1]

DIO CHRYSOSTOM, the "golden-mouthed," was
born in Bithynia about A.D. 40. Exiled for fourteen
years by his fear of Domitian, he acquired the
peculiar knowledge of the coast towns of the Black
Sea and of the savage Getae that is shown in his
writings. We have eighty of his speeches, or rather
essays; they are partly moral lectures or sermons
delivered both during and after his exile, which
ended in 96 with the accession of his friend Nerva.
He denounces the "god-forsaken" sophists, but for
part at least of his life he was a professed sophist,
and many of his essays are purely sophistic. Dio
labelled himself a philosopher, and he was one of
Plutarch's type, borrowing the best from all the
schools. He wrote the "plain" style and Xenophon
and Plato were his favourite models. Next to Lucian
he is the most successful and the most agreeable to

---

[1] *Palatine Anthology* vii. 645. The "foreigners" are
Romans, and Ostrakine is a desert village between Egypt
and Palestine.

read of all the Atticizing writers with sophistic
tendencies.

FAVORINUS (A.D. 80–150) was a Gaul who came to
Rome to study Greek and Latin letters in the second
Christian century; he spent much of his professional
life in Asia Minor. He became the intimate friend
of Plutarch, Fronto, and other distinguished men,
and had a powerful patron in the Emperor Hadrian.
He wrote Greek treatises on history, philosophy, and
geography. A statue of him was set up in the public
library of Corinth to encourage the youth of Corinth
to imitate his eloquence. He was regarded as a sort
of encyclopaedia, and his learning is praised by
Cassius Dio, Galen, and Aulus Gellius. He belonged
to the Academic school of philosophy, but composed
numerous sophistic speeches including paradoxical
panegyrics, *e.g.* an *Encomium of Quartan Fever.*
Lucian[1] speaks of him disparagingly as " a certain
eunuch of the school of the Academy who came
from Gaul and became famous in Greece a little
before my time." He was an Asianist in his use of
broken and excessive rhythms. We can judge of
his style from his *Corinthian Oration,* which survives
among the *Orations* of Dio Chrysostom. It is the
longest extant piece of Asianic prose of the early
second century.[2] The *Universal History* of Favorinus
was probably the chief source used by Athenaeus for
his *Deipnosophists,* and was freely borrowed from by
Diogenes Laertius.

GORGIAS of Leontini in Sicily came to Athens in
427 B.C., at the age of about fifty-five, on an embassy
from Leontini, and that date marks a turning-point

---

[1] *Eunuch* 7; *cf. Demonax* 12.
[2] Norden, *Kunst-Prosa,* p. 422.

in the history of prose-writing. The love of
parallelism and antithesis was innate in the Greeks,
and the so-called "Gorgianic" figures, antithesis,
similar endings (homoioteleuta), and symmetrical,
carefully balanced clauses were in use long before
the time of Gorgias. They are to be found in
Heracleitus and Empedocles, and in the plays of
Euripides that appeared before 427. But by his
exaggerated use of these figures and his deliberate
adoption for prose of effects that had been held to
be the property of poetry, Gorgias set a fashion that
was never quite discarded in Greek prose, though it
was often condemned as frigid and precious. He is
the founder of epideictic oratory, and his influence
lasted to the end. But the surer taste of Athenian
prose writers rejected the worst of his exaggerations,
and later, when Aristotle or Cicero or Longinus points
out the dangers of making one's prose "metrical" by
abuse of rhythms, or condemns short and jerky clauses,
minuta et versiculorum similia (Cicero, *Orator* 39), they
cite the mannerisms of Gorgias. A fragment of his
Funeral Oration survives, and, though scholars are not
agreed as to the genuineness of the *Helen* and the
Palamedes which have come down under his name,
these are useful as showing the characteristic features
of his style. We have the inscription that was composed for the statue of Gorgias dedicated at Olympia
by his grand-nephew Eumolpus; in it he defends
Gorgias from the charge of ostentation in having
in his lifetime dedicated a gold statue of himself at
Delphi.

PROTAGORAS of Abdera in Thrace was born about
480 B.C. and came to Athens about 450. His agnostic
utterances about the gods led to his prosecution for

impiety by the Athenians who would not tolerate a professed sceptic. He may be called the founder of grammar, since he is said to have been the first to distinguish the three genders by name, and he divided the form of the verb into categories which were the foundation of our moods. In speech he was a purist. His philosophy was Heracleitean, and to him is ascribed the famous phrase " Man is the measure of all things." His aim was to train statesmen in civic virtue, by which he meant an expert knowledge how to get the better of an opponent in any sort of debate. We have no writings that are certainly his, but can judge of his style by Plato's imitation in the *Protagoras.* A treatise on medicine called *On the Art,* which has come down to us among the works of Hippocrates, has been assigned by some to Protagoras. For his *Life* Philostratus used Diogenes Laertius.

HIPPIAS of Elis was the most many-sided of the early sophists, the polymath or encyclopaedist. He professed to have made all that he wore, taught astronomy and geography, and was a politician rather than a professed teacher of rhetoric. In the two Platonic dialogues that bear his name he appears as a vain and theatrical improvisator. In the *Protagoras* his preference for teaching scientific subjects is ridiculed, in passing, by Protagoras. Philostratus derives his account of Hippias from Plato, *Hippias Maior* 282-286, where Socrates draws out Hippias and encourages him to boast of his versatility and success in making money.

PRODICUS of Ceos was a slightly younger contemporary of Protagoras. He was famous for his study of synonyms and their precise use, and may

be regarded as the father of the art of using the inevitable word, *le mot juste*. Plato speaks of him with a mixture of scorn and respect, but perhaps Prodicus showed him the way to his own nice distinction of terms. " Cleverer than Prodicus " became a proverbial phrase.

POLUS of Sicily, "colt by name and colt by nature," is the respondent to Socrates in the second part of Plato's *Gorgias*, and on that dialogue and the *Phaedrus* we rely mainly for our knowledge of this young and ardent disciple of Gorgias. He had composed an *Art of Rhetoric* which Socrates had just read, and he provokes Socrates to attack rhetoric as the counterfeit of an art, like cookery. In the *Phaedrus* 267 B, he is ridiculed as a Euphuist who had invented a number of technical rhetorical terms and cared chiefly for fine writing; but he is far inferior, we are told, to his teacher Gorgias, and exaggerates his faults.

THRASYMACHUS of Chalcedon is said to have been the first to develop periodic prose, and hence he may be said to have founded rhythmic prose. In the *Phaedrus* 267 c, D Plato parodies his excessive use of rhythm and poetical words. In the First Book of the *Republic* Plato makes him play the part of a violent and sophistic interlocutor whom Socrates easily disconcerts with his dialectic. He wrote handbooks of rhetoric, and according to the *Phaedrus* he was a master of the art of composing pathetic commonplaces (τόποι), *miserationes*, " piteous whinings," as Plato calls them. Like Polus, his name, " hot-headed fighter," indicates the temperament of the man.

ANTIPHON of the Attic deme Rhamnus was born

soon after 480 B.C., and was a celebrated teacher of
rhetoric at Athens. He was deeply influenced by
Sicilian rhetoric. Thucydides says that no man of
his time was superior to Antiphon in conceiving and
expressing an argument and in training a man to
speak in the courts or the assembly. He was an
extreme oligarch, and was deeply implicated in the
plot that placed the Four Hundred in power in 411.
When they fell he was condemned to death and
drank hemlock, his fortune was confiscated, and his
house pulled down. We have his *Tetralogies,* fifteen
speeches all dealing with murder cases; twelve of
these are in groups of four, hence the name, and
give two speeches each for the plaintiff and the
defendant in fictitious cases. He uses the commonplaces of the sophists, but his style is severe and
archaic. The only other authority for the generally
discredited statement of Philostratus that he increased
the Athenian navy is pseudo-Plutarch, *Lives of the
Ten Orators.* Recently there have been found in
Egypt four fragments of his *Apology,* that defence
which Thucydides[1] called "the most beautiful
apologetic discourse ever given." Antiphon tries
to prove that his motives in bringing the oligarchs
into power were unselfish. He reminds the judges
of his family, whom he did not want to abandon,
and without whom he could easily have made his
escape. I assume that Antiphon was both orator
and sophist, though some maintain that throughout
the *Life* Philostratus has confused two separate
Antiphons.

CRITIAS, "the handsome," son of Callaeschrus, is
remembered chiefly for his political career as a

[1] viii. 68

leader of the oligarchy, a pro-Spartan, and one of the Thirty Tyrants. He was exiled from Athens in 407 B.C., and returned in 405. It was Xenophon who said [1] that he degenerated during his stay in Thessaly. He was killed fighting against Thrasybulus and the democrats a year later. Critias was a pupil of Socrates and also of the sophists. He wrote tragedies, elegies, and prose works, of which not enough has survived for any sure estimate to be made of his talent. He was greatly admired by the later sophists, especially by Herodes Atticus.

Isocrates (436-338) was trained by the sophists, by Prodicus certainly, and perhaps Protagoras, for a public career, but a weak voice and an incurable diffidence barred him from this, and after studying in Thessaly with Gorgias he became a professional rhetorician at Athens, where he opened his school about 393. In that school, which Cicero calls an "oratorical laboratory," were trained the most distinguished men of the fourth century at Athens. It was his fixed idea that the Greeks must forget their quarrels and unite against Persia, and towards the end of his life he believed that Philip of Macedon might reconcile the Greek states and lead them to this great enterprise. The tradition that, when Philip triumphed over Greece at Chaeronea, Isocrates, disillusioned, refused to survive, has been made popular by Milton's sonnet, *To the Lady Margaret Ley*. Isocrates did in fact die in 338, but he was ninety-eight, and it is not certain that he would have despaired at the success of Philip. He was a master of epideictic prose, and brought the period to perfection in long and lucid sentences. Since Cicero's

[1] *Memorabilia* i. 3. 24.

INTRODUCTION

style is based on Isocrates, the latter may be said to have influenced, through Cicero, the prose of modern Europe.

AESCHINES was born in 389 B.C. of an obscure family, and after being an actor and then a minor clerk, raised himself to the position of leading politician, ambassador, and rival of Demosthenes. He supported Philip of Macedon, and in 343 defended himself successfully in his speech *On the False Embassy*, from an attack by Demosthenes, whom he attacked in turn without success in the speech *Against Ctesiphon* in 330; to this Demosthenes retorted with his speech *On the Crown*. After this failure, Aeschines withdrew to Rhodes, where he spent the rest of his life in teaching, and it is because he taught rhetoric that Philostratus includes him here and calls him a sophist.

NICETES flourished in the latter half of the first Christian century under the Emperors Vespasian, Domitian, and Nerva. After the *Life* of Aeschines Philostratus skips four centuries and passes to a very different type of orator. He is the first important representative of Asianic oratory in the *Lives*. Philostratus calls this the Ionian type, and it was especially associated with the coast towns of Asia Minor, and above all Smyrna and Ephesus. Nicetes is mentioned in passing by Tacitus,[1] as having travelled far from the style of Aeschines and Demosthenes; Pliny the Younger says[2] that he heard him lecture. Nothing of his is extant. There was another sophist of the same name whom Seneca quotes, but he lived earlier and flourished under Tiberius.

[1] *Dialogus* 15.   [2] *Epistles* vi. 6.

INTRODUCTION

Isaeus will always be remembered, but he does not owe his immortality to Philostratus, but rather to the fact that Pliny[1] praised his eloquence in a letter to Trajan, and Juvenal,[2] in his scathing description of the hungry Greekling at Rome, said that not even Isaeus could pour forth such a torrent of words. He came to Rome about A.D. 97 and made a great sensation there.

Scopelian of Clazomenae lived under Domitian, Nerva, and Trajan. His eloquence was of the Asianic type, as was natural in a pupil of Nicetes. In the letter addressed to him by Apollonius of Tyana,[3] Scopelian is apparently warned not to imitate even the best, but to develop a style of his own; this was shockingly heterodox advice. For Philostratus, his popularity with the crowd was the measure of his ability.

Dionysius of Miletus is mentioned in passing by Cassius Dio lxix. 789, who says that he offended the Emperor Hadrian. Nothing of his survives, for he almost certainly did not write the treatise *On the Sublime* which has been attributed to him, as to other writers of the same name, though on the very slightest grounds. He was inclined to Asianism, if we may trust the anecdote of his rebuke by Isaeus; see p. 513.

Lollianus of Ephesus, who lived under Hadrian and Antoninus, is ridiculed by Lucian, *Epigram* 26, for his volubility, and his diction is often criticized by Phrynichus. He wrote handbooks on rhetoric which have perished. From the quotations of Philostratus it is evident that he was an Asianist. He made the New Sophistic popular in

[1] *Epistles* ii. 3.   [2] *Satire* iii. 24.   [3] *Letter* 19.

Athens. He was *curator annonae*, an office which in Greek is represented by στρατοπεδάρχης or στρατηγὸς ἐπὶ τῶν ὅπλων; the title had lost its military significance.[1] We have the inscription[2] composed for the statue of Lollianus in the agora at Athens; it celebrates his ability in the lawcourts and as a declaimer, but in a brief phrase, while the rest of the inscription aims at securing the immortal renown of the "well-born pupils" who dedicated the statue.

POLEMO of Laodicea was born about A.D. 85 and lived under Trajan, Hadrian, and Antoninus. There have survived two of his declamations in which two fathers of Marathon heroes dispute the honour of pronouncing the funeral oration on those who fell at Marathon. We can judge from them of the Asianic manner of the time, with its exaggerated tropes, tasteless similes, short and antithetic clauses, and, in general, its obvious straining after effect and lack of coherent development of ideas. Polemo makes an attempt at Attic diction, but is full of solecisms and late constructions. These compositions seem to us to lack charm and force, but his improvisations may have been very different. Even as late as the fourth century he was admired and imitated, *e.g.* by Gregory Nazianzen.

HERODES ATTICUS, the most celebrated sophist of the second century, was born about A.D. 100 at Marathon, and died about 179; he was consul in 143. With him begins an important development of Sophistic, for he and his followers at least strove to

[1] See for this office the *Lives* of Eunapius, especially the *Life* of Prohaeresius.
[2] Kaibel, *Epigrammata Graeca* 877.

be thorough Atticists and were diligent students of the writers of the classical period. They set up a standard of education that makes them respectable, and we may say of them, as of some of the sophists of the fourth Christian century, that never has there been shown a more ardent appreciation of the glorious past of Greece, never a more devoted study of the classical authors, to whatever sterile ends. But it is evident that Herodes, who threw all his great influence on the side of a less theatrical and more scholarly rhetoric than Scopelian's, failed to win any such popularity as his. For the main facts of his life we rely on Philostratus. Of all his many-sided literary activities only one declamation remains, in which a young Theban oligarch urges his fellow-citizens to make war on Archelaus of Macedonia. But its authenticity is disputed, and it shows us only one side of his rhetoric. Its rather frigid correctness is certainly not typical of the New Sophistic, nor has it the pathos for which he was famed. There are many admiring references to Herodes in Lucian, Aulus Gellius, and Plutarch. In the *Lives* that follow his it will be seen how deeply he influenced his numerous pupils, and, through them, the trend of the New Sophistic.[1] The notice of Herodes in Suidas is independent of Philostratus. If we accept the theory of Rudolph, Athenaeus in his *Deipnosophists* (*Banquet of the Learned*), has given us a characterization of Herodes as the host, disguised under the name Larensius.

There are extant two long Greek inscriptions[2]

---

[1] See Schmid, *Atticismus* 201.
[2] Kaibel, *Epigrammata Graeca* 1046, gives a useful commentary on the dates in the life of Herodes.

found at Rome, composed for Regilla, the wife of
Herodes, one for her heroum or shrine on the Appian
Way, the other for her statue in the temple of
Minerva and Nemesis. Her brother Braduas was
consul in 160. The inscription for the Appian Way
must have been composed before 171, the date of
the encounter at Sirmium of Herodes and Marcus
Aurelius related by Philostratus, since in it Elpinice
his daughter is named as still alive; it was partly
grief for her death that made Herodes indifferent to
his fate at Sirmium.

ARISTOCLES, the pupil of Herodes, wrote philosophical treatises and rhetorical handbooks which
have all perished. He was evidently a thorough
Atticist. His conversion from philosophy to sophistic
and his personal habits are described by Synesius,
Dio 35 D. Synesius says that, whereas Dio was converted from sophistic to philosophy, Aristocles in his
old age became a dissipated sophist and competed with
his declamations in the theatres of Italy and Asia.

ALEXANDER the Cilician probably derived his love
of philosophy from his teacher Favorinus, but his
nickname " Clay Plato " implies that his pretensions
were not taken seriously. However sound may have
been the studies of these more scholarly sophists of
the type of Herodes, they evidently resorted to the
trivial devices and excessive rhythms that the crowd
had been taught by the Asianists to expect from a
declaimer. If Alexander really declaimed more
soberly than Scopelian, as Herodes said, the quotations from him in Philostratus do not show any real
difference of style. Alexander was, however, something more than a mere expert in the etiquette of
Sophistic.

INTRODUCTION

HERMOGENES of Tarsus is the most famous technical writer on rhetoric in the second century, though one would not infer this from Philostratus. His career as a declaimer was brief, but it is improbable that, as Suidas says, his mind became deranged at twenty-four. He was a youthful prodigy, a boy orator, who turned to the composition of treatises when his knack of declamation forsook him in early manhood. We have his *Preparatory Exercises*, Προγυμνάσματα, his treatise, *On the Constitution of Cases*, Περὶ τῶν στάσεων, *On Invention*, Περὶ εὑρέσεως, and, best known of all, *On the Types of Style*, Περὶ ἰδεῶν. For him Demosthenes is the perfect orator who displays all the seventeen qualities of good oratory, such as clearness, beauty, the grand manner, and the rest. Hermogenes defines and classifies them, together with the formal elements of a speech. His categories are quoted by all the technical rhetoricians who succeed him. All his work was intended to lead to the scientific imitation of the classical writers, though he admired also a few later authors, especially the Atticist Aristeides, the strictest of the archaists. Philostratus, who can admire only the declaimer, says nothing of his success as a technical writer.

AELIUS ARISTEIDES, surnamed Theodorus, was born in Mysia, in 117. According to Suidas, he studied under Polemo, but no doubt he owed more to the teaching of Herodes. He is the chief representative of the religious and literary activity of the sophists and their revival of Atticism in the second century, and we must judge of that revival mainly from his works which are in great part extant. We have fifty-five *Orations* of various kinds, and two treatises on rhetoric in which he shows himself inferior in

INTRODUCTION

method and thoroughness to Hermogenes. He was proverbially unpopular as a teacher of rhetoric, and though the epigram on *the seven pupils of Aristeides, four walls and three benches,* which is quoted in the anonymous argument to his *Panathenaic Oration,* is there said to have been composed for a later rhetorician of the same name, it somehow clung to his memory, and a denial was felt to be necessary. His six *Sacred Discourses,* in which he discusses the treatment by Asclepius of a long illness of thirteen years with which he was afflicted, are one of the curiosities of literature. They mark the close association of Sophistic and religion in the second century, and it is to be observed that Polemo, Antiochus, and Hermocrates also frequented the temple of Asclepius. The sophists constantly opposed the irreligion of the contemporary philosophers, but it is hard to believe that an educated man of that time could seriously describe his interviews with Asclepius and the god's fulsome praises of his oratory. It is less surprising when Eunapius, in the fourth century, reports, apparently in good faith, the conversations of his contemporaries with Asclepius at Pergamon, for superstition, fanned by the theurgists, had by that time made great headway.

For the later sophists described by Eunapius, Aristeides ranks with Demosthenes as a model of Greek prose, and he was even more diligently read; it was the highest praise to say that one of them resembled "the divine Aristeides." For them he was the ideal sophist, and he did indeed defend Sophistic with all his energy against the philosophers, whom he despised. He even carried on a polemic against Plato, and made a formal defence of Gorgias whom

INTRODUCTION

Plato had attacked in the *Gorgias*. In spite of his lack of success as a declaimer, he was an epideictic orator. He rebuked his fellow sophists for their theatrical methods, and his Oration *Against the Dancing Sophists* is the bitterest invective against Asianic emotional eloquence that we possess. But he was no less emotional than they, when there was a chance for pathos. When Smyrna was destroyed by an earthquake in 178 he wrote a *Monody on Smyrna* which has all the faults of Asianism. There is little real feeling in this speech over which Marcus Aurelius shed conventional tears. Yet he was in the main an Atticist, who dreamed of reproducing the many-sided eloquence of Demosthenes and pursued this ideal at the cost of popularity with the crowd. He had his reward in being for centuries rated higher than Demosthenes by the critics and writers on rhetoric. Libanius, in the fourth century, was his devout imitator, though he himself practised a more flexible style of oratory. Aristeides died in the reign of Commodus, about A.D. 187.

HADRIAN, the Phoenician pupil of Herodes, is hardly known except through Philostratus. He can scarcely have been as old as eighty when he died, for, as Commodus himself died in 190, that is the latest year in which he can have sent an appointment to the dying Hadrian, as Philostratus relates. Now Herodes had died about 180 at the age of seventy, and Philostratus makes it clear that Hadrian was a much younger man. This is of small importance in itself, but it illustrates the carelessness of Philostratus as a chronicler.

JULIUS POLLUX of Naucratis came to Rome in the reign of Antoninus or Marcus Aurelius, and taught

xxxviii

rhetoric to the young Commodus to whom he dedicated his *Onomasticon*. His speeches, which even Philostratus found it impossible to praise, are lost, but we have the *Onomasticon*, a valuable thesaurus of Greek words and synonyms, and especially of technical terms of rhetoric. It was designed as a guide to rhetoric for Commodus, but Pollux was to be more useful than he knew. He is bitterly satirized by Lucian in his *Rhetorician's Guide*, where he is made to describe with the most shameless effrontery the ease with which a declaimer may gull his audience and win a reputation. How far this satire was justified we cannot tell, but we may assume that Pollux had made pretensions to shine as a declaimer, and Lucian, always hostile to that type, chose to satirize one who illustrated the weaknesses rather than the brilliance of that profession. Nevertheless the passage quoted from a declamation of Pollux by Philostratus is not inferior to other such extracts in the *Lives*.

PAUSANIAS the sophist is assumed by some scholars to be the famous archaeologist and traveller. But the latter was not a native of Lycia, and though he speaks of Herodes, he nowhere says that he had studied with him. Nor does Suidas in his list of the sophist's works mention the famous *Description of Greece*. The Pausanias of Philostratus is perhaps the author of the *Attic Lexicon* praised by Photius. We have some fragments of this work.

ANTIPATER the Syrian was one of the teachers of Philostratus. At the court of Septimius Severus he had great influence, perhaps due in part to his Syrian birth, for the compatriots of the Empress Julia were under her special patronage. At Athens he had

been the pupil of Hadrian, Pollux, and a certain Zeno, a writer on rhetoric whom Philostratus does not include in the *Lives*. He educated the Emperor's sons, Caracalla and Geta, received the consulship, and was for a short time Governor of Bithynia. Galen, the court physician, praises Severus for the favour shown to Antipater. He starved himself to death after Caracalla's favour was withdrawn. This was about 212. We may therefore place his birth about 144. Philostratus studied with him before he became an official. Antipater's marriage with the plain daughter of Hermocrates took place when the court was in the East, but whether Philostratus in his account of this event means the first or the second Eastern expedition of Severus he does not say, so that we cannot precisely date Antipater's appointment as Imperial Secretary; it occurred about 194 or 197; Kayser prefers the later date. We learn from Suidas that Antipater was attacked by Philostratus the First in an essay, *On the Name*, or *On the Noun*. This statement is useful as fixing the date of the father of our Philostratus. The Antipater of the *Lives* must not be confused with an earlier sophist of the same name mentioned by Dio Chrysostom.

CLAUDIUS AELIAN, the "honey-tongued," as Suidas tells us he was called, is the most important of the learned sophists of the third century. He was born at Praeneste towards the close of the second century, and was a Hellenized Roman who, like Marcus Aurelius, preferred to write Greek. He was an industrious collector of curious facts and strange tales, but, in spite of the statement of Philostratus as to the purity of his dialect, he hardly deserves to rank as a writer of Greek prose. Though he claims

xl

to write for "educated ears," his language is a strange mixture of Homeric, tragic, and Ionic Greek, with the "common" dialect as a basis. He is erudite in order to interest his readers and with no purpose of preserving a literary tradition; and in his extant works he observes none of the rules of rhetorical composition as they were handed down by the sophists. He aims at simplicity, ἀφέλεια, but is intolerably artificial. We have his treatise in seventeen books, *On Animals*, a curious medley of facts and anecdotes designed to prove that animals display the virtues and vices of human beings; and the less well preserved *Varied History*, a collection of anecdotes about famous persons set down without any attempt at orderly sequence or connexion. Two religious treatises survive in fragments. In choosing to be a mere writer rather than an epideictic orator he really forfeited the high privilege of being called a sophist.

BIBLIOGRAPHY

Manuscripts.

THERE are a number of MSS. of the *Lives*, of which the following are the most important : *Vaticanus* 99, eleventh century ; *Vaticanus* 64, fourteenth century ; *Vaticanus* 140, fifteenth or sixteenth century (contains also the *Lives* of Eunapius); *Laurentianus* 59, twelfth century; *Marcianus*, 391, fifteenth century. Cobet's emendations are in *Mnemosyne*, 1873, Jahn's notes and emendations in his *Symbolae ad Philostrati librum de vitis sophistarum*, Berne, 1837.

Editions.

Aldine, 1502. Juntine, 1517, 1535. Morell, 1608. Olearius, Leipzig, 1709. Westermann, Didot, Paris, 1822, reprinted 1849 and 1878 (with a Latin version, often incorrect). Heyne and Jacobs, 1797. Kayser, Heidelberg, 1838, with notes. Kayser, Zürich, 1842–1846, 1853. Kayser, Teubner, Leipzig, 1871.[1] Bendorf, Leipzig, 1893.

POLEMO : Hinck, Leipzig, 1873. HERODES ATTICUS : In *Oratores Attici*, Paris, 1868. Hass, *De H. A. oratione περὶ πολιτείας*, Kiel, 1880. ARISTEIDES : Dindorf, Leipzig, 1829. Keil, Berlin, 1897.

Literature.

Fertig, *De Philostrati sophistis*, Bamberg, 1894. Schmid, *Atticismus*, vol. iv. Stuttgart, 1896, on the style of Philostratus ; vol. i. on the style of Aristeides, 1887.

---

[1] The text of the present edition is that of Kayser, revised. The paging is that of Olearius.

xlii

BIBLIOGRAPHY

Baumgart, *Aelius Aristeides*, Leipzig, 1874. Jüttner, *De Polemone*, Breslau, 1898. Rohde, *Der griechische Roman*, Leipzig. 1876, 1900. Norden, *Antike Kunst-Prosa*, Leipzig, 1898. Leo, *Griechisch-römische Biographie*, Leipzig, 1901. Bruns, *Die atticistischen Bestrebungen*, Kiel, 1896. Volkmann, *Die Rhetorik der Griechen und Römer*, 2nd edition, Leipzig, 1885. Kohl, *De scholasticarum declamationum argumentis ex historia petitis*, Paderborn, 1915. Rohde in *Rheinisches Museum*, xli. Kaibel in *Hermes*, xx. Radermacher in *Rheinisches Museum*, lii., liv. (the last three articles are discussions of the historical development of the New Sophistic). Münscher, "Die Philostrate" in *Philologus*, Supplement 10, 1907 (this is the best discussion of the identity and the ascription of the works of the Philostrati), Wilamowitz in *Hermes* xxxv. (on Atticism and Asianism). Stock, *De prolaliarum usu rhetorico*, Königsberg, 1911. Burgess, *Epideictic Literature*, Chicago, 1902. *Philologische Abhandlungen*, Breslau, 1901, *Quaestiones rhetoricae* (articles on the lives and works of second and fourth century rhetoricians). A. Boulanger, *Aelius Aristide et la sophistique dans la province d'Asie au II*[e]* siècle de notre ère*, Paris, 1923. P. Graindor, *Un milliardaire antique : Hérode Atticus et sa famille*, Cairo, 1930. E. Groag, "Cn. Claudius Severus und der Sophist Hadrian," in *Wiener Studien*, 24 (1902), pp. 261 ff. F. Solmsen, "Philostratos," in *Pauly-Wissowa, Realencycl.*, 20. 1, cols. 125–174. J. Keil, "Vertreter der Zweiten Sophistik in Ephesos," in *Jahreshefte d. öster. arch. Inst.*, 40, 1953, pp. 5 ff. C. Behr, *Aelius Aristides and the Sacred Tales*, 1968.

ΦΙΛΟΣΤΡΑΤΟΥ

ΒΙΟΙ ΣΟΦΙΣΤΩΝ

ΤΩΙ ΛΑΜΠΡΟΤΑΤΩΙ ΥΠΑΤΩΙ ΑΝΤΩΝΙΩΙ ΓΟΡΔΙΑΝΩΙ
ΦΛΑΥΙΟΣ ΦΙΛΟΣΤΡΑΤΟΣ

Τοὺς φιλοσοφήσαντας ἐν δόξῃ τοῦ σοφιστεῦσαι
καὶ τοὺς οὕτω κυρίως προσρηθέντας σοφιστὰς ἐς
δύο βιβλία ἀνέγραψά σοι, γιγνώσκων μέν, ὅτι καὶ
γένος ἐστί σοι πρὸς τὴν τέχνην ἐς ᾿Ηρώδην τὸν
480 σοφιστὴν ἀναφέροντι, μεμνημένος δὲ καὶ τῶν
κατὰ τὴν ᾿Αντιόχειαν σπουδασθέντων ποτὲ ἡμῖν
ὑπὲρ σοφιστῶν ἐν τῷ τοῦ Δαφναίου ἱερῷ. πατέρας
δὲ οὐ προσέγραψα, μὰ Δί᾿ οὔ, πᾶσιν,[1] ἀλλὰ τοῖς
ἀπ᾿ εὐδοκίμων· οἶδα γὰρ δὴ καὶ Κριτίαν τὸν
σοφιστὴν οὐκ ἐκ πατέρων ἀρξάμενον,[2] ἀλλὰ ῾Ομή-
ρου δὴ μόνου σὺν τῷ πατρὶ ἐπιμνησθέντα, ἐπειδὴ
θαῦμα δηλώσειν ἔμελλε πατέρα ῾Ομήρῳ ποταμὸν
εἶναι. καὶ ἄλλως οὐκ εὐτυχὲς τῷ βουλομένῳ

---

[1] μὰ Δία, οὐ πᾶσιν Kayser ; μὰ Δί᾿ οὔ, πᾶσιν Richards.
[2] ἀρξάμενον add. Richards.

---

[1] See Introduction, p. xii.
[2] On the famous temple of Apollo in the suburb of Daphne
cf. Julian, Misopogon 346 ; Philostratus, Life of Apollonius
of Tyana i. 16.

PHILOSTRATUS

LIVES OF THE SOPHISTS

Dedicated by Flavius Philostratus to the most illustrious Antonius Gordianus, Consul[1]

PREFACE

I HAVE written for you in two Books an account of certain men who, though they pursued philosophy, ranked as sophists, and also of the sophists properly so called; partly because I know that your own family is connected with that profession, since Herodes the sophist was your ancestor; but I remembered, too, the discussions we once held about the sophists at Antioch, in the temple of Daphnean Apollo.[2] Their fathers' names I have not added in all cases, God forbid! but only for those who were the sons of illustrious men. For one thing I am aware that the sophist Critias also did not begin with the father's name as a rule, but only in the case of Homer mentioned his father, because the thing he had to relate was a marvel, namely, that Homer's father was a river.[3] And further it would be no great piece of luck for one who desired to be really

---

[3] There was a tradition that Homer's father was the river Meles, near Smyrna.

πολλὰ εἰδέναι πατέρα μὲν τοῦ δεῖνος ἐξεπίστασθαι
καὶ μητέρα, τὰς δὲ περὶ αὐτὸν ἀρετάς τε καὶ
κακίας οὐ γιγνώσκειν, μηδ' ὅ τι κατώρθωσέ τε
οὗτος καὶ ἐσφάλη ἢ τύχῃ ἢ γνώμῃ. τὸ δὲ φρόντισμα τοῦτο, ἄριστε ἀνθυπάτων, καὶ τὰ ἄχθη σοι
κουφιεῖ τῆς γνώμης, ὥσπερ ὁ κρατὴρ τῆς Ἑλέ-
νης τοῖς Αἰγυπτίοις φαρμάκοις. ἔρρωσο Μουσ-
ηγέτα.

Α'

Τὴν ἀρχαίαν σοφιστικὴν ῥητορικὴν ἡγεῖσθαι
χρὴ φιλοσοφοῦσαν· διαλέγεται μὲν γὰρ ὑπὲρ ὧν
οἱ φιλοσοφοῦντες, ἃ δὲ ἐκεῖνοι τὰς ἐρωτήσεις
ὑποκαθήμενοι καὶ τὰ σμικρὰ τῶν ζητουμένων
προβιβάζοντες οὔπω φασὶ γιγνώσκειν, ταῦτα ὁ
παλαιὸς σοφιστὴς ὡς εἰδὼς λέγει. προοίμια γοῦν
ποιεῖται τῶν λόγων τὸ " οἶδα " καὶ τὸ " γιγνώ-
σκω " καὶ " πάλαι διέσκεμμαι " καὶ " βέβαιον
ἀνθρώπῳ οὐδέν." ἡ δὲ τοιαύτη ἰδέα τῶν προ-
οιμίων εὐγένειάν τε προηχεῖ τῶν λόγων καὶ φρόνημα καὶ κατάληψιν σαφῆ τοῦ ὄντος. ἥρμοσται
481 δὲ ἡ μὲν τῇ ἀνθρωπίνῃ μαντικῇ, ἣν Αἰγύπτιοί
τε καὶ Χαλδαῖοι καὶ πρὸ τούτων Ἰνδοὶ ξυνέθεσαν,
μυρίοις ἀστέρων στοχαζόμενοι τοῦ ὄντος, ἡ δὲ
τῇ θεσπιῳδῷ τε καὶ χρηστηριώδει· καὶ γὰρ δὴ
καὶ τοῦ Πυθίου ἐστὶν ἀκούειν

---

[1] A sophistic commonplace from *Odyssey* iv. 220; *cf. Life
of Apollonius* vii. 22, and note on Julian, *Oration* viii.
240 c, vol. ii.
[2] For Plato's criticism of sophistic assurance *cf. Meno* 70,
Symposium 208 c, *Theaetetus* 180 A.

4

well informed, to know precisely who was So-and-so's father and mother, yet fail to learn what were the man's own virtues and vices, and in what he succeeded or failed, whether by luck or judgement. This essay of mine, best of proconsuls, will help to lighten the weight of cares on your mind, like Helen's cup with its Egyptian drugs.[1] Farewell, leader of the Muses!

BOOK I

We must regard the ancient sophistic art as philosophic rhetoric. For it discusses the themes that philosophers treat of, but whereas they, by their method of questioning, set snares for knowledge, and advance step by step as they confirm the minor points of their investigations, but assert that they have still no sure knowledge, the sophist of the old school assumes a knowledge of that whereof he speaks. At any rate, he introduces his speeches with such phrases as " I know," or " I am aware," or " I have long observed," or " For mankind there is nothing fixed and sure." This kind of introduction gives a tone of nobility and self-confidence to a speech and implies a clear grasp of the truth.[2] The method of the philosophers resembles the prophetic art which is controlled by man and was organized by the Egyptians and Chaldeans and, before them, by the Indians, who used to conjecture the truth by the aid of countless stars; the sophistic method resembles the prophetic art of soothsayers and oracles. For indeed one may hear the Pythian oracle say:

οἶδα δ' ἐγὼ ψάμμου τ' ἀριθμὸν καὶ μέτρα θαλάσσης

καὶ

τεῖχος Τριτογενεῖ ξύλινον διδοῖ εὐρύοπα Ζεύς

καὶ

Νέρων Ὀρέστης Ἀλκμαίων μητροκτόνοι
καὶ πολλὰ τοιαῦτα, ὥσπερ σοφιστοῦ, λέγοντος.

Ἡ μὲν δὴ ἀρχαία σοφιστικὴ καὶ τὰ φιλοσοφού-
μενα ὑποτιθεμένη διῄει αὐτὰ ἀποτάδην καὶ ἐς
μῆκος, διελέγετο μὲν γὰρ περὶ ἀνδρείας, διελέγετο
δὲ περὶ δικαιότητος, ἡρώων τε πέρι καὶ θεῶν καὶ
ὅπη ἀπεσχημάτισται ἡ ἰδέα τοῦ κόσμου. ἡ δὲ
μετ' ἐκείνην, ἣν οὐχὶ νέαν, ἀρχαία γάρ, δευτέραν
δὲ μᾶλλον προσρητέον, τοὺς πένητας ὑπετυπώ-
σατο καὶ τοὺς πλουσίους καὶ τοὺς ἀριστέας καὶ
τοὺς τυράννους καὶ τὰς ἐς ὄνομα ὑποθέσεις, ἐφ'
ἃς ἡ ἱστορία ἄγει. ἦρξε δὲ τῆς μὲν ἀρχαιοτέρας
Γοργίας ὁ Λεοντῖνος ἐν Θετταλοῖς, τῆς δὲ δευτέρας Αἰσχίνης ὁ Ἀτρομήτου τῶν μὲν Ἀθήνησι
πολιτικῶν ἐκπεσών, Καρίᾳ δὲ ἐνομιλήσας καὶ
Ῥόδῳ, καὶ μετεχειρίζοντο τὰς ὑποθέσεις οἱ μὲν
κατὰ τέχνην, οἱ δὲ ἀπὸ Γοργίου κατὰ τὸ δόξαν.

482 Σχεδίων δὲ πηγὰς λόγων οἱ μὲν ἐκ Περικλέους
ῥυῆναι πρῶτον φασίν. ὅθεν καὶ μέγας ὁ Περι-
κλῆς ἐνομίσθη τὴν γλῶτταν, οἱ δὲ ἀπὸ τοῦ Βυζαντίου Πύθωνος, ὃν Δημοσθένης μόνος Ἀθηναίων

---

[1] Herodotus i. 147; *Life of Apollonius* vi. 11.

[2] *i.e.* Athene, whose city Athens is protected by the
wooden wall of her navy.

[3] Suetonius, *Nero* 39; *Life of Apollonius* iv. 38; the
enigmatic or bombastic phraseology of the oracles reminds
Philostratus of the oracular manner and obscurity of certain
sophists.

6

I know the number of the sands of the sea and the measure
thereof,[1]

and

Far-seeing Zeus gives a wooden wall to the Trito-Born,[2]

and

Nero, Orestes, Alcmaeon, matricides,[3]

and many other things of this sort, just like a sophist.

Now ancient sophistic, even when it propounded
philosophical themes, used to discuss them diffusely
and at length;[4] for it discoursed on courage, it
discoursed on justice, on the heroes and gods, and
how the universe has been fashioned into its present
shape. But the sophistic that followed it, which we
must not call "new," for it is old, but rather
"second," sketched the types of the poor man and
the rich, of princes and tyrants, and handled arguments that are concerned with definite and special
themes for which history shows the way. Gorgias
of Leontini founded the older type in Thessaly,[5] and
Aeschines, son of Atrometus, founded the second,
after he had been exiled from political life at Athens
and had taken up his abode in Caria and Rhodes;
and the followers of Aeschines handled their themes
according to the rules of art, while the followers of
Gorgias handled theirs as they pleased.

The fountains of extempore eloquence flowed,
some say, from Pericles their source, and hence
Pericles has won his great reputation as an orator;
but others say that it arose with Python of
Byzantium, of whom Demosthenes says[6] that he

---

[4] Plato, *Sophist* 217 c.   [5] Plato, *Meno* 70 B.

[6] Demosthenes, *On the Crown* 136; the same account is
given by Philostratus, *Life of Apollonius* vii. 37. Python
came to Athens as the agent of Philip of Macedon.

ἀνασχεῖν φησι θρασυνόμενον καὶ πολὺν ῥέοντα, οἱ
δὲ Αἰσχίνου φασὶ τὸ σχεδιάζειν εὕρημα, τοῦτον
γὰρ πλεύσαντα ἐκ Ῥόδου παρὰ τὸν Κᾶρα Μαύ-
σωλον σχεδίῳ αὐτὸν λόγῳ ᾖσαι. ἐμοὶ δὲ πλεῖστα μὲν ἀνθρώπων Αἰσχίνης δοκεῖ σχεδιάσαι
πρεσβεύων τε καὶ ἀποπρεσβεύων συνηγορῶν τε
καὶ δημηγορῶν, καταλιπεῖν δὲ μόνους τοὺς συγ-
γεγραμμένους τῶν λόγων, ἵνα τῶν Δημοσθένους
φροντισμάτων μὴ πολλῷ λείποιτο, σχεδίου δὲ
λόγου Γοργίας ἄρξαι — παρελθὼν γὰρ οὗτος ἐς
τὸ Ἀθήνησι [1] θέατρον ἐθάρρησεν εἰπεῖν '' προ-
βάλλετε '' καὶ τὸ κινδύνευμα τοῦτο πρῶτος ἀνεφθέγξατο, ἐνδεικνύμενος δήπου πάντα μὲν εἰδέναι,
περὶ παντὸς δ' ἂν εἰπεῖν ἐφιεὶς τῷ καιρῷ — τοῦτο
δ' ἐπελθεῖν τῷ Γοργίᾳ διὰ τόδε· Προδίκῳ τῷ
Κείῳ συνεγέγραπτό τις οὐκ ἀηδὴς λόγος· ἡ
ἀρετὴ καὶ ἡ κακία φοιτῶσαι παρὰ τὸν Ἡρακλέα
ἐν εἴδει γυναικῶν, ἐσταλμέναι ἡ μὲν ἀπατηλῷ τε
καὶ ποικίλῳ, ἡ δὲ ὡς ἔτυχεν, καὶ προτείνουσαι
τῷ Ἡρακλεῖ νέῳ ἔτι ἡ μὲν ἀργίαν καὶ τρυφήν, ἡ
δὲ αὐχμὸν καὶ πόνους· καὶ τοῦ ἐπὶ πᾶσι διὰ
πλειόνων συντεθέντος, τοῦ λόγου ἔμμισθον ἐπί-
483 δειξιν ἐποιεῖτο Πρόδικος περιφοιτῶν τὰ ἄστη καὶ
θέλγων αὐτὰ τὸν Ὀρφέως τε καὶ Θαμύρου τρό-

---

[1] Ἀθηναίων Kayser; Ἀθήνησι Cobet.

[1] For an account of Prodicus and his famous fable see
below, p. 496.
[2] An echo of Plato, *Protagoras* 315 A, where it is said of
Protagoras.

8

alone of the Athenians was able to check Python's insolent and overpowering flow of words; while yet others say that extempore speaking was an invention of Aeschines; for after he sailed from Rhodes to the court of Mausolus of Caria, he delighted the king by an improvised speech. But my opinion is that Aeschines did indeed improvise more often than any other speaker, when he went on embassies and gave reports of these missions, and when he defended clients in the courts and delivered political harangues; but I think that he left behind him only such speeches as he had composed with care, for fear that he might fall far short of the elaborate speeches of Demosthenes, and that it was Gorgias who founded the art of extempore oratory. For when he appeared in the theatre at Athens he had the courage to say, " Do you propose a theme " ; and he was the first to risk this bold announcement, whereby he as good as advertised that he was omniscient and would speak on any subject whatever, trusting to the inspiration of the moment; and I think that this idea occurred to Gorgias for the following reason. Prodicus of Ceos [1] had composed a certain pleasant fable in which Virtue and Vice came to Heracles in the shape of women, one of them dressed in seductive and many-coloured attire, the other with no care for effect; and to Heracles, who was still young, Vice offered idleness and sensuous pleasures, while Virtue offered squalor and toil on toil. For this story Prodicus wrote a rather long epilogue, and then he toured the cities and gave recitations of the story in public, for hire, and charmed them after the manner of Orpheus [2] and Thamyris. For these recitations he won a great

9

πον, ἐφ' οἷς μεγάλων μὲν ἠξιοῦτο παρὰ Θηβαίοις,
πλειόνων δὲ παρὰ Λακεδαιμονίοις, ὡς ἐς τὸ
συμφέρον τῶν νέων ἀναδιδάσκων ταῦτα· ὁ δὴ
Γοργίας ἐπισκώπτων τὸν Πρόδικον, ὡς ἕωλά τε
καὶ πολλάκις εἰρημένα ἀγορεύοντα, ἐπαφῆκεν
ἑαυτὸν τῷ καιρῷ. οὐ μὴν φθόνου γε ἥμαρτεν·
ἦν γάρ τις Χαιρεφῶν Ἀθήνησιν, οὐχ ὃν ἡ κωμῳδία
πύξινον ἐκάλει, ἐκεῖνος μὲν γὰρ ὑπὸ φροντισμάτων ἐνόσει τὸ αἷμα, ὃν δὲ νυνὶ λέγω, ὕβριν
ἤσκει καὶ ἀναιδῶς ἐτώθαζεν. οὗτος ὁ Χαιρεφῶν
τὴν σπουδὴν τοῦ Γοργίου διαμασώμενος "διὰ
τί" ἔφη "ὦ Γοργία, οἱ κύαμοι τὴν μὲν γαστέρα
φυσῶσι, τὸ δὲ πῦρ οὐ φυσῶσιν;" ὁ δὲ οὐδὲν
ταραχθεὶς ὑπὸ τοῦ ἐρωτήματος "τουτὶ μὲν"
ἔφη "σοὶ καταλείπω σκοπεῖν, ἐγὼ δὲ ἐκεῖνο
πάλαι οἶδα, ὅτι ἡ γῆ τοὺς νάρθηκας ἐπὶ τοὺς
τοιούτους φύει."

Δεινότητα δὲ οἱ Ἀθηναῖοι περὶ τοὺς σοφιστὰς
ὁρῶντες ἐξεῖργον αὐτοὺς τῶν δικαστηρίων, ὡς
ἀδίκῳ λόγῳ τοῦ δικαίου κρατοῦντας καὶ ἰσχύον-
τας παρὰ τὸ εὐθύ, ὅθεν Αἰσχίνης καὶ Δημοσθένης
προὔφερον μὲν αὐτὸ ἀλλήλοις, οὐχ ὡς ὄνειδος
δέ, ἀλλὰ ὡς διαβεβλημένον τοῖς δικάζουσιν, ἰδίᾳ

---

[1] Chaerephon was a favourite butt of Comedy and was
thus nicknamed on account of his sallow complexion, as one
should say "tallow-faced"; cf. Eupolis, *Kolakes*, fr. 165
Kock; scholiast on *Wasps* 1408 and on *Clouds* 496; Athenaeus
iv. 164. He was also called the "bat."

[2] There is a play on the verb, which means both "inflate"
and "blow the bellows." The same question is asked in
Athenaeus 408; in both passages "fire" seems to mean
"the intelligence" as opposed to material appetite. The
comic poets satirized the sophists for investigating such
questions.

reputation at Thebes and a still greater at Sparta, as one who benefited the young by making this fable widely known. Thereupon Gorgias ridiculed Prodicus for handling a theme that was stale and hackneyed, and he abandoned himself to the inspiration of the moment. Yet he did not fail to arouse envy. There was at Athens a certain Chaerephon, not the one who used to be nicknamed "Boxwood" in Comedy,[1] because he suffered from anaemia due to hard study, but the one I now speak of had insolent manners and made scurrilous jokes; he rallied Gorgias for his ambitious efforts, and said : " Gorgias, why is it that beans blow out my stomach, but do not blow up the fire ? "[2] But he was not at all disconcerted by the question and replied: "This I leave for you to investigate ; but here is a fact which I have long known, that the earth grows canes[3] for such as you."

The Athenians when they observed the too great cleverness of the sophists, shut them out of the law-courts on the ground that they could defeat a just argument by an unjust, and that they used their power to warp men's judgement. That is the reason why Aeschines[4] and Demosthenes[5] branded each other with the title of sophist, not because it was a disgrace, but because the very word was suspect in the eyes of the jury; for in their career outside the courts they claimed consideration and applause on

---

[3] The jest lies in the ambiguity of the meaning and also the application here of this word, which is originally " hollow reed," such as that used by Prometheus to steal fire from heaven, but was also the regular word for a rod for chastisement ; it has the latter meaning in the *Life of Apollonius* viii. 3.

[4] *e.g. Against Timarchus* 170.   [5] *e.g. On the Crown* 276.

γὰρ ἠξίουν ἀπ' αὐτοῦ θαυμάζεσθαι. καὶ Δημοσθένης μέν, εἰ πιστέα Αἰσχίνῃ, πρὸς τοὺς γνωρίμους ἐκόμπαζεν, ὡς τὴν τῶν δικαστῶν ψῆφον
484 πρὸς τὸ δοκοῦν ἑαυτῷ μεταγαγών, Αἰσχίνης δὲ
οὐκ ἄν μοι δοκεῖ πρεσβεῦσαι παρὰ Ῥοδίοις, ἃ
μήπω ἐγίγνωσκον, εἰ μὴ καὶ Ἀθήνησιν αὐτὰ
ἐσπουδάκει.

Σοφιστὰς δὲ οἱ παλαιοὶ ἐπωνόμαζον οὐ μόνον
τῶν ῥητόρων τοὺς ὑπερφωνοῦντάς τε καὶ λαμ-
προύς, ἀλλὰ καὶ τῶν φιλοσόφων τοὺς ξὺν εὐροίᾳ
ἑρμηνεύοντας, ὑπὲρ ὧν ἀνάγκη προτέρων λέγειν,
ἐπειδὴ οὐκ ὄντες σοφισταί, δοκοῦντες δὲ παρ-
ῆλθον ἐς τὴν ἐπωνυμίαν ταύτην.

α'. Εὔδοξος μὲν γὰρ ὁ Κνίδιος τοὺς ἐν Ἀκαδημίᾳ λόγους ἱκανῶς ἐκφροντίσας ὅμως ἐνεγράφη
τοῖς σοφισταῖς ἐπὶ τῷ κόσμῳ τῆς ἀπαγγελίας καὶ
τῷ σχεδιάζειν εὖ, καὶ ἠξιοῦτο τῆς τῶν σοφιστῶν
ἐπωνυμίας καθ' Ἑλλήσποντον καὶ Προποντίδα
κατά τε Μέμφιν καὶ τὴν ὑπὲρ Μέμφιν Αἴγυπτον,
ἣν Αἰθιοπία τε ὁρίζει καὶ τῶν ἐκείνῃ σοφῶν οἱ
Γυμνοί.

485 β'. Λέων δὲ ὁ Βυζάντιος νέος μὲν ὢν ἐφοίτα
Πλάτωνι, ἐς δὲ ἄνδρας ἥκων σοφιστὴς προσερ-
ρήθη πολυειδῶς ἔχων τοῦ λόγου καὶ πιθανῶς
τῶν ἀποκρίσεων. Φιλίππῳ μὲν γὰρ στρατεύοντι
ἐπὶ Βυζαντίους προαπαντήσας '' εἰπέ μοι, ὦ
Φίλιππε,'' ἔφη '' τί παθὼν πολέμου ἄρχεις; ''

---

[1] *Against Timarchus* 170.
[2] Aeschines founded a school of rhetoric at Rhodes.
[3] A full account of the Gymnosophists is given by Philostratus, *Life of Apollonius of Tyana* vi. 5.

the very ground that they were sophists. In fact, Demosthenes, if we may believe Aeschines,[1] used to boast to his friends that he had won over the votes of the jury to his own views; while Aeschines at Rhodes[2] would not, I think, have given the first place to a study of which the Rhodians knew nothing before his coming, unless he had already devoted serious attention to it at Athens.

The men of former days applied the name "sophist," not only to orators whose surpassing eloquence won them a brilliant reputation, but also to philosophers who expounded their theories with ease and fluency. Of these latter, then, I must speak first, because, though they were not actually sophists, they seemed to be so, and hence came to be so called.

1. EUDOXUS OF CNIDUS, though he devoted considerable study to the teachings of the Academy, was nevertheless placed on the list of sophists because his style was ornate and he improvised with success. He was honoured with the title of sophist in the Hellespont and the Propontis, at Memphis, and in Egypt beyond Memphis where it borders on Ethiopia and the region inhabited by those wise men who are called Naked Philosophers.[3]

2. LEON OF BYZANTIUM was in his youth a pupil of Plato, but when he reached man's estate he was called a sophist because he employed so many different styles of oratory, and also because his repartees were so convincing. For example, when Philip brought an army against Byzantium, Leon went out to meet him and said: "Tell me, Philip, what moved you to begin war on us?" And when

13

τοῦ δὲ εἰπόντος " ἡ πατρὶς ἡ σὴ καλλίστη πόλεων
οὖσα ὑπηγάγετό με ἐρᾶν αὐτῆς καὶ διὰ τοῦτο
ἐπὶ θύρας τῶν ἐμαυτοῦ παιδικῶν ἥκω," ὑπολαβὼν
ὁ Λέων " οὐ φοιτῶσιν " ἔφη " μετὰ ξιφῶν ἐπὶ
τὰς τῶν παιδικῶν θύρας οἱ ἄξιοι τοῦ ἀντερᾶσθαι,
οὐ γὰρ πολεμικῶν ὀργάνων, ἀλλὰ μουσικῶν οἱ
ἐρῶντες δέονται." καὶ ἠλευθεροῦτο [1] Βυζάντιον
Δημοσθένους μὲν πολλὰ πρὸς Ἀθηναίους εἰπόντος, Λέοντος δὲ ὀλίγα πρὸς αὐτὸν τὸν [2] Φίλιππον.
καὶ πρεσβεύων δὲ παρ' Ἀθηναίους οὗτος ὁ Λέων,
ἐστασίαζε μὲν πολὺν ἤδη χρόνον ἡ πόλις καὶ
παρὰ τὰ ἤθη ἐπολιτεύετο, παρελθὼν δ' ἐς τὴν
ἐκκλησίαν προσέβαλεν αὐτοῖς ἀθρόον γέλωτα ἐπὶ
τῷ εἴδει, ἐπειδὴ πίων ἐφαίνετο καὶ περιττὸς τὴν
γαστέρα, ταραχθεὶς δὲ οὐδὲν ὑπὸ τοῦ γέλωτος
" τί," ἔφη " ὦ Ἀθηναῖοι, γελᾶτε; ἢ ὅτι παχὺς
ἐγὼ καὶ τοσοῦτος; ἔστι μοι καὶ γυνὴ πολλῷ
παχυτέρα, καὶ ὁμονοοῦντας μὲν ἡμᾶς χωρεῖ ἡ
κλίνη, διαφερομένους δὲ οὐδὲ ἡ οἰκία," καὶ ἐς
ἓν ἦλθεν ὁ τῶν Ἀθηναίων δῆμος ἁρμοσθεὶς ὑπὸ
τοῦ Λέοντος σοφῶς ἐπισχεδιάσαντος τῷ καιρῷ.

γʹ. Δίας δὲ ὁ Ἐφέσιος τὸ μὲν πεῖσμα τῆς ἑαυτοῦ φιλοσοφίας ἐξ Ἀκαδημίας ἐβέβλητο, σοφιστὴς δὲ ἐνομίσθη διὰ τόδε· τὸν Φίλιππον ὁρῶν
χαλεπὸν ὄντα τοῖς Ἕλλησιν ἐπὶ τὴν Ἀσίαν στρα-
486 τεύειν ἔπεισε, καὶ πρὸς τοὺς Ἕλληνας διεξῆλθε
λέγων, ὡς δέον ἀκολουθεῖν στρατεύοντι, καλὸν

---

[1] ἠλευθέρου τὸ Kayser; ἠλευθεροῦτο Valckenaer.
[2] τὸν add. Kayser.

---

[1] cf. Life of Apollonius vii. 42.
[2] Diogenes Laertius iv. 37 tells the same story about
Arcesilaus the head of the Academy. Athenaeus 550

he replied: "Your birthplace, the fairest of cities, lured me on to love her, and that is why I have come to my charmer's door," Leon retorted: "They come not with swords to the beloved's door who are worthy of requited love. For lovers need not the instruments of war but of music." [1] And Byzantium was freed, after Demosthenes had delivered many speeches to the Athenians on her behalf, while Leon had said but these few words to Philip himself. When this Leon came on an embassy to Athens, the city had long been disturbed by factions and was being governed in defiance of established customs. When he came before the assembly he excited universal laughter, since he was fat and had a prominent paunch, but he was not at all embarrassed by the laughter. "Why," said he, "do ye laugh, Athenians? Is it because I am so stout and so big? I have a wife at home who is much stouter than I, and when we agree the bed is large enough for us both, but when we quarrel not even the house is large enough." Thereupon the citizens of Athens came to a friendly agreement, thus reconciled by Leon, who had so cleverly improvised to meet the occasion. [2]

3. DIAS OF EPHESUS made fast the cable [3] of his philosophy to the Academy, but he was held to be a sophist for the following reason. When he saw that Philip was treating the Greeks harshly, he persuaded him to lead an expedition against Asia, and went to and fro telling the Greeks that they ought to accompany Philip on his expedition, since it was no

says that Leon told this anecdote not about himself but Python.
[3] For this figure cf. *Life of Apollonius* vi. 12.

γὰρ εἶναι καὶ τὸ ἔξω δουλεύειν ἐπὶ τῷ οἴκοι ἐλευθεροῦσθαι.

δ′. Καὶ Καρνεάδης δὲ ὁ Ἀθηναῖος ἐν σοφισταῖς ἐγράφετο, φιλοσόφως μὲν γὰρ κατεσκεύαστο τὴν γνώμην, τὴν δὲ ἰσχὺν τῶν λόγων ἐς τὴν ἄγαν ἤλαυνε δεινότητα.

ε′. Οἶδα καὶ Φιλόστρατον τὸν Αἰγύπτιον Κλεοπάτρα μὲν συμφιλοσοφοῦντα τῇ βασιλίδι, σοφιστὴν δὲ προσρηθέντα, ἐπειδὴ λόγου ἰδέαν πανηγυρικὴν ἥρμοστο καὶ ποικίλην, γυναικὶ ξυνών, ᾗ καὶ αὐτὸ τὸ φιλολογεῖν τρυφὴν εἶχεν, ὅθεν καὶ παρῴδουν τινὲς ἐπ᾽ αὐτῷ τόδε τὸ ἐλεγεῖον·

πανσόφου ὀργὴν ἴσχε Φιλοστράτου, ὃς Κλεοπάτρα
    νῦν προσομιλήσας τοῖος ἰδεῖν ἐφάνη.[1]

ϛ′. Καὶ Θεόμνηστον δὲ τὸν Ναυκρατίτην ἐπιδήλως φιλοσοφήσαντα ἡ περιβολὴ τῶν λόγων ἐς τοὺς σοφιστὰς ἀπήνεγκεν.

ζ′. Δίωνα δὲ τὸν Προυσαῖον οὐκ οἶδ᾽ ὅ τι χρὴ προσειπεῖν διὰ τὴν ἐς πάντα ἀρετήν, Ἀμαλθείας γὰρ κέρας ἦν, τὸ τοῦ λόγου, ξυγκείμενος μὲν τῶν ἄριστα εἰρημένων τοῦ ἀρίστου, βλέπων δὲ πρὸς τὴν Δημοσθένους ἠχὼ καὶ Πλάτωνος, ᾗ, καθάπερ αἱ μαγάδες τοῖς ὀργάνοις, προσηχεῖ ὁ Δίων τὸ ἑαυτοῦ ἴδιον ξὺν ἀφελείᾳ ἐπεστραμμένῃ. ἀρί-

---

[1] πέφαται Kayser; ἐφάνη Cobet.

---

[1] The original of this parody is Theognis 215 where he advises men to be as adaptable as the polypus which takes on the colour of its rock. It became a proverb: Athenaeus 317; Julian, *Misopogon* 349 D.

[2] We know nothing of Theomnestus, unless he be the Academician mentioned by Plutarch, *Brutus* 24, as a teacher at Athens.

dishonour to endure slavery abroad in order to secure
freedom at home.

4. CARNEADES OF ATHENS was also enrolled among
the sophists, for though his mind had been equipped
for the pursuit of philosophy, yet in virtue of the
force and vigour of his orations he attained to an
extraordinarily high level of eloquence.

5. I am aware that PHILOSTRATUS THE EGYPTIAN
also, though he studied philosophy with Queen
Cleopatra, was called a sophist. This was because he
adopted the panegyrical and highly-coloured type of
eloquence; which came of associating with a woman
who regarded even the love of letters as a sensuous
pleasure. Hence the following elegiac couplet was
composed as a parody aimed at him:

Acquire the temperament of that very wise man, Philostratus, who, fresh from his intimacy with Cleopatra, has
taken on colours like hers.[1]

6. THEOMNESTUS [2] OF NAUCRATIS was by profession a
philosopher, but the elaborate and rhetorical style of
his speeches caused him to be classed with the
sophists.

7. As for DIO OF PRUSA, I do not know what one
ought to call him, such was his excellence in all
departments; for, as the proverb says, he was a
" horn of Amalthea," [3] since in him is compounded
the noblest of all that has been most nobly expressed.
His style has the ring of Demosthenes and Plato,
but Dio has besides a peculiar resonance of his own,
which enhances theirs as the bridge enhances the
tone of musical instruments; and it was combined
with a serious and direct simplicity of expression.

[3] The horn of plenty, or cornucopia, was said to have
belonged to a goat named Amalthea which suckled the
infant Zeus.

17

στη δὲ ἐν τοῖς Δίωνος λόγοις καὶ ἡ τοῦ ἤθους
κρᾶσις· ὑβριζούσαις τε γὰρ πόλεσι πλεῖστα
ἐπιπλήξας οὐ φιλολοίδορος οὐδὲ ἀηδὴς ἔδοξεν,
ἀλλ' οἷον ἵππων ὕβριν χαλινῷ καταρτύων μᾶλλον
ἢ μάστιγι, πόλεών τε εὐνομουμένων ἐς ἐπαίνους
καταστὰς οὐκ ἐπαίρειν αὐτὰς ἔδοξεν, ἀλλ' ἐπι-
στρέφειν μᾶλλον ὡς ἀπολουμένας, εἰ μεταβαλοῖντο.[1]
ἦν δὲ αὐτῷ καὶ τὸ τῆς ἄλλης φιλοσοφίας ἦθος οὐ
κοινὸν οὐδὲ εἰρωνικόν, ἀλλὰ ἐμβριθῶς μὲν ἐγκεί-
μενον, κεχρωσμένον δέ, οἷον ἡδύσματι, τῇ πρᾳό-
τητι. ὡς δὲ καὶ ἱστορίαν ἱκανὸς ἦν ξυγγράφειν,
δηλοῖ τὰ Γετικά, καὶ γὰρ δὴ καὶ ἐς Γέτας ἦλθεν,
ὁπότε ἠλᾶτο. τὸν δὲ Εὐβοέα καὶ τὸν τοῦ ψιτ-
τακοῦ ἔπαινον καὶ ὁπόσα οὐχ ὑπὲρ μεγάλων
ἐσπούδασται τῷ Δίωνι, μὴ μικρὰ ἡγώμεθα, ἀλλὰ
σοφιστικά, σοφιστοῦ γὰρ τὸ καὶ ὑπὲρ τοιούτων
σπουδάζειν.

Γενόμενος δὲ κατὰ τοὺς χρόνους, οὓς Ἀπολλώ-
488 νιός τε ὁ Τυανεὺς καὶ Εὐφράτης ὁ Τύριος ἐφιλο-
σόφουν, ἀμφοτέροις ἐπιτηδείως εἶχε καίτοι δια-
φερομένοις πρὸς ἀλλήλους ἔξω τοῦ φιλοσοφίας
ἤθους. τὴν δὲ ἐς τὰ Γετικὰ ἔθνη πάροδον τοῦ
ἀνδρὸς φυγὴν μὲν οὐκ ἀξιῶ ὀνομάζειν, ἐπεὶ μὴ
προσετάχθη αὐτῷ φυγεῖν, οὐδὲ ἀποδημίαν, ἐπειδὴ
τοῦ φανεροῦ ἐξέστη κλέπτων ἑαυτὸν ὀφθαλμῶν

---

[1] μεταβάλοιντο Kayser ; μεταβαλοῖντο Cobet.

---

[1] This work is lost.
[2] This charming idyl of pastoral life in Euboea as witnessed
by a shipwrecked traveller is included with the *Orations* of
Dio Chrysostom, the "Golden-mouthed" as he is usually
called.
[3] See *Life of Apollonius* v. 33 and 37. The quarrel was

Again, in Dio's orations the elements of his own noble character were admirably displayed. For though he very often rebuked licentious cities, he did not show himself acrimonious or ungracious, but like one who restrains an unruly horse with the bridle rather than the whip; and when he set out to praise cities that were well governed, he did not seem to extol them, but rather to guide their attention to the fact that they would be ruined if they should change their ways. In other connexions also the temper of his philosophy was never vulgar or ironical; and though his attacks were made with a heavy hand, they were tempered and as it were seasoned with benevolence. That he had also a talent for writing history is proved by his treatise *On the Getae*[1]; he did in fact travel as far as the Getae during his wandering as an exile. As for his *Tale of Euboea*,[2] the *Encomium of a Parrot,* and all those writings in which he handled themes of no great importance, we must not regard them as mere trifles, but rather as sophistic compositions; for it is characteristic of a sophist to devote serious study to themes even so slight as these.

He lived at a time when Apollonius of Tyana and Euphrates[3] of Tyre were teaching their philosophy, and he was intimate with both men, though in their quarrel with one another they went to extremes that are alien to the philosophic temper. His visit to the Getic tribes I cannot rightly call exile, since he had not been ordered to go into exile, yet it was not merely a traveller's tour, for he vanished from men's sight, hiding himself from their eyes and ears, and

kept up in the *Letters of Apollonius.* Euphrates is praised by Pliny, *Epistles* i. 10.

τε καὶ ὤτων καὶ ἄλλα ἐν ἄλλῃ γῇ πράττων δέει
τῶν κατὰ τὴν πόλιν τυραννίδων, ὑφ' ὧν ἠλαύνετο
φιλοσοφία πᾶσα. φυτεύων δὲ καὶ σκάπτων καὶ
ἐπαντλῶν βαλανείοις τε καὶ κήποις καὶ πολλὰ
τοιαῦτα ὑπὲρ τροφῆς ἐργαζόμενος οὐδὲ τοῦ
σπουδάζειν ἠμέλει, ἀλλ' ἀπὸ[1] δυοῖν βιβλίοιν ἑαυτὸν
ξυνεῖχεν· ταυτὶ δὲ ἦν ὅ τε Φαίδων ὁ τοῦ Πλάτωνος καὶ Δημοσθένους ὁ κατὰ τῆς πρεσβείας.
θαμίζων δὲ ἐς τὰ στρατόπεδα, ἐν οἷσπερ εἰώθει
τρύχεσι,[2] καὶ τοὺς στρατιώτας ὁρῶν ἐς νεώτερα
ὁρμῶντας ἐπὶ Δομετιανῷ ἀπεσφαγμένῳ οὐκ ἐφεί-
σατο ἀταξίαν ἰδὼν ἐκραγεῖσαν, ἀλλὰ γυμνὸς ἀναπηδήσας ἐπὶ βωμὸν ὑψηλὸν ἤρξατο τοῦ λόγου ὧδε·

" αὐτὰρ ὁ γυμνώθη ῥακέων πολύμητις Ὀδυσσεύς,"

καὶ εἰπὼν ταῦτα καὶ δηλώσας ἑαυτόν, ὅτι μὴ
πτωχός, μηδὲ ὃν ᾤοντο, Δίων δὲ εἴη ὁ σοφός, ἐπὶ
μὲν τὴν κατηγορίαν τοῦ τυράννου πολὺς ἔπνευσεν,
τοὺς δὲ στρατιώτας ἐδίδαξεν ἄμεινον[3] φρονεῖν τὰ
δοκοῦντα Ῥωμαίοις πράττοντας. καὶ γὰρ ἡ
πειθὼ τοῦ ἀνδρὸς οἷα καταθέλξαι καὶ τοὺς μὴ
τὰ Ἑλλήνων ἀκριβοῦντας· Τραιανὸς γοῦν ὁ
αὐτοκράτωρ ἀναθέμενος αὐτὸν ἐπὶ τῆς Ῥώμης
ἐς τὴν χρυσῆν ἅμαξαν, ἐφ' ἧς οἱ βασιλεῖς τὰς ἐκ
τῶν πολέμων πομπὰς πομπεύουσιν, ἔλεγε θαμὰ
ἐπιστρεφόμενος ἐς τὸν Δίωνα " τί μὲν λέγεις,
οὐκ οἶδα, φιλῶ δέ σε ὡς ἐμαυτόν."

[1] Cobet would read ἐπί.
[2] τρύχεσθαι Kayser ; τρύχεσι Cobet.
[3] ἀμείνω Kayser ; ἄμεινον Cobet.

---

[1] Rome.   [2] *Life of Apollonius* vii. 4.
[3] Suetonius, *Domitian* 23.   [4] *Odyssey* xxii. 1.
[5] This incident is improbable and is not elsewhere

occupying himself in various ways in various lands, through fear of the tyrants in the capital[1] at whose hands all philosophy was suffering persecution.[2] But while he planted and dug, drew water for baths and gardens, and performed many such menial tasks for a living, he did not neglect the study of letters, but sustained himself with two books; these were the *Phaedo* of Plato, and Demosthenes *On the False Embassy.* He often visited the military camps in the rags he was wont to wear, and after the assassination of Domitian, when he saw that the troops were beginning to mutiny,[3] he could not contain himself at the sight of the disorder that had broken out, but stripped off his rags, leaped on to a high altar, and began his harangue with the verse:

Then Odysseus of many counsels stripped him of his rags,[4]

and having said this and thus revealed that he was no beggar, nor what they believed him to be, but Dio the sage, he delivered a spirited and energetic indictment of the tyrant; and he convinced the soldiers that they would be wiser if they acted in accordance with the will of the Roman people. And indeed the persuasive charm of the man was such as to captivate even men who were not versed in Greek letters. An instance of this is that the Emperor Trajan in Rome set him by his side on the golden chariot in which the Emperors ride in procession when they celebrate their triumphs in war, and often he would turn to Dio and say: "I do not understand what you are saying, but I love you as I love myself."[5]

recorded. That Trajan understood Greek is probable from Cassius Dio lxviii. 3, where Nerva in a letter exhorts him with a quotation from Homer; *cf.* also Cassius Dio lxviii. 7, and Pliny's *Panegyric* xlvii. 1.

Σοφιστικώταται δὲ τοῦ Δίωνος αἱ τῶν λόγων
εἰκόνες, ἐν αἷς εἰ καὶ πολύς, ἀλλὰ καὶ ἐναργὴς
καὶ τοῖς ὑποκειμένοις ὅμοιος.

489   η΄. Ὁμοίως καὶ Φαβωρῖνον τὸν φιλόσοφον ἡ
εὐγλωττία ἐν σοφισταῖς ἐκήρυττεν. ἦν μὲν γὰρ
τῶν ἑσπερίων Γαλατῶν οὗτος, Ἀρελάτου πόλεως,
ἣ ἐπὶ Ῥοδανῷ [1] ποταμῷ ᾤκισται, διφυὴς δὲ
ἐτέχθη καὶ ἀνδρόθηλυς, καὶ τοῦτο ἐδηλοῦτο μὲν
καὶ παρὰ τοῦ εἴδους, ἀγενείως γὰρ τοῦ προσώπου καὶ γηράσκων εἶχεν, ἐδηλοῦτο δὲ καὶ τῷ
φθέγματι, ὀξυηχὲς γὰρ ἠκούετο καὶ λεπτὸν καὶ
ἐπίτονον, ὥσπερ ἡ φύσις τοὺς εὐνούχους ἥρμοκεν.
θερμὸς δὲ οὕτω τις ἦν τὰ ἐρωτικά, ὡς καὶ μοιχοῦ
λαβεῖν αἰτίαν ἐξ ἀνδρὸς ὑπάτου. διαφορᾶς δὲ
αὐτῷ πρὸς Ἀδριανὸν βασιλέα γενομένης οὐδὲν
ἔπαθεν. ὅθεν ὡς παράδοξα ἐπεχρησμῴδει τῷ
ἑαυτοῦ βίῳ τρία ταῦτα· Γαλάτης ὢν ἑλληνίζειν,
εὐνοῦχος ὢν μοιχείας κρίνεσθαι, βασιλεῖ διαφέ-
ρεσθαι καὶ ζῆν. τουτὶ δὲ Ἀδριανοῦ ἔπαινος εἴη
ἂν μᾶλλον, εἰ βασιλεὺς ὢν ἀπὸ τοῦ ἴσου διεφέ-
ρετο πρὸς ὃν ἐξῆν ἀποκτεῖναι. βασιλεὺς δὲ κρείττων,

  "ὅτε χώσεται ἀνδρὶ χέρηι,"

ἦν ὀργῆς κρατῇ, καὶ

  "θυμὸς δὲ μέγας ἐστὶ διοτρεφέων βασιλήων,"

ἦν λογισμῷ κολάζηται. βέλτιον δὲ ταῦτα ταῖς

----

[1] Ἠριδανῷ Kayser; Ῥοδανῷ Cobet.

----

[1] Arles.
[2] *Iliad* i. 80. Philostratus interprets κρείσσων as "morally
superior" whereas in the original it simply means
"stronger."
22

The images employed by Dio in his orations are entirely in the sophistic manner, but though he abounds in them his style is nevertheless clear and in keeping with the matter in hand.

8. FAVORINUS the philosopher, no less than Dio, was proclaimed a sophist by the charm and beauty of his eloquence. He came from the Gauls of the West, from the city of Arelate[1] which is situated on the river Rhone. He was born double-sexed, a hermaphrodite, and this was plainly shown in his appearance; for even when he grew old he had no beard; it was evident too from his voice which sounded thin, shrill, and high-pitched, with the modulations that nature bestows on eunuchs also. Yet he was so ardent in love that he was actually charged with adultery by a man of consular rank. Though he quarrelled with the Emperor Hadrian, he suffered no ill consequences. Hence he used to say in the ambiguous style of an oracle, that there were in the story of his life these three paradoxes: Though he was a Gaul he led the life of a Hellene; a eunuch, he had been tried for adultery; he had quarrelled with an Emperor and was still alive. But this must rather be set down to the credit of Hadrian, seeing that, though he was Emperor, he disagreed on terms of equality with one whom it was in his power to put to death. For a prince is really superior if he controls his anger

> When he is wrath with a lesser man,[2]

and

> Mighty is the anger of Zeus-nurtured kings,

if only it be kept in check by reason. Those who

23

τῶν ποιητῶν δόξαις προσγράφειν τοὺς εὖ τιθε-
μένους τὰ τῶν βασιλέων ἤθη.

490 Ἀρχιερεὺς δὲ ἀναρρηθεὶς ἐς τὰ οἴκοι πάτρια
ἐφῆκε μὲν κατὰ τοὺς ὑπὲρ τῶν τοιούτων νόμους,
ὡς ἀφειμένος τοῦ λειτουργεῖν, ἐπειδὴ ἐφιλοσόφει,
τὸν δὲ αὐτοκράτορα ὁρῶν ἐναντίαν ἑαυτῷ θέσθαι
διανοούμενον, ὡς μὴ φιλοσοφοῦντι, ὑπετέμετο
αὐτὸν ὧδε· " ἐνύπνιόν μοι," ἔφη " ὦ βασιλεῦ,
γέγονεν, ὃ καὶ πρὸς σὲ χρὴ εἰρῆσθαι· ἐπιστὰς
γάρ μοι Δίων ὁ διδάσκαλος ἐνουθέτει με ὑπὲρ
τῆς δίκης λέγων, ὅτι μὴ ἑαυτοῖς μόνον, ἀλλὰ καὶ
ταῖς πατρίσι γεγόναμεν· ὑποδέχομαι δή, ὦ βασιλεῦ, τὴν λειτουργίαν καὶ τῷ διδασκάλῳ πείθομαι."
ταῦτα ὁ μὲν αὐτοκράτωρ διατριβὴν ἐπεποίητο,
καὶ διῆγε τὰς βασιλείους φροντίδας ἀπονεύων ἐς
σοφιστάς τε καὶ φιλοσόφους, Ἀθηναίοις δὲ δεινὰ
ἐφαίνετο καὶ συνδραμόντες αὐτοὶ μάλιστα οἱ ἐν
τέλει Ἀθηναῖοι χαλκῆν εἰκόνα κατέβαλον τοῦ
ἀνδρὸς ὡς πολεμιωτάτου τῷ αὐτοκράτορι· ὁ δέ,
ὡς ἤκουσεν, οὐδὲν σχετλιάσας οὐδὲ ἀγριάνας
ὑπὲρ ὧν ὕβριστο " ὤνητ᾽ ἄν" ἔφη " καὶ Σωκράτης εἰκόνα χαλκῆν ὑπ᾽ Ἀθηναίων ἀφαιρεθεὶς
μᾶλλον ἢ πιὼν κώνειον."

Ἐπιτηδειότατος μὲν οὖν Ἡρώδη τῷ σοφιστῇ
ἐγένετο διδάσκαλόν τε ἡγουμένῳ καὶ πατέρα καὶ
πρὸς αὐτὸν γράφοντι " πότε σε ἴδω καὶ πότε σου
περιλείξω τὸ στόμα; " ὅθεν καὶ τελευτῶν κληρο-

---

[1] The high priest was president of the public games in the
cities of his district and provided them at his own expense
as a " liturgy."

[2] An echo of Demosthenes, On the Crown 205, and
perhaps also of Plato, Crito 50.

endeavour to guide and amend the morals of princes would do well to add this saying to the sentiments expressed by the poets.

He was appointed high priest,[1] whereupon he appealed to the established usage of his birthplace, pleading that, according to the laws on such matters, he was exempt from public services because he was a philosopher. But when he saw that the Emperor intended to vote against him on the ground that he was not a philosopher, he forestalled him in the following way. " O Emperor," he cried, " I have had a dream of which you ought to be informed. My teacher Dio appeared to me, and with respect to this suit admonished and reminded me that we come into the world not for ourselves alone, but also for the country of our birth.[2] Therefore, O Emperor, I obey my teacher, and I undertake this public service." Now the Emperor had acted thus merely for his own diversion, for by turning his mind to philosopher and sophists he used to lighten the responsibilities of Empire. The Athenians however took the affair seriously, and, especially the Athenian magistrates themselves, hastened in a body to throw down the bronze statue of Favorinus as though he were the Emperor's bitterest enemy. Yet on hearing of it Favorinus showed no resentment or anger at the insult, but observed : "Socrates himself would have been the gainer, if the Athenians had merely deprived him of a bronze statue, instead of making him drink hemlock."

He was very intimate with Herodes the sophist who regarded him as his teacher and father, and wrote to him : " When shall I see you, and when shall I lick the honey from your lips?"[3] Accord-

[3] An echo of Aristophanes *frag.* 231 preserved in Dio Chrysostom, *Oration* 52 Arnim.

νόμον Ἡρώδην ἀπέφηνε τῶν τε βιβλίων, ὁπόσα
ἐκέκτητο, καὶ τῆς ἐπὶ τῇ Ῥώμῃ οἰκίας καὶ τοῦ
Αὐτοληκύθου. ἦν δὲ οὗτος Ἰνδὸς μὲν καὶ ἱκανῶς
μέλας, ἄθυρμα δὲ Ἡρώδου τε καὶ Φαβωρίνου,
ξυμπίνοντας γὰρ αὐτοὺς διῆγεν ἐγκαταμιγνὺς
Ἰνδικοῖς Ἀττικὰ καὶ πεπλανημένῃ τῇ γλώττῃ
βαρβαρίζων.

Ἡ δὲ γενομένη πρὸς τὸν Πολέμωνα τῷ Φα-
βωρίνῳ διαφορὰ ἤρξατο μὲν ἐν Ἰωνίᾳ προσθε-
μένων αὐτῷ τῶν Ἐφεσίων, ἐπεὶ τὸν Πολέμωνα
ἡ Σμύρνα ἐθαύμαζεν, ἐπέδωκε δὲ ἐν τῇ Ῥώμῃ,
ὕπατοι γὰρ καὶ παῖδες ὑπάτων οἱ μὲν τὸν ἐπαινοῦντες, οἱ δὲ τόν, ἦρξαν αὐτοῖς φιλοτιμίας, ἢ πολὺν
ἐκκαίει φθόνον καὶ σοφοῖς ἀνδράσιν. συγγνω-
στοὶ μὲν οὖν τῆς φιλοτιμίας, τῆς ἀνθρωπείας φύ-
491 σεως τὸ φιλότιμον ἀγήρων ἡγουμένης,[1] μεμπτέοι
δὲ τῶν λόγων, οὓς ἐπ᾽ ἀλλήλους ξυνέθεσαν, ἀσελ-
γὴς γὰρ λοιδορία, κἂν ἀληθὴς τύχῃ, οὐκ ἀφίησιν
αἰσχύνης οὐδὲ τὸν ὑπὲρ τοιούτων εἰπόντα. τοῖς
μὲν οὖν σοφιστὴν τὸν Φαβωρῖνον καλοῦσιν ἀπέχρη
ἐς ἀπόδειξιν καὶ αὐτὸ τὸ διενεχθῆναι αὐτὸν σοφιστῇ, τὸ γὰρ φιλότιμον, οὗ ἐμνήσθην, ἐπὶ τοὺς
ἀντιτέχνους φοιτᾷ.

Ἥρμοσται δὲ τὴν γλῶτταν ἀνειμένως μέν,
σοφῶς δὲ καὶ ποτίμως. ἐλέγετο δὲ σὺν εὐροίᾳ
σχεδιάσαι. τὰ μὲν δὴ ἐς Πρόξενον μήτ᾽ ἂν ἐνθυ-

---

[1] Cobet suggests κεκτημένης to improve the sense.

---

[1] The name means "he who carries his own oil-flask"
which was the mark of a slave. It was a mannerism of the
Atticists to use words compounded with "auto," *cf.* Lucian,
Lexiphanes ii. 9 ; in the latter passage the word occurs
which is here used as a proper name. In the *Life of*

ingly at his death he bequeathed to Herodes all the books that he had collected, his house in Rome, and Autolecythus.[1] This was an Indian, entirely black, a pet of Herodes and Favorinus, for as they drank their wine together he used to divert them by sprinkling his Indian dialect with Attic words and by speaking barbarous Greek with a tongue that stammered and faltered.

The quarrel that arose between Polemo and Favorinus began in Ionia, where the Ephesians favoured Favorinus, while Smyrna admired Polemo; and it became more bitter in Rome; for there consulars and sons of consulars by applauding either one or the other started between them a rivalry such as kindles the keenest envy and malice even in the hearts of wise men. However they may be forgiven for that rivalry, since human nature holds that the love of glory never grows old;[2] but they are to be blamed for the speeches that they composed assailing one another; for personal abuse is brutal, and even if it be true, that does not acquit of disgrace even the man who speaks about such things. And so when people called Favorinus a sophist, the mere fact that he had quarrelled with a sophist was evidence enough; for that spirit of rivalry of which I spoke is always directed against one's competitors in the same craft.[3]

His style of eloquence was careless in construction, but it was both learned and pleasing. It is said that he improvised with ease and fluency. As for the speeches against Proxenus, we must conclude that

Apollonius iii. 11 this slave is referred to as Meno and is called an Ethiopian.   [2] An echo of Thuc. ii. 44.
    [3] Hesiod, *Works and Days* 25.

μηθῆναι τὸν Φαβωρῖνον ἡγώμεθα μήτ' ἂν ξυνθεῖναι, ἀλλ' εἶναι αὐτὰ μειρακίου φρόντισμα μεθύοντος, μᾶλλον δὲ ἐμοῦντος, τὸν δὲ ἐπὶ τῷ ἀώρῳ καὶ
τὸν ὑπὲρ τῶν μονομάχων καὶ τὸν ὑπὲρ τῶν βαλανείων γνησίους τε ἀποφαινόμεθα καὶ εὖ ξυγκειμένους, καὶ πολλῷ μᾶλλον τοὺς φιλοσοφουμέ-
νους αὐτῷ τῶν λόγων, ὧν ἄριστοι οἱ Πυρρώνειοι·
τοὺς γὰρ Πυρρωνείους ἐφεκτικοὺς ὄντας οὐκ
ἀφαιρεῖται καὶ τὸ δικάζειν δύνασθαι.

Διαλεγομένου δὲ αὐτοῦ κατὰ τὴν Ῥώμην μεστὰ
ἦν σπουδῆς πάντα, καὶ γὰρ δὴ καὶ ὅσοι τῆς Ἑλλήνων φωνῆς ἀξύνετοι ἦσαν, οὐδὲ τούτοις ἀφ' ἡδονῆς ἡ
ἀκρόασις ἦν, ἀλλὰ κἀκείνους ἔθελγε τῇ τε ἠχῇ τοῦ
φθέγματος καὶ τῷ σημαίνοντι τοῦ βλέμματος καὶ τῷ
492 ῥυθμῷ τῆς γλώττης· ἔθελγε δὲ αὐτοὺς τοῦ λόγου
καὶ τὸ ἐπὶ πᾶσιν, ὃ ἐκεῖνοι μὲν ᾠδὴν ἐκάλουν, ἐγὼ
δὲ φιλοτιμίαν, ἐπειδὴ τοῖς ἀποδεδειγμένοις ἐφυμνεῖ-
ται. Δίωνος μὲν οὖν ἀκοῦσαι λέγεται, τοσοῦτον δὲ
ἀφέστηκεν, ὅσον οἱ μὴ ἀκούσαντες.

Τοσαῦτα μὲν ὑπὲρ τῶν φιλοσοφησάντων ἐν δόξῃ
τοῦ σοφιστεῦσαι. οἱ δὲ κυρίως προσρηθέντες σοφισταὶ ἐγένοντο οἵδε·

θ΄. Σικελία Γοργίαν ἐν Λεοντίνοις ἤνεγκεν,
ἐς ὃν ἀναφέρειν ἡγώμεθα τὴν τῶν σοφιστῶν τέχνην,
ὥσπερ ἐς πατέρα· εἰ γὰρ τὸν Αἰσχύλον ἐνθυμη-
θείημεν, ὡς πολλὰ τῇ τραγῳδίᾳ ξυνεβάλετο ἐσθῆτί
τε αὐτὴν κατασκευάσας καὶ ὀκρίβαντι ὑψηλῷ καὶ

---

[1] cf. the saying of Aristeides below, p. 583.
[2] This work was called On the Tropes of Pyrrho.
[3] On this sophistic mannerism see below, p. 513. Dio,
Oration xxxii. 68, ridicules this habit of singing instead of
speaking, which, he says, has invaded even the law courts;
cf. Cicero, Orator 18.

Favorinus would neither have conceived nor composed them, but that they are the work of an immature youth who was intoxicated at the time, or rather he vomited them.[1] But the speeches *On One Untimely Dead*, and *For the Gladiators*, and *For the Baths*, I judge to be genuine and well written; and this is far more true of his dissertations on philosophy, of which the best are those on the doctrines of Pyrrho[2]; for he concedes to the followers of Pyrrho the ability to make a legal decision, though in other matters they suspend their judgement.

When he delivered discourses in Rome, the interest in them was universal, so much so that even those in his audience who did not understand the Greek language shared in the pleasure that he gave; for he fascinated even them by the tones of his voice, by his expressive glance and the rhythm of his speech. They were also enchanted by the epilogue of his orations, which they called "The Ode,"[3] though I call it mere affectation, since it is arbitrarily added at the close of an argument that has been logically proved. He is said to have been a pupil of Dio, but he is as different from Dio as any who never were his pupils. This is all I have to say about the men who, though they pursued philosophy, had the reputation of sophists. But those who were correctly styled sophists were the following.

9. Sicily produced GORGIAS OF LEONTINI, and we must consider that the art of the sophists carries back to him as though he were its father. For if we reflect how many additions Aeschylus made to tragedy when he furnished her with her proper costume and the buskin that gave the actor's height, with the types

29

ἡρώων εἴδεσιν ἀγγέλοις τε καὶ ἐξαγγέλοις καὶ οἷς
ἐπὶ σκηνῆς τε καὶ ὑπὸ σκηνῆς χρὴ πράττειν, τοῦτο
ἂν εἴη καὶ ὁ Γοργίας τοῖς ὁμοτέχνοις. ὁρμῆς τε γὰρ
τοῖς σοφισταῖς ἦρξε καὶ παραδοξολογίας καὶ πνεύματος καὶ τοῦ τὰ μεγάλα μεγάλως ἑρμηνεύειν,
ἀποστάσεών τε καὶ προσβολῶν, ὑφ' ὧν ὁ λόγος
ἡδίων ἑαυτοῦ γίγνεται καὶ σοβαρώτερος, περιεβάλλετο δὲ καὶ ποιητικὰ ὀνόματα ὑπὲρ κόσμου καὶ
σεμνότητος. ὡς μὲν οὖν καὶ ῥᾷστα ἀπεσχεδίαζεν,
εἴρηταί μοι κατὰ ἀρχὰς τοῦ λόγου, διαλεχθεὶς δὲ
Ἀθήνησιν ἤδη γηράσκων εἰ μὲν ὑπὸ τῶν πολλῶν
ἐθαυμάσθη, οὔπω θαῦμα, ὁ δέ, οἶμαι, καὶ τοὺς
ἐλλογιμωτάτους ἀνηρτήσατο, Κριτίαν μὲν καὶ
493 Ἀλκιβιάδην νέω ὄντε, Θουκυδίδην δὲ καὶ Περικλέα
ἤδη γηράσκοντε. καὶ Ἀγάθων δὲ ὁ τῆς τραγῳδίας ποιητής, ὃν ἡ κωμῳδία σοφόν τε καὶ καλλιεπῆ
οἶδε, πολλαχοῦ τῶν ἰάμβων γοργιάζει.

Ἐμπρέπων δὲ καὶ ταῖς τῶν Ἑλλήνων πανηγύ-
ρεσι τὸν μὲν λόγον τὸν Πυθικὸν ἀπὸ τοῦ βωμοῦ
ἤχησεν, ἀφ' οὗ καὶ χρυσοῦς ἀνετέθη, ἐν τῷ τοῦ
Πυθίου ἱερῷ, ὁ δὲ Ὀλυμπικὸς λόγος ὑπὲρ τοῦ
μεγίστου αὐτῷ ἐπολιτεύθη. στασιάζουσαν γὰρ τὴν
Ἑλλάδα ὁρῶν ὁμονοίας ξύμβουλος αὐτοῖς ἐγένετο
τρέπων ἐπὶ τοὺς βαρβάρους καὶ πείθων ἆθλα ποιεῖ-

---

[1] For this term see Glossary.
[2] See p. 482.
[3] This is one of the most obvious errors of Philostratus.
Pericles had been dead for two years when Gorgias came to
Athens.
[4] Aristophanes, *Thesmophoriazusae* 49. Plato, *Symposium*
195 foll., with satirical intention makes Agathon speak in the
style of Gorgias.

of heroes, with messengers who tell what has happened at home and abroad, and with the conventions as to what must be done both before and behind the scenes, then we find that this is what Gorgias in his turn did for his fellow-craftsmen. For he set an example to the sophists with his virile and energetic style, his daring and unusual expressions, his inspired impressiveness, and his use of the grand style for great themes; and also with his habit of breaking off his clauses and making sudden transitions,[1] by which devices a speech gains in sweetness and sublimity; and he also clothed his style with poetic words for the sake of ornament and dignity. That he also improvised with the greatest facility I have stated at the beginning of my narrative;[2] and when, already advanced in years, he delivered discourses at Athens, there is nothing surprising in the fact that he won applause from the crowd; but he also, as is well known, enthralled the most illustrious men, not only Critias and Alcibiades, who were both young men, but also Thucydides and Pericles[3] who were by that time well on in years. Agathon also, the tragic poet, whom Comedy calls a clever poet and "lovely in his speech,"[4] often imitates Gorgias in his iambics.

Moreover, he played a distinguished part at the religious festivals of the Greeks, and declaimed his *Pythian Oration* from the altar; and for this his statue was dedicated in gold and was set up in the temple of the Pythian god. His *Olympian Oration* dealt with a theme of the highest importance to the state. For, seeing that Greece was divided against itself, he came forward as the advocate of reconciliation, and tried to turn their energies against the barbarians

31

σθαι τῶν ὅπλων μὴ τὰς ἀλλήλων πόλεις, ἀλλὰ τὴν
τῶν βαρβάρων χώραν. ὁ δὲ ἐπιτάφιος, ὃν διῆλθεν
᾿Αθήνησιν, εἴρηται μὲν ἐπὶ τοῖς ἐκ τῶν πολέμων,
οὓς ᾿Αθηναῖοι δημοσίᾳ ξὺν ἐπαίνοις ἔθαψαν, σοφίᾳ
δὲ ὑπερβαλλούσῃ ξύγκειται· παροξύνων τε γὰρ
τοὺς ᾿Αθηναίους ἐπὶ Μήδους τε καὶ Πέρσας καὶ
τὸν αὐτὸν νοῦν τῷ ᾿Ολυμπικῷ ἀγωνιζόμενος ὑπὲρ
ὁμονοίας μὲν τῆς πρὸς τοὺς ῞Ελληνας οὐδὲν διῆλθεν, ἐπειδὴ πρὸς ᾿Αθηναίους ἦν ἀρχῆς ἐρῶντας, ἣν
οὐκ ἦν κτήσασθαι μὴ τὸ δραστήριον αἱρουμένους,
ἐνδιέτριψε δὲ τοῖς τῶν Μηδικῶν τροπαίων ἐπαίνοις,
494 ἐνδεικνύμενος αὐτοῖς, ὅτι τὰ μὲν κατὰ τῶν βαρβάρων τρόπαια ὕμνους ἀπαιτεῖ, τὰ δὲ κατὰ τῶν
῾Ελλήνων θρήνους.

Λέγεται δὲ ὁ Γοργίας ἐς ὀκτὼ καὶ ἑκατὸν
ἐλάσας ἔτη μὴ καταλυθῆναι τὸ σῶμα ὑπὸ τοῦ
γήρως, ἀλλ᾿ ἄρτιος καταβιῶναι καὶ τὰς αἰσθήσεις
ἡβῶν.

ιʹ. Πρωταγόρας δὲ ὁ Ἀβδηρίτης σοφιστὴς Δημοκρίτου μὲν ἀκροατὴς οἴκοι ἐγένετο, ὡμίλησε δὲ
καὶ τοῖς ἐκ Περσῶν μάγοις κατὰ τὴν Ξέρξου ἐπὶ
τὴν ῾Ελλάδα ἔλασιν. πατὴρ γὰρ ἦν αὐτῷ Μαίαν-
δρος πλούτῳ κατεσκευασμένος παρὰ πολλοὺς τῶν
ἐν τῇ Θρᾴκῃ, δεξάμενος δὲ καὶ τὸν Ξέρξην οἰκίᾳ τε
καὶ δώροις τὴν ξυνουσίαν τῶν μάγων τῷ παιδὶ παρ᾿
αὐτοῦ εὕρετο. οὐ γὰρ παιδεύουσι τοὺς μὴ Πέρσας
Πέρσαι μάγοι, ἢν μὴ ὁ βασιλεὺς ἐφῇ. τὸ δὲ
ἀπορεῖν φάσκειν, εἴτε εἰσὶ θεοί, εἴτε οὐκ εἰσί, δοκεῖ

---

[1] cf. Isocrates, Panegyric 42.
[2] This is a lapse of memory on the part of Philostratus.
Diogenes Laertius tells this story of Democritus, not of
Protagoras. For the father of Democritus as the host of
Xerxes cf. Valerius Maximus viii. 7.

and to persuade them not to regard one another's cities as the prize to be won by their arms, but rather the land of the barbarians.[1] The *Funeral Oration*, which he delivered at Athens, was spoken in honour of those who had fallen in the wars, to whom the Athenians awarded public funerals and panegyrics, and it is composed with extraordinary cleverness. For though he incited the Athenians against the Medes and Persians, and was arguing with the same purpose as in the *Olympian Oration*, he said nothing about a friendly agreement with the rest of the Greeks, for this reason, that it was addressed to Athenians who had a passion for empire, and that could not be attained except by adopting a drastic line of policy. But he dwelt openly on their victories over the Medes and praised them for these, making it evident to them the while that victories over barbarians call for hymns of praise, but victories over Greeks for dirges.

It is said that though Gorgias attained to the age of 108, his body was not weakened by old age, but to the end of his life he was in sound condition, and his senses were the senses of a young man.

10. PROTAGORAS OF ABDERA, the sophist, was a pupil of Democritus in the city of his birth, and he also associated with the Persian magi [2] when Xerxes led his expedition against Greece. For his father was Maeander, who had amassed wealth beyond most men in Thrace; he even entertained Xerxes in his house, and, by giving him presents, obtained his permission for his son to study with the magi. For the Persian magi do not educate those that are not Persians, except by command of the Great King. And when he says that he has no knowledge whether

μοι Πρωταγόρας ἐκ τῆς Περσικῆς παιδεύσεως
παρανομῆσαι· μάγοι γὰρ ἐπιθειάζουσι μὲν οἷς
ἀφανῶς δρῶσι, τὴν δὲ ἐκ φανεροῦ δόξαν τοῦ θείου
καταλύουσιν οὐ βουλόμενοι δοκεῖν παρ' αὐτοῦ
δύνασθαι. διὰ μὲν δὴ τοῦτο πάσης γῆς ὑπὸ Ἀθηναίων ἠλάθη, ὡς μέν τινες, κριθείς, ὡς δὲ ἐνίοις
δοκεῖ, ψήφου ἐπενεχθείσης μὴ κριθέντι. νήσους δὲ
ἐξ ἠπείρων ἀμείβων καὶ τὰς Ἀθηναίων τριήρεις
φυλαττόμενος πάσαις θαλάτταις ἐνεσπαρμένας
κατέδυ πλέων ἐν ἀκατίῳ μικρῷ.

Τὸ δὲ μισθοῦ διαλέγεσθαι πρῶτος εὗρε, πρῶτος
δὲ παρέδωκεν Ἕλλησι πρᾶγμα οὐ μεμπτόν, ἃ γὰρ
σὺν δαπάνῃ σπουδάζομεν, μᾶλλον ἀσπαζόμεθα τῶν
προῖκα. γνοὺς δὲ τὸν Πρωταγόραν ὁ Πλάτων
σεμνῶς μὲν ἑρμηνεύοντα, ἐνυπτιάζοντα δὲ τῇ
195 σεμνότητι καί που καὶ μακρολογώτερον τοῦ συμ-
μέτρου, τὴν ἰδέαν αὐτοῦ μύθῳ μακρῷ ἐχαρακτή-
ρισεν.

ια'. Ἱππίας δὲ ὁ σοφιστὴς ὁ Ἠλεῖος τὸ μὲν
μνημονικὸν οὕτω τι καὶ γηράσκων ἔρρωτο, ὡς καὶ
πεντήκοντα ὀνομάτων ἀκούσας ἅπαξ ἀπομνημονεύ-
ειν αὐτὰ καθ' ἣν ἤκουσε τάξιν, ἐσήγετο δὲ ἐς τὰς
διαλέξεις γεωμετρίαν ἀστρονομίαν μουσικὴν ῥυθμούς, διελέγετο δὲ καὶ περὶ ζωγραφίας καὶ περὶ
ἀγαλματοποιίας. ταῦτα ἑτέρωθι, ἐν Λακεδαίμονι

---

[1] For these triremes, sixty in number, cf. Plutarch,
Pericles 11.
[2] Protagoras 349 A and Gorgias 520 c.
[3] This is the myth of Prometheus and Epimetheus in the
Protagoras.

the gods exist or not, I think that Protagoras derived this heresy from his Persian education. For though the magi invoke the gods in their secret rites, they avoid any public profession of belief in a deity, because they do not wish it to be thought that their own powers are derived from that source. It was for this saying that he was outlawed from the whole earth by the Athenians, as some say after a trial, but others hold that the decree was voted against him without the form of a trial. And so he passed from island to island and from continent to continent, and while trying to avoid the Athenian triremes [1] which were distributed over every sea, he was drowned when sailing in a small boat.

He was the first to introduce the custom of charging a fee for lectures, and so was the first to hand down to the Greeks a practice which is not to be despised, since the pursuits on which we spend money we prize more than those for which no money is charged. Plato recognized [2] that though Protagoras had a dignified style of eloquence, that dignity was a mask for his real indolence of mind, and that he was at times too long-winded and lacked a sense of proportion, and so, in a long myth, he hit off the main characteristics of the other's style. [3]

11. HIPPIAS OF ELIS, the sophist, had such extraordinary powers of memory, even in his old age, that after hearing fifty names only once he could repeat them from memory in the order in which he had heard them. He introduced into his discourses discussions on geometry, astronomy, music, and rhythms, and he also lectured on painting and the art of sculpture. These were the subjects that he handled in other parts of Greece, but in Sparta he

δὲ γένη τε διήει πόλεων καὶ ἀποικίας καὶ ἔργα,
ἐπειδὴ οἱ Λακεδαιμόνιοι διὰ τὸ βούλεσθαι ἄρχειν τῇ
ἰδέᾳ ταύτῃ ἔχαιρον. ἔστιν δὲ αὐτῷ καὶ Τρωικὸς
διάλογος, οὐ λόγος· ὁ Νέστωρ ἐν Τροίᾳ ἁλούσῃ
ὑποτίθεται Νεοπτολέμῳ τῷ Ἀχιλλέως, ἃ χρὴ
ἐπιτηδεύοντα ἄνδρ’ ἀγαθὸν φαίνεσθαι.[1] πλεῖστα δὲ
Ἑλλήνων πρεσβεύσας ὑπὲρ τῆς Ἤλιδος οὐδαμοῦ
κατέλυσε τὴν ἑαυτοῦ δόξαν δημηγορῶν τε καὶ
διαλεγόμενος, ἀλλὰ καὶ χρήματα πλεῖστα ἐξέλεξε
καὶ φυλαῖς ἐνεγράφη πόλεων μικρῶν τε καὶ μειζόνων. παρῆλθε καὶ ἐς τὴν Ἰνυκὸν ὑπὲρ χρημάτων,
τὸ δὲ πολίχνιον τοῦτο Σικελικοί εἰσιν, οὓς ὁ Πλάτων
ἐπισκώπτει. εὐδοκιμῶν δὲ καὶ τὸν ἄλλον χρόνον
496 ἔθελγε τὴν Ἑλλάδα ἐν Ὀλυμπίᾳ λόγοις ποικίλοις
καὶ πεφροντισμένοις εὖ. ἑρμήνευε δὲ οὐκ ἐλλιπῶς,
ἀλλὰ περιττῶς καὶ κατὰ φύσιν, ἐς ὀλίγα κατα-
φεύγων τῶν ἐκ ποιητικῆς ὀνόματα.

ιβ΄. Προδίκου δὲ τοῦ Κείου ὄνομα τοσοῦτον
ἐπὶ σοφίᾳ ἐγένετο, ὡς καὶ τὸν Γρύλλου ἐν Βοιωτοῖς
δεθέντα ἀκροᾶσθαι διαλεγομένου, καθιστάντα ἐγ-
γυητὴν τοῦ σώματος. πρεσβεύων δὲ παρὰ Ἀθηναίους παρελθὼν ἐς τὸ βουλευτήριον ἱκανώτατος
ἔδοξεν ἀνθρώπων, καίτοι δυσήκοον καὶ βαρὺ φθεγ-
γόμενος. ἀνίχνευε δὲ οὗτος τοὺς εὐπατρίδας τῶν
νέων καὶ τοὺς ἐκ τῶν βαθέων οἴκων, ὡς καὶ προξέ-

---

[1] Cobet would read γίγνεσθαι.

[1] i.e. he was given the privileges of a citizen.
[2] In Plato *Hippias Maior* 282 ε Hippias says that at
Inycus alone, a small city, he made more than twenty
minae, i.e. about £80; Plato scoffs at the luxurious Sicilians
for paying to learn virtue, whereas at Sparta Hippias made
nothing.
[3] Xenophon.

described the different types of states and colonies and their activities, because the Spartans, owing to their desire for empire, took pleasure in this kind of discourse. There is also extant by him a Trojan dialogue which is not an oration—Nestor in Troy, after it has been taken, expounds to Neoptolemus the son of Achilles what course one ought to pursue in order to win a good name. On behalf of Elis he went on more embassies than any other Greek, and in no case did he fail to maintain his reputation, whether when making public speeches or lecturing, and at the same time he amassed great wealth and was enrolled in the tribes [1] of cities both great and small. In order to make money he also visited Inycus, a small town in Sicily, to whose people Plato alludes sarcastically.[2] In the rest of his time also he won renown for himself, and used to charm the whole of Greece at Olympia by his ornate and carefully studied orations. His style was never meagre, but copious and natural, and he seldom had to take refuge in the vocabulary of the poets.

12. PRODICUS OF CEOS had so great a reputation for wisdom that even the son of Gryllus,[3] when he was a prisoner in Boeotia,[4] used to attend his lectures, after procuring bail for himself. When he came on an embassy to Athens and appeared before the Senate, he proved to be the most capable ambassador possible, though he was hard to hear and had a very deep bass voice.[5] He used to hunt out well-born youths and those who came from wealthy families,[6]

---

[4] There is no other evidence for this imprisonment of Xenophon, but it may have occurred in 412 when the Boeotians took Oropus ; cf. Thucydides viii. 60.

[5] Probably an echo of Plato, *Protagoras* 316 A.

[6] Plato, *Sophist* 231 D.

νους ἐκτῆσθαι ταύτης τῆς θήρας, χρημάτων τε γὰρ
ἥττων ἐτύγχανε καὶ ἡδοναῖς ἐδεδώκει. τὴν δὲ Ἡρα-
κλέους αἵρεσιν τὸν τοῦ Προδίκου λόγον οὗ κατ᾽
ἀρχὰς ἐπεμνήσθην, οὐδὲ Ξενοφῶν ἀπηξίωσε μὴ
οὐχὶ ἑρμηνεῦσαι. καὶ τί ἂν χαρακτηρίζοιμεν τὴν
τοῦ Προδίκου γλῶτταν, Ξενοφῶντος αὐτὴν ἱκανῶς
ὑπογράφοντος;

497 ιγ'. Πῶλον δὲ τὸν Ἀκραγαντῖνον Γοργίας
σοφιστὴν ἐξεμελέτησε πολλῶν, ὥς φασι, χρημάτων,
καὶ γὰρ δὴ καὶ τῶν πλουτούντων ὁ Πῶλος. εἰσὶ
δέ, οἵ φασι καὶ τὰ πάρισα καὶ τὰ ἀντίθετα καὶ τὰ
ὁμοιοτέλευτα Πῶλον εὑρηκέναι πρῶτον, οὐκ ὀρθῶς
λέγοντες, τῇ γὰρ τοιᾷδε ἀγλαΐᾳ τοῦ λόγου Πῶλος
εὑρημένῃ κατεχρήσατο, ὅθεν ὁ Πλάτων διαπτύων
αὐτὸν ἐπὶ τῇ φιλοτιμίᾳ ταύτῃ φησίν· "ὦ λῷστε
Πῶλε, ἵνα σε προσείπω κατὰ σέ."

ιδ'. Οἱ δὲ καὶ Θρασύμαχον τὸν Καλχηδόνιον
ἐν σοφισταῖς γράφοντες δοκοῦσί μοι παρακούειν
Πλάτωνος λέγοντος [1] ταὐτὸν εἶναι λέοντα ξυρεῖν
καὶ συκοφαντεῖν Θρασύμαχον· δικογραφίαν γὰρ
αὐτῷ προφέροντός ἐστί που ταῦτα καὶ τὸ ἐν δικαστηρίοις συκοφαντοῦντα τρίβεσθαι.

498 ιε'. Ἀντιφῶντα δὲ τὸν Ῥαμνούσιον οὐκ οἶδ᾽,
εἴτε χρηστὸν δεῖ προσειπεῖν, εἴτε φαῦλον. χρη-
στὸς μὲν γὰρ προσειρήσθω διὰ τάδε· ἐστρατήγησε
πλεῖστα, ἐνίκησε πλεῖστα, ἑξήκοντα τριήρεσι πε-
πληρωμέναις ηὔξησεν Ἀθηναίοις τὸ ναυτικόν, ἱκανώτατος ἀνθρώπων ἔδοξεν εἰπεῖν τε καὶ γνῶναι· διὰ

[1] λέγοντος Cobet adds.

---

[1] *Memorabilia* ii. 1. 21.
[2] *Gorgias* 467 в. In the Greek the sentence contains two
jingles of sound such as Polus and his school employed.
cf. Plato, *Symposium*, 185.   [3] *Republic*, 341 c.

so much so that he even had agents employed in this pursuit; for he had a weakness for making money and was addicted to pleasure. Even Xenophon [1] did not disdain to relate the fable of Prodicus called *The Choice of Heracles*, which I mentioned when I began my narrative. As for the language of Prodicus, why should I describe its characteristics, when Xenophon has given so complete a sketch of it?

13. POLUS OF AGRIGENTUM, the sophist, was trained in the art by Gorgias, and for this he paid, as we are told, very high fees; for in fact Polus was a wealthy man. Some say that Polus was the first to use clauses that exactly balance, antitheses, and similar endings; but they are mistaken in so saying; for rhetorical ornament of this kind was already invented, and Polus merely employed it to excess. Hence Plato, to express his contempt for Polus because of this affectation, says: "O polite Polus! to address you in your own style." [2]

14. Those who include THRASYMACHUS OF CHALCEDON among the sophists fail, in my opinion, to understand Plato when he says [3] that shaving a lion is the same thing as trying to get the law of Thrasymachus. For this saying really amounts to taunting him with writing legal speeches for clients, and spending his time in the law courts trumping up cases for the prosecution.

15. As for ANTIPHON OF RHAMNUS, I am uncertain whether one ought to call him a good or a bad man. On the one hand he may be called a good man, for the following reasons. Very often he held commands in war, very often he was victorious; he added to the Athenian navy sixty fully equipped triremes; he was held to be the most able of men, both in the art of speaking and in the invention

μὲν δὴ ταῦτα ἐμοί τε ἐπαινετέος καὶ ἑτέρῳ. κακὸς
δ' ἂν εἰκότως διὰ τάδε φαίνοιτο· κατέλυσε τὴν
δημοκρατίαν, ἐδούλωσε τὸν Ἀθηναίων δῆμον,
ἐλακώνισε κατ' ἀρχὰς μὲν ἀφανῶς, ὕστερον δ'
ἐπιδήλως, τυράννων τετρακοσίων δῆμον ἐπαφῆκε
τοῖς Ἀθηναίων πράγμασιν.

Ῥητορικὴν δὲ τὸν Ἀντιφῶντα οἱ μὲν οὐκ οὖσαν
εὑρεῖν, οἱ δ' εὑρημένην αὐξῆσαι, γενέσθαι τε αὐτὸν
οἱ μὲν αὐτομαθῶς σοφόν, οἱ δὲ ἐκ πατρός. πατέρα
γὰρ εἶναι δὴ αὐτῷ Σώφιλον διδάσκαλον ῥητορικῶν
λόγων, ὃς ἄλλους τε τῶν ἐν δυνάμει καὶ τὸν τοῦ
Κλεινίου ἐπαίδευσεν. πιθανώτατος δὲ ὁ Ἀντιφῶν
γενόμενος καὶ προσρηθεὶς Νέστωρ ἐπὶ τῷ περὶ
παντὸς εἰπὼν ἂν πεῖσαι νηπενθεῖς ἀκροάσεις ἐπήγ-
γειλεν, ὡς οὐδὲν οὕτω δεινὸν ἐρούντων ἄχος, ὃ μὴ
499 ἐξελεῖν τῆς γνώμης. καθάπτεται δὲ ἡ κωμῳδία
τοῦ Ἀντιφῶντος ὡς δεινοῦ τὰ δικανικὰ καὶ λόγους
κατὰ τοῦ δικαίου ξυγκειμένους ἀποδιδομένου πολλῶν χρημάτων αὐτοῖς μάλιστα τοῖς κινδυνεύουσιν.
τουτὶ ὁποίαν ἔχει φύσιν, ἐγὼ δηλώσω· ἄνθρωποι
κατὰ μὲν τὰς ἄλλας ἐπιστήμας καὶ τέχνας τιμῶσι
τοὺς ἐν ἑκάστῃ αὐτῶν προὔχοντας καὶ θαυμάζουσι
τῶν ἰατρῶν τοὺς μᾶλλον παρὰ τοὺς ἧττον, θαυμάζουσι δ' ἐν μαντικῇ καὶ μουσικῇ τὸν σοφώτερον,

---

[1] This account of Antiphon as the contriver of the whole
scheme of the oligarchic revolution, and of his rhetorical
ability, is probably derived from Thucydides viii. 68.

[2] Alcibiades.

[3] Νηπενθής is an epic word and the reference is to the
φάρμακον νηπενθές used by Helen, Odyssey iv. 221.

[4] A paraphrase of Euripides, Orestes 1-3:

> οὐκ ἔστιν οὐδὲν δεινὸν ὧδ' εἰπεῖν ἔπος
> οὐδὲ πάθος οὐδὲ συμφορὰ θεήλατος
> ἧς οὐκ ἂν ἄραιτ' ἄχθος ἀνθρώπου φύσις.

of themes. On these grounds, then, he deserves praise from me or any other. But on the other hand there are evidently good reasons for regarding him as a bad man, and they are the following. He broke up the democracy; he enslaved the Athenian people; he sided with Sparta, secretly at first, but openly later on; and he let loose on the public life of Athens the mob of the Four Hundred Tyrants.[1]

Some say that Antiphon invented rhetoric which before him did not exist, others that it was already invented, but that he widened its scope; some say that he was self-taught, others that he owed his erudition to his father's teaching. For, say they, his father was Sophilus who taught the art of composing rhetorical speeches and educated the son of Cleinias,[2] as well as other men of great influence. Antiphon achieved an extraordinary power of persuasion, and having been nicknamed " Nestor " because of his ability to convince his hearers, whatever his theme, he announced a course of "sorrow-assuaging[3]" lectures, asserting that no one could tell him of a grief so terrible that he could not expel it from the mind.[4] Antiphon is attacked in Comedy for being too clever in legal matters, and for selling for large sums of money speeches composed in defiance of justice for the use of clients whose case was especially precarious. The nature of this charge I will proceed to explain. In the case of other branches of science and the arts, men pay honour to those who have won distinction in any one of these fields; that is to say, they pay more honour to physicians who are skilful than to those who are less skilful; in the arts of divination and music they admire the expert, and

τὴν αὐτὴν καὶ περὶ τεκτονικῆς καὶ πασῶν βαναύσων τιθέμενοι ψῆφον, ῥητορικὴν δὲ ἐπαινοῦσι μέν, ὑποπτεύουσι δὲ ὡς πανοῦργον καὶ φιλοχρήματον καὶ κατὰ τοῦ δικαίου ξυγκειμένην. γιγνώσκουσι δ' οὕτω περὶ τῆς τέχνης οὐχ οἱ πολλοὶ μόνον,[1] ἀλλὰ καὶ τῶν σπουδαίων οἱ ἐλλογιμώτατοι· καλοῦσι γοῦν δεινοὺς ῥήτορας τοὺς ἱκανῶς μὲν συνιέντας, ἱκανῶς δὲ ἑρμηνεύοντας, οὐκ εὔφημον ἐπωνυμίαν τιθέμενοι τῷ πλεονεκτήματι. τούτου δὲ φύσιν τοιαύτην ἔχοντος οὐκ ἀπεικὸς ἦν, οἶμαι, γενέσθαι καὶ τὸν Ἀντιφῶντα κωμῳδίας λόγον αὐτὰ μάλιστα κωμῳδούσης τὰ λόγου ἄξια.

Ἀπέθανε μὲν οὖν περὶ Σικελίαν ὑπὸ Διονυσίου τοῦ τυράννου, τὰς δ' αἰτίας, ἐφ' αἷς ἀπέθανεν, Ἀντιφῶντι μᾶλλον ἢ Διονυσίῳ προσγράφομεν· διε-
500 φαύλιζε γὰρ τὰς τοῦ Διονυσίου τραγῳδίας, ἐφ' αἷς ὁ Διονύσιος ἐφρόνει μεῖζον ἢ ἐπὶ τῷ τυραννεύειν, σπουδάζοντος δὲ τοῦ τυράννου περὶ εὐγενείας χαλκοῦ καὶ ἐρομένου τοὺς παρόντας, τίς ἤπειρος ἢ νῆσος, τὸν ἄριστον χαλκὸν φύει, παρατυχὼν ὁ Ἀντιφῶν τῷ λόγῳ "ἐγὼ ἄριστον" ἔφη "οἶδα τὸν Ἀθήνησιν, οὗ γεγόνασιν αἱ[2] Ἁρμοδίου καὶ Ἀριστογείτονος εἰκόνες." ἐπὶ μὲν δὴ τούτοις ἀπέθανεν, ὡς ὑφέρπων τὸν Διονύσιον καὶ τρέπων ἐπ' αὐτὸν τοὺς Σικελιώτας. ἥμαρτε δὲ ὁ Ἀντιφῶν πρῶτον

---

[1] μᾶλλον Kayser; μόνον Cobet.
[2] αἱ Cobet adds.

---

[1] Since the regular meaning of λόγου ἄξια is "noteworthy," perhaps Philostratus intended nothing but a compliment to Antiphon.

[2] Philostratus confuses the orator Antiphon with a poet of the same name, who is said by Plutarch, *On the Flatterer*, to have been put to death for his rash epigram. The

for carpentering and all the inferior trades they cast the same sort of vote; only in the case of rhetoric, even while they praise it they suspect it of being rascally and mercenary and constituted in despite of justice. And it is not only the crowd who so regard this art, but also the most distinguished among the men of sound culture. At any rate they apply the term "clever rhetorician" to those who show skill in the invention of themes and their exposition, thus attaching a far from flattering label to this particular excellence. Seeing that such conditions exist, it was, I think, not unnatural that Antiphon like the rest should become a theme for Comedy; for it is just the things which deserve to be a theme that Comedy makes fun of.[1]

He was put to death in Sicily by Dionysius the tyrant,[2] and I ascribe to Antiphon himself rather than to Dionysius the responsibility for his death. For he used to run down the tragedies of Dionysius, though Dionysius prided himself more on these than on his power as a tyrant; and once when the tyrant was interested in finding out where the best kind of bronze was produced, and asked the bystanders what continent or island produced the best bronze, Antiphon, who happened to be there, said "The best I know of is at Athens, of which the statues of Harmodius and Aristogeiton[3] have been made." The result of this behaviour was that he was put to death on the charge of plotting against Dionysius and turning the Sicilians against him. And Antiphon was in the wrong, in the first place,

Athenian orator was executed in 411 and the tyranny of Dionysius did not begin till about 404.

[3] Who overthrew the tyrants at Athens.

μὲν τυράννῳ προσκρούων, ὑφ' ᾧ ζῆν ᾔρητο μᾶλλον
ἢ οἴκοι δημοκρατεῖσθαι, ἔπειτα Σικελιώτας μὲν
ἐλευθερῶν, 'Αθηναίους δὲ δουλούμενος. καὶ μὴν
καὶ τοῦ τραγῳδίαν ποιεῖν ἀπάγων τὸν Διονύσιον
ἀπῆγεν αὐτὸν τοῦ ῥᾳθυμεῖν, αἱ γὰρ τοιαίδε σπουδαὶ
ῥᾴθυμοι, καὶ οἱ τύραννοι δὲ αἱρετώτεροι τοῖς
ἀρχομένοις ἀνιέμενοι [1] μᾶλλον ἢ ξυντείνοντες, εἰ γὰρ
ἀνήσουσιν, ἧττον μὲν ἀποκτενοῦσιν, ἧττον δὲ
βιάσονταί [2] τε καὶ ἁρπάσονται, τύραννος δὲ τραγῳ-
δίαις ἐπιτιθέμενος ἰατρῷ εἰκάσθω νοσοῦντι μέν,
ἑαυτὸν δὲ θεραπεύοντι· αἱ γὰρ μυθοποιίαι καὶ αἱ
μονῳδίαι καὶ οἱ ῥυθμοὶ τῶν χορῶν καὶ ἡ τῶν ἠθῶν
μίμησις, ὧν ἀνάγκη τὰ πλείω χρηστὰ φαίνεσθαι,
μετακαλεῖ [3] τοὺς τυράννους τοῦ ἀπαραιτήτου καὶ
σφοδροῦ, καθάπερ αἱ φαρμακοποσίαι τὰς νόσους.
ταῦτα μὴ κατηγορίαν 'Αντιφῶντος, ἀλλὰ ξυμβου-
λίαν ἐς πάντας ἡγώμεθα τοῦ μὴ ἐκκαλεῖσθαι τὰς
τυραννίδας, μηδὲ ἐς ὀργὴν ἄγειν ἤθη ὠμά.

Λόγοι δ' αὐτοῦ δικανικοὶ μὲν πλείους, ἐν οἷς
ἡ δεινότης καὶ πᾶν τὸ ἐκ τέχνης ἔγκειται, σοφισ-
τικοὶ δὲ καὶ ἕτεροι μέν, σοφιστικώτερος δὲ ὁ
ὑπὲρ τῆς ὁμονοίας, ἐν ᾧ γνωμολογίαι τε λαμπραὶ
καὶ φιλόσοφοι σεμνή τε ἀπαγγελία καὶ ἐπηνθισ-
μένη ποιητικοῖς ὀνόμασι καὶ τὰ ἀποτάδην ἑρμη-
νευόμενα παραπλήσια τῶν πεδίων τοῖς λείοις.

501 ιϛ'. Κριτίας δὲ ὁ σοφιστὴς εἰ μὲν κατέλυσε

---

[1] ἀνειμένοι Kayser; ἀνιέμενοι Richards.
[2] δράσονται mss., Kayser; δράξονται Jahn; βιάσονται Cobet;
cf. Plato, Republic, 574 в; διασπάσονται Richards.
[3] μεταβάλλει Kayser; μετακαλεῖ Cobet.

for provoking a collision with a tyrant under whom he had chosen to live rather than be under a democracy at home; secondly he was wrong in trying to free the Sicilians, whereas he had tried to enslave the Athenians. Furthermore, in diverting Dionysius from writing tragedy he really diverted him from being easy-going; for pursuits of that sort belong to an easy temper, and their subjects may well prefer tyrants when they are slack rather than when they are strung up. For when they slacken their energies they will put fewer men to death, they will do less violence and plunder less; so that a tyrant who occupies himself with tragedies may be likened to a physician who is sick, but is trying to heal himself. For the writing of myths and monodies and choric rhythms and the representation of characters, the greater part of which necessarily present what is morally good, diverts tyrants from their own implacable and violent temper as taking medicines diverts the course of disease. What I have just said we must not regard as an indictment of Antiphon, but rather as advice to all men not to provoke tyrants against themselves, or excite to wrath their savage dispositions.

A good many of his legal speeches are extant, and they show his great oratorical power and all the effects of art. Of the sophistic type there are several, but more sophistic than any is the speech *On Concord*, in which are brilliant philosophical maxims and a lofty style of eloquence, adorned moreover with the flowers of poetical vocabulary; and their diffuse style makes them seem like smooth plains.

16. CRITIAS the sophist, even though he did over-

τὸν 'Αθηναίων δῆμον, οὔπω κακός — καταλυθείη
γὰρ ἂν καὶ ὑφ' ἑαυτοῦ δῆμος οὕτω τι ἐπηρμένος,
ὡς μηδὲ τῶν κατὰ νόμους ἀρχόντων ἀκροᾶσθαι —
ἀλλ' ἐπεὶ λαμπρῶς μὲν ἐλακώνισε, προὐδίδου δὲ
τὰ ἱερά, καθῄρει δὲ διὰ Λυσάνδρου τὰ τείχη, οὓς
δ' ἤλαυνε τῶν 'Αθηναίων τὸ στῆναί ποι τῆς Ἑλλάδος ἀφῃρεῖτο πόλεμον Λακωνικὸν ἀνειπὼν ἐς
πάντας, εἴ τις τὸν 'Αθηναῖον φεύγοντα δέξοιτο,
ὠμότητι δὲ καὶ μιαιφονίᾳ τοὺς τριάκοντα ὑπερε-
βάλλετο βουλεύματός τε ἀτόπου τοῖς Λακεδαιμονίοις ξυνελάμβανεν, ὡς μηλόβοτος ἡ 'Αττικὴ
ἀποφανθείη τῆς τῶν ἀνθρώπων ἀγέλης ἐκκενω-
θεῖσα, κάκιστος ἀνθρώπων ἔμοιγε φαίνεται ξυμ-
πάντων, ὧν ἐπὶ κακίᾳ ὄνομα. καὶ εἰ μὲν ἀπαίδευτος ὢν ἐς τάδε ὑπήχθη, ἔρρωτο ἂν ὁ λόγος
τοῖς φάσκουσιν ὑπὸ Θετταλίας καὶ τῆς ἐκείνῃ
ὁμιλίας παρεφθορέναι αὐτόν, τὰ γὰρ ἀπαίδευτα
ἤθη εὐπαράγωγα πάντως ἐς βίου αἵρεσιν· ἐπεὶ
δὲ ἄριστα μὲν ἦν πεπαιδευμένος, γνώμας δὲ πλείστας ἑρμηνεύων, ἐς Δρωπίδην δ' ἀναφέρων, ὃς
μετὰ Σόλωνα 'Αθηναίοις ἦρξεν, οὐκ ἂν διαφύγοι
παρὰ τοῖς πολλοῖς αἰτίαν τὸ μὴ οὐ κακίᾳ φύσεως
ἁμαρτεῖν ταῦτα. καὶ γὰρ αὖ κἀκεῖνο ἄτοπον
Σωκράτει μὲν τῷ Σωφρονίσκου μὴ ὁμοιωθῆναι
αὐτόν, ᾧ πλεῖστα δὴ συνεφιλοσόφησε σοφωτάτῳ

---

[1] A favourite oratorical theme; cf. Thucydides iii. 58.

[2] For the disorder and licence of the Thessalians cf. Plato,
Crito 53 D, and the proverb "Thessalian forcible persuasion"
in Julian and Eunapius.

throw democratic government at Athens, was not thereby proved to be a bad man; for the democracy might well have been overthrown from within, since it had become so overbearing and insolent that it would not heed even those who governed according to the established laws. But seeing that he conspicuously sided with Sparta, and betrayed the holy places[1] to the enemy; that he pulled down the walls by the agency of Lysander; that he deprived the Athenians whom he drove into exile of any place of refuge in Greece by proclaiming that Sparta would wage war on any that should harbour an Athenian exile; that in brutality and bloodthirstiness he surpassed even the Thirty; that he shared in the monstrous design of Sparta to make Attica look like a mere pasture for sheep by emptying her of her human herd; for all this I hold him to be the greatest criminal of all who are notorious for crime. Now if he had been an uneducated man, led astray into these excesses, there would be some force in the explanation of those who assert that he was demoralized by Thessaly[2] and the society that he frequented there; for characters that lack education are easily led to choose any sort of life. But since he had been highly educated and frequently delivered himself of philosophical maxims, and his family dated back to Dropides who was archon at Athens next after Solon, he cannot be acquitted in the sight of most men of the charge that these crimes were due to his own natural wickedness. Then again it is a strange thing that he did not grow to be like Socrates, the son of Sophroniscus, with whom above all others he studied philosophy and who had the reputation of being the wisest and the most just

τε καὶ δικαιοτάτῳ τῶν ἐφ᾽ ἑαυτοῦ δόξαντι, Θετταλοῖς δ᾽ ὁμοιωθῆναι, παρ᾽ οἷς ἀγερωχία καὶ
ἄκρατος καὶ τυραννικὰ ἐν οἴνῳ σπουδάζεται.
ἀλλ᾽ ὅμως οὐδὲ Θετταλοὶ σοφίας ἠμέλουν, ἀλλ᾽
ἐγοργίαζον ἐν Θετταλίᾳ μικραὶ καὶ μείζους πό-
502 λεις ἐς Γοργίαν ὁρῶσαι τὸν Λεοντῖνον, μετέβαλον
δ᾽ ἂν καὶ ἐς τὸ κριτιάζειν, εἴ τινα τῆς ἑαυτοῦ
σοφίας ἐπίδειξιν ὁ Κριτίας παρ᾽ αὐτοῖς ἐποιεῖτο·
ὁ δὲ ἠμέλει μὲν τούτου, βαρυτέρας δ᾽ αὐτοῖς
ἐποίει τὰς ὀλιγαρχίας διαλεγόμενος τοῖς ἐκεῖ
δυνατοῖς καὶ καθαπτόμενος μὲν δημοκρατίας ἁ-
πάσης, διαβάλλων δ᾽ Ἀθηναίους, ὡς πλεῖστα ἀνθρώπων ἁμαρτάνοντας, ὥστε ἐνθυμουμένῳ ταῦτα
Κριτίας ἂν εἴη Θετταλοὺς διεφθορὼς μᾶλλον ἢ
Κριτίαν Θετταλοί.

Ἀπέθανε μὲν οὖν ὑπὸ τῶν ἀμφὶ Θρασύβουλον,
οἳ κατῆγον ἀπὸ Φυλῆς[1] τὸν δῆμον, δοκεῖ δ᾽ ἐνίοις
ἀνὴρ ἀγαθὸς γενέσθαι παρὰ τὴν τελευτήν, ἐπειδὴ
ἐνταφίῳ τῇ τυραννίδι ἐχρήσατο· ἐμοὶ δὲ ἀποπεφάνθω μηδένα ἀνθρώπων καλῶς δὴ ἀποθανεῖν
ὑπὲρ ὧν οὐκ ὀρθῶς εἵλετο, δι᾽ ἅ μοι δοκεῖ καὶ ἡ
σοφία τοῦ ἀνδρὸς καὶ τὰ φροντίσματα ἧττον
σπουδασθῆναι τοῖς Ἕλλησιν· εἰ γὰρ μὴ ὁμολο-
γήσει ὁ λόγος τῷ ἤθει, ἀλλοτρίᾳ τῇ γλώττῃ δό-
ξομεν φθέγγεσθαι, ὥσπερ οἱ αὐλοί.

Τὴν δὲ ἰδέαν τοῦ λόγου δογματίας ὁ Κριτίας
καὶ πολυγνώμων σεμνολογῆσαί τε ἱκανώτατος οὐ

---

[1] φυγῆς Kayser ; Φυλῆς Bentley, Cobet.

---

[1] *i.e.* he lost his life in its cause. For this favourite figure
cf. p. 590 and *Gymnasticus* 34 ; it is derived from Isocrates,
Archidamus 45.

[2] An echo of Aeschines, *Against Ctesiphon* 623 ; *cf.*

of his times; but did grow to be like the Thessalians, who maintain by force an insolent arrogance, and practise tyrannical customs even in their wine-drinking. However, not even the Thessalians neglected learning, but all the cities great and small in Thessaly tried to write like Gorgias and looked to Gorgias of Leontini; and they would have changed over and tried to write like Critias, if Critias had made any public display in their country of his own peculiar skill. But for this kind of success he cared nothing, and instead he tried to make the oligarchies more oppressive to the people, by conversing with the men in power there and assailing all popular government, and by falsely accusing the Athenians of an unheard of number of crimes; so that, taking all this into consideration, it would seem that Critias corrupted the Thessalians, rather than the Thessalians Critias.

He was put to death by Thrasybulus and his party who restored the democracy from Phyle, and there are those who think that he played an honourable part at the last, because his tyranny became his shroud.[1] But let me declare my opinion that no human being can be said to have died nobly for a cause that he took up in defiance of the right. And I believe that this is the reason why this man's wisdom and his writings are held in slight esteem by the Greeks; for unless our public utterances and our moral character are in accord, we shall seem, like flutes, to speak with a tongue that is not our own.[2]

As regards the style of his oratory, Critias abounded in brief and sententious sayings, and he

[1] *Corinthians*, xiii. 1 ; " I am become as sounding brass or a tinkling cymbal."

49

τὴν διθυραμβώδη σεμνολογίαν, οὐδὲ καταφεύγου-
σαν ἐς τὰ ἐκ ποιητικῆς ὀνόματα, ἀλλ' ἐκ τῶν
503 κυριωτάτων συγκειμένην καὶ κατὰ φύσιν ἔχουσαν. ὁρῶ τὸν ἄνδρα καὶ βραχυλογοῦντα ἱκανῶς
καὶ δεινῶς καθαπτόμενον ἐν ἀπολογίας ἤθει, ἀτ-
τικίζοντά τε οὐκ ἀκράτως, οὐδὲ ἐκφύλως — τὸ
γὰρ ἀπειρόκαλον ἐν τῷ ἀττικίζειν βάρβαρον —
ἀλλ' ὥσπερ ἀκτίνων αὐγαὶ τὰ Ἀττικὰ ὀνόματα
διαφαίνεται τοῦ λόγου. καὶ τὸ ἀσυνδέτως δὲ
χωρίῳ προσβαλεῖν Κριτίου ὥρα, καὶ τὸ παραδόξως μὲν ἐνθυμηθῆναι, παραδόξως δ' ἀπαγγεῖ-
λαι Κριτίου ἀγών, τὸ δὲ τοῦ λόγου πνεῦμα ἐλ-
λιπέστερον μέν, ἡδὺ δὲ καὶ λεῖον, ὥσπερ τοῦ
Ζεφύρου ἡ αὔρα.

ιζ'. Ἡ δὲ Σειρὴν ἡ ἐφεστηκυῖα τῷ Ἰσοκράτους τοῦ σοφιστοῦ σήματι, ἐφέστηκε δὲ καὶ οἷον
ᾄδουσα, πειθὼ κατηγορεῖ τοῦ ἀνδρός, ἣν συνε-
βάλετο ῥητορικοῖς νόμοις καὶ ἤθεσι, πάρισα καὶ
ἀντίθετα καὶ ὁμοιοτέλευτα οὐχ εὑρὼν πρῶτος,
ἀλλ' εὑρημένοις εὖ χρησάμενος, ἐπεμελήθη δὲ καὶ
περιβολῆς καὶ ῥυθμοῦ καὶ συνθήκης καὶ κρότου.
ταυτὶ δ' ἡτοίμασέ που καὶ τὴν Δημοσθένους
504 γλῶτταν· Δημοσθένης γὰρ μαθητὴς μὲν Ἰσαίου,
ζηλωτὴς δὲ Ἰσοκράτους γενόμενος ὑπερεβάλετο
αὐτὸν θυμῷ καὶ ἐπιφορᾷ καὶ περιβολῇ καὶ ταχυ-

---

[1] Lucian, *Lexiphanes* 24, satirizes the hyperatticism which
consists in using obsolete or rare words ; on the Atticism of
the Sophists see Introduction.

[2] On the invention of προσβολαί by Gorgias see Glossary.

[3] For περιβολή see Glossary.

was most skilful in the use of elevated language, but not of the dithyrambic sort, nor did he have recourse to words borrowed from poetry; but his was the kind of elevated language that is composed of the most appropriate words and is not artificial. I observe, moreover, that he was a master of concise eloquence, and that even when he maintained the tone proper to a speech in defence, he used to make vigorous attacks on his opponent; and that he Atticized, but in moderation, nor did he use outlandish words[1]—for bad taste in Atticizing is truly barbarous—but his Attic words shine through his discourse like the gleams of the sun's rays. Critias also secures a charming effect by passing without connectives from one part of his speech to another.[2] Then, too, Critias strives for the daring and unusual both in thought and expression, yet his eloquence is somewhat lacking in virility, though it is agreeable and smooth, like the breath of the west wind.

17. The Siren which stands on the tomb of Isocrates the sophist—its pose is that of one singing —testifies to the man's persuasive charm, which he combined with the conventions and customs of rhetoric. For though he was not the inventor of clauses that exactly balance, antitheses, and similar endings, since they had already been invented, nevertheless he employed those devices with great skill. He also paid great attention to rhetorical amplification,[3] rhythm, structure, and a striking effect, and in fact it was by his study of these very things that Demosthenes achieved his eloquence. For though Demosthenes was a pupil of Isaeus, it was on Isocrates that he modelled himself, but he surpassed him in fire and impetuosity, in amplification,

τῆτι λόγου τε καὶ ἐννοίας. σεμνότης δ᾽ ἡ μὲν
Δημοσθένους ἐπεστραμμένη μᾶλλον, ἡ δὲ Ἰσοκράτους ἁβροτέρα τε καὶ ἡδίων. παράδειγμα δὲ
ποιώμεθα τῆς Δημοσθένους σεμνότητος· " πέ-
ρας μὲν γὰρ ἅπασιν ἀνθρώποις ἐστὶ τοῦ βίου
θάνατος, κἂν ἐν οἰκίσκῳ τις αὐτὸν καθείρξας
τηρῇ, δεῖ δὲ τοὺς ἀγαθοὺς ἄνδρας ἐγχειρεῖν μὲν
ἅπασιν ἀεὶ τοῖς καλοῖς τὴν ἀγαθὴν προβαλλομέ-
νους ἐλπίδα, φέρειν δέ, ἃ ἂν ὁ θεὸς διδῷ, γενναίως." ἡ δὲ Ἰσοκράτους σεμνότης ὧδε κεκό-
σμηται· " τῆς γὰρ γῆς ἁπάσης τῆς ὑπὸ τῷ κόσμῳ κειμένης δίχα τετμημένης, καὶ τῆς μὲν
Ἀσίας, τῆς δὲ Εὐρώπης καλουμένης, τὴν ἡμί-
σειαν ἐκ τῶν συνθηκῶν εἴληφεν, ὥσπερ πρὸς
τὸν Δία τὴν χώραν νεμόμενος."

505   Τὰ μὲν οὖν πολιτικὰ ὤκνει καὶ ἀπεφοίτα τῶν
ἐκκλησιῶν διά τε τὸ ἐλλιπὲς τοῦ φθέγματος, διά
τε τὸν Ἀθήνησιν φθόνον ἀντιπολιτευόμενον αὐτοῖς μάλιστα τοῖς σοφώτερόν τι ἑτέρου ἀγο-
ρεύουσιν. ὅμως δ᾽ οὐκ ἀπεσπούδαζε τῶν κοινῶν·
τόν τε γὰρ Φίλιππον, ἐν οἷς πρὸς αὐτὸν ἔγραφεν,
Ἀθηναίοις δήπου διωρθοῦτο, καὶ οἷς περὶ τῆς
εἰρήνης συνέγραφεν, ἀνεσκεύαζε τοὺς Ἀθηναίους
τῆς θαλάττης, ὡς κακῶς ἐν αὐτῇ ἀκούοντας,
πανηγυρικός τ᾽ ἐστὶν αὐτῷ λόγος, ὃν διῆλθεν
Ὀλυμπίασι τὴν Ἑλλάδα πείθων ἐπὶ τὴν Ἀσίαν
στρατεύειν παυσαμένους τῶν οἴκοι ἐγκλημάτων.
οὗτος ὶ ἐν οὖν εἰ καὶ κάλλιστος λόγων, αἰτίαν

---

[1] On the Crown 97. This is a favourite passage with the
rhetoricians; cf. Lucian, Encomium of Demosthenes 5;
Hermogenes, On the Types of Oratory 222 Walz.
[2] Panegyricus 179. Note the "similar endings" of the
participles.

and in rapidity both of speech and thought. Again, the grand style in Demosthenes is more vigorous, while in Isocrates it is more refined and suave. Let me give a specimen of the grand style of Demosthenes : " For to all mankind the end of life is death, though a man keep himself shut up in a closet ; yet it is the duty of brave men ever to set their hands to all honourable tasks, setting their good hope before them as their shield, and endure nobly whatever comes from the hand of God." [1] With Isocrates on the other hand, the grand style is ornate, as in the following : " For since the whole earth that lies beneath the heavens is divided into two parts, and one is called Asia, the other Europe, he has received by the treaty one half thereof, as though he were dividing the territory with Zeus." [2]

He shrank from political life and did not attend political assemblies, partly because his voice was not strong enough, partly because of the jealous distrust that in politics at Athens was always especially opposed to those who had a talent above the average for public speaking.[3] Yet in spite of this he took a strong interest in public affairs. Hence in the letters that he addressed to Philip he tried to reconcile him with the Athenians ; in his writings on peace he tried to wean the Athenians from their maritime policy, on the ground that they thereby injured their reputation ; and there is also his *Panegyric* which he delivered at Olympia, when he tried to persuade Greece to cease from domestic quarrels and make war on Asia. This oration, though it is the finest of all, nevertheless gave rise to the charge that it had

[3] For this *cf.* Thucydides iii. 38, Cleon's attack on plausible orators.

ὅμως παρέδωκεν, ὡς ἐκ τῶν Γοργίᾳ σπουδασθέντων ἐς τὴν αὐτὴν ὑπόθεσιν συντεθείη. ἄριστα
δὲ τῶν Ἰσοκράτους φροντισμάτων ὅ τε Ἀρχίδαμος
ξύγκειται καὶ ὁ Ἀμάρτυρος, τοῦ μὲν γὰρ διήκει
φρόνημα τῶν Λευκτρικῶν ἀναφέρον καὶ οὐκ ἀκριβῆ
μόνον τὰ ὀνόματα, ἀλλὰ καὶ ἡ ξυνθήκη λαμπρά,
ἐναγώνιος δὲ ὁ λόγος, ὡς καὶ τὸ μυθῶδες αὐτοῦ
μέρος, τὸ περὶ τὸν Ἡρακλέα καὶ τὰς βοῦς σὺν
ἐπιστροφῇ ἑρμηνεῦσθαι, ὁ δὲ Ἀμάρτυρος ἰσχὺν
ἐνδείκνυται κεκολασμένην ἐς ῥυθμούς, νόημα γὰρ
ἐκ νοήματος ἐς περιόδους ἰσοκώλους τελευτᾷ.

506 Ἀκροαταὶ τοῦ ἀνδρὸς τούτου πολλοὶ μέν, ἐλλογιμώτατος δὲ Ὑπερείδης ὁ ῥήτωρ, Θεόπομπον
γὰρ τὸν ἐκ τῆς Χίου καὶ τὸν Κυμαῖον Ἔφορον
οὔτ' ἂν διαβάλοιμι οὔτ' ἂν θαυμάσαιμι. οἱ δὲ
ἡγούμενοι τὴν κωμῳδίαν καθάπτεσθαι τοῦ ἀνδρός, ὡς αὐλοποιοῦ, ἁμαρτάνουσιν, πατὴρ μὲν γὰρ
αὐτῷ Θεόδωρος ἦν, ὃν ἐκάλουν αὐλοποιὸν Ἀθήνησιν, αὐτὸς δὲ οὔτε αὐλοὺς ἐγίγνωσκεν οὔτε
ἄλλο τι τῶν ἐν βαναυσίοις, οὐδὲ γὰρ ἂν οὐδὲ τῆς
ἐν Ὀλυμπίᾳ εἰκόνος ἔτυχεν, εἴ τι τῶν εὐτελῶν
εἰργάζετο. ἀπέθανε μὲν οὖν Ἀθήνησιν ἀμφὶ τὰ
ἑκατὸν ἔτη, ἕνα δὲ αὐτὸν ἡγώμεθα τῶν ἐν πολέμῳ
ἀποθανόντων, ἐπειδὴ μετὰ Χαιρώνειαν ἐτελεύτα
μὴ καρτερήσας τὴν ἀκρόασιν τοῦ Ἀθηναίων
πταίσματος.

---

[1] This is the sub-title of the speech *Against Euthynous*,
and was so called because the plaintiff had no evidence to
produce and depended on logical argument.

[2] Heracles carried off the oxen of Geryon.

[3] These minor historians were fellow-pupils in the school
which Isocrates opened at Chios.

been compiled from the works of Gorgias on the same subject. The most skilfully composed of all the works of Isocrates are the *Archidamus* and the speech called *Without Witnesses*.[1] For the former is animated throughout by the desire to revive men's courage and spirit after the defeat at Leuctra, and not only is its language exquisitely chosen, but its composition is brilliant also, and the whole speech is in the style of a legal argument; so that even the myth in it, the story of Heracles and the oxen,[2] is expressed with vigour and energy. Again, the speech *Without Witnesses* in its rhythms displays a well-restrained energy, for it is composed of periods of equal length, as one idea follows another.

Isocrates had many pupils, but the most illustrious was the orator Hypereides; for as for Theopompus of Chios and Ephorus[3] of Cumae, I will neither criticize nor commend them. Those who think that Comedy aimed her shafts at Isocrates because he was a maker of flutes,[4] are mistaken; for though his father was Theodorus, who was known in Athens as a flute-maker, Isocrates himself knew nothing about flute-making or any other sordid trade; and he certainly would not have been honoured with the statue at Olympia if he had ever been employed in any low occupation. He died at Athens, aged about one hundred years, and we must reckon him among those who perished in war, seeing that he died after the battle of Chaeronea because he could not support the tidings of the Athenian defeat.[5]

[4] Strattis, *frag.* 712 Kock, refers to Isocrates as "the flute-borer"; *cf.* pseudo-Plutarch, *Isocrates* 836 E.

[5] *cf.* Milton, Sonnet—

As that dishonest victory,
At Chaeronea, fatal to liberty,
Killed with report that old man eloquent.

507 ιη΄. Περὶ δὲ Αἰσχίνου τοῦ ᾿Ατρομήτου, ὃν
φαμεν τῆς δευτέρας σοφιστικῆς ἄρξαι, τάδε χρὴ
ἐπεσκέφθαι· ἡ ᾿Αθήνησι δημαγωγία διειστήκει
πᾶσα, καὶ οἱ μὲν βασιλεῖ ἐπιτήδειοι ἦσαν, οἱ
δὲ Μακεδόσιν, ἐφέροντο δὲ ἄρα τὴν πρώτην τῶν
μὲν βασιλεῖ χαριζομένων ὁ Παιανιεὺς Δημοσθένης, τῶν δὲ ἐς Φίλιππον ὁρώντων ὁ Κοθωκίδης
Αἰσχίνης, καὶ χρήματα παρ᾿ ἀμφοῖν ἐφοίτα σφίσι,
βασιλέως μὲν ἀσχολοῦντος δι᾿ ᾿Αθηναίων Φίλιππον τὸ μὴ ἐπὶ ᾿Ασίαν ἐλάσαι, Φιλίππου δὲ πειρω-
μένου διαλύειν τὴν ἰσχὺν ᾿Αθηναίων, ὡς ἐμπόδισμα
τῆς διαβάσεως.

Διαφορᾶς δ᾿ ἦρξεν Αἰσχίνῃ καὶ Δημοσθένει καὶ
αὐτὸ μὲν τὸ ἄλλον ἄλλῳ βασιλεῖ πολιτεύειν, ὡς
δ᾿ ἐμοὶ φαίνεται, τὸ ἐναντίως ἔχειν καὶ τῶν ἠθῶν,
ἐξ ἠθῶν γὰρ ἀλλήλοις ἀντιξόων φύεται μῖσος
αἰτίαν οὐκ ἔχον. ἀντιξόω δ᾿ ἤστην καὶ διὰ τάδε·
ὁ μὲν Αἰσχίνης φιλοπότης τε ἐδόκει καὶ ἡδὺς καὶ
ἀνειμένος καὶ πᾶν τὸ ἐπίχαρι ἐκ Διονύσου ᾐρη-
κώς, καὶ γὰρ δὴ καὶ τοῖς βαρυστόνοις ὑποκρι-
ταῖς τὸν ἐν μειρακίῳ χρόνον ὑπετραγῴδησεν, ὁ δ᾿
508 αὖ συννενοφώς τε ἐφαίνετο καὶ βαρὺς τὴν ὀφρὺν
καὶ ὕδωρ πίνων, ὅθεν δυσκόλοις τε καὶ δυσ-
τρόποις ἐνεγράφετο, καὶ πολλῷ πλέον, ἐπειδὴ
πρεσβεύοντε ξὺν ἑτέροις παρὰ τὸν Φίλιππον καὶ

---

[1] Demosthenes, *On the Crown* 262 ; Aeschines was only a
tritagonist.

LIVES OF THE SOPHISTS

18. AESCHINES, the son of Atrometus, we are accustomed to call the founder of the Second Sophistic, and with respect to him the following facts must be borne in mind. The whole government at Athens was divided into two parties, of which one was friendly to the Persian king, the other to the Macedonians. Now among those who favoured the Persian king, Demosthenes of the deme Paeania was the recognized leader, while Aeschines of the deme Kothokidai led those who looked to Philip; and sums of money used to arrive regularly from both these, from the king because with the aid of Athenians he kept Philip too busy to invade Asia; and from Philip in the attempt to destroy the power of Athens which hindered him from crossing over into Asia.

The quarrel between Aeschines and Demosthenes arose partly because of this very fact that the former was working in the interests of one king and the latter in the interests of another; but also, in my opinion, because they were of wholly opposite temperaments. For between temperaments that are antagonistic to one another there grows up a hatred that has no other grounds. And naturally antagonistic the two men were, for the following reasons. Aeschines was a lover of wine, had agreeable and easy manners, and was endowed with all the charm of a follower of Dionysus; and in fact while he was still a mere boy, he actually played minor parts for ranting tragic actors.[1] Demosthenes, on the other hand, had a gloomy expression and an austere brow, and was a water-drinker; hence he was reckoned an ill-tempered and unsociable person, and especially so when the two men along with others went on an embassy to Philip, and as messmates the one showed

PHILOSTRATUS

ὁμοδιαίτω ὄντε ὁ μὲν διακεχυμένος τε καὶ ἡδὺς
ἐφαίνετο τοῖς συμπρέσβεσιν, ὁ δὲ κατεσκληκώς
τε καὶ ἀεὶ σπουδάζων. ἐπέτεινε δὲ αὐτοῖς τὴν
διαφορὰν ὁ ὑπὲρ ᾿Αμφιπόλεως ἐπὶ τοῦ Φιλίππου
λόγος, ὅτε δὴ ἐξέπεσε τοῦ λόγου ὁ Δημοσθένης,
ὁ δ᾿ Αἰσχίνης . . . οὐδὲ τῶν ἀποβεβλημένων ποτὲ
τὴν ἀσπίδα ἐνθυμουμένῳ τὸ ἐν Ταμύναις ἔργον,[1] ἐν
ᾧ Βοιωτοὺς ἐνίκων ᾿Αθηναῖοι· ἀριστεῖα τούτου
δημοσίᾳ ἐστεφανοῦτο τά τε ἄλλα καὶ χρησάμενος
ἀμηχάνῳ τάχει περὶ τὰ εὐαγγέλια τῆς νίκης. διαβάλλοντος δὲ αὐτὸν Δημοσθένους, ὡς αἴτιον τοῦ
Φωκικοῦ πάθους, ἀπέγνωσαν ᾿Αθηναῖοι τὴν αἰτίαν, ἐπὶ δὲ τῷ καταψηφισθέντι ᾿Αντιφῶντι ἥλω
μὴ κριθείς, καὶ ἀφείλοντο αὐτὸν οἱ ἐξ ᾿Αρείου
πάγου τὸ μὴ οὐ συνειπεῖν σφισιν ὑπὲρ τοῦ ἱεροῦ
τοῦ ἐν Δήλῳ. καὶ μὴν καὶ πυλαγόρας ἀναρρηθεὶς οὔπω παρὰ τοῖς πολλοῖς διαπέφευγε τὸ μὴ
509 οὐκ αὐτὸς ᾿Ελατείᾳ ἐπιστῆσαι τὸν Φίλιππον τὴν
Πυλαίαν συνταράξας εὐπροσώποις λόγοις καὶ
μύθοις. ᾿Αθηνῶν δὲ ὑπεξῆλθεν οὐχὶ φεύγειν προσ-
ταχθείς, ἀλλ᾿ ἀτιμίᾳ ἐξιστάμενος, ᾗ ὑπήγετο

[1] Some words have dropped out which confuses the
construction though the meaning is clear.

[1] The incident is described by Aeschines, *On the False
Embassy* 34.
[2] The text is corrupt and the meaning is not clear.
[3] The Athenian general Phocion won the battle of
Tamynae in Euboea in 354 in an attempt to recover the
cities which had revolted from Athens; *cf.* Aeschines, *On
the False Embassy* 169.
[4] Demosthenes, *On the Crown* 142; Demosthenes, *On the
False Embassy* throughout makes Aeschines responsible for
the crushing defeat of the Phocians by Philip when he seized

58

himself pliant and amiable to his fellow-ambassadors, while the other was stiff and dry and took everything too seriously. And their quarrel was intensified by the discussions about Amphipolis in Philip's presence, when Demosthenes broke down in his speech [1]; but Aeschines . . . [2] was not one of those who ever throw away the shield, as is evident when one considers the battle of Tamynae,[3] when the Athenians defeated the Boeotians. As a reward for his part in this he was crowned by the state, both for his conduct in general and because he had conveyed the good news of the victory with extraordinary speed. When Demosthenes accused him of being responsible for the Phocian disaster,[4] the Athenians acquitted him of the charge, but just as Antiphon had been condemned Aeschines was found guilty without a trial, and the court of the Areopagus deprived him of the right to join them in pleading for the temple on Delos.[5] And after he had been nominated as a deputy to Pylae [6] he did not escape suspicion from most men of having himself prompted Philip to seize Elatea, by his action in stirring up the synod at Pylae with his specious words and fables.[7] He secretly left Athens, not because he had been ordered to go into exile, but in order to avoid the political disgrace which he had incurred when he failed to secure the necessary votes in his

Delphi in 346. Aeschines had assured the Athenians that Philip would not deal harshly with the Phocians.

[5] The Athenians were defending their right to control the sanctuary of Apollo on Delos.

[6] *On the Crown* 149. This was in 346.

[7] Demosthenes, *On the Crown* 143, brings this charge; Philostratus borrows freely from this speech in his account of the political life of Aeschines.

ὑπὸ Δημοσθένει καὶ Κτησιφῶντι ἐκπεσὼν τῶν
ψήφων. ἡ μὲν δὴ ὁρμὴ τῆς ἀποδημίας αὐτῷ
παρὰ τὸν Ἀλέξανδρον ἦν, ὡς αὐτίκα ἥξοντα ἐς
Βαβυλῶνά τε καὶ Σοῦσα, καθορμισθεὶς δὲ ἐς τὴν
Ἔφεσον καὶ τὸν μὲν τεθνάναι ἀκούων, τὰ δὲ τῆς
Ἀσίας οὕτω ξυγκεκλυσμένα πράγματα, Ῥόδου
εἴχετο, ἡ δὲ νῆσος ἀγαθὴ ἐνσπουδάσαι, καὶ σοφιστῶν φροντιστήριον ἀποφήνας τὴν Ῥόδον αὐτοῦ διῃτᾶτο θύων ἡσυχίᾳ τε καὶ Μούσαις καὶ
Δωρίοις ἤθεσιν ἐγκαταμιγνὺς Ἀττικά.

Τὸν δὲ αὐτοσχέδιον λόγον ξὺν εὐροίᾳ καὶ θείως
διατιθέμενος τὸν ἔπαινον τοῦτον πρῶτος ἠνέγ-
κατο. τὸ γὰρ θείως λέγειν οὔπω μὲν ἐπεχω-
ρίασε σοφιστῶν σπουδαῖς, ἀπ' Αἰσχίνου δ' ἤρξατο
θεοφορήτῳ ὁρμῇ ἀποσχεδιάζοντος, ὥσπερ οἱ τοὺς
χρησμοὺς ἀναπνέοντες. ἀκροατὴς δὲ Πλάτωνός
τε καὶ Ἰσοκράτους γενόμενος πολλὰ καὶ παρὰ
510 τῆς ἑαυτοῦ φύσεως ἠγάγετο. σαφηνείας τε γὰρ
φῶς ἐν τῷ λόγῳ καὶ ἁβρὰ σεμνολογία καὶ τὸ
ἐπίχαρι σὺν δεινότητι καὶ καθάπαξ ἡ ἰδέα τοῦ
λόγου κρείττων ἢ μιμήσει ὑπαχθῆναι.

Λόγοι δ' Αἰσχίνου γ'[1] κατ' ἐνίους μὲν καὶ τέ-
ταρτός τις Δηλιακὸς καταψευδόμενος τῆς ἐκείνου
γλώττης. οὐ γὰρ ἄν ποτε τοὺς μὲν περὶ τὴν
Ἄμφισσαν λόγους, ὑφ' ὧν ἡ Κιρραία χώρα καθιε-
ρώθη, εὐπροσώπως τε καὶ ξὺν ὥρᾳ διέθετο κακὰ

[1] γ' Richards inserts.

[1] Philostratus ignores the fact that seven years elapsed between the departure of Aeschines from Athens in 330 and the death of Alexander in 323.
[2] This may be an echo of Longinus, *On the Sublime* xiii. 2.
[3] This is not true.
[4] An allusion to Aeschines, *Against Ctesiphon* 119 foll.,

suit against Demosthenes and Ctesiphon. It was his purpose, when he set out on his journey, to go to Alexander, since the latter was on the point of arriving at Babylon and Susa. But when he touched at Ephesus he learned that Alexander was dead,[1] and that therefore things were greatly disturbed in Asia, so he took up his abode at Rhodes, for the island is well adapted to literary pursuits, and having transformed Rhodes into a Reflectory for sophists, he continued to live there, sacrificing to peace and the Muses, and introducing Attic customs into the Dorian mode of life.

As an extempore speaker he was easy and fluent and employed the inspired manner, in fact he was the first to win applause by this means. For hitherto the inspired manner in oratory had not become a regular device of the sophists, but it dates from Aeschines, who extemporized as though he were carried away by a divine impulse, like one who exhales oracles.[2] He was a pupil of Plato,[3] and Isocrates, but his success was due in great part to natural talent. For in his orations shines the light of perfect lucidity, he is at once sublime and seductive, energetic and delightful, and in a word his sort of eloquence defies the efforts of those who would imitate it.

There are three orations of Aeschines; but some ascribe to him a fourth besides, On Delos, though it does no credit to his eloquence. Nor is it at all likely that after having composed so plausibly and with such charm those speeches about Amphissa, the people by whom the plain of Cirrha was consecrated to the god,[4] when his design was to injure Athens,

where he quotes his accusation against Amphissa, made in 340.

PHILOSTRATUS

βουλεύων 'Αθηναίοις, ὥς φησι Δημοσθένης, ἐπὶ
δὲ τοὺς Δηλιακοὺς μύθους, ἐν οἷς θεολογία τε
καὶ θεογονία καὶ ἀρχαιολογία, φαύλως οὕτως
ὥρμησε καὶ τοῦτο προαγωνιζόμενος 'Αθηναίων
οὐ μικρὸν ἀγώνισμα ἡγουμένων τὸ μὴ ἐκπεσεῖν
τοῦ ἐν Δήλῳ ἱεροῦ. τρισὶ δὴ λόγοις περιωρίσθω
ἡ Αἰσχίνου γλῶττα· τῷ τε κατὰ Τιμάρχου καὶ
τῇ ἀπολογίᾳ τῆς πρεσβείας καὶ τῇ τοῦ Κτησιφῶντος κατηγορίᾳ. ἔστι δὲ καὶ τέταρτον αὐτοῦ
φρόντισμα, ἐπιστολαί, οὐ πολλαὶ μέν, εὐπαιδευ-
σίας δὲ μεσταὶ καὶ ἤθους. τοῦ δὲ ἠθικοῦ καὶ
'Ροδίοις ἐπίδειξιν ἐποιήσατο· ἀναγνοὺς γάρ ποτε
δημοσίᾳ τὸν κατὰ Κτησιφῶντος οἱ μὲν ἐθαύμαζον,
ὅπως ἐπὶ τοιούτῳ λόγῳ ἡττήθη καὶ καθήπτοντο
τῶν 'Αθηναίων ὡς παρανοούντων, ὁ δὲ " οὐκ ἂν "
ἔφη " ἐθαυμάζετε, εἰ Δημοσθένους λέγοντος πρὸς
ταῦτα ἠκούσατε," οὐ μόνον ἐς ἔπαινον ἐχθροῦ καθιστάμενος, ἀλλὰ καὶ τοὺς δικαστὰς ἀφιεὶς αἰτίας.

ιθ'. Ὑπερβάντες δ' 'Αριοβαρζάνην τὸν Κίλικα
511 καὶ Ξενόφρονα τὸν Σικελιώτην καὶ Πειθαγόραν τὸν
ἐκ Κυρήνης, οἳ μήτε γνῶναι ἱκανοὶ ἔδοξαν, μήθ'
ἑρμηνεῦσαι τὰ γνωσθέντα, ἀλλ' ἀπορίᾳ γενναίων
σοφιστῶν ἐσπουδάσθησαν τοῖς ἐφ' ἑαυτῶν Ἕλλησιν, ὅν που τρόπον τοῖς σίτου ἀπορῦσιν οἱ ὄροβοι,
ἐπὶ Νικήτην ἴωμεν τὸν Σμυρναῖον. οὗτος γὰρ ὁ
Νικήτης παραλαβὼν τὴν ἐπιστήμην ἐς στενὸν ἀπει-
λημμένην ἔδωκεν αὐτῇ παρόδους πολλῷ λαμπρο-
τέρας ὧν αὐτὸς τῇ Σμύρνῃ ἐδείματο, συνάψας τὴν

---

[1] These are not extant.
[2] Libanius, *Oration* i. 8, says that in his education he had
to put up with inferior sophists, *as men eat bread made of
barley for lack of a better sort.*

62

as Demosthenes says, he would have handled so un-
skilfully the myths about Delos, which are concerned
with the nature and descent of the gods and the
story of bygone times, and that too when he was
arguing the case of the Athenians, who considered
it of the utmost importance not to fail to maintain
the custody of the temple at Delos. Accordingly we
must limit the eloquence of Aeschines to three
orations, which are: *Against Timarchus, In Defence
of the Embassy,* and the speech *Against Ctesiphon.*
There is also extant a fourth work of his, the
Letters,[1] which, though they are few, are full of
learning and character. What that character was
he clearly showed at Rhodes. For once after he
had read in public his speech *Against Ctesiphon,* they
were expressing their surprise that he had been
defeated after so able a speech, and were criticizing
the Athenians as out of their senses, but Aeschines
said: "You would not marvel thus if you had heard
Demosthenes in reply to these arguments." Thus
he not only praised his enemy but also acquitted the
jury from blame.

19. We will pass over Ariobarzanes of Cilicia,
Xenophron of Sicily, and Peithagoras of Cyrene, who
showed no skill either in invention or in the expression of their ideas, though in the scarcity of first-rate
sophists they were sought after by the Greeks of
their day, as men seek after pulse when they are short
of corn;[2] and we will proceed to NICETES of Smyrna.
For this Nicetes found the science of oratory reduced
to great straits, and he bestowed on it approaches
far more splendid even than those which he himself
built for Smyrna, when he connected the city with

πόλιν ταῖς ἐπὶ τὴν Ἔφεσον πύλαις καὶ διὰ μέγεθος
ἀντεξάρας λόγοις ἔργα. ὁ δὲ ἀνὴρ οὗτος τοῖς μὲν
δικανικοῖς ἀμείνων ἐδόκει τὰ δικανικά, τοῖς δὲ
σοφιστικοῖς τὰ σοφιστικὰ ὑπὸ τοῦ περιδεξίως τε
καὶ πρὸς ἅμιλλαν ἐς ἄμφω ἡρμόσθαι. τὸ μὲν γὰρ
δικανικὸν σοφιστικῇ περιβολῇ ἐκόσμησεν, τὸ δὲ
σοφιστικὸν κέντρῳ δικανικῷ ἐπέρρωσεν. ἡ δὲ
ἰδέα τῶν λόγων τοῦ μὲν ἀρχαίου καὶ πολιτικοῦ
ἀποβέβηκεν, ὑπόβακχος δὲ καὶ διθυραμβώδης, τὰς
δ᾽ ἐννοίας ἰδίας τε καὶ παραδόξους ἐκδίδωσιν,
ὥσπερ "οἱ βακχεῖοι θύρσοι" τὸ μέλι καὶ "τοὺς
ἐσμοὺς τοῦ γάλακτος."

Μεγάλων δ᾽ ἀξιούμενος τῆς Σμύρνης τί οὐκ ἐπ᾽
αὐτῷ βοώσης ὡς ἐπ᾽ ἀνδρὶ θαυμασίῳ καὶ ῥήτορι,
οὐκ ἐθάμιζεν ἐς τὸν δῆμον, ἀλλ᾽ αἰτίαν παρὰ τοῖς
πολλοῖς ἔχων φόβου "φοβοῦμαι" ἔφη "δῆμον
ἐπαίροντα μᾶλλον ἢ λοιδορούμενον." τελώνου δὲ
θρασυναμένου ποτὲ πρὸς αὐτὸν ἐν δικαστηρίῳ καὶ
εἰπόντος "παῦσαι ὑλακτῶν με" μάλα ἀστείως ὁ
Νικήτης "νὴ Δία," εἶπεν "ἢν καὶ σὺ παύσῃ
δάκνων με."

512 Ἡ δὲ ὑπὲρ Ἄλπεις τε καὶ Ῥῆνον ἀποδημία τοῦ
ἀνδρὸς ἐγένετο μὲν ἐκ βασιλείου προστάγματος,
αἰτία δὲ αὐτῆς ἥδε· ἀνὴρ ὕπατος, ᾧ ὄνομα Ῥοῦφος,
τοὺς Σμυρναίους ἐλογίστευε πικρῶς καὶ δυστρόπως.
τούτῳ τι προσκρούσας ὁ Νικήτης "ἔρρωσο," εἶπεν,
καὶ οὐκέτι προσῄει δικάζοντι. τὸν μὲν δὴ χρόνον,

---

[1] For this word see Glossary.
[2] Both these phrases are echoes of Euripides, *Bacchae* 710-11.
[3] *i.e.* like a noxious insect; this seems to have been a favourite retort. *cf.* p. 588.

the gate that looks to Ephesus, and by this great
structure raised his deeds to the same high level as
his words. He was a man who, when he dealt with
legal matters, seemed to be a better lawyer than
anything else, and again when he dealt with
sophistic themes he seemed to do better as a
sophist, because of the peculiar skill and the keen
spirit of competition with which he adapted himself
to both styles. For he adorned the legal style with
sophistic amplification,[1] while he reinforced the
sophistic style with the sting of legal argument.
His type of eloquence forsook the antique political
convention and is almost bacchic and like a dithyramb,
and he produces phrases that are peculiar and
surprise by their daring, like " the thyrsi of Dionysus " in reference to honey, and " swarms of milk." [2]

Though he was deemed worthy of the highest
honour in Smyrna, which left nothing unsaid in its
loud praise of him as a marvellous man and a great
orator, he seldom came forward to speak in the public
assembly ; and when the crowd accused him of being
afraid : " I am more afraid," said he, " of the public
when they praise than when they abuse me." And
once when a tax-collector behaved insolently to him
in the law court, and said : " Stop barking at me,"
Nicetes replied with ready wit : " I will, by Zeus, if
you too will stop biting [3] me."

His journey beyond the Alps and the Rhine was
made at the command of the Emperor, and the reason
for it was as follows. A consular named Rufus was
regulating the finances of Smyrna with great harsh-
ness and malevolence, and Nicetes having come into
collision with him in a certain matter, said " Good
day " to him and did not again appear before his

ὃν μιᾶς πόλεως ἦρξεν, οὔπω δεινὰ πεπονθέναι
ᾤετο, ἐπιτραπεὶς δὲ τὰ Κελτικὰ στρατόπεδα ὀργῆς
ἀνεμνήσθη — αἱ γὰρ εὐπραγίαι τά τε ἄλλα τοὺς
ἀνθρώπους ἐπαίρουσι καὶ τὸ μηκέτι καρτερεῖν, ἃ
πρὶν εὖ πράττειν ἀνθρωπίνῳ λογισμῷ ἐκαρτέρουν —
καὶ γράφει πρὸς τὸν αὐτοκράτορα Νέρωνα πολλὰ
ἐπὶ τὸν Νικήτην καὶ σχέτλια, καὶ ὁ αὐτοκράτωρ
"αὐτὸς" εἶπεν "ἀκροάσει ἀπολογουμένου, κἂν
ἀδικοῦντα εὕρῃς, ἐπίθες δίκην." ταυτὶ δὲ ἔγραφεν
οὐ τὸν Νικήτην ἐκδιδούς, ἀλλὰ τὸν Ῥοῦφον ἐς
συγγνώμην ἑτοιμάζων, οὐ γὰρ ἄν ποτε ἄνδρα τοιοῦτον ἐφ' ἑαυτῷ γεγονότα οὔτ' ἂν ἀποκτεῖναι ὁ Ῥοῦφος, οὔτ' ἂν ἕτερον ζημιῶσαι οὐδέν, ὡς μὴ φανείη
βαρὺς τῷ καθιστάντι αὐτὸν δικαστὴν ἐχθροῦ. διὰ
μὲν δὴ ταῦτα ἐπὶ Ῥῆνόν τε καὶ Κελτοὺς ἦλθεν,
παρελθὼν δὲ ἐπὶ τὴν ἀπολογίαν οὕτω τι κατέπληξε
τὸν Ῥοῦφον, ὡς πλείω μὲν ἀφεῖναι ἐπὶ τῷ Νικήτῃ
δάκρυα οὗ διεμέτρησεν αὐτῷ ὕδατος,[1] ἀποπέμψαι
δὲ οὐκ ἄτρωτον μόνον, ἀλλὰ περίβλεπτον καὶ ἐν
τοῖς ζηλωτοῖς Σμυρναίων. τὸν δὲ ἄνδρα τοῦτον
χρόνοις ὕστερον Ἡρακλείδης ὁ Λύκιος σοφιστὴς
διορθούμενος ἐπέγραψε Νικήτην τὸν κεκαθαρμένον,
ἠγνόησε δὲ ἀκροθίνια Πυγμαῖα κολοσσῷ ἐφαρ-
μόζων.[2]

κ΄. Ἰσαῖος δὲ ὁ σοφιστὴς ὁ Ἀσσύριος τὸν μὲν
ἐν μειρακίῳ χρόνον ἡδοναῖς ἐδεδώκει, γαστρός τε
513 γὰρ καὶ φιλοποσίας ἥττητο καὶ λεπτὰ ἠμπίσχετο

---

[1] i.e. in the clepsydra, the water-clock.
[2] Heracleides ventured to rewrite the speech delivered by
Nicetes before Rufus ; see pp. 612–613 for Heracleides.

court. Now so long as Rufus had charge of only one city, he did not take serious offence at this behaviour; but when he received the command of the armies in Gaul his anger revived in his memory; for men are uplifted by success in various ways, but especially they refuse any longer to tolerate things that, before their success, when they used ordinary human standards, they used to tolerate. Accordingly he wrote to the Emperor Nero, bringing many serious charges against Nicetes, to which the Emperor replied: " You shall yourself hear him in his own defence, and if you find him guilty do you fix the penalty." Now in writing thus he was not abandoning Nicetes, but rather preparing the mind of Rufus for forgiveness, since he thought that he would never put to death so worthy a man if the decision were in his hands, nor indeed inflict any other penalty on him, lest he should appear harsh and vindictive to him who had appointed him his enemy's judge. It was therefore on this account that Nicetes went to the Rhine and to Gaul, and when he came forward to make his defence he impressed Rufus so profoundly that the tears he shed over Nicetes amounted to more than the water that had been allotted[1] to him for his defence; and he sent him away not only unscathed, but singled out for honour even among the most illustrious of the citizens of Smyrna. In latter times Heracleides,[2] the Lycian sophist, attempted to correct the writings of this great man and called his work *Nicetes Revised*, but he failed to see that he was fitting the spoils of the Pygmies on to a colossus.

20. ISAEUS, the Assyrian sophist, had devoted the period of his early youth to pleasure, for he was the slave of eating and drinking, dressed himself in elegant

καὶ θαμὰ ἤρα καὶ ἀπαρακαλύπτως ἐκώμαζεν, ἐς δὲ
ἄνδρας ἥκων οὕτω τι μετέβαλεν, ὡς ἕτερος ἐξ
ἑτέρου νομισθῆναι, τὸ μὲν γὰρ φιλόγελων ἐπι-
πολάζειν αὐτῷ δοκοῦν ἀφεῖλε καὶ προσώπου καὶ
γνώμης, λυρῶν τε καὶ αὐλῶν κτύποις οὐδ᾽ ἐπὶ
σκηνῆς ἔτι παρετύγχανεν, ἀπέδυ δὲ καὶ τὰ λήδια
καὶ τὰς τῶν ἐφεστρίδων βαφὰς καὶ τράπεζαν
ἐκόλασε καὶ τὸ ἐρᾶν μεθῆκεν,[1] ὥσπερ τοὺς προ-
τέρους ὀφθαλμοὺς ἀποβαλών· Ἄρδυος γοῦν τοῦ
ῥήτορος ἐρομένου αὐτόν, εἰ ἡ δεῖνα αὐτῷ καλὴ
φαίνοιτο, μάλα σωφρόνως ὁ Ἰσαῖος "πέπαυμαι"
εἶπεν "ὀφθαλμιῶν." ἐρομένου δὲ αὐτὸν ἑτέρου,
τίς ἄριστος τῶν ὀρνίθων καὶ τῶν ἰχθύων ἐς βρῶσιν,
"πέπαυμαι" ἔφη ὁ Ἰσαῖος "ταῦτα σπουδάζων,
ξυνῆκα γὰρ τοὺς Ταντάλου κήπους τρυγῶν,"
ἐνδεικνύμενος δήπου τῷ ἐρομένῳ ταῦτα, ὅτι σκιὰ
καὶ ὀνείρατα αἱ ἡδοναὶ πᾶσαι.

Τῷ δὲ Μιλησίῳ Διονυσίῳ ἀκροατῇ ὄντι τὰς μελέτας ξὺν ᾠδῇ ποιουμένῳ ἐπιπλήττων ὁ Ἰσαῖος
"μειράκιον" ἔφη "Ἰωνικόν, ἐγὼ δέ σε ᾄδειν οὐκ
ἐπαίδευσα." νεανίσκου δὲ Ἰωνικοῦ θαυμάζοντος
πρὸς αὐτὸν τὸ τοῦ Νικήτου μεγαλοφώνως ἐπὶ τοῦ
Ξέρξου εἰρημένον "ἐκ τῆς βασιλείου νεὼς Αἴ-
γιναν ἀναδησώμεθα" καταγελάσας πλατὺ ὁ
Ἰσαῖος "ἀνόητε," εἶπεν, "καὶ πῶς ἀναχθήσῃ;"
Τὰς δὲ μελέτας οὐκ αὐτοσχεδίους ἐποιεῖτο, ἀλλ᾽
ἐπεσκεμμένος[2] τὸν ἐξ ἕω ἐς μεσημβρίαν καιρόν.

514

[1] μετέθηκεν Kayser; μεθῆκεν Cobet.
[2] ἐπεσκεμμένας Kayser; ἐπεσκεμμένος Cobet.

---

[1] A proverb of fleeting joys; cf. p. 595 and Life of Apollonius iv. 25.

stuffs, was often in love, and openly joined in drunken revels. But when he attained to manhood he so transformed himself as to be thought to have become another person, for he discarded both from his countenance and his mind the frivolity that had seemed to come to the surface in him; no longer did he, even in the theatre, hearken to the sounds of the lyre and the flute; he put off his transparent garments and his many-coloured cloaks, reduced his table, and left off his amours as though he had lost the eyes he had before. For instance, when Ardys the rhetorician asked him whether he considered some woman or other handsome, Isaeus replied with much discretion: "I have ceased to suffer from eye trouble." And when someone asked him what sort of bird and what sort of fish were the best eating: "I have ceased," replied Isaeus, "to take these matters seriously, for I now know that I used to feed on the gardens of Tantalus."[1] Thus he indicated to his questioner that all pleasures are a shadow and a dream.

When Dionysius of Miletus, who had been his pupil, delivered his declamations in a sing-song, Isaeus rebuked him, saying: "Young man from Ionia, I did not train you to sing."[2] And when a youth from Ionia admired in his presence the grandiloquent saying of Nicetes in his *Xerxes*, "Let us fasten Aegina to the king's ship," Isaeus burst into a loud laugh and said: "Madman, how will you put to sea?"

His declamations were not actually extempore, but he deliberated from daybreak till midday. The

[2] The Ionian rhetoricians were especially fond of such vocal effects.

69

ἰδέαν δ' ἐπήσκησε λόγων οὔτ' ἐπιβεβλημένην,[1] οὔτ' αὖον, ἀλλ' ἀπέριττον καὶ κατὰ φύσιν καὶ ἀποχρῶσαν τοῖς πράγμασιν. καὶ τὸ βραχέως ἑρμηνεύειν, τοῦτό τε καὶ πᾶσαν ὑπόθεσιν συνελεῖν ἐς βραχὺ Ἰσαίου εὕρημα, ὡς ἐν πλείοσι μὲν ἑτέροις, μάλιστα δὲ ἐν τοῖσδε ἐδηλώθη· τοὺς μὲν γὰρ Λακεδαιμονίους ἀγωνιζόμενος τοὺς βουλευομένους περὶ τοῦ τείχους ἀπὸ τῶν Ὁμήρου ἐβραχυλόγησε τοσοῦτον·

" ἀσπὶς ἄρ' ἀσπίδ' ἔρειδε, κόρυς κόρυν, ἀνέρα δ'
    ἀνήρ·

οὕτω στῆτέ μοι, Λακεδαιμόνιοι, καὶ τετειχίσμεθα." κατηγορῶν δὲ τοῦ Βυζαντίου Πύθωνος, ὡς δεθέντος μὲν ἐκ χρησμῶν ἐπὶ προδοσίᾳ, κεκριμένης δὲ τῆς προδοσίας, ὡς ἀνέζευξεν ὁ Φίλιππος, ξυνέλαβε τὸν ἀγῶνα τοῦτον ἐς τρεῖς ἐννοίας, ἔστι γὰρ τὰ εἰρημένα ἐν τρισὶ τούτοις· " ἐλέγχω Πύθωνα προδεδωκότα τῷ χρήσαντι θεῷ, τῷ δήσαντι δήμῳ, τῷ ἀναζεύξαντι Φιλίππῳ, ὁ μὲν γὰρ οὐκ ἂν ἔχρησεν, εἰ μή τις ἦν, ὁ δὲ οὐκ ἂν ἔδησεν, εἰ μὴ τοιοῦτος ἦν, ὁ δὲ οὐκ ἂν ἀνέζευξεν, εἰ μὴ δι' ὃν ἦλθεν, οὐχ εὗρεν."

κα'. Ὑπὲρ Σκοπελιανοῦ τοῦ σοφιστοῦ διαλέξομαι καθαψάμενος πρότερον τῶν κακίζειν αὐτὸν

---

[1] Cobet would read περιβεβλημένην, but this is unnecessary.

---

[1] *Iliad* xvi. 215. On the later fortification of Sparta *cf.* Pausanias i. 13. This was a famous theme and was inspired by the saying *Non est Sparta lapidibus circumdata* (Seneca, *Suasoriae* ii. 3); *cf.* below, p. 584.

[2] For Python *cf.* p. 482 note. But here as elsewhere, Python is probably confused with Leon of Byzantium, of

style of eloquence that he practised was neither exuberant nor meagre, but simple and natural and suited to the subject matter. Moreover, a concise form of expression and the summing up of every argument into a brief statement was peculiarly an invention of Isaeus, as was clearly shown in many instances, but especially in the following. He had to represent the Lacedaemonians debating whether they should fortify themselves by building a wall, and he condensed his argument into these few words from Homer:

"And shield pressed on shield, helm on helm, man on man.[1]

Thus stand fast, Lacedaemonians, these are our fortifications!" When he took for his theme the indictment of Python[2] of Byzantium, imprisoned for treason at the command of an oracle and on his trial for treason after Philip's departure, he confined his case to three points to be considered; for what he said is summed up in these three statements: "I find Python guilty of treason by the evidence of the god who gave the oracle, of the people who put him in prison, of Philip who has departed. For the first would not have given the oracle if there were no traitor; the second would not have imprisoned him if he were not that sort of man; the third would not have departed if he had not failed to find the man who had caused him to come." [3]

21. I will now speak of the sophist Scopelian, but first I will deal with those who try to calumniate

whom Suidas relates this story. For this theme as used in declamations *cf.* the third-century rhetorician Apsines ix. 479 Walz.

[3] This is an example of antithesis combined with *ἰσόκωλα*, clauses of equal length.

πειρωμένων, ἀπαξιοῦσι γὰρ δὴ τὸν ἄνδρα τοῦ τῶν
σοφιστῶν κύκλου διθυραμβώδη καλοῦντες καὶ ἀκό-
515 λαστον καὶ πεπαχυσμένον. ταυτὶ περὶ αὐτοῦ λέγου-
σιν οἱ λεπτολόγοι καὶ νωθροὶ καὶ μηδὲν ἀπ' αὐτο-
σχεδίου γλώττης ἀναπνέοντες· φύσει μὲν γὰρ ἐπί-
φθονον χρῆμα ἄνθρωπος.[1] διαβάλλουσι γοῦν τοὺς
μὲν εὐμήκεις οἱ μικροί, τοὺς δὲ εὐειδεῖς οἱ πονηροὶ
τὸ εἶδος, τοὺς δὲ κούφους τε καὶ δρομικοὺς οἱ
βραδεῖς καὶ ἑτερόποδες, τοὺς θαρσαλέους οἱ δειλοὶ
καὶ οἱ ἄμουσοι τοὺς λυρικούς, τοὺς δ' ἀμφὶ παλαίστραν οἱ ἀγύμναστοι, καὶ οὐ χρὴ θαυμάζειν, εἰ
πεπηδημένοι τὴν γλῶττάν τινες καὶ βοῦν ἀφωνίας
ἐπ' αὐτὴν βεβλημένοι καὶ μήτ' ἂν αὐτοί τι ἐνθυ-
μηθέντες μέγα, μήτ' ἂν ἐνθυμηθέντος ἑτέρου
ξυμφήσαντες διαπτύοιέν τε καὶ κακίζοιεν τὸν
ἑτοιμότατα δὴ καὶ θαρραλεώτατα καὶ μεγαλειότατα
τῶν ἐφ' ἑαυτοῦ Ἑλλήνων ἑρμηνεύσαντα. ὡς δὲ
ἠγνοήκασι τὸν ἄνδρα, ἐγὼ δηλώσω, καὶ ὁποῖον
αὐτῷ καὶ τὸ τοῦ οἴκου σχῆμα.

Ἀρχιερεὺς μὲν γὰρ ἐγένετο τῆς Ἀσίας αὐτός τε
καὶ οἱ πρόγονοι αὐτοῦ παῖς ἐκ πατρὸς πάντες, ὁ δὲ
στέφανος οὗτος πολὺς καὶ ὑπὲρ πολλῶν χρημάτων.
δίδυμός τε ἀποτεχθεὶς ἄμφω μὲν ἤστην ἐν σπαρ-
γάνοις, πεμπταίων δὲ ὄντων κεραυνῷ μὲν ἐβλήθη
ὁ ἕτερος, ὁ δὲ οὐδεμίαν ἐπηρώθη τῶν αἰσθήσεων
ξυγκατακείμενος τῷ βληθέντι. καίτοι τὸ τῶν σκη-
πτῶν πῦρ οὕτω δριμὺ καὶ θειῶδες, ὡς τῶν ἀγχοῦ
τοὺς μὲν ἀποκτείνειν κατ' ἔκπληξιν, τῶν δὲ ἀκοάς

[1] ἄνθρωποι Kayser; ἄνθρωπος Cobet.

---

[1] A proverb for silence first found in Theognis 651 ; cf.
Aeschylus, Agamemnon 36 ; Philostratus, Life of Apollonius
vi. 11 ; its precise origin is not clear, but it may refer to the

him. For they say that he is unworthy of the sophistic circle and call him dithyrambic, intemperate in his style, and thick-witted. Those who say this about him are quibblers and sluggish and are not inspired with extempore eloquence; for man is by nature a creature prone to envy. At any rate the short disparage the tall, the ill-favoured the good-looking, those who are slow and lame disparage the light-footed swift runner, cowards the brave, the unmusical the musical, those who are unathletic disparage athletes. Hence we must not be surprised if certain persons who are themselves tongue-tied, and have set on their tongues the "ox of silence,"[1] who could not of themselves conceive any great thought or sympathize with another who conceived it, should sneer at and revile one whose style of eloquence was the readiest, the boldest, and the most elevated of any Greek of his time. But since they have failed to understand the man, I will make known what he was and how illustrious was his family.

For he was himself high-priest of Asia and so were his ancestors before him, all of them, inheriting the office from father to son. And this is a great crown of glory and more than great wealth. He was one of twins, and as both were lying in one cradle, when they were five days old, one of them was struck by lightning, but the other, though he was lying with the stricken child, was not maimed in any one of his senses. And yet, so fierce and sulphurous was the fire of the thunderbolt that some of those who stood near were killed by the shock, others suffered

---

weight of the ox, or to coins engraved with an ox and laid on the tongue *e.g.* of a victim. The Latin proverb *bos in lingua*, "he is bribed," must refer to an engraved coin.

τε καὶ ὀφθαλμοὺς σίνεσθαι, τῶν δὲ ἐς τοὺς νοῦς
ἀποσκήπτειν. ἀλλ' οὐδενὶ τούτων ὁ Σκοπελιανὸς
ἥλω, διετέλεσε γὰρ δὴ καὶ ἐς γῆρας βαθὺ ἀκέραιός
τε καὶ ἄρτιος. τουτὶ δὲ ὁπόθεν θαυμάζω, δηλῶσαί
σοι βούλομαι· ἐδείπνουν μὲν κατὰ τὴν Λῆμνον ὑπὸ
δρυὶ μεγάλῃ θερισταὶ ὀκτὼ περὶ τὸ καλούμενον
Κέρας τῆς νήσου, τὸ δὲ χωρίον τοῦτο λιμήν ἐστιν
516 ἐς κεραίας ἐπιστρέφων λεπτάς, νέφους δὲ τὴν δρῦν
περισχόντος καὶ σκηπτοῦ ἐς αὐτὴν ἐκδοθέντος ἡ
μὲν ἐβέβλητο, οἱ θερισταὶ δὲ ἐκπλήξεως αὐτοῖς
ἐμπεσούσης, ἐφ' οὗπερ ἔτυχεν ἕκαστος πράττων,
οὕτως ἀπέθανεν, ὁ μὲν γὰρ κύλικα ἀναιρούμενος, ὁ
δὲ πίνων, ὁ δὲ μάττων, ὁ δὲ ἐσθίων, ὁ δὲ ἕτερόν τι [1]
ποιῶν τὰς ψυχὰς ἀφῆκαν ἐπιτεθυμμένοι καὶ μέλανες,
ὥσπερ οἱ χαλκοῖ τῶν ἀνδριάντων περὶ τὰς ἐμπύ-
ρους τῶν πηγῶν κεκαπνισμένοι. ὁ δὲ οὕτω τι οὐκ
ἀθεεὶ ἐτρέφετο, ὡς διαφυγεῖν μὲν τὸν ἐκ τοῦ
σκηπτοῦ θάνατον, ὃν μηδὲ οἱ σκληρότατοι τῶν
ἀγροίκων διέφυγον, ἄτρωτος δὲ μεῖναι τὰς αἰσθήσεις καὶ τὸν νοῦν ἕτοιμος καὶ ὕπνου κρείττων, καὶ
γὰρ δὴ καὶ τὸ νωθρὸν αὐτοῦ ἀπῆν.

Ἐφοίτησε δὲ τοὺς ῥητορικοὺς τῶν λόγων παρὰ
τὸν Σμυρναῖον Νικήτην μελετήσαντα μὲν ἐπιφανῶς,
πολλῷ δὲ μεῖζον ἐν δικαστηρίοις πνεύσαντα. δεο-
μένων δὲ τῶν Κλαζομενίων τὰς μελέτας αὐτὸν οἴκοι
ποιεῖσθαι καὶ προβήσεσθαι τὰς Κλαζομενὰς ἐπὶ
μέγα ἡγουμένων, εἰ τοιοῦτος δὴ ἀνὴρ ἐμπαιδεύσοι
σφίσιν, τουτὶ μὲν οὐκ ἀμούσως παρῃτήσατο τὴν

[1] δέ τι Kayser ; δὲ ἕτερόν τι Cobet.

injury to their ears and eyes, while the minds of others were affected by the shock of the bolt. But Scopelian was afflicted by none of these misfortunes, for he remained healthy and sound far on into old age. I will explain the reason why I marvel at this. Once, in Lemnos, eight harvesters were eating their meal beneath a great oak, near that part of the island called the Horn—this place is a harbour curved in the shape of slender horns—when a cloud covered the oak and a bolt was hurled on to it, so that the tree itself was struck, and the harvesters, when the stroke fell on them, were killed every one of them in the act of doing whatever it might be, one as he lifted a cup, one drinking, one kneading bread, one while eating, in fact, whatever else it might be that they were engaged on, thus in the act they lost their lives; and they were covered with smoke and blackened like bronze statues that are near hot springs and so become darkened by fumes. But Scopelian was reared under the protection of the gods so carefully that he not only escaped death from the thunderbolt, though not even the most robust of those field-labourers escaped it, but remained with his senses unimpaired, keen-witted, and independent of sleep, and in fact he was never subject even to a feeling of torpor.

He frequented the rhetoricians' schools of oratory as a pupil of Nicetes of Smyrna, who had conspicuous success as a declaimer, though in the law courts he was an even more vigorous orator. When the city of Clazomenae begged Scopelian to declaim in his native place, because they thought it would greatly benefit Clazomenae if so talented a man should open a school there, he declined politely, saying that the

ἀηδόνα φήσας ἐν οἰκίσκῳ μὴ ᾄδειν, ὥσπερ δὲ ἄλσος
τι τῆς ἑαυτοῦ εὐφωνίας τὴν Σμύρναν ἐσκέψατο καὶ
τὴν ἠχὼ τὴν ἐκεῖ πλείστου ἀξίαν ᾠήθη. πάσης
γὰρ τῆς Ἰωνίας οἷον μουσείου πεπολισμένης
ἀρτιωτάτην ἐπέχει τάξιν ἡ Σμύρνα, καθάπερ ἐν
τοῖς ὀργάνοις ἡ μαγάς.

Αἱ δὲ αἰτίαι, δι' ἃς ὁ πατὴρ ἐξ ἡμέρου τε καὶ
πράου χαλεπὸς αὐτῷ ἐγένετο, λέγονται μὲν ἐπὶ
πολλά, καὶ γὰρ ἡ δεῖνα καὶ ἡ δεῖνα καὶ πλείους,
ἀλλ' ἐγὼ τὴν ἀληθεστάτην δηλώσω· μετὰ γὰρ τὴν
τοῦ Σκοπελιανοῦ μητέρα γυναῖκα ὁ πρεσβύτης
ἤγετο ἡμίγαμόν τε καὶ οὐ κατὰ νόμους, ὁ δὲ ὁρῶν
517 ταῦτα ἐνουθέτει καὶ ἀπῆγεν, τουτὶ δὲ τοῖς ἐξώροις
ἀηδές. ἡ δ' αὖ ξυνετίθει κατ' αὐτοῦ λόγον, ὡς
ἐρῶντος μὲν αὐτῆς, τὴν διαμαρτίαν δὲ μὴ καρτε-
ροῦντος. ξυνελάμβανε δὲ αὐτῇ τῶν διαβολῶν καὶ
οἰκέτης τοῦ πρεσβύτου μάγειρος, ᾧ ἐπωνυμία
Κύθηρος, ὑποθωπεύων, ὥσπερ ἐν δράματι, τὸν
δεσπότην καὶ τοιαυτὶ λέγων· "ὦ δέσποτα, βού-
λεταί σε ὁ υἱὸς τεθνάναι ἤδη, οὐδὲ τὸν αὐτόματον
καὶ μετ' οὐ πολὺ θάνατον ἐνδιδοὺς τῷ σῷ γήρᾳ,
ἀλλὰ καὶ αὐτουργῶν μὲν τὴν ἐπιβουλήν, μισθούμενος δὲ καὶ τὰς ἐμὰς χεῖρας. ἔστι γὰρ αὐτῷ
φάρμακα ἀνδροφόνα ἐπὶ σέ, ὧν τὸ καιριώτατον
κελεύει με ἐμβαλεῖν ἐς ἕν τι τῶν ὄψων ἐλευθερίαν τε
ὁμολογῶν καὶ ἀγροὺς καὶ οἰκίας καὶ χρήματα καὶ
πᾶν ὅ τι βουλοίμην ἔχειν τοῦ σοῦ οἴκου, καὶ ταυτὶ
μὲν πειθομένῳ εἶναι, ἀπειθοῦντι δὲ μαστίγωσίν τε
καὶ στρέβλωσιν καὶ παχείας πέδας καὶ κύφωνα

---

[1] For the same figure cf. p. 487.

nightingale does not sing in a cage; and he regarded Smyrna as, so to speak, a grove in which
he could practise his melodious voice, and thought
it best worth his while to let it echo there. For
while all Ionia is, as it were, an established seat of
the Muses, Smyrna holds the most important position,
like the bridge in musical instruments.[1]

The reasons why his father, after being kind and
indulgent to him, treated him harshly, are told in
many different versions, for they allege now this
reason, now that, then more than one, but I shall
relate the truest version. After the death of
Scopelian's mother, the old man was preparing to
bring home a woman as a concubine and not in legal
wedlock, and when the son perceived this he
admonished him and tried to deter him, which is
always an annoying thing to older men. The woman
thereupon trumped up a tale against him to the
effect that he was in love with her, and could not
endure his lack of success. In this calumny she had
also a slave as accomplice, the old man's cook whose
name was Cytherus, and he used to flatter his master,
like a slave in a play, and say things of this sort:
" Master, your son wishes you to die now at once, nor
will he allow to your old age a natural death, such as
must needs be, not long hence; and he himself is
preparing the plot, but he is trying to hire the help
of my hands as well. For he has poisonous drugs
destined for you, and he orders me to put the most
deadly of them in one of my dishes, promising me
my freedom, lands, houses, money, and whatever I
may please to have from your house; and this, if I
obey; but if I disobey he promises me the lash,
torture, stout fetters, and the cruel pillory." And

βαρύν." καὶ τοιοῖσδε θωπεύμασι περιελθὼν τὸν
δεσπότην τελευτῶντος μετ᾽ οὐ πολὺ καὶ πρὸς
διαθήκαις ὄντος γράφεται κληρονόμος, υἱός τε
προσρηθεὶς καὶ ὀφθαλμοὶ καὶ ψυχὴ πᾶσα. καὶ
οὐχὶ ταυτὶ χρὴ θαυμάζειν, ἐπεὶ πρεσβύτην ἐρῶντα
ἔθελξεν ἴσως που καὶ παραπαίοντα ὑπὸ ἡλικίας καὶ
αὐτοῦ τοῦ ἐρᾶν — καὶ γὰρ δὴ καὶ νέοι ἐρῶντες οὐκ
ἔστιν ὅστις αὐτῶν τὸν ἑαυτοῦ νοῦν ἔχει — ἀλλ᾽ ὅτι
καὶ τῆς τοῦ Σκοπελιανοῦ δεινότητος τε καὶ τῆς ἐν
τοῖς δικαστηρίοις ἀκμῆς κρείττων ἔδοξεν ἀγωνισάμενος μὲν περὶ τῶν διαθηκῶν πρὸς αὐτόν, ἀντεκ-
τείνας δὲ τῇ ἐκείνου δεινότητι τὸν ἐκείνου πλοῦτον·
ἀπαντλῶν γὰρ τῆς οὐσίας καὶ μισθούμενος ὑπερβολαῖς χρημάτων γλώττας ὁμοῦ πάσας καὶ δικαστῶν ψήφους πανταχοῦ τὴν νικῶσαν ἀπηνέγκατο,
ὅθεν ὁ Σκοπελιανὸς τὰ μὲν Ἀναξαγόρου μηλόβοτα
εἶναι, τὰ δὲ αὑτοῦ δουλόβοτα ἔλεγεν. ἐπιφανὴς δὲ
καὶ τὰ πολιτικὰ ὁ Κύθηρος γενόμενος γηράσκων
ἤδη καὶ τὴν οὐσίαν ὁρῶν ὑποδιδοῦσαν καταφρονού-
μενός τε ἱκανῶς καί που καὶ πληγὰς λαβὼν πρὸς
ἀνδρός, ὃν χρήματα ἀπαιτῶν ἐτύγχανεν, ἱκέτης τοῦ
518 Σκοπελιανοῦ γίγνεται μνησικακίαν τε αὐτῷ παρεῖναι καὶ ὀργὴν ἀπολαβεῖν τε τὸν τοῦ πατρὸς οἶκον
ἀνέντα μὲν αὐτῷ μέρος τῆς οἰκίας πολλῆς οὔσης,
ὡς μὴ ἀνελευθέρως ἐνδιαιτήσηται, συγχωρήσαντα
δὲ ἀγροὺς δύο τῶν ἐπὶ θαλάττῃ. καὶ Κυθήρου
οἶκος ἐπωνόμασται νῦν ἔτι τὸ μέρος τῆς οἰκίας, ἐν
ᾧ κατεβίω. ταυτὶ μέν, ὡς μὴ ἀγνοεῖν αὐτά,

---

[1] Anaxagoras when exiled from Athens lost his property,
which was then neglected ; the story is told by Diogenes
Laertius ii. 9 ; cf. Plato, Hippias maior 283 A ; Philostratus,
Life of Apollonius i. 13.

by wheedling him in this way he got round his
master, so that when the latter was dying not long
after, and came to make a will, he was appointed
heir and was therein styled his son, his eyes, and his
whole soul.   And this indeed need not surprise us,
since he whom he beguiled was an amorous old man,
who was perhaps feeble-minded besides, from old age
and from that same passion—for even when young
men are in love there is not one of them that keeps
his wits—but the surprising thing is that he showed
himself more than a match for the oratorical talent of
Scopelian, and his high reputation, in the law courts ;
for he went to law with him over the will, and used
Scopelian's own fortune to counteract the latter's
talent.   For by drawing deeply on the estate and
bribing with extravagant sums the tongues of all men,
and at the same time the votes of the jury, he won a
complete victory on every point, and hence Scopelian
used to say that, whereas the property of Anaxagoras
had become a sheep pasture, his own was a slave
pasture.[1]   Cytherus became prominent in public life
also, and when he was now an old man and saw that
his estate was growing less and that he himself was
greatly despised, nay had even received blows at the
hands of a man from whom he tried to recover
money, he implored Scopelian to lay aside the
memory of his wrongs and his anger, and to take
back his father's property, only giving up to himself
a part of the house, which was spacious, so that he
might live in it without too great squalor ; and to
yield to him also two fields out of those near the sea.
And to this day, that part of the house in which he
lived till his death is called the dwelling of Cytherus.
All these facts I have related that they may not

συνιέναι δὲ κἀκ τούτων, ὅτι οἱ ἄνθρωποι μὴ θεοῦ μόνον, ἀλλὰ καὶ ἀλλήλων παίγνια.

Σκοπελιανοῦ δὲ σπουδάζοντος ἐν τῇ Σμύρνῃ ξυμφοιτᾶν μὲν ἐς αὐτὴν Ἴωνάς τε καὶ Λυδοὺς καὶ Κᾶρας καὶ Μαίονας Αἰολέας τε καὶ τοὺς ἐκ Μυσῶν Ἕλληνας καὶ Φρυγῶν οὔπω μέγα, ἀγχί-θυρος γὰρ τοῖς ἔθνεσι τούτοις ἡ Σμύρνα καιρίως ἔχουσα τῶν γῆς καὶ θαλάττης πυλῶν, ὁ δὲ ἦγε μὲν Καππαδόκας τε καὶ Ἀσσυρίους, ἦγε δὲ Αἰ-γυπτίους καὶ Φοίνικας Ἀχαιῶν τε τοὺς εὐδο-κιμωτέρους καὶ νεότητα τὴν ἐξ Ἀθηνῶν ἅπασαν. δόξαν μὲν οὖν ἐς τοὺς πολλοὺς παραδεδώκει ῥα-στώνης τε καὶ ἀμελείας, ἐπειδὴ τὸν πρὸ τῆς μελέ-της καιρὸν ξυνῆν ὡς ἐπὶ πολὺ τοῖς τῶν Σμυρναίων τέλεσιν ὑπὲρ τῶν πολιτικῶν, ὁ δὲ ἀπεχρῆτο μὲν καὶ τῇ φύσει λαμπρᾷ τε οὔσῃ καὶ μεγαλογνώμονι, καὶ τὸν μεθ᾽ ἡμέραν καιρὸν ἧττον ἐσπούδαζεν, ἀυπνότατος δ᾽ ἀνθρώπων γενόμενος "ὦ νύξ," ἔλεγε "σὺ γὰρ δὴ πλεῖστον σοφίας μετέχεις μέρος θεῶν," ξυνεργὸν δὲ αὐτὴν ἐποιεῖτο τῶν ἑαυτοῦ φροντισμάτων. λέγεται γοῦν καὶ ἐς ὄρ-θρον ἀποτεῖναι σπουδάζων ἀπὸ ἑσπέρας.

Προσέκειτο μὲν οὖν ἅπασι ποιήμασι, τραγῳ-δίας δὲ ἐνεφορεῖτο, ἀγωνιζόμενος πρὸς τὴν τοῦ διδασκάλου μεγαλοφωνίαν—ἀπὸ γὰρ τούτου τοῦ μέρους ὁ Νικήτης σφόδρα ἐθαυμάζετο—ὁ δὲ οὕτω τι μεγαλοφωνίας ἐπὶ μεῖζον ἤλασεν, ὡς καὶ Γιγαντίαν ξυνθεῖναι παραδοῦναί τε Ὁμηρί-

---

[1] Plato, *Laws* 644 D. The saying became a proverb, *cf.* *Life of Apollonius* iv. 36.

remain unknown, and that from them we may learn that men are the playthings not only of God [1] but of one another.

It is no great wonder that, while Scopelian taught at Smyrna, Ionians, Lydians, Carians, Maeonians, Aeolians also and Hellenes from Mysia and Phrygia flocked thither to his school; for Smyrna is next door to these peoples and is a convenient gateway both by land and sea. But besides these he attracted Cappadocians and Assyrians, he attracted also Egyptians and Phoenicians, the more illustrious of the Achaeans, and all the youth of Athens. To the crowd he no doubt gave an impression of indolence and negligence, since during the period before a declamation he was generally in the society of the magistrates of Smyrna transacting public business, but he was able to rely on his own genius, which was brilliant and of a lofty kind; and in fact during the daytime he did not work much, but he was the most sleepless of men, and hence he used to say: "O Night, thy share of wisdom is greater than that of the other gods!" [2] and he made her the collaborator in his studies. Indeed it is said that he used to work continuously from evening until dawn.

He devoted himself to all kinds of poetry, but tragedies he devoured in his endeavour to rival the grand style of his teacher; for in this branch Nicetes was greatly admired. But Scopelian went so much further in magniloquence that he even composed an *Epic of the Giants*, and furnished the Homerids [3] with

[2] Menander, *frag.* 789 Koerte; Scopelian adapted the line by substituting *wisdom* for *love*.

[3] The allusion is to certain epic poets of the day who imitated Scopelian's epic and are hence sarcastically called "Sons of Homer."

δαις ἀφορμὰς ἐς τὸν λόγον. ὡμίλει δὲ σοφιστῶν μὲν μάλιστα Γοργίᾳ τῷ Λεοντίνῳ, ῥητόρων δὲ 519 τοῖς λαμπρὸν ἠχοῦσιν. τὸ δὲ ἐπίχαρι φύσει μᾶλλον εἶχεν ἢ μελέτῃ, πρὸς φύσεως μὲν γὰρ τοῖς Ἰωνικοῖς τὸ ἀστείζεσθαι, τῷ δ' αὖ καὶ ἐπὶ τῶν λόγων τοῦ φιλόγελω περιῆν, τὸ γὰρ κατηφὲς δυσξύμβολόν τε καὶ ἀηδὲς ἡγεῖτο. παρῄει δὲ καὶ ἐς τοὺς δήμους ἀνειμένῳ τε καὶ διακεχυμένῳ τῷ προσώπῳ, καὶ πολλῷ πλέον, ὅτε ξὺν ὀργῇ ἐκ- κλησιάζοιεν, ἀνιεὶς αὐτοὺς καὶ διαπραΰνων τῇ τοῦ εἴδους εὐθυμίᾳ. τὸ δὲ ἐν τοῖς δικαστηρίοις ἦθος οὔτε φιλοχρήματος οὔτε φιλολοίδορος· προῖ- κα μὲν γὰρ ξυνέταττεν ἑαυτὸν τοῖς ὑπὲρ ψυχῆς κινδυνεύουσι, τοὺς δὲ λοιδορουμένους ἐν τοῖς λόγοις καὶ θυμοῦ τινα ἐπίδειξιν ἡγουμένους ποιεῖ- σθαι γραΐδια ἐκάλει μεθύοντα καὶ λυττῶντα. τὰς δὲ μελέτας μισθοῦ μὲν ἐποιεῖτο, ὁ δὲ μισθὸς ἦν ἄλλος ἄλλου καὶ ὡς ἕκαστος οἴκου εἶχεν, παρῄει τε ἐς αὐτοὺς οὔθ' ὑπερφρονῶν καὶ σεσοβημένος, οὔθ' ὥσπερ οἱ δεδιότες, ἀλλ' ὡς εἰκὸς ἦν τὸν ἀγωνιῶντα μὲν ὑπὲρ τῆς ἑαυτοῦ δόξης, θαρροῦντα δὲ τῷ μὴ ἂν σφαλῆναι. διελέγετο δὲ ἀπὸ μὲν τοῦ θρόνου ξὺν ἁβρότητι, ὅτε δὲ ὀρθὸς διαλέγοιτο, ἐπιστροφήν τε εἶχεν ὁ λόγος καὶ ἔρρωτο. καὶ ἐπεσκοπεῖτο οὐκ ἔνδον, οὐδ' ἐν τῷ ὁμίλῳ, ἀλλ' ὑπεξιὼν ἐν βραχεῖ τοῦ καιροῦ διεώρα πάντα. περιῆν δὲ αὐτῷ καὶ εὐφωνίας, καὶ τὸ φθέγμα

material for their poetry. Of the sophists he studied most carefully Gorgias of Leontini, and of the orators those that have a splendid ring. But his charm was natural rather than studied, for with the Ionians urbanity and wit are a gift of nature. For example, even in his orations he abounded in jests, for he held that to be over-serious is unsociable and disagreeable. And even when he appeared in the public assembly it was with a cheerful and lively countenance, and all the more when the meeting was excited by anger, for then he relaxed the tension and calmed their minds by his own good-tempered demeanour. In the law courts he displayed a temper neither avaricious nor malevolent. For without a fee he would champion the cause of those who were in danger of their lives, and when men became abusive in their speeches, and thought fit to make a great display of indignation, he used to call them tipsy and frenzied old hags. Though he charged a fee for declaiming, it was not the same for every pupil, and depended on the amount of property possessed by each. And he used to appear before his audience with no arrogance or conceited airs, nor again with the bearing of a timid speaker, but as befitted one who was entering the lists to win glory for himself and was confident that he could not fail. He would argue with suavity, so long as he was seated, but when he stood up to speak his oration became more impressive and gained in vigour. He meditated his theme neither in private nor before his audience, but he would withdraw and in a very short time would review all his arguments. He had an extremely melodious voice and a charming pronunciation, and he would often

ἡδονὴν εἶχε τόν τε μηρὸν θαμὰ ἔπληττεν ἑαυτόν
τε ὑπεγείρων καὶ τοὺς ἀκροωμένους. ἄριστος
μὲν οὖν καὶ σχηματίσαι λόγον καὶ ἐπαμφοτέρως
εἰπεῖν, θαυμασιώτερος δὲ περὶ τὰς ἀκμαιοτέρας
τῶν ὑποθέσεων καὶ πολλῷ πλέον περὶ τὰς Μηδι-
κάς, ἐν αἷς οἱ Δαρεῖοί τέ εἰσι καὶ οἱ Ξέρξαι, ταύ-
520 τας γὰρ αὐτός τέ μοι δοκεῖ ἄριστα σοφιστῶν
ἑρμηνεῦσαι παραδοῦναί τε τοῖς ἐπιγιγνομένοις
ἑρμηνεύειν, καὶ γὰρ φρόνημα ἐν αὐταῖς ὑπεκρίνετο καὶ κουφότητα τὴν ἐν τοῖς βαρβάροις ἤθεσιν.
ἐλέγετο καὶ σείεσθαι μᾶλλον ἐν ταύταις, ὥσπερ
βακχεύων, καί τινος τῶν ἀμφὶ τὸν Πολέμωνα
τυμπανίζειν αὐτὸν φήσαντος λαβόμενος ὁ Σκοπελιανὸς τοῦ σκώμματος " τυμπανίζω μέν," εἶπεν
" ἀλλὰ τῇ τοῦ Αἴαντος ἀσπίδι."

Βασίλειοι δὲ αὐτοῦ πρεσβεῖαι πολλαὶ μέν, καὶ
γάρ τις καὶ ἀγαθὴ τύχη ξυνηκολούθει πρεσβεύ-
οντι, ἀρίστη δὲ ἡ ὑπὲρ τῶν ἀμπέλων· οὐ γὰρ
ὑπὲρ Σμυρναίων μόνων, ὥσπερ αἱ πλείους, ἀλλ'
ὑπὲρ τῆς Ἀσίας ὁμοῦ πάσης ἐπρεσβεύθη. τὸν
δὲ νοῦν τῆς πρεσβείας ἐγὼ δηλώσω· ἐδόκει τῷ
βασιλεῖ μὴ εἶναι τῇ Ἀσίᾳ ἀμπέλους, ἐπειδὴ ἐν
οἴνῳ στασιάζειν ἔδοξαν, ἀλλ' ἐξῃρῆσθαι μὲν τὰς
ἤδη πεφυτευμένας, ἄλλας δὲ μὴ φυτεύειν ἔτι.
ἔδει δὴ πρεσβείας ἀπὸ τοῦ κοινοῦ καὶ ἀνδρός, ὃς
ἔμελλεν ὥσπερ Ὀρφεύς τις ἢ Θάμυρις ὑπὲρ αὐτῶν
θέλξειν. αἱροῦνται τοίνυν Σκοπελιανὸν πάντες, ὁ

---

[1] For this type of rhetoric see Glossary.
[2] Domitian; *cf. Life of Apollonius* vi. 42; and Suetonius,
Domitian, who gives another reason for this edict.

smite his thigh in order to arouse both himself and his hearers. He excelled also in the use of "covert allusion"[1] and ambiguous language, but he was even more admirable in his treatment of the more vigorous and grandiloquent themes, and especially those relating to the Medes, in which occur passages about Darius and Xerxes; for in my opinion he surpassed all the other sophists, both in phrasing these allusions and in handing down that sort of eloquence for his successors to use; and in delivering them he used to represent dramatically the arrogance and levity that are characteristic of the barbarians. It is said that at these times he would sway to and fro more than usual, as though in a Bacchic frenzy, and when one of Polemo's pupils said of him that he beat a loud drum, Scopelian took to himself the sneering jest and retorted: "Yes, I do beat a drum, but it is the shield of Ajax."

He went on many embassies to the Emperor, and while a peculiar good luck ever accompanied his missions as ambassador, his most successful was that on behalf of the vines. For this embassy was sent, not as in most cases on behalf of Smyrna alone, but on behalf of all Asia in general. I will relate the aim of the embassy. The Emperor[2] resolved that there should be no vines in Asia, because it appeared that the people when under the influence of wine plotted revolution; those that had been already planted were to be pulled up, and they were to plant no more in future. There was clearly need of an embassy to represent the whole commune, and of a man who in their defence, like another Orpheus or Thamyris, would charm his hearer. Accordingly they unanimously selected Scopelian, and on this

δ' οὕτω τι ἐκ περιουσίας ἐκράτει τὴν πρεσβείαν, ὡς μὴ μόνον τὸ ἐξεῖναι φυτεύειν ἐπανελθεῖν ἔχων, ἀλλὰ καὶ ἐπιτίμια κατὰ τῶν μὴ φυτευόντων. ὡς δὲ ηὐδοκίμησε τὸν ἀγῶνα τὸν ὑπὲρ τῶν ἀμπέλων, δηλοῖ μὲν καὶ τὰ εἰρημένα, ὁ γὰρ λόγος ἐν τοῖς θαυμασιωτάτοις, δηλοῖ δὲ καὶ τὰ ἐπὶ τῷ λόγῳ, δώρων τε γὰρ ἐπ' αὐτῷ ἔτυχεν, ἃ νομίζεται παρὰ βασιλεῖ, πολλῶν τε προσρήσεών τε καὶ ἐπαίνων, νεότης τε αὐτῷ λαμπρὰ ξυνηκολούθησεν ἐς Ἰωνίαν σοφίας ἐρῶντες.

Ἐπεὶ δὲ Ἀθήνησιν ἐγένετο, ποιεῖται αὐτὸν ξένον ὁ Ἡρώδου τοῦ σοφιστοῦ πατὴρ Ἀττικὸς θαυμάζων ἐπὶ ῥητορικῇ μᾶλλον ἢ τὸν Γοργίαν ποτὲ Θετταλοί. ὁπόσοι γοῦν τῶν πάλαι ῥητόρων ἑρμαῖ ἦσαν ἐν τοῖς τῆς οἰκίας δρόμοις, ἐκέλευε τούτους βάλλεσθαι λίθοις, ὡς διεφθορότας αὐτῷ τὸν υἱόν. μειράκιον μὲν δὴ ἐτύγχανεν ὢν ὁ Ἡρώδης τότε καὶ ὑπὸ τῷ πατρὶ ἔτι, τοῦ δὲ αὐτοσχεδιάζειν ἤρα μόνου, οὐ μὴν ἐθάρρει γε αὐτό, οὐδὲ γὰρ τῷ Σκοπελιανῷ ξυγγεγονὼς ἦν ἐς ἐκεῖνό πω τοῦ χρόνου, οὐδ' ἥτις ἡ τῶν αὐτοσχεδίων ὁρμὴ γιγνώσκων, ὅθεν ἀσμένῳ οἱ ἐγένετο ἡ ἐπιδημία τοῦ ἀνδρός· ἐπειδὴ γὰρ λέγοντος ἤκουσε καὶ διατιθεμένου τὸν αὐτοσχέδιον, ἐπτερώθη ὑπ' αὐτοῦ καὶ ἡτοιμάσθη, καὶ τὸν πατέρα δὲ ἧσαι διανοηθεὶς ἀπαγγέλλει οἱ μελέτην ἐς τὴν ἰδέαν τοῦ ξένου. ὁ πατὴρ δὲ ἠγάσθη τε αὐτὸν τῆς μιμήσεως καὶ πεντήκοντα [1] ἔδωκεν αὐτῷ τάλαντα, ἔδωκε δὲ καὶ αὐτῷ τῷ Σκοπελιανῷ πεντεκαίδεκα, ὁ δέ, ὅσαπερ

---

[1] πεντακόσια Kayser; πεντήκοντα Valckenaer in order to reduce the improbably large sum.

mission he succeeded so far beyond their hopes that he returned bringing not only the permission to plant, but actually the threat of penalties for those who should neglect to do so. How great a reputation he won in this contest on behalf of the vines is evident from what he said, for the oration is among the most celebrated; and it is evident too from what happened as a result of the oration. For by it he won such presents as are usually given at an imperial court, and also many compliments and expressions of praise, and moreover a brilliant band of youths fell in love with his genius and followed him to Ionia.

While he was at Athens he was entertained by Atticus, the father of Herodes the sophist, who admired him for his eloquence more than the Thessalians once admired Gorgias. Atticus accordingly gave orders that all the busts of the ancient orators that were in the porticoes of his house should be pelted with stones, because they had corrupted his son's talent. Herodes at the time was only a stripling and still under his father's control, but he cared only for extempore speaking, though he had not enough confidence for it, since he had not yet studied with Scopelian, nor learned the vigour that extempore eloquence requires. For this reason he rejoiced at Scopelian's visit. For when he heard him speak and handle an extempore discourse, by his example he became fledged and fully equipped, and with the idea of pleasing his father he invited him to hear him give a declamation in the same style as their guest. His father greatly admired his imitation and gave him fifty talents, while to Scopelian himself he gave fifteen; but Herodes besides gave him from

ὁ πατήρ, τοσαῦτα ἀπὸ τῆς ἑαυτοῦ δωρεᾶς προσ-
έδωκεν αὐτῷ, ἔτι καὶ διδάσκαλον ἑαυτοῦ προσειπών. τουτὶ δὲ συνιέντι Ἡρώδου καὶ τῶν τοῦ
Πακτωλοῦ πηγῶν ἥδιον.

Τὴν δὲ εὐτυχίαν, ᾗ περὶ τὰς πρεσβείας ἐχρῆτο,
ξυμβάλλειν ἐστὶ καὶ τοῖσδε· ἔδει μὲν γὰρ τοῖς
Σμυρναίοις τοῦ πρεσβεύσοντος ὑπὲρ αὐτῶν ἀνδρός,
ἡ πρεσβεία δὲ ἦν ὑπὲρ τῶν μεγίστων. ὁ μὲν δὴ
ἐγήρασκεν ἤδη καὶ τοῦ ἀποδημεῖν ἐξώρως εἶχεν,
ἐχειροτονεῖτο δὲ ὁ Πολέμων οὔπω πεπρεσβευκὼς
πρότερον. εὐξάμενος οὖν ὑπὲρ τῆς ἀγαθῆς τύχης
ἐδεῖτο γενέσθαι οἱ τὴν τοῦ Σκοπελιανοῦ πειθώ,
καὶ περιβαλὼν αὐτὸν ἐπὶ τῆς ἐκκλησίας μάλα
ἀστείως ὁ Πολέμων τὰ ἐκ Πατροκλείας ἐπεῖπεν
τῷ ἀνδρί.[1]

δὸς δέ μοι ὤμοιιν τὰ σὰ τεύχεα θωρηχθῆναι,
αἴ κ' ἐμὲ σοὶ ἴσκωσι,

καὶ Ἀπολλώνιος δὲ ὁ Τυανεὺς ὑπερενεγκὼν σοφίᾳ
τὴν ἀνθρωπίνην φύσιν τὸν Σκοπελιανὸν ἐν θαυμασίοις τάττει.

κβ'. Διονύσιος δὲ ὁ Μιλήσιος εἴθ', ὡς ἔνιοί
φασι, πατέρων ἐπιφανεστάτων ἐγένετο, εἴθ', ὥς
τινες, αὐτὸ τοῦτο ἐλευθέρων, ἀφείσθω τούτου
522 τοῦ μέρους, ἐπειδὴ οἰκείᾳ ἀρετῇ ἐλαμπρύνετο, τὸ
γὰρ καταφεύγειν ἐς τοὺς ἄνω ἀποβεβληκότων
ἐστὶ τὸν ἐφ' ἑαυτῶν ἔπαινον. Ἰσαίου δὲ ἀκροατὴς γενόμενος ἀνδρός, ὡς ἔφην, κατὰ φύσιν ἑρμη-
νεύοντος τουτὶ μὲν ἱκανῶς ἀπεμάξατο καὶ πρὸς

---

[1] μάλα . . . ἀνδρὶ in mss. and Kayser precede the quotation;
Cobet transposes.

his own present the same sum as had been bestowed by his father, and called him his teacher. And when he heard this title from Herodes it was sweeter to him than the springs of Pactolus.

The good fortune that attended his embassies we may gather also from the following. The citizens of Smyrna needed someone to go on an embassy for them, and the mission was on affairs of the greatest moment. But he was now growing old and was past the age for travelling, and therefore Polemo was elected, though he had never before acted as ambassador. So in offering up prayers for good luck, Polemo begged that he might be granted the persuasive charm of Scopelian, embraced him before the assembly, and applied very aptly to him the verses from the exploits of Patroclus:

Give me thy harness to buckle about my shoulders, if perchance they may take me for.thee.[1]

Apollonius of Tyana also, who in wisdom surpassed mere human achievement, ranks Scopelian among the men to be admired.[2]

22. With regard to DIONYSIUS OF MILETUS, whether, as some say, he was born of highly distinguished parentage, or, as others say, was merely of free birth, let him not be held responsible on this head, seeing that he achieved distinction by his own merits. For to have recourse to one's ancestors is the mark of those who despair of applause for themselves. He was a pupil of Isaeus, that is of one who, as I have said, employed a natural style, and of this style he successfully took the impress, and the orderly arrange-

---

[1] *Iliad* xvi. 40, Patroclus to Achilles.
[2] *Life of Apollonius* i. 23, 24.

τούτῳ τὴν εὐταξίαν τῶν νοημάτων, καὶ γὰρ δὴ
καὶ τοῦτο Ἰσαίου. μελιχρότατος δὲ περὶ τὰς
ἐννοίας γενόμενος οὐκ ἐμέθυε περὶ τὰς ἡδονάς,
ὥσπερ ἔνιοι τῶν σοφιστῶν, ἀλλ' ἐταμιεύετο λέγων
ἀεὶ πρὸς τοὺς γνωρίμους, ὅτι χρὴ τοῦ μέλιτος
ἄκρῳ δακτύλῳ, ἀλλὰ μὴ κοίλῃ χειρὶ γεύεσθαι,
ὡς ἐν ἅπασι μὲν τοῖς εἰρημένοις δεδήλωται τῷ
Διονυσίῳ, λογικοῖς τε καὶ νομικοῖς καὶ ἠθικοῖς
ἀγῶσι, μάλιστα δὲ ἐν τῷ ἐπὶ Χαιρωνείᾳ θρήνῳ.
διεξιὼν γὰρ τὸν Δημοσθένην τὸν μετὰ Χαιρώνειαν προσαγγέλλοντα [1] τῇ βουλῇ ἑαυτὸν ἐς τήνδε
τὴν μονῳδίαν τοῦ λόγου ἐτελεύτησεν· " ὦ Χαι-
ρώνεια πονηρὸν χωρίον." καὶ πάλιν " ὦ αὐτο-
μολήσασα πρὸς τοὺς βαρβάρους Βοιωτία. στε-
νάξατε οἱ κατὰ γῆς ἥρωες, ἐγγὺς Πλαταιῶν
νενικήμεθα." καὶ πάλιν ἐν τοῖς κρινομένοις ἐπὶ τῷ
μισθοφορεῖν Ἀρκάσιν " Ἀγορὰ πολέμου πρόκειται
καὶ τὰ τῶν Ἑλλήνων κακὰ τὴν Ἀρκαδίαν τρέφει,"
καὶ " ἐπέρχεται πόλεμος αἰτίαν οὐκ ἔχων."

Τοιάδε μὲν ἡ ἐπίπαν ἰδέα τοῦ Διονυσίου, καθ'
ἣν τὰ τῆς μελέτης αὐτῷ προὔβαινεν ἐπισκοπου-
523 μένῳ καιρόν, ὅσονπερ ὁ Ἰσαῖος, ὁ δὲ λόγος ὁ
περὶ τοῦ Διονυσίου λεγόμενος, ὡς Χαλδαίοις
τέχναις τοὺς ὁμιλητὰς τὸ μνημονικὸν ἀναπαι-
δεύοντος πόθεν εἴρηται, ἐγὼ δηλώσω· τέχναι
μνήμης οὔτε εἰσὶν οὔτ' ἂν γένοιντο, μνήμη μὲν
γὰρ δίδωσι τέχνας, αὐτὴ δὲ ἀδίδακτος καὶ οὐδε-

---

[1] προσάγοντα Kayser ; προσαγγέλλοντα Cobet.

---

[1] A proverb ; cf. Lucian, How to write History 4.
[2] This imaginary situation was a favourite theme ; cf.
Life of Polemo, p. 542 ; Syrianus ii. 165 ; Apsines ix. 471.
[3] This perhaps echoes Aeschines, Against Ctesiphon 648.

ment of his thoughts besides; for this too was characteristic of Isaeus. And though he presented his ideas
with honeyed sweetness, he was not intemperate in
the use of pleasing effects, like some of the sophists,
but was economical with them, and would always say
to his pupils that honey should be tasted with the
finger-tip [1] and not by the handful. This indeed
is clearly shown in all the speeches delivered by
Dionysius, whether critical works or forensic or
moral disputations, but above all in the *Dirge for
Chaeronea*. For when representing Demosthenes
as he denounced himself before the Senate after
Chaeronea, [2] he ended his speech with this monody:
"O Chaeronea, wicked city!" and again: "O Boeotia
that hast deserted to the barbarians! Wail, ye
heroes beneath the earth! We have been defeated
near Plataea!" [3] And again in the passage where the
Arcadians are on trial for being mercenaries, he said:
"War is bought and sold in the market-place, and
the woes of the Greeks fatten Arcadia," and "A war
for which there is no cause is upon us." [4]

Such was in general the style of Dionysius,
thus his declamations proceeded, and he used to
meditate his themes about as long as Isaeus. As
for the story that is told about him that he used
to train his pupils in mnemonics by the help of
Chaldean arts, [5] I will show the source of the tradition.
There is no such thing as an art of memory, nor
could there be, for though memory gives us the arts,
it cannot itself be taught, nor can it be acquired by

[4] On the Asianic rhythms in these quotations see Norden,
Antike Kunst-Prosa i. 413. The Arcadians were *notorious*
mercenaries; *cf.* Xenophon, *Hellenica* vii. 1. 23.
[5] For Chaldean astrology *cf.* Julian, vol. i. *Oration* 4.
156 B; 5. 172 D, note; here it is regarded as a kind of magic.

μιᾷ τέχνῃ ἁλωτός, ἔστι γὰρ πλεονέκτημα φύσεως
ἢ τῆς ἀθανάτου ψυχῆς μοῖρα. οὐ γὰρ ἄν ποτε
ἀθάνατα [1] νομισθείη τὰ ἀνθρώπεια, οὐδὲ διδακτά,
ἃ ἐμάθομεν, εἰ μὴ [2] μνήμη συνεπολιτεύετο ἀνθρώποις, ἣν εἴτε μητέρα δεῖ χρόνου καλεῖν, εἴτε
παῖδα, μὴ διαφερώμεθα πρὸς τοὺς ποιητάς, ἀλλ'
ἔστω, ὅ τι βούλονται. πρὸς δὲ τούτοις τίς οὕτως
εὐήθης κατὰ τῆς ἑαυτοῦ δόξης ἐν σοφοῖς γραφόμενος, ὡς γοητεύων ἐν μειρακίοις διαβάλλειν καὶ
ἃ ὀρθῶς ἐπαιδεύθη; πόθεν οὖν τὸ μνημονικὸν
τοῖς ἀκροωμένοις; ἄπληστα τὴν ἡδονὴν ἐδόκει
τὰ τοῦ Διονυσίου καὶ πολλάκις ἐπαναλαμβάνειν
αὐτὰ ἠναγκάζετο, ἐπειδὴ ξυνίει σφῶν χαιρόντων
τῇ ἀκροάσει. οἱ δὴ εὐμαθέστεροι τῶν νέων ἐν-
ετυποῦντο αὐτὰ ταῖς γνώμαις καὶ ἀπήγγελλον
ἑτέροις μελέτῃ μᾶλλον ἢ μνήμῃ ξυνειληφότες,
ὅθεν μνημονικοί τε ὠνομάζοντο καὶ τέχνην αὐτὸ
524 πεποιημένοι. ἔνθεν ὁρμώμενοί τινες τὰς τοῦ Διονυσίου μελέτας ἐσπερματολογῆσθαί φασιν, ὡς δὴ
ἄλλο ἄλλου ξυνενεγκόντων ἐς αὐτάς, ἐν ᾧ ἐβρα-
χυλόγησεν.

Μεγάλων μὲν οὖν ἠξιοῦτο κἀκ τῶν πόλεων,
ὁπόσαι αὐτὸν ἐπὶ σοφίᾳ ἐθαύμαζον, μεγίστων δὲ
ἐκ βασιλέως· Ἀδριανὸς γὰρ σατράπην μὲν αὐτὸν
ἀπέφηνεν οὐκ ἀφανῶν ἐθνῶν, ἐγκατέλεξε δὲ
τοῖς δημοσίᾳ ἱππεύουσι καὶ τοῖς ἐν τῷ Μουσείῳ
σιτουμένοις, τὸ δὲ Μουσεῖον τράπεζα Αἰγυπτία

---

[1] θνητὰ Kayser; ἀθάνατα Jahn.　　[2] μὴ Cobet adds.

[1] An allusion to the Platonic doctrine of reminiscence,
and especially to *Meno* 81 c D.

[2] Philostratus refers to the *Hymn to Memory* by Apollonius
of Tyana; see his *Life* i. 14. The sophists certainly taught
some sort of mnemonics; *cf.* Volkmann, *Rhetorik* 567 foll.

any method or system, since it is a gift of nature or a part of the immortal soul. For never could human beings be regarded as endowed with immortality, nor could what we have learned be taught, did not Memory inhabit the minds of men.[1] And I will not dispute with the poets whether we ought to call her the mother of Time or the daughter, but let that be as they please.[2] Moreover, who that is enrolled among the wise would be so foolishly careless of his own reputation as to use magic arts with his pupils, and so bring into disrepute also what has been taught by correct methods? How was it then that his pupils had a peculiar gift of memory? It was because the declamations of Dionysius gave them a pleasure of which they could never have enough, and he was compelled to repeat them very often, since he knew that they were delighted to hear them. And so the more ready-witted of these youths used to engrave them on their minds, and when, by long practice rather than by sheer memory, they had thoroughly grasped them, they used to recite them to the rest; and hence they came to be called " the memory-artists," and men who made it into an art. It is on these grounds that some people say that the declamations of Dionysius are a collection of odds and ends, for they say one person added this, another that, where he had been concise.

Great honours were paid him by the cities that admired his talent, but the greatest was from the Emperor. For Hadrian appointed him satrap [3] over peoples by no means obscure, and enrolled him in the order of the knights and among those who had free meals in the Museum. (By the Museum I mean

---

[3] *i.e.* procurator. An Ephesian inscription refers to D. as ἐπίτροπον τοῦ Σεβαστοῦ.

ξυγκαλοῦσα τοὺς ἐν πάσῃ τῇ γῇ ἐλλογίμους.
πλείστας δὲ ἐπελθὼν πόλεις καὶ πλείστοις ἐνομιλήσας ἔθνεσιν οὔτε ἐρωτικήν ποτε αἰτίαν ἔλαβεν
οὔτε ἀλαζόνα ὑπὸ τοῦ σωφρονέστατός τε φαίνεσθαι καὶ ἐφεστηκώς. οἱ δὲ ἀνατιθέντες Διονυσίῳ τὸν Ἀράσπαν τὸν τῆς Πανθείας ἐρῶντα
ἀνήκοοι μὲν τῶν τοῦ Διονυσίου ῥυθμῶν, ἀνήκοοι
δὲ τῆς ἄλλης ἑρμηνείας, ἄπειροι δὲ τῆς τῶν ἐνθυμημάτων τέχνης· οὐ γὰρ Διονυσίου τὸ φρόντισμα
τοῦτο, ἀλλὰ Κέλερος τοῦ τεχνογράφου, ὁ δὲ
Κέλερ βασιλικῶν μὲν ἐπιστολῶν ἀγαθὸς προστάτης, μελέτῃ δὲ οὐκ ἀποχρῶν, Διονυσίῳ δὲ
τὸν ἐκ μειρακίου χρόνον διάφορος.

Μηδ' ἐκεῖνα παρείσθω μοι Ἀρισταίου γε ἠκροα-
μένῳ αὐτὰ πρεσβυτάτου τῶν κατ' ἐμὲ Ἑλλήνων καὶ
πλεῖστα ὑπὲρ σοφιστῶν εἰδότος· ἐγήρασκε μὲν ὁ
Διονύσιος ἐν δόξῃ λαμπρᾷ, παρήει δ' ἐς ἀκμὴν ὁ
Πολέμων οὔπω γιγνωσκόμενος τῷ Διονυσίῳ καὶ
ἐπεδήμει ταῖς Σάρδεσι ἀγορεύσων [1] δίκην ἐν τοῖς
ἑκατὸν ἀνδράσιν, ὑφ' ὧν ἐδικαιοῦτο ἡ Λυδία.
ἑσπέρας οὖν ἐς τὰς Σάρδεις ἥκων ὁ Διονύσιος ἤρετο
525 Δωρίωνα τὸν κριτικὸν ξένον ἑαυτοῦ· " εἰπέ μοι,"
ἔφη " ὦ Δωρίων, τί Πολέμων ἐνταῦθα;" καὶ ὁ
Δωρίων " ἀνὴρ" ἔφη " πλουσιώτατος τῶν ἐν
Λυδίᾳ κινδυνεύων περὶ τῆς οὐσίας ἄγει συνήγορον
τὸν Πολέμωνα ἀπὸ τῆς Σμύρνης πείσας διταλάντῳ

---

[1] ἀγορεύων Kayser; ἀγορεύσων Cobet.

[1] Founded by the first Ptolemy at Alexandria in connexion with the Library.
[2] Panthea, wife of the Persian king Abradatas, was taken
captive by the Elder Cyrus and placed in charge of the

a dining-table in Egypt[1] to which are invited the most distinguished men of all countries.) He visited very many cities and lived among many peoples, yet he never incurred the charge of licentious or insolent conduct, being most temperate and sedate in his behaviour. Those who ascribe to Dionysius the piece called *Araspes the Lover of Panthea*,[2] are ignorant not only of his rhythms but of his whole style of eloquence, and moreover they know nothing of the art of ratiocination. For this work is not by Dionysius, but by Celer[3] the writer on rhetoric; and Celer, though he was a good Imperial Secretary, lacked skill in declamation and was on unfriendly terms with Dionysius from their earliest youth.

I must not omit the following facts which I heard direct from Aristaeus who was the oldest of all the educated Greeks in my time and knew most about the sophists. When Dionysius was beginning to grow old and enjoyed the most distinguished reputation, and Polemo, on the other hand, was attaining to the height of his career, though he was not yet personally known to Dionysius, Polemo paid a visit to Sardis to plead a case before the Centumviri who had jurisdiction over Lydia. And towards evening Dionysius came to Sardis and asked Dorion the critic, who was his host: "Tell me, Dorion, what is Polemo doing here?" And Dorion replied: "A very wealthy man, a Lydian, is in danger of losing his property, and hence he has brought Polemo from Smyrna to be his advocate by the inducement of a fee of two talents, and he will defend the suit

Mede Araspes who fell in love with her; *cf.* Xenophon, *Cyropaedia* v. 1. 4; Philostratus, *Imagines* ii. 9.

[3] Probably the teacher of Marcus Aurelius; *cf. To Himself* viii. 25.

μισθῷ, καὶ ἀγωνιεῖται τὴν δίκην αὔριον." καὶ ὁ
Διονύσιος " οἷον " ἔφη " ἔρμαιον εἴρηκας, εἰ καὶ
ἀκοῦσαί μοι ἔσται Πολέμωνος οὔπω ἐς πεῖραν
αὐτοῦ ἀφιγμένῳ." " ἔοικεν " εἶπεν ὁ Δωρίων
" στρέφειν σε ὁ νεανίας ἐς ὄνομα ἤδη προβαίνων
μέγα." " καὶ καθεύδειν γε οὐκ ἐᾷ, μὰ τὴν Ἀθηνᾶν,
ἦ δ' ὁ Διονύσιος " ἀλλ' ἐς πήδησιν ἄγει τὴν καρδίαν καὶ τὴν γνώμην ἐνθυμουμένῳ, ὡς πολλοὶ οἱ
ἐπαινέται αὐτοῦ, καὶ τοῖς μὲν δωδεκάκρουνον [1]
δοκεῖ τὸ στόμα, οἱ δὲ καὶ πήχεσι διαμετροῦσιν
αὐτοῦ τὴν γλῶτταν, ὥσπερ τὰς τοῦ Νείλου ἀνα-
βάσεις. σὺ δ' ἂν [2] ταύτην ἰάσαιό μοι τὴν φροντίδα
εἰπών, τί μὲν πλέον, τί δὲ ἧττον ἐν ἐμοί τε κἀκείνῳ
καθεώρακας." καὶ ὁ Δωρίων μάλα σωφρόνως
" αὐτός," εἶπεν " ὦ Διονύσιε, σεαυτῷ τε κἀκείνῳ
δικάσεις ἄμεινον, σὺ γὰρ ὑπὸ σοφίας οἷος σαυτόν τε
γιγνώσκειν, ἕτερόν τε μὴ ἀγνοῆσαι." ἤκουσεν ὁ
Διονύσιος ἀγωνιζομένου τὴν δίκην καὶ ἀπιὼν τοῦ
δικαστηρίου " ἰσχὺν " ἔφη " ὁ ἀθλητὴς ἔχει, ἀλλ'
οὐκ ἐκ παλαίστρας." ταῦτα ὡς ἤκουσεν ὁ Πολέμων,
ἦλθε μὲν ἐπὶ θύρας τοῦ Διονυσίου μελέτην αὐτῷ
ἐπαγγέλλων, ἀφικομένου δὲ διαπρεπῶς ἀγωνιζό-
526 μενος προσῆλθε τῷ Διονυσίῳ καὶ ἀντερείσας τὸν
ὦμον, ὥσπερ οἱ τῆς σταδιαίας πάλης ἐμβιβάζοντες,
μάλα ἀστείως ἐπετώθασεν εἰπὼν

ἦσάν ποτ', ἦσαν ἄλκιμοι Μιλήσιοι.

[1] δωδεκάκρουνος Kayser; δωδεκάκρουνον Cobet; cf. Cratinus,
Putine frag. 7 δωδεκάκρουνον τὸ στόμα.
[2] αὖ Kayser; ἂν Cobet.

[1] The epithet indicates the volume and variety of his
oratory.

to-morrow." "What a stroke of luck is this!" cried Dionysius, "that I shall actually be able to hear Polemo, for I have never yet had a chance to judge of him." Dorion remarked: "The young man seems to make you uneasy by his rapid advance to a great reputation." "Yes, by Athene," said Dionysius, "he does not even allow me to sleep. He makes my heart palpitate, and my mind too, when I think how many admirers he has. For some think that from his lips flow twelve springs,[1] others measure his tongue by cubits, like the risings of the Nile. But you might cure this anxiety for me by telling me what are the respective superiorities and defects that you have observed in us both." Dorion replied with great discretion: "You yourself, Dionysius, will be better able to judge between yourself and him, for you are well qualified by your wisdom not only to know yourself but also to observe another accurately." Dionysius heard Polemo defend the suit, and as he left the court he remarked: "This athlete possesses strength, but it does not come from the wrestling-ground." When Polemo heard this he came to Dionysius' door and announced that he would declaim before him. And when he had come and Polemo had sustained his part with conspicuous success, he went up to Dionysius, and leaning shoulder to shoulder with him, like those who begin a wrestling match standing, he wittily turned the laugh against him by quoting

Once O once they were strong, the men of Miletus.[2]

[2] For this iambic response of Apollo which became a proverb for the degenerate cf. Aristophanes, *Plutus* 1003. It occurs also as a fragment of Anacreon.

Ἀνδρῶν μὲν οὖν ἐπιφανῶν πᾶσα γῆ τάφος,
Διονυσίῳ δὲ σῆμα ἐν τῇ ἐπιφανεστάτῃ Ἐφέσῳ,
τέθαπται γὰρ ἐν τῇ ἀγορᾷ κατὰ τὸ κυριώτατον τῆς
Ἐφέσου, ἐν ᾗ κατεβίω παιδεύσας τὸν πρῶτον βίον
ἐν τῇ Λέσβῳ.

κγ΄. Λολλιανὸς δὲ ὁ Ἐφέσιος προύστη μὲν
τοῦ Ἀθήνησι θρόνου πρῶτος, προύστη δὲ καὶ τοῦ
Ἀθηναίων δήμου στρατηγήσας αὐτοῖς τὴν ἐπὶ τῶν
ὅπλων, ἡ δὲ ἀρχὴ αὕτη πάλαι μὲν κατέλεγέ τε καὶ
ἐξῆγεν ἐς τὰ πολέμια, νυνὶ δὲ τροφῶν ἐπιμελεῖται
καὶ σίτου ἀγορᾶς. θορύβου δὲ καθεστηκότος παρὰ
τὰ ἀρτοπώλια καὶ τῶν Ἀθηναίων βάλλειν αὐτὸν
ὡρμηκότων Παγκράτης ὁ κύων ὁ μετὰ ταῦτα ἐν
Ἰσθμῷ φιλοσοφήσας παρελθὼν ἐς τοὺς Ἀθηναίους
καὶ εἰπὼν " Λολλιανὸς οὐκ ἔστιν ἀρτοπώλης, ἀλλὰ
λογοπώλης " διέχεεν οὕτω τοὺς Ἀθηναίους, ὡς
μεθεῖναι τοὺς λίθους διὰ χειρὸς αὐτοῖς ὄντας. σίτου
δὲ ἐκ Θετταλίας ἐσπεπλευκότος καὶ χρημάτων
δημοσίᾳ οὐκ ὄντων ἐπέτρεψεν ὁ Λολλιανὸς ἔρανον
τοῖς αὐτοῦ γνωρίμοις, καὶ χρήματα συχνὰ ἠθροίσθη.
καὶ τοῦτο μὲν ἀνδρὸς εὐμηχάνου δόξει καὶ σοφοῦ
τὰ πολιτικά, ἐκεῖνο δὲ δικαίου τε καὶ εὐγνώμονος·
τὰ γὰρ χρήματα ταῦτα τοῖς ξυμβαλομένοις ἀπέδωκεν ἐπανεὶς τὸν μισθὸν τῆς ἀκροάσεως.

Ἔδοξε δὲ ὁ σοφιστὴς οὗτος τεχνικώτατός τε καὶ
φρονιμώτατος τὸ ἐπιχειρηματικὸν ἐν ἐπινοίᾳ τεχ-
νικῇ κείμενον ἱκανῶς ἐκπονῆσαι, καὶ ἑρμηνεῦσαι

---

[1] From Thucydides ii. 43.
[2] *i.e.* the municipal, as distinct from the Imperial chair.

Famous men have the whole earth for their sepulchre,[1] but the actual tomb of Dionysius is in the most conspicuous part of Ephesus, for he was buried in the market-place, on the most important spot in Ephesus, in which city he ended his life; though during the earlier period of his career he had taught in Lesbos.

23. LOLLIANUS OF EPHESUS was the first to be appointed to the chair of rhetoric[2] at Athens, and he also governed the Athenian people, since he held the office of hoplite general in that city. The functions of this office were formerly to levy troops and lead them to war, but now it has charge of the food-supplies and the provision-market. Once when a riot arose in the bread-sellers' quarter, and the Athenians were on the point of stoning Lollianus, Pancrates the Cynic, who later professed philosophy at the Isthmus, came forward before the Athenians, and by simply remarking: "Lollianus does not sell bread but words," he so diverted the Athenians that they let fall the stones that were in their hands. Once when a cargo of grain came by sea from Thessaly and there was no money in the public treasury to pay for it, Lollianus bade his pupils contribute, and a large sum was collected. This device proves him to have been a very ingenious man and prudent in public affairs, but what followed proved that he was both just and magnanimous. For by remitting the fee for his lectures he repaid this money to those who had subscribed it.

This sophist was considered to be deeply versed in his art and very clever in working out successfully the train of reasoning that depends on skill in invention. His style was admirable, and in the invention

μὲν ἀποχρῶν, νοῆσαι δὲ καὶ τὰ νοηθέντα τάξαι ἀπέριττος. διαφαίνονται δὲ τοῦ λογου καὶ λαμπρό-τητες λήγουσαι ταχέως, ὥσπερ τὸ τῆς ἀστραπῆς σέλας. δηλοῦται δὲ τοῦτο ἐν πᾶσι μέν, μάλιστα δὲ ἐν τοῖσδε· κατηγορῶν μὲν γὰρ τοῦ Λεπτίνου διὰ τὸν νόμον, ἐπεὶ μὴ ἐφοίτα τοῖς Ἀθηναίοις ἐκ τοῦ Πόντου σῖτος, ὧδε ἥκμασεν· " κέκλεισται τὸ στόμα τοῦ Πόντου νόμῳ καὶ τὰς Ἀθηναίων τροφὰς ὀλίγαι κωλύουσι συλλαβαί, καὶ ταυτὸν δύναται Λύσανδρος ναυμαχῶν καὶ Λεπτίνης νομομαχῶν" ἀντιλέγων δὲ τοῖς Ἀθηναίοις ἀπορία χρημάτων βουλευομένοις πωλεῖν τὰς νήσους ὧδε ἔπνευσεν· " λῦσον, ὦ Πόσειδον, τὴν ἐπὶ Δήλῳ χάριν, συγ-χώρησον αὐτῇ πωλουμένῃ φυγεῖν." ἐσχεδίαζε μὲν οὖν κατὰ τὸν Ἰσαῖον, οὗ δὴ καὶ ἠκροάσατο, μισθοὺς δὲ γενναίους ἐπράττετο τὰς συνουσίας οὐ μελε-τηρὰς μόνον, ἀλλὰ καὶ διδασκαλικὰς παρέχων. εἰκόνες δὲ αὐτοῦ Ἀθήνησι μία μὲν ἐπ᾽ ἀγορᾶς, ἑτέρα δὲ ἐν τῷ ἄλσει τῷ μικρῷ, ὃ αὐτὸς λέγεται ἐκφυτεῦσαι.

κδ'. Οὐδὲ τὸν Βυζάντιον σοφιστὴν παραλείψω Μάρκον, ὑπὲρ οὗ κἂν ἐπιπλήξαιμι τοῖς Ἕλλησιν, εἰ 528 τοιόσδε γενόμενος, ὁποῖον δηλώσω, μήπω τυγχάνοι τῆς ἑαυτοῦ δόξης. Μάρκῳ τοίνυν ἦν ἀναφορὰ τοῦ

---

[1] This fictitious theme is based on Demosthenes, *Leptines* 30, delivered in 355, and assumes that the law of Leptines to abolish exemptions from public services was in force, and that the evils foreboded by Demosthenes had come about; *cf.* Apsines 232 for the same theme.

[2] Norden, p. 410, quotes this passage for its "similar endings."

[3] We do not know whether this theme is based on historical fact or is purely fictitious.

and arrangement of his ideas he was free from affectation and redundancy. In his oratory brilliant passages flare out and suddenly come to an end like a flash of lightning. This is evident in all that he wrote, but especially in the example that I now quote. His theme was to denounce Leptines on account of his law, because the supply of corn had failed to reach the Athenians from the Pontus;[1] and he wound up as follows: "The mouth of the Pontus has been locked up by a law, and a few syllables keep back the food supply of Athens; so that Lysander fighting with his ships and Leptines fighting with his law have the same power."[2] Again, when his theme was to oppose the Athenians, when in a scarcity of funds they were planning to sell the islands,[3] he declaimed with energy the following: "Take back, Poseidon, the favour that you granted to Delos![4] Permit her, while we are selling her, to make her escape!" In his extempore speeches he imitated Isaeus, whose pupil he had been. He used to charge handsome fees, and in his classes he not only declaimed but also taught the rules of the art. There are two statues of him at Athens, one in the agora, the other in the small grove which he is said to have planted himself.

24. Nor must I omit to speak of MARCUS OF BYZANTIUM,[5] on whose behalf I will bring this reproach against the Greeks, that though he was as talented as I shall show, he does not as yet receive the honour that he deserves. The genealogy of Marcus dated back as

[4] Delos was once a "floating" island and was made stationary by Poseidon; cf. Ovid, *Metamorphoses* vi. 191.
[5] We know nothing more about Marcus, unless he is the Annius Marcus mentioned by Capitolinus, *Life of Marcus Aurelius*, as one of that Emperor's teachers.

γένους ἐς τὸν ἀρχαῖον Βύζαντα, πατὴρ δὲ ὁμώνυμος
ἔχων θαλαττουργοὺς οἰκέτας ἐν Ἱερῷ, τὸ δὲ Ἱερὸν
παρὰ τὰς ἐκβολὰς τοῦ Πόντου. διδάσκαλος δὲ
αὐτοῦ Ἰσαῖος ἐγένετο, παρ᾽ οὗ καὶ τὸ κατὰ φύσιν
ἑρμηνεύειν μαθὼν ἐπεκόσμησεν αὐτὸ ὡραισμένῃ
πραότητι. καὶ παράδειγμα ἱκανώτατον τῆς Μάρκου ἰδέας ὁ Σπαρτιάτης ὁ ξυμβουλεύων τοῖς
Λακεδαιμονίοις μὴ παραδέχεσθαι τοὺς ἀπὸ Σφακ-
τηρίας γυμνοὺς ἥκοντας. τῇδε γὰρ τῆς ὑποθέσεως
ἤρξατο ὧδε· " ἀνὴρ Λακεδαιμόνιος μέχρι γήρως
φυλάξας τὴν ἀσπίδα ἡδέως μὲν ἂν τοὺς γυμνοὺς
τούτους ἀπέκτεινα." ὅστις δὲ καὶ τὰς διαλέξεις
ὅδε ὁ ἀνὴρ ἐγένετο, ξυμβαλεῖν ἐστιν ἐκ τῶνδε·
διδάσκων γὰρ περὶ τῆς τῶν σοφιστῶν τέχνης, ὡς
πολλὴ καὶ ποικίλη, παράδειγμα τοῦ λόγου τὴν ἶριν
ἐποιήσατο καὶ ἤρξατο τῆς διαλέξεως ὧδε· " ὁ τὴν
ἶριν ἰδών, ὡς ἓν χρῶμα, οὐκ εἶδεν ὡς θαυμάσαι, ὁ
δέ, ὅσα χρώματα, μᾶλλον ἐθαύμασεν." οἱ δὲ
τὴν διάλεξιν ταύτην Ἀλκινόῳ τῷ Στωικῷ ἀνατιθέντες διαμαρτάνουσι μὲν ἰδέας λόγου, διαμαρτάνουσι δὲ ἀληθείας, ἀδικώτατοι δ᾽ ἀνθρώπων εἰσὶ
προσαφαιρούμενοι τὸν σοφιστὴν καὶ τὰ οἰκεῖα.

Τὸ δὲ τῶν ὀφρύων ἦθος καὶ ἡ τοῦ προσώπου
σύννοια σοφιστὴν ἐδήλου τὸν Μάρκον, καὶ γὰρ
ἐτύγχανεν ἀεί τι ἐπισκοπῶν τῇ γνώμῃ καὶ ἀνα-
παιδεύων ἑαυτὸν τοῖς ἐς τὸ σχεδιάζειν ἄγουσι.
καὶ τοῦτο ἐδηλοῦτο μὲν τῇ τῶν ὀφθαλμῶν στάσει

---

[1] The legendary founder of Byzantium, said to have been
the son of Poseidon.

[2] The punishment of these men by Sparta is described by
Thucydides v. 34.

[3] Iris was the daughter of Thaumas whose name means

far as the original Byzas,[1] and his father, who had the
same name, owned slaves who were fishermen at
Hieron. (Hieron is near the entrance to the Pontus.)
His teacher was Isaeus, and from him he learned the
natural style of oratory, but he adorned it with a
charming suavity. The most characteristic example
of the style of Marcus is his speech of the Spartan
advising the Lacedaemonians not to receive the men
who had returned from Sphacteria without their
weapons.[2] He began this argument as follows: " As
a citizen of Lacedaemon who till old age has kept
his shield, I would gladly have slain these men who
have lost theirs." His style in his discourses may be
gathered from the following. He was trying to
show how rich and how many-sided is the art of the
sophists, and taking the rainbow as the image of an
oration, he began his discourse thus : " He who sees
the rainbow only as a single colour does not see a
sight to marvel at, but he who sees how many
colours it has, marvels more." [3] Those who ascribe
this discourse to Alcinous the Stoic fail to observe
the style of his speech, they fail to observe the truth,
and are most dishonest men, in that they try to rob
the sophist even of what he wrote about his own art.

The expression of his brows and the gravity of
his countenance proclaimed Marcus a sophist, and
indeed his mind was constantly brooding over some
theme, and he was always training himself in the
methods that prepare one for extempore speaking.
This was evident from the steady gaze of his eyes

" Wonder." The play on the word θαυμάζειν, " to wonder,"
seems to echo Plato, *Theaetetus* 155 c d : " philosophy begins
in wonder." Plato goes on to apply the image of the rainbow (Iris) to philosophy.

πεπηγότων τὰ πολλὰ ἐς ἀπορρήτους ἐννοίας, ὡμο-
λογήθη δὲ καὶ ὑπὸ τοῦ ἀνδρός· ἐρομένου γάρ τινος
αὐτὸν τῶν ἐπιτηδείων, ὅπως χθὲς ἐμελέτα " ἐπ'
529 ἐμαυτοῦ μὲν " ἔφη " λόγου ἀξίως, ἐπὶ δὲ τῶν γνωρίμων ἧττον." θαυμάσαντος δὲ τὴν ἀπόκρισιν
" ἐγὼ " ἔφη ὁ Μάρκος " καὶ τῇ σιωπῇ ἐνεργῷ
χρῶμαι καὶ γυμνάζουσί με δύο ὑποθέσεις καὶ τρεῖς
ὑπὸ τὴν μίαν, ἣν ἐς τὸ κοινὸν ἀγωνίζομαι."
γενειάδος δὲ καὶ κόμης αὐχμηρῶς εἶχεν, ὅθεν
ἀγροικότερος ἀνδρὸς πεπνυμένου ἐδόκει τοῖς πολλοῖς. τουτὶ δὲ καὶ Πολέμων ὁ σοφιστὴς πρὸς
αὐτὸν ἔπαθεν· παρῆλθε μὲν γὰρ ἐς τὴν τοῦ
Πολέμωνος διατριβὴν ὀνομαστὸς ἤδη ὤν, ξυγ-
καθημένων δὲ τῶν ἐς τὴν ἀκρόασιν ἀπηντηκότων
ἀναγνούς τις αὐτὸν τῶν ἐς τὸ Βυζάντιον πεπλευ-
κότων διεμήνυσε τῷ πέλας, ὁ δὲ τῷ πλησίον, καὶ
διεδόθη ἐς πάντας, ὅτι ὁ Βυζάντιος εἴη σοφιστής,
ὅθεν τοῦ Πολέμωνος αἰτοῦντος τὰς ὑποθέσεις
ἐπεστρέφοντο πάντες ἐς τὸν Μάρκον, ἵνα προβάλοι.
τοῦ δὲ Πολέμωνος εἰπόντος " τί ἐς τὸν ἄγροικον
ὁρᾶτε; οὐ γὰρ δώσει γε οὗτος ὑπόθεσιν," ὁ
Μάρκος ἐπάρας τὴν φωνήν, ὥσπερ εἰώθει, καὶ
ἀνακύψας " καὶ προβαλῶ[1]" ἔφη " καὶ μελετασεῦμαι." ἔνθεν ἑλὼν ὁ Πολέμων καὶ ξυνιεὶς
δωριάζοντος διελέχθη ἐς τὸν ἄνδρα πολλά τε καὶ
θαυμάσια ἐφιεὶς τῷ καιρῷ, μελετήσας δὲ καὶ
μελετῶντος ἀκροασάμενος καὶ ἐθαυμάσθη καὶ
ἐθαύμασεν.

Μετὰ ταῦτα δὲ ἧκων ὁ Μάρκος ἐς τὰ Μέγαρα,
οἰκισταὶ δὲ οὗτοι Βυζαντίων, ἐστασίαζον μὲν οἱ

---

[1] προβαλοῦμαι . . . μελετήσομαι Kayser; προβαλῶ . . .
μελετασεῦμαι Cobet, to give the Doric dialect.

which were usually intent on secret thoughts, and, moreover, it was admitted by the man himself. For when one of his friends asked him how he declaimed the day before, he replied : " To myself, well enough, but to my pupils not so well." And when the other expressed surprise at the answer, Marcus said: " I work even when I am silent, and I keep myself in practice with two or three arguments beside the one that I maintain in public." His beard and hair were always unkempt, and hence most people thought that he looked too boorish to be a learned man. And this was the impression of him that Polemo the sophist had. For, when he had already made his reputation, he once visited Polemo's school, and when the pupils who had come to attend the lecture had taken their seats, one of those who had made the voyage to Byzantium recognized him and pointed him out to the man next him, and he in turn to his neighbour, and so word was handed on to them all that he was the sophist from Byzantium. Accordingly, when Polemo asked for themes to be proposed, they all turned towards Marcus that he might propose one. And when Polemo asked: " Why do you look to the rustic? This fellow will not give you a theme," Marcus, speaking as he always did at the top of his voice, and throwing his head up, retorted : " I will propose a subject and will myself declaim." Thereupon Polemo, who recognized him partly by his Doric dialect, addressed himself to Marcus in a long and wonderful speech on the spur of the moment, and when he had declaimed and heard the other declaim he both admired and was admired.

When, later on, Marcus went to Megara (Byzantium was originally a Megarian colony), the Megarians

Μεγαρεῖς πρὸς τοὺς Ἀθηναίους ἀκμαζούσαις ταῖς
γνώμαις, ὥσπερ ἄρτι τοῦ πινακίου ἐπ' αὐτοὺς γε-
γραμμένου, καὶ οὐκ ἐδέχοντο σφᾶς ἐς τὰ Πύθια τὰ
μικρὰ ἥκοντας. παρελθὼν δὲ ἐς μέσους ὁ Μάρκος
οὕτω τι μεθήρμοσε τοὺς Μεγαρέας, ὡς ἀνοῖξαι
πεῖσαι τὰς οἰκίας καὶ δέξασθαι τοὺς Ἀθηναίους ἐπὶ
γυναῖκάς τε καὶ παῖδας. ἠγάσθη αὐτὸν καὶ
530 Ἀδριανὸς ὁ αὐτοκράτωρ πρεσβεύοντα ὑπὲρ Βυζαντίων, ἐπιτηδειότατος τῶν πάλαι βασιλέων γενόμενος ἀρετὰς αὐξῆσαι.

κε΄. Πολέμων δὲ ὁ σοφιστὴς οὔθ', ὡς οἱ πολλοὶ
δοκοῦσι, Σμυρναῖος, οὔθ', ὥς τινες, ἐκ Φρυγῶν,
ἀλλὰ ἤνεγκεν αὐτὸν Λαοδίκεια ἡ ἐν Καρίᾳ, ποταμῷ
πρόσοικος Λύκῳ, μεσογεία μέν, δυνατωτέρα δὲ
τῶν ἐπὶ θαλάττῃ. ἡ μὲν δὴ τοῦ Πολέμωνος οἰκία
πολλοὶ ὕπατοι καὶ ἔτι, ἐρασταὶ δὲ αὐτοῦ πολλαὶ μὲν
πόλεις, διαφερόντως δὲ ἡ Σμύρνα· οὗτοι γὰρ ἐκ
μειρακίου κατιδόντες τι ἐν αὐτῷ μέγα πάντας τοὺς
οἴκοι στεφάνους ἐπὶ τὴν τοῦ Πολέμωνος κεφαλὴν
συνήνεγκαν, αὐτῷ τε ψηφισάμενοι καὶ γένει τὰ
οἴκοι ζηλωτά, προκαθῆσθαι γὰρ τῶν Ἀδριανῶν
Ὀλυμπίων ἔδοσαν τῷ ἀνδρὶ καὶ ἐγγόνοις, καὶ τῆς
531 ἱερᾶς τριήρους ἐπιβατεύειν. πέμπεται γάρ τις μηνὶ
Ἀνθεστηριῶνι μεταρσία τριήρης ἐς ἀγοράν, ἣν ὁ
τοῦ Διονύσου ἱερεύς, οἷον κυβερνήτης, εὐθύνει πεί-
σματα ἐκ θαλάττης λύουσαν.

Ἐνσπουδάζων δὲ τῇ Σμύρνῃ τάδε αὐτὴν ὤνησεν·
πρῶτα μὲν τὴν πόλιν πολυανθρωποτάτην αὑτῆς

---

[1] This was the decree by which the Megarians were
proscribed by the Athenians in the fifth century B.C.
[2] These games were held at Smyrna.
[3] February.

were still keeping up their quarrel with the Athenians with the utmost energy of their minds, just as if the famous decree[1] against them had been lately drawn up; and they did not admit them when they came to the Lesser Pythian games. Marcus, however, came among them, and so changed the hearts of the Megarians that he persuaded them to throw open their houses and to admit the Athenians to the society of their wives and children. The Emperor Hadrian too admired him when he came on an embassy for Byzantium, for of all the Emperors in the past he was the most disposed to foster merit.

25. POLEMO the sophist was neither a native of Smyrna, as is commonly supposed, nor from Phrygia as some say, but he was born at Laodicea in Caria, a city which lies on the river Lycus and, though far inland, is more important than those on the sea-coast. Polemo's family has produced many men of consular rank, and still does, and many cities were in love with him, but especially Smyrna. For the people having from his boyhood observed in him a certain greatness, heaped on the head of Polemo all the wreaths of honour that were theirs to give, decreeing for himself and his family the distinctions most sought after in Smyrna; for they bestowed on him and his descendants the right to preside over the Olympic games founded by Hadrian,[2] and to go on board the sacred trireme. For in the month Anthesterion[3] a trireme in full sail is brought in procession to the agora, and the priest of Dionysus, like a pilot, steers it as it comes from the sea, loosing its cables.

By opening his school at Smyrna he benefited the city in the following ways. In the first place he made her appear far more populous than before,

φαίνεσθαι, νεότητος αὐτῇ ἐπιρρεούσης ἐξ ἠπείρων
τε καὶ νήσων οὐκ ἀκολάστου καὶ ξυγκλύδος, ἀλλ'
ἐξειλεγμένης τε καὶ καθαρῶς [1] Ἑλλάδος, ἔπειτα
ὁμονοοῦσαν καὶ ἀστασίαστον πολιτεύειν, τὸν γὰρ
πρὸ τοῦ χρόνον ἐστασίαζεν ἡ Σμύρνα καὶ διεστή-
κεσαν οἱ ἄνω πρὸς τοὺς ἐπὶ θαλάττῃ. πλείστου δὲ
ἄξιος τῇ πόλει καὶ τὰ πρεσβευτικὰ ἐγένετο φοιτῶν
παρὰ τοὺς αὐτοκράτορὰς καὶ προαγωνιζόμενος τῶν
ἠθῶν. Ἀδριανὸν γοῦν προσκείμενον τοῖς Ἐφεσίοις
οὕτω τι μετεποίησε τοῖς Σμυρναίοις, ὡς ἐν ἡμέρᾳ
μιᾷ μυριάδας χιλίας ἐπαντλῆσαι αὐτὸν τῇ Σμύρνῃ,
ἀφ' ὧν τά τε τοῦ σίτου ἐμπόρια ἐξεποιήθη καὶ
γυμνάσιον τῶν κατὰ τὴν Ἀσίαν μεγαλοπρεπέστατον
καὶ νεὼς τηλεφανὴς ὁ ἐπὶ τῆς ἄκρας ἀντικεῖσθαι
δοκῶν τῷ Μίμαντι. καὶ μὴν καὶ τοῖς ἁμαρτα-
νομένοις δημοσίᾳ ἐπιπλήττων καὶ κατὰ σοφίαν
πλεῖστα νουθετῶν ὠφέλει, ὕβριν τε ὁμοίως ἐξῆρει
καὶ ἀγερωχίαν πᾶσαν, τοσούτῳ πλέον, ὅσῳ μηδὲ
532 τοῦ Ἰωνικοῦ ἀπεθίζειν ἦν.[2] ὠφέλει δὲ κἀκεῖνα
δήπου· τὰς δίκας τὰς πρὸς ἀλλήλους οὐκ ἄλλοσέ
ποι ἐκφοιτᾶν εἴα, ἀλλ' οἴκοι ἔπαυεν· λέγω δὲ τὰς
ὑπὲρ χρημάτων, τὰς γὰρ ἐπὶ μοιχοὺς καὶ ἱεροσύλους
καὶ σφαγέας, ὧν ἀμελουμένων ἄγη φύεται, οὐκ
ἐξάγειν παρεκελεύετο μόνον, ἀλλὰ καὶ ἐξωθεῖν τῆς
Σμύρνης, δικαστοῦ γὰρ δεῖσθαι αὐτὰς ξίφος ἔχοντος.
Καὶ ἡ αἰτία δέ, ἣν ἐκ τῶν πολλῶν εἶχεν, ὡς

---

[1] καθαρᾶς Kayser; καθαρῶς Cobet.
[2] Lacuna in mss.; ἦν Kayser suggests.

---

[1] "Windy Mimas" (*Odyssey* iii. 172) is a headland
opposite Chios. This temple was destroyed by an earthquake and rebuilt by Marcus Aurelius.

since the youth flowed into her from both continents and the islands; nor were they a dissolute and promiscuous rabble, but select and genuinely Hellenic. Secondly, he brought about a harmonious government free from faction. For, before that, Smyrna was rent by factions, and the inhabitants of the higher district were at variance with those on the sea-shore. Also he proved to be of great value to the city by going on embassies to the Emperors and defending their ways at home. Hadrian, at any rate, had hitherto favoured Ephesus, but Polemo so entirely converted him to the cause of Smyrna that in one day he lavished ten million drachmae on the city, and with this the corn-market was built, a gymnasium which was the most magnificent of all those in Asia, and a temple that can be seen from afar, the one on the promontory that seems to challenge Mimas.[1] Moreover, when they made mistakes in their public policy, Polemo would rebuke them, and often gave them wise advice; thus he was of great use to them, and at the same time he cured them of arrogance and every kind of insolence, an achievement that was all the greater because it was not like the Ionian to reform his ancient customs. He helped them also in the following manner. The suits which they brought against one another he did not allow to be carried anywhere abroad, but he would settle them at home. I mean the suits about money, for those against adulterers, sacrilegious persons and murderers, the neglect of which breeds pollution, he not only urged them to carry them out of Smyrna but even to drive them out. For he said that they needed a judge with a sword in his hand.

Though he excited the disapproval of many,

ὁδοιποροῦντι αὐτῷ πολλὰ μὲν σκευοφόρα ἔποιτο,
πολλοὶ δὲ ἵπποι, πολλοὶ δὲ οἰκέται, πολλὰ δὲ ἔθνη
κυνῶν ἄλλα ἐς ἄλλην θήραν, αὐτὸς δὲ ἐπὶ ζεύγους
ἀργυροχαλίνου Φρυγίου τινὸς ἢ Κελτικοῦ πορεύοιτο,
εὔκλειαν τῇ Σμύρνῃ ἔπραττεν· πόλιν γὰρ δὴ
λαμπρύνει μὲν ἀγορὰ καὶ κατασκευὴ μεγαλοπρεπὴς
οἰκοδομημάτων, λαμπρύνει δὲ οἰκία εὖ πράττουσα,
οὐ γὰρ μόνον δίδωσι πόλις ἀνδρὶ ὄνομα, ἀλλὰ καὶ
αὐτὴ ἄρνυται ἐξ ἀνδρός. ἐπεσκοπεῖτο δὲ καὶ τὴν
Λαοδίκειαν ὁ Πολέμων θαμίζων ἐς τὸν ἑαυτοῦ
οἶκον καὶ δημοσίᾳ ὠφελῶν ὅ τι ἠδύνατο.

Τὰ δὲ ἐκ βασιλέων αὐτῷ τοιαῦτα· Τραιανὸς
μὲν αὐτοκράτωρ ἀτελῆ πορεύεσθαι διὰ γῆς καὶ
θαλάττης, Ἀδριανὸς δὲ καὶ τοῖς ἀπ' αὐτοῦ πᾶσιν,
ἐγκατέλεξε δὲ αὐτὸν καὶ τῷ τοῦ Μουσείου κύκλῳ
ἐς τὴν Αἰγυπτίαν σίτησιν, ἐπί τε τῆς Ῥώμης
ἀπαιτουμένου πέντε καὶ εἴκοσι μυριάδας ὑπερ-
απέδωκε ταῦτα τὰ χρήματα οὔτε εἰπόντος, ὡς
δέοιτο, οὔτε προειπών, ὡς δώσοι. αἰτιωμένης δὲ
αὐτὸν τῆς Σμύρνης, ὡς πολλὰ τῶν ἐπιδοθέντων
σφίσιν ἐκ βασιλέως χρημάτων ἐς τὸ ἑαυτοῦ ἡδὺ
καταθέμενον ἔπεμψεν ὁ αὐτοκράτωρ ἐπιστολὴν
ὧδε ξυγκειμένην· "Πολέμων τῶν ἐπιδοθέντων
ὑμῖν χρημάτων ὑπ' ἐμοῦ ἐμοὶ τοὺς λογισμοὺς
ἔδωκεν." ταῦτα δὲ εἰ καὶ συγγνώμην ἐρεῖ τις,
οὐκ ἦν δήπου συγγνώμην αὐτὸν τὴν ἐπὶ τοῖς
χρήμασι μὴ οὐκ ἐς τὸ προὔχον τῆς ἄλλης ἀρετῆς
εὑρέσθαι. τὸ δὲ Ἀθήνησιν Ὀλυμπίειον [1] δι' ἐξή-

---

[1] Ὀλύμπιον Kayser ; Ὀλυμπίειον Cobet.

---

[1] A favourite saying with Pindar ; cf. Thucydides vi. 16.
[2] See above, p. 524.

because when he travelled he was followed by a long train of baggage-animals and many horses, many slaves and many different breeds of dogs for various kinds of hunting, while he himself would ride in a chariot from Phrygia or Gaul, with silver-mounted bridles, by all this he acquired glory for Smyrna. For just as its market-place and a splendid array of buildings reflect lustre on a city, so does an opulent establishment; for not only does a city give a man renown, but itself acquires it from a man.[1] Polemo administered the affairs of Laodicea as well, for he often visited his relatives there, and gave what assistance he could in public affairs.

The following privileges were bestowed on him by the Emperors. By the Emperor Trajan the right to travel free of expense by land and sea, and Hadrian extended this to all his descendants, and also enrolled him in the circle of the Museum, with the Egyptian right of free meals.[2] And when he was in Rome and demanded 250,000 drachmae,[3] he gave him that sum and more, though Polemo had not said that he needed it, nor had the Emperor said beforehand that he would give it. When the people of Smyrna accused him of having expended on his own pleasures a great part of the money that had been given by the Emperor for them, the Emperor sent a letter to the following effect: "Polemo has rendered me an account of the money given to you by me." And though one may say that this was an act of clemency, nevertheless it would not have been possible for him to win clemency in the affair of the money, had he not won pre-eminence for virtue of another kind. The temple of Olympian Zeus at Athens had been

---

[3] The drachma was worth about ninepence [in 1921].

PHILOSTRATUS

κοντα καὶ πεντακοσίων ἐτῶν ἀποτελεσθὲν καθιε-
ρώσας ὁ αὐτοκράτωρ, ὡς χρόνου μέγα ἀγώνισμα,
ἐκέλευσε καὶ τὸν Πολέμωνα ἐφυμνῆσαι τῇ θυσίᾳ.
ὁ δέ, ὥσπερ εἰώθει, στήσας τοὺς ὀφθαλμοὺς ἐπὶ
τὰς ἤδη παρισταμένας ἐννοίας ἐπαφῆκεν ἑαυτὸν
τῷ λόγῳ καὶ ἀπὸ τῆς κρηπῖδος τοῦ νεὼ διελέχθη
πολλὰ καὶ θαυμάσια, προοίμιον ποιούμενος τοῦ
λόγου τὸ μὴ ἀθεεὶ τὴν περὶ αὐτοῦ ὁρμὴν γενέσθαι
οἱ.

Διήλλαξε δὲ αὐτῷ καὶ τὸν ἑαυτοῦ παῖδα Ἀν-
534 τωνῖνον ὁ αὐτοκράτωρ ἐν τῇ τοῦ σκήπτρου παρα-
δόσει θεὸς ἐκ θνητοῦ γιγνόμενος. τουτὶ δὲ ὁποῖον,
ἀνάγκη δηλῶσαι· ἦρξε μὲν γὰρ δὴ πάσης ὁμοῦ
Ἀσίας ὁ Ἀντωνῖνος, καὶ κατέλυσεν ἐν τῇ τοῦ
Πολέμωνος οἰκίᾳ ὡς ἀρίστῃ τῶν κατὰ τὴν Σμύρναν καὶ ἀρίστου ἀνδρός, νύκτωρ δὲ ἐξ ἀποδημίας
ἥκων ὁ Πολέμων ἐβόα ἐπὶ θύραις, ὡς δεινὰ πάσχοι
τῶν ἑαυτοῦ εἰργόμενος, εἶτα συνηνάγκασε τὸν
Ἀντωνῖνον ἐς ἑτέραν οἰκίαν μετασκευάσασθαι.
ταῦτα ἐγίγνωσκε μὲν ὁ αὐτοκράτωρ, ἠρώτα δὲ
ὑπὲρ αὐτῶν οὐδέν, ὡς μὴ ἀναδέροιτο, ἀλλ' ἐνθυμη-
θεὶς τὰ μετ' αὐτὸν καὶ ὅτι πολλάκις καὶ τὰς ἡμέ-
ρους ἐκκαλοῦνται φύσεις οἱ προσκείμενοί τε καὶ
παροξύνοντες, ἔδεισε περὶ τῷ Πολέμωνι, ὅθεν ἐν
ταῖς ὑπὲρ τῆς βασιλείας διαθήκαις " καὶ Πολέμων
ὁ σοφιστὴς " ἔφη " ξύμβουλος τῆς διανοίας ἐμοὶ
ταύτης ἐγένετο," τῷ καὶ χάριν ὡς εὐεργέτῃ πράττειν τὴν συγγνώμην ἐκ περιουσίας ἑτοιμάζων.

---

[1] The original Olympieion, begun about 530 B.C. by
Peisistratus, was never completed. The existing temple was
begun about 174 B.C. by Antiochus Epiphanes, was completed
by the Emperor Hadrian and dedicated A.D. 130.

completed at last after an interval of five hundred and sixty years,[1] and when the Emperor consecrated it as a marvellous triumph of time, he invited Polemo also to make an oration at the sacrifice. He fixed his gaze, as was his custom, on the thoughts that were already taking their place in his mind, and then flung himself into his speech, and delivered a long and admirable discourse from the base of the temple. As the prooemium of his speech he declared that not without a divine impulse was he inspired to speak on that theme.

Moreover, the Emperor reconciled his own son Antoninus with Polemo, at the time when he handed over his sceptre and became a god instead of a mortal. I must relate how this happened. Antoninus was proconsul of the whole of Asia without exception, and once he took up his lodging in Polemo's house because it was the best in Smyrna and belonged to the most notable citizen. However, Polemo arrived home at night from a journey and raised an outcry at the door that he was outrageously treated in being shut out of his own house, and next he compelled Antoninus to move to another house. The Emperor was informed of this, but he held no inquiry into the affair, lest he should reopen the wound. But in considering what would happen after his death, and that even mild natures are often provoked by persons who are too aggressive and irritating, he became anxious about Polemo. Accordingly in his last testament on the affairs of the Empire, he wrote: "And Polemo, the sophist, advised me to make this arrangement." By this means he opened the way for him to win favour as a benefactor, and forgiveness enough and to spare. And in fact Antoninus used

113

καὶ ὁ Ἀντωνῖνος ἠστείζετο μὲν πρὸς τὸν Πολέμωνα περὶ τῶν κατὰ τὴν Σμύρναν ἐνδεικνύμενός που τὸ μὴ ἐκλελῆσθαι, ταῖς δὲ ἑκάστοτε τιμαῖς ἐπὶ μέγα ἦρεν ἐγγυώμενός που τὸ μὴ μεμνῆσθαι. ἠστείζετο δὲ τάδε· ἐς τὴν πόλιν ἥκοντος τοῦ Πολέμωνος περιβαλὼν αὐτὸν Ἀντωνῖνος "δότε" ἔφη "Πολέμωνι καταγωγήν, καὶ μηδεὶς αὐτὸν ἐκβάλῃ." ὑποκριτοῦ δὲ τραγῳδίας ἀπὸ τῶν κατὰ τὴν Ἀσίαν Ὀλυμπίων, οἷς ἐπεστάτει ὁ Πολέμων,
535 ἐφιέναι φήσαντος, ἐξελαθῆναι γὰρ παρ' αὐτοῦ κατ' ἀρχὰς τοῦ δράματος, ἤρετο ὁ αὐτοκράτωρ τὸν ὑποκριτήν, πηνίκα εἴη, ὅτε τῆς σκηνῆς ἠλάθη, τοῦ δὲ εἰπόντος, ὡς μεσημβρία τυγχάνοι οὖσα, μάλα ἀστείως ὁ αὐτοκράτωρ "ἐμὲ δὲ" εἶπεν "ἀμφὶ μέσας νύκτας ἐξήλασε τῆς οἰκίας, καὶ οὐκ ἐφῆκα."

Ἐχέτω μοι καὶ ταῦτα δήλωσιν βασιλέως τε πράου καὶ ἀνδρὸς ὑπέρφρονος. ὑπέρφρων γὰρ δὴ οὕτω τι ὁ Πολέμων, ὡς πόλεσι μὲν ἀπὸ τοῦ προὔχοντος, δυνάσταις δὲ ἀπὸ τοῦ μὴ ὑφειμένου, θεοῖς δὲ ἀπὸ τοῦ ἴσου διαλέγεσθαι. Ἀθηναίοις μὲν γὰρ ἐπιδεικνύμενος αὐτοσχεδίους λόγους, ὅτε καὶ πρῶτον Ἀθήναζε ἀφίκετο, οὐκ ἐς ἐγκώμια κατέστησεν ἑαυτὸν τοῦ ἄστεος, τοσούτων ὄντων, ἃ τις ὑπὲρ Ἀθηναίων ἂν εἴποι, οὐδ' ὑπὲρ τῆς ἑαυτοῦ δόξης ἐμακρηγόρησε, καίτοι καὶ τῆς τοιᾶσδε ἰδέας ὠφελούσης τοὺς σοφιστὰς ἐν ταῖς ἐπιδείξεσιν, ἀλλ' εὖ γιγνώσκων, ὅτι τὰς Ἀθηναίων φύσεις ἐπικόπτειν χρὴ μᾶλλον ἢ ἐπαίρειν διελέχθη ὧδε· "φασὶν ὑμᾶς, ὦ Ἀθηναῖοι, σοφοὺς

to jest with Polemo about what had happened in Smyrna, thus showing that he had by no means forgotten it, though by the honours with which he exalted him on every occasion he seemed to pledge himself not to bear it in mind. This is the sort of jest he would make. When Polemo came to Rome, Antoninus embraced him, and then said: "Give Polemo a lodging and do not let anyone turn him out of it." And once when a tragic actor who had performed at the Olympic games in Asia, over which Polemo presided, declared that he would prosecute him, because Polemo had expelled him at the beginning of the play, the Emperor asked the actor what time it was when he was expelled from the theatre, and when he replied that it happened to be at noon, the Emperor made this witty comment: "But it was midnight when he expelled *me* from his house, and I did not prosecute him."

Let this suffice to show how mild an Emperor could be, and how arrogant a mere man. For in truth Polemo was so arrogant that he conversed with cities as his inferiors, Emperors as not his superiors, and the gods as his equals. For instance, when he gave a display to the Athenians of extempore speeches on first coming to Athens, he did not condescend to utter an encomium on the city, though there were so many things that one might say in honour of the Athenians; nor did he make a long oration about his own renown, although this style of speech is likely to win favour for sophists in their public declamations. But since he well knew that the natural disposition of the Athenians needs to be held in check rather than encouraged to greater pride, this was his introductory speech: "Men say, Athenians,

εἶναι ἀκροατὰς λόγων· εἴσομαι." ἀνδρὸς δέ, ὃς ἦρχε μὲν Βοσπόρου, πᾶσαν δὲ Ἑλληνικὴν παίδευσιν ἥρμοστο, καθ' ἱστορίαν τῆς Ἰωνίας ἐς τὴν Σμύρναν ἥκοντος οὐ μόνον οὐκ ἔταξεν ἑαυτὸν ἐν τοῖς θεραπεύουσιν, ἀλλὰ καὶ δεομένου ξυνεῖναί οἱ θαμὰ ἀνεβάλλετο, ἕως ἠνάγκασε τὸν βασιλέα ἐπὶ θύρας ἀφικέσθαι ἀπάγοντα μισθοῦ δέκα τάλαντα. ἥκων δὲ ἐς τὸ Πέργαμον, ὅτε δὴ τὰ ἄρθρα ἐνόσει, κατέδαρθε μὲν ἐν τῷ ἱερῷ, ἐπιστάντος δὲ αὐτῷ τοῦ Ἀσκληπιοῦ καὶ προειπόντος ἀπέχεσθαι ψυχροῦ ποτοῦ ὁ Πολέμων " βέλτιστε," εἶπεν " εἰ δὲ βοῦν ἐθεράπευες; "

Τὸ δὲ μεγαλόγνωμον τοῦτο καὶ φρονηματῶδες ἐκ Τιμοκράτους ἔσπασε τοῦ φιλοσόφου, συγγε-
536 νόμενος αὐτῷ ἥκοντι ἐς Ἰωνίαν ἐτῶν τεττάρων. οὐ χεῖρον δὲ καὶ τὸν Τιμοκράτην δηλῶσαι· ἦν μὲν γὰρ ἐκ τοῦ Πόντου ὁ ἀνὴρ οὗτος καὶ ἦν αὐτῷ πατρὶς Ἡράκλεια τὰ Ἑλλήνων ἐπαινοῦντες, ἐφιλοσόφει δὲ κατ' ἀρχὰς μὲν τοὺς ἰατρικοὺς τῶν λόγων, εἰδὼς εὖ τὰς Ἱπποκράτους τε καὶ Δημοκρίτου δόξας, ἐπεὶ δὲ ἤκουσεν Εὐφράτου τοῦ Τυρίου, πλήρεσιν ἱστίοις ἐς τὴν ἐκείνου φιλοσοφίαν ἀφῆκεν. ἐπιχολώτερος δὲ οὕτω τι ἦν τοῦ ξυμμέτρου, ὡς ὑπανίστασθαι αὐτῷ διαλεγομένῳ τήν τε γενειάδα καὶ τὰς ἐν τῇ κεφαλῇ χαίτας, ὥσπερ τῶν λεόντων ἐν ταῖς ὁρμαῖς. τῆς δὲ γλώττης εὐφόρως εἶχε καὶ σφοδρῶς καὶ ἑτοίμως, διὸ καὶ τῷ Πολέμωνι πλείστου ἦν ἄξιος ἀσπαζομένῳ τὴν τοιάνδε ἐπιφορὰν τοῦ λόγου. διαφορᾶς γοῦν τῷ

---

[1] At this date there were kings of the Bosporus under the protectorate of Rome.

[2] Lucian, *Demonax* 3, praises Timocrates.

that as an audience you are accomplished judges of oratory. I shall soon find out." And once when the ruler of the Bosporus, a man who had been trained in all the culture of Greece, came to Smyrna in order to learn about Ionia, Polemo not only did not take his place among those who went to salute him, but even when the other begged him to visit him he postponed it again and again, until he compelled the king[1] to come to his door with a fee of ten talents. Again, when he came to Pergamon suffering from a disease of the joints, he slept in the temple, and when Asclepius appeared to him and told him to abstain from drinking anything cold, "My good sir," said Polemo, "but what if you were doctoring a cow?"

This proud and haughty temper he contracted from Timocrates[2] the philosopher, with whom he associated for four years when he came to Ionia. It would do no harm to describe Timocrates also. This man came from the Pontus and his birthplace was Heraclea whose citizens admire Greek culture. At first he devoted himself to the study of writings on medicine and was well versed in the theories of Hippocrates and Democritus. But when he had once heard Euphrates[3] of Tyre, he set full sail for his kind of philosophy. He was irascible beyond measure, so much so that while he was arguing his beard and the hair on his head stood up like a lion's when it springs to the attack. His language was fluent, vigorous and ready, and it was on this account that Polemo, who loved this headlong style of oratory, valued him so highly. At any rate, when a quarrel arose between Timocrates

[3] cf. p. 488 and *Life of Apollonius, passim*. Euphrates had much influence with Vespasian.

Τιμοκράτει πρὸς τὸν Σκοπελιανὸν γενομένης ὡς
ἐκδεδωκότα ἑαυτὸν πίττῃ καὶ παρατιλτρίαις διέ-
στη μὲν ἡ ἐνομιλοῦσα νεότης τῇ Σμύρνῃ, ὁ δὲ
Πολέμων ἀμφοῖν ἀκροώμενος τῶν τοῦ Τιμοκράτους στασιωτῶν ἐγένετο πατέρα καλῶν αὐτὸν τῆς
ἑαυτοῦ γλώττης. ἀπολογούμενος δὲ αὐτῷ καὶ ὑπὲρ
τῶν πρὸς Φαβωρῖνον λόγων εὐλαβῶς ὑπέστειλε
καὶ ὑφειμένως, ὥσπερ τῶν παίδων οἱ τὰς ἐκ τῶν
διδασκάλων πληγάς, εἴ τι ἀτακτήσειαν, δεδιότες.

Τῷ δὲ ὑφειμένῳ τούτῳ καὶ πρὸς τὸν Σκοπελιανὸν ἐχρήσατο χρόνῳ ὕστερον, πρεσβεύειν μὲν
χειροτονηθεὶς ὑπὲρ τῶν Σμυρναίων, ὡς ὅπλα δὲ
Ἀχίλλεια τὴν ἐκείνου πειθὼ αἰτήσας. Ἡρώδῃ
δὲ τῷ Ἀθηναίῳ πῇ μὲν ἀπὸ τοῦ ὑφειμένου, πῇ
δὲ ἀπὸ τοῦ ὑπεραίροντος ξυνεγένετο. ὅπως δὲ
καὶ ταῦτα ἔσχε, δηλῶσαι βούλομαι, καλὰ γὰρ καὶ
μεμνῆσθαι ἄξια· ἦρα μὲν γὰρ τοῦ αὐτοσχεδιάζειν ὁ Ἡρώδης μᾶλλον ἢ τοῦ ὑπατός τε καὶ ἐξ
ὑπάτων δοκεῖν, τὸν Πολέμωνα δὲ οὔπω γιγνώ-
537 σκων ἀφῖκτο μὲν ἐς τὴν Σμύρναν ἐπὶ ξυνουσίᾳ
τοῦ ἀνδρὸς κατὰ χρόνους, οὓς τὰς ἐλευθέρας τῶν
πόλεων αὐτὸς διωρθοῦτο, περιβαλὼν δὲ καὶ ὑπερ-
ασπασάμενος ὁμοῦ τῷ τὸ στόμα ἀφελεῖν τοῦ
στόματος " πότε," εἶπεν " ὦ πάτερ, ἀκροασό-
μεθά σου; " καὶ ὁ μὲν δὴ ᾤετο ἀναβαλεῖσθαι
αὐτὸν τὴν ἀκρόασιν ὀκνεῖν φήσαντα ἐπ' ἀνδρὸς
τοιούτου ἀποκινδυνεύειν, ὁ δὲ οὐδὲν πλασάμενος
" τήμερον " ἔφη " ἀκρῶ, καὶ ἴωμεν." τοῦτο
ἀκούσας ὁ Ἡρώδης ἐκπλαγῆναί φησι τὸν ἄνδρα,

---

[1] This was a mark of effeminacy and foppishness.
[2] This incident is described above, p. 521.
[3] See p. 548.

and Scopelian, because the latter had become addicted to the use of pitch-plasters and professional "hair-removers,"[1] the youths who were then residing in Smyrna took different sides, but Polemo, who was the pupil of both men, became one of the faction of Timocrates and called him "the father of my eloquence." And when he was defending himself before Timocrates for his speeches against Favorinus, he cowered before him in awe and submission, like boys who fear blows from their teachers when they have been disobedient.

This same humility Polemo showed also towards Scopelian somewhat later, when he was elected to go on an embassy on behalf of Smyrna, and begged for Scopelian's power of persuasion as though it were the arms of Achilles.[2] His behaviour to Herodes the Athenian was in one way submissive and in another arrogant. I wish to relate how this came about, for it is a good story and worth remembering. Herodes, you must know, felt a keener desire to succeed in extempore speaking than to be called a consular and the descendant of consulars, and so, before he was acquainted with Polemo, he came to Smyrna in order to study with him. It was at the time when Herodes alone[3] was regulating the status of the free cities. When he had embraced Polemo and saluted him very affectionately by kissing him on the mouth, he asked: "Father, when shall I hear you declaim?" Now Herodes thought that he would put off the declamation and would say that he hesitated to run any risks in the presence of so great a man, but Polemo, without any such pretext, replied: "Hear me declaim to-day, and let us be going." Herodes says that when he heard this, he was struck with admiration

119

ὡς καὶ τὴν γλῶτταν αὐτοσχέδιον καὶ τὴν γνώμην. ταῦτα μὲν οὖν φρόνημα ἐνδείκνυται τοῦ ἀνδρὸς καί, νὴ Δία, σοφίαν, ᾗ ἐς τὴν ἔκπληξιν ἐχρήσατο, ἐκεῖνα δὲ σωφροσύνην τε καὶ κόσμον· ἀφικόμενον γὰρ ἐς τὴν ἐπίδειξιν ἐδέξατο ἐπαίνῳ μακρῷ καὶ ἐπαξίῳ τῶν Ἡρώδου λόγων τε καὶ ἔργων.

Τὴν δὲ σκηνὴν τοῦ ἀνδρός, ᾗ ἐς τὰς μελέτας ἐχρήσατο, ἔστι μὲν καὶ Ἡρώδου μαθεῖν ἐν μιᾷ τῶν πρὸς τὸν Βάρβαρον ἐπιστολῶν εἰρημένον,[1] δηλώσω δὲ κἀγὼ ἐκεῖθεν· παρῄει μὲν ἐς τὰς ἐπιδείξεις διακεχυμένῳ τῷ προσώπῳ καὶ τεθαρρηκότι, φοράδην δὲ ἐσεφοίτα διεφθορότων αὐτῷ ἤδη τῶν ἄρθρων. καὶ τὰς ὑποθέσεις οὐκ ἐς τὸ κοινὸν ἐπεσκοπεῖτο, ἀλλ᾽ ἐξιὼν τοῦ ὁμίλου βραχὺν καιρόν. φθέγμα δὲ ἦν αὐτῷ λαμπρὸν καὶ ἐπίτονον καὶ κρότος θαυμάσιος οἷος ἀπεκτύπει τῆς γλώττης. φησὶ δὲ αὐτὸν ὁ Ἡρώδης καὶ ἀναπηδᾶν τοῦ θρόνου περὶ τὰς ἀκμὰς τῶν ὑποθέσεων, τοσοῦτον αὐτῷ περιεῖναι ὁρμῆς, καὶ ὅτε ἀποτορνεύοι περίοδον, τὸ ἐπὶ πᾶσιν αὐτῆς κῶλον σὺν μειδιάματι φέρειν, ἐνδεικνύμενον πολὺ τὸ ἀλύπως φράζειν, καὶ κροαίνειν ἐν τοῖς τῶν ὑποθέσεων χωρίοις 538 οὐδὲν μεῖον τοῦ Ὁμηρικοῦ ἵππου. ἀκροᾶσθαι δὲ αὐτοῦ τὴν μὲν πρώτην, ὡς οἱ δικάζοντες, τὴν δὲ ἐφεξῆς, ὡς οἱ ἐρῶντες, τὴν δὲ τρίτην, ὡς οἱ θαυμάζοντες, καὶ γὰρ δὴ καὶ τριῶν ἡμερῶν ξυγγενέσθαι οἱ. ἀναγράφει καὶ τὰς ὑποθέσεις ὁ Ἡρώδης, ἐφ᾽ αἷς ξυνεγένετο· ἦν τοίνυν ἡ μὲν πρώτη Δημο-

---

[1] ἐπιστολῇ εἰρημένων Kayser; ἐπιστολῶν εἰρημένον Cobet.

---

[1] See Glossary s.v. σκηνή.
[2] Cf. Hesperia 26, 1957, 1220, no. 78.
[3] Iliad vi. 507.

of the man and the ready facility both of his tongue and brain. This incident illustrates Polemo's pride and, by Zeus, the cleverness with which he was wont to dazzle his hearers, but the following shows equally his modesty and sense of propriety. For when the other arrived to hear him declaim, he received him with a long and appropriate panegyric on the words and deeds of Herodes.

The scenic effects [1] which he employed in his declamations we may learn from Herodes, since they are described in one of the letters that he wrote to Barbarus,[2] and I will relate them from that source. He would come forward to declaim with a countenance serene and full of confidence, and he always arrived in a litter, because his joints were already diseased. When a theme had been proposed, he did not meditate on it in public but would withdraw from the crowd for a short time. His utterance was clear and incisive, and there was a fine ringing sound in the tones of his voice. Herodes says also that he used to rise to such a pitch of excitement that he would jump up from his chair when he came to the most striking conclusions in his argument, and whenever he rounded off a period he would utter the final clause with a smile, as though to show clearly that he could deliver it without effort, and at certain places in the argument he would stamp the ground just like the horse in Homer.[3] Herodes adds that he listened to his first declamation like an impartial judge, to the second like one who longs for more, to the third as one who can but admire ; and that he attended his lectures for three days. Moreover, Herodes has recorded the themes of the declamations at which he was present. The first was :

σθένης ἐξομνύμενος ταλάντων πεντήκοντα δωρο-
δοκίαν, ἣν ἦγεν ἐπ' αὐτὸν Δημάδης, ὡς 'Αλεξάν-
δρου τοῦτο 'Αθηναίοις ἐκ τῶν Δαρείου λογισμῶν
ἐπεσταλκότος, ἡ δὲ ἐφεξῆς τὰ τρόπαια κατέλυε
τὰ 'Ελληνικὰ τοῦ Πελοποννησίου πολέμου ἐς διαλ-
λαγὰς ἥκοντος, ἡ δὲ τρίτη τῶν ὑποθέσεων τοὺς
'Αθηναίους μετὰ Αἰγὸς ποταμοὺς ἐς τοὺς δήμους
ἀνεσκεύαζεν· ὑπὲρ οὗ φησιν ὁ 'Ηρώδης πέμψαι
οἱ πεντεκαίδεκα μυριάδας προσειπὼν αὐτὰς μισθὸν τῆς ἀκροάσεως, μὴ προσεμένου δὲ αὐτὸς μὲν
ὑπερῴφθαι οἴεσθαι, ξυμπίνοντα δὲ αὐτῷ Μουνά-
τιον τὸν κριτικόν, ὁ δὲ ἀνὴρ οὗτος ἐκ Τραλλέων,
" ὦ 'Ηρώδη," φάναι " δοκεῖ μοι Πολέμων ὀνειρο-
πολήσας πέντε καὶ εἴκοσι μυριάδας παρὰ τοῦτ'
ἔλαττον ἔχειν ἡγεῖσθαι, παρ' ὃ μὴ τοσαύτας ἔπεμ-
ψας." προσθεῖναί φησιν ὁ 'Ηρώδης τὰς δέκα
καὶ τὸν Πολέμωνα προθύμως λαβεῖν, ὥσπερ
ἀπολαμβάνοντα. ἔδωκε τῷ Πολέμωνι ὁ 'Ηρώ-
539 δης καὶ τὸ μὴ παρελθεῖν ἐπ' αὐτῷ ἐς λόγων ἐπίδειξιν, μηδ' ἐπαγωνίσασθαί οἱ, νύκτωρ δὲ ἐξελά-
σαι τῆς Σμύρνης, ὡς μὴ βιασθείη, θρασὺ γὰρ καὶ
τὸ βιασθῆναι ᾤετο. διετέλει δὲ καὶ τὸν ἄλλον
χρόνον ἐπαινῶν τὸν Πολέμωνα καὶ ὑπερθαυμάζων.[1]
'Αθήνῃσι μὲν γὰρ διαπρεπῶς ἀγωνισάμενος τὸν
περὶ τῶν τροπαίων ἀγῶνα καὶ θαυμαζόμενος ἐπὶ

---

[1] ὑπὲρ θαῦμα ἄγων Kayser; ὑπερθαυμάζων Cobet.

---

[1] Apsines 219 mentions this theme, and it was also declaimed by Herodes, cf. p. 539. The argument was that
there must not be permanent monuments of Greek victories
over Greeks.
[2] This theme is similar to that of Isocrates mentioned

"Demosthenes swears that he did not take the bribe of fifty talents," the charge which Demades brought against him, on the ground that Alexander had communicated this fact to the Athenians, having learned it from the account-books of Darius. In the second, on the conclusion of peace after the Peloponnesian war, he urged: "That the trophies erected by the Greeks should be taken down."[1] The third argument was to persuade the Athenians to return to their demes after the battle of Aegos Potami.[2] Herodes says that in payment for this he sent him 150,000 drachmae, and called this the fee for his lectures. But since he did not accept it, Herodes thought that he had been treated with contempt, but Munatius the critic, when drinking with him (this man came from Tralles), remarked: "Herodes, I think that Polemo dreamed of 250,000 drachmae, and so thinks that he is being stinted because you did not send so large a sum." Herodes says that he added the 100,000 drachmae, and that Polemo took the money without the least hesitation, as though he were receiving only what was his due. Herodes gave Polemo leave not to appear after him to give an exhibition of his oratory, and not to have to maintain a theme after him, and allowed him to depart from Smyrna by night, lest he should be compelled to do this, since Polemo thought it outrageous to be compelled to do anything. And from that time forward he never failed to commend Polemo, and to think him beyond praise. For instance, in Athens, when Herodes had brilliantly maintained the argument about the war trophies, and was being complimented on the fluency and

above, p. 505 ; it was designed to induce the Athenians to renounce their empire of the sea.

τῇ φορᾷ τοῦ λόγου " τὴν Πολέμωνος " ἔφη " μελέτην ἀνάγνωτε καὶ εἴσεσθε ἄνδρα." Ὀλυμπίασι δὲ
βοησάσης ἐπ' αὐτῷ τῆς Ἑλλάδος " εἷς ὡς Δημοσθένης," " εἴθε γὰρ " ἔφη " ὡς ὁ Φρύξ," τὸν
Πολέμωνα ὧδε ἐπονομάζων, ἐπειδὴ τότε ἡ Λαοδίκεια τῇ Φρυγίᾳ συνετάττετο. Μάρκου δὲ τοῦ
αὐτοκράτορος πρὸς αὐτὸν εἰπόντος " τί σοι δοκεῖ
ὁ Πολέμων ; " στήσας τοὺς ὀφθαλμοὺς ὁ Ἡρώδης

ἵππων μ'

ἔφη

ὠκυπόδων ἀμφὶ κτύπος οὔατα βάλλει,

ἐνδεικνύμενος δὴ τὸ ἐπίκροτον καὶ τὸ ὑψηχὲς τῶν
λόγων. ἐρομένου δὲ αὐτὸν καὶ Βαρβάρου τοῦ
ὑπάτου, τίσι καὶ διδασκάλοις ἐχρήσατο, " τῷ δεῖνι
μὲν καὶ τῷ δεῖνι " ἔφη " παιδευόμενος, Πολέμωνι
δὲ ἤδη παιδεύων."

Φησὶν ὁ Πολέμων ἠκροᾶσθαι καὶ Δίωνα[1] ἀποδημίαν ὑπὲρ τούτου στείλας ἐς τὸ τῶν Βιθυνῶν
ἔθνος. ἔλεγε δὲ ὁ Πολέμων τὰ μὲν τῶν κατα-
λογάδην ὤμοις[2] δεῖν ἐκφέρειν, τὰ δὲ τῶν ποιητῶν
ἁμάξαις. κἀκεῖνα τῶν Πολέμωνι τιμὴν ἐχόντων·
ἤριζεν ἡ Σμύρνα ὑπὲρ τῶν ναῶν καὶ τῶν ἐπ'
αὐτοῖς δικαίων, ξύνδικον πεποιημένη τὸν Πολέμωνα ἐς τέρμα ἤδη τοῦ βίου ἥκοντα. ἐπεὶ δὲ ἐν
ὁρμῇ τῆς ὑπὲρ τῶν δικαίων ἀποδημίας ἐτελεύτησεν,
ἐγένετο μὲν ἐπ' ἄλλοις ξυνδίκοις ἡ πόλις, πονηρῶς
540 δὲ αὐτῶν ἐν τῷ βασιλείῳ δικαστηρίῳ διατιθεμένων
τὸν λόγον βλέψας ὁ αὐτοκράτωρ ἐς τοὺς τῶν

---

[1] Δίωνος Kayser ; Δίωνα Schmid.
[2] ὄνοις, "on the backs of asses," Prof. Margoliouth
suggests.

vigour of his speech, he said: "Read Polemo's declamation, and then you will know a great man." And at the Olympic games when all Greece acclaimed him, crying: "You are the equal of Demosthenes!" he replied: "I wish I were the equal of the Phrygian," applying this name to Polemo because in those days Laodicea counted as part of Phrygia. When the Emperor Marcus asked him: "What is your opinion of Polemo?" Herodes gazed fixedly before him and said:

The sound of swift-footed horses strikes upon mine ears;[1] thus indicating how resonant and far-echoing was his eloquence. And when Barbarus the consul asked him what teachers he had had, he replied: "This man and that, while I was being taught, but Polemo, when I was teaching others."

Polemo says that he studied also with Dio, and that in order to do so he paid a visit to the people of Bithynia. He used to say that the works of prose writers needed to be brought out[2] by armfuls, but the works of poets by the wagon-load. Among the honours that he received were also the following. Smyrna was contending on behalf of her temples and their rights, and when he had already reached the last stage of his life, appointed Polemo as one of her advocates. But since he died at the very outset of the journey to defend those rights, the city was entrusted to other advocates. Before the imperial tribunal they presented their case very badly, whereupon the Emperor looked towards the counsel from

[1] *Iliad* x. 535.

[2] The meaning of the verb is obscure, but as "bury" and "publish" are improbable, Polemo seems to mean that the student, for his training as a sophist, must take out from his store of books more poets than prose writers.

Σμυρναίων ξυνηγόρους " οὐ Πολέμων" εἶπεν
" τουτουὶ τοῦ ἀγῶνος ξύνδικος ὑμῖν ἀπεδέδεικτο; "
" ναί," ἔφασαν " εἴ γε τὸν σοφιστὴν λέγεις." καὶ
ὁ αὐτοκράτωρ " ἴσως οὖν" ἔφη " καὶ λόγον τινὰ
ξυνέγραψεν ὑπὲρ τῶν δικαίων, οἷα δὴ ἐπ' ἐμοῦ τε
ἀγωνιούμενος καὶ ὑπὲρ τηλικούτων." " ἴσως,"
ἔφασαν, " ὦ βασιλεῦ, οὐ μὴν ἡμῖν γε εἰδέναι." καὶ
ἔδωκεν ἀναβολὰς ὁ αὐτοκράτωρ τῇ δίκῃ, ἔστ' ἂν
διακομισθῇ ὁ λόγος, ἀναγνωσθέντος δὲ ἐν τῷ
δικαστηρίῳ κατ' αὐτὸν ἐψηφίσατο ὁ βασιλεύς, καὶ
ἀπῆλθεν ἡ Σμύρνα τὰ πρωτεῖα νικῶσα καὶ τὸν
Πολέμωνα αὐτοῖς ἀναβεβιωκέναι φάσκοντες.

Ἐπεὶ δὲ ἀνδρῶν ἐλλογίμων ἀξιομνημόνευτα οὐ
μόνον τὰ μετὰ σπουδῆς λεχθέντα, ἀλλὰ καὶ τὰ ἐν
ταῖς παιδιαῖς, ἀναγράψω καὶ τοὺς ἀστεισμοὺς τοῦ
Πολέμωνος, ὡς μηδὲ οὗτοι παραλελειμμένοι φαί-
νοιντο. μειράκιον Ἰωνικὸν ἐτρύφα κατὰ τὴν Σμύρναν ὑπὲρ τὰ Ἰώνων ἤθη, καὶ ἀπώλλυ αὐτὸ πλοῦτος
βαθύς, ὅσπερ ἐστὶ πονηρὸς διδάσκαλος τῶν ἀκολάστων φύσεων. ὄνομα μὲν δὴ τῷ μειρακίῳ Οὔαρος,
διεφθορὸς δὲ ὑπὸ κολάκων ἐπεπείκει αὐτὸ ἑαυτὸ
ὡς καλῶν τε εἴη ὁ κάλλιστος καὶ μέγας ὑπὲρ τοὺς
εὐμήκεις καὶ τῶν ἀμφὶ παλαίστραν γενναιότατός τε
καὶ τεχνικώτατος καὶ μηδ' ἂν τὰς Μούσας ἀναβάλ-
λεσθαι αὐτοῦ ἥδιον, ὁπότε πρὸς τὸ ᾄδειν τράποιτο.
παραπλήσια δὲ τούτοις καὶ περὶ τῶν σοφιστῶν
ᾤετο, παριππεῦσαι γὰρ ἂν καὶ τὰς ἐκείνων γλώττας,
ὁπότε μελετῴη, καὶ γὰρ δὴ καὶ ἐμελέτα, καὶ οἱ

Smyrna and said: "Had not Polemo been appointed as your public advocate in this suit?" "Yes," they replied, "if you mean the sophist." "Then, perhaps," said the Emperor, "he wrote down some speech in defence of your rights, inasmuch as he was to speak for the defence in my presence and on behalf of such great issues." "Perhaps, O Emperor," they replied, "but not as far as we know." Whereupon the Emperor adjourned the case until the speech could be brought, and when it had been read aloud in court the Emperor gave his decision in accordance with it; and so Smyrna carried off the victory, and the citizens departed declaring that Polemo had come to life to help them.

Now inasmuch as, when men have become illustrious, not only what they said in earnest but also what they said in jest is worthy of record, I will write down Polemo's witticisms also, so that I may not seem to have neglected even them. There was an Ionian youth who was indulging in a life of dissipation at Smyrna to a degree not customary with the Ionians, and was being ruined by his great wealth, which is a vicious teacher of ill-regulated natures. Now the youth's name was Varus, and he had been so spoiled by parasites that he had convinced himself that he was the fairest of the fair, the tallest of the tall, and the noblest and most expert of the youths at the wrestling-ground, and that not even the Muses could strike up a prelude more sweetly than he, whenever he had a mind to sing. He had the same notions about the sophists; that is to say, that he could outstrip even their tongues whenever he declaimed—and he actually used to declaim—and those who borrowed money

δανειζόμενοι παρ' αὐτοῦ χρήματα τὸ καὶ μελετῶντος ἀκροάσασθαι προσέγραφον τῷ τόκῳ. ὑπήγετο δὲ καὶ ὁ Πολέμων τῷ δασμῷ τούτῳ νέος ὢν
541 ἔτι καὶ οὔπω νοσῶν, δεδάνειστο γὰρ παρ' αὐτοῦ
χρήματα, καὶ ἐπεὶ μὴ ἐθεράπευε, μηδὲ ἐς τὰς
ἀκροάσεις ἐφοίτα, χαλεπὸν ἦν τὸ μειράκιον καὶ
ἠπείλει τύπους. οἱ δὲ τύποι γράμμα εἰσὶν ἀγορᾶς,
ἐρήμην ἐπαγγέλλον τῷ οὐκ ἀποδιδόντι. αἰτιωμένων οὖν τὸν Πολέμωνα τῶν οἰκείων, ὡς ἀηδῆ καὶ
δύστροπον, εἰ παρὸν αὐτῷ μὴ ἀπαιτεῖσθαι καὶ τὸ
μειράκιον ἐκκαρποῦσθαι παρέχοντα αὐτῷ νεῦμα
εὔνουν μὴ ποιεῖ τοῦτο, ἀλλ' ἐκκαλεῖται αὐτὸ καὶ
παροξύνει, τοιαῦτα ἀκούων ἀπήντησε μὲν ἐπὶ τὴν
ἀκρόασιν, ἐπεὶ δὲ ἐς δείλην ἤδη ὀψίαν τὰ τῆς
μελέτης αὐτῷ προὔβαινε καὶ οὐδεὶς ὅρμος ἐφαίνετο
τοῦ λόγου, σολοικισμῶν τε καὶ βαρβαρισμῶν καὶ
ἐναντιώσεων πλέα ἦν πάντα, ἀναπηδήσας ὁ Πολέμων καὶ ὑποσχὼν τὼ χεῖρε "Οὔαρε," εἶπεν
" φέρε τοὺς τύπους." λῃστὴν δὲ πολλαῖς αἰτίαις
ἑαλωκότα στρεβλοῦντος ἀνθυπάτου καὶ ἀπορεῖν
φάσκοντος, τίς γένοιτ' ἂν ἐπ' αὐτῷ τιμωρία τῶν
εἰργασμένων ἀξία, παρατυχὼν ὁ Πολέμων " κέλευσον " ἔφη " αὐτὸν ἀρχαῖα ἐκμανθάνειν." καίτοι
γὰρ πλεῖστα ἐκμαθὼν ὁ σοφιστὴς οὗτος ὅμως ἐπι-
πονώτατον ἡγεῖτο τῶν ἐν ἀσκήσει τὸ ἐκμανθάνειν.
ἰδὼν δὲ μονόμαχον ἱδρῶτι ῥεόμενον καὶ δεδιότα
τὸν ὑπὲρ τῆς ψυχῆς ἀγῶνα " οὕτως " εἶπεν " ἀγω-

from him used to reckon their attendance at his
declamations as part of the interest. Even Polemo,
when he was still a young man and not yet an
invalid, was induced to pay this tribute, for he had
borrowed money from him, and when he did not
pay court to him or attend his lectures, the youth
resented it and threatened him with a summons to
recover the debt. This summons is a writ issued by the
law court proclaiming judgement by default against
the debtor who fails to pay. Thereupon his friends
reproached Polemo with being morose and dis-
courteous, seeing that when he could avoid being
sued and could profit by the young man's money by
merely giving him an amiable nod of approval, he
would not do this, but provoked and irritated him.
Hearing this sort of thing said, he did indeed come
to the lecture, but when, late in the evening, the
youth's declamation was still going on, and no place
of anchorage for his speech was in sight, and everything he said was full of solecisms, barbarisms, and
inconsistencies, Polemo jumped up, and stretching out
his hands, cried : " Varus, bring your summons." On
another occasion, when the proconsul was putting
to the torture a bandit who had been convicted on
several charges, and declared that he could not
think of any penalty for him that would match his
crimes, Polemo who was present said : " Order him
to learn by heart some antiquated stuff." For
though this sophist had learned by heart a great
number of passages, he nevertheless considered that
this is the most wearisome of all exercises. Again,
on seeing a gladiator dripping with sweat out of
sheer terror of the life-and-death struggle before
him, he remarked : " You are in as great an agony

νιᾶς, ὡς μελετᾶν μέλλων." σοφιστῇ δὲ ἐντυχὼν
ἀλλᾶντας ὠνουμένῳ καὶ μαινίδας καὶ τὰ εὐτελῆ
ὄψα " ὦ λῷστε," εἶπεν " οὐκ ἔστι τὸ Δαρείου καὶ
Ξέρξου φρόνημα καλῶς ὑποκρίνασθαι ταῦτα σιτου-
μένῳ." Τιμοκράτους δὲ τοῦ φιλοσόφου πρὸς
αὐτὸν εἰπόντος, ὡς λάλον χρῆμα ὁ Φαβωρῖνος
γένοιτο, ἀστειότατα ὁ Πολέμων " καὶ πᾶσα " ἔφη
" γραῦς " τὸ εὐνουχῶδες αὐτοῦ διασκώπτων.
ἀγωνιστοῦ δὲ τραγῳδίας ἐν τοῖς κατὰ τὴν Σμύρναν
Ὀλυμπίοις τὸ " ὦ Ζεῦ " ἐς τὴν γῆν δείξαντος, τὸ
δὲ " καὶ γᾶ " ἐς τὸν οὐρανὸν ἀνασχόντος, προκαθ-
ήμενος τῶν Ὀλυμπίων ὁ Πολέμων ἐξέωσεν αὐτὸν
542 τῶν ἄθλων εἰπὼν " οὗτος τῇ χειρὶ ἐσολοίκισεν."
μὴ πλείω ὑπὲρ τούτων, ἀπόχρη γὰρ καὶ ταῦτα τὸ
ἐπίχαρι τοῦ ἀνδρὸς δηλῶσαι.

Ἡ δὲ ἰδέα τῶν Πολέμωνος λόγων θερμὴ καὶ
ἐναγώνιος καὶ τορὸν ἠχοῦσα, ὥσπερ ἡ Ὀλυμπιακὴ
σάλπιγξ, ἐπιπρέπει δὲ αὐτῇ καὶ τὸ Δημοσθενικὸν
τῆς γνώμης, καὶ ἡ σεμνολογία οὐχ ὑπτία, λαμπρὰ
δὲ καὶ ἔμπνους, ὥσπερ ἐκ τρίποδος. διαμαρτάνουσι μέντοι τοῦ ἀνδρὸς φάσκοντες αὐτὸν τὰς μὲν
ἐπιφορὰς ἄριστα σοφιστῶν μεταχειρίσασθαι, τὰς δὲ
ἀπολογίας ἧττον, ἐλέγχει γὰρ τὸν λόγον τοῦτον ὡς
οὐκ ἀληθῆ καὶ ἡ δεῖνα μὲν καὶ ἡ δεῖνα τῶν ὑποθέσεων, ἐν αἷς ἀπολογεῖται, μάλιστα δὲ ὁ Δημοσθένης
ὁ τὰ πεντήκοντα τάλαντα ἐξομνύμενος. ἀπολογίαν
γὰρ οὕτω χαλεπὴν διαθέμενος ἤρκεσε τῷ λόγῳ ξὺν
περιβολῇ καὶ τέχνῃ. τὴν αὐτὴν ὁρῶ διαμαρτίαν καὶ

---

[1] From Euripides, *Orestes* 1496.
[2] *i.e.* by an oracle.
[3] For this theme *cf.* Apsines ix. 535.

as though you were going to declaim." Again, when he met a sophist who was buying sausages, sprats, and other cheap dainties of that sort, he said : " My good sir, it is impossible for one who lives on this diet to act convincingly the arrogance of Darius and Xerxes." When Timocrates the philosopher remarked to him that Favorinus had become a chatterbox, Polemo said wittily : " And so is every old woman," thus making fun of him for being like a eunuch. Again, when a tragic actor at the Olympic games in Smyrna pointed to the ground as he uttered the words, " O Zeus ! " [1] then raised his hands to heaven at the words, " and Earth ! " Polemo, who was presiding at the Olympic games, expelled him from the contest, saying : " The fellow has committed a solecism with his hand." I will say no more on this subject, for this is enough to illustrate the charming wit of the man.

Polemo's style of eloquence is passionate, combative, and ringing to the echo, like the trumpet at the Olympic games. The Demosthenic cast of his thought lends it distinction and a gravity which is not dull or inert but brilliant and inspired, as though delivered from the tripod.[2] But they fail to understand the man who say that he handles invective more skilfully than any other sophist, but is less skilful in making a defence. Such a criticism is proved to be untrue by this and that declamation in which he speaks for the defence, but especially by the speech in which Demosthenes swears that he did not accept the fifty talents.[3] For in establishing a defence so difficult to make, his ornate rhetoric and technical skill were fully equal to the argument. I observe the same error in the case of those who

131

περὶ τοὺς ἡγουμένους αὐτὸν ἐκφέρεσθαι τῶν ἐσχη-
ματισμένων ὑποθέσεων εἰργόμενον τοῦ δρόμου,
καθάπερ ἐν δυσχωρίᾳ ἵππον, παραιτούμενόν τε
αὐτὰς τὰς Ὁμηρείους γνώμας εἰπεῖν

ἐχθρὸς γάρ μοι κεῖνος ὁμῶς Ἀΐδαο πύλῃσιν,
ὅς χ᾽ ἕτερον μὲν κεύθῃ ἐνὶ φρεσίν, ἄλλο δὲ εἴπῃ,

ταῦτα γὰρ ἴσως ἔλεγεν αἰνιττόμενος καὶ παραδηλῶν
τὸ δύστροπον τῶν τοιούτων ὑποθέσεων, ἄριστα
δὲ κἀκεῖνα ἠγωνίσατο, ὡς δηλοῦσιν ὅ τε μοιχὸς ὁ
ἐκκεκαλυμμένος [1] καὶ ὁ Ξενοφῶν ὁ ἀξιῶν ἀποθνήσκειν ἐπὶ Σωκράτει καὶ ὁ Σόλων ὁ αἰτῶν ἀπα-
λείφειν τοὺς νόμους λαβόντος τὴν φρουρὰν τοῦ
Πεισιστράτου καὶ οἱ Δημοσθένεις τρεῖς, ὁ μετὰ
Χαιρώνειαν προσαγγέλλων [2] ἑαυτὸν καὶ ὁ δοκῶν
543 θανάτου ἑαυτῷ τιμᾶσθαι ἐπὶ τοῖς Ἁρπαλείοις καὶ
ὁ ξυμβουλεύων ἐπὶ τῶν τριήρων φεύγειν ἐπιόντος
μὲν Φιλίππου, νόμον δὲ Αἰσχίνου κεκυρωκότος
ἀποθνήσκειν τὸν πολέμου μνημονεύσαντα. ἐν γὰρ
ταύταις μάλιστα τῶν ὑπ᾽ αὐτοῦ κατὰ σχῆμα προ-
ηγμένων ἡνία τε ἐμβέβληται τῷ λόγῳ καὶ τὸ
ἐπαμφότερον αἱ διάνοιαι σώζουσιν.

Ἰατροῖς δὲ θαμὰ ὑποκείμενος λιθιώντων αὐτῷ
τῶν ἄρθρων παρεκελεύετο αὐτοῖς ὀρύττειν καὶ τέ-
μνειν τὰς Πολέμωνος λιθοτομίας. Ἡρώδῃ δὲ ἐπι-

---

[1] Cobet suggests ἐγκεκαλυμμένος, "veiled," as more suitable
for an "ambiguous" speech.
[2] προσάγων Kayser; προσαγγέλλων Wright, cf. p. 522.

---

[1] See Glossary.
[2] Iliad ix. 312.
[3] Solon's efforts to check the tyranny of Peisistratus are
described by Aristotle, Constitution of Athens xiv. 2,
Plutarch, Solon, and elsewhere; but this precise incident is
not recorded. For the bodyguard see Herodotus i. 59.

hold that he was not qualified to sustain simulated arguments,[1] but was forced off the course like a horse for whom the ground is too rough, and that he deprecated the use of these themes when he quoted the maxim of Homer :

> For hateful to me even as the gates of hell is he that hideth one thing in his heart and uttereth another.[2]

Perhaps he used to say this with a double meaning, and to illustrate by this allusion how intractable are such themes ; nevertheless, these too he sustained with great skill, as is evident from his *Adulterer Unmasked* or his *Xenophon refuses to survive Socrates ;* or his *Solon demands that his laws be rescinded after Peisistratus has obtained a bodyguard.*[3]   Then there are the three on Demosthenes, the first where he denounced himself after Chaeronea,[4] the second in which he pretends that he ought to be punished with death for the affair of Harpalus, lastly that in which he advises the Athenians to flee on their triremes at the approach of Philip,[5] though Aeschines had carried a law that anyone who mentioned the war should be put to death.   For in these more than any other of the simulated themes that he produced, he has given free reins to the argument, and yet the ideas preserve the effect of presenting both sides.

When the doctors were regularly attending him for hardening of the joints, he exhorted them to " dig and carve in the stone-quarries of Polemo." And in writing to Herodes about this disease he

---

[4] For this theme, a " simulated argument " like the one that follows, see p. 522.

[5] This was perhaps modelled on the famous rhetorical theme in which Themistocles gives similar advice in the Persian war.

στέλλων ὑπὲρ τῆς νόσου ταύτης ὧδε ἐπέστειλεν·
" δεῖ ἐσθίειν, χεῖρας οὐκ ἔχω· δεῖ βαδίζειν, πόδες
οὐκ εἰσί μοι· δεῖ ἀλγεῖν, τότε καὶ πόδες εἰσί μοι
καὶ χεῖρες."

Ἐτελεύτα μὲν περὶ τὰ ἓξ καὶ πεντήκοντα ἔτη,
τὸ δὲ μέτρον τῆς ἡλικίας τοῦτο ταῖς μὲν ἄλλαις
ἐπιστήμαις γήρως ἀρχή, σοφιστῇ δὲ νεότης ἔτι,
γηράσκουσα γὰρ ἤδε ἡ ἐπιστήμη σοφίαν ἀρτύνει.

Τάφος δὲ αὐτῷ κατὰ τὴν Σμύρναν οὐδείς, εἰ καὶ
πλείους λέγονται· οἱ μὲν γὰρ ἐν τῷ κήπῳ τοῦ τῆς
Ἀρετῆς ἱεροῦ ταφῆναι αὐτόν, οἱ δὲ οὐ πόρρω τούτου ἐπὶ θαλάττῃ, νεὼς δέ τίς ἐστι βραχὺς καὶ
ἄγαλμα ἐν αὐτῷ Πολέμωνος ἐσταλμένον, ὡς ἐπὶ
τῆς τριήρους ὠργίαζεν, ὑφ' ᾧ κεῖσθαι τὸν ἄνδρα, οἱ
δὲ ἐν τῇ τῆς οἰκίας αὐλῇ ὑπὸ τοῖς χαλκοῖς ἀν-
δριᾶσιν. ἔστι δὲ οὐδὲν τούτων ἀληθές, εἰ γὰρ
ἐτελεύτα κατὰ τὴν Σμύρναν, οὐδενὸς ἂν τῶν
θαυμασίων παρ' αὐτοῖς ἱερῶν ἀπηξιώθη τὸ μὴ οὐκ
ἐν αὐτῷ κεῖσθαι. ἀλλ' ἐκεῖνα ἀληθέστερα, κεῖσθαι
μὲν αὐτὸν ἐν τῇ Λαοδικείᾳ παρὰ τὰς Συρίας πύλας,
οὗ δὴ καὶ τῶν προγόνων αὐτοῦ θῆκαι, ταφῆναι δὲ
αὐτὸν ζῶντα ἔτι, τουτὶ γὰρ τοῖς φιλτάτοις ἐπι-
544 σκῆψαι, κείμενόν τε ἐν τῷ σήματι παρακελεύεσθαι
τοῖς συγκλείουσι τὸν τάφον " ἔπειγε, ἔπειγε,[1] μὴ
γὰρ ἴδοι με σιωπῶντα ἥλιος." πρὸς δὲ τοὺς
οἰκείους ὀλοφυρομένους αὐτὸν ἀνεβόησε· " δότε
μοι σῶμα καὶ μελετήσομαι."

Μέχρι Πολέμωνος τὰ Πολέμωνος, οἱ γὰρ ἐπ'

---

[1] ἔπαγε, ἔπαγε Kayser; ἔπειγε, ἔπειγε Cobet.

sent this bulletin: "I must eat, but I have no hands; I must walk, but I have no feet; I must endure pain, and then I find I have both feet and hands."

When he died he was about fifty-six years old, but this age-limit, though for the other learned professions it is the beginning of senility, for a sophist still counts as youthfulness, since in this profession a man's knowledge grows more adaptable with advancing age.

He has no tomb in Smyrna, though several there are said to be his. For some say that he was buried in the garden of the temple of Virtue; others, not far from that place near the sea, and there is a small temple thereabouts with a statue of Polemo in it, arrayed as he was when he performed the sacred rites on the trireme, and beneath his statue they say that the man himself lies; while others say that he was buried in the courtyard of his house under the bronze statues. But none of these accounts is true, for if he had died in Smyrna there is not one of the marvellous temples in that city in which he would have been deemed unworthy to lie. But yet another version is nearer the truth, namely that he lies at Laodicea near the Syrian gate, where, in fact, are the sepulchres of his ancestors; that he was buried while still alive, for so he had enjoined on his nearest and dearest; and that, as he lay in the tomb, he thus exhorted those who were shutting up the sepulchre: "Make haste, make haste! Never shall the sun behold me reduced to silence!" And when his friends wailed over him, he cried with a loud voice: "Give me a body and I will declaim!"

With Polemo ended the house of Polemo, for his

αὐτῷ γενόμενοι ξυγγενεῖς μέν, οὐ μὴν οἷοι πρὸς
τὴν ἐκείνου ἀρετὴν ἐξετάζεσθαι, πλὴν ἑνὸς ἀνδρός,
περὶ οὗ μικρὸν ὕστερον λέξω.

κϛ'. Μηδὲ Σεκούνδου τοῦ Ἀθηναίου ἀμνη-
μονῶμεν, ὃν ἐκάλουν ἐπίουρόν τινες ὡς τέκτονος
παῖδα. Σεκοῦνδος τοίνυν ὁ σοφιστὴς γνῶναι μὲν
περιττός, ἑρμηνεῦσαι δὲ ἀπέριττος, Ἡρώδην δὲ
ἐκπαιδεύσας ἐς διαφορὰν αὐτῷ ἀφίκετο παι-
δεύοντι ἤδη, ὅθεν ὁ Ἡρώδης διετώθαζεν αὐτὸν
ἐκεῖνο ἐπιλέγων·

καὶ κεραμεὺς κεραμεῖ κοτέει καὶ ῥήτορι τέκτων,

ἀλλ' ἀποθανόντι καὶ λόγον ἐπεφθέγξατο καὶ δάκρυα
ἐπέδωκε καίτοι γηραιῷ τελευτήσαντι.

545 Μνήμης δὲ ἄξια τοῦ ἀνδρὸς τούτου καὶ πλείω
μέν, μάλιστα δὲ ἥδε ἡ ὑπόθεσις· " ὁ ἄρξας στάσεως ἀποθνησκέτω καὶ ὁ παύσας στάσιν ἐχέτω
δωρεάν· ὁ αὐτὸς καὶ ἄρξας καὶ παύσας αἰτεῖ τὴν
δωρεάν." τήνδε τὴν ὑπόθεσιν ὧδε ἐβραχυλόγησεν·
" οὐκοῦν " ἔφη " τί πρότερον; τὸ κινῆσαι στάσιν.
τί δεύτερον; τὸ παῦσαι. δοὺς οὖν τὴν ἐφ' οἷς
ἠδίκεις τιμωρίαν, τὴν ἐφ' οἷς εὖ πεποίηκας δωρεάν,
εἰ δύνασαι, λάβε." τοιόσδε μὲν ὁ ἀνὴρ οὗτος,
τέθαπται δὲ πρὸς τῇ Ἐλευσῖνι ἐν δεξιᾷ τῆς Μέγα-
ράδε ὁδοῦ.

---

[1] This is Polemo's great-grandson Hermocrates, whose
Life Philostratus gives below, p. 608.

descendants, though they were his kindred, were not the sort of men who could be compared with his surpassing merit, with the exception of one, of whom I shall speak a little later.[1]

26. I must not fail to mention SECUNDUS THE ATHENIAN whom some called "Wooden Peg," because he was the son of a carpenter. Secundus the sophist was varied and abundant in invention, but plain and simple in his style. Though he taught Herodes, he quarrelled with him while he was still his pupil, and therefore Herodes ridiculed him, and quoted at his expense the verse :

> And the potter envies the potter and the carpenter
> the orator.[2]

Nevertheless, when he died Herodes not only spoke his funeral oration, but shed a tribute of tears over him, though he died an old man.

Several of this man's compositions are worthy of mention, but above all the following theme for a disputation : "Suppose that he who instigates a revolt is to die, and he who suppresses it is to receive a reward. Now the same man both instigated a revolt and suppressed it, and he demands the reward." Secundus summed up this argument as follows. "Which of the two," he asked, "came first ? The instigation to revolt. Which second ? The suppression thereof. Therefore first pay the penalty for trying to do wrong, then, if you can, receive the reward for your good deed." Such was Secundus. He is buried near Eleusis, on the right of the road that leads to Megara.

[2] Hesiod, *Works and Days* 25. Herodes changed the word τέκτονι to ῥήτορι, the orator being himself.

Β'.

α'. Περὶ δὲ Ἡρώδου τοῦ Ἀθηναίου τάδε χρὴ
εἰδέναι· ὁ σοφιστὴς Ἡρώδης ἐτέλει μὲν ἐκ πατέρων ἐς τοὺς δισυπάτους, ἀνέφερε δὲ ἐς τὸν τῶν Αἰακι-
546 δῶν, οὓς ξυμμάχους ποτὲ ἡ Ἑλλὰς ἐπὶ τὸν Πέρσην
ἐποιεῖτο, ἀπηξίου δὲ οὐδὲ τὸν Μιλτιάδην, οὐδὲ τὸν
Κίμωνα, ὡς ἄνδρε ἀρίστω καὶ πολλοῦ ἀξίω Ἀθη-
547 ναίοις τε καὶ τοῖς ἄλλοις Ἕλλησι περὶ τὰ Μηδικά,
ὁ μὲν γὰρ ἦρξε τροπαίων Μηδικῶν, ὁ δὲ ἀπήτησε
δίκας τοὺς βαρβάρους ὧν μετὰ ταῦτα ὕβρισαν.

Ἄριστα δὲ ἀνθρώπων πλούτῳ ἐχρήσατο. τουτὶ
δὲ μὴ τῶν εὐμεταχειρίστων ἡγώμεθα, ἀλλὰ τῶν
παγχαλέπων τε καὶ δυσκόλων, οἱ γὰρ πλούτῳ
μεθύοντες ὕβριν τοῖς ἀνθρώποις ἐπαντλοῦσιν. προσ-
διαβάλλουσι δὲ ὡς καὶ τυφλὸν τὸν Πλοῦτον, ὃς εἰ
καὶ τὸν ἄλλον χρόνον ἐδόκει τυφλός, ἀλλ' ἐπὶ
Ἡρώδου ἀνέβλεψεν, ἔβλεψε μὲν γὰρ ἐς φίλους,
ἔβλεψε δὲ ἐς πόλεις, ἔβλεψε δὲ ἐς ἔθνη, πάντων
περιωπὴν ἔχοντος τοῦ ἀνδρὸς καὶ θησαυρίζοντος

---

[1] Herodotus viii. 64 describes the invocation by the
Athenians of the Aeacids Ajax and Telamon; cf. Philostratus, *Heroicus* 743.

[2] They were descended from Aeacus. Philostratus seems
to reprove Plato, who disparaged them in the *Gorgias* 515.

138

BOOK II

1. Concerning HERODES THE ATHENIAN the following facts ought to be known. Herodes the sophist
on his father's side belonged to a family which twice
held consulships and also dated back to the house of
the Aeacids,[1] whom Greece once enlisted as allies
against the Persian. Nor did he fail to be proud of
Miltiades and Cimon,[2] seeing that they were two very
illustrious men and did great service to the Athenians
and the rest of Greece in the wars with the Medes.
For the former was the first to triumph over the
Medes and the latter inflicted punishment on the
barbarians for their insolent acts afterwards.[3]

No man employed his wealth to better purpose.
And this we must not reckon a thing easy to achieve,
but very difficult and arduous. For men who are
intoxicated with wealth are wont to let loose a flood
of insults on their fellow-men. And moreover they
bring this reproach on Plutus[4] that he is blind ; but
even if at all other times he appeared to be blind,
yet in the case of Herodes he recovered his sight.
For he had eyes for his friends, he had eyes for
cities, he had eyes for whole nations, since the man
watched over them all, and laid up the treasures

---

[3] In 466 Cimon defeated the Persians by sea and land,
and, later, expelled them from the Thracian Chersonese.
[4] Plutus was the god of wealth.

τὸν πλοῦτον ἐν ταῖς τῶν μετεχόντων αὐτοῦ
γνώμαις. ἔλεγε γὰρ δή, ὡς προσήκοι τὸν ὀρθῶς
πλούτῳ χρώμενον τοῖς μὲν δεομένοις ἐπαρκεῖν, ἵνα
μὴ δέωνται, τοῖς δὲ μὴ δεομένοις, ἵνα μὴ δεηθῶσιν,
ἐκάλει τε τὸν μὲν ἀσύμβολον πλοῦτον καὶ φειδοῖ
κεκολασμένον νεκρὸν πλοῦτον, τοὺς δὲ θησαυρούς,
ἐς οὓς ἀποτίθενται τὰ χρήματα ἔνιοι, πλούτου
δεσμωτήρια, τοὺς δὲ καὶ θύειν ἀξιοῦντας ἀποθέτοις
χρήμασιν Ἀλωάδας ἐπωνόμαζε θύοντας Ἄρει μετὰ
τὸ δῆσαι αὐτόν.

Πηγαὶ δὲ αὐτῷ τοῦ πλούτου πολλαὶ μὲν κἀκ
πολλῶν οἴκων, μέγισται δὲ ἥ τε πατρῷα καὶ ἡ
μητρόθεν. ὁ μὲν γὰρ πάππος αὐτοῦ Ἵππαρχος
ἐδημεύθη τὴν οὐσίαν ἐπὶ τυραννικαῖς αἰτίαις, ἃς
Ἀθηναῖοι μὲν οὐκ ἐπῆγον, ὁ δὲ αὐτοκράτωρ οὐκ
ἠγνόησεν, Ἀττικὸν δὲ τὸν μὲν ἐκείνου παῖδα,
Ἡρώδου δὲ πατέρα οὐ περιεῖδεν ἡ Τύχη πένητα
ἐκ πλουσίου γενόμενον, ἀλλ' ἀνέδειξεν αὐτῷ
θησαυροῦ χρῆμα ἀμύθητον ἐν μιᾷ τῶν οἰκιῶν, ἃς
πρὸς τῷ θεάτρῳ ἐκέκτητο, οὗ διὰ μέγεθος εὐ-
548 λαβὴς μᾶλλον ἢ περιχαρὴς γενόμενος ἔγραψε πρὸς
τὸν αὐτοκράτορα ἐπιστολὴν ὧδε ξυγκειμένην·
" θησαυρόν, ὦ βασιλεῦ, ἐπὶ τῆς ἐμαυτοῦ οἰκίας
εὕρηκα· τί οὖν περὶ αὐτοῦ κελεύεις; " καὶ ὁ
αὐτοκράτωρ, Νερούας δὲ ἦρχε τότε, " χρῶ " ἔφη
" οἷς εὕρηκας." τοῦ δὲ Ἀττικοῦ ἐπὶ τῆς αὐτῆς
εὐλαβείας μείναντος καὶ γράψαντος ὑπὲρ ἑαυτὸν
εἶναι τὰ τοῦ θησαυροῦ μέτρα " καὶ παραχρῶ "

---

[1] cf. Matthew vi. 20.
[2] Iliad v. 385; Otus and Ephialtes, the Aloadae, imprisoned Ares for thirteen months; he was released by
Hermes.
[3] Suetonius, Vespasian 13, refers to the trial of Hipparchus.

of his riches [1] in the hearts of those who shared them with him. For indeed he used to say that he who would use his wealth aright ought to give to the needy that they might cease to be in need, and to those that needed it not, lest they should fall into need; and he used to call riches that did not circulate and were tied up by parsimony "dead riches," and the treasure-chambers in which some men hoard their money "prison-houses of wealth"; and those who thought they must actually sacrifice to their hoarded money he nicknamed "Aloadae," [2] for they sacrificed to Ares after they had imprisoned him.

The sources of his wealth were many and derived from several families, but the greatest were the fortunes that came from his father and mother. For his grandfather Hipparchus suffered the confiscation of his estate on the charge of aspiring to a tyranny, of which the Emperor was not ignorant, though the Athenians did not bring it forward.[3] His son Atticus, however, the father of Herodes, was not overlooked by Fortune after he had lost his wealth and become poor, but she revealed to him a prodigious treasure in one of the houses which he had acquired near the theatre. And since, on account of its vastness, it made him cautious rather than overjoyed, he wrote the following letter to the Emperor: "O Emperor, I have found a treasure in my own house. What commands do you give about it?" To which the Emperor (Nerva at that time was on the throne) replied: "Use what you have found." But Atticus did not abandon his caution and wrote that the extent of the treasure was beyond his station. "Then misuse your windfall," replied the

ἔφη " τῷ ἑρμαίῳ, σὸν γάρ ἐστιν." ἐντεῦθεν
μέγας μὲν ὁ Ἀττικός, μείζων δὲ ὁ Ἡρώδης,
πρὸς γὰρ τῷ πατρῴῳ πλούτῳ καὶ ὁ μητρῷος
αὐτῷ πλοῦτος οὐ παρὰ πολὺ τούτου ἐπερρύη.

Μεγαλοψυχία δὲ λαμπρὰ καὶ περὶ τὸν Ἀττικὸν
τοῦτον· ἦρχε μὲν γὰρ τῶν κατὰ τὴν Ἀσίαν ἐλευθέρων πόλεων ὁ Ἡρώδης, ἰδὼν δὲ τὴν Τρῳάδα
βαλανείων τε πονήρως ἔχουσαν καὶ γεῶδες ὕδωρ
ἐκ φρεάτων ἀνιμῶντας ὀμβρίων τε ὑδάτων θήκας
ὀρύττοντας ἐπέστειλεν Ἀδριανῷ αὐτοκράτορι μὴ
περιιδεῖν πόλιν ἀρχαίαν καὶ εὐθάλαττον αὐχμῷ
φθαρεῖσαν, ἀλλ᾽ ἐπιδοῦναί σφισι τριακοσίας μυριάδας ἐς ὕδωρ, ὧν πολλαπλασίους ἤδη καὶ κώμαις
ἐπιδεδώκοι. ἐπήνεσεν ὁ αὐτοκράτωρ τὰ ἐπεσ-
ταλμένα ὡς πρὸς τρόπου ἑαυτῷ ὄντα καὶ τὸν
Ἡρώδην αὐτὸν ἐπέταξε τῷ ὕδατι. ἐπεὶ δὲ ἐς
ἑπτακοσίας μυριάδας ἡ δαπάνη προὔβαινεν ἐπ-
έστελλόν τε τῷ αὐτοκράτορι οἱ τὴν Ἀσίαν ἐπι-
τροπεύοντες, ὡς δεινὸν πεντακοσίων πόλεων φόρον
ἐς μιᾶς πόλεως δαπανᾶσθαι κρήνην, ἐμέμψατο
πρὸς τὸν Ἀττικὸν ὁ αὐτοκράτωρ ταῦτα, καὶ ὁ
Ἀττικὸς μεγαλοφρονέστατα ἀνθρώπων " ὦ βασιλεῦ," εἶπεν " ὑπὲρ μικρῶν μὴ παροξύνου, τὸ γὰρ
ὑπὲρ τὰς τριακοσίας μυριάδας ἀναλωθὲν ἐγὼ μὲν
τῷ υἱῷ ἐπιδίδωμι, ὁ δὲ υἱὸς τῇ πόλει ἐπιδώσει.¹ "
549 καὶ αἱ διαθῆκαι δέ, ἐν αἷς τῷ Ἀθηναίων δήμῳ
κατέλειπε καθ᾽ ἕκαστον ἔτος μνᾶν καθ᾽ ἕνα, μεγα-
λοφροσύνην κατηγοροῦσι τοῦ ἀνδρός, ᾗ καὶ ἐς τὰ

¹ ἐπιδίδωσι Kayser ; ἐπιδώσει Cobet.

---

¹ Suidas tells the story of Herodes himself.
² This is the later city known as Alexandria Troas.

Emperor, "for yours it is." [1] Hence Atticus became powerful, but Herodes still more so, for besides his father's fortune his mother's also, which was not much less, helped to make him affluent.

This same Atticus was also distinguished for his lordly spirit. As an instance, at a time when Herodes was governor of the free cities in Asia, he observed that Troy [2] was ill-supplied with baths, and that the inhabitants drew muddy water from their wells, and had to dig cisterns to catch rain water. Accordingly he wrote to the Emperor Hadrian to ask him not to allow an ancient city, conveniently near the sea, to perish from drought, but to give them three million drachmae to procure a water-supply, since he had already bestowed on mere villages many times that sum. The Emperor approved of the advice in the letter as in accordance with his own disposition, and appointed Herodes himself to take charge of the water-supply. But when the outlay had reached the sum of seven million drachmae,[3] and the officials who governed Asia kept writing to the Emperor that it was a scandal that the tribute received from five hundred cities should be spent on the fountain of one city, the Emperor expressed his disapproval of this to Atticus, whereupon Atticus replied in the most lordly fashion in the world : " Do not, O Emperor, allow yourself to be irritated on account of so trifling a sum. For the amount spent in excess of the three millions I hereby present to my son, and my son will present it to the town." His will, moreover, in which he bequeathed to the people of Athens a mina [4] annually for every citizen, proclaims the magnificence of the man ; and he practised it in

[3] About £280,000 [in 1921].
[4] A little over £4 [in 1921].

ἄλλα ἐχρῆτο, ἑκατὸν μὲν βοῦς τῇ θεῷ θύων ἐν
ἡμέρᾳ μιᾷ πολλάκις, ἑστιῶν δὲ τῇ θυσίᾳ τὸν
Ἀθηναίων δῆμον κατὰ φυλὰς καὶ γένη, ὁπότε δὲ
ἥκοι Διονύσια καὶ κατίοι ἐς Ἀκαδημίαν τὸ τοῦ Διονύσου ἕδος, ἐν Κεραμεικῷ ποτίζων ἀστοὺς ὁμοίως
καὶ ξένους κατακειμένους ἐπὶ στιβάδων κιττοῦ.

Ἐπεὶ δὲ τῶν τοῦ Ἀττικοῦ διαθηκῶν ἐπεμνήσθην, ἀνάγκη καὶ τὰς αἰτίας ἀναγράψαι, δι᾽ ἃς
προσέκρουσεν Ἡρώδης Ἀθηναίοις· εἶχον μὲν γὰρ
αἱ διαθῆκαι, ὡς εἶπον, ἔγραψε δὲ αὐτὰς ξυμ-
βουλίᾳ τῶν ἀμφ᾽ ἑαυτὸν ἀπελευθέρων, οἳ χαλεπὴν
ὁρῶντες τὴν Ἡρώδου φύσιν ἀπελευθέροις τε καὶ
δούλοις ἀποστροφὴν ἐποιοῦντο τὸν Ἀθηναίων
δῆμον,[1] ὡς τῆς δωρεᾶς αὐτοὶ αἴτιοι. καὶ ὁποῖα
μὲν τῶν ἀπελευθέρων τὰ πρὸς τὸν Ἡρώδην,
δηλούτω ἡ κατηγορία, ἣν πεποίηται σφῶν πᾶν
κέντρον ἠρμένος τῆς ἑαυτοῦ γλώττης. ἀναγνω-
σθεισῶν δὲ τῶν διαθηκῶν ξυνέβησαν οἱ Ἀθηναῖοι πρὸς τὸν Ἡρώδην πέντε μνᾶς αὐτὸν ἐσάπαξ
ἑκάστῳ καταβαλόντα[2] πρίασθαι παρ᾽ αὐτῶν τὸ
μὴ ἀεὶ διδόναι· ἀλλ᾽ ἐπεὶ προσῄεσαν μὲν ταῖς
τραπέζαις ὑπὲρ τῶν ὡμολογημένων, ἐπανεγιγνώ-
σκετο δὲ αὐτοῖς ξυμβόλαια πατέρων τε καὶ πάπ-
πων ὡς ὀφειλόντων τοῖς Ἡρώδου γονεῦσιν ἀντι-
λογισμοῖς τε ὑπήγοντο καὶ οἱ μὲν μικρὰ ἠριθμοῦντο,
οἱ δὲ οὐδέν, οἱ δὲ συνείχοντο ἐπ᾽ ἀγορᾶς ὡς καὶ

[1] τοῦ ... δήμου Kayser; τὸν ... δῆμον Valckenaer and
others.
[2] καταβάλλοντα Kayser; καταβαλόντα Cobet.

[1] cf. Pausanias i. 29. 2.   The image of Dionysus of Eleu-

144

other ways also. He would often sacrifice a hundred oxen to the goddess in a single day, and entertain at the sacrificial feast the whole population of Athens by tribes and families. And whenever the festival of Dionysus came round and the image of Dionysus descended to the Academy,[1] he would furnish wine to drink for citizens and strangers alike, as they lay in the Cerameicus on couches of ivy leaves.

Since I have mentioned the will of Atticus, I must also record the reasons why Herodes offended the Athenians. The terms of the will were as I have stated, and Atticus drew it up by the advice of his freedmen, who since they saw that Herodes was by nature prone to deal harshly with his freedmen and slaves, tried in this way to prepare a haven for themselves among the people of Athens, by appearing responsible for the legacy. What sort of relation existed between the freedmen and Herodes may be plainly seen in the invective which he composed against them. For in it he shot forth at them every weapon that his tongue could command. When the will had been read, the Athenians made a compact with Herodes that by paying them each five minae down he should redeem his obligation to keep up continued payments. But when they came to the banks to get the sum that had been agreed upon, then and there they had to listen to the recital of contracts made by their fathers and grandfathers, showing that they were in debt to the parents of Herodes, and they were held liable for counter-payments, with the result that some received payment of only a small sum, others nothing at all, while some were detained in

therae was taken in procession once a year to the god's small temple near the Academy.

ἀποδώσοντες, παρώξυνε ταῦτα τοὺς Ἀθηναίους
ὡς ἡρπασμένους τὴν δωρεὰν καὶ οὐκ ἐπαύσαντο
μισοῦντες, οὐδὲ ὁπότε τὰ μέγιστα εὐεργετεῖν ᾤετο.
τὸ οὖν στάδιον ἔφασαν εὖ ἐπωνομάσθαι Παναθη-
ναϊκόν, κατεσκευάσθαι γὰρ αὐτὸ ἐξ ὧν ἀπεστε-
ροῦντο Ἀθηναῖοι πάντες.

Καὶ μὴν καὶ ἐλειτούργησεν Ἀθηναίοις τήν τε
ἐπώνυμον καὶ τὴν τῶν Πανελληνίων, στεφανω-
θεὶς δὲ καὶ τὴν τῶν Παναθηναίων " καὶ ὑμᾶς,"
550 εἶπεν " ὦ Ἀθηναῖοι, καὶ τῶν Ἑλλήνων τοὺς
ἥξοντας καὶ τῶν ἀθλητῶν τοὺς ἀγωνιουμένους
ὑποδέξομαι σταδίῳ λίθου λευκοῦ." καὶ εἰπὼν
ταῦτα τὸ στάδιον τὸ ὑπὲρ τὸν Ἰλισσὸν ἔσω τεττάρων ἐτῶν ἀπετέλεσεν ἔργον ξυνθεὶς ὑπὲρ πάντα
τὰ θαύματα, οὐδὲν γὰρ θέατρον αὐτῷ ἁμιλλᾶται.
κἀκεῖνα περὶ τῶν Παναθηναίων τούτων ἤκουον·
πέπλον μὲν ἀνῆφθαι τῆς νεὼς ἡδίῳ γραφῆς ξὺν
οὐρίῳ τῷ κόλπῳ, δραμεῖν δὲ τὴν ναῦν οὐχ ὑπο-
ζυγίων ἀγόντων, ἀλλ' ὑπογείοις μηχαναῖς ἐπολι-
σθάνουσαν, ἐκ Κεραμεικοῦ δὲ ἄρασαν χιλίᾳ κώπῃ
ἀφεῖναι ἐπὶ τὸ Ἐλευσίνιον καὶ περιβαλοῦσαν
αὐτὸ παραμεῖψαι τὸ Πελασγικὸν κομιζομένην τε
παρὰ τὸ Πύθιον ἐλθεῖν, οἷ νῦν ὥρμισται. τὸ δὲ
ἐπὶ θάτερα τοῦ σταδίου νεὼς ἐπέχει Τύχης καὶ

---

[1] The chief archon at Athens gave his name to the current
year.
[2] A marble stadium has been built recently on the site
of the stadium of Herodes.
[3] The Athenians dedicated a robe, " peplos," to Athene
annually and displayed it on a ship constructed for this
purpose and dragged in a procession.
[4] This is probably not the Pythium near the Olympieion

the market-place as debtors who must pay. This treatment exasperated the Athenians, who felt they had been robbed of their legacy, and they never ceased to hate Herodes, not even at the time when he thought he was conferring on them the greatest benefits. Hence they declared the Panathenaic stadium was well named, since he had built it with money of which all the Athenians were being deprived.

Furthermore he held the office of archon eponymus [1] at Athens, and the curatorship of the pan-Hellenic festival; and when he was offered the crowning honour of the charge of the Panathenaic festival he made this announcement: "I shall welcome you, O Athenians, and those Hellenes that shall attend, and the athletes who are to compete, in a stadium of pure white marble." In accordance with this promise he completed within four years the stadium [2] on the other side of the Ilissus, and thus constructed a monument that is beyond all other marvels, for there is no theatre that can rival it. Moreover, I have been told the following facts concerning this Panathenaic festival. The robe of Athene that was hung on the ship [3] was more charming than any painting, with folds that swelled before the breeze, and the ship, as it took its course, was not hauled by animals, but slid forward by means of underground machinery. Setting sail at the Cerameicus with a thousand rowers, it arrived at the Eleusinium, and after circling it, passed by the Pelasgicum: and thus escorted came by the Pythium,[4] to where it is now moored. The other end of the stadium is occupied by a temple of Fortune with

but, according to Dörpfeld, is the old shrine of Apollo near Pan's Cave.

ἄγαλμα ἐλεφάντινον ὡς κυβερνώσης πάντα. μετεκόσμησε δὲ καὶ τοὺς Ἀθηναίων ἐφήβους ἐς τὸ νῦν σχῆμα χλαμύδας πρῶτος ἀμφιέσας λευκάς, τέως γὰρ δὴ μελαίνας ἐνημμένοι τὰς ἐκκλησίας περιεκάθηντο καὶ τὰς πομπὰς ἔπεμπον πενθούντων δημοσίᾳ τῶν Ἀθηναίων τὸν κήρυκα τὸν Κοπρέα, ὃν αὐτοὶ ἀπέκτειναν τοὺς Ἡρακλείδας τοῦ βωμοῦ ἀποσπῶντα.

551 Ἀνέθηκε δὲ Ἡρώδης Ἀθηναίοις καὶ τὸ ἐπὶ Ῥηγίλλῃ θέατρον κέδρου ξυνθεὶς τὸν ὄροφον, ἡ δὲ ὕλη καὶ ἐν ἀγαλματοποιίαις σπουδαία· δύο μὲν δὴ ταῦτα Ἀθήνησιν, ἃ οὐχ ἑτέρωθι τῆς ὑπὸ Ῥωμαίοις, ἀξιούσθω δὲ λόγου καὶ τὸ ὑπωρόφιον θέατρον, ὃ ἐδείματο Κορινθίοις, παρὰ πολὺ μὲν τοῦ Ἀθήνησιν, ἐν ὀλίγοις δὲ τῶν παρ' ἄλλοις ἐπαινουμένων, καὶ τὰ Ἰσθμοῖ ἀγάλματα ὅ τε τοῦ Ἰσθμίου κολοσσὸς καὶ ὁ τῆς Ἀμφιτρίτης καὶ τὰ ἄλλα, ὧν τὸ ἱερὸν ἐνέπλησεν, οὐδὲ τὸν τοῦ Μελικέρτου παρελθὼν δελφῖνα. ἀνέθηκε δὲ καὶ τῷ Πυθίῳ τὸ Πυθοῖ στάδιον καὶ τῷ Διὶ τὸ ἐν τῇ Ὀλυμπίᾳ ὕδωρ, Θετταλοῖς τε καὶ τοῖς περὶ Μηλιακὸν κόλπον Ἕλλησι τὰς ἐν Θερμοπύλαις κολυμβήθρας τοῖς νοσοῦσι παιωνίους. ᾤκισε δὲ καὶ τὸ ἐν τῇ Ἠπείρῳ Ὠρικὸν ὑποδεδωκὸς ἤδη καὶ τὸ ἐν τῇ Ἰταλίᾳ Κανύσιον ἡμερώσας ὕδατι

---

[1] *Iliad* xv. 639 ; for this custom *cf.* Plutarch, *Aratus* 53 ; Pausanias ii. 3. 6 ; Philostratus, *Heroicus* 740. Copreus was the herald of Eurystheus, the task-master of Heracles.

[2] The Odeum or Theatre of Music, of which considerable remains exist ; Pausanias vii. 20. 6. Regilla was the wife of Herodes.

[3] Pausanias i. 44. 11. The corpse of Melicertes or Palaemon, who was drowned by his mother Ino Leucothea,

her statue in ivory to show that she directs all contests. Herodes also changed the dress of the Athenian youths to its present form, and was the first to dress them in white cloaks, for before that time they had worn black cloaks whenever they sat in a group at public meetings, or marched in festal processions, in token of the public mourning of the Athenians for the herald Copreus,[1] whom they themselves had slain when he was trying to drag the sons of Heracles from the altar.

Herodes also dedicated to the Athenians the theatre in memory of Regilla,[2] and he made its roof of cedar wood, though this wood is considered costly even for making statues. These two monuments, then, are at Athens, and they are such as exist nowhere else in the Roman Empire; but I must not neglect to mention also the roofed theatre which he built for the Corinthians, which is far inferior indeed to the one at Athens but there are not many famous things elsewhere which equal it; and there are also the statues at the Isthmus and the colossal statue of the Isthmian god, and that of Amphitrite, and the other offerings with which he filled the temple; nor must I pass over the dolphin sacred to Melicertes.[3] He also dedicated the stadium at Pytho to the Pythian god, and the aqueduct at Olympia to Zeus, and for the Thessalians and the Greeks who dwell around the Maliac gulf, the bathing pools at Thermopylae that heal the sick. Further he colonized Oricum in Epirus, which by this time had fallen into decay, and Canusium in Italy, and made it habitable by giving it a water-supply, since it was

was carried by dolphins to the shore near Corinth, and games were celebrated in his honour at the Isthmus.

μάλα τούτου δεόμενον, ὤνησε δὲ καὶ τὰς ἐν Εὐβοίᾳ καὶ Πελοποννήσῳ καὶ Βοιωτίᾳ πόλεις ἄλλο ἄλλην. καὶ τοσοῦτος ὢν ἐν μεγαλουργίᾳ μέγα οὐδὲν εἰργάσθαι ᾤετο, ἐπεὶ μὴ τὸν Ἰσθμὸν ἔτεμεν, λαμπρὸν ἡγούμενος ἤπειρον ἀποτεμεῖν καὶ πελάγη ξυνάψαι διττὰ καὶ ἐς περίπλουν σταδίων ἓξ καὶ εἴκοσι θαλάττης ξυνελεῖν μήκη. καὶ τούτου ἤρα μέν, οὐκ ἐθάρρει δὲ αὐτὸ αἰτεῖν ἐκ βασιλέως, ὡς μὴ διαβληθείη διανοίας δοκῶν ἅπτεσθαι, ᾗ μηδὲ Νέρων ἤρκεσεν. ἐξελάλησε δὲ αὐτὸ ὧδε· ὡς γὰρ
552 ἐγὼ Κτησιδήμου τοῦ Ἀθηναίου ἤκουον, ἤλαυνε μὲν τὴν ἐπὶ Κορίνθου ὁ Ἡρώδης ξυγκαθημένου τοῦ Κτησιδήμου, γενόμενος δὲ κατὰ τὸν Ἰσθμὸν "Πόσειδον," εἶπεν "βούλομαι μέν, ξυγχωρήσει δὲ οὐδείς." θαυμάσας οὖν ὁ Κτησίδημος τὸ εἰρημένον ἤρετο αὐτὸν τὴν αἰτίαν τοῦ λόγου. καὶ ὁ Ἡρώδης "ἐγὼ" ἔφη "πολὺν χρόνον ἀγωνίζομαι σημεῖον ὑπολείπεσθαι τοῖς μετ' ἐμὲ ἀνθρώποις διανοίας δηλούσης ἄνδρα καὶ οὔπω δοκῶ μοι τῆς δόξης ταύτης τυγχάνειν." ὁ μὲν δὴ Κτησίδημος ἐπαίνους διῄει τῶν τε λόγων αὐτοῦ καὶ τῶν ἔργων ὡς οὐκ ἐχόντων ὑπερβολὴν ἑτέρῳ, ὁ δὲ Ἡρώδης "φθαρτὰ" ἔφη "λέγεις ταῦτα, καὶ γάρ ἐστι χρόνῳ ἁλωτά, καὶ τοὺς λόγους ἡμῶν τοιχωρυχοῦσιν ἕτεροι ὁ μὲν τὸ μεμφόμενος, ὁ δὲ τό, ἡ δὲ τοῦ Ἰσθμοῦ τομὴ ἔργον ἀθάνατον καὶ ἀπιστούμενον τῇ φύσει, δοκεῖ γάρ μοι τὸ ῥῆξαι τὸν Ἰσθμὸν Ποσειδῶνος δεῖσθαι ἢ ἀνδρός."

---

[1] Of Corinth.

greatly in need of this. And he endowed the cities of Euboea and the Peloponnese and Boeotia with various gifts. And yet, though he had achieved such great works, he held that he had done nothing important because he had not cut through the Isthmus.[1] For he regarded it as a really brilliant achievement to cut away the mainland to join two seas, and to contract lengths of sea into a voyage of twenty-six stades. This then he longed to do, but he never had the courage to ask the Emperor to grant him permission, lest he should be accused of grasping at an ambitious plan to which not even Nero had proved himself equal. But in conversation he did let out that ambition in the following way. For as I have been told by Ctesidemus the Athenian, Herodes was driving to Corinth with Ctesidemus sitting by his side, and when he arrived at the Isthmus Herodes cried: "Poseidon, I aspire to do it, but no one will let me!" Ctesidemus was surprised at what he had said and asked him why he had made the remark. Whereupon Herodes replied: "For a long time I have been striving to bequeath to men that come after me some proof of an ambition that reveals me for the man I am, and I consider that I have not yet attained to this reputation." Then Ctesidemus recited praises of his speeches and his deeds which no other man could surpass. But Herodes replied: "All this that you speak of must decay and yield to the hand of time, and others will plunder my speeches and criticize now this, now that. But the cutting of the Isthmus is a deathless achievement and more than one would credit to human powers, for in my opinion to cleave through the Isthmus calls for Poseidon rather than a mere man."

Ὃν δ' ἐκάλουν οἱ πολλοὶ Ἡρώδου Ἡρακλέα, νεανίας οὗτος ἦν ἐν ὑπήνη πρώτῃ Κελτῷ μεγάλῳ ἴσος καὶ ἐς ὀκτὼ πόδας τὸ μέγεθος. διαγράφει δὲ αὐτὸν ὁ Ἡρώδης ἐν μιᾷ τῶν πρὸς τὸν Ἰουλιανὸν ἐπιστολῶν, κομᾶν τε ξυμμέτρως καὶ τῶν ὀφρύων λασίως ἔχειν, ἃς καὶ ξυμβάλλειν ἀλλήλαις οἷον μίαν, χαροπήν τε ἀκτῖνα ἐκ τῶν ὀμμάτων ἐκδίδοσθαι παρεχομένην τι ὁρμῆς ἦθος καὶ γρυπὸν εἶναι καὶ εὐτραφῶς ἔχοντα τοῦ αὐχένος, τουτὶ δὲ ἐκ πόνων ἥκειν αὐτῷ μᾶλλον ἢ σίτου. εἶναι δὲ αὐτῷ καὶ στέρνα εὐπαγῆ καὶ ξὺν ὥρᾳ κατεσκληκότα, καὶ κνήμην μικρὸν ἐς τὰ ἔξω κυρτουμένην καὶ παρέχουσαν τῇ βάσει τὸ εὖ
553 βεβηκέναι. ἐνῆφθαι δὲ αὐτὸν καὶ δορὰς λύκων, ῥαπτὸν ἔσθημα, ἄθλους τε ποιεῖσθαι τοὺς ἀγρίους τῶν συῶν καὶ τοὺς θῶας καὶ τοὺς λύκους καὶ τῶν ταύρων τοὺς ὑβρίζοντας, καὶ ὠτειλὰς δὲ δεικνύναι τούτων τῶν ἀγώνων. γενέσθαι δὲ τὸν Ἡρακλέα τοῦτον οἱ μὲν γηγενῆ φασιν ἐν τῷ Βοιωτίῳ δήμῳ, Ἡρώδης δὲ ἀκοῦσαι λέγοντός φησιν, ὡς μήτηρ μὲν αὐτῷ γένοιτο γυνὴ οὕτω τι ἐρρωμένη,[1] ὡς βουκολεῖν, πατὴρ δὲ Μαραθών, οὗ τὸ ἐν Μαραθῶνι ἄγαλμα, ἔστι δὲ ἥρως γεωργός. ἤρετό τε τὸν Ἡρακλέα τοῦτον ὁ Ἡρώδης, εἰ καὶ ἀθάνατος εἴη, ὁ δὲ " θνητοῦ " ἔφη " μακροημερώτερος." ἤρετο αὐτὸν καὶ ὅ τι σιτοῖτο, ὁ δὲ " γαλακτοφαγῶ " ἔφη " τὸν πλείω τοῦ χρόνου καί με βόσκουσιν αἶγές τε καὶ ποῖμναι[2] τῶν τε βοῶν καὶ τῶν ἵππων αἱ τοκάδες, ἐκδίδοται δέ τι καὶ θηλῆς ὄνων γάλα εὔποτόν τε καὶ κοῦφον, ἐπειδὰν δὲ ἀλφίτοις

---

[1] ἐπερρωμένη Kayser ; ἐρρωμένη Cobet.
[2] ποιμένες Kayser ; ποῖμναι Cobet.

As to the being whom most men used to call the
Heracles of Herodes, this was a youth in early manhood,[1] as tall as a tall Celt, and in fact about eight
feet high. Herodes describes him in one of his
letters to Julian.[2] He says that his hair grew evenly
on his head, his eyebrows were bushy and they met
as though they were but one, and his eyes gave out a
brilliant gleam which betrayed his impulsive temperament; he was hook-nosed, and had a solidly built
neck, which was due rather to work than to diet.
His chest, too, was well formed and beautifully slim,
and his legs were slightly bowed outwards, which
made it easy for him to stand firmly planted. He
was draped in wolf-skins sewed together to make a
garment, and he used to contend against wild boars,
jackals, wolves, and mad bulls, and would exhibit
the scars from these combats. Some say that this
Heracles was " earth-born " and sprang from the folk
in Boeotia, but Herodes says that he heard him say
that his mother was a woman so strong that she
herded cattle, and his father was Marathon whose
statue is at Marathon, and he is a rustic hero. Herodes
asked this Heracles whether he also was immortal.
To which he replied : " I am only longer lived than a
mortal." Then he asked him what he lived on, and
he said : " I live chiefly on milk, and am fed by goats
and herds of cows and brood mares, and the she-ass
also provides a sweet sort of milk and light to digest.
But when I meet with barley meal, I eat ten quarts,[3]

---

[1] *Odyssey* x. 279 πρῶτον ὑπηνήτῃ, τοῦ περ χαριεστάτη ἥβη;
Lucian, *Demonax* 1, calls him Sostratus.

[2] Antonius Julianus is mentioned by Aulus Gellius, *Attic
Nights*, xix. 9. Perhaps Claudius Julianus, cos. *c.* 159,
Fronto's correspondent, is meant.

[3] One quart was regarded as a day's ration for an ordinary
man.

προσβάλλω, δέκα σιτοῦμαι χοίνικας, καὶ ξυμφέρουσί μοι τὸν ἔρανον τοῦτον γεωργοὶ Μαραθώνιοί τε καὶ Βοιώτιοι, οἵ με καὶ Ἀγαθίωνα ἐπονομάζουσιν, ἐπειδὴ καὶ εὐξύμβολος αὐτοῖς φαίνομαι." "τὴν δὲ δὴ γλῶτταν" ἔφη ὁ Ἡρώδης "πῶς ἐπαιδεύθης καὶ ὑπὸ τίνων; οὐ γάρ μοι τῶν ἀπαιδεύτων φαίνῃ." καὶ ὁ Ἀγαθίων "ἡ μεσογεία" ἔφη "τῆς Ἀττικῆς ἀγαθὸν διδασκαλεῖον ἀνδρὶ βουλομένῳ διαλέγεσθαι, οἱ μὲν γὰρ ἐν τῷ ἄστει Ἀθηναῖοι μισθοῦ δεχόμενοι Θρᾴκια καὶ Ποντικὰ μειράκια καὶ ἐξ ἄλλων ἐθνῶν βαρβάρων ξυνερρυηκότα παραφθείρονται παρ' αὐτῶν τὴν φωνὴν μᾶλλον ἢ ξυμβάλλονταί τι αὐτοῖς ἐς εὐγλωττίαν, ἡ μεσογεία δὲ ἄμικτος βαρβάροις οὖσα ὑγιαίνει αὐτοῖς ἡ φωνὴ καὶ ἡ γλῶττα τὴν ἄκραν Ἀτθίδα ἀποψάλλει." "πανηγύρει δὲ" ἦ δ' ὁ Ἡρώδης "παρέτυχες;" καὶ ὁ Ἀγαθίων "τῇ γε Πυθοῖ" ἔφη "οὐκ ἐπιμιγνὺς τῷ ὁμίλῳ, ἀλλ' ἐκ περιωπῆς τοῦ Παρνασοῦ ἀκούων τῶν τῆς μουσικῆς ἀγωνιστῶν, ὅτε Παμμένης ἐπὶ τραγῳδίᾳ ἐθαυμάσθη, καὶ
554 μοι ἔδοξαν οἱ σοφοὶ Ἕλληνες οὐ χρηστὸν πρᾶγμα ἐργάζεσθαι τὰ τῶν Πελοπιδῶν καὶ τὰ τῶν Λαβδακιδῶν κακὰ ξὺν ἡδονῇ ἀκούοντες, ξύμβουλοι γὰρ σχετλίων ἔργων μῦθοι μὴ ἀπιστούμενοι." φιλοσοφοῦντα δὲ αὐτὸν ἰδὼν ὁ Ἡρώδης ἤρετο καὶ περὶ τῆς γυμνικῆς ἀγωνίας ὅπως γιγνώσκοι, καὶ ὃς "ἐκείνων" ἔφη "καταγελῶ μᾶλλον ὁρῶν τοὺς ἀνθρώπους διαγωνιζομένους ἀλλήλοις παγκράτιον καὶ πυγμὴν καὶ δρόμον καὶ πάλην καὶ στεφανουμένους ὑπὲρ τούτου· στεφανούσθω δὲ ὁ μὲν δρομικὸς ἀθλητὴς ἔλαφον παρελθὼν ἢ ἵππον,

---

[1] "Goodfellow." [2] cf. Life of Aelian, below, p. 624.

and the farmers of Marathon and Boeotia supply
me with this feast; they also nickname me Agathion,[1] because they think that I bring them luck."
"And what about your speech?" asked Herodes.
"How were you educated, and by whom? For you
do not seem to be an uneducated man." "The
interior of Attica educated me," Agathion replied,
"a good school for a man who wishes to be able to
converse. For the Athenians in the city admit as
hirelings youths who come in like a flood from Thrace
and the Pontus and from other barbarian peoples,
and their own speech deteriorates from the influence
of these barbarians to a greater extent than they can
contribute to the improvement of the speech of the
newcomers. But the central district is untainted by
barbarians, and hence its language remains uncor-
rupted and its dialect sounds the purest strain of
Atthis."[2] "Were you ever at a public festival?"
inquired Herodes. "Yes, at Pytho," replied
Agathion, "but I did not mingle with the crowd,
but from the summit of Parnassus I listened to the
musical competitions when Pammenes won applause
in tragedy, and it seemed to me that the wise Greeks
were doing an immoral thing when they listened
with delight to the criminal deeds of the houses of
Pelops and Labdacus; for when myths are not discredited they may be the counsellors of evil deeds."
When Herodes saw that he had a philosophic bent,
he asked him also what was his opinion about the
gymnastic contests, and he replied: "Even more do
I laugh at them when I see men struggling with
one another in the pancratium, and boxing, running,
wrestling, and winning crowns for all this. Let the
athlete who is a runner receive a crown for running

PHILOSTRATUS

ὁ δὲ τὰ βαρύτερα ἀσκῶν ταύρῳ συμπλακεὶς ἢ
ἄρκτῳ, ὃ ἐγὼ ὁσημέραι πράττω μέγαν ἆθλον
ἀφῃρημένης μοι τῆς τύχης, ἐπεὶ μηκέτι βόσκει
λέοντας Ἀκαρνανία."

Ἀγασθεὶς οὖν ὁ Ἡρώδης ἐδεῖτο αὐτοῦ ξυσ-
σιτῆσαί οἱ. καὶ ὁ Ἀγαθίων " αὔριον " ἔφη
" ἀφίξομαί σοι κατὰ μεσημβρίαν ἐς τὸ τοῦ Κανώ-
βου ἱερόν, ἔστω δὲ σοι κρατὴρ ὁ μέγιστος τῶν ἐν
τῷ ἱερῷ γάλακτος πλέως, ὃ μὴ γυνὴ ἤμελξεν."
καὶ ἀφίκετο μὲν ἐς τὴν ὑστεραίαν καθ᾽ ὃν ὡμολόγησε καιρόν, τὴν δὲ ῥῖνα ἐρείσας ἐς τὸν κρατῆρα
" οὐ καθαρὸν " ἔφη " τὸ γάλα, προσβάλλει γάρ
με χεὶρ γυναικός." καὶ εἰπὼν ταῦτα ἀπῆλθε μὴ
ἐπισπασάμενος τοῦ γάλακτος. ἐπιστήσας οὖν ὁ
Ἡρώδης τῷ περὶ τῆς γυναικὸς λόγῳ ἔπεμψεν ἐς
τὰ ἐπαύλια τοὺς ἐπισκεψομένους τἀληθές, καὶ
μαθὼν αὐτὸ οὕτως ἔχον, ξυνῆκεν ὡς δαιμονία
φύσις εἴη περὶ τὸν ἄνδρα.

Οἱ δὲ ποιούμενοι κατηγορίαν τῶν Ἡρώδου χειρῶν ὡς ἐπενεχθεισῶν Ἀντωνίνῳ ἐν τῇ Ἴδῃ τῷ ὄρει
κατὰ χρόνους, οὓς ὁ μὲν τῶν ἐλευθέρων πόλεων, ὁ
δὲ πασῶν τῶν κατὰ τὴν Ἀσίαν ἦρχον, ἠγνοηκέναι
555 μοι δοκοῦσι τὸν Δημοστράτου πρὸς τὸν Ἡρώδην
ἀγῶνα, ἐν ᾧ πλεῖστα διαβάλλων αὐτὸν οὐδαμοῦ τῆς
παροινίας ταύτης ἐπεμνήσθη, ἐπεὶ μηδὲ ἐγένετο.
ὠθισμὸς μὲν γάρ τις αὐτοῖς ξυνέπεσεν, ὡς ἐν δυσχωρίᾳ καὶ στενοῖς, αἱ δὲ χεῖρες οὐδὲν παρηνόμησαν,

---

[1] Canobus or Canopus was the helmsman of Menelaus, who
died in Egypt, and a city was named after him at the mouth
of the Nile. His cult was often confused with that of
Serapis, who had long been worshipped at Athens, and it is
possible that the latter's temple is meant here (Pausanias
i. 34).

156

faster than a deer or a horse, and let him who
trains for a weightier contest be crowned for wrestling with a bull or bear, a thing which I do every
day; for fortune has robbed me of a really great
encounter, now that Acarnania no longer breeds
lions."

On this Herodes admired him greatly and begged
him to dine with him. "To-morrow," replied
Agathion, "I will come to you at noon at the temple of
Canobus,[1] and do you have there the largest bowl that
is in the temple full of milk that has not been milked
by a woman." Accordingly he came next day at the
time agreed upon, but when he had raised the bowl to
his nose, he said : " The milk is not pure, for the odour
of a woman's hand assails my senses." When he had
said this he went away without tasting the milk.
Then Herodes gave heed to what he had said about
the woman, and sent to the cow-sheds to find out the
truth ; and on hearing that thus the matter actually
stood, he recognized that there was a superhuman
character about the man.

Those who accused Herodes of having lifted his
hand against Antoninus[2] on Mount Ida, at the time
when the former was the governor of the free cities,
and the latter of all the cities in Asia, were, in my
opinion, unaware of the action brought by Demostratus against Herodes, in which he made many
charges against him, but nowhere mentioned this
insolent act, for the reason that it never took place.
For though they did in a manner shove one another
aside, as happens in a rough place and a narrow road,
still they did not break the law by coming to blows,

[2] Later the Emperor Antoninus Pius ; for his quarrel with
Polemo about the same time see p. 534.

καίτοι[1] οὐκ ἂν παρῆκεν ὁ Δημόστρατος διελθεῖν αὐτὰ ἐν τῇ πρὸς τὸν Ἡρώδην δίκῃ πικρῶς οὕτω καθαψάμενος τοῦ ἀνδρός, ὡς διαβάλλειν αὐτοῦ καὶ τὰ ἐπαινούμενα.

Ἦλθεν ἐπὶ τὸν Ἡρώδην καὶ φόνου δίκη ὧδε ξυντεθεῖσα· κύειν μὲν αὐτῷ τὴν γυναῖκα Ῥήγιλλαν ὀγδοόν που μῆνα, τὸν δὲ Ἡρώδην οὐχ ὑπὲρ μεγάλων Ἀλκιμέδοντι ἀπελευθέρῳ προστάξαι τυπτῆσαι αὐτήν, πληγεῖσαν δὲ ἐς τὴν γαστέρα τὴν γυναῖκα ἀποθανεῖν ἐν ὠμῷ τῷ τόκῳ. ἐπὶ τούτοις ὡς ἀληθέσι γράφεται αὐτὸν φόνου Βραδούας ὁ τῆς Ῥηγίλλης ἀδελφὸς εὐδοκιμώτατος ὢν ἐν ὑπάτοις καὶ τὸ ξύμβολον τῆς εὐγενείας περιηρτημένος τῷ ὑποδήματι, τοῦτο δέ ἐστιν ἐπισφύριον ἐλεφάντινον μηνοειδές, καὶ παρελθὼν ἐς τὸ Ῥωμαίων βουλευτήριον πιθανὸν μὲν οὐδὲν διῄει περὶ τῆς αἰτίας, ἣν ἐπῆγεν, ἑαυτοῦ δὲ ἔπαινον ἐμακρηγόρει περὶ τοῦ γένους, ὅθεν ἐπισκώπτων αὐτὸν ὁ Ἡρώδης " σὺ " ἔφη " τὴν εὐγένειαν ἐν τοῖς ἀστραγάλοις ἔχεις." μεγαλαυχουμένου δὲ τοῦ κατηγόρου καὶ ἐπ' εὐεργεσίᾳ μιᾶς τῶν ἐν Ἰταλίᾳ πόλεων μάλα γενναίως
556 ὁ Ἡρώδης " κἀγὼ " ἔφη " πολλὰ τοιαῦτα περὶ ἐμαυτοῦ διῄειν ἄν, εἰ ἐν ἁπάσῃ τῇ γῇ ἐκρινόμην." ξυνήρατο δὲ αὐτῷ τῆς ἀπολογίας πρῶτον μὲν τὸ μηδὲν προστάξαι τοιοῦτον ἐπὶ τὴν Ῥήγιλλαν, ἔπειτα τὸ ὑπερπενθῆσαι ἀποθανοῦσαν· διεβάλλετο μὲν γὰρ καὶ ταῦτα ὡς πλάσμα, ἀλλ' ὅμως τἀληθὲς

---

[1] ὥστε Kayser; καίτοι he suggests.

---

[1] Roman patricians and senators wore a half moon as a badge on their shoes; cf. Juvenal vii. 191. In the inscription to Regilla, "starry sandals" are mentioned as her family's hereditary insignia.

and indeed Demostratus would not have neglected to describe the incident in his suit against Herodes, when he attacked the man so bitterly that he actually censured those acts of his which are regularly applauded.

A charge of murder was also brought against Herodes, and it was made up in this way. His wife Regilla, it was said, was in the eighth month of her pregnancy, and Herodes ordered his freedman Alcimedon to beat her for some slight fault, and the woman died in premature childbirth from a blow in the belly. On these grounds, as though true, Regilla's brother Braduas brought a suit against him for murder. He was a very illustrious man of consular rank, and the outward sign of his high birth, a crescent-shaped ivory buckle, was attached to his sandal.[1] And when Braduas appeared before the Roman tribunal he brought no convincing proof of the charge that he was making, but delivered a long panegyric on himself dealing with his own family. Whereupon Herodes jested at his expense and said: "You have your pedigree on your toe-joints."[2] And when his accuser boasted too of his benefactions to one of the cities of Italy, Herodes said with great dignity: "I too could have recited many such actions of my own in whatever part of the earth I were now being tried." Two things helped him in his defence. First that he had given orders for no such severe measures against Regilla; secondly, his extraordinary grief at her death. Even this was regarded as a pretence and made a charge against him, but nevertheless the

[2] *i.e.* there was no need to talk about it.

ἴσχυεν, οὐ γάρ ποτε οὔτ' ἂν θέατρον αὐτῇ ἀναθεῖναι
τοιοῦτον, οὔτ' ἂν δευτέραν κλήρωσιν τῆς ὑπάτου
ἀρχῆς ἐπ' αὐτῇ ἀναβαλέσθαι μὴ καθαρῶς ἔχοντα
τῆς αἰτίας, οὔτ' ἂν τὸν κόσμον αὐτῆς ἐς τὸ ἐν
Ἐλευσῖνι ἱερὸν ἀναθεῖναι φέροντα φόνῳ μεμια-
σμένον, τουτὶ γὰρ τιμωροὺς τοῦ φόνου ποιοῦντος
ἦν τὰς θεὰς μᾶλλον ἢ ξυγγνώμονας. ὁ δὲ καὶ τὸ
σχῆμα τῆς οἰκίας ἐπ' αὐτῇ ὑπήλλαξε μελαίνων τὰ
τῶν οἴκων ἄνθη παραπετάσμασι καὶ χρώμασι καὶ
λίθῳ Λεσβίῳ — κατηφὴς δὲ ὁ λίθος καὶ μέλας —
ὑπὲρ ὧν λέγεται καὶ Λούκιος ἀνὴρ σοφὸς ἐς ξυμ-
βουλίαν τῷ Ἡρώδῃ καθιστάμενος, ὡς οὐκ ἔπειθε
μεταβαλεῖν αὐτὸν διασκῶψαι. ἄξιον δὲ μηδὲ τοῦτο
παρελθεῖν λόγου παρὰ τοῖς σπουδαίοις ἀξιούμενον·
ἦν μὲν γὰρ ἐν τοῖς φανεροῖς σπουδαῖος ὁ ἀνὴρ οὗτος,
Μουσωνίῳ δὲ τῷ Τυρίῳ προσφιλοσοφήσας εὐ-
σκόπως εἶχε τῶν ἀποκρίσεων καὶ τὸ ἐπίχαρι σὺν
καιρῷ ἐπετήδευεν, ἐπιτηδειότατος δὲ ὢν τῷ
557 Ἡρώδῃ παρῆν αὐτῷ πονήρως διατιθεμένῳ τὸ
πένθος καὶ ἐνουθέτει τοιαῦτα λέγων· "ὦ Ἡρώδη,
πᾶν τὸ ἀποχρῶν μεσότητι ὥρισται, καὶ ὑπὲρ τούτου πολλὰ μὲν ἤκουσα Μουσωνίου διαλεγομένου,
πολλὰ δὲ αὐτὸς διείλεγμαι, καὶ σοῦ δὲ ἠκροώμην ἐν
Ὀλυμπίᾳ ἐπαινοῦντος αὐτὸ πρὸς τοὺς Ἕλληνας,
ὅτε δὴ καὶ τοὺς ποταμοὺς ἐκέλευες μέσους τῆς
ὄχθης ῥεῖν. ἀλλὰ μὴν νῦν ποῦ ταῦτα; σεαυτοῦ

truth prevailed. For he never would have dedicated
to her memory so fine a theatre nor would he have
postponed for her sake the casting of lots for his
second consulship, if he had not been innocent
of the charge; nor again would he have made an
offering of her apparel at the temple of Eleusis, if he
had been polluted by a murder when he brought it,
for this was more likely to turn the goddesses into
avengers of the murder than to win their pardon.
He also altered the appearance of his house in her
honour by making the paintings and decorations of
the rooms black by means of hangings, dyes, and
Lesbian marble, which is a gloomy and dark marble.
And they say that Lucius, a wise man, tried to give
Herodes advice about this, and since he could not
persuade him to alter it, he turned him into ridicule.
And this incident must not be omitted from my
narrative, since it is held worthy of mention by learned
writers. For this Lucius ranked among men renowned for learning, and since he had been trained in
philosophy by Musonius of Tyre, his repartees were
apt to hit the mark, and he practised a wit well suited
to the occasion. Now, as he was very intimate with
Herodes, he was with him when he was most deeply
afflicted by his grief, and used to give him good
advice to the following effect: "Herodes, in every
matter that which is enough is limited by the golden
mean, and I have often heard Musonius argue on this
theme, and have often discoursed on it myself; and,
moreover, I used to hear you also, at Olympia, com-
mending the golden mean to the Greeks, and at that
time you would even exhort rivers to keep their
course in mid channel between their banks. But
what has now become of all this advice? For you

γὰρ ἐκπεσὼν ἄξια τοῦ πενθεῖσθαι πράττεις περὶ τῇ
δόξῃ κινδυνεύων ’’ καὶ πλείω ἕτερα. ὡς δὲ οὐκ
ἔπειθεν, ἀπῄει δυσχεράνας. ἰδὼν δὲ παῖδας ἐν
κρήνῃ τινὶ τῶν κατὰ τὴν οἰκίαν ῥαφανῖδας πλύ-
νοντας ἤρετο αὐτούς, ὅτου εἴη τὸ δεῖπνον, οἱ δὲ
ἔφασαν Ἡρώδῃ εὐτρεπίζειν αὐτό. καὶ ὁ Λούκιος
‘‘ ἀδικεῖ ’’ ἔφη ‘‘ Ῥήγιλλαν Ἡρώδης λευκὰς ῥαφανῖδας σιτούμενος ἐν μελαίνῃ οἰκίᾳ.’’ ταῦτα ὡς
ἤκουσεν ἐσαγγελθέντα ὁ Ἡρώδης ἀφεῖλε τὴν
ἀχλὺν τῆς οἰκίας, ὡς μὴ ἄθυρμα γένοιτο ἀνδρῶν
σπουδαίων.

Λουκίου τούτου κἀκεῖνο θαυμάσιον· ἐσπούδαζε
μὲν ὁ αὐτοκράτωρ Μάρκος περὶ Σέξτον τὸν ἐκ
Βοιωτίας φιλόσοφον, θαμίζων αὐτῷ καὶ φοιτῶν
ἐπὶ θύρας, ἄρτι δὲ ἥκων ἐς τὴν Ῥώμην ὁ Λούκιος
ἤρετο τὸν αὐτοκράτορα προϊόντα, ποῖ βαδίζοι καὶ
ἐφ’ ὅ τι, καὶ ὁ Μάρκος ‘‘ καλὸν ’’ ἔφη ‘‘ καὶ γηρά-
σκοντι τὸ μανθάνειν· εἶμι δὴ πρὸς Σέξτον τὸν
φιλόσοφον μαθησόμενος, ἃ οὔπω οἶδα.’’ καὶ ὁ
Λούκιος ἐξάρας τὴν χεῖρα ἐς τὸν οὐρανὸν ‘‘ ὦ
Ζεῦ,’’ ἔφη ‘‘ ὁ Ῥωμαίων βασιλεὺς γηράσκων ἤδη
δέλτον ἐξαψάμενος ἐς διδασκάλου φοιτᾷ, ὁ δὲ ἐμὸς
βασιλεὺς Ἀλέξανδρος δύο καὶ τριάκοντα ὢν [1]
ἀπέθανεν.’’ ἀπόχρη καὶ τὰ εἰρημένα δεῖξαι τὴν
ἰδέαν, ἣν ἐφιλοσόφει Λούκιος, ἱκανὰ γάρ που ταῦτα
δηλῶσαι τὸν ἄνδρα, καθάπερ τὸν ἀνθοσμίαν τὸ
γεῦμα.

Τὸ μὲν δὴ ἐπὶ Ῥηγίλλῃ πένθος ὧδε ἐσβέσθη,

[1] ἐτῶν Kayser; ὢν Cobet.

---

[1] For a curious modern parallel see *Punch* 1916 : “In
Paris they are serving a half-mourning salad consisting
mainly of potatoes, artichokes, and pickled walnuts . . . he

have lost your self-control, and are acting in a way that we must needs deplore, since you risk your great reputation." He said more to the same effect. But since he could not convince him, he went away in anger. And he saw some slaves at a well that was in the house, washing radishes, and asked them for whose dinner they were intended. They replied that they were preparing them for Herodes. At this Lucius remarked: "Herodes insults Regilla by eating white radishes[1] in a black house." This speech was reported indoors to Herodes, and when he heard it he removed the signs of mourning from his house, for fear he should become the laughing-stock of wise men.

Here is another admirable saying of this Lucius. The Emperor Marcus was greatly interested in Sextus the Boeotian philosopher, attending his classes and going to his very door. Lucius had just arrived in Rome, and asked the Emperor, whom he met going out, where he was going and for what purpose. Marcus answered: "It is a good thing even for one who is growing old to acquire knowledge. I am going to Sextus the philosopher to learn what I do not yet know." At this Lucius raised his hand to heaven, and exclaimed: "O Zeus! The Emperor of the Romans is already growing old, but he hangs a tablet round his neck and goes to school, while my Emperor Alexander died at thirty-two!" What I have quoted is enough to show the kind of philosophy cultivated by Lucius, for these speeches suffice to reveal the man as a sip reveals the bouquet of wine.

Thus, then, his grief for Regilla was quenched,

expressed surprise at their failure to add a few radishes to the dish."

PHILOSTRATUS

τὸ δὲ ἐπὶ Παναθηναΐδι τῇ θυγατρὶ Ἀθηναῖοι ἐπράυ-
558 ναν ἐν ἄστει τε αὐτὴν θάψαντες καὶ ψηφισάμενοι
τὴν ἡμέραν, ἐφ' ἧς ἀπέθανεν, ἐξαιρεῖν τοῦ ἔτους.
ἀποθανούσης δὲ αὐτῷ καὶ τῆς ἄλλης θυγατρός, ἣν
Ἐλπινίκην ὠνόμαζεν, ἔκειτο μὲν ἐν τῷ δαπέδῳ τὴν
γῆν παίων καὶ βοῶν " τί σοι, θύγατερ, καθαγίσω;
τί σοι ξυνθάψω; " παρατυχὼν δὲ αὐτῷ Σέξτος ὁ
φιλόσοφος " μεγάλα " ἔφη " τῇ θυγατρὶ δώσεις
ἐγκρατῶς αὐτὴν πενθήσας." ἐπένθει δὲ ταῖς
ὑπερβολαῖς ταύταις τὰς θυγατέρας, ἐπειδὴ Ἀττικὸν
τὸν υἱὸν ἐν ὀργῇ εἶχεν. διεβέβλητο δὲ πρὸς αὐτὸν
ὡς ἠλιθιώδη καὶ δυσγράμματον καὶ παχὺν τὴν
μνήμην· τὰ γοῦν πρῶτα γράμματα παραλαβεῖν
μὴ δυνηθέντος ἦλθεν ἐς ἐπίνοιαν τῷ Ἡρώδῃ ξυν-
τρέφειν αὐτῷ τέτταρας παῖδας καὶ εἴκοσιν ἰσήλικας
ὠνομασμένους ἀπὸ τῶν γραμμάτων, ἵνα ἐν τοῖς τῶν
παίδων ὀνόμασι τὰ γράμματα ἐξ ἀνάγκης αὐτῷ
μελετῷτο. ἑώρα δὲ αὐτὸν καὶ μεθυστικὸν καὶ
ἀνοήτως ἐρῶντα, ὅθεν ζῶν μὲν ἐπεχρησμῴδει τῇ
ἑαυτοῦ οἰκίᾳ[1] ἐκεῖνο τὸ ἔπος·

εἷς δ' ἔτι που μωρὸς καταλείπεται εὐρεῖ οἴκῳ,

τελευτῶν δὲ τὰ μὲν μητρῷα αὐτῷ ἀπέδωκεν, ἐς
ἑτέρους δὲ κληρονόμους τὸν ἑαυτοῦ οἶκον μετέστησεν. ἀλλ' Ἀθηναίοις ἀπάνθρωπα ἐδόκει ταῦτα οὐκ
ἐνθυμουμένοις τὸν Ἀχιλλέα καὶ τὸν Πολυδεύκην
καὶ τὸν Μέμνονα, οὓς ἴσα γνησίοις ἐπένθησε τροφί-
μους ὄντας, ἐπειδὴ καλοὶ μάλιστα καὶ ἀγαθοὶ ἦσαν

---

[1] οὐσίᾳ Kayser; οἰκίᾳ Cobet.

[1] The original of this verse, often parodied by the sophists, and several times by Dionysius of Halicarnassus, is *Odyssey* iv. 498:

164

while his grief for his daughter Panathenais was mitigated by the Athenians, who buried her in the city, and decreed that the day on which she died should be taken out of the year. But when his other daughter, whom he called Elpinice, died also, he lay on the floor, beating the earth and crying aloud: "O my daughter, what offerings shall I consecrate to thee? What shall I bury with thee?" Then Sextus the philosopher who chanced to be present said: "No small gift will you give your daughter if you control your grief for her." He mourned his daughters with this excessive grief because he was offended with his son Atticus. He had been misrepresented to him as foolish, bad at his letters, and of a dull memory. At any rate, when he could not master his alphabet, the idea occurred to Herodes to bring up with him twenty-four boys of the same age named after the letters of the alphabet, so that he would be obliged to learn his letters at the same time as the names of the boys. He saw too that he was a drunkard and given to senseless amours, and hence in his lifetime he used to utter a prophecy over his own house, adapting a famous verse as follows:

One fool methinks is still left in the wide house,[1]

and when he died he handed over to him his mother's estate, but transferred his own patrimony to other heirs. The Athenians, however, thought this inhuman, and they did not take into consideration his foster-sons Achilles, Polydeuces, and Memnon, and that he mourned them as though they had been his own children, since they were highly honourable youths,

εἰς δ' ἔτι που ζωὸς κατερύκεται εὐρέι πόντῳ.
Herodes substitutes "house" for "deep."

γενναῖοί τε καὶ φιλομαθεῖς καὶ τῇ παρ' αὐτῷ
τροφῇ πρέποντες. εἰκόνας γοῦν ἀνετίθει σφῶν
559 θηρώντων καὶ τεθηρακότων καὶ θηρασόντων τὰς
μὲν ἐν δρυμοῖς, τὰς δὲ ἐπ' ἀγροῖς, τὰς δὲ πρὸς
πηγαῖς, τὰς δὲ ὑπὸ σκιαῖς πλατάνων, οὐκ ἀφανῶς,
ἀλλὰ ξὺν ἀραῖς τοῦ περικόψοντος ἢ κινήσοντος, οὓς
οὐκ ἂν ἐπὶ τοσοῦτον ἦρεν, εἰ μὴ ἐπαίνων ἀξίους
ἐγίγνωσκεν. Κυντιλίων δέ, ὁπότε ἦρχον τῆς Ἑλλάδος, αἰτιωμένων αὐτὸν ἐπὶ ταῖς τῶν μειρακίων
τούτων εἰκόσιν ὡς περιτταῖς " τί δὲ ὑμῖν " ἔφη
" διενήνοχεν, εἰ ἐγὼ τοῖς ἐμοῖς ἐμπαίζω λιθαρίοις; "

Ἦρξε δὲ αὐτῷ τῆς πρὸς τοὺς Κυντιλίους διαφορᾶς, ὡς μὲν οἱ πολλοί φασι, Πυθικὴ πανήγυρις,
ἐπειδὴ ἑτεροδόξως τῆς μουσικῆς ἠκροῶντο, ὡς δὲ
ἔνιοι, τὰ παισθέντα περὶ αὐτῶν Ἡρώδῃ πρὸς
Μάρκον· ὁρῶν γὰρ αὐτοὺς Τρῶας μέν, μεγάλων δὲ
ἀξιουμένους παρὰ τοῦ βασιλέως " ἐγὼ " ἔφη " καὶ
τὸν Δία μέμφομαι τὸν Ὁμηρικόν, ὅτι τοὺς Τρῶας
φιλεῖ." ἡ δὲ ἀληθεστέρα αἰτία ἥδε· τὼ ἄνδρε
τούτω, ὁπότε ἄμφω τῆς Ἑλλάδος ἠρχέτην, καλέ-
σαντες ἐς τὴν ἐκκλησίαν Ἀθηναῖοι φωνὰς ἀφῆκαν
τυραννευομένων πρὸς τὸν Ἡρώδην ἀποσημαίνον-
τες καὶ δεόμενοι ἐπὶ πᾶσιν ἐς τὰ βασίλεια ὦτα
παραπεμφθῆναι τὰ εἰρημένα. τῶν δὲ Κυντιλίων
παθόντων τι πρὸς τὸν δῆμον καὶ ξὺν ὁρμῇ ἀναπεμ-
ψάντων ἃ ἤκουσαν, ἐπιβουλεύεσθαι παρ' αὐτῶν ὁ
Ἡρώδης ἔφασκεν ὡς ἀναθολούντων ἐπ' αὐτὸν τοὺς
Ἀθηναίους. μετ' ἐκείνην γὰρ τὴν ἐκκλησίαν Δημό-

---

[1] These brothers are mentioned by Cassius Dio lxxi. 33.

noble-minded and fond of study, a credit to their upbringing in his house. Accordingly he put up statues of them hunting, having hunted, and about to hunt, some in his shrubberies, others in the fields, others by springs or in the shade of plane-trees, not hidden away, but inscribed with execrations on any one who should pull down or move them. Nor would he have exalted them thus, had he not known them to be worthy of his praises. And when the Quintilii during their proconsulship of Greece censured him for putting up the statues of these youths on the ground that they were an extravagance, he retorted: "What business is it of yours if I amuse myself with my poor marbles?"

His quarrel with the Quintilii [1] began, as most people assert, over the Pythian festival, when they held different views about the musical competition; but some say that it began with the jests that Herodes made to Marcus at their expense. For when he saw that, though they were Trojans, the Emperor thought them worthy of the highest honours, he said: "I blame Homer's Zeus also, for loving the Trojans." But the following reason is nearer the truth. When these two men were both governing Greece, the Athenians invited them to a meeting of the assembly, and made speeches to the effect that they were oppressed by a tyrant, meaning Herodes; and finally begged that what they had said might be forwarded to the Emperor's ears. And when the Quintilii felt pity for the people and without delay reported what they had heard, Herodes asserted that they were plotting against him, for they were inciting the Athenians to attack him. Certainly, after that meeting of the assembly there sprang into

στρατοὶ ἀνέφυσαν καὶ Πραξαγόραι καὶ Μαμερ-
τῖνοι καὶ ἕτεροι πλείους ἐς τὸ ἀντίξοον τῷ Ἡρώδῃ
560 πολιτεύοντες. γραψάμενος δὲ αὐτοὺς Ἡρώδης ὡς
ἐπισυνιστάντας αὐτῷ τὸν δῆμον ἦγεν ἐπὶ τὴν ἡγε-
μονίαν, οἱ δὲ ὑ ᾿εξῆλθον ἀφανῶς παρὰ τὸν αὐτοκράτορα Μάρκ ν, θαρροῦντες τῇ τε φύσει τοῦ
βασιλέως δημοκρατέρᾳ οὔσῃ καὶ τῷ καιρῷ· ὧν
γὰρ ὑπώπτευσε Λούκιον κοινωνὸν αὐτῷ τῆς ἀρχῆς
γενόμενον, οὐδὲ τὸν Ἡρώδην ἠφίει τοῦ μὴ οὐ
ξυμμετέχειν αὐτῷ. ὁ μὲν δὴ αὐτοκράτωρ ἐκάθητο
ἐς τὰ Παιόνια ἔθνη ὁρμητηρίῳ τῷ Σιρμίῳ χρώμενος,
κατέλυον δὲ οἱ μὲν ἀμφὶ τὸν Δημόστρατον περὶ τὰ
βασίλεια, παρέχοντος αὐτοῖς ἀγορὰν τοῦ Μάρκου
καὶ θαμὰ ἐρωτῶντος, εἴ του δέοιντο. φιλανθρώπως
δὲ πρὸς αὐτοὺς ἔχειν αὐτός τε ἑαυτὸν ἐπεπείκει καὶ
τῇ γυναικὶ ἐπέπειστο καὶ τῷ θυγατρίῳ ψελλιζομένῳ
ἔτι, τοῦτο γὰρ μάλιστα ξὺν πολλοῖς θωπεύμασι
περιπῖπτον τοῖς γόνασι τοῦ πατρὸς ἐδεῖτο σῶσαί οἱ
τοὺς Ἀθηναίους. ὁ δὲ Ἡρώδης ἐν προαστείῳ
ἐσκήνου, ἐν ᾧ πύργοι ἐξῳκοδόμηντο καὶ ἡμιπύργια,
καὶ δὴ ξυναπεδήμουν αὐτῷ καὶ δίδυμοι κόραι πρὸς
ἀκμῇ γάμων θαυμαζόμεναι ἐπὶ τῷ εἴδει, ἃς ἐκνη-
πιώσας ὁ Ἡρώδης οἰνοχόους ἑαυτῷ καὶ ὀψοποιοὺς
ἐπεποίητο θυγάτρια ἐπονομάζων καὶ ὧδε ἀσπαζό-
μενος — Ἀλκιμέδοντος μὲν δὴ αὗται θυγατέρες, ὁ
δὲ Ἀλκιμέδων ἀπελεύθερος τοῦ Ἡρώδου — καθευ-

---

[1] Lucius Verus, the Emperor's son-in-law and colleague;
cf. Cassius Dio lxxi. 1–2.

activity men like Demostratus, Praxagoras and
Mamertinus, and many others whose public policy
was opposed to Herodes. Thereupon Herodes indicted them on the charge of a conspiracy to set the
people against him, and tried to bring them before
the proconsular court. But they escaped secretly
and went to the Emperor Marcus, relying both on
the Emperor's disposition, which was somewhat
democratic, and also on the favourable moment.
For the Emperor did not acquit Herodes of being
an accomplice in the treasonable plots of which he
had suspected Lucius,[1] after the latter had become
his consort in the Empire. Now the Emperor had
his head-quarters among the tribes of Pannonia, with
Sirmium for his base, and Demostratus and his
friends lodged near the Emperor's head-quarters,
where Marcus furnished them with supplies, and
often asked them whether they needed anything.
Not only was he himself convinced that he ought to
treat them with this benevolence, but also he was
induced to do so by his wife and by his little
daughter who could not yet speak plainly; for she
above all used to fall at her father's knees with
many blandishments and implore him to save the
Athenians for her. But Herodes lodged in a suburb
in which towers had been erected, some of full height
and others half-towers; and there had travelled
with him from home two girls, twins just of marriage-
able age, who were greatly admired for their beauty.
Herodes had brought them up from childhood, and
appointed them to be his cupbearers and cooks,
and used to call them his little daughters and loved
them as though they were. They were the daughters
of Alcimedon, and he was a freedman of Herodes.

δούσας δὲ αὐτὰς ἐν ἑνὶ τῶν πύργων, ὃς ἦν
ἐχυρώτατος, σκηπτὸς ἐνεχθεὶς νύκτωρ ἀπέκτεινεν.
ὑπὸ τούτου δὴ τοῦ πάθους ἔκφρων ὁ Ἡρώδης
ἐγένετο καὶ παρῆλθεν ἐς τὸ βασίλειον δικαστήριον
561 οὔτε ἔννους καὶ θανάτου ἐρῶν. παρελθὼν γὰρ
καθίστατο ἐς διαβολὰς τοῦ αὐτοκράτορος οὐδὲ
σχηματίσας τὸν λόγον, ὡς εἰκὸς ἦν ἄνδρα γεγυμνα-
σμένον τῆς τοιᾶσδε ἰδέας μεταχειρίσασθαι τὴν
ἑαυτοῦ χολήν, ἀλλ' ἀπηγκωνισμένῃ τῇ γλώττῃ καὶ
γυμνῇ διετείνετο λέγων " ταῦτά μοι ἡ Λουκίου
ξενία, ὃν σύ μοι ἔπεμψας· ὅθεν δικάζεις, γυναικί με
καὶ τριετεῖ παιδίῳ καταχαριζόμενος." Βασσαίου
δὲ τοῦ πεπιστευμένου τὸ ξίφος θανατᾶν αὐτὸν [1]
φήσαντος ὁ Ἡρώδης " ὦ λῷστε," ἔφη " γέρων
ὀλίγα φοβεῖται." ὁ μὲν οὖν Ἡρώδης ἀπῆλθε τοῦ
δικαστηρίου εἰπὼν ταῦτα καὶ μετέωρον καταλείψας
πολὺ τοῦ ὕδατος, ἡμεῖς δὲ τῶν ἐπιδήλως τῷ Μάρκῳ
φιλοσοφηθέντων καὶ τὰ περὶ τὴν δίκην ταύτην
ἡγώμεθα· οὐ γὰρ ξυνήγαγε τὰς ὀφρῦς, οὐδὲ
ἔτρεψε τὸ ὄμμα, ὃ κἂν διαιτητής τις ἔπαθεν, ἀλλ'
ἐπιστρέψας ἑαυτὸν ἐς τοὺς Ἀθηναίους " ἀπολο-
γεῖσθε," ἔφη, " ὦ Ἀθηναῖοι, εἰ καὶ μὴ ξυγχωρεῖ
Ἡρώδης." καὶ ἀκούων ἀπολογουμένων ἐπὶ πολλοῖς μὲν ἀφανῶς ἤλγησεν, ἀναγιγνωσκομένης δὲ
αὐτῷ καὶ Ἀθηναίων ἐκκλησίας, ἐν ᾗ ἐφαίνοντο
καθαπτόμενοι τοῦ Ἡρώδου, ὡς τοὺς ἄρχοντας τῆς

---

[1] θάνατον αὐτῷ Kayser; θανατᾶν αὐτὸν Cobet.

---

[1] i.e. it was a lost opportunity for a speech of " covert
allusion "; see Glossary.
[2] This is the only place where ἐκκλησία, " assembly," is
used as the equivalent of ψήφισμα, " decree voted."

Now while they were asleep in one of the towers which was very strongly built, a thunderbolt struck them in the night and killed them. Herodes was driven frantic by this misfortune, and when he came before the Emperor's tribunal he was not in his right mind but longed for death. For when he came forward to speak he launched into invectives against the Emperor, and did not even use figures of speech [1] in his oration, though it might have been expected that a man who had been trained in this type of oratory would have had his own anger under control. But with an aggressive and unguarded tongue he persisted in his attack, and cried : " This is what I get for showing hospitality to Lucius, though it was you who sent him to me ! These are the grounds on which you judge men, and you sacrifice me to the whim of a woman and a three-year-old child ! " And when Bassaeus, the pretorian prefect, said that he evidently wished to die, Herodes replied : " My good fellow, an old man fears few things ! " With these words Herodes left the court, leaving much of his allowance of water in the clock still to run. But among the eminently philosophic actions of Marcus we must include his behaviour in this trial. For he never frowned or changed his expression, as might have happened even to an umpire, but he turned to the Athenians and said : " Make your defence, Athenians, even though Herodes does not give you leave." And as he listened to the speeches in defence he was greatly pained, though without showing it, by many things that he heard. But when the decree [2] of the Athenian assembly was recited to him, in which they openly attacked Herodes for trying to corrupt the magis-

Ἑλλάδος ὑποποιουμένου πολλῷ τῷ μέλιτι καί που καὶ βεβηκότες " ὦ πικροῦ μέλιτος " καὶ πάλιν " μακάριοι οἱ ἐν τῷ λοιμῷ ἀποθνήσκοντες " οὕτως ἐσείσθη τὴν καρδίαν ὑφ' ὧν ἤκουσεν, ὡς ἐς δάκρυα φανερὰ ὑπαχθῆναι. τῆς δὲ τῶν Ἀθηναίων ἀπολογίας ἐχούσης κατηγορίαν τοῦ τε Ἡρώδου καὶ τῶν ἀπελευθέρων τὴν ὀργὴν ὁ Μάρκος ἐς τοὺς ἀπελευθέρους ἔτρεψε κολάσει χρησάμενος ὡς οἷόν τε ἐπιεικεῖ, οὕτω γὰρ αὐτὸς χαρακτηρίζει τὴν ἑαυτοῦ κρίσιν, μόνῳ δὲ Ἀλκιμέδοντι τὴν τιμωρίαν ἐπανῆκεν ἀποχρῶσαν εἶναί οἱ φήσας τὴν ἐπὶ τοῖς τέκνοις συμφοράν. ταῦτα μὲν δὴ ὧδε ἐφιλοσοφεῖτο τῷ Μάρκῳ.

562 Ἐπιγράφουσι δὲ ἔνιοι καὶ φυγὴν οὐ φυγόντι καί φασιν αὐτὸν οἰκῆσαι τὸ ἐν τῇ Ἠπείρῳ Ὠρικόν, ὃ καὶ πολίσαι αὐτόν, ὡς εἴη δίαιτα ἐπιτηδεία τῷ σώματι. ὁ δὲ Ἡρώδης ᾤκησε μὲν τὸ χωρίον τοῦτο νοσήσας ἐν αὐτῷ καὶ θύσας ἐκβατήρια τῆς νόσου, φυγεῖν δὲ οὔτε προσετάχθη οὔτε ἔτλη. καὶ μάρτυρα τοῦ λόγου τούτου ποιήσομαι τὸν θεσπέσιον Μάρκον· μετὰ γὰρ τὰ ἐν τῇ Παιονίᾳ διῃτᾶτο μὲν ὁ Ἡρώδης ἐν τῇ Ἀττικῇ περὶ τοὺς φιλτάτους ἑαυτῷ δήμους Μαραθῶνα καὶ Κηφισίαν ἐξηρτημένης αὐτοῦ τῆς πανταχόθεν νεότητος, οἳ κατ' ἔρωτα τῶν ἐκείνου λόγων ἐφοίτων Ἀθήναζε, πεῖραν δὲ ποιούμενος, μὴ χαλεπὸς αὐτῷ εἴη διὰ τὰ ἐν τῷ δικαστηρίῳ πέμπει πρὸς αὐτὸν ἐπιστολὴν οὐκ ἀπολογίαν ἔχουσαν, ἀλλ' ἔγκλημα, θαυμάζειν γὰρ ἔφη, τοῦ χάριν οὐκέτι

---

[1] See p. 551.

trates of Greece with the honeyed strains of his eloquence, and when they exclaimed: "Alas, what bitter honey!" and again, "Happy they who perished in the plague!" his feelings were so profoundly affected by what he heard that he burst into tears without concealment. But since the Athenian defence contained an indictment not of Herodes only but also of his freedmen, Marcus turned his anger against the freedmen, employing a punishment which was "as mild as possible"; for by this phrase he himself describes his judgement. Only in the case of Alcimedon he remitted the penalty, saying that the loss of his children was enough. Thus did Marcus conduct this affair in a manner worthy of a philosopher.

Some place on record the exile of Herodes, though exiled he was not, and they say that he lived at Oricum in Epirus and that he in fact founded the city [1] in order that it might be a residence suited to his constitution. But though Herodes did actually live in this place and fell ill there, and offered sacrifices in return for his recovery from sickness, still he was never condemned to exile nor did he suffer this penalty. And as a witness to the truth of this statement I will employ the divine Marcus. For after the affair in Pannonia, Herodes lived in Attica in the demes that he loved best, Marathon and Cephisia. And youths from all parts of the world hung on his lips, and they flocked to Athens in their desire to hear his eloquence. But he put it to the test whether the Emperor was offended with him on account of what had happened in the court, by sending him a letter which so far from being an apology was a complaint. For he said that he

173

αὐτῷ ἐπιστέλλοι καίτοι τὸν πρὸ τοῦ χρόνον θαμὰ
οὕτω γράφων, ὡς καὶ τρεῖς γραμματοφόρους
ἀφικέσθαι ποτὲ παρ' αὐτὸν ἐν ἡμέρᾳ μιᾷ κατὰ
πόδας ἀλλήλων. καὶ ὁ αὐτοκράτωρ διὰ πλειόνων
μὲν καὶ ὑπὲρ πλειόνων, θαυμάσιον δὲ ἦθος ἐγκαταμίξας τοῖς γράμμασιν ἐπέστειλε πρὸς τὸν Ἡρώδην, ὧν ἐγὼ τὰ ξυντείνοντα ἐς τὸν παρόντα μοι
λόγον ἐξελὼν τῆς ἐπιστολῆς δηλώσω· τὸ μὲν δὴ
προοίμιον τῶν ἐπεσταλμένων "χαῖρέ μοι, φίλε
Ἡρώδη." διαλεχθεὶς δὲ ὑπὲρ τῶν τοῦ πολέμου
χειμαδίων, ἐν οἷς ἦν τότε, καὶ τὴν γυναῖκα ὀλο-
φυράμενος ἄρτι αὐτῷ τεθνεῶσαν¹ εἰπών τέ τι καὶ
περὶ τῆς τοῦ σώματος ἀσθενείας ἐφεξῆς γράφει
"σοὶ δὲ ὑγιαίνειν τε εὔχομαι καὶ περὶ ἐμοῦ ὡς
εὔνου σοι διανοεῖσθαι, μηδὲ ἡγεῖσθαι ἀδικεῖσθαι,
εἰ καταφωράσας τινὰς τῶν σῶν πλημμελοῦντας
κολάσει ἐπ' αὐτοὺς ἐχρησάμην ὡς οἷόν τε ἐπιεικεῖ.
διὰ μὲν δὴ ταῦτα μή μοι ὀργίζου, εἰ δέ τι λελύ-
563 πηκά σε ἢ λυπῶ, ἀπαίτησον παρ' ἐμοῦ δίκας ἐν
τῷ ἱερῷ τῆς ἐν ἄστει Ἀθηνᾶς ἐν μυστηρίοις.
ηὐξάμην γάρ, ὁπότε ὁ πόλεμος μάλιστα ἐφλέγ-
μαινε, καὶ μυηθῆναι, εἴη δὲ καὶ σοῦ μυσταγω-
γοῦντος." τοιάδε ἡ ἀπολογία τοῦ Μάρκου καὶ
οὕτω φιλάνθρωπος καὶ ἐρρωμένη. τίς ἂν οὖν
ποτε ἢ ὃν φυγῇ περιέβαλεν οὕτω προσεῖπεν ἢ τὸν
ἄξιον οὕτω προσειρῆσθαι φεύγειν προσέταξεν;

Ἔστι δέ τις λόγος, ὡς νεώτερα μὲν ὁ τὴν ἑῴαν
ἐπιτροπεύων Κάσσιος ἐπὶ τὸν Μάρκον βουλεύοι,²

---

¹ The Empress Faustina died suddenly at the foot of
Mount Taurus, about A.D. 175.
² For the conspiracy and death of Cassius in Syria see
Cassius Dio lxxi. 22.

wondered why the Emperor no longer wrote to him, though in former times he had written to him so often that three letter-carriers had once arrived at his house in a single day, treading in one another's footsteps. Thereupon the Emperor wrote to Herodes at some length and on several subjects, tempering what he wrote with an admirable urbanity, and from this letter I will extract all that bears on my present narrative, and publish it. The letter began with these words: " I greet you, friend Herodes!" Then after discussing the military winter quarters where he was at the time, and lamenting his wife of whom he had recently been bereaved by death,[1] and after some remarks on his own bad health, he continued the letter as follows: " For yourself I wish you good health, and that you should think of me as well disposed to you. And do not regard yourself as unjustly treated, if after I detected the crimes of some of your household I chastised them with a punishment as mild as possible. Do not, I say, feel resentment against me on this account, but if I have annoyed you in aught, or am still annoying you, demand reparation from me in the temple of Athene in your city at the time of the Mysteries. For I made a vow, when the war began to blaze highest, that I too would be initiated, and I could wish that you yourself should initiate me into those rites." Such was the apology of Marcus, so benignant and so firm. Who would ever have addressed in these terms one whom he had cast into exile, or who would have imposed exile on one whom he held worthy to be so addressed?

Moreover, the story is told that when Cassius [2] the governor of the Eastern provinces was plotting treason

ὁ δὲ Ἡρώδης ἐπιπλήξειεν αὐτῷ δι' ἐπιστολῆς
ὧδε ξυγκειμένης " Ἡρώδης Κασσίῳ· ἐμάνης."
τήνδε τὴν ἐπιστολὴν μὴ μόνον ἐπίπληξιν ἡγώμεθα,
ἀλλὰ καὶ ῥώμην ἀνδρὸς ὑπὲρ τοῦ βασιλέως τιθε-
μένου τὰ τῆς γνώμης ὅπλα.

Ὁ δὲ λόγος, ὃν διῆλθε πρὸς τὸν Ἡρώδην ὁ
Δημόστρατος, ἐν θαυμασίοις δοκεῖ. ἰδέα δὲ αὐτοῦ ἡ μὲν τοῦ ἤθους μία, τὸ γὰρ ἐμβριθὲς ἐκ προ-
οιμίων ἐς τέλος διήκει τοῦ λόγου, αἱ δὲ τῆς ἑρμηνείας ἰδέαι πολλαὶ καὶ ἀνόμοιαι μὲν ἀλλήλαις,
λόγου δὲ ἄξιαι. ἔστω που καὶ τὸ δι' Ἡρώδην
παρὰ τοῖς βασκάνοις εὐδοκιμεῖν τὸν λόγον, ἐπειδὴ
ἀνὴρ τοιοῦτος ἐν αὐτῷ κακῶς ἤκουσεν. ἀλλ'
ὅπως γε καὶ πρὸς τὰς λοιδορίας ἔρρωτο, δηλώσει
καὶ τὰ πρὸς τὸν κύνα Πρωτέα λεχθέντα ποτὲ ὑπ'
αὐτοῦ Ἀθήνησιν· ἦν μὲν γὰρ τῶν οὕτω θαρραλέως φιλοσοφούντων ὁ Πρωτεὺς οὗτος, ὡς καὶ
ἐς πῦρ ἑαυτὸν ἐν Ὀλυμπίᾳ ῥῖψαι, ἐπηκολούθει
δὲ τῷ Ἡρώδῃ κακῶς ἀγορεύων αὐτὸν ἡμιβαρ-
βάρῳ γλώττῃ· ἐπιστραφεὶς οὖν ὁ Ἡρώδης
" ἔστω," ἔφη " κακῶς με ἀγορεύεις, πρὸς τί
καὶ οὕτως;" ἐπικειμένου δὲ τοῦ Πρωτέως ταῖς
λοιδορίαις " γεγηράκαμεν" ἔφη " σὺ μὲν κακῶς
564 με ἀγορεύων, ἐγὼ δὲ ἀκούων" ἐνδεικνύμενος
δήπου τὸ ἀκούειν μέν, καταγελᾶν δὲ ὑπὸ τοῦ
πεπεῖσθαι τὰς ψευδεῖς λοιδορίας μὴ περαιτέρω
ἀκοῆς ἥκειν.

Ἑρμηνεύσω καὶ τὴν γλῶτταν τοῦ ἀνδρὸς ἐς
χαρακτῆρα ἰὼν τοῦ λόγου· ὡς μὲν δὴ Πολέμωνα

---

[1] Lucian in his *Peregrinus* gives a full account of the self-
immolation, of which he was an eyewitness, of Peregrinus
Proteus the Cynic philosopher. This took place in A.D. 165.

against Marcus, Herodes rebuked him in a letter
that ran thus : " Herodes to Cassius. You have gone
mad." We must regard this letter as not merely a
rebuke but also as a strong demonstration by one
who, to defend the Emperor, took up the weapons
of the intelligence.

The speech which Demostratus delivered against
Herodes is, I think, admirable. In regard to its style,
its characterization is even throughout, for the impressive manner is sustained from the opening sentences
to the end of the speech. But the formal modes
of expression are manifold and never alike, but are
worthy of all praise. I grant that the speech has
become famous among the malicious partly on
account of Herodes, because it attacked one so
distinguished. But how stoutly Herodes bore himself in the face of abuse will appear also from what
he once said to the Cynic Proteus [1] at Athens. For
this Proteus was one of those who have the courage
of their philosophy, so much so that he threw himself
into a bonfire at Olympia ; and he used to dog the
steps of Herodes and insult him in a semi-barbarous
dialect. So once Herodes turned round and said :
" You speak ill of me, so be it, but why in such bad
Greek ? " And when Proteus became still more per-
sistent with his accusations, he said : " We two have
grown old, you in speaking ill of me and I in hearing
you." By which he implied that, though he heard
him, he laughed him to scorn, because he was convinced that false accusations reach the ears but
wound no deeper. [2]

I will describe also the eloquence of Herodes and
proceed to the main characteristics of his oratory. I

[2] An echo of Aeschines, *On the False Embassy*, 149.

καὶ Φαβωρῖνον καὶ Σκοπελιανὸν ἐν διδασκάλοις
ἑαυτοῦ ἦγε καὶ ὡς Σεκούνδῳ τῷ Ἀθηναίῳ ἐφοίτησεν, εἰρημένον μοι ἤδη, τοὺς δὲ κριτικοὺς τῶν
λόγων Θεαγένει τε τῷ Κνιδίῳ καὶ Μουνατίῳ τῷ
ἐκ Τραλλέων συνεγένετο καὶ Ταύρῳ τῷ Τυρίῳ
ἐπὶ ταῖς Πλάτωνος δόξαις. ἡ δὲ ἁρμονία τοῦ
λόγου ἱκανῶς κεκολασμένη καὶ ἡ δεινότης ὑφέρ-
πουσα μᾶλλον ἢ ἐγκειμένη κρότος τε σὺν ἀφελείᾳ
καὶ κριτιάζουσα ἠχὼ καὶ ἔννοιαι οἷαι μὴ ἑτέρῳ
ἐνθυμηθῆναι κωμική τε εὐγλωττία οὐκ ἐπέσακτος,
ἀλλ᾽ ἐκ τῶν πραγμάτων, καὶ ἡδὺς ὁ λόγος καὶ
πολυσχήματος καὶ εὐσχήμων καὶ σοφῶς ἐξαλ-
λάττων τὸ πνεῦμά τε οὐ σφοδρόν, ἀλλὰ λεῖον καὶ
καθεστηκὸς καὶ ἡ ἐπίπαν ἰδέα τοῦ λόγου χρυσοῦ
ψῆγμα ποταμῷ ἀργυροδίνῃ ὑπαύγαζον. προσέκειτο μὲν γὰρ πᾶσι τοῖς παλαιοῖς, τῷ δὲ Κριτίᾳ
καὶ προσετετήκει καὶ παρήγαγεν αὐτὸν ἐς ἤθη
Ἑλλήνων τέως ἀμελούμενον καὶ περιορώμενον.
βοώσης δὲ ἐπ᾽ αὐτῷ τῆς Ἑλλάδος καὶ καλούσης
αὐτὸν ἕνα τῶν δέκα οὐχ ἡττήθη τοῦ ἐπαίνου μεγάλου δοκοῦντος, ἀλλ᾽ ἀστειότατα πρὸς τοὺς ἐπαινέ-
565 σαντας " Ἀνδοκίδου μὲν " ἔφη " βελτίων εἰμί."
εὐμαθέστατος δὲ ἀνθρώπων γενόμενος οὐδὲ τοῦ
μοχθεῖν ἠμέλησεν, ἀλλὰ καὶ παρὰ πότον ἐσπούδαζε καὶ νύκτωρ ἐν τοῖς διαλείμμασι τῶν ὕπνων,
ὅθεν ἐκάλουν αὐτὸν σιτευτὸν ῥήτορα οἱ ὀλίγωροι

---

[1] From Aristophanes, *Frogs* 1003 :

ἡνίκ᾽ ἂν τὸ πνεῦμα λεῖον καὶ καθεστηκὸς λάβῃς.

[2] The same figure is used by Lucian, *Dialogues of the Sea-Gods* 3.

have already said that he counted Polemo, Favorinus, and Scopelian among his teachers, that he attended the lectures of Secundus the Athenian, but for the critical branch of oratory he studied with Theagenes of Cnidos and Munatius of Tralles; and for the doctrines of Plato, with Taurus of Tyre. The structure of his work was suitably restrained, and its strength lay in subtlety rather than in vigour of attack. He was impressive in the plain style, sonorous after the manner of Critias; his ideas were such as would not occur to the mind of another; he had an easy and urbane wit which was not dragged in, but inspired by the subjects themselves; his diction was pleasing and abounded in figures and had grace and beauty; he was skilful in varying his constructions; his tone was not vehement but smooth and steady,[1] and, speaking generally, his type of eloquence is like gold dust shining beneath the waters of a silvery eddying river.[2] For while he devoted himself to the study of all the older writers, from Critias he was inseparable, and he made the Greeks better acquainted with him, since he had hitherto been neglected and overlooked. And when all Greece was loud in applause of Herodes and called him one of the Ten,[3] he was not abashed by such a compliment, though it seems magnificent enough, but replied to his admirers with great urbanity: "Well at any rate I am better than Andocides." Though no man ever learned more easily than he, he did not neglect hard work, but used to study even while he drank his wine, and at night in his wakeful intervals. Hence the lazy and light-minded used to call him the "Stuffed Orator."

[3] The Ten Attic Orators of the canon.

τε καὶ λεπτοί. ἄλλος μὲν οὖν ἄλλο ἀγαθὸς καὶ
ἄλλος ἐν ἄλλῳ βελτίων ἑτέρου, ὁ μὲν γὰρ σχεδιάσαι θαυμάσιος, ὁ δὲ ἐκπονῆσαι λόγον, ὁ δὲ τὰ
ξύμπαντα ἄριστα τῶν σοφιστῶν διέθετο καὶ τὸ
παθητικὸν οὐκ ἐκ τῆς τραγῳδίας μόνον, ἀλλὰ
κἀκ τῶν ἀνθρωπίνων συνελέξατο.

Ἐπιστολαὶ δὲ πλεῖσται Ἡρώδου καὶ διαλέξεις
καὶ ἐφημερίδες ἐγχειρίδιά τε καὶ καίρια τὴν
ἀρχαίαν πολυμάθειαν ἐν βραχεῖ ἀπηνθισμένα. οἱ
δὲ προφέροντες αὐτῷ νέῳ ἔτι τὸ λόγου τινὸς ἐν
Παιονίᾳ ἐκπεσεῖν ἐπὶ τοῦ αὐτοκράτορος ἡγνοη-
κέναι μοι δοκοῦσιν, ὅτι καὶ Δημοσθένης ἐπὶ Φιλίππου λέγων ταὐτὸν ἔπαθεν· κἀκεῖνος μὲν ἥκων
Ἀθήναζε τιμὰς προσῄει καὶ στεφάνους ἀπολω-
λυίας Ἀθηναίοις Ἀμφιπόλεως, Ἡρώδης δέ, ἐπεὶ
τοῦτο ἔπαθεν, ἐπὶ τὸν Ἴστρον ἦλθεν ὡς ῥίψων
ἑαυτόν, τοσοῦτον γὰρ αὐτῷ περιῆν τοῦ ἐν λόγοις
βούλεσθαι ὀνομαστῷ εἶναι, ὡς θανάτου τιμᾶσθαι
τὸ σφαλῆναι.

Ἐτελεύτα μὲν οὖν ἀμφὶ τὰ ἓξ καὶ ἑβδομήκοντα
ξυντακὴς γενόμενος. ἀποθανόντος δὲ αὐτοῦ ἐν τῷ
Μαραθῶνι καὶ ἐπισκήψαντος τοῖς ἀπελευθέροις
ἐκεῖ θάπτειν, Ἀθηναῖοι ταῖς τῶν ἐφήβων χερσὶν
ἁρπάσαντες ἐς ἄστυ ἤνεγκαν προαπαντῶντες τῷ
λέχει πᾶσα ἡλικία δακρύοις ἅμα καὶ ἀνευφημοῦν-
566 τες, ὅσα παῖδες χρηστοῦ πατρὸς χηρεύσαντες,
καὶ ἔθαψαν ἐν τῷ Παναθηναϊκῷ ἐπιγράψαντες
αὐτῷ βραχὺ καὶ πολὺ ἐπίγραμμα τόδε·

Different men excel in different ways and this or that man is superior to another in this or that, since one is admirable as an extempore speaker, another at elaborating a speech, but our friend surpassed every other sophist in his grasp of all these methods; and when he wished to move his hearers he drew not only on tragedy but also on the life of every day.

There are extant by Herodes very many letters, discourses and diaries, handbooks and collections of suitable passages in which the flowers of antique erudition have been collected in a small volume. And those who cast in his teeth the fact that while he was yet a youth he broke down in a speech before the Emperor in Pannonia, are, I think, not aware that the same thing happened to Demosthenes also, when he spoke before Philip. And Demosthenes returned to Athens and demanded honours and crowns, though the Athenians never recovered Amphipolis[1]; but Herodes after that humiliation rushed to the river Danube as though he would throw himself in; for so overwhelming was his desire to become famous as an orator, that he assessed the penalty of failure at death.

He died at the age of about seventy-six, of a wasting sickness. And though he expired at Marathon and had left directions to his freedmen to bury him there, the Athenians carried him off by the hands of the youths and bore him into the city, and every age went out to meet the bier with tears and pious ejaculations, as would sons who were bereft of a good father. They buried him in the Panathenaic stadium, and inscribed over him this brief and noble

[1] Philip had taken Amphipolis in 357, eleven years before this embassy, and the failure of Demosthenes had nothing to do with its retention by him.

Ἀττικοῦ Ἡρώδης Μαραθώνιος, οὗ τάδε πάντα
κεῖται τῷδε τάφῳ, πάντοθεν εὐδόκιμος.

τοσαῦτα περὶ Ἡρώδου τοῦ Ἀθηναίου, τὰ μὲν εἰρημένα, τὰ δὲ ἠγνοημένα ἑτέροις.

β΄. Ἐπὶ τὸν σοφιστὴν Θεόδοτον καλεῖ με ὁ
λόγος. Θεόδοτος μὲν προὔστη καὶ τοῦ Ἀθηναίων
δήμου κατὰ χρόνους, οὓς προσέκρουον Ἡρώδῃ
Ἀθηναῖοι, καὶ ἐς ἀπέχθειαν φανερὰν οὐδεμίαν τῷ
ἀνδρὶ ἀφίκετο, ἀλλ᾽ ἀφανῶς αὐτὸν ὑπεκάθητο
δεινὸς ὢν χρῆσθαι τοῖς πράγμασιν, καὶ γὰρ δὴ
καὶ τῶν ἀγοραίων εἷς οὗτος· τοῖς γοῦν ἀμφὶ τὸν
Δημόστρατον οὕτω ξυνεκέκρατο, ὡς καὶ ξυνά-
ρασθαί σφισι τῶν λόγων, οὓς ἐξεπόνουν πρὸς τὸν
Ἡρώδην. προὔστη δὲ καὶ τῆς Ἀθηναίων νεότητος πρῶτος ἐπὶ ταῖς ἐκ βασιλέως μυρίαις. καὶ
οὐ τοῦτό πω λόγου ἄξιον, οὐδὲ γὰρ πάντες οἱ
ἐπιβατεύοντες τοῦ θρόνου τούτου λόγου ἄξιοι,
ἀλλ᾽ ὅτι τοὺς μὲν Πλατωνείους καὶ τοὺς ἀπὸ τῆς
Στοᾶς καὶ τοὺς ἀπὸ τοῦ Περιπάτου καὶ ἀπὸ τοῦ
Ἐπικούρου προσέταξεν ὁ Μάρκος τῷ Ἡρώδῃ
κρῖναι, τὸν δὲ ἄνδρα τοῦτον ἀπὸ τῆς περὶ αὐτὸν
567 δόξης αὐτὸς ἐπέκρινε τοῖς νέοις ἀγωνιστὴν τῶν
πολιτικῶν προσειπὼν λόγων καὶ ῥητορικῆς ὄφελος.
ὁ ἀνὴρ οὗτος Λολλιανοῦ μὲν ἀκροατής, Ἡρώδου
δὲ οὐκ ἀνήκοος. ἐβίω μὲν οὖν ὑπὲρ τὰ πεντήκοντα δυοῖν ἐτοῖν κατασχὼν τὸν θρόνον, τὴν δὲ
ἰδέαν τῶν λόγων ἀποχρῶν καὶ τοῖς δικανικοῖς
καὶ τοῖς ὑπερσοφιστεύουσιν.

γ΄. Ὀνομαστὸς ἐν σοφισταῖς καὶ Ἀριστοκλῆς

---

[1] Nothing more of any importance is known about this
sophist.
[2] He was " king archon " at Athens.

epitaph: "Here lies all that remains of Herodes, son of Atticus, of Marathon, but his glory is world-wide." That is all I have to say concerning Herodes the Athenian; part of it has been told already by others, but part was hitherto unknown.

2. My narrative calls me to consider the sophist THEODOTUS.[1] Theodotus was a chief magistrate[2] of the Athenian people at the time when the Athenians had their quarrel with Herodes, and though he never reached the stage of open hostility towards him, he plotted against him in secret, since he had a talent for profiting by any turn of affairs; and indeed he was one of the baser sort. At any rate he became so thoroughly mixed up with Demostratus and his friends that he collaborated with them in the speeches that they were carefully preparing against Herodes. Also he was appointed to the chair of rhetoric to educate the youth of Athens, and was the first to receive a salary of ten thousand drachmae from the Emperor. Yet this fact alone would not be worth mentioning; for not all who ascend this chair are worthy of mention, but I do so because Marcus assigned to Herodes the task of choosing the Platonic philosophers and the Stoics, Peripatetics, and Epicureans, but this man he himself chose from the opinion that he had formed of him to direct the education of the youth and called him a past master of political oratory and an ornament to rhetoric. This man was a pupil of Lollianus, but he had also attended the lectures of Herodes. He lived to be over fifty, held the chair for two years, and both in the forensic and purely sophistic branches of oratory the style of his speeches was sufficiently good.

3. ARISTOCLES of Pergamon also won renown among

183

ὁ ἐκ τοῦ Περγάμου, ὑπὲρ οὗ δηλώσω, ὁπόσα τῶν
πρεσβυτέρων ἤκουον· ἐτέλει μὲν γὰρ ἐς ὑπάτους
ὁ ἀνὴρ οὗτος, τὸν δὲ ἐκ παίδων ἐς ἥβην χρόνον
τοὺς ἀπὸ τοῦ Περιπάτου φιλοσοφήσας λόγους ἐς
τοὺς σοφιστὰς μετερρύη θαμίζων ἐν τῇ Ῥώμῃ
τῷ Ἡρώδῃ διατιθεμένῳ σχεδίους λόγους. ὃν δὲ
ἐφιλοσόφει χρόνον αὐχμηρὸς δοκῶν καὶ τραχὺς τὸ
εἶδος καὶ δυσπινὴς τὴν ἐσθῆτα, ἥβρυνε καὶ τὸν
αὐχμὸν ἀπετρίψατο, ἡδονάς τε, ὁπόσαι λυρῶν τε
καὶ αὐλῶν καὶ εὐφωνίας εἰσί, πάσας ἐσηγάγετο
ἐπὶ τὴν δίαιταν, ὥσπερ ἐπὶ θύρας αὐτῷ ἡκούσας,
τὸν γὰρ πρὸ τοῦ χρόνον οὕτω κεκολασμένος ἀτάκ-
τως ἐς τὰ θέατρα ἐφοίτα καὶ ἐπὶ τὴν τούτων ἠχώ.
εὐδοκιμοῦντι δὲ αὐτῷ κατὰ τὸ Πέργαμον κἀξηρ-
τημένῳ πᾶν τὸ ἐκείνῃ Ἑλληνικὸν ἐξελαύνων ὁ
Ἡρώδης ἐς Πέργαμον ἔπεμψε τοὺς ἑαυτοῦ ὁμιλη-
568 τὰς πάντας καὶ τὸν Ἀριστοκλέα ᾖρεν, ὥσπερ τις
Ἀθηνᾶς ψῆφος. ἡ δὲ ἰδέα τοῦ λόγου διαυγὴς μὲν
καὶ ἀττικίζουσα, διαλέγεσθαι δὲ ἐπιτηδεία μᾶλλον ἢ ἀγωνίζεσθαι, χολή τε γὰρ ἄπεστι τοῦ λόγου
καὶ ὁρμαὶ πρὸς βραχύ, αὐτή τε ἡ ἀττίκισις, εἰ
παρὰ τὴν τοῦ Ἡρώδου γλῶτταν βασανίζοιτο, λεπ-
τολογεῖσθαι δόξει μᾶλλον ἢ κρότου τε καὶ ἠχοῦς
ξυγκεῖσθαι. ἐτελεύτα δὲ ὁ Ἀριστοκλῆς μεσαι-
πόλιος, ἄρτι προσβαίνων τῷ γηράσκειν.

δ΄. Ἀντίοχον δὲ τὸν σοφιστὴν αἱ Κιλίκων
Αἰγαὶ ἤνεγκαν οὕτω τι εὐπατρίδην, ὡς νῦν ἔτι
τὸ ἀπ᾽ αὐτοῦ γένος ὑπάτους εἶναι. αἰτίαν δὲ ἔχων

---

[1] An echo of Plato, *Republic* 489 B ; *Phaedrus* 233 E.
[2] The vote of Athene given in the trial of Orestes in
Aeschylus, *Eumenides*, became a proverb.
[3] The Greek epithet is from *Iliad* xiii. 361.

<s/># LIVES OF THE SOPHISTS

the sophists, and I will relate all that I have heard
about him from men older than myself. This man
belonged to a family of consular rank, and though
from boyhood to early manhood he had devoted
himself to the teachings of the Peripatetic school, he
went over entirely to the sophists, and at Rome
regularly attended the lectures of Herodes on extempore oratory. Now, so long as he was a student of
philosophy he was slovenly in appearance, unkempt
and squalid in his dress, but now he began to be
fastidious, discarded his slovenly ways, and admitted
into his house all the pleasures that are afforded by
the lyre, the flute, and the singing voice, as though
they had come begging to his doors.[1] For though
hitherto he had lived with such austerity he now
began to be immoderate in his attendance at theatres
and their loud racket. When he was beginning to
be famous at Pergamon, and all the Hellenes in that
region hung on his oratory, Herodes travelled to Pergamon and sent all his own pupils to hear him, thereby
exalting the reputation of Aristocles as though
Athene[2] herself had cast her vote. His style of
eloquence was lucid and Attic, but it was more
suited to formal discourse than to forensic argument,
for his language is without acrimony or impulsive
outbreaks on the spur of the moment. And even
his Atticism, tested by comparison with the language
of Herodes, will seem over-subtle and deficient in the
qualities of magnificence and sonorousness. Aristocles
died when his hair was streaked with grey,[3] on the
very threshold of old age.

4. ANTIOCHUS the sophist was born at Aegae in
Cilicia of so distinguished a family that even now
his descendants are made consuls. When he was

185

PHILOSTRATUS

δειλίας, ἐπεὶ μὴ παρήει ἐς τὸν δῆμον, μηδὲ ἐς τὸ
κοινὸν ἐπολίτευεν, " οὐχ ὑμᾶς," εἶπεν " ἀλλ'
ἐμαυτὸν δέδοικα," εἰδώς που τὴν ἑαυτοῦ χολὴν
ἄκρατόν τε καὶ οὐ καθεκτὴν οὖσαν. ἀλλ' ὅμως
ὠφέλει τοὺς ἀστοὺς ἀπὸ τῆς οὐσίας, ὅ τι εἴη
δυνατός, σῖτόν τε ἐπιδιδούς, ὁπότε τούτου δεομένους αἴσθοιτο, καὶ χρήματα ἐς τὰ πεπονηκότα
τῶν ἔργων. τὰς δὲ πλείους τῶν νυκτῶν ἐς τὸ
τοῦ Ἀσκληπιοῦ ἱερὸν ἀπεκάθευδεν ὑπέρ τε ὀνει-
ράτων ὑπέρ τε ξυνουσίας, ὁπόση ἐγρηγορότων τε
καὶ διαλεγομένων ἀλλήλοις, διελέγετο γὰρ αὐτῷ
ἐγρηγορότι ὁ θεὸς καλὸν ἀγώνισμα ποιούμενος τῆς
ἑαυτοῦ τέχνης τὸ τὰς νόσους ἐρύκειν τοῦ Ἀντιόχου.

Ἀκροατὴς ὁ Ἀντίοχος ἐν παισὶ μὲν Δαρδάνου
τοῦ Ἀσσυρίου, προϊὼν δὲ ἐς τὰ μειράκια Διονυσίου ἐγένετο τοῦ Μιλησίου κατέχοντος ἤδη τὴν
Ἐφεσίων. διελέγετο μὲν οὖν οὐκ ἐπιτηδείως —
φρονιμώτατος δ' ἀνθρώπων γενόμενος διέβαλλεν
569 αὐτὸ ὡς μειρακιῶδες, ἵνα ὑπερεωρακὼς αὐτοῦ
μᾶλλον ἢ ἀπολειπόμενος φαίνοιτο — τὰ δὲ ἀμφὶ
μελέτην ἐλλογιμώτατος· ἀσφαλὴς μὲν γὰρ ἐν ταῖς
κατὰ σχῆμα προηγμέναις τῶν ὑποθέσεων, σφοδρὸς δὲ ἐν ταῖς κατηγορίαις καὶ ἐπιφοραῖς, εὐ-
πρεπὴς δὲ τὰς ἀπολογίας καὶ τῷ ἠθικῷ ἰσχύων,
καὶ καθάπαξ τὴν ἰδέαν τοῦ λόγου δικανικῆς μὲν
σοφιστικώτερος, σοφιστικῆς δὲ δικανικώτερος. καὶ
τὰ πάθη ἄριστα σοφιστῶν μετεχειρίσατο, οὐ γὰρ

accused of cowardice in not appearing to speak before the assembly and taking no part in public business, he said: " It is not you but myself that I fear." No doubt that was because he knew that he had a bitter and violent temper, and that he could not control it. But nevertheless he used to aid the citizens from his private means as far as he was able, and furnished them not only with corn whenever he saw they were in need, but also with money to restore their dilapidated buildings.[1] He used to spend very many nights in the temple of Asclepius,[2] both on account of the dreams that he had there, and also on account of all the intercourse there is between those who are awake and converse with one another, for in his case the god used to converse with him while awake, and held it to be a triumph of his healing art to ward off disease from Antiochus.

As a boy, Antiochus was a pupil of Dardanus the Assyrian, and as he grew to early manhood he studied with Dionysius of Miletus, who was already living in Ephesus. He had no talent for formal discourse, and since he was the shrewdest of men he used to run down this branch of the art as childish, so that he might appear to despise it rather than to be unequal to it. But in declamation he won great fame, for he had a sure touch in simulated arguments, was energetic in accusation and invective, brilliant in defence, strong in characterization, and, in a word, his style of eloquence was somewhat too sophistic for the forensic branch and more forensic than sophistic usually is.[3] He handled the emotions more skilfully than any other sophist, for he did not

[3] The same is said of Nicetes, p. 511, of Damianus, p. 606 ; cf. Cicero, Brutus 31.

μονῳδίας ἀπεμήκυνεν, οὐδὲ θρήνους ὑποκειμέ-
νους, ἀλλ' ἐβραχυλόγει αὐτὰ ξὺν διανοίαις λόγου
κρείττοσιν, ὡς ἔκ τε τῶν ἄλλων ὑποθέσεων δηλοῦται καὶ μάλιστα ἐκ τῶνδε· κόρη βιασθεῖσα θάνατον ᾔρηται τοῦ βιασαμένου· μετὰ ταῦτα γέγονε
παιδίον ἐκ τῆς βίας καὶ διαμιλλῶνται οἱ πάπποι,
παρ' ὁποτέρῳ τρέφοιτο τὸ παιδίον. ἀγωνιζόμενος οὖν ὑπὲρ τοῦ πρὸς πατρὸς πάππου " ἀπόδος " ἔφη " τὸ παιδίον, ἀπόδος ἤδη, πρὶν γεύση-
ται μητρῴου γάλακτος." ἡ δὲ ἑτέρα ὑπόθεσις
τοιαύτη· τύραννον καταθέμενον τὴν ἀρχὴν ἐπὶ
τῷ ἐκλελύσθαι ἀπέκτεινέ τις εὐνοῦχος ὑπ' αὐτοῦ
γεγονὼς καὶ ἀπολογεῖται ὑπὲρ τοῦ φόνου. ἐνταῦθα τὸ μάλιστα ἐρρωμένον τῆς κατηγορίας τὸν
περὶ τῶν σπονδῶν λόγον ἀπεώσατο περίνοιαν
ἐγκαταμίξας τῷ πάθει· " τίσι γὰρ " ἔφη " ταῦτα
ὡμολόγησε; παισὶ γυναίοις μειρακίοις πρεσβύ-
ταις ἀνδράσιν· ἐγὼ δὲ ὄνομα ἐν ταῖς συνθήκαις
οὐκ ἔχω." ἄριστα δὲ καὶ ὑπὲρ τῶν Κρητῶν
ἀπολελόγηται τῶν κρινομένων ἐπὶ τῷ τοῦ Διὸς
σήματι φυσιολογίᾳ τε καὶ θεολογίᾳ πάσῃ ἐναγω-
νισάμενος λαμπρῶς. τὰς μὲν οὖν μελέτας αὐτο-
570 σχεδίους ἐποιεῖτο, ἔμελε δὲ αὐτῷ καὶ φροντισμάτων,
ὡς ἕτερά τε δηλοῖ τῶν ἐκείνου καὶ μάλιστα ἡ
ἱστορία, ἐπίδειξιν γὰρ ἐν αὐτῇ πεποίηται λέξεώς
τε καὶ θεωρίας,[1] ἐσποιῶν ἑαυτὸν καὶ τῷ φιλο-

---

[1] ῥητορείας Kayser, but suggests θεωρίας or ἱστορίας.

---

[1] i.e. she had the alternative of marrying him; for a
dilemma arising out of a similar case cf. Hermogenes,
Περὶ στάσεων iii. 15.
[2] The theme presented the arguments for the Cretan
claim that the tomb of Zeus was in Crete.

spin out long monodies or abject lamentations, but expressed them in a few words and adorned them with ideas better than I can describe, as is evident in other cases that he pleaded, but especially in the following. A girl has been ravished, and has chosen that her ravisher shall be put to death [1]; later a child is born of this rape, and the grandfathers dispute as to which one of them shall bring up the child. Antiochus was pleading on behalf of its paternal grandfather, and exclaimed : "Give up the child! Give it up this instant before it can taste its mother's milk!" The other theme is as follows. A tyrant abdicates on condition of immunity for himself. He is slain by one whom he has caused to be made a eunuch, and the latter is on his defence for the murder. In this case Antiochus refuted the strongest point made by the prosecution when they quoted the compact between the people and the tyrant; and threw in an ingenious argument while he set forth the eunuch's personal grievance : "With whom, pray," cried he, "did he make this agreement? With children, weak women, boys, old men, and men. But there is no description of me in that contract." Most skilful, too, was his defence of the Cretans, standing their trial in the matter of the tomb of Zeus [2]; when he made brilliant use of arguments drawn from natural philosophy and all that is taught concerning the gods. He delivered extempore declamations, but he also took pains with written compositions, as others of his works make evident, but above all, his *History*. For in this he has displayed to the full both his powers of language and of thought, and, moreover, he devotes himself to

καλεῖν. περὶ δὲ τῆς τελευτῆς τοῦ ἀνδρός, οἱ
μὲν ἑβδομηκοντούτην τεθνάναι αὐτόν, οἱ δὲ οὔπω,
καὶ οἱ μὲν οἴκοι, οἱ δὲ ἑτέρωθι.

εʹ. Ἀλεξάνδρῳ δέ, ὃν Πηλοπλάτωνα οἱ πολλοὶ
ἐπωνόμαζον, πατρὶς μὲν ἦν Σελεύκεια πόλις οὐκ
ἀφανὴς ἐν Κιλικίᾳ, πατὴρ δὲ ὁμώνυμος καὶ τοὺς
ἀγοραίους λόγους ἱκανώτατος, μήτηρ δὲ περιττὴ
τὸ εἶδος, ὡς αἱ γραφαὶ ἑρμηνεύουσι, καὶ προσ-
φερὴς τῇ τοῦ Εὐμήλου Ἑλένῃ· Εὐμήλῳ γάρ τις
Ἑλένη γέγραπται οἷα ἀνάθεμα εἶναι τῆς Ῥωμαίων ἀγορᾶς. ἐρασθῆναι τῆς γυναικὸς ταύτης
καὶ ἑτέρους μέν, ἐπιδήλως δὲ Ἀπολλώνιόν φασι
τὸν Τυανέα, καὶ τοὺς μὲν ἄλλους ἀπαξιῶσαι, τῷ
δὲ Ἀπολλωνίῳ ξυγγενέσθαι δι᾽ ἔρωτα εὐπαιδίας,
ἐπειδὴ θειότερος ἀνθρώπων. τοῦτο μὲν δὴ ὁπό-
σοις τρόποις ἀπίθανον, εἴρηται σαφῶς ἐν τοῖς ἐς
Ἀπολλώνιον. θεοειδὴς δὲ ὁ Ἀλέξανδρος καὶ
περίβλεπτος ξὺν ὥρᾳ, γενειάς τε γὰρ ἦν αὐτῷ
βοστρυχώδης καὶ καθειμένη τὸ μέτριον ὄμμα τε
ἁβρὸν καὶ μέγα καὶ ῥὶς ξύμμετρος καὶ ὀδόντες
λευκότατοι δάκτυλοί τε εὐμήκεις καὶ τῇ τοῦ
λόγου ἡνία ἐπιπρέποντες. ἦν δὲ αὐτῷ καὶ πλοῦτος δαπανώμενος ἐς ἡδονὰς οὐ μεμπτάς.

Ἐς δὲ ἄνδρας ἥκων ἐπρέσβευε μὲν ὑπὲρ τῆς
Σελευκείας παρὰ τὸν Ἀντωνῖνον, διαβολαὶ δὲ ἐπ᾽
αὐτὸν ἐφοίτησαν, ὡς νεότητα ἐπιποιοῦντα τῷ εἴδει.
ἧττον δὲ αὐτῷ προσέχειν δοκοῦντος τοῦ βασιλέως
571 ἐπάρας τὴν φωνὴν ὁ Ἀλέξανδρος "πρόσεχέ μοι,"

---

¹ *Life of Apollonius* i. 13, vi. 42.

the love of the beautiful. Concerning the end of Antiochus, some say that he died at the age of seventy, others that he was not so old; again, some say that he died at home, others abroad.

5. ALEXANDER, who was generally nicknamed "Clay-Plato," was born at Seleucia, a famous city in Cilicia. His father had the same name as himself and was very talented in forensic oratory, while his mother, as her portraits show, was extraordinarily beautiful, and in fact resembled the Helen of Eumelus. (Now Eumelus painted a picture of Helen that was thought worthy to be dedicated in the Roman Forum.) They say that among others who fell in love with her was Apollonius of Tyana, and that he made no secret of it; that she rejected the others, but gave herself to Apollonius because of her desire for noble offspring, since he more than ordinary men had in him something divine. In my work on Apollonius [1] I have stated clearly on how many grounds this story is incredible. But it is true that Alexander had a godlike appearance, and was conspicuous for his beauty and charm. For his beard was curly and of moderate length, his eyes large and melting, his nose well shaped, his teeth very white, his fingers long and slender, and well fitted to hold the reins of eloquence. He had, moreover, a large fortune, which he used to spend on pleasures that were above reproach.

After he had reached manhood he went on an embassy to Antoninus on behalf of Seleucia, and malicious gossip became current about him, that to make himself look younger he used artificial means. Now the Emperor seemed to be paying too little attention to him, whereupon Alexander raised his voice and said: "Pay attention to me, Caesar."

ἔφη " Καῖσαρ." καὶ ὁ αὐτοκράτωρ παροξυνθεὶς
πρὸς αὐτὸν ὡς θρασυτέρᾳ τῇ ἐπιστροφῇ χρησά-
μενον " προσέχω " ἔφη " καὶ ξυνίημί σου· σύ
γὰρ " ἔφη " ὁ τὴν κόμην ἀσκῶν καὶ τοὺς ὀδόντας
λαμπρύνων καὶ τοὺς ὄνυχας ξέων καὶ τοῦ μύρου
ἀεὶ πνέων."

Τὸν μὲν δὴ πλεῖστον τοῦ βίου τῇ τε Ἀντιοχείᾳ
ἐνεσπούδαζε καὶ τῇ Ῥώμῃ καὶ τοῖς Ταρσοῖς καὶ νὴ
Δία Αἰγύπτῳ πάσῃ, ἀφίκετο γὰρ καὶ ἐς τὰ τῶν
Γυμνῶν ἤθη. αἱ δὲ Ἀθήνησι διατριβαὶ τοῦ ἀνδρὸς
ὀλίγαι μέν, οὐκ ἄξιαι δὲ ἀγνοεῖσθαι. ἐβάδιζε μὲν
γὰρ ἐς τὰ Παιονικὰ ἔθνη μετακληθεὶς ὑπὸ Μάρκου
βασιλέως ἐκεῖ στρατεύοντος καὶ δεδωκότος αὐτῷ τὸ
ἐπιστέλλειν Ἕλλησιν, ἀφικόμενος δὲ ἐς τὰς Ἀθήνας, ὁδοῦ δὲ μῆκος τοῦτο οὐ μέτριον τῷ ἐκ τῆς
ἑῴας ἐλαύνοντι, " ἐνταῦθα " ἔφη " γόνυ κάμψω-
μεν." καὶ εἰπὼν τοῦτο ἐπήγγειλε τοῖς Ἀθηναίοις
αὐτοσχεδίους λόγους ἐρῶσιν αὐτοῦ τῆς ἀκροάσεως.
ἀκούων δὲ τὸν Ἡρώδην ἐν Μαραθῶνι διαιτώμενον
καὶ τὴν νεότητα ἐπακολουθοῦσαν αὐτῷ πᾶσαν
γράφει πρὸς αὐτὸν ἐπιστολὴν αἰτῶν τοὺς Ἕλληνας,
καὶ ὁ Ἡρώδης " ἀφίξομαι " ἔφη " μετὰ τῶν Ἑλλήνων καὶ αὐτός." ξυνελέγοντο μὲν δὴ ἐς τὸ ἐν τῷ
Κεραμεικῷ θέατρον, ὃ δὴ ἐπωνόμασται Ἀγριπ-
πεῖον, προϊούσης δὲ ἤδη τῆς ἡμέρας καὶ τοῦ
Ἡρώδου βραδύνοντος ἤσχαλλον οἱ Ἀθηναῖοι ὡς
ἐκλυομένης τῆς ἀκροάσεως καὶ τέχνην αὐτὸ ᾤοντο,

---

[1] For the Gymnosophists see *Life of Apollonius* vi. 6.
This sect of naked ascetics and miracle-workers had
migrated from India to Egypt and Ethiopia.

[2] For this phrase *cf.* Aeschylus, *Prometheus Vinctus* 32 ;
in tragedy, as here, it means " sit," or " rest," but not
" kneel."

The Emperor, who was much irritated with him for using so unceremonious a form of address, retorted: "I am paying attention, and I know you well. You are the fellow who is always arranging his hair, cleaning his teeth, and polishing his nails, and always smells of perfume."

For the greater part of his life he carried on his profession at Antioch, Rome, Tarsus, and, by Zeus, in the whole of Egypt, for he travelled even to the place where is the sect of the Naked Philosophers.[1] His visits to Athens were few, but it would not be proper to ignore them. He journeyed to the tribes of Pannonia at the summons of the Emperor Marcus, who was conducting the war there and bestowed on him the title of Imperial Secretary for the Greeks. When he reached Athens—and it is a journey of no ordinary length for one travelling from the East— "Here," said he, "let us bend the knee in repose."[2] After saying this he announced to the Athenians that he would deliver extempore speeches, since they were very eager to hear him. But when he was told that Herodes was living at Marathon, and that all the Athenian youth had followed him there, he wrote him a letter asking him for his Hellenes; to which Herodes replied: "I will come myself too with my Hellenes." They were accordingly assembled in the Cerameicus, in the theatre which has been called the Theatre of Agrippa,[3] and as the day was already far advanced and Herodes still tarried, the Athenians complained that the lecture was being given up, and they thought that it was a trick;

[3] For this theatre see below, p. 580. On the identity of this building with the Odeum in the agora see *Hesperia*, 19, 1950.

572 ὅθεν ἀνάγκη τῷ Ἀλεξάνδρῳ ἐγένετο παρελθεῖν ἐπὶ
τὴν διάλεξιν καὶ πρὶν ἥκειν τὸν Ἡρώδην. ἡ μὲν
δὴ διάλεξις ἔπαινοι ἦσαν τοῦ ἄστεος καὶ ἀπολογία
πρὸς τοὺς Ἀθηναίους ὑπὲρ τοῦ μήπω πρότερον παρ᾽
αὐτοὺς ἀφῖχθαι, εἶχε δὲ καὶ τὸ ἀποχρῶν μῆκος,
Παναθηναϊκοῦ γὰρ λόγου ἐπιτομῇ εἴκαστο. εὐ-
σταλὴς δὲ οὕτω τοῖς Ἀθηναίοις ἔδοξεν, ὡς καὶ
βόμβον διελθεῖν αὐτῶν ἔτι σιωπῶντος ἐπαινεσάντων
αὐτοῦ τὸ εὔσχημον. ἡ μὲν δὴ νενικηκυῖα ὑπόθεσις
ὁ τοὺς Σκύθας ἐπανάγων ἐς τὴν προτέραν πλάνην,
ἐπειδὴ πόλιν οἰκοῦντες νοσοῦσι, καιρὸν δ᾽ ἐπισχὼν
βραχὺν ἀνεπήδησε τοῦ θρόνου φαιδρῷ τῷ προσώπῳ,
καθάπερ εὐαγγέλια ἐπάγων τοῖς ἀκροωμένοις ὧν
εἰπεῖν ἔχοι. προϊόντος δὲ αὐτῷ τοῦ λόγου ἐπέστη
ὁ Ἡρώδης Ἀρκάδι πίλῳ τὴν κεφαλὴν σκιάζων,
ὡς ἐν ὥρᾳ θέρους εἰώθει Ἀθήνησιν, ἴσως δέ που
καὶ ἐνδεικνύμενος αὐτῷ τὸ ἐκ τῆς ὁδοῦ ἥκειν. καὶ
ὁ Ἀλέξανδρος ἔνθεν ἑλὼν διελέχθη μὲν ἐς τὴν
παρουσίαν τοῦ ἀνδρὸς ὑποσέμνῳ τῇ λέξει καὶ
ἠχούσῃ, ἐπ᾽ αὐτῷ δὲ ἔθετο, εἴτε βούλοιτο τῆς ἤδη
σπουδαζομένης ὑποθέσεως ἀκροᾶσθαι, εἴτε ἑτέραν
αὐτὸς δοῦναι. τοῦ δὲ Ἡρώδου ἀναβλέψαντος ἐς
τοὺς ἀκροωμένους καὶ εἰπόντος, ὡς ποιήσοι, ὅπερ
ἂν ἐκείνοις δόξῃ, πάντες ξυνεπένευσαν ἐς τὴν τῶν
Σκυθῶν ἀκρόασιν, καὶ γὰρ δὴ καὶ λαμπρῶς διῄει
τὸν ἀγῶνα, ὡς δηλοῖ τὰ εἰρημένα. θαυμασίαν δὲ
ἰσχὺν ἐνεδείξατο καὶ ἐν τοῖσδε· τὰς γὰρ διανοίας

---

[1] A favourite theme was the comparison of nomadic with
city life, with the Scythians to point the moral; cf. below,
p. 575, 620; Apsines 228, 247.

so that it became necessary for Alexander to come forward and make the introductory speech before the arrival of Herodes. Now his introductory speech was a panegyric of the city and an apology to the Athenians for not having visited them before, and it was of the appropriate length, for it was like an epitome of a Panathenaic oration. The Athenians thought his appearance and costume so exquisite that before he spoke a word a low buzz of approval went round as a tribute to his perfect elegance. Now the theme that they chose was this: " The speaker endeavours to recall the Scythians to their earlier nomadic life, since they are losing their health by dwelling in cities." [1] After pausing for a brief space he sprang from his seat with a look of gladness on his face, like one who brings good news to those who shall listen to what he has to tell them. While his speech was proceeding, Herodes made his appearance, wearing a shady Arcadian hat as was the fashion in the summer season at Athens, but perhaps also to show Alexander that he had just arrived from a journey. Thereupon Alexander adapted his speech so as to take note of the famous man's presence in impressive and sonorous language; and he put it to him whether he would prefer to listen to the argument that was already being discussed or to propose another himself. Herodes glanced towards the audience, saying that he would do whatever they decided, and they unanimously agreed that they would hear *The Scythians*; for indeed Alexander was making out his case with brilliant success, as the anecdote shows. But he made a further wonderful display of his marvellous powers in what now took place. For the sentiments that he had so brilliantly

195

τὰς πρὶν ἥκειν τὸν Ἡρώδην λαμπρῶς αὐτῷ εἰρημένας μετεχειρίσατο ἐπιστάντος οὕτω τι ἑτέρᾳ λέξει
καὶ ἑτέροις ῥυθμοῖς, ὡς τοῖς δεύτερον ἀκροωμένοις
μὴ διλογεῖν δόξαι. τὸ γοῦν εὐδοκιμώτατα τῶν
πρὶν ἐπιστῆναι τὸν Ἡρώδην εἰρημένων " ἑστὸς καὶ
τὸ ὕδωρ νοσεῖ " μετὰ ταῦτα ἐπιστάντος ἑτέρᾳ
573 δυνάμει μεταλαβὼν " καὶ ὑδάτων " εἶπεν " ἡδίω τὰ
πλανώμενα." κἀκεῖνα τῶν Ἀλεξάνδρου Σκυθῶν·
" καὶ πηγνυμένου μὲν Ἴστρου πρὸς μεσημβρίαν
ἤλαυνον, λυομένου δὲ ἐχώρουν πρὸς ἄρκτον ἀκέραιος
τὸ σῶμα καὶ οὐχ ὥσπερ νυνὶ κείμενος. τί γὰρ ἂν
πάθοι δεινὸν ἄνθρωπος ταῖς ὥραις ἑπόμενος; " ἐπὶ
τελευτῇ δὲ τοῦ λόγου διαβάλλων τὴν πόλιν ὡς
πνιγηρὸν οἰκητήριον τὸ ἐπὶ πᾶσιν ὧδε ἀνεφθέγξατο·
" ἀλλ' ἀναπέτασον τὰς πύλας, ἀναπνεῦσαι θέλω."
προσδραμὼν δὲ τῷ Ἡρώδῃ καὶ περισχὼν αὐτὸν
" ἀντεφεστίασόν με " ἔφη, καὶ ὁ Ἡρώδης " τί δὲ
οὐ μέλλω " εἶπεν " λαμπρῶς οὕτως ἑστιάσαντα; "
διαλυθείσης δὲ τῆς ἀκροάσεως καλέσας ὁ Ἡρώδης
τῶν ἑαυτοῦ γνωρίμων τοὺς ἐν ἐπιδόσει ἠρώτα,
ποῖός τις αὐτοῖς ὁ σοφιστὴς φαίνοιτο, Σκέπτου δὲ
τοῦ ἀπὸ τῆς Κορίνθου τὸν μὲν πηλὸν εὑρηκέναι
φήσαντος, τὸν δὲ Πλάτωνα ζητεῖν, ἐπικόπτων
αὐτὸν ὁ Ἡρώδης " τουτὶ " ἔφη " πρὸς μηδένα
εἴπῃς ἕτερον, σεαυτὸν γὰρ " ἔφη " διαβαλεῖς ὡς
ἀμαθῶς κρίνοντα, ἐμοὶ δὲ ἔπου μᾶλλον ἡγουμένῳ
αὐτὸν Σκοπελιανὸν νήφοντα." ταυτὶ δὲ ὁ Ἡρώδης
ἐχαρακτήριζε καθεωρακὼς τὸν ἄνδρα κεκραμένην

---

[1] See p. 619, where Hippodromus recasts his declamation,
and, for Plato's scorn of this device, *Phaedrus* 235 B.

[2] Euripides, *Phoenician Women* 297; the phrase from
tragedy, the iambic metre and ἀνα- repeated are marks of
Asianism.

expressed before Herodes came he now recast in his presence, but with such different words and different rhythms, that those who were hearing them for the second time could not feel that he was repeating himself.[1] For example, before Herodes appeared, the epigram that won the greatest applause was this: " When it is stagnant, even water goes bad." But after his arrival he gave it a different force, by saying: " Even those waters are sweeter that keep on the move." Here are some more quotations from *The Scythians* of Alexander. " When the Danube froze I would travel South, but when it thawed I would go North, always in perfect health, not as I am now, an invalid. For what harm can come to a man who follows the seasons in their course ? " In the last part of his speech he denounced the city as a cramped and suffocating dwelling, and for the closing sentence he cried out very loud: " Come fling open the gates,[2] I must breathe the air ! " Then he hastened up to Herodes, embraced him and said: " Pray regale me in return." " Why not indeed," said Herodes, " when you have regaled me so splendidly ? " When the declamation was over, Herodes called together the more advanced of his own pupils and asked them what was their opinion of the sophist ; and when Sceptus of Corinth said that he had found the clay but had still to find the Plato, Herodes cut him short, and said: " Do not talk like that to anyone else, for," said he, " you will incriminate yourself as an illiterate critic. Nay rather follow me in thinking him a more sober Scopelian."[3] Herodes thus characterized him because he had observed that the sophist knew how to

[3] For Scopelian's style see above, pp. 518, 519.

ἑρμηνείαν ἐφαρμόζοντα τῇ περὶ τὰς σοφιστικὰς
ἐννοίας τόλμῃ. ἐπιδεικνύμενος δὲ τῷ Ἀλεξάνδρῳ
τήν τε ἠχὼ τῆς διαλέξεως προσῆρεν, ἐπειδὴ ἐγίγνωσκε τούτῳ καὶ μάλιστα χαίροντα αὐτὸν τῷ τόνῳ,
ῥυθμούς τε ποικιλωτέρους αὐλοῦ καὶ λύρας ἐσηγάγετο ἐς τὸν λόγον, ἐπειδὴ πολὺς αὐτῷ καὶ περὶ τὰς
574 ἐξαλλαγὰς ἔδοξεν. ἡ δὲ σπουδασθεῖσα ὑπόθεσις οἱ
ἐν Σικελίᾳ τρωθέντες ἦσαν αἰτοῦντες τοὺς ἀπαν-
ισταμένους ἐκεῖθεν Ἀθηναίους τὸ ὑπ' αὐτῶν ἀπο-
θνῄσκειν. ἐπὶ ταύτης τῆς ὑποθέσεως τὸ θρυλούμενον
ἐκεῖνο ἱκέτευσεν ἐπιτέγξας τοὺς ὀφθαλμοὺς δακρύοις
" ναὶ Νικία, ναὶ πάτερ, οὕτως Ἀθήνας ἴδοις," ἐφ'
ᾧ τὸν Ἀλέξανδρόν φασιν ἀναβοῆσαι· " ὦ Ἡρώδη,
τεμάχιά σου ἐσμὲν οἱ σοφισταὶ πάντες," καὶ τὸν
Ἡρώδην ὑπερησθέντα τῷ ἐπαίνῳ καὶ τῆς ἑαυτοῦ
φύσεως γενόμενον δοῦναί οἱ δέκα μὲν σκευοφόρα,
δέκα δὲ ἵππους, δέκα δὲ οἰνοχόους, δέκα δὲ σημείων
γραφέας, τάλαντα δὲ εἴκοσι χρυσοῦ, πλεῖστον δὲ
ἄργυρον, δύο δὲ ἐκ Κολλυτοῦ παιδία ψελλιζόμενα,
ἐπειδὴ ἤκουεν αὐτὸν χαίροντα νέαις φωναῖς.
τοιαῦτα μὲν οὖν αὐτῷ τὰ Ἀθήνησιν.

Ἐπεὶ δὲ καὶ ἑτέρων σοφιστῶν ἀπομνημονεύματα
παρεθέμην, δηλούσθω καὶ ὁ Ἀλέξανδρος ἐκ πλειόνων, οὐδὲ γὰρ ἐς πλῆρές πω τῆς ἑαυτοῦ δόξης
ἀφῖκται παρὰ τοῖς Ἕλλησιν. ὡς μὲν δὴ σεμνῶς τε
καὶ ξὺν ἡδονῇ διελέγετο, δηλοῦσι τῶν διαλέξεων

---

[1] This is the technical term to describe the theme voted
for by the audience when several had been proposed.
[2] This theme is based on the narrative of Thucydides
vii. 75.
[3] An echo of the famous saying of Aeschylus that his
plays were " slices," τεμάχη, from Homer's splendid feasts.

combine a sober and tempered eloquence with a bold use of sophistic modes of thought; and when he himself declaimed before Alexander he raised his eloquence to a higher pitch, because he knew that Alexander took the keenest pleasure in intensity and force; and he introduced into his speech rhythms more varied than those of the flute and the lyre, because he considered that Alexander was especially skilful in elaborate variations. The theme elected [1] by his audience was, "The wounded in Sicily implore the Athenians who are retreating thence to put them to death with their own hands." [2] In the course of this argument, with tears in his eyes, he uttered that famous and often quoted supplication: "Ah, Nicias! Ah, my father! As you hope to see Athens once more!" Whereupon they say that Alexander exclaimed: "O Herodes, we sophists are all of us merely small slices of yourself!" [3] And that Herodes was delighted beyond measure by this eulogy, and yielding to his innate generosity presented him with ten pack-animals, ten horses, ten cup-bearers, ten shorthand writers, twenty talents of gold, a great quantity of silver, and two lisping children from the deme Collytus, since he was told that Alexander liked to hear childish voices. This, then, is what happened to Alexander at Athens.

Now since I have set before my readers certain memorable sayings of the other sophists, I must make Alexander also known to them by quoting several sayings of his. For among the Greeks he has never yet attained to the full measure of the renown that is his due. The following quotations from his discourses show how sublime and at the same time

αἵδε· " Μαρσύας ἤρα 'Ολύμπου καὶ "Ολυμπος
τοῦ αὐλεῖν " καὶ πάλιν " 'Αραβία γῆ δένδρα πολλά,
πεδία κατάσκια, γυμνὸν οὐδέν, φυτὰ ἡ γῆ, τὰ ἄνθη.
οὐδὲ φύλλον 'Αράβιον ἐκβαλεῖς, οὐδὲ κάρφος ἀπορ-
ρίψεις οὐδὲν ἐκεῖ φυέν, τοσοῦτον ἡ γῆ περὶ τοὺς
ἰδρῶτας εὐτυχεῖ." καὶ πάλιν " ἀνὴρ πένης ἀπ'
'Ιωνίας, ἡ δὲ 'Ιωνία "Ελληνές εἰσιν οἰκήσαντες ἐν
τῇ βαρβάρων." τὴν δὲ ἰδέαν ταύτην διατωθάζων
ὁ 'Αντίοχος καὶ διαπτύων αὐτὸν ὡς τρυφῶντα ἐς
τὴν τῶν ὀνομάτων ὥραν, παρελθὼν ἐς τὴν 'Αντιό-
χειαν διελέχθη ὧδε· " 'Ιωνίαι Λυδίαι Μαρσύαι
μωρίαι, δότε προβλήματα." τὰ δὲ ἐν τῇ μελέτῃ
575 πλεονεκτήματα δεδήλωται μὲν καὶ ἐπὶ τούτων,
δηλούσθω δὲ καὶ ἐπ' ἄλλων ὑποθέσεων· διεξιὼν
μὲν γὰρ τὸν Περικλέα τὸν κελεύοντα ἔχεσθαι τοῦ
πολέμου καὶ μετὰ τὸν χρησμόν, ἐν ᾧ καὶ καλού-
μενος καὶ ἄκλητος ὁ Πύθιος ἔφη τοῖς Λακεδαιμονίοις συμμαχήσειν, ὧδε ἀπήντησε τῷ χρησμῷ·
" ἀλλ' ὑπισχνεῖταί, φησι, τοῖς Λακεδαιμονίοις
βοηθήσειν ὁ Πύθιος· ψεύδεται· οὕτως αὐτοῖς καὶ
Τεγέαν ἐπηγγείλατο." διεξιὼν δὲ τὸν ξυμβου-
λεύοντα τῷ Δαρείῳ ζεῦξαι τὸν "Ιστρον· " ὑπορ-
ρείτω σοι ὁ Σκυθῶν "Ιστρος, κἂν εὔρους τὴν

---

[1] Quoted by Norden, p. 411, to illustrate the excessive
use of rhythm in prose.

[2] The point lies in the magniloquent use of the plural and
the hackneyed allusions.

[3] Thucydides i. 118 speaks of this oracle, but not in connexion with Pericles.

[4] Herodotus i. 66 describes the misleading oracle which
refused the Spartans the conquest of Arcadia, but promised
that they should take Tegea; they were defeated and
captured by the Tegeans.

how delightful was his style of eloquence. "Marsyas was in love with Olympus, and Olympus with flute-playing." And again : " Arabia is a land of abundant woods, well-shaded plains, there is no barren spot, her soil is all plants and flowers. Not a leaf that Arabia grows would one ever throw aside, no stem or stalk that grew there would one ever cast away ; so happy is her soil in all that exudes therefrom." [1] And again : "I am a poor man from Ionia, yet Ionia consists of pure Hellenes who colonized the land of the barbarians." Antiochus made fun of this style, and despised Alexander for in-dulging too much in the luxury of fine-sounding words ; and so when he came before the public at Antioch he began his speech with the words : "Ionias, Lydias, Marsyases, foolishness, propose me themes." [2]

In these quotations I have shown Alexander's peculiar talent for declamation, but I must go on to show it in themes of another kind. For instance, when his theme was this : "Pericles urges that they should keep up the war, even after the oracle in which the Pythian god declared that, whether summoned to their aid or not summoned, he would be the ally of the Lacedaemonians," [3] he withstood the oracle with these words : " But the Pythian god, you say, promises to aid the Lacedaemonians. He is deceiving them. Even so did he promise them Tegea." [4] And again, when representing the man who advised Darius to throw a bridge over the Danube,[5] he said : " Let the Danube of the Scythians flow beneath your feet, and if he gives your army a

[5] In Herodotus iv. 89 is a passage which may have inspired this theme.

στρατιὰν διαγάγῃ, τίμησον αὐτὸν ἐξ αὐτοῦ πιών."
τὸν δὲ Ἀρτάβαζον ἀγωνιζόμενος τὸν ἀπαγορεύοντα
τῷ Ξέρξῃ μὴ τὸ δεύτερον στρατεύειν ἐπὶ τὴν
Ἑλλάδα ὧδε ἐβραχυλόγησεν· " τὰ μὲν δὴ Περσῶν
τε καὶ Μήδων τοιαῦτά σοι, βασιλεῦ, κατὰ χώραν
μένοντι, τὰ δὲ Ἑλλήνων γῆ λεπτὴ θάλαττα στενὴ
καὶ ἄνδρες ἀπονενοημένοι καὶ θεοὶ βάσκανοι."
τοὺς δὲ ἐν τοῖς πεδίοις νοσοῦντας ἐς τὰ ὄρη ἀνοικί-
ζεσθαι πείθων ὧδε ἐφυσιολόγησεν· " δοκεῖ δέ μοι
καὶ ὁ τοῦ παντὸς δημιουργὸς τὰ μὲν πεδία, ὥσπερ
ἀτιμοτέρας[1] ὕλης, ῥῖψαι κάτω, ἐπαίρειν δὲ τὰ ὄρη,
576 ὥσπερ ἀξιώματα. ταῦτα πρῶτα μὲν ἥλιος ἀσπάζεται, τελευταῖα δὲ ἀπολείπει. τίς οὐκ ἀγαπήσει
τόπον μακροτέρας ἔχοντα τὰς ἡμέρας ; "

Διδάσκαλοι τῷ Ἀλεξάνδρῳ ἐγένοντο Φαβωρῖνός
τε καὶ Διονύσιος· ἀλλὰ Διονυσίου μὲν ἡμιμαθὴς
ἀπῆλθε μεταπεμφθεὶς ὑπὸ τοῦ πατρὸς νοσοῦντος,
ὅτε δὴ καὶ ἐτελεύτα, Φαβωρίνου δὲ γνησιώτατα
ἠκροάσατο, παρ' οὗ μάλιστα καὶ τὴν ὥραν τοῦ
λόγου ἔσπασεν. τελευτῆσαι τὸν Ἀλέξανδρον οἱ μὲν
ἐν Κελτοῖς φασιν ἔτι ἐπιστέλλοντα, οἱ δ' ἐν Ἰταλίᾳ
πεπαυμένον τοῦ ἐπιστέλλειν, καὶ οἱ μὲν ἑξηκοντού-
την, οἱ δὲ καὶ οὔπω, καὶ οἱ μὲν ἐπὶ υἱῷ, οἱ δ' ἐπὶ
θυγατρί, ὑπὲρ ὧν οὐδὲν εὗρον λόγου ἄξιον.

ϛ΄. Ἀξιούσθω λόγου καὶ Οὔαρος ὁ ἐκ τῆς
Πέργης. Οὐάρῳ πατὴρ μὲν Καλλικλῆς ἐγένετο
ἀνὴρ ἐν τοῖς δυνατωτάτοις τῶν Περγαίων, διδά-

---

[1] ἀτιμότερα Kayser ; ἀτιμοτέρας Cobet.

---

[1] cf. Herodotus vii. 10. In Philostratus, as in Hermogenes,
On the Types of Style 396, the name should be Artabanus,
not Artabazus.
[2] This is a variant of *The Scythians* ; see p. 572.
[3] Nothing more is known of this sophist.

smooth crossing, do him the honour of drinking of
his waters." Again, when he sustained the part of
Artabazus trying to dissuade Xerxes from making a
second expedition against Greece,[1] he summed up
the argument as follows: " Now the condition of the
Persians and Medes is as I have said, O King, if you
stay where you are. But the soil of the Greeks is
poor, their sea is narrow, their men are foolhardy,
their gods are jealous gods." When he was trying
to persuade those who had bad health in the plains
to migrate to the mountains,[2] he thus discoursed on
nature: " I believe the Creator of the universe
hurled down the plains as being of less precious
material, and raised up the mountains as worthy of
regard. These the sun greets first and abandons
last. Who would not love a place where the days
are longer than elsewhere?"

Alexander's teachers were Favorinus and Dionysius.
But he left Dionysius when his education was only
half completed, because he had been summoned by
his father who was ill. Then, when his father was
dead, Alexander became the genuine disciple of
Favorinus, and it was from him above all that he
caught the charm and beauty of his eloquence.
Some say that Alexander died in Gaul while he was
still an Imperial Secretary, others that he died in
Italy after he had ceased to be Secretary. Again
some say that he was sixty, others that he had not
reached that age. Some say that he left a son,
others a daughter, but on these points I could
discover nothing worth mentioning.

6. I must not omit to mention VARUS[3] who came
from Perge. The father of Varus was Callicles, one
of Perge's most important citizens. His teacher

σκαλος δὲ Κοδρατίων ὁ ὕπατος ἀποσχεδιάζων τὰς
θετικὰς ὑποθέσεις καὶ τὸν Φαβωρίνου τρόπον
σοφιστεύων. πελαργὸν δὲ τὸν Οὔαρον οἱ πολλοὶ
ἐπωνόμαζον διὰ τὸ πυρσὸν τῆς ῥινὸς καὶ ῥαμφῶδες,
καὶ τοῦτο μὲν ὡς οὐκ ἀπὸ δόξης ἠστείζοντο, ἔξεστι
συμβαλεῖν ταῖς εἰκόσιν, αἳ ἀνάκεινται ἐν τῷ τῆς
Περγαίας ἱερῷ. ὁ δὲ χαρακτὴρ τοῦ λόγου τοιοῦτος·
" ἐφ' Ἑλλήσποντον ἐλθὼν ἵππον αἰτεῖς; ἐπ' Ἄθω
δὲ ἐλθὼν πλεῦσαι θέλεις; οὐκ οἶδας, ἄνθρωπε, τὰς
ὁδούς; ἀλλ' Ἑλλησπόντῳ γῆν ὀλίγην ἐπιβαλὼν
577 ταύτην οἴει σοι μενεῖν,[1] τῶν ὀρῶν μὴ μενόντων; "
ἐλέγετο δὲ ἀπαγγέλλειν ταῦτα λαμπρᾷ τῇ φωνῇ
καὶ ἠσκημένῃ. ἐτελεύτα μὲν οὖν οἴκοι οὔπω
γηράσκων καὶ ἐπὶ παισί, τὸ δὲ ἀπ' αὐτοῦ γένος
εὐδόκιμοι πάντες ἐν τῇ Πέργῃ.

ζ'. Ἑρμογένης δέ, ὃν Ταρσοὶ ἤνεγκαν, πεντεκαίδεκα ἔτη γεγονὼς ἐφ' οὕτω μέγα προὔβη τῆς
τῶν σοφιστῶν δόξης, ὡς καὶ Μάρκῳ βασιλεῖ παρασχεῖν ἔρωτα ἀκροάσεως· ἐβάδιζε γοῦν ἐπὶ τὴν
ἀκρόασιν αὐτοῦ ὁ Μάρκος καὶ ἥσθη μὲν διαλεγομένου, ἐθαύμαζε δὲ σχεδιάζοντος, δωρεὰς δὲ
λαμπρὰς ἔδωκεν. ἐς δὲ ἄνδρας ἥκων ἀφῃρέθη τὴν
ἕξιν ὑπ' οὐδεμιᾶς φανερᾶς νόσου, ὅθεν ἀστεισμοῦ
λόγον παρέδωκε τοῖς βασκάνοις, ἔφασαν γὰρ τοὺς
λόγους ἀτεχνῶς καθ' Ὅμηρον πτερόεντας εἶναι,
ἀποβεβληκέναι γὰρ αὐτοὺς τὸν Ἑρμογένην καθάπερ

----

[1] μένειν Kayser; μενεῖν Cobet.

----

[1] Quadratus was proconsul of Asia A.D. 165; Aristeides
calls him a sophist.
[2] Artemis.
[3] This hackneyed antithesis was ridiculed by Lucian.

was Quadratus[1] the consular, who used to argue extempore on abstract philosophical themes, and as a sophist followed the fashion set by Favorinus. Varus was commonly nicknamed " the stork," because of the fiery hue and beaked shape of his nose, and that this witticism was not far-fetched we may gather from the likenesses of him which are dedicated in the temple of the goddess[2] of Perge. The following is characteristic of his eloquence : " When you arrive at the Hellespont do you call for a horse ? When you arrive at Athos do you wish to navigate it ?[3] Man, do you not know the regular routes ? You throw this handful of earth on the Hellespont, and think you that it will remain, when mountains do not remain ? " It is said that he used to declaim these words in a magnificent and well-trained voice. For the rest, he died at home while still a young man, leaving children, and his descendants are all highly esteemed in Perge.

7. HERMOGENES, who was born at Tarsus, by the time he was fifteen had attained such a reputation as a sophist that even the Emperor Marcus became eager to hear him. At any rate Marcus made the journey to hear him declaim, and was delighted with his formal discourse, but marvelled at him when he declaimed extempore, and gave him splendid presents. But when Hermogenes arrived at manhood his powers suddenly deserted him, though this was not due to any apparent disease, and this provided the envious with an occasion for their wit. For they declared that his words were in very truth "winged," as Homer says, and that Hermogenes had moulted

The Rhetorician's Guide 18 ; *cf.* Cicero, *De finibus* ii. 34; Dio Chrysostom, *Oration* iii. 31 Arnim.

πτερά. καὶ Ἀντίοχος δὲ ὁ σοφιστὴς ἀποσκώπτων
ποτὲ ἐς αὐτὸν " οὗτος " ἔφη " Ἑρμογένης, ὁ ἐν
578 παισὶ μὲν γέρων, ἐν δὲ γηράσκουσι παῖς." ἡ δὲ
ἰδέα τοῦ λόγου, ἣν ἐπετήδευε, τοιάδε τις ἦν· ἐπὶ
γὰρ τοῦ Μάρκου διαλεγόμενος " ἰδοὺ ἥκω σοι,"
ἔφη " βασιλεῦ, ῥήτωρ παιδαγωγοῦ δεόμενος, ῥήτωρ
ἡλικίαν περιμένων " καὶ πλείω ἕτερα διελέχθη καὶ
ὧδε βωμόλοχα. ἐτελεύτα μὲν οὖν ἐν βαθεῖ γήρᾳ,
εἷς δὲ τῶν πολλῶν νομιζόμενος, κατεφρονήθη γὰρ
ἀπολιπούσης αὐτὸν τῆς τέχνης.

η'. Φίλαγρος δὲ ὁ Κίλιξ Λολλιανοῦ μὲν ἀκροατὴς ἐγένετο, σοφιστῶν δὲ θερμότατος καὶ ἐπιχο-
λώτατος, λέγεται γὰρ δὴ νυστάζοντά ποτε ἀκροατὴν
καὶ ἐπὶ κόρρης πλῆξαι, καὶ ὁρμῇ δὲ λαμπρᾷ ἐκ μειρακίου χρησάμενος οὐκ ἀπελείφθη αὐτῆς οὐδ' ὁπότε
ἐγήρασκεν, ἀλλ' οὕτω τι ἐπέδωκεν, ὡς καὶ σχῆμα
τοῦ διδασκάλου νομισθῆναι. πλείστοις δὲ ἐπιμίξας
ἔθνεσι καὶ δοκῶν ἄριστα μεταχειρίζεσθαι τὰς ὑποθέσεις οὐ μετεχειρίσατο Ἀθήνησιν εὖ τὴν αὐτοῦ
χολήν, ἀλλ' ἐς ἀπέχθειαν Ἡρώδῃ κατέστησεν
ἑαυτόν, καθάπερ τούτου ἀφιγμένος ἕνεκα. ἐβάδιζε
μὲν γὰρ δείλης ἐν Κεραμεικῷ μετὰ τεττάρων, οἷοι
Ἀθήνησιν οἱ τοὺς σοφιστὰς θηρεύοντες, ἰδὼν δὲ
νεανίαν ἐκ δεξιᾶς ἀναστρέφοντα μετὰ πλειόνων
σκώπτεσθαί τι ὑπ' αὐτοῦ δόξας " ἀλλ' ἦ σὺ " ἔφη
" τίς; " " Ἀμφικλῆς ἐγώ," ἔφη " εἰ δὴ τὸν Χαλ-

---

[1] A parody of Pindar, *Nem.* iii. 72.
[2] Nothing more is known of this sophist.

them, like wing-feathers. And once Antiochus the sophist, jesting at his expense, said : " Lo, here is that fellow Hermogenes, who among boys was an old man, but among the old is a boy." [1] The following will show the kind of eloquence that he affected. In a speech that he was delivering before Marcus, he said, " You see before you, Emperor, an orator who still needs an attendant to take him to school, an orator who still looks to come of age." He said much more of this sort and in the same facetious vein. He died at a ripe old age, but accounted as one of the rank and file, for he became despised when his skill in his art deserted him.

8. PHILAGRUS OF CILICIA [2] was a pupil of Lollianus, and was the most excitable and hot-tempered of the sophists. For instance it is said that when someone in his audience began to go to sleep, he gave him a blow in the face with his open hand. After making a brilliant start in his career while still a mere boy, he did not fall short of it even when he began to grow old, but made such progress that he was regarded as the model of what a teacher should be. But though he lived among many peoples and won a great reputation among them for his dexterity in handling arguments, at Athens he showed no skill in handling his own hot temper, but picked a quarrel with Herodes just as though he had come there for that very purpose. For he was walking towards evening in the Cerameicus with four men of the sort that at Athens chase after the sophists, and saw a young man on his right, with several others, keep turning round, and imagining that he was making some jest at his expense he called out : " Well, and who may you be ? " " I am Amphicles,"

κιδέα ἀκούεις." "ἀπέχου τοίνυν" ἔφη "τῶν
ἐμῶν ἀκροάσεων, οὐ γάρ μοι δοκεῖς ὑγιαίνειν."
τοῦ δὲ ἐρομένου "τίς δὲ ὢν ταῦτα κηρύττεις;"
δεινὰ πάσχειν ἦ δ' ὁ Φίλαγρος, εἰ ἀγνοεῖταί ποι.
ἐκφύλου δὲ αὐτὸν ῥήματος ὡς ἐν ὀργῇ διαφυγόντος
λαβόμενος ὁ Ἀμφικλῆς, καὶ γὰρ δὴ καὶ ἐτύγχανε
τῶν Ἡρώδου γνωρίμων τὴν πρώτην φερόμενος,
"παρὰ τίνι τῶν ἐλλογίμων" ἔφη "τοῦτο εἴρηται;"
καὶ ὃς "παρὰ Φιλάγρῳ" ἔφη. αὕτη μὲν δὴ ἡ
579 παροινία ἐς τὰ τοιαῦτα προὔβη, τῆς δὲ ὑστεραίας
μαθὼν τὸν Ἡρώδην ἐν τῷ προαστείῳ διαιτώμενον
γράφει πρὸς αὐτὸν ἐπιστολὴν καθαπτόμενος τοῦ
ἀνδρὸς ὡς ἀμελοῦντος τοῦ τῶν ἀκροατῶν κόσμου.
καὶ ὁ Ἡρώδης "δοκεῖς μοι" ἔφη "οὐ καλῶς
προοιμιάζεσθαι" ἐπιπλήττων αὐτῷ ὡς μὴ κτω-
μένῳ ἀκροατῶν εὔνοιαν, ἣν προοίμιον ἡγεῖσθαι χρὴ
τῶν ἐπιδείξεων. ὁ δὲ ὥσπερ οὐ ξυνιεὶς τοῦ αἰνίγματος, ἢ ξυνιεὶς μέν, ἐν γέλωτι δὲ τὴν τοῦ Ἡρώδου
γνώμην βελτίστην οὖσαν τιθέμενος ἐψεύσθη τῆς
ἐπιδείξεως παρελθὼν ἐς ἀκροατὰς οὐκ εὔνους. ὡς
γὰρ τῶν πρεσβυτέρων ἤκουον, προσέκρουσε μὲν
ἡ διάλεξις νεαροηχὴς δόξασα καὶ διεσπασμένη[1] τὰς
ἐννοίας, ἔδοξε δὲ καὶ μειρακιώδης, γυναικὸς γὰρ
θρῆνος ἐγκατεμέμικτο τοῖς Ἀθηναίων ἐγκωμίοις
τεθνώσης αὐτῷ ἐν Ἰωνίᾳ, τὴν δὲ μελέτην οὕτως
ἐπεβουλεύθη· ἠγώνιστό τις αὐτῷ κατὰ τὴν Ἀσίαν

----

[1] ἐσπασμένη Kayser; διεσπασμένη Cobet.

----

[1] The second-century sophists, when purists, carefully
avoided "barbarisms" and Latinisms. The most striking
instance of this is *Life of Apollonius* iv. 5. Aristeides in his
panegyric of Rome used no Roman name. Dio Chrysostom,
Oration xxi. 11, defends his allusions to the Emperor Nero
and others who are "modern and despised."

he replied, "if indeed you have heard of that citizen of Chalcis." "Then keep away from my lectures," said Philagrus, "for you do not appear to me to have any sense." "And who are you?" inquired the other, "to issue that edict?" Whereupon Philagrus said that it was an insult to him not to be recognized wherever he might be. An outlandish word [1] escaped him in the heat of his anger, and Amphicles pounced on it, for he was in fact the most distinguished of the pupils of Herodes, and asked: "In what classic is that word to be found?" "In Philagrus," was the answer. Now this foolish brawl went no further at the time; but on the next day he learned that Herodes was living in his suburban villa, and wrote him a letter accusing him of neglecting to teach his pupils decent manners. To this Herodes replied: "It seems to me that you are not very successful with your prooemium." This was to censure him for not trying to win the goodwill of his hearers, which one must regard as the true prooemium of a declamation. But Philagrus, as though he did not understand the conundrum, or understood, but regarded the advice of Herodes as absurd, though it was in fact excellent, was disappointed in his declamation because he came before an audience that was ill-disposed towards him. For as I have heard from men older than myself, his introductory speech gave offence, because they thought it had a new-fangled ring and was disconnected in its ideas; nay they even thought it childish. For into his encomium of the Athenians he inserted a lament for his wife who had died in Ionia. So when he came to deliver his declamation a plot was formed against him, as follows. In Asia he had already

ὑπόθεσις οἱ παραιτούμενοι τὴν τῶν ἀκλήτων συμ-
μαχίαν· ταύτης ἐκδεδομένης ἤδη τῆς ὑποθέσεως
μνήμην ξυνελέξατο, καὶ γὰρ δὴ καὶ εὐδοκιμηκὼς
ἐπ' αὐτῇ ἐτύγχανε, λόγου δὲ ἥκοντος ἐς τοὺς ἀμφὶ
τὸν Ἡρώδην, ὡς ὁ Φίλαγρος τὰς μὲν πρῶτον ὁριζο-
μένας ὑποθέσεις αὐτοσχεδιάζοι, τὰς δὲ καὶ δεύτερον
οὐκέτι ἀλλ' ἕωλα μελετῴη καὶ ἑαυτῷ προειρημένα
προὔβαλον μὲν αὐτῷ τοὺς ἀκλήτους τούτους, δο-
κοῦντι δὲ ἀποσχεδιάζειν ἀντανεγιγνώσκετο ἡ μελέτη.
θορύβου δὲ πολλοῦ καὶ γέλωτος τὴν ἀκρόασιν κατα-
σχόντος βοῶν ὁ Φίλαγρος καὶ κεκραγώς, ὡς δεινὰ
πάσχοι τῶν ἑαυτοῦ εἰργόμενος οὐ διέφυγε τὴν ἤδη
πεπιστευμένην αἰτίαν. ταῦτα μὲν οὖν ἐν τῷ Ἀγριπ-
πείῳ ἐπράχθη, διαλιπὼν δὲ ἡμέρας ὡς τέτταρας
580 παρῆλθεν ἐς τὸ τῶν τεχνιτῶν βουλευτήριον, ὃ δὴ
ᾠκοδόμηται παρὰ τὰς τοῦ Κεραμεικοῦ πύλας οὐ
πόρρω τῶν ἱππέων. εὐδοκιμώτατα δὲ ἀγωνιζόμενος τὸν Ἀριστογείτονα τὸν ἀξιοῦντα κατηγορεῖν
τοῦ μὲν Δημοσθένους Μηδισμόν,[1] τοῦ δὲ Αἰσχίνου
Φιλιππισμόν, ὑπὲρ ὧν καὶ γεγραμμένοι ἀλλήλους
ἐτύγχανον, ἐσβέσθη τὸ φθέγμα ὑπὸ τῆς χολῆς
ἐπισκοτοῦντος φύσει τοῖς ἐπιχόλοις τὴν φωνὴν τοῦ
φωνητικοῦ πνεύματος. χρόνῳ μὲν οὖν ὕστερον ἐπ-

---

[1] Μηδισμοῦ . . . Φιλιππισμοῦ Kayser; Μηδισμόν . . . Φιλιππισμόν Cobet.

---

[1] This theme is probably derived from Thucydides viii.
86, where Alcibiades declines the aid of the Argives.

[2] There was a similar guild of *artifices scaenici* at Rome ;
see below, p. 596. This guild, one of the earliest instances
of organized labour, had extraordinary power and even
political influence.

[3] Diogenes Laertius vii. 182 mentions equestrian statues
in the Cerameicus, but nothing more is known about them.

argued a certain theme entitled : " They reject as allies those whom they have not invited to their aid." [1]   This argument had already been published, and had attracted notice, in fact it had greatly enhanced his reputation.   Now a rumour reached the pupils of Herodes that Philagrus, when a theme was proposed to him, used to improvise the first time, but did not do so on a second occasion, but would declaim stale arguments that he had used before. Accordingly they proposed to him this same theme " The Uninvited," and when he pretended to be improvising they retaliated by reading the declamation aloud.   Then the lecture became the scene of uproar and laughter, with Philagrus shouting and vociferating that it was an outrage on him not to be allowed to use what was his own ; but he failed to win acquittal of a charge that was so fully proven. Now all this took place in the theatre of Agrippa, and after an interval of about four days he came forward to declaim in the council-chamber of the theatrical artisans,[2] the building which stands near the gates of the Cerameicus not far from the equestrian statues.[3]   But when he was winning universal approval in the character of Aristogeiton demanding the right to denounce Demosthenes for conspiring with Persia and Aeschines for conspiring with Philip—accusations which they had in fact brought against one another [4]—his very utterance was stifled by his wrath.   For with choleric persons the breath on which the voice depends is apt to obscure and check the power of speech.   It is true that, somewhat later, he was promoted to the chair

[4] For this obviously fictitious theme see Marcellinus iv. 472 Walz.

βάτευσε τοῦ κατὰ τὴν ˈΡώμην θρόνου, ᾿Αθήνησι δὲ ἀπηνέχθη τῆς ἑαυτοῦ δόξης δι᾽ ἃς εἴρηκα αἰτίας.

Χαρακτὴρ τῶν τοῦ Φιλάγρου λόγων ὁ μὲν ἐν ταῖς διαλέξεσι τοιοῦτος· " εἶτα οἴει ἥλιον ἑσπέρῳ φθονεῖν ἢ μέλειν αὐτῷ, εἴ τίς ἐστιν ἀστὴρ ἄλλος ἐν οὐρανῷ; οὐχ οὕτως ἔχει τὰ τοῦ μεγάλου τούτου πυρός. ἐμοὶ μὲν γὰρ δοκεῖ καὶ ποιητικῶς ἑκάστῳ διανέμειν, σοὶ μὲν ἄρκτον δίδωμι, λέγοντα, σοὶ δὲ μεσημβρίαν,[1] σοὶ δὲ ἑσπέραν, πάντες δὲ ἐν νυκτί, πάντες, ὅταν ἐγὼ μὴ βλέπωμαι·

᾿Ήλιος δ᾽ ἀνόρουσε λιπὼν περικαλλέα λίμνην

καὶ ἀστέρες οὐδαμοῦ." τίνες δὲ καὶ οἱ τῆς μελέτης αὐτῷ ῥυθμοὶ ἦσαν, δηλώσει τὰ πρὸς τοὺς ἀκλήτους εἰρημένα, καὶ γὰρ καὶ χαίρειν αὐτοῖς ἐλέγετο· " φίλε, τήμερόν σε τεθέαμαι καὶ τήμερον ἐν ὅπλοις καὶ μετὰ ξίφους μοι λαλεῖς " καὶ " τὴν ἀπὸ τῆς ἐκκλησίας μόνην οἶδα φιλίαν. ἄπιτε οὖν, ἄνδρες φίλοι, τοῦτο γὰρ ὑμῖν τηροῦμεν τοὔνομα, κἂν δεηθῶμέν ποτε συμμάχων, ἐφ᾽ ὑμᾶς πέμψομεν, εἴ ποτε δήπου."

Μέγεθος μὲν οὖν ὁ Φίλαγρος μετρίου μείων, τὴν δὲ ὀφρὺν πικρὸς καὶ τὸ ὄμμα ἕτοιμος καὶ ἐς 581 ὀργὴν ἐκκληθῆναι πρόθυμος, καὶ τὸ ἐν αὐτῷ δύστροπον οὐδ᾽ αὐτὸς ἠγνόει· ἐρομένου γοῦν αὐτὸν ἑνὸς τῶν ἑταίρων, τί παθὼν[2] παιδοτροφίᾳ οὐ χαίροι, " ὅτι " ἔφη " οὐδ᾽ ἐμαυτῷ χαίρω." ἀπο-

---

[1] Cobet would insert σοὶ δὲ ἐῴαν "to thee the East" for symmetry.

[2] μαθὼν Kayser; παθὼν Cobet.

---

[1] An allusion to *Iliad* xv. 190 foll., where Poseidon describes the partition of the universe among Zeus, Hades

of rhetoric at Rome, nevertheless at Athens, for the reasons I have stated, he was deprived of the credit that was his due.

The following quotation shows the characteristic style of Philagrus' oratory in his introductory speeches : " And so you think that the sun is jealous of the evening-star, or that it matters to him what star beside is in the sky ? Not thus is it with this mighty fire. For it seems to me that, like the poet,[1] he assigns his portion to each, saying : To thee I give the North and to thee the South, to thee the evening, but in the darkness of night are ye all, yea all, when I am invisible ;

Then the sun rises leaving the fair waters of the sea,[2]

and the stars are nowhere." The rhythms that he used in his declamations may be seen in his speech " The Uninvited"; and indeed he is said to have delighted in such rhythms : " Friend, to-day I have seen thee as thou art, to-day thou speakest to me in arms and sword in hand." And again : " The only friendship that I recognize springs from the assembly of the people. Therefore depart, friends, since for you we preserve this title, and if ever we need allies, we will send for you ; if ever, that is to say !"

In height Philagrus was below the average, his brow was stern, his eye alert and easily roused to anger, and he was himself conscious of his morose temper. Hence when one of his friends asked him why he did not enjoy bringing up a family, he replied : " Because I do not even enjoy myself."

and himself; but possibly the meaning is "like a poet assigning their parts to the actors."

[2] *Odyssey* iii. 1. This speech is quoted by Norden, p. 413, as an example of the metrical rhythms of Sophistic.

θανεῖν δὲ αὐτὸν οἱ μὲν ἐν τῇ θαλάττῃ, οἱ δὲ ἐν
Ἰταλίᾳ περὶ πρῶτον γῆρας.

θ΄. Ἀριστείδην δὲ τὸν εἴτε Εὐδαίμονος εἴτε
Εὐδαίμονα Ἀδριανοὶ μὲν ἤνεγκαν, οἱ δὲ Ἀδριανοὶ
πόλις οὐ μεγάλη ἐν Μυσοῖς, Ἀθῆναι δὲ ἤσκησαν
κατὰ τὴν Ἡρώδου ἀκμὴν καὶ τὸ ἐν τῇ Ἀσίᾳ
Πέργαμον κατὰ τὴν Ἀριστοκλέους γλῶτταν.
νοσώδης δὲ ἐκ μειρακίου γενόμενος οὐκ ἠμέλησε
τοῦ πονεῖν. τὴν μὲν οὖν ἰδέαν τῆς νόσου καὶ ὅτι
τὰ νεῦρα αὐτῷ ἐπεφρίκει, ἐν Ἱεροῖς βιβλίοις αὐτὸς
φράζει, τὰ δὲ βιβλία ταῦτα ἐφημερίδων ἐπέχει
τινὰ αὐτῷ λόγον, αἱ δὲ ἐφημερίδες ἀγαθαὶ διδάσκαλοι τοῦ περὶ παντὸς εὖ διαλέγεσθαι. ἐπὶ δὲ
582 τὸ σχεδιάζειν μὴ ἑπομένης αὐτῷ τῆς φύσεως
ἀκριβείας ἐπεμελήθη καὶ πρὸς τοὺς παλαιοὺς
ἔβλεψεν ἱκανῶς τε τῷ γονίμῳ ἴσχυσε κουφολο-
γίαν ἐξελὼν τοῦ λόγου. ἀποδημίαι δὲ Ἀριστείδου οὐ πολλαί, οὔτε γὰρ ἐς χάριν τῶν πολλῶν
διελέγετο οὔτε ἐκράτει χολῆς ἐπὶ τοὺς μὴ ξὺν
ἐπαίνῳ ἀκροωμένους, ἃ δέ γε ἐπῆλθεν ἔθνη, Ἰταλοί τέ εἰσι καὶ Ἑλλὰς καὶ ἡ πρὸς τῷ Δέλτα κατω-
κημένη Αἴγυπτος, οἳ χαλκοῦν ἔστησαν αὐτὸν ἐπὶ
τῆς κατὰ τὴν Σμύρναν ἀγορᾶς.

Οἰκιστὴν δὲ καὶ τὸν Ἀριστείδην τῆς Σμύρνης
εἰπεῖν οὐκ ἀλαζὼν ἔπαινος, ἀλλὰ δικαιότατός τε
καὶ ἀληθέστατος· τὴν γὰρ πόλιν ταύτην ἀφανισ-
θεῖσαν ὑπὸ σεισμῶν τε καὶ χασμάτων οὕτω τι
ὠλοφύρατο πρὸς τὸν Μάρκον, ὡς τῇ μὲν ἄλλῃ

---

[1] This is perhaps merely a foolish play on the word
εὐδαίμων, " happy."
[2] Aristeides i. 514.
[3] Quoted by Synesius, On Dreams 155 B.

214

Some say that he died at sea, others in Italy when he was on the eve of old age.

9. ARISTEIDES, whether he was the son of Eudaemon. or is himself to be so called,[1] was born at Hadriani. a town of no great size in Mysia. But he was educated at Athens when Herodes was at the height of his fame, and at Pergamon in Asia when Aristocles was teaching oratory there. Though he had poor health from his boyhood, he did not fail to work hard. The nature of his disease and the fact that he suffered from a palsy of the muscles he tells us himself in his *Sacred Discourses*.[2] These discourses served him in some sort as a diary, and such diaries are excellent teachers of the art of speaking well on any subject.[3] And since his natural talent was not in the line of extempore eloquence, he strove after extreme accuracy, and turned his attention to the ancient writers; he was well endowed with native ability and purified his style of any empty verbosity. Aristeides made few journeys, for he did not discourse with the aim of pleasing the crowd, and he could not control his anger against those who did not applaud his lectures. But the countries that he actually visited were Italy, Greece, and that part of Egypt which is situated near the Delta; and the people of this region set up a bronze statue [4] of him in the market-place of Smyrna.

To say that Aristeides founded Smyrna is no mere boastful eulogy but most just and true. For when this city had been blotted out by earthquakes and chasms that opened in the ground, he lamented its fate to Marcus in such moving words that the

---

[4] The inscription for this statue is preserved in the Museum at Verona.

μονωδίᾳ θαμὰ ἐπιστενάξαι τὸν βασιλέα, ἐπὶ δὲ
τῷ " ζέφυροι δὲ ἐρήμην καταπνέουσι " καὶ δάκρυα τῷ βιβλίῳ ἐπιστάξαι τὸν βασιλέα ξυνοικίαν
τε τῇ πόλει ἐκ τῶν τοῦ Ἀριστείδου ἐνδοσίμων
νεῦσαι. ἐτύγχανε δὲ καὶ ξυγγεγονὼς ἤδη τῷ
Μάρκῳ ὁ Ἀριστείδης ἐν Ἰωνίᾳ, ὡς γὰρ τοῦ
Ἐφεσίου Δαμιανοῦ ἤκουον, ἐπεδήμει μὲν ὁ αὐτοκράτωρ ἤδη τῇ Σμύρνῃ τρίτην ἡμέραν, τὸν δὲ
Ἀριστείδην οὔπω γιγνώσκων ἤρετο τοὺς Κυντιλίους, μὴ ἐν τῷ τῶν ἀσπαζομένων ὁμίλῳ παρ-
εωραμένος αὐτῷ ὁ ἀνὴρ εἴη, οἱ δὲ οὐδὲ αὐτοὶ ἔφασαν
ἑωρακέναι αὐτόν, οὐ γὰρ ἂν παρεῖναι τὸ μὴ οὐ
ξυστῆσαι, καὶ ἀφίκοντο τῆς ὑστεραίας τὸν Ἀριστείδην ἄμφω δορυφοροῦντες. προσειπὼν δὲ αὐτὸν ὁ αὐτοκράτωρ " διὰ τί σε " ἔφη " βραδέως
εἴδομεν; " καὶ ὁ Ἀριστείδης " θεώρημα," ἔφη
" ὦ βασιλεῦ, ἠσχόλει, γνώμη δὲ θεωροῦσά τι μὴ
ἀποκρεμαννύσθω οὗ ζητεῖ." ὑπερησθεὶς δὲ ὁ
αὐτοκράτωρ τῷ ἤθει τἀνδρὸς ὡς ἁπλοικωτάτῳ τε
καὶ σχολικωτάτῳ " πότε " ἔφη " ἀκροάσομαί
583 σου; " καὶ ὁ Ἀριστείδης " τήμερον " εἶπεν
" πρόβαλε καὶ αὔριον ἀκροῶ· οὐ γὰρ ἐσμὲν τῶν
ἐμούντων, ἀλλὰ τῶν ἀκριβούντων. ἐξέστω δέ,
ὦ βασιλεῦ, καὶ τοὺς γνωρίμους παρεῖναι τῇ ἀκροάσει." " ἐξέστω " ἦ δ᾽ ὁ Μάρκος, " δημοτικὸν
γάρ." εἰπόντος δὲ τοῦ Ἀριστείδου " δεδόσθω δὲ

---

[1] This monody or lament is extant.
[2] Either the Emperor was easily moved, or the rhythmical
effect of this sentence is lost on us.
[3] Literally " keynote."
[4] See above p. 559 and Athenaeus xiv. 649 D.
[5] This saying was later echoed by other sophists; cf.
Eunapius, *Life of Prohaeresius* p. 488; Synesius, *Dio* 56 c;

Emperor frequently groaned at other passages in the monody,[1] but when he came to the words: "She is a desert through which the west winds blow"[2] the Emperor actually shed tears over the pages, and in accordance with the impulse[3] inspired by Aristeides, he consented to rebuild the city. Now Aristeides had, as it happened, met Marcus once at an earlier time in Ionia. For as I was told by Damianus of Ephesus, the Emperor was visiting Smyrna and when three days had gone by without his having as yet made the acquaintance of Aristeides, he asked the brothers Quintilii[4] whether he had by chance overlooked the man in the throng of those who came to welcome him. But they said that they too had not seen him, for otherwise they would not have failed to present him; and next day they both arrived to escort Aristeides in state. The Emperor addressed him, and inquired: "Why did we have to wait so long to see you?" To which Aristeides replied: "A subject on which I was meditating kept me busy, and when the mind is absorbed in meditation it must not be distracted from the object of its search." The Emperor was greatly pleased with the man's personality, so unaffected was it and so devoted to study, and he asked: "When shall I hear you declaim?" "Propose the theme to-day," he replied, "and to-morrow come and hear me, for I am one of those who do not vomit their speeches but try to make them perfect.[5] Permit my students also, O Emperor, to be in the audience."

"They have my permission," said Marcus, "for that is democratic." And when Aristeides added:

Aristeides perhaps echoed Cicero, *Epist. ad Div.* xii. 2 "omnibus est visus vomere suo more, non dicere."

αὐτοῖς, ὦ βασιλεῦ, καὶ βοᾶν καὶ κροτεῖν, ὁπόσον
δύνανται," μειδιάσας ὁ αὐτοκράτωρ " τοῦτο "
ἔφη " ἐπὶ σοὶ κεῖται." οὐκ ἔγραψα τὴν μελετη-
θεῖσαν ὑπόθεσιν, ἐπειδὴ ἄλλοι ἄλλην φασίν, ἐκεῖνό γε μὴν πρὸς πάντων ὁμολογεῖται, τὸν Ἀριστείδην ἀρίστῃ φορᾷ ἐπὶ τοῦ Μάρκου χρήσασθαι
πόρρωθεν τῇ Σμύρνῃ ἑτοιμαζούσης τῆς τύχης τὸ
δι᾽ ἀνδρὸς τοιούτου δὴ ἀνοικισθῆναι. καὶ οὐ
φημὶ ταῦτα, ὡς οὐχὶ καὶ τοῦ βασιλέως ἀνοικί-
σαντος ἂν ἀπολωλυῖαν πόλιν, ἣν οὖσαν ἐθαύμασεν,
ἀλλ᾽ ὅτι αἱ βασίλειοί τε καὶ θεσπέσιοι φύσεις,
ἣν προσεγείρῃ αὐτὰς ξυμβουλία καὶ λόγος, ἀνα-
λάμπουσι μᾶλλον καὶ πρὸς τὸ ποιεῖν εὖ ξὺν ὁρμῇ
φέρονται.

Δαμιανοῦ κἀκεῖνα ἤκουον, τὸν σοφιστὴν τοῦτον
διαβάλλειν μὲν τοὺς αὐτοσχεδίους ἐν ταῖς διαλέξεσι, θαυμάζειν δὲ οὕτω τὸ σχεδιάζειν, ὡς καὶ
ἰδίᾳ ἐκπονεῖν αὐτὸ ἐν δωματίῳ ἑαυτὸν καθειργ-
νύντα, ἐξεπόνει δὲ κῶλον ἐκ κώλου καὶ νόημα
ἐκ νοήματος ἐπανακυκλῶν. τουτὶ δὲ ἡγώμεθα
μασωμένου μᾶλλον ἢ ἐσθίοντος, αὐτοσχέδιος γὰρ
γλώττης εὐροούσης ἀγώνισμα. κατηγοροῦσι δὲ
τοῦ Ἀριστείδου τινὲς ὡς εὐτελὲς εἰπόντος προοίμιον ἐπὶ τῶν μισθοφόρων τῶν ἀπαιτουμένων
τὴν γῆν, ἄρξασθαι γὰρ δὴ αὐτὸν τῆς ὑποθέσεως
ταύτης ὧδε· " οὐ παύσονται οὗτοι οἱ ἄνθρωποι
παρέχοντες ἡμῖν πράγματα." ἐπιλαμβάνονται δέ
τινες καὶ ἀκμῆς τοῦ ἀνδρὸς ἐπὶ τοῦ παραιτου-

---

[1] A scholiast on Hermogenes explains that lands had been
assigned instead of pay to certain mercenaries; after they
had founded a city they were ordered to take their pay and
give up the land.

" Grant them leave, O Emperor, to shout and applaud
as loud as they can," the Emperor smiled and
retorted : " That rests with you." I have not given
the theme of this declamation, because the accounts
of its title vary, but in this at least all agree, that
Aristeides in speaking before Marcus employed an
admirable impetuosity of speech, and that far ahead
fate was preparing for Smyrna to be rebuilt through
the efforts of this gifted man. And when I say
this I do not imply that the Emperor would not of
his own accord have restored the ruined city which
he had admired when it was still flourishing, but I
say it because even dispositions that are truly royal
and above the ordinary, when incited by good advice
and by eloquence, shine out more brightly and press
on with ardour to noble deeds.

This too I have heard from Damianus, that though
in his discourses this sophist used to disparage extempore speakers, nevertheless he so greatly admired
extempore eloquence that he used to shut himself
up in a room and practise it in private. And he
used to work it out by evolving it clause by clause
and thought by thought. But this process we must
regard as chewing rather than eating, for extempore
eloquence is the crowning achievement of a fluent
and facile tongue. There are some who accuse
Aristeides of having made a weak and ineffective
prooemium when his theme was : " The mercenaries
are ordered to give back their lands." [1] They say
that he began the argument with these words :
" These persons will never cease to make trouble
for us." And some criticize the man's vigorous
language [2] when he spoke in the rôle of the Spartan

[2] For this technical term see Glossary.

584 μένου τὸν τειχισμὸν τῆς Λακεδαίμονος, εἴρηται
δὲ ὧδε· "μὴ γὰρ δὴ ἐν τείχει ἐπιπτήξαιμεν
ὀρτύγων ἐναψάμενοι[1] φύσιν." ἐπιλαμβάνονται καὶ
παροιμίας ὡς ταπεινῶς προσερριμμένης, ἐπιδια-
βάλλων γὰρ τὸν Ἀλέξανδρον ὡς πατρῴζοντα τὴν
ἐν τοῖς πράγμασι δεινότητα, τοῦ πατρὸς ἔφη τὸ
παιδίον εἶναι. οἱ αὐτοὶ κατηγοροῦσι καὶ σκώμματος, ἐπειδὴ τοὺς Ἀριμασποὺς τοὺς μονομμά-
τους ἔφη ξυγγενεῖς εἶναι τοῦ Φιλίππου, καίτοι
καὶ τοῦ Δημοσθένους ἀπολελογημένου τοῖς Ἕλλησιν πρὸς τὸν τραγικὸν πίθηκον καὶ τὸν ἀρου-
ραῖον Οἰνόμαον. ἀλλὰ μὴ ἐκ τούτων τὸν Ἀριστείδην, δηλούτω δὲ αὐτὸν ὅ τε Ἰσοκράτης ὁ τοὺς
Ἀθηναίους ἐξάγων τῆς θαλάττης καὶ ὁ ἐπιτιμῶν
τῷ Καλλιξείνῳ ἐπὶ τῷ μὴ θάπτειν τοὺς δέκα καὶ
οἱ βουλευόμενοι περὶ τῶν ἐν Σικελίᾳ καὶ ὁ μὴ
λαβὼν Αἰσχίνης παρὰ τοῦ Κερσοβλέπτου τὸν
585 σῖτον, καὶ οἱ παραιτούμενοι τὰς σπονδὰς μετὰ τὸ
κτεῖναι τὰ γένη, ἐν ᾗ μάλιστα ὑποθέσεων ἀνα-
διδάσκει ἡμᾶς, πῶς ἄν τις ἀσφαλῶς κεκινδυνευ-
μένας τε καὶ τραγικὰς ἐννοίας μεταχειρίσαιτο.
καὶ πλείους ἑτέρας ὑποθέσεις οἶδα εὐπαιδευσίαν
ἐνδεικνυμένας τοῦ ἀνδρὸς τούτου καὶ ἰσχὺν καὶ

---

[1] ἀναψάμενοι Kayser; ἐναψάμενοι Cobet.

---

[1] For this theme see above, p. 514.
[2] Philip had lost an eye at the siege of Methone 352 B.C.
The fabulous Arismaspi are described by Herodotus iv. 27.
[3] *On the Crown* 242. "Tragic ape" was a proverbial
phrase for an arrogant person. Oenomaus was the hero of a
lost play of Sophocles, and these were sneering references to
the career of Aeschines as a travelling actor.
[4] This theme is based on Isocrates, *On the Peace* 64.
[5] This favourite theme is based on a fictitious situation in

who deprecated the fortifying of Lacedaemon.[1]
What he said was this : " May we never take on the
nature of quails and cower within walls." They also
criticize a proverbial phrase of his, on the ground
that he had thrown it in casually with an effect of
vulgarity.   I mean that, when attacking Alexander
for merely imitating his father's energy in affairs, he
said : " He is a chip of the old block."   These same
critics also condemn a jest of his when he said that
the one-eyed Arimaspi were Philip's kinsmen.[2]
And yet even Demosthenes defended his policy
to the Greeks against one whom he called "the
tragic ape," and " the rustic Oenomaus." [3]   But do
not judge of Aristeides from these extracts, but
rather estimate his powers in such speeches as
" Isocrates tries to wean the Athenians from their
empire of the sea" [4] ; or "The speaker upbraids
Callixenus for not having granted burial to the
Ten " [5] ; or " The deliberations on the state of affairs
in Sicily " [6] ; or " Aeschines, when he had not
received the corn from Cersobleptes " [7] ; or "They
reject the treaty of alliance after their children have
been murdered." [8]   It is in this last argument above
all that he teaches us how, without making any slip,
one may handle daring and tragic conceptions.
And I know several other arguments of his that
demonstrate the man's erudition, force and power
of characterization, and it is by these that he ought

which Callixenus advises the Athenians not to bury the
generals who were executed after the battle of Arginusae.
It is quoted by Hermogenes and Syrianus.
  [6] This theme is quoted by Hermogenes.
  [7] Apsines states this theme rather differently ; it is
apparently based on Polyaenus vii. 32.
  [8] This theme is described more fully below, p. 593.

ἦθος, ἀφ' ὧν μᾶλλον αὐτὸν θεωρητέον, ἢ εἴ που
καὶ παρέπτυσέ τι ἐς φιλοτιμίαν ἐκπεσών. καὶ
τεχνικώτατος δὲ σοφιστῶν ὁ Ἀριστείδης ἐγένετο
καὶ πολὺς ἐν θεωρήμασι, ὅθεν καὶ τοῦ σχεδιάζειν
ἀπηνέχθη, τὸ γὰρ κατὰ θεωρίαν βούλεσθαι προ-
άγειν πάντα ἀσχολεῖ τὴν γνώμην καὶ ἀπαλλάττει
τοῦ ἑτοίμου.

Ἀποθανεῖν δὲ τὸν Ἀριστείδην οἱ μὲν οἴκοι
γράφουσιν, οἱ δὲ ἐν Ἰωνίᾳ ἔτη βιώσαντα οἱ μὲν
ἑξήκοντά φασιν, οἱ δὲ ἀγχοῦ τῶν ἑβδομήκοντα.

ιʹ. Ἀδριανὸν δὲ τὸν Φοίνικα Τύρος μὲν ἤνεγκεν, Ἀθῆναι δὲ ἤσκησαν. ὡς γὰρ τῶν ἐμαυτοῦ
διδασκάλων ἤκουον, ἀφίκετο μὲν ἐς αὐτὰς κατὰ
Ἡρώδην, φύσεως δὲ ἰσχὺν σοφιστικωτάτην ἐνδεικνύμενος καὶ οὐκ ἄδηλος ὢν ὡς ἐπὶ μέγα ἥξοι·
ἐφοίτησε μὲν γὰρ τῷ Ἡρώδῃ ὀκτὼ καὶ δέκα
ἴσως γεγονὼς ἔτη καὶ ταχέως ἀξιωθείς, ὧν Σκέ-
πτος τε καὶ Ἀμφικλῆς ἠξιοῦντο, ἐνεγράφη καὶ
τῇ τοῦ Κλεψυδρίου ἀκροάσει. τὸ δὲ Κλεψύδριον
ὧδε εἶχεν· τῶν τοῦ Ἡρώδου ἀκροατῶν δέκα οἱ
ἀρετῆς ἀξιούμενοι ἐπεσιτίζοντο τῇ ἐς πάντας
ἀκροάσει κλεψύδραν ξυμμεμετρημένην [1] ἐς ἑκατὸν
ἔπη, ἃ διῄει ἀποτάδην ὁ Ἡρώδης παρῃτημένος
τὸν ἐκ τῶν ἀκροατῶν ἔπαινον καὶ μόνου γεγονὼς
τοῦ λέγειν. παραδεδωκότος δὲ αὐτοῦ τοῖς γνω-

---

[1] Schmid, *Atticismus* 194, suggests ξυμμεμετρημένοι ὅσον.

---

[1] Two brief declamations ascribed to Hadrian are extant
[2] "A lecture timed by the clock," cp. p. 594. Rohde
thinks that the meal is figurative, and that it was a feast
of reason.

to be estimated rather than by passages in which he has drivelled somewhat and has fallen into affectation. Moreover, Aristeides was of all the sophists most deeply versed in his art, and his strength lay in the elaborate cogitation of a theme; for which reason he refrained from extempore speaking. For the desire not to produce anything except after long cogitation keeps the mind too busy and robs it of alertness.

Some writers record that Aristeides died at home, others say that it was in Ionia; again some say that he reached the age of sixty, others that he was nearly seventy.

10. HADRIAN [1] the Phoenician was born at Tyre, but he was trained in rhetoric at Athens. For, as I used to hear from my own teachers, he came to Athens in the time of Herodes and there displayed a great natural talent for sophistic, and it was generally held that he would rise to greatness in his profession. For he began to attend the school of Herodes when he was perhaps eighteen years old, was very soon admitted to the same privileges as Sceptus and Amphicles, and was enrolled among the pupils belonging to the Clepsydrion. Now the Clepsydrion was conducted in the following manner. After the general lecture which was open to all, ten of the pupils of Herodes, that is to say those who were proved worthy of a reward for excellence, used to dine for a period limited by a water-clock [2] timed to last through a hundred verses; and these verses Herodes used to expound with copious comments, nor would he allow any applause from his hearers, but was wholly intent on what he was saying. And since he had enjoined on his pupils not to be idle

586 ρίμοις τὸ μηδὲ τὸν τοῦ πότου καιρὸν ἀνιέναι,
ἀλλὰ κἀκεῖ τι ἐπισπουδάζειν τῷ οἴνῳ ξυνέπινε
μὲν ὁ Ἀδριανὸς τοῖς ἀπὸ τῆς κλεψύδρας ὡς κοι-
νωνὸς μεγάλου ἀπορρήτου, λόγου δὲ αὐτοῖς περὶ
τῆς ἑκάστου τῶν σοφιστῶν ἰδέας προβαίνοντος
παρελθὼν ἐς μέσους ὁ Ἀδριανὸς " ἐγὼ " ἔφη
" ὑπογράψω τοὺς χαρακτῆρας οὐ κομματίων ἀπο-
μνημονεύων ἢ νοιδίων ἢ κώλων ἢ ῥυθμῶν, ἀλλ'
ἐς μίμησιν ἐμαυτὸν καθιστὰς καὶ τὰς ἁπάντων
ἰδέας ἀποσχεδιάζων σὺν εὐροίᾳ καὶ ἐφιεὶς τῇ
γλώττῃ." παραλιπόντος δὲ αὐτοῦ τὸν Ἡρώδην
ὁ μὲν Ἀμφικλῆς ἤρετο τοῦ χάριν τὸν διδάσκαλον
αὐτῶν παρέλθοι αὐτός τε ἐρῶν τῆς ἰδέας ἐκείνους
τε ἰδὼν ἐρῶντας " ὅτι " ἔφη " οὗτοι μὲν οἷοι
καὶ μεθύοντι παραδοῦναι μίμησιν, Ἡρώδην δὲ
τὸν βασιλέα τῶν λόγων ἀγαπητὸν ἦν ἄοινός τε
καὶ νήφων ὑποκρίνωμαι." ταῦτα ἀπαγγελθέντα
τῷ Ἡρώδῃ διέχεεν αὐτὸν ὄντα καὶ ἄλλως ἥττω
εὐδοξίας. ἐπήγγειλε δὲ τῷ Ἡρώδῃ καὶ ἀκρόασιν
σχεδίου λόγου νεάζων ἔτι, καὶ ὁ Ἡρώδης οὐχ, ὡς
διαβάλλουσί τινες, βασκαίνων τε καὶ τωθάζων,
ἀλλ' ἀπὸ τοῦ διακειμένου τε καὶ ἵλεω ἀκροασάμενος ἐπέρρωσε τὸν νεανίαν εἰπὼν ἐπὶ πᾶσιν
" κολοσσοῦ ταῦτα μεγάλα σπαράγματ' ἂν εἴη,"
ἅμα μὲν διορθούμενος αὐτὸν ὡς ὑφ' ἡλικίας δι-
εσπασμένον τε καὶ μὴ ξυγκείμενον, ἅμα δὲ ἐπαινῶν ὡς μεγαλόφωνόν τε καὶ μεγαλογνώμονα.

even when it was the hour for drinking, but at that time also to pursue some sort of study over their wine, Hadrian used to drink with the pupils of the clepsydra as their partner in a great and mysterious rite. Now a discussion was once going on about the style of all the sophists, when Hadrian came forward in their midst, and said: "I will now give a sketch of their types of style, not by quoting from memory brief phrases of theirs or smart sayings, or clauses or rhythmical effects. But I will undertake to imitate them, and will reproduce extempore the style of every one of them, with an easy flow of words and giving the rein to my tongue." But in doing this he left out Herodes, and Amphicles asked him to explain why he had omitted their own teacher, seeing that he himself was enamoured of his style of eloquence, and saw that they were likewise enamoured. "Because," said he, "these fellows are the sort that lend themselves to imitation, even when one is drunk. But as for Herodes, the prince of eloquence, I should be thankful if I could mimic him when I have had no wine and am sober." When this was reported to Herodes it gave him the keenest pleasure, naturally, since he never could resist his longing for approbation. When he was still a mere youth Hadrian invited Herodes to hear him make a speech extempore. Herodes listened to him, not as some people unjustly accuse him, in an envious or scoffing spirit, but with his usual calm and kindly bearing, and afterwards he encouraged the youth, and ended by saying: "These might well be great fragments of a colossus." Thus while he tried to correct his disjointed and ill-constructed style as a fault of youth, he applauded the grandeur both of his words and

καὶ λόγον τῷ Ἡρώδῃ ἀποθανόντι ἐπεφθέγξατο
ἐπάξιον τοῦ ἀνδρός, ὡς ἐς δάκρυα ἐκκληθῆναι
τοὺς Ἀθηναίους ἐν τῇ τοῦ λόγου ἀκροάσει.

Μεστὸς δὲ οὕτω παρρησίας ἐπὶ τὸν θρόνον
παρῆλθε τὸν Ἀθήνησιν, ὡς προοίμιόν οἱ γενέσθαι
τῆς πρὸς αὐτοὺς διαλέξεως μὴ τὴν ἐκείνων σοφίαν,
587 ἀλλὰ τὴν ἑαυτοῦ, ἤρξατο γὰρ δὴ ὧδε· " πάλιν
ἐκ Φοινίκης γράμματα." τὸ μὲν δὴ προοίμιον
τοῦτο ὑπερπνέοντος ἦν τοὺς Ἀθηναίους καὶ διδόντος τι αὐτοῖς ἀγαθὸν μᾶλλον ἢ λαμβάνοντος,
μεγαλοπρεπέστατα δὲ τοῦ Ἀθήνησι θρόνου ἐπεμελήθη ἐσθῆτα μὲν πλείστου ἀξίαν ἀμπεχόμενος,
ἐξηρτημένος δὲ τὰς θαυμασιωτέρας τῶν λίθων καὶ
κατιὼν μὲν ἐπὶ τὰς σπουδὰς ἐπ' ἀργυροχαλίνου
ὀχήματος, ἐπεὶ δὲ σπουδάσειε, ζηλωτὸς αὖ ἐπ-
ανιὼν ξὺν πομπῇ τοῦ πανταχόθεν Ἑλληνικοῦ.
ἤδη¹ γὰρ ἐθεράπευον αὐτόν, ὥσπερ τὰ γένη τῆς
Ἐλευσῖνος ἱεροφάντην λαμπρῶς ἱερουργοῦντα.
ὑπεποιεῖτο δὲ αὐτοὺς καὶ παιδιαῖς καὶ πότοις
καὶ θήραις καὶ κοινωνίᾳ πανηγύρεων Ἑλληνικῶν,
ἄλλα ἄλλῳ ξυννεάζων, ὅθεν διέκειντο πρὸς αὐτὸν
ὡς πρὸς πατέρα παῖδες ἡδύ τε καὶ πρᾶον καὶ
ξυνδιαφέροντα αὐτοῖς τὸ Ἑλληνικὸν σκίρτημα.
ἐγώ τοι καὶ δακρύοντας αὐτῶν ἐνίους οἶδα, ὁπότε
ἐς μνήμην τοῦ ἀνδρὸς τούτου καθίσταιντο, καὶ
τοὺς μὲν τὸ φθέγμα ὑποκοριζομένους, τοὺς δὲ
τὸ βάδισμα, τοὺς δὲ τὸ εὔσχημον τῆς στολῆς.

¹ οἶδε Kayser; ἤδη Jahn.

---

¹ " Letters " in a double sense ; the Greek alphabet was
supposed to have come from Phoenicia.

his ideas. When Herodes died Hadrian delivered a funeral oration which did full justice to the man, so that the Athenians were moved to tears while they listened to his speech.

So full of self-confidence was Hadrian when he ascended the chair of rhetoric at Athens, that in the prooemium of his address to the Athenians he dilated not on their wisdom but on his own, for he began by announcing: "Once again letters have come from Phoenicia."[1] In fact his prooemium was in the tone of one who breathed on a higher plane than the Athenians and bestowed a benefit on them rather than received it. He performed the duties of the chair at Athens with the greatest ostentation, wore very expensive clothes, bedecked himself with precious gems, and used to go down to his lectures in a carriage with silver-mounted bridles; and always after the lecture he would go home envied of all, escorted by those who loved Hellenic culture, from all parts of the world. They went so far as to reverence him just as the tribes of Eleusis reverence the initiating priest when he is ceremoniously performing the rites. Then, too, he won them over by giving games and wine-parties and hunts, and by sharing with them the Hellenic festivals; thus adapting himself to their youthfulness and all its varied interests, so that they felt towards him as sons feel towards a father who is amiable and indulgent, and with them keeps up the most boisterous Greek dance. Indeed I myself know that some of them used actually to shed tears when they remembered this sophist, and that some would try to imitate his accent, others his walk, or the elegance of his attire.

Ἐπαχθεῖσαν δὲ αὐτῷ καὶ φονικὴν αἰτίαν ὧδε
ἀπέφυγεν· ἦν Ἀθήνησιν ἀνθρώπιον οὐκ ἀγύ-
μναστον τοῦ περὶ τοὺς σοφιστὰς δρόμου· τούτῳ
ἀμφορέα μέν τις οἴνου προσάγων ἢ ὄψα ἢ ἐσθῆτα
ἢ ἀργύριον εὐμεταχειρίστῳ ἐχρῆτο, καθάπερ οἱ
τὰ πεινῶντα τῶν θρεμμάτων τῷ θαλλῷ ἄγοντες,
εἰ δὲ ἀμελοῖτο, φιλολοιδόρως εἶχε καὶ ὑλάκτει.
588 τῷ μὲν οὖν Ἀδριανῷ προσκεκρούκει διὰ τὴν
εὐχέρειαν τοῦ ἤθους, Χρῆστον δὲ τὸν ἐκ τοῦ Βυζαντίου σοφιστὴν ἐθεράπευεν, καὶ ὁ μὲν Ἀδριανὸς ἐκαρτέρει τὰ ἐξ αὐτοῦ πάντα, δήγματα κόρεων
τὰς ἐκ τῶν τοιούτων λοιδορίας καλῶν, οἱ γνώριμοι δὲ οὐκ ἐνεγκόντες παρεκελεύσαντο τοῖς
ἑαυτῶν οἰκέταις παίειν αὐτόν, καὶ ἀνοιδησάντων
αὐτῷ τῶν σπλάγχνων ἐν ἡμέρᾳ τριακοστῇ ἀπέθανε παρασχών τινα καὶ αὐτὸς τῷ θανάτῳ λόγον,
ἐπειδὴ ἀκράτου νοσῶν ἔσπασεν. οἱ δὲ προσήκοντες τῷ τεθνεῶτι γράφονται τὸν σοφιστὴν
φόνου παρὰ τῷ τῆς Ἑλλάδος ἄρχοντι ὡς ἕνα
Ἀθηναίων, ἐπειδὴ φυλή τε ἦν αὐτῷ καὶ δῆμος
Ἀθήνησιν, ὁ δὲ ἀπέγνω τὴν αἰτίαν ὡς μήτε ταῖς
ἑαυτοῦ χερσὶ μήτε ταῖς τῶν ἑαυτοῦ δούλων τετυ-
πτηκότος τὸν τεθνάναι λεγόμενον. ξυνήρατο δὲ
αὐτῷ τῆς ἀπολογίας πρῶτον μὲν τὸ Ἑλληνικὸν
τίνας οὐχὶ ἀφιέντες ὑπὲρ αὐτοῦ φωνὰς δακρύοις
ἅμα, ἔπειτα ἡ τοῦ ἰατροῦ μαρτυρία ἡ ἐπὶ τῷ
οἴνῳ.

Κατὰ δὲ τοὺς χρόνους, οὓς ὁ αὐτοκράτωρ Μάρ-

---

¹ An echo of Plato, *Phaedrus* 230 D. Socrates says that
Phaedrus has enticed him into the country by the promise
of hearing a discourse read, as men wave branches to entice
hungry animals to follow them.

A charge of murder was brought against him, but he escaped it in the following way. There was in Athens a fellow of no account who had had some training in the curriculum of the sophists. One could easily keep him in a good humour by bestowing on him a jar of wine or a dainty dish, or clothes, or silver, just as men entice hungry animals by waving a branch[1] before them; but if he was ignored he would indulge in abuse and bark like a dog. He had fallen foul of Hadrian who disliked him for the levity of his manners, but he was the devoted disciple of Chrestus the sophist, of Byzantium. Hadrian used to put up with all his insults, and would call the slanders of such men "flea-bites"; but his pupils could not tolerate the behaviour of the man and gave orders to their own slaves to thrash him. This brought on a swelling of the intestines, and thirty days later he died, but not without having himself contributed to cause his own death, since during his illness he drank greedily of undiluted wine. But the relatives of the dead man charged the sophist with murder in the court of the proconsul of Greece, as being an Athenian citizen, since both his tribe and his deme were at Athens. He however denied the charge, alleging that neither with his own hands or the hands of any of his slaves had he struck the man who was said to have died. He was assisted in his defence, first by the whole crowd of Hellenes who made every possible plea[2] in his behalf, weeping the while, and secondly by the evidence of the doctor about the wine.

Now at the time when the Emperor Marcus

[2] An echo of Demosthenes, *On the Crown* 195.

κος Ἀθήναζε ὑπὲρ μυστηρίων ἐστάλη, ἐκράτει
μὲν ἤδη τοῦ τῶν σοφιστῶν θρόνου ὁ ἀνὴρ οὗτος,
ἐν μέρει δὲ ὁ Μάρκος τῆς τῶν Ἀθηνῶν ἱστορίας
ἔθετο μηδὲ τὴν ἐκείνου σοφίαν ἀγνοῆσαι· καὶ
γὰρ δὴ καὶ ἐπέταξεν αὐτὸν τοῖς νέοις οὐκ ἀκροάσει βασανίσας, ἀλλὰ ξυνθέμενος τῇ περὶ αὐτοῦ
φήμῃ. Σεβήρου δὲ ἀνδρὸς ὑπάτου διαβάλλοντος
αὐτὸν ὡς τὰς σοφιστικὰς ὑποθέσεις ἐκβακχεύοντα
διὰ τὸ ἐρρῶσθαι πρὸς τοὺς ἀγῶνας, ἔλεγχον τούτου ποιούμενος ὁ Μάρκος προὔβαλε μὲν αὐτῷ
τὸν Ὑπερείδην τὸν ἐς μόνας ἐπιστρέφοντα τὰς
589 Δημοσθένους γνώμας, ὅτε δὴ ἐν Ἐλατείᾳ Φίλιππος ἦν, ὁ δὲ οὕτως τὸν ἀγῶνα εὐηνίως διέθετο,
ὡς μηδὲ τοῦ Πολέμωνος ῥοίζου λείπεσθαι δόξαι.
ἀγασθεὶς δὲ αὐτὸν ὁ αὐτοκράτωρ ἐπὶ μέγα ἦρε
δωρεαῖς τε καὶ δώροις. καλῶ δὲ δωρεὰς μὲν
τάς τε σιτήσεις καὶ τὰς προεδρίας καὶ τὰς ἀτελείας καὶ τὸ ἱερᾶσθαι καὶ ὅσα ἄλλα λαμπρύνει
ἄνδρας, δῶρα δὲ χρυσὸν ἄργυρον ἵππους ἀνδράποδα καὶ ὅσα ἑρμηνεύει πλοῦτον, ὧν αὐτόν τε
ἐνέπλησε καὶ γένος τὸ ἐκείνου πάντας.

Κατασχὼν δὲ καὶ τὸν ἄνω θρόνον οὕτως τὴν
Ῥώμην ἐς ἑαυτὸν ἐπέστρεψεν, ὡς καὶ τοῖς ἀξυνέτοις
γλώττης Ἑλλάδος ἔρωτα παρασχεῖν ἀκροάσεως.
ἠκροῶντο δὲ ὥσπερ εὐστομούσης ἀηδόνος, τὴν

---

[1] See above, p. 563.

[2] This was probably Claudius Severus the teacher of
Marcus Aurelius, consul for the second time in 173. For an
inscription in which Hadrian honours Severus in elegiacs *cf.*
E. Groag, in *Wien. St.* 24 (1902), pp. 261 ff.

[3] A similar theme is mentioned by Apsines 219 ; it has no
historical basis ; *cf.* Demosthenes, *On the Crown* 169-179.

[4] This phrase always means the chair at Rome.

[5] An echo of Sophocles, *Oedipus at Colonus* 18.

travelled to Athens to be initiated into the Mysteries,[1] this sophist was already in possession of the chair of rhetoric at Athens, and among the things that Marcus wished to investigate at Athens he counted this, that he would inform himself as to the professional skill of Hadrian. For he had indeed appointed him to lecture to the Athenian youth without testing him by hearing him lecture, but in acquiescence with the general rumour about him. Now the consular Severus[2] was attacking Hadrian for putting too much passion and frenzy into his purely sophistic arguments, because his real strength lay in forensic pleading. Therefore Marcus, who wished to put this to the proof, proposed as the theme for declamation " Hypereides, when Philip is at Elatea, pays heed only to the counsels of Demosthenes."[3] Whereupon Hadrian guided the reins of the argument so skilfully that he proved himself fully equal to Polemo in force and vigour. The Emperor admired him greatly, and exalted him to the skies by grants and gifts. By grants, I mean the right to dine at the expense of the state, a seat of honour at the public games, immunity from taxes, priestly offices, and all else that sheds a lustre on men ; and by gifts I mean gold and silver, horses, slaves, and all the outward signs of wealth with which he lavishly endowed not only Hadrian but his family also, one and all.

When he was promoted to the higher chair[4] of rhetoric he so successfully drew the attention of all Rome to himself that he inspired even those who did not know the Greek language with an ardent desire to hear him declaim. And they listened to him as to a sweet-voiced nightingale,[5] struck with

231

εὐγλωττίαν ἐκπεπληγμένοι καὶ τὸ σχῆμα καὶ τὸ
εὔστροφον τοῦ φθέγματος καὶ τοὺς πεζῇ τε καὶ ξὺν
ᾠδῇ ῥυθμούς. ὁπότε οὖν σπουδάζοιεν περὶ τὰς
ἐγκυκλίους θέας, ὀρχηστῶν δὲ αὗται τὸ ἐπίπαν,
φανέντος ἂν περὶ τὴν σκηνὴν τοῦ τῆς ἀκροάσεως
ἀγγέλου ἐξανίσταντο μὲν οἱ[1] ἀπὸ τῆς συγκλήτου
βουλῆς, ἐξανίσταντο δὲ τῶν δημοσίᾳ ἱππευόντων
οὐχ οἱ τὰ Ἑλλήνων σπουδάζοντες μόνον, ἀλλὰ καὶ
ὁπόσοι τὴν ἑτέραν γλῶτταν ἐπαιδεύοντο ἐν τῇ
Ῥώμῃ καὶ δρόμῳ ἐχώρουν ἐς τὸ Ἀθήναιον ὁρμῆς
μεστοὶ καὶ τοὺς βάδην πορευομένους κακίζοντες.

Νοσοῦντι δὲ αὐτῷ κατὰ τὴν Ῥώμην, ὅτε δὴ καὶ
590 ἐτελεύτα, ἐψηφίσατο μὲν τὰς ἐπιστολὰς ὁ Κόμ-
μοδος ξὺν ἀπολογίᾳ τοῦ μὴ καὶ θᾶττον, ὁ δὲ
ἐπιθειάσας μὲν ταῖς Μούσαις, ὥσπερ εἰώθει, προσ-
κυνήσας δὲ τὰς βασιλείους δέλτους τὴν ψυχὴν
πρὸς αὐταῖς ἀφῆκεν ἐνταφίῳ τῇ τιμῇ χρησάμενος·
ἐτελεύτα δὲ ἀμφὶ τὰ ὀγδοήκοντα ἔτη, οὕτω τι
εὐδόκιμος, ὡς καὶ πολλοῖς γόης δόξαι· ὅτι μὲν οὖν
ἀνὴρ πεπαιδευμένος οὐκ ἄν ποτε ἐς γοήτων ὑπαχ-
θείη τέχνας, ἱκανῶς ἐν τοῖς ὑπὲρ Διονυσίου λόγοις
εἴρηκα, ὁ δέ, οἶμαι, τερατευόμενος ἐν ταῖς ὑποθέ-
σεσι περὶ τὰ τῶν μάγων ἤθη τὴν ἐπωνυμίαν ταύτην
παρ' αὐτῶν ἔσπασεν. διαβάλλουσι δὲ αὐτὸν ὡς καὶ
ἀναιδῆ τὸ ἦθος, πέμψαι μὲν γὰρ αὐτῷ τινα τῶν
γνωρίμων ἰχθῦς διακειμένους ἐπὶ δίσκου ἀργυροῦ

---

[1] οἱ Cobet adds.

---

[1] For this *canticum* at the close of a speech see Glossary,
s.v. ᾠδή.
[2] Latin; the Athenaeum at Rome was a school founded
by the Emperor Hadrian.

admiration of his facile tongue, his well-modulated
and flexible voice, and his rhythms, whether in prose
or when he sang in recitative.[1] So much so, that,
when they were attending shows in which the vulgar
delight—these were, generally speaking, perform-
ances of dancers—a messenger had only to appear
in the theatre to announce that Hadrian was going
to declaim, when even the members of the Senate
would rise from their sitting, and the members of
the equestrian order would rise, not only those who
were devoted to Hellenic culture, but also those
who were studying the other language[2] at Rome;
and they would set out on the run to the Athenaeum,
overflowing with enthusiasm, and upbraiding those
who were going there at a walking pace.

When he lay ill at Rome and was in fact dying,
Commodus appointed him Imperial Secretary, and
made excuses for not having done so sooner, whereupon Hadrian invoked the Muses, as was his wont,
saluted reverently the Emperor's rescript, and
breathed out his soul over it, thus making of that
honour his funeral shroud. He was about eighty
when he died, and had attained to such high honour
that many actually believed him to be a magician.
But in my account of Dionysius I have said enough
to show that a well-educated man would never be
led astray into the practice of magic arts. But I
suppose it was because he used to tell marvellous
tales in his declamations about the customs of the
magicians that he drew down on himself from his
hearers this sort of appellation. They slander him
too in saying that he had shameless manners because,
when one of his pupils sent him a present of fish
lying on a silver plate embossed with gold, he was

πεποικιλμένου χρυσῷ, τὸν δὲ ὑπερησθέντα τῷ
δίσκῳ μήτε ἀποδοῦναι καὶ ἀποκρίνασθαι τῷ πέμ-
ψαντι " εὖγε, ὅτι καὶ τοὺς ἰχθῦς." τουτὶ δὲ
διατριβῆς μὲν ἔνεκα παῖξαι λέγεται πρός τινα τῶν
ἑαυτοῦ γνωρίμων, ὃν ἤκουε μικροπρεπῶς τῷ
πλούτῳ χρώμενον, τὸν δὲ ἄργυρον ἀποδοῦναι
σωφρονίσας τὸν ἀκροατὴν τῷ ἀστεισμῷ.

Ὁ δὲ σοφιστὴς οὗτος πολὺς μὲν περὶ τὰς ἐννοίας
καὶ λαμπρὸς καὶ τὰς διασκευὰς τῶν ὑποθέσεων
ποικιλώτατος ἐκ τῆς τραγῳδίας τοῦτο ᾑρηκώς, οὐ
μὴν τεταγμένος γε, οὐδὲ τῇ τέχνῃ ἑπόμενος, τὴν δὲ
παρασκευὴν τῆς λέξεως ἀπὸ τῶν ἀρχαίων σοφιστῶν
περιεβάλλετο ἤχῳ προσάγων μᾶλλον ἢ κρότῳ. πολλαχοῦ δὲ τῆς μεγαλοφωνίας ἐξέπεσεν ἀταμιεύτως
τῇ τραγῳδίᾳ χρησάμενος.

ιαʹ. Τὸν δὲ Βυζάντιον σοφιστὴν Χρῆστον
ἀδικεῖ ἡ Ἑλλὰς ἀμελοῦντες ἀνδρός, ὃς ἄριστα μὲν
591 Ἑλλήνων ὑπὸ Ἡρώδου ἐπαιδεύθη, πολλοὺς δὲ
ἐπαίδευσε καὶ θαυμασίους ἄνδρας, ὧν ἐγένετο
Ἱππόδρομός τε ὁ σοφιστὴς καὶ Φιλίσκος καὶ
Ἰσαγόρας ὁ τῆς τραγῳδίας ποιητὴς ῥήτορές τε
εὐδόκιμοι Νικομήδης ὁ ἐκ τοῦ Περγάμου καὶ
Ἀκύλας ὁ ἐκ τῆς ἑῴου Γαλατίας καὶ Ἀρισταίνετος
ὁ Βυζάντιος καὶ τῶν ἐλλογίμως φιλοσοφησάντων
Κάλλαισχρός τε ὁ Ἀθηναῖος καὶ ὁ ἐπὶ βωμῷ
Σῶσπις καὶ πλείους ἕτεροι λόγου ἄξιοι. παιδεύ-
οντι δὲ αὐτῷ κατὰ τοὺς Ἀδριανοῦ τοῦ σοφιστοῦ
καιροὺς ἑκατὸν ἔμμισθοι ἀκροαταὶ ἦσαν καὶ ἄριστοι
τούτων, οὓς εἶπον. Ἀδριανοῦ δὲ καθιδρυθέντος

---

[1] Nothing more is known of this sophist.
[2] He was priest at the sacrifices, perhaps at the public
games.

enchanted with the plate and so did not return it, and in acknowledging the present to the sender, he said: " It was indeed kind of you to send the fish as well." But it is said that he made this jest as a sarcasm against one of his pupils who had been reported to him as using his wealth in a miserly fashion, and that he gave back the piece of silver after he had castigated the student in this witty manner.

This sophist had a copious flow of ideas and handled them brilliantly, and also in the disposition of his themes he showed the utmost variety, which he had acquired from his study of tragedy. He did not observe the conventional arrangement or follow the rules of the art, but he furnished himself with the diction of the ancient sophists and clothed his style therewith as with a garment, with sonorousness rather than striking effects. But in the grand style he often failed, because he employed tragedy with too prodigal a hand.

11. To CHRESTUS[1] OF BYZANTIUM, the sophist, Greece does less than justice, since it neglects a man who received from Herodes the best education of any Hellene, and himself educated many remarkable men. Among these were Hippodromus the sophist, Philiscus, Isagoras the tragic poet, famous rhetoricians, namely Nicomedes of Pergamon, Aquila from Galatia, and Aristaenetus of Byzantium ; and among well-known philosophers, Callaeschrus the Athenian, Sospis the curator of the altar,[2] and several others worthy of mention. He taught in the days of the sophist Hadrian and had then a hundred pupils who paid fees, the best of them those whom I have mentioned. After Hadrian had been installed in the

ἐς τὴν Ῥώμην ἐψηφίζοντο μὲν οἱ Ἀθηναῖοι πρε-
σβεύεσθαι ὑπὲρ Χρήστου τὸν Ἀθήνησιν αὐτῷ
θρόνον ἐκ βασιλέως αἰτοῦντες, ὁ δὲ παρελθὼν ἐς
αὐτοὺς ἐκκλησιάζοντας διέλυσε τὴν πρέσβευσιν
ἄλλα τε διαλεχθεὶς ἀξιόλογα καὶ ἐπὶ πᾶσιν εἰπὼν
" οὐχ αἱ μύριαι τὸν ἄνδρα."

Οἴνου δὲ ἡττώμενος παροινίας ἐκράτει καὶ εὐχε-
ρείας καὶ ἀγερωχίας, ἣν ὁ οἶνος ἐπὶ τὰς γνώμας
τῶν ἀνθρώπων ἐσάγει, τοσοῦτον δὲ αὐτῷ περιῆν
τοῦ νήφειν, ὡς καὶ ἐς ἀλεκτρυόνων ᾠδὰς προβάντος
τοῦ πότου σπουδῆς αὐτὸν ἅπτεσθαι, πρὶν ὕπνου
σπάσαι. διεβέβλητο δὲ μάλιστα πρὸς τοὺς ἀλα-
ζόνας τῶν νέων καίτοι χρησιμωτέρους τῶν ἄλλων
ὄντας ἐς τὰς ξυμβολὰς τοῦ μισθοῦ. Διογένη γοῦν
592 τὸν Ἀμαστριανὸν ὁρῶν τετυφωμένον ἐκ μειρακίου
καὶ περινοοῦντα μὲν σατραπείας, περινοοῦντα δὲ
αὐλὰς καὶ τὸ ἀγχοῦ βασιλέων ἐστήξειν, λέγοντα δέ,
ὡς ὁ δεῖνα Αἰγύπτιος προειρήκοι αὐτῷ ταῦτα, ὁ
Χρῆστος ἐνουθέτει[1] μηδὲ τὰ ἑαυτοῦ σιωπῶν.

Τὴν δὲ ἰδέαν τῶν λόγων πεποίκιλται μὲν ἐκ
τῶν Ἡρώδου πλεονεκτημάτων, λείπεται δὲ αὐτῶν
τοῦ ἑτοίμου, καθάπερ ἐν ζωγραφίᾳ ἡ ἄνευ χρω-
μάτων ἐσκιαγραφημένη μίμησις, προὔβη δὲ ἂν
καὶ ἐς τὸ ἴσον τῆς ἀρετῆς, εἰ μὴ πεντηκοντούτης
ἀπέθανεν.

ιβ΄. Πολυδεύκη δὲ τὸν Ναυκρατίτην οὐκ οἶδα,
εἴτε ἀπαίδευτον δεῖ καλεῖν εἴτε πεπαιδευμένον,
εἴθ᾽, ὅπερ εὔηθες δόξει, καὶ ἀπαίδευτον καὶ πε-
παιδευμένον· ἐνθυμουμένῳ γὰρ αὐτοῦ τὰ ὀνόματα

---

[1] For the lacuna after ὁ Kayser suggests Χρῆστος ἐνουθέτει.

---

[1] This was the salary of the chair.

chair at Rome, the Athenians voted to send an embassy on behalf of Chrestus to ask for him from the Emperor the chair at Athens. But he came before them in the assembly and broke up the embassy, saying many memorable things in his discourse, and he ended with these words: "The ten thousand drachmae [1] do not make a man."

He had a weakness for wine, but he kept in check the drunken insolence, levity, and arrogance which wine induces in the minds of men; and his ability to keep sober was so extraordinary that, though his potations went on till cockcrow, he would then attack his studies before he had snatched any sleep. He made himself especially obnoxious to youths of the foolish boasting sort, in spite of the fact that they are more profitable than the rest for the payment of fees. At any rate, when he perceived that Diogenes of Amastris was from his earliest youth puffed up with pride, dreaming ever of satrapies and courts and of being one day the right hand of emperors, and moreover that he asserted that a certain Egyptian had foretold all this to him, Chrestus admonished him and told his own story.

He varied and enriched the style of his oratory with the peculiar excellences of Herodes, but he falls short of these in alertness of mind, just as in the painter's art a likeness falls short that is done in outline without colours.[2] But he would have progressed even to an equal level of merit, had he not died at the age of fifty.

12. I am not sure whether one ought to call Pollux of Naucratis unlearned or learned, or, absurd as it will seem, both learned and unlearned. For when one

---

[2] An echo of Plato, *Politicus* 277 c.

ἱκανῶς ἐγεγύμναστο τὴν γλῶτταν τῆς ἀττικιζούσης
λέξεως, διορῶντι δὲ τὸ ἐν ταῖς μελέταις εἶδος
οὐδὲν βέλτιον ἑτέρου ἠττίκισεν. τάδε οὖν χρὴ περὶ
αὐτοῦ εἰδέναι· Πολυδεύκης τὰ μὲν κριτικὰ ἱκανῶς
ἤσκητο, πατρὶ ξυγγενόμενος τοὺς κριτικοὺς λόγους
εἰδότι, τοὺς δὲ σοφιστικοὺς τῶν λόγων τόλμῃ μᾶλλον ἢ τέχνῃ ξυνέβαλλε θαρρήσας τῇ φύσει, καὶ γὰρ
δὴ καὶ ἄριστα ἐπεφύκει. Ἀδριανοῦ δὲ ἀκροατὴς
γενόμενος ἴσον ἀφέστηκεν αὐτοῦ καὶ τῶν πλεονεκτημάτων καὶ τῶν ἐλαττωμάτων, ἥκιστα μὲν γὰρ
πίπτει, ἥκιστα δὲ αἴρεται, πλὴν ἀλλ' εἰσί τινες
ἡδονῶν λιβάδες διακεκραμέναι τοῦ λόγου. ἰδέα δὲ
αὐτοῦ διαλεγομένου μὲν ἥδε· " ὁ Πρωτεὺς ὁ
Φάριος τὸ θαῦμα τὸ Ὁμηρικὸν πολλαὶ μὲν αὐτοῦ
593 καὶ πολυειδεῖς αἱ μορφαί, καὶ γὰρ ἐς ὕδωρ αἴρεται
καὶ ἐς πῦρ ἅπτεται καὶ ἐς λέοντα θυμοῦται καὶ
ἐς σῦν ὁρμᾷ καὶ ἐς δράκοντα χωρεῖ καὶ ἐς πάρδαλιν
πηδᾷ καὶ δένδρον ἢν γένηται, κομᾷ." μελετῶντος
δὲ αὐτοῦ χαρακτῆρα ποιώμεθα τοὺς νησιώτας τοὺς
τὰ γένη πιπράσκοντας ἐς τὴν ἀπαγωγὴν τῶν
φόρων, ἐπειδὴ βούλονται καὶ ἄριστα εἰρῆσθαι τήνδε
τὴν ὑπόθεσιν, ἧς τὸ ἐπὶ πᾶσιν ὧδε εἴρηται· " παῖς
ἠπειρώτης ἀπὸ Βαβυλῶνος πατρὶ νησιώτῃ γράφει·
δουλεύω βασιλεῖ δῶρον ἐκ σατράπου δοθείς, οὔτε
δὲ ἵππον ἀναβαίνω Μηδικὸν οὔτε τόξον λαμβάνω
Περσικόν, ἀλλ' οὐδὲ ἐπὶ πόλεμον ἢ θήραν, ὡς
ἀνήρ, ἐξέρχομαι, ἐν γυναικωνίτιδι δὲ κάθημαι καὶ
τὰς βασιλέως θεραπεύω παλλακάς, καὶ βασιλεὺς

---

[1] *Odyssey* iv. 456 foll. Pollux seems to have been declaiming on the versatility of the sophists. Note the short
balanced clauses and the similar endings in the Greek.
Himerius, *Oration* xxi. 9, imitates this passage of Philostratus
and calls Proteus a sophist.

considers his studies in words it seems that his tongue had been well trained in the Attic dialect, yet, when one observes closely the type of his style in his declamations, he was as an Atticist no more skilful than the average. In his case, then, we must take into account the following facts. Pollux had been sufficiently well trained in the science of criticism, because he was the pupil of his father, who was an expert in the art of criticism; but he composed his purely sophistic speeches with the aid of audacity rather than art, relying on his natural talents, for he was indeed very high endowed by nature. He was a pupil of Hadrian, and represents the mean between that sophist's excellences and defects. For while he never sinks too low, he never soars, except that rivulets, so to speak, of sweetness permeate his oratory. Here is an example of his style in a discourse: "Proteus of Pharos, that marvel in Homer [1] puts on many and manifold shapes, for he rises up into water, blazes into fire, rages into a lion, makes a rush into a boar, crawls into a serpent, springs into a panther, and when he turns into a tree, grows leaves for hair." To show the characteristics of his style in declamation, let me quote the theme "The islanders who sell their children in order to pay their taxes"; for they claim that this is his most successful argument. The words of the epilogue are as follows: "A boy on the mainland writes from Babylon to his father on an island: 'I am a king's slave; I was given to him as a present from a satrap; yet I never mount a horse of the Medes or handle a Persian bow, nay I never even go forth to war or the chase like a man, but I sit in the women's quarters and wait on the king's concubines. Nor does the king

239

οὐκ ὀργίζεται, εὐνοῦχος γάρ εἰμι. εὐδοκιμῶ δὲ
παρ' αὐταῖς θάλατταν Ἑλληνικὴν διηγούμενος καὶ
τὰ τῶν Ἑλλήνων μυθολογῶν καλά, πῶς Ἠλεῖοι
πανηγυρίζουσι, πῶς Δελφοὶ θεσπίζουσι, τίς ὁ παρ'
Ἀθηναίοις Ἐλέου βωμός. ἀλλὰ καὶ σύ, πάτερ,
μοι γράφε, πότε παρὰ Λακεδαιμονίοις Ὑακίνθια
καὶ παρὰ Κορινθίοις Ἴσθμια καὶ παρὰ Δελφοῖς
Πύθια καὶ εἰ νικῶσιν Ἀθηναῖοι ναυμαχοῦντες.
ἔρρωσο καὶ τὸν ἀδελφόν μοι προσαγόρευσον, εἰ
μήπω πέπραται." ταῦτα μὲν δὴ ὁποῖα τοῦ
ἀνδρὸς τούτου σκοπεῖν ἔξεστι τοῖς ἀδεκάστως
ἀκροωμένοις. ἀδεκάστους δὲ ἀκροατὰς καλῶ τοὺς
μήτε εὔνους μήτε δύσνους. ἐλέγετο δὲ ταῦτα καὶ
μελιχρᾷ τῇ φωνῇ ἀπαγγέλλειν, ᾗ καὶ βασιλέα
Κόμμοδον θέλξας τὸν Ἀθήνησι θρόνον παρ' αὐτοῦ
εὕρετο. ἐβίω μὲν οὖν ἐς ὀκτὼ καὶ πεντήκοντα ἔτη,
ἐτελεύτα δὲ ἐπὶ παιδὶ γνησίῳ μέν, ἀπαιδεύτῳ δέ.

ιγ'. Καισάρεια δὲ ἡ Καππαδοκῶν ὄρει Ἀργαίῳ
πρόσοικος Παυσανίου τοῦ σοφιστοῦ οἶκος. ὁ δὲ
594 Παυσανίας ἐπαιδεύθη μὲν ὑπὸ Ἡρώδου καὶ τῶν
τοῦ Κλεψυδρίου μετεχόντων εἷς ἐγένετο, οὓς
ἐκάλουν οἱ πολλοὶ διψῶντας, ἐς πολλὰ δὲ ἀναφέρων
τῶν Ἡρώδου πλεονεκτημάτων καὶ μάλιστα τὸ
αὐτοσχεδιάζειν ἀπήγγελλε δὲ αὐτὰ παχείᾳ τῇ
γλώττῃ καὶ ὡς Καππαδόκαις ξύνηθες, ξυγκρούων
μὲν τὰ σύμφωνα τῶν στοιχείων, συστέλλων δὲ τὰ
μηκυνόμενα καὶ μηκύνων τὰ βραχέα, ὅθεν ἐκάλουν
αὐτὸν οἱ πολλοὶ μάγειρον πολυτελῆ ὄψα πονήρως

---

[1] i.e. thirsty for knowledge ; cf. Life of Apollonius iv. 24,
for the same metaphor.

[2] Lucian, Epigram 43, says that it would be easier to find
white crows and flying tortoises than a Cappadocian who

resent this, for I am a eunuch. And I win their favour by describing to them the seas of Greece, and telling them tales of all the fine things that the Greeks do; how they hold the festivals at Elis, how oracles are given at Delphi, and which is the altar of Pity at Athens. But pray, father, write back to me and say when the Lacedaemonians celebrate the Hyacinthia and the Corinthians the Isthmian games; when are the Pythian games held at Delphi, and whether the Athenians are winning their naval battles. Farewell, and greet my brother for me, if he has not yet been sold.'" Impartial hearers may estimate the quality of this man's speeches as here quoted. And by impartial I mean hearers who are prejudiced neither for nor against. It is said that he used to deliver these declamations in a mellifluous voice, with which he so charmed the Emperor Commodus that he won from him the chair at Athens. He lived to the age of fifty-eight, and died leaving a son who was legitimate but uneducated.

13. Caesarea in Cappadocia, near neighbour to Mount Argaeus, was the birthplace of PAUSANIAS the sophist. He was educated by Herodes, and was one of the members of the Clepsydrion, who were vulgarly called " the thirsty ones." [1] But though he inherited many of the peculiar excellences of Herodes, and especially his skill in extempore oratory, yet he used to deliver his declamations with a coarse and heavy accent, as is the way with the Cappadocians.[2] He would make his consonants collide, would shorten the long syllables and lengthen the short. Hence he was commonly spoken of as a cook who spoiled expensive

was a reputable orator. For the bad accent of the Cappadocians *cf. Life of Apollonius* i. 7.

ἀρτύοντα. ἡ δὲ ἰδέα τῆς μελέτης ὑπτιωτέρα, ἔρρωται δὲ ὅμως καὶ οὐχ ἁμαρτάνει τοῦ ἀρχαίου, ὡς ὑπάρχει ταῖς μελέταις ξυμβαλεῖν, πολλαὶ γὰρ τοῦ Παυσανίου κατὰ τὴν Ῥώμην, οἳ δὴ καὶ καταβιοὺς ἀπέθανε γηράσκων ἤδη, τοῦ θρόνου μετέχων, μετεῖχε δὲ καὶ τοῦ Ἀθήνησιν, ὅτε δὴ καὶ ἀπιὼν ἐκεῖθεν ἐπὶ πᾶσιν, οἷς πρὸς τοὺς Ἀθηναίους διεξῆλθε, καιριώτατα τὸ τοῦ Εὐριπίδου ἐπεφθέγξατο

Θησεῦ, πάλιν με στρέψον, ὡς ἴδω πόλιν.

ιδ'. Ἀθηνόδωρος δὲ ὁ σοφιστὴς τὸ μὲν ἐς πατέρας [1] ἧκον ἐπιφανέστατος ἦν τῶν κατὰ τὴν Αἶνον, τὸ δὲ ἐς διδασκάλους καὶ παίδευσιν φανερώτατος τοῦ Ἑλληνικοῦ. Ἀριστοκλέους μὲν γὰρ ἤκουσε παῖς ἔτι, Χρήστου δὲ ἤδη ξυνιείς, ὅθεν ἀπ' ἀμφοῖν ἐκράθη τὴν γλῶτταν ἀττικίζων τε κἀκ περιβολῆς ἑρμηνεύων. παιδεύων δὲ Ἀθήνησι κατὰ τοὺς χρόνους, οὓς καὶ Πολυδεύκης ἐπαίδευσεν, ἐπέσκωπτεν αὐτὸν ταῖς διαλέξεσιν ὡς μειρακιώδη 595 λέγων " οἱ Ταντάλου κῆποι " δοκεῖν ἐμοὶ τὸ κοῦφον τοῦ λόγου καὶ ἐπιπόλαιον φαντασίᾳ προσεικάζων οὔσῃ τε καὶ οὐκ οὔσῃ. ἐμβριθὴς δὲ καὶ τὸ ἦθος γενόμενος ἐτελεύτα ἡβῶν ἔτι ἀφαιρεθεὶς ὑπὸ τῆς τύχης τὸ καὶ πρόσω ἐλάσαι δόξης.

---

[1] πατέρα Kayser ; πατέρας Cobet.

[1] Plato, *Phaedrus*, 265 E.
[2] *Mad Heracles*, 1406 ; Pausanias substituted " city " for the " children " of the original.
[3] Nothing more is known of this sophist.
[4] A town in Thrace ; *cf.* Vergil, *Aeneid*, iii. 18.
[5] He reached a compromise between the Attic and Asianic types of rhetorical prose.
[6] This proverb for the unsubstantial is based on the

delicacies in the preparation.[1]   His style in declamation was somewhat sluggish, nevertheless it has force, and succeeds in giving a flavour of antiquity, as we may gather from the declamations that are extant.   For there are many of these by Pausanias, delivered at Rome where he spent the latter part of his life; and there he died when he was already growing old and was still holding the chair of rhetoric. He also held the chair at Athens, and on the occasion of his leaving it he concluded his address to the Athenians by quoting very appropriately the verse of Euripides

> Theseus, turn me round that I may behold the city.[2]

14. ATHENODORUS [3] the sophist was, by virtue of his ancestors, the most illustrious of the citizens of Aenus,[4] and by virtue of his teachers and his education the most notable of all the educated Greeks in that city.   For he was educated by Aristocles while still a mere boy, and by Chrestus when his intelligence began to mature; and from these two he derived his well-tempered dialect, for he both Atticized and employed an ornate style of eloquence.[5]   He taught at Athens at the time when Pollux also was teaching there, and in his discourses he used to ridicule him as puerile and would quote " The gardens of Tantalus," [6] by which I think he meant to compare his light and superficial style of eloquence with some visionary image which both is and is not. He was a man of great weight and seriousness of character, but he died in the flower of early manhood, robbed by fate of the chance to push on to still greater fame.

description of the vanishing fruits which mocked Tantalus in *Odyssey*, xi. 588.

ιε΄. Λαμπρὸν ἐν σοφισταῖς καὶ Πτολεμαῖος ὁ
Ναυκρατίτης ἤχησεν. ἦν μὲν γὰρ τῶν μετεχόντων
τοῦ ἱεροῦ τοῦ περὶ Ναύκρατιν ὀλίγοις Ναυκρα-
τιτῶν ὑπάρχων, Ἡρώδου δὲ ἀκροατὴς μέν, οὐ μὴν
ζηλωτὴς ἐγένετο, ἀλλ᾽ ἐς τὸν Πολέμωνα μᾶλλον
ὑπηνέχθη, τὸν γὰρ ῥοῖζον τοῦ λόγου καὶ τὸ πνεῦμα
καὶ τὸ ἐκ περιβολῆς φράζειν ἐκ τῆς Πολέμωνος
σκηνῆς ἐσηγάγετο, λέγεται δὲ καὶ αὐτοσχεδιάσαι
σὺν εὐροίᾳ ἀμηχάνῳ. δικῶν τε καὶ δικαστηρίων
παρέτραγε μέν, οὐ μήν, ὡς ὄνομα ἐντεῦθεν ἄρασθαι.
Μαραθῶνα δὲ αὐτὸν ἐπωνόμαζον, ὡς μέν τινες,
ἐπειδὴ τῷ Μαραθῶνι δήμῳ ἐνεγράφη Ἀθήνησιν,
ὡς δὲ ἐνίων ἤκουον, ἐπειδὴ ἐν ταῖς Ἀττικαῖς τῶν
ὑποθέσεων τῶν Μαραθῶνι προκινδυνευσάντων θαμὰ
ἐμνημόνευεν.

Κατηγοροῦσι δὲ τοῦ Πτολεμαίου τινὲς ὡς μὴ
διορῶντος τὰς ὑποθέσεις, μηδὲ ὅπῃ ξυνεστᾶσί τε
καὶ μή, τεκμήριον τόδε τιθέμενοι τῆς κατηγορίας
ταύτης· τοὺς Μεσσηνίους οἱ Θηβαῖοι γράφονται τὴν
596 τῶν ἀχαριστησάντων, ἐπεὶ τοὺς φεύγοντας αὐτῶν
μὴ ἐδέξαντο, ὅτε καὶ αἱ Θῆβαι ὑπὸ Ἀλεξάνδρου
ἥλωσαν. ταύτην γὰρ ἐπιφανῶς αὐτῷ εἰρημένην τὴν
ὑπόθεσιν καὶ σοφῶς, ὡς οἷόν τε, συκοφαντοῦσι
λέγοντες, ὡς εἰ μὲν ζῶντος Ἀλεξάνδρου κρίνονται,
τίς οὕτω θρασύς, ὡς καταψηφίσασθαι Μεσσηνίων;
εἰ δὲ τεθνεῶτος, τίς οὕτω πρᾷος, ὡς ἀπογνῶναι τὴν

---

[1] Nothing more is known of this sophist.
[2] An echo of Demosthenes, *On the Crown* 208.
[3] This theme seems to be based on Diodorus xv. 66,
though it is nowhere stated that the Messenians acted as is

15. PTOLEMY [1] OF NAUCRATIS also had a brilliant reputation among sophists. For he was one of those who were admitted to dine at the public expense in the temple of Naucratis, an honour paid to few of her citizens. Moreover, he was a pupil of Herodes, but he did not desire to imitate him, but came rather under the influence of Polemo. For the impetus and force of his style and the ample use of rhetorical ornament he borrowed from the equipment of Polemo. Also it is said that he spoke extempore with marvellous ease and fluency. He nibbled at legal cases and the courts, but not enough to win fame for himself thereby. They used to call him "Marathon." Some say that this was because he was enrolled in the deme Marathon at Athens, but I have been told by others that it was because in his Attic themes he so often mentioned those who were forward to brave death at Marathon.[2]

Ptolemy is sometimes accused of having failed to comprehend clearly his controversial themes so as to see where they were consistent and where not; and as evidence for this accusation they quote the following instance: "The Thebans accuse the Messenians of ingratitude because they refused to receive the Theban refugees when Thebes was taken by Alexander."[3] For though he handled this argument brilliantly, and with the greatest possible skill, they make out an unfair case against it by saying: If the Messenians were being tried while Alexander was still alive, who would be so foolhardy as to give a verdict against them? But if it was after his death, who would be so lenient as to acquit them of the

assumed; it is mentioned by Marcellinus iv. 249; Sopater viii. 239 quotes a similar theme; cf. Schmid, Atticismus 65.

αἰτίαν; οὐ γὰρ ξυνιᾶσιν οἱ ταῦτα διαβάλλοντες, ὅτι ἡ τῶν Μεσσηνίων ἀπολογία κατὰ ξυγγνώμην ἵσταται τὸν Ἀλέξανδρον προϊσχομένων καὶ τὸν ἐκείνου φόβον, οὗ μηδὲ ἡ ἄλλη Ἑλλὰς ἀπείρως εἶχεν. ταῦτά μοι ἀπολελογήσθω ὑπὲρ τοῦ ἀνδρὸς παραιτουμένῳ αὐτὸν ἀδίκου καὶ πεπανουργημένης αἰτίας· καὶ γὰρ δὴ καὶ εὐφημότατος σοφιστῶν οὗτος. πλεῖστα δὲ ἐπελθὼν ἔθνη καὶ πλείσταις ἐνομιλήσας πόλεσιν οὐδαμοῦ διέβαλε τὸ ἑαυτοῦ κλέος, οὐδὲ ἥττων ἢ προσεδοκήθη ἔδοξεν, ἀλλ' ὥσπερ ἐπὶ λαμπροῦ ὀχήματος τῆς φήμης πορευόμενος διῄει τὰ ἄστη. ἐτελεύτα δὲ γηραιὸς ἐν Αἰγύπτῳ τοὺς ὀφθαλμοὺς οὐκ ἀφαιρεθεὶς μὲν ὑπὸ τοῦ τῆς κεφαλῆς ῥεύματος, ἐπικοπεὶς δέ.

ιϛ'. Εὐοδιανὸν δὲ τὸν Σμυρναῖον τὸ μὲν γένος ἐς Νικήτην τὸν σοφιστὴν ἀνῆγεν, αἱ δὲ οἴκοι τιμαὶ ἐς τοὺς ἀρχιερέας τε καὶ στεφανουμένους τὴν ἐπὶ τῶν ὅπλων, τὰ δὲ τῆς φωνῆς ἆθλα ἐς τὴν Ῥώμην καὶ τὸν ἐκείνῃ θρόνον. ἐπιταχθεὶς δὲ καὶ τοῖς ἀμφὶ τὸν Διόνυσον τεχνίταις, τὸ δὲ ἔθνος τοῦτο ἀγέρωχοι καὶ χαλεποὶ ἀρχθῆναι, ἐπιτηδειότατος τὴν ἀρχὴν ἔδοξε καὶ κρείττων ἢ λαβεῖν αἰτίαν. υἱοῦ δὲ αὐτῷ τελευτήσαντος ἐν τῇ Ῥώμῃ οὐδὲν θῆλυ οὐδὲ ἀγεννὲς ἀνεφθέγξατο, ἀλλ' " ὦ τέκνον " 597 τρὶς ἀνακαλέσας ἔθαψεν. ἀποθνήσκοντι δὲ αὐτῷ κατὰ τὴν Ῥώμην παρῆσαν μὲν οἱ ἐπιτήδειοι πάντες, βουλὴν δὲ αὐτῶν ποιουμένων ὑπὲρ τοῦ σώματος, εἴτε χρὴ καταθάπτειν αὐτόθι, εἴτε ταριχεύσαντας πορθμεύειν ἐς τὴν Σμύρναν ἀναβοήσας ὁ Εὐοδιανὸς

---

[1] Nothing more is known of this sophist.
[2] See above, p. 580 ; and, for the bad character of these *thymelici*, Aulus Gellius xx. 4.

charge? For those who make these severe criticisms do not understand that the defence made by the Messenians is framed as a plea for pardon, since they shield themselves by making Alexander their excuse, and that dread of him from which the rest of Greece also was not immune. So much let me say in defence of Ptolemy, that I may ward off from him an unfair and maliciously manufactured accusation; for indeed this man was of all the sophists the most moderate and temperate in his speech and though he visited very many nations and was conversant with many cities, nowhere did he bring reproach on his own fame or fall below their expectations of him; but he passed on from one city to another, borne as it were on the shining car of his own renown. He died in Egypt, well on in years; a catarrh of the head had not indeed destroyed his eyesight, but had seriously impaired it.

16. EUODIANUS OF SMYRNA [1] by birth ranked as a descendant of Nicetes the sophist, but the honours won by his house ranked him with high-priests and those crowned as generals in charge of supplies, and the achievements of his oratory carried him to Rome and the chair of rhetoric in that city. He was appointed also to supervise the artisans of Dionysus,[2] a very arrogant class of men and hard to keep in order; but he proved himself most capable in this office, and above all criticism. When his son died at Rome he gave vent to no womanish or ignoble laments, but thrice cried aloud, "O my child!" and then laid him in the grave. When he was at the point of death in Rome, all his most intimate friends were by his bedside and were consulting about his body, whether they ought to bury it there or embalm it and ship it to Smyrna, when

"οὐ καταλείπω" ἔφη "τὸν υἱὸν μόνον." ὧδε μὲν δὴ σαφῶς¹ ἐπέσκηψε τὸ τῷ παιδὶ ξυνταφῆναι. ἀκροατὴς δὲ Ἀριστοκλέους γενόμενος πανηγυρικῆς ἰδέας ἥψατο ἐν στρυφνῷ κρατῆρι συγκεράσας οἷον νᾶμα πότιμον. εἰσὶ δὲ οἵ φασι καὶ Πολέμωνος ἠκροᾶσθαι αὐτόν.

ιζ'. Ῥοῦφον δὲ τὸν ἐκ τῆς Περίνθου σοφιστὴν μὴ ἀπὸ τῆς οὐσίας, μηδὲ εἰ πολλοὶ ὕπατοι τὸ ἐκείνου γένος, μηδὲ εἰ τὴν τῶν Πανελληνίων Ἀθήνησιν εὐκλεῶς ἦρξεν, ταυτὶ γὰρ εἰ καὶ πλείω λέγοιτο, οὔπω τῇ σοφίᾳ τοῦ ἀνδρὸς παραβεβλῆσθαι ἄξια, ἀλλ' ἡ γλῶττα δηλούτω αὐτὸν καὶ ἡ ξύνεσις, ᾗ περὶ τὰς ἐσχηματισμένας μάλιστα τῶν ὑποθέσεων ἐχρήσατο. τὴν δὲ ἰδέαν ταύτην ἐθαυμάσθη πρῶτον μέν, ὅτι χαλεπὴ ἑρμηνεῦσαι, δεῖ γὰρ ἐν ταῖς κατὰ σχῆμα ξυγκειμέναις τῶν ὑποθέσεων τοῖς μὲν λεγομένοις ἡνίας, τοῖς δὲ σιωπωμένοις κέντρου, ἔπειτα, οἶμαι, καὶ διὰ τὴν ἑαυτοῦ φύσιν, ἐκκειμένως γὰρ τοῦ ἤθους καὶ ἀπανούργως ἔχων ὑπεκρίνετο εὖ, καὶ ἃ μὴ ἐπεφύκει. πλουσιώτατος δὲ τῶν κατὰ τὸν
598 Ἑλλήσποντον καὶ Προποντίδα γενόμενος καὶ δόξης αὐτῷ ἐπὶ τῷ σχεδιάζειν πολλῆς μὲν ὑπαρχούσης Ἀθήνησι, πολλῆς δὲ ἐν Ἰωνίᾳ τε καὶ Ἰταλίᾳ, οὐδαμοῦ κατέστησεν ἑαυτὸν ἐς ἀπέχθειαν ἢ πόλεως ἢ ἀνδρός, ἀλλὰ πραότητος ἦν χρηματιστής.

¹ σοφῶς Kayser ; σαφῶς Cobet.

---

¹ This is a commonplace in sophistic prose and the Christian Fathers. Three Platonic passages seem to be echoed ; *Phaedrus* 235 c, *Timaeus* 75 ε. but especially *Phaedrus* 213 ᴅ ἐπιθυμῶ ποτίμῳ λόγῳ οἷον ἁλμυρὰν ἀκοὴν ἀποκλύσασθαι ; *cf.* Libanius, *Oration*, xiii. 67 Foerster ; Himerius, *Eclogues*, x. 76.

² Nothing more is known of this sophist.

³ See Glossary *s.v.* σχηματίζειν and above, pp. 542, 561.

Euodianus exclaimed in a loud voice : " I will not leave
my son behind alone." Thus did he clearly enjoin on
them that he should be buried in the same grave as
his son. Having been a pupil of Aristocles he devoted
himself to the panegyrical type of oratory, but he
poured as it were sweet spring water into that bitter
bowl.[1] Some say that he studied with Polemo also.

17. It is not for his wealth that I shall hand down
to fame the name of RUFUS OF PERINTHUS,[2] the sophist,
or because his family produced many men of consular
rank, or because he presided over the Pan-Hellenic
festival at Athens with great distinction. For
though I might recount even more honours of this
sort, they would yet not be worthy of comparison
with the man's skill and learning. But rather let
his eloquent tongue be his passport to fame, and
that keen intelligence which he employed by preference in simulated arguments.[3] For this type of
eloquence he was much admired ; in the first place
because it is a difficult kind of oratory, since in
themes that are composed as simulated arguments
one needs to put a curb on what one actually says,
but to apply the spur to what one leaves unsaid.
Then too I think he was admired because his own
natural disposition was taken into account. For
though his character was naturally open and without
guile, he was clever in portraying characters that were
not at all suited to his natural bent. And though
he became the wealthiest man in the region of the
Hellespont and the Propontis, though he won a
great reputation at Athens for extempore eloquence
and in Ionia and Italy also, yet he nowhere incurred
the enmity of any city or individual, but made
money out of his benevolent disposition. It is said

ἐλέγετο δὲ καὶ γυμναστικῇ κρατύνειν τὸ σῶμα
ἀναγκοφαγῶν ἀεὶ καὶ διαπονῶν αὐτὸ παραπλησίως
τοῖς ἀγωνιζομένοις. ἀκροατὴς δὲ Ἡρώδου μὲν ἐν
παισίν, Ἀριστοκλέους δὲ ἐν μειρακίοις γενόμενος,
καὶ μεγάλων ὑπ' αὐτοῦ ἀξιωθεὶς ἐλαμπρύνετο τῷ
Ἡρώδῃ μᾶλλον δεσπότην τε αὐτὸν καλῶν καὶ
Ἑλλήνων γλῶτταν καὶ λόγων βασιλέα καὶ πολλὰ
τοιαῦτα. ἐτελεύτα δὲ οἴκοι ἓν καὶ ἑξήκοντα ἔτη
γενόμενος καὶ ἐπὶ παισίν, ὑπὲρ ὧν γε μέγα οὐδὲν
ἔχω εἰπεῖν, πλήν γε δὴ ὅτι ἀπ' ἐκείνου.

ιη΄. Ὀνόμαρχος δὲ ὁ ἐκ τῆς Ἄνδρου σοφιστὴς
οὐκ ἐθαυμάζετο μέν, οὐ μεμπτὸς δὲ ἐφαίνετο.
ἐπαίδευσε μὲν γὰρ κατὰ χρόνους, οὓς Ἀδριανός
τε καὶ Χρῆστος Ἀθήνησι, πρόσοικος δὲ ὢν τῆς
Ἀσίας τῆς Ἰωνικῆς ἰδέας οἷον ὀφθαλμίας ἔσπασε,
σπουδαζομένης μάλιστα τῇ Ἐφέσῳ, ὅθεν ἐδόκει
τισὶν οὐδ' ἠκροᾶσθαι Ἡρώδου καταψευδομένοις
τοῦ ἀνδρός· τὸ μὲν γὰρ τῆς ἑρμηνείας παρέφθορεν
ἔσθ' ὅπῃ δι' ἣν εἴρηκα αἰτίαν, αἱ δὲ ἐπιβολαὶ τῶν
νοημάτων Ἡρώδειοί τε καὶ ἀπορρήτως γλυκεῖαι.
ἔξεστι δὲ αὐτὸν θεωρεῖν ἐπὶ τοῦ τῆς εἰκόνος ἐρῶντος, εἰ μὴ μειρακιεύεσθαι δόξω. εἴρηται δὲ ὧδε·
" ὦ κάλλος ἔμψυχον ἐν ἀψύχῳ σώματι, τίς ἄρα
σε δαιμόνων ἐδημιούργησεν; πειθώ τις ἢ χάρις ἢ
αὐτὸς ὁ Ἔρως, ὁ τοῦ κάλλους πατήρ; ὡς πάντα
σοι πρόσεστιν ἐν ἀληθείᾳ προσώπου στάσις χρόας
ἄνθος βλέμματος κέντρον μειδίαμα κεχαρισμένον

---

[1] Nothing more is known of this sophist.

of him that he used to harden his body by athletics, that he always followed a rigid diet, and exercised himself like a regular athlete. As a boy he studied with Herodes, with Aristocles when he was a stripling, and he was greatly esteemed by the latter; but he took more pride in Herodes, and used to call him the master, the tongue of the Hellenes, the prince of eloquence, and much more of the same sort. He died at home aged sixty-one years, and left sons about whom I have nothing important to relate, except indeed that they were his offspring.

18. ONOMARCHUS[1] OF ANDROS, the sophist, was not greatly admired, yet he was evidently not to be despised. He taught in the days when Hadrian and Chrestus were lecturing at Athens, and living as he did so near to the coast of Asia, he contracted, as one might ophthalmia, the Ionian manner of oratory, which flourished especially at Ephesus. On this account there were some who did not believe that he had ever so much as attended a lecture by Herodes, but in this they did him an injustice. For though he did debase his style to some extent, from the cause that I have mentioned, nevertheless his abundant use of synonyms was like Herodes, and they were pleasing beyond words. If I shall not be thought too frivolous, we can observe his style in his speech · "The man who fell in love with a statue." Here is a quotation from it : "O living loveliness in a lifeless body, what deity fashioned thee? Was some goddess of Persuasion, or a Grace, or Eros himself the parent of thy loveliness? For truly nothing is lacking in thee, the expression of the face, the bloom on the skin, the sting in the glance, the charming smile, the blush on the cheeks,

παρειῶν ἔρευθος ἀκοῆς ἴχνος. ἔχεις δὲ καὶ φωνὴν
μέλλουσαν ἀεί. τάχα τι καὶ λαλεῖς, ἀλλ' ἐμοῦ
μὴ παρόντος, ἀνέραστε καὶ βάσκανε, πρὸς πιστὸν
ἐραστὴν ἄπιστε. οὐδενός μοι μετέδωκας ῥήμα-
τος· τοιγαροῦν τὴν φρικωδεστάτην ἅπασιν ἀεὶ
τοῖς καλοῖς ἀρὰν ἐπὶ σοὶ θήσομαι· εὔχομαί σοι
γηρᾶσαι."

Τελευτῆσαι δὲ αὐτὸν οἱ μὲν 'Αθήνησι, οἱ δὲ
οἴκοι, μεσαιπόλιόν τε καὶ παριόντα ἐς γῆρας,
γενέσθαι δὲ ἀγροικότερον τὸ εἶδος καὶ κατὰ τὸν
Μάρκου τοῦ Βυζαντίου αὐχμόν.

ιθ'. 'Απολλώνιος δὲ ὁ Ναυκρατίτης 'Ηρακλεί-
δῃ μὲν ἐναντία ἐπαίδευσε τὸν 'Αθήνησι θρόνον
κατειληφότι, λόγου δὲ ἐπεμελήθη πολιτικοῦ καὶ
εὖ κεκολασμένου, ἧττον δὲ ἀγωνιζομένου, περιβολὴ γὰρ ἄπεστιν αὐτοῦ καὶ πνεῦμα. ὄντι δὲ
αὐτῷ κακῷ τὰ ἐρωτικὰ γίγνεται παῖς ἐξ ἀδίκων
γάμων 'Ρουφῖνος ὁ ἐπ' αὐτῷ σοφιστεύσας οὐδὲν
γόνιμον, οὐδὲ ἐκ καρδίας, ἀλλὰ τῶν ἐκείνου κομματίων τε καὶ νοιδίων ἐχόμενος, ἐφ' ᾧ καὶ λαβὼν
αἰτίαν ἐξ ἀνδρὸς σοφοῦ " οἱ νόμοι " ἔφη " διδόασί
μοι χρῆσθαι τοῖς πατρῴοις," καὶ ὃς " διδόασι
μέν," εἶπεν " ἀλλὰ τοῖς κατὰ νόμους γεγονόσι."
καθάπτονται δὲ αὐτοῦ τινες καὶ τὸ σταλῆναι ἐς
600 Μακεδονίαν μισθωτὸν οἰκίας οὐδὲ εὖ πραττούσης.
ἀλλ' ἀφείσθω τῶν τοιούτων· εὕροις μὲν γὰρ ἂν
καὶ τῶν πολὺ[1] σοφῶν ἐνίους πολλὰ καὶ ἀνελεύ-
θερα ὑπὲρ χρημάτων πράξαντας, οὐ μὴν τόν γε

---

[1] Valckenaer suggests πάλαι, "the wise men of old."

---

[1] Nothing more is known of this sophist.

signs that thou canst hear me. Yea and thou hast
a voice ever about to speak. And one day it may
be that thou wilt even speak, but I shall be far
away. O unloving and unkind! O faithless to thy
faithful lover! To me thou hast granted not one
word. Therefore I will lay on thee that curse at
which all fair ones always shudder most : I pray that
thou mayest grow old."

Some say that he died at Athens, others at home,
when his hair was beginning to grow grey and he
was on the verge of old age ; they say too that he
was somewhat rustic in appearance and squalid and
unkempt, like Marcus of Byzantium.

19. Apollonius[1] of Naucratis taught rhetoric as
the rival of Heracleides, when the latter held the chair
at Athens. He devoted himself to political oratory
of a type restrained and moderate, but little suited
to controversy ; for it lacks rhetorical amplitude and
force. He was a libertine in love, and from one of
his lawless intrigues he had a son named Rufinus who
succeeded him as a sophist, but produced nothing
that was his own or from the heart, but always clung
to his father's phrases and epigrams. When he was
criticized for this by a learned man, he said : " The
laws allow me to use my patrimony." " The laws
allow it, certainly," said the other, " but only to
those that are born within the law." Some people
blame him for going to Macedonia as the hireling
of a certain family that was not even in good circumstances. But let us acquit him of any such
charge. For though even among the most learned
men you would easily find those who for the sake
of gain have done much that is unworthy of a
free-born man, yet this is not true of our Apollonius

Ἀπολλώνιον τοῦτον, κοινήν τε γὰρ παρέσχε τὴν
οὐσίαν τῶν Ἑλλήνων τοῖς δεομένοις, καὶ οὐ βαρὺς
ἦν ὑπὲρ μισθοῦ ξυμβῆναι. ἐτελεύτα δὲ ἑβδομηκοντούτης Ἀθήνησιν ἔχων ἐντάφιον τὴν ἐξ ἁπάντων Ἀθηναίων εὔνοιαν. Ἀδριανοῦ μὲν καὶ Χρήστου τῶν σοφιστῶν ἀκροατὴς ἐγένετο, ἀμφοῖν
δὲ ἀφέστηκεν, ὅσον οἱ μὴ ἀκούσαντες. ἐφεώρα
δὲ τὰς ὑποθέσεις ὑπεξιὼν μὲν τοῦ κοινοῦ, καιρὸν
δὲ πλείω τοῦ ξυμμέτρου.

κ΄. Ὁ δὲ Ἀπολλώνιος ὁ Ἀθηναῖος ὀνόματος
μὲν ἠξιώθη καθ᾽ Ἕλληνας, ὡς ἱκανὸς τὰ δικανικὰ καὶ τὰ ἀμφὶ μελέτην οὐ μεμπτός, ἐπαίδευσε
δὲ Ἀθήνησι καθ᾽ Ἡρακλείδην τε καὶ τὸν ὁμώ-
νυμον τοῦ πολιτικοῦ θρόνου προεστὼς ἐπὶ ταλάντῳ.
διαπρεπὴς δὲ καὶ τὰ πολιτικὰ γενόμενος ἔν τε
πρεσβείαις ὑπὲρ τῶν μεγίστων ἐπρέσβευσεν ἔν
τε λειτουργίαις, ἃς μεγίστας Ἀθηναῖοι νομίζουσι,
τήν τε ἐπώνυμον καὶ τὴν ἐπὶ τῶν ὅπλων ἐπετράπη
καὶ τὰς ἐξ ἀνακτόρου φωνὰς ἤδη γηράσκων,
601 Ἡρακλείδου μὲν καὶ Λογίμου καὶ Γλαύκου καὶ
τῶν τοιούτων ἱεροφαντῶν εὐφωνίᾳ μὲν ἀποδέων,
σεμνότητι δὲ καὶ μεγαλοπρεπείᾳ καὶ κόσμῳ παρὰ
πολλοὺς δοκῶν τῶν ἄνω.

Πρεσβεύων δὲ παρὰ Σεβῆρον ἐν Ῥώμῃ τὸν
αὐτοκράτορα ἀπεδύσατο πρὸς Ἡρακλείδην τὸν
σοφιστὴν τὸν ὑπὲρ μελέτης ἀγῶνα, καὶ ἀπῆλθεν

---

[1] For this metaphor cf. pp. 502, 590.
[2] Nothing more is known of this sophist.
[3] Apollonius of Naucratis.
[4] Or " the municipal chair " as opposed to the imperial;
but there is no clear evidence that Athens maintained a
second salaried chair of rhetoric.

at any rate. For he shared his estate with any Hellenes that were in need, nor was he hard to deal with in the matter of lecture fees. He died at Athens, aged seventy, and for his winding-sheet [1] he had the goodwill of all the Athenians. He was a pupil of the sophists Hadrian and Chrestus, but he was as different from them both as any who had not studied with them. He used to retire from the public view to meditate on the themes of his declamations, and would spend an inordinate length of time on this.

20. APOLLONIUS OF ATHENS [2] won a name for himself among the Greeks as an able speaker in the legal branch of oratory, and as a declaimer he was not to be despised. He taught at Athens at the same time as Heracleides and his own namesake,[3] and held the chair of political oratory [4] at a salary of one talent. He also won distinction in public affairs, and not only was he sent as ambassador on missions of the greatest importance, but also performed the public functions which the Athenians rank highest, being appointed both archon and food controller, and when already well on in years hierophant [5] of the temple of Demeter. In beauty of enunciation he fell short of Heracleides, Logimus, Glaucus, and other hierophants of that sort, but in dignity, magnificence, and in his attire he showed himself superior to many of his predecessors.

While he was on an embassy to the Emperor Severus at Rome,[6] he entered the lists against the sophist Heracleides to compete in declamation, and Heracleides came out of the encounter with the loss

---

[5] The hierophant delivered the mystic utterances at the Eleusinian rites, and was often a sophist.

[6] In A.D. 196 or 197.

ὁ μὲν τὴν ἀτέλειαν ἀφαιρεθείς, ὁ δὲ Ἀπολλώνιος
δῶρα ἔχων. διαδόντος δὲ τοῦ Ἡρακλείδου λόγον
οὐκ ἀληθῆ ὑπὲρ τοῦ Ἀπολλωνίου, ὡς αὐτίκα δὴ
βαδιουμένου ἐς Λιβύην, ἡνίκα ἦν ὁ αὐτοκράτωρ
ἐκεῖ καὶ τὰς ἐξ ἁπάσης γῆς ἀρετὰς συνῆγεν, καὶ
πρὸς αὐτὸν εἰπόντος " ὥρα σοι ἀναγιγνώσκειν τὸν
πρὸς Λεπτίνην" " σοὶ μὲν οὖν," ἦ δ' ὁ Ἀπολλώνιος, " καὶ γὰρ δὴ καὶ ὑπὲρ τῆς ἀτελείας γέγραπται."

Βαλβῖδα μὲν δὴ τοῦ λόγου ὁ Ἀπολλώνιος ἐκ
τῆς Ἀδριανοῦ ἰδέας βέβληται ἅτε δὴ καὶ ἀκροατὴς γενόμενος, παραλλάττει δὲ ὅμως ἐς ῥυθμοὺς
ἐμμέτρους τε καὶ ἀναπαίοντας, οὓς εἰ φυλάξαιτο,
σεμνοπρεπὴς τὴν ἀπαγγελίαν δοκεῖ καὶ βεβηκώς.
τουτὶ δέ ἐστιν εὑρεῖν καὶ ἐπ' ἄλλων μὲν ὑποθέσεων,
μάλιστα δὲ ἐπὶ τοῦ Καλλίου, ὃς ἀπαγορεύει τοῖς
Ἀθηναίοις πυρὶ μὴ θάπτειν· " ὑψηλὴν ἆρον, ἄν-
602 θρωπε, τὴν δᾷδα. τί βιάζῃ καὶ κατάγεις κάτω
καὶ βασανίζεις τὸ πῦρ; οὐράνιόν ἐστιν, αἰθέριόν
ἐστιν, πρὸς τὸ ξυγγενὲς ἔρχεται τὸ πῦρ. οὐ κατά-
γει νεκρούς, ἀλλ' ἀνάγει θεούς. ἰὼ Προμηθεῦ
δᾳδοῦχε καὶ πυρφόρε, οἷά σου τὸ δῶρον ὑβρίζεται·
νεκροῖς ἀναισθήτοις ἀναμίγνυται. ἐπάρηξον βοή-
θησον κλέψον, εἰ δυνατόν, κἀκεῖθεν τὸ πῦρ."

Παρεθέμην δὲ ταῦτα οὐ παραιτούμενος αὐτὸν
τῶν ἀκολάστων ῥυθμῶν, ἀλλὰ διδάσκων, ὅτι
μηδὲ τοὺς σωφρονεστέρους ῥυθμοὺς ἠγνόει. ἐτε-

---

[1] From certain taxes and expensive public services,
i.e. "liturgies."
[2] The law of Leptines abolished all exemptions from
public charges. In 355 B.C. Demosthenes by his speech
Against Leptines secured the repeal of the law. Heracleides may be punning on the word Leptis where the

of his privileges of exemption,[1] while Apollonius carried off gifts. Heracleides spread a false report about Apollonius that he was to set out forthwith to Libya, when the Emperor was staying there and was gathering about him the talented from all parts, and he said to Apollonius: " It is a good time for you to read the speech *Against Leptines*."[2] " Nay for you rather," retorted Apollonius, " for indeed it also was written on behalf of exemptions."

Apollonius took as the starting-point and basis of his eloquence the style of Hadrian, whose pupil he had in fact been. But in spite of this he slips into rhythms that belong to verse, and anapaestic effects ; but whenever he avoided these his style has great impressiveness and a stately march. This may be observed in others also of his arguments, but especially in that called " Callias tries to dissuade the Athenians from burning the dead": " Lift the torch on high, man ! Why do you do violence to its fire and abase it to the earth and torment it ? Fire belongs to the sky, it is ethereal, it tends towards that which is akin to itself. It does not lead the dead down below, but leads the gods up to the skies. Alas, Prometheus, torch-bearer and fire-bringer, see how thy gift is insulted ! It is polluted by the senseless corpse. Come to its help, give it aid, and, if thou canst, even from where thou art steal this fire ! "[3]

I have not quoted this passage in order to excuse him for his licence in the use of rhythms, but to show that he also knew how to use the more sober

Emperor was born. Philostratus here includes Egypt under the word Libya and refers to the visit of Severus to Egypt.

[3] Quoted by Norden, p. 414, for its dochmiac rhythm which was one of the marks of Asianism.

λεύτα μὲν οὖν ἀμφὶ τὰ πέντε καὶ ἑβδομήκοντα
ἔτη πολὺς καὶ ἐν τῷ Ἀθηναίων δήμῳ πνεύσας,
ἐτάφη δὲ ἐν τῷ προαστείῳ τῆς Ἐλευσῖνάδε λεω-
φόρου. ὄνομα μὲν δὴ τῷ προαστείῳ Ἱερὰ συκῆ,
τὰ δὲ Ἐλευσινόθεν ἱερά, ἐπειδὰν ἐς ἄστυ ἄγωσιν,
ἐκεῖ ἀναπαύουσιν.

κα΄. Ἀναγράψω καὶ Πρόκλον τὸν Ναυκρατίτην εἰδὼς εὖ τὸν ἄνδρα, καὶ γὰρ δὴ καὶ τῶν ἐμῶν
διδασκάλων εἷς οὗτος. Πρόκλος τοίνυν ἦν μὲν
603 τῶν οὐκ ἀφανῶν κατ᾽ Αἴγυπτον, στασιάζουσαν
δὲ ἰδὼν τὴν Ναύκρατιν καὶ παρὰ τὰ ἤθη πολι-
τεύοντας τὴν Ἀθήνησιν ἡσυχίαν ἠσπάσατο καὶ
ὑπεκπλεύσας ἐκεῖ ἔζη πολλὰ μὲν ἀγαγὼν χρήματα, πολλοὺς δὲ οἰκέτας καὶ τὴν ἄλλην κατα-
σκευὴν μεγαλοπρεπῶς κεκοσμημένην. εὖ δὲ ἀκούων Ἀθήνησι καὶ τὸν ἐν μειρακίῳ χρόνον ηὐδοκίμησε πολλῷ μᾶλλον ἀνὴρ γενόμενος, πρῶτον
μὲν ἐπὶ τῇ τοῦ βίου αἱρέσει, ἔπειτα, οἶμαι, καὶ
ἐπὶ εὐεργετήματι γενομένῳ μὲν περὶ ἕνα Ἀθηναῖον, δήλωσιν δὲ παρασχομένῳ χρηστοῦ ἤθους·
ἐς γὰρ τὸν Πειραιᾶ ἐσπλεύσας ἤρετό τινα τῶν
αὐτόθεν, εἰ ὁ δεῖνα καλῶς Ἀθήνησι ζῇ καὶ εὖ
πράττει, ἠρώτα δὲ ταῦτα ὑπὲρ τοῦ ξένου, ᾧ προσ-
έμιξεν Ἀθήνησι νέος ὤν, ὅτε δὴ καὶ Ἀδριανῷ
ἐφοίτα. μαθὼν δὲ αὐτὸν εἶναί τε καὶ ζῆν, ἐκπε-

---

[1] Pausanias i. 37; Athenaeus 74 D.
[2] Nothing more is known of this sophist.

sort. For the rest he died aged about seventy-five, after a career of great energy as a speaker at Athens, and was buried in the suburbs near the highway that leads to Eleusis. This suburb is called the "Sacred Fig-tree," [1] and when the sacred emblems from Eleusis are carried in procession to the city they halt here to rest.

21. I will proceed to record the life of PROCLUS OF NAUCRATIS [2] also, for I knew the man well, indeed he was one of my own teachers. Proclus, then, was a person of some importance in Egypt, but since he saw that Naucratis was rent by factions and that the State was administered with no regard to law and order, he desired to embrace the peace and quiet of Athens. So he sailed away secretly, and spent his life in that city. He brought with him a large sum of money, many slaves and other household gear, all splendid and ornate. Even while yet a stripling he was well thought of at Athens, but after he had attained to manhood he became far more renowned. This was due in the first place to the manner of life that he elected, but also I think it was because of a beneficent act of his, which, though it concerned only one Athenian citizen, yet furnished clear proof of a noble and generous disposition. For when he had arrived by ship at the Piraeus, he inquired of one of the inhabitants of that place whether a certain person still lived at Athens, and whether his affairs were going well. Now these inquiries concerned a friend and host of his with whom he had been intimate as a young man at Athens, at the time, that is, when he was attending the lectures of Hadrian. He was told that he still survived and lived there, but that he was on the point of being evicted from

σεῖσθαι δὲ αὐτίκα τῆς οἰκίας διακηρυττομένης ἐπ'
ἀγορᾶς πρὸς δραχμὰς μυρίας, ἃς ἐπ' αὐτῇ ἐδεδά-
νειστο, ἔπεμψεν αὐτῷ τὰς μυρίας μηδὲ ἀνελθών
πω ἐς τὸ ἄστυ εἰπὼν " ἐλευθέρωσον τὴν οἰκίαν, ἵνα
μή σε κατηφῆ ἴδω." ταῦτα μὴ πλουσίου μόνον
ἡγώμεθα, ἀλλὰ καὶ τῷ πλούτῳ καλῶς χρωμένου
πεπαιδευμένου τε ἱκανῶς καὶ τὰ φιλικὰ ἀκριβοῦντος.
    Ἐκτήσατο δὲ καὶ οἰκίας δ',[1] δύο μὲν ἐν ἄστει,
μίαν δὲ ἐν Πειραιεῖ καὶ ἄλλην Ἐλευσῖνι. ἐφοίτα
δὲ αὐτῷ καὶ ἀπ' Αἰγύπτου λιβανωτὸς ἐλέφας
μύρον βίβλος βιβλία καὶ πᾶσα ἡ τοιάδε ἀγορά,
καὶ ἀποδιδόμενος αὐτὰ τοῖς διατιθεμένοις τὰ
τοιαῦτα οὐδαμοῦ φιλοχρήματος ἔδοξεν οὐδὲ ἀν-
ελεύθερος, οὐδὲ ἐραστὴς τοῦ πλείονος, οὐδὲ ἐπικέρδειαν[2] μαστεύων ἢ τόκους, ἀλλ' αὐτὸ ἀγαπῶν
τὸ ἀρχαῖον. υἱῷ τε ἀσώτῳ περὶ ἀλεκτρυόνων
τροφὴν περί τε ὀρτύγων κυνῶν τε καὶ κυνιδίων
καὶ ἵππων ξυννεάζων μᾶλλον ἢ ἐπιπλήττων καὶ
παρὰ τοῖς πολλοῖς ἔχων αἰτίαν " θᾶττον" ἔφη
" μεταβαλεῖ τὸ μετὰ γερόντων παίζειν ἢ μετὰ
ἡλίκων." ἀποθανόντος δὲ αὐτῷ τοῦ παιδὸς καὶ
τῆς γυναικὸς ἐπὶ παλλακῇ ἐγένετο διὰ τὸ καὶ
604 γηράσκοντας ὀφθαλμοὺς ἐπάγεσθαι, θηλυτάτῃ δὲ
αὐτῇ γενομένῃ πᾶσαν ἐφιεὶς ἡνίαν οὐκ ἀγαθὸς
ἔδοξε προστάτης τοῦ οἴκου.
    Τὰ δὲ τῆς μελέτης πάτρια τῷ ἀνδρὶ τούτῳ διέ-
κειτο ὧδε· ἑκατὸν δραχμὰς ἅπαξ καταβαλόντι

---

[1] δ' Richards adds, cf. p. 510.
[2] ἐπικέρδια Kayser; ἐπικέρδειαν Valckenaer, Cobet; so
correct Heroicus 740.

---

[1] The book trade has passed from Athens to Alexandria
and Rome.

his house, and that it was being advertised for sale in the market-place, for ten thousand drachmae, for which sum he had mortgaged it. Thereupon, before he himself even went up to the city, he sent the man the sum named, with this message ; " Free your house, that I may not see you depressed." We are to consider this the act not of a rich man merely, but of one who knew how to use his riches to good purpose, one whom education had made truly humane, and who had an exact understanding of the claims of friendship.

He bought four houses, two in Athens itself, one at the Piraeus, and another at Eleusis. He used to receive direct from Egypt regular supplies of incense, ivory, myrrh, papyrus, books,[1] and all such merchandise, and would sell them to those who traded in such things, but on no occasion did he show himself avaricious or illiberal or a lover of gain ; for he did not seek after profits or usury, but was content with his actual principal. He had a son who dissipated his fortune in breeding fighting-cocks, quails, dogs, puppies, and horses, but instead of rebuking him he used to join him in these youthful pursuits. And when many people blamed him for this, he said : " He will stop playing with old men sooner than he will with those of his own age." When his son died and then his wife, he became attached to a mistress, since even eyes that are growing old can be captivated, and as she had all the feminine vices he gave her the rein in all matters, and showed himself a very poor guardian of his own estate.

Proclus laid down the following rules for attendance at his school of declamation. One hundred

ἐξῆν ἀκροᾶσθαι τὸν ἀεὶ χρόνον. ἦν δὲ αὐτῷ καὶ
θήκη βιβλίων ἐπὶ τῆς οἰκίας, ὧν μετῆν τοῖς ξυλ-
λεγομένοις ἐς τὸ πλήρωμα τῆς ἀκροάσεως. ὡς
δὲ μὴ συρίττοιμεν ἀλλήλους, μηδὲ σκώπτοιμεν,
ἃ ἐν ταῖς τῶν σοφιστῶν ξυνουσίαις φιλεῖ γίγνεσθαι, ἀθρόοι ἐσεκαλούμεθα καὶ ἐκαθήμεθα ἐσ-
κληθέντες οἱ μὲν παῖδες καὶ οἱ παιδαγωγοὶ μέσοι,[1]
τὰ μειράκια δὲ αὐτοί. τὸ μὲν οὖν διαλεχθῆναι
αὐτὸν ἐν σπανιστοῖς ἔκειτο, ὅτε δὲ ὁρμήσειεν ἐς
διάλεξιν, ἱππιάζοντί τε ἐῴκει καὶ γοργιάζοντι.
ἡ μελέτη δὲ τῆς προτεραίας προεωραμένη ἐσεκυ-
κλεῖτο. τὸ δὲ μνημονικὸν ἐνενηκοντούτης ἤδη
γηράσκων καὶ ὑπὲρ τὸν Σιμωνίδην ἔρρωτο, καὶ
ἑρμήνευε μὲν κατὰ φύσιν, Ἀδριάνειοι δὲ ἦσαν αἱ
ἐπιβολαὶ τῶν νοημάτων.

κβ΄. Φοῖνιξ δὲ ὁ Θετταλὸς οὐδὲ θαυμάσαι ἄξιος,
οὐδὲ αὖ διαβαλεῖν πάντα. ἦν μὲν γὰρ τῶν Φιλάγρῳ πεφοιτηκότων, γνῶναι δὲ ἀμείνων ἢ ἑρμηνεῦσαι, τάξιν τε γὰρ τὸ νοηθὲν εἶχε καὶ οὐθὲν
ἔξω καιροῦ ἐνοεῖτο, ἡ δὲ ἑρμηνεία διεσπάσθαι τε
ἐδόκει καὶ ῥυθμοῦ ἀφεστηκέναι. ἐδόκει δὲ ἐπι-
τηδειότερος γεγονέναι τοῖς ἀρχομένοις τῶν νέων
ἢ τοῖς ἕξιν τινὰ ἤδη κεκτημένοις, τὰ γὰρ πράγματα γυμνὰ ἐξέκειτο καὶ οὐ περιήμπισχεν αὐτὰ
ἡ λέξις. ἑβδομηκοντούτης δὲ ἀποθανὼν Ἀθήνησιν ἐτάφη οὐκ ἀφανῶς, κεῖται γὰρ πρὸς τοῖς

---

[1] *i.e.* the attendants who had brought the boys to the
school.

[2] In his *Life of Apollonius* Philostratus says precisely the
same of Apollonius of Tyana at the age of one hundred.
Simonides the fifth-century lyric poet was famous for his
good memory.

[3] Nothing more is known of this sophist.

drachmae paid down gave one the right to attend his lectures at all times. Moreover, he had a library at his own house which was open to his pupils and supplemented the teaching in his lectures. And to prevent us from hissing or jeering at one another, as so often happens in the schools of the sophists, we were summoned to come in all together, and when we had obeyed the summons we sat down, first the boys, then the pedagogues[1] in the middle, and the youths by themselves. It was the rarest thing for him to deliver a formal prooemium, but whenever he did embark on such an address, Hippias and Gorgias were the men whom he resembled. He used to review his declamations on the day before he delivered them in public. Even when he was an old man, aged ninety years, in his powers of memory he surpassed even Simonides.[2] The style of his eloquence was natural, but in his abundant use of synonyms he imitated Hadrian.

22. PHOENIX[3] THE THESSALIAN deserves neither to be admired, nor on the other hand to be wholly slighted. He was one of the pupils of Philagrus, but he had more talent for oratorical invention than for eloquence. For though his ideas were disposed in the proper order, and he never uttered any that were unsuited to the occasion, yet his style of eloquence seemed disjointed and destitute of rhythm. He was thought to be better suited to teach youths who were beginners than those who had already acquired some grasp of their studies; for his subject matter was displayed in the barest terms, and his diction failed to clothe it with rhetoric. He died at Athens at the age of seventy, and was buried in no obscure place, for he lies near the graves of

ἐκ τῶν πολέμων ἐν δεξιᾷ τῆς Ἀκαδημίανδε καθόδου.

605 κγ'. Ἄγει με ὁ λόγος ἐπ' ἄνδρα ἐλλογιμώτατον Δαμιανὸν τὸν ἐκ τῆς Ἐφέσου, ὅθεν ἐξηρήσθων Σωτῆροί τε καὶ Σῶσοι καὶ Νίκανδροι καὶ Φαῖδροι Κῦροί τε καὶ Φύλακες, ἀθύρματα γὰρ τῶν Ἑλλήνων μᾶλλον οὗτοι προσρηθεῖεν ἂν ἢ σοφισταὶ λόγου ἄξιοι. Δαμιανῷ τοίνυν ἐλλογιμώτατον μὲν καὶ τὸ ἄνω γένος καὶ πλείστου ἄξιον τῇ Ἐφέσῳ, εὐδοκιμώτατοι δὲ καὶ οἱ ἀπ' αὐτοῦ φύντες, ξυγκλήτου γὰρ βουλῆς ἀξιοῦνται πάντες ἐπ' εὐδοξίᾳ θαυμαζόμενοι καὶ ὑπεροψίᾳ χρημάτων, αὐτός τε πλούτῳ ποικίλῳ καὶ πολυπρεπεῖ κατεσκευασμένος ἐπήρκει μὲν καὶ τοῖς δεομένοις τῶν Ἐφεσίων, πλεῖστα δὲ ὠφέλει τὸ κοινὸν χρήματά τε ἐπιδιδοὺς καὶ τὰ ὑποδεδωκότα τῶν δημοσίων ἔργων ἀνακτώμενος. συνῆψε δὲ καὶ τὸ ἱερὸν τῇ Ἐφέσῳ κατατείνας ἐς αὐτὸ τὴν διὰ τῶν Μαγνητικῶν κάθοδον. ἔστι δὲ αὕτη στοὰ ἐπὶ στάδιον λίθου πᾶσα, νοῦς δὲ τοῦ οἰκοδομήματος μὴ ἀπεῖναι τοῦ ἱεροῦ τοὺς θεραπεύοντας,[1] ὁπότε ὕοι. τοῦτο μὲν δὴ τοὖργον ἀπὸ πολλῶν χρημάτων ἀποτελεσθὲν ἐπέγραψεν ἀπὸ τῆς ἑαυτοῦ γυναικός, τὸ δὲ ἐν τῷ ἱερῷ ἑστιατήριον αὐτὸς ἀνέθηκε μεγέθει τε ἐξάρας ὑπὲρ πάνθ' ὁμοῦ τὰ παρ' ἑτέροις καὶ λόγου κρείττω περιβαλὼν κό-

---

[1] θεραπεύσοντας Richards suggests.

---

[1] Nothing more is known of this sophist.

[2] Soter was an Athenian by birth, though he was educated at Ephesus. We have the inscription found there, in which he is made to boast that the Ephesians twice honoured him with the title of "leading sophist"; this was probably set

those who died in the wars, on the right of the road that goes down to the Academy.

23. In the course of my narrative I now come to a man who became most illustrious, DAMIANUS[1] OF EPHESUS. But let me omit from it such persons as Soter,[2] Sosus, Nicander, Phaedrus, Cyrus, and Phylax, since these men would more properly be called the playthings of the Greeks than sophists worthy of mention. Damianus, then, was descended from the most distinguished ancestors who were highly esteemed at Ephesus, and his offspring likewise were held in high repute, for they are all honoured with seats in the Senate, and are admired both for their distinguished renown and because they do not set too much store by their money. Damianus was himself magnificently endowed with wealth of various sorts, and not only maintained the poor of Ephesus, but also gave most generous aid to the State by contributing large sums of money and by restoring any public buildings that were in need of repair. Moreover, he connected the temple[3] with Ephesus by making an approach to it along the road that runs through the Magnesian gate. This work is a portico a stade in length, all of marble, and the idea of this structure is that the worshippers need not stay away from the temple in case of rain. When this work was completed at great expense, he inscribed it with a dedication to his wife, but the banqueting-hall in the temple he dedicated in his own name, and in size he built it to surpass all that exist elsewhere put together. He decorated it with an elegance beyond words, for it is adorned

up by the eleven pupils whose names precede the inscription: *Jahreshefte öst. arch. Inst.*, 1953, p. 16.   [3] Of Artemis.

σμον, ὡράισται γὰρ Φρυγίῳ λίθῳ, οἷος οὔπω
ἐτμήθη. πλούτῳ δὲ χρῆσθαι καλῶς ἐκ μειρακίου ἤρξατο· Ἀριστείδου γὰρ δὴ καὶ Ἀδριανοῦ
κατειληφότοιν τοῦ μὲν τὴν Σμύρναν, τοῦ δὲ τὴν
Ἔφεσον, ἠκροάσατο ἀμφοῖν ἐπὶ μυρίαις εἰπὼν
πολλῷ ἥδιον ἐς τοιαῦτα δαπανᾶν παιδικὰ ἢ ἐς
καλούς τε καὶ καλάς, ὥσπερ ἔνιοι. καὶ ὁπόσα
ὑπὲρ τῶν ἀνδρῶν τούτων ἀναγέγραφα Δαμιανοῦ
μαθὼν εὕρηκα εὖ τὰ ἀμφοῖν εἰδότος. πλούτου δὲ
606 ἐπίδειξιν τῷ ἀνδρὶ τούτῳ κἀκεῖνα εἶχεν· πρῶτα
μὲν ἡ γῆ πᾶσα, ὁπόσην ἐκέκτητο, ἐκπεφυτευμένη
δένδρεσι καρπίμοις τε καὶ εὐσκίοις, ἐν δὲ τοῖς
ἐπὶ θαλάττῃ καὶ νῆσοι χειροποίητοι καὶ λιμένων
προσχώσεις[1] βεβαιοῦσαι τοὺς ὅρμους καταιροῦ-
σαις τε καὶ ἀφιείσαις ὁλκάσιν, οἰκίαι τε ἐν προ-
αστείοις αἱ μὲν κατεσκευασμέναι τὸν ἐν ἄστει
τρόπον, αἱ δὲ ἀντρώδεις, ἔπειτα αὐτοῦ τοῦ ἀνδρὸς
τὸ ἐν τῇ ἀγορᾷ ἦθος οὐ πᾶν ἀσπαζομένου κέρδος,
οὐδὲ ἐπαινοῦντος τὸ ἐξ ἅπαντος λαμβάνειν, ἀλλ'
οὓς αἴσθοιτο ἀποροῦντας προῖκα τούτοις τὴν
ἑαυτοῦ φωνὴν διδόντος. παραπλήσιον δὲ ἦν κἂν
τοῖς σοφιστικοῖς τῶν λόγων, οὓς γὰρ αἴσθοιτο
ἀποροῦντας ἐξ ὑπερορίων ἐθνῶν ἥκοντας, ἠφίει
τούτοις τὸν μισθὸν τῆς ἀκροάσεως, μὴ λάθοιεν
δαπανώμενοι.

[1] προσχώσεις Kayser ; προσχώσεις Cobet.

with Phrygian marble such as had never before been quarried. Even when a stripling he began to spend his wealth to good purpose. For when Aristeides and Hadrian held sway, the former at Smyrna, the latter at Ephesus, he attended the lectures of both men, and paid them fees of ten thousand drachmae, declaring that he found it more agreeable to spend money on favourites of that sort than on handsome boys and girls, as some prefer to do. And in fact all that I have recorded above about those sophists I stated on the authority of Damianus, who was well acquainted with the careers of both. The wealth of Damianus was displayed also in what I shall now describe. In the first place all the land that he had acquired was planted with trees, both to bear fruit and to give abundant shade. And for his estate by the sea-shore he made artificial islands and moles for harbours to secure safe anchorage for cargo-boats when they put in or set sail; then his residences in the suburbs were in some cases furnished and equipped like town houses, while others were more like grottoes. In the next place the man's own disposition, as he showed it in legal affairs, was that of one who did not embrace every chance of making a profit or approve of taking what he could get from any and every one. On the contrary, whenever he saw that people were in difficulties, he would offer to speak for them himself without payment. It was much the same with his sophistic lectures; for whenever he saw that pupils who had come from remote peoples were embarrassed for money, he used to remit the fee for his lectures, that they might not be led unawares into spending too much.

Ἦν δὲ δικανικοῦ μὲν σοφιστικώτερος, σοφιστικοῦ δὲ δικανικώτερος. προϊὼν δὲ ἐς γῆρας μεθῆκεν ἄμφω τὰς σπουδὰς τὸ σῶμα καταλυθεὶς μᾶλλον ἢ τὴν γνώμην· τοῖς γοῦν κατὰ κλέος αὐτοῦ
φοιτῶσιν ἐς τὴν Ἔφεσον παρέχων ἑαυτὸν ἀνέθηκε κἀμοί τινα ξυνουσίαν πρώτην τε καὶ δευτέραν καὶ τρίτην, καὶ εἶδον ἄνδρα παραπλήσιον
τῷ Σοφοκλείῳ ἵππῳ, νωθρὸς γὰρ ὑφ᾽ ἡλικίας
δοκῶν νεάζουσαν ὁρμὴν ἐν ταῖς σπουδαῖς ἀνε-
κτᾶτο. ἐτελεύτα δὲ οἴκοι ἔτη βιοὺς ἑβδομήκοντα
καὶ ἐτάφη ἐν προαστείῳ τινὶ τῶν ἑαυτοῦ, ᾧ μάλιστα ἐνεβίωσεν.

κδ´. Ἀντιπάτρῳ δὲ τῷ σοφιστῇ πατρὶς μὲν
ἦν Ἱεράπολις, ἐγκαταλεκτέα δὲ αὕτη ταῖς κατὰ
τὴν Ἀσίαν εὖ πραττούσαις, πατὴρ δὲ Ζευξίδημος
τῶν ἐπιφανεστάτων ἐκείνῃ, Ἀδριανῷ δὲ καὶ
607 Πολυδεύκει φοιτήσας ἀπὸ τοῦ Πολυδεύκους μᾶλλον ἥρμοσται, τὰς ὁρμὰς τῶν νοημάτων ἐκλύων
τοῖς τῆς ἑρμηνείας ῥυθμοῖς. ἀκροασάμενος δὲ
καὶ Ζήνωνος τοῦ Ἀθηναίου τὸ περὶ τὴν τέχνην
ἀκριβὲς ἐκείνου ἔμαθεν. αὐτοσχέδιος δὲ ὢν οὐδὲ
φροντισμάτων ἠμέλει, ἀλλ᾽ Ὀλυμπικούς τε ἡμῖν
διῄει καὶ Παναθηναϊκοὺς καὶ ἐς ἱστορίαν ἔβαλε [1]
τὰ Σεβήρου τοῦ βασιλέως ἔργα, ὑφ᾽ οὗ μάλιστα
ταῖς βασιλείοις ἐπιστολαῖς ἐπιταχθεὶς λαμπρόν τι
ἐν αὐταῖς ἤχησεν. ἐμοὶ μὲν γὰρ δὴ ἀποπεφάνθω
μελετῆσαι μὲν καὶ ξυγγράψαι τοῦ ἀνδρὸς τούτου

_____
[1] ἔλαβε Kayser; ἔβαλε Cobet.

_____
[1] See above, pp. 511, 569, where the same is said of Nicetes
and Antiochus.
[2] *Electra* 25.
He was appointed by Severus independently of his son
and *consors imperii*, Caracalla.

His style was more sophistic than is usual in a legal orator, and more judicial than is usual in a sophist.[1] As old age came on he gave up both these pursuits, from weakness of body rather than of mind. At any rate when students were attracted to Ephesus by his renown he still allowed them access to himself, and so it was that he honoured me also with one interview, then with a second and a third. And so I beheld a man who resembled the horse in Sophocles.[2] For though he seemed sluggish from old age, nevertheless in our discussions he recovered the vigour of youth. He died at home aged seventy years, and was buried in one of his own suburban villas in which he had spent most of his life.

24. The birthplace of ANTIPATER the sophist was Hierapolis, which must be reckoned among the flourishing cities of Asia, and his father was Zeuxidemus, one of the most distinguished men in that place. Though he studied under Hadrian and Pollux, he modelled himself rather on Pollux, and hence he weakened the force of his ideas by the rhythmical effects of his style. He also attended the lectures of Zeno of Athens, and from him learned the subtleties of his art. Though he had a talent for speaking extempore, he nevertheless did not neglect written work, but used to recite to us Olympic and Panathenaic orations and wrote an historical account of the achievements of the Emperor Severus. For it was by the latter's independent[3] appointment that he was made Imperial Secretary, a post in which he was brilliantly successful. For my part let me here openly express my opinion that, though there were many men who both declaimed and wrote historical narrative better than Antipater,

πολλοὺς βέλτιον, ἐπιστεῖλαι δὲ μηδένα ἄμεινον,
ἀλλ' ὥσπερ τραγῳδίας λαμπρὸν ὑποκριτὴν τοῦ
δράματος εὖ ξυνιέντα ἐπάξια τοῦ βασιλείου προσώπου φθέγξασθαι. σαφήνειάν τε γὰρ τὰ λεγόμενα εἶχε καὶ γνώμης μέγεθος καὶ τὴν ἑρμηνείαν
ἐκ τῶν παρόντων καὶ ξὺν ἡδονῇ τὸ ἀσύνδετον, ὃ
δὴ μάλιστα ἐπιστολὴν λαμπρύνει.

Ὑπάτοις δὲ ἐγγραφεὶς ἦρξε μὲν τοῦ τῶν Βιθυνῶν ἔθνους, δόξας δὲ ἑτοιμότερον χρῆσθαι τῷ ξίφει
τὴν ἀρχὴν παρελύθη. βίου μὲν δὴ ὀκτὼ καὶ ἑξήκοντα ἔτη τῷ Ἀντιπάτρῳ ἐγένετο καὶ ἐτάφη οἴκοι,
λέγεται δὲ ἀποθανεῖν καρτερίᾳ μᾶλλον ἢ νόσῳ· διδάσκαλος μὲν γὰρ τῶν Σεβήρου παίδων ἐνομίσθη
καὶ θεῶν διδάσκαλον ἐκαλοῦμεν αὐτὸν ἐν τοῖς ἐπαίνοις τῆς ἀκροάσεως, ἀποθανόντος δὲ τοῦ νεωτέ-
ρου σφῶν ἐπ' αἰτίᾳ, ὡς τῷ ἀδελφῷ ἐπιβουλεύοι,
γράφει πρὸς τὸν πρεσβύτερον ἐπιστολὴν μονῳδίαν
περιέχουσαν[1] καὶ θρῆνον, ὡς εἷς μὲν αὐτῷ ὀφθαλ-
μὸς ἐκ δυοῖν, χεὶρ δὲ μία, καὶ οὓς ἐπαίδευσεν
ὅπλα ὑπὲρ ἀλλήλων αἴρεσθαι, τούτους ἀκούοι κατ'
ἀλλήλων ἠρμένους. ὑφ' ὧν παροξυνθῆναι τὸν
βασιλέα μὴ ἀπιστῶμεν, καὶ γὰρ ἂν καὶ ἰδιώτην
ταῦτα παρώξυνε βουλόμενόν γε τὸ δοκεῖν ἐπιβεβου-
λεῦσθαι μὴ ἀπιστεῖσθαι.

608   κε'. Πολὺς ἐν σοφιστῶν κύκλῳ καὶ Ἑρμοκρά-

---

[1] ἐπέχουσαν Kayser; περιέχουσαν Cobet.

[1] Secretaries were appointed by the Roman emperors to
write their letters, under which title rescripts and other
public documents were included. The secretary's title was
ab epistulis, or ἐπὶ τῶν ἐπιστολῶν, and sophists were often
appointed; cf. p. 590, and Eunapius, Nymphidianus 497.
[2] For this device see what is said of Critias, p. 503.

270

yet no one composed letters[1] better than he, but like a brilliant tragic actor who has a thorough knowledge of his profession, his utterances were always in keeping with the Imperial rôle. For what he said was always clear, the sentiments were elevated, the style was always well adapted to the occasion, and he secured a pleasing effect by the use of asyndeton,[2] a device that, in a letter above all, enhances the brilliance of the style.

He was elevated to the rank of consul, and governed the people of Bithynia, but as he showed himself too ready with the sword he was relieved of the office. Antipater lived to be sixty-eight, and was buried in his native place. It is said that he died of voluntary fasting rather than of any disease. For he had been appointed as tutor to the sons of Severus—in fact we used to call him "Tutor of the Gods" when we applauded his lectures—and when the younger of the two[3] was put to death on the charge that he was plotting against his brother, he wrote to the elder a letter which contained a monody and a dirge, lamenting that Caracalla now had but one eye left and one hand, and that those whom he had taught to take up arms for one another had now, he heard, taken them up against one another. We may well believe that the Emperor[4] was greatly incensed by this, and indeed these remarks would have incensed even a private person, at any rate if he were anxious to gain credence for an alleged plot against himself.

25. HERMOCRATES[5] OF PHOCAEA was a member of

---

[3] Geta; he was assassinated by Caracalla A.D. 212.
[4] Caracalla.
[5] Nothing more is known of this sophist.

της ὁ Φωκαεὺς ᾄδεται φύσεως ἰσχὺν δηλώσας
παρὰ πάντας, οὓς ἑρμηνεύω, οὐδενὶ γὰρ θαυμασίῳ σοφιστῇ ξυγγενόμενος, ἀλλὰ Ῥουφίνου τοῦ
Σμυρναίου ἀκηκοὼς τὰ σοφιστικὰ τολμῶντος
μᾶλλον ἢ κατορθοῦντος ἑρμήνευσε ποικιλώτατα
609 Ἑλλήνων καὶ ἔγνω καὶ ἔταξεν, οὐ τὰς μὲν τῶν
ὑποθέσεων, τὰς δὲ οὐχί, ἅπαξ δ' ἁπάσας[1] τὰς
μελετωμένας, καὶ γὰρ δὴ καὶ τὰς ἐσχηματισμένας
εὖ διέθετο ἀμφιβολίας τε πλείστας ἐπινοήσας καὶ
τὸ σημαινόμενον ἐγκαταμίξας τῷ ὑφειμένῳ.

Πάππος μὲν δὴ αὐτῷ ἐγένετο Ἄτταλος ὁ Πολέμωνος τοῦ σοφιστοῦ παῖς, πατὴρ δὲ Ῥουφινιανὸς
ὁ ἐκ Φωκαίας, ἀνὴρ ὕπατος Καλλιστὼ γήμας τὴν
610 Ἀττάλου. τελευτήσαντος δὲ αὐτῷ τοῦ πατρὸς ἐς
διαφορὰν κατέστη πρὸς τὴν ἑαυτοῦ μητέρα οὕτω τι
ἀπαραίτητον, ὡς μηδὲ δάκρυον ἐπ' αὐτῷ τὴν Καλλιστὼ ἀφεῖναι ἐν μειρακίῳ ἀποθανόντι, ὅτε δὴ καὶ
τοῖς πολεμιωτάτοις ἐλεεινὰ τὰ τῆς ἡλικίας φαίνεται.
καὶ τοῦτο οὑτωσὶ μὲν ἀκούσαντι κακίᾳ τοῦ μειρακίου προσκείσεται μᾶλλον, εἰ μηδὲ μήτηρ ἐπ' αὐτῷ
τι ἔπαθεν, λογιζομένῳ δὲ τὴν αἰτίαν καὶ ὅτι τὴν
μητέρα ἀπέστερξεν ἐπὶ δούλου ἔρωτι, ὁ μὲν ξυμ-
βαίνων τοῖς νόμοις φαίνοιτο ἄν, οἳ δεδώκασι τὸ
ἐπὶ ταῖς τοιαῖσδε αἰτίαις καὶ ἀποκτείνειν, ἡ δὲ ἀξία
μισεῖν καὶ τοῖς οὐ προσήκουσιν ὑπὲρ ὧν ἑαυτήν τε
καὶ τὸν υἱὸν ᾔσχυνεν.

Ὥσπερ δὲ ταύτην ὁ Ἑρμοκράτης διαφεύγει τὴν

[1] δὲ πάσας Kayser; δ' ἁπάσας Cobet.

---

[1] See Glossary and p. 597.　　　[2] See above, p. 543.

the sophistic circle who became very celebrated and showed greater natural powers than any whom I describe here. For though he was not trained by any sophist of great repute, but was a pupil of Rufinus of Smyrna who in the sophistic art displayed more audacity than felicity, he easily surpassed all the Greeks of his day in variety, whether of eloquence or invention or arrangement; and it was not that he excelled thus in some kinds of arguments and not in others, but in all, without exception, to which he devoted his attention. For indeed he was very skilful also in handling speeches with simulated arguments,[1] devised many ambiguous expressions, and inserted among his veiled allusions a hint of the true meaning. His grandfather was Attalus, son of Polemo[2] the sophist, and his father was Rufinianus of Phocaea, a man of consular rank who had married Callisto, the daughter of Attalus. After his father's death he quarrelled with his own mother so irrevocably that Callisto did not even shed a tear for him when he died in the flower of his youth, though on such an occasion even to the bitterest enemies it seems piteous to die at that age. One who hears this and only this, will be inclined to impute it to the youth's own evil disposition that not even his mother felt any grief for his loss. But if one takes into account the real reason, and that he ceased to love his mother because of her low passion for a slave, it will appear that the son conformed to the laws, which actually give him the right to put a woman to death for a reason of that sort; whereas the woman deserves to be detested even by those outside the family for the disgrace that she brought upon herself and her son.

But while we acquit Hermocrates of this charge, it

αἰτίαν, οὕτως ἐκείνην οὐκ ἂν διαφύγοι· τὸν γὰρ
πατρῷον οἶκον βαθὺν αὐτῷ παραδοθέντα κατεδα-
πάνησεν οὐκ ἐς ἱπποτροφίας οὐδὲ ἐς λειτουργίας,
ἀφ' ὧν καὶ ὄνομά ἐστιν ἄρασθαι, ἀλλ' ἐς ἄκρατον
καὶ ἑταίρους οἵους παρασχεῖν καὶ κωμῳδίᾳ λόγον,
οἷον παρέσχον λόγον οἱ Καλλίαν ποτὲ τὸν Ἱππονί-
κου κολακεύσαντες.

Ἀντιπάτρου δὲ παρεληλυθότος ἐς τὰς βασιλείους
ἐπιστολὰς ἤδη ἀσπαζομένου τε ἁρμόσαι οἱ τὴν ἑαυτοῦ θυγατέρα πονήρως ἔχουσαν τοῦ εἴδους οὐκ
ἐπήδησε πρὸς τὴν ἐκείνου εὐπραγίαν, ἀλλὰ καὶ τῆς
προμνηστρίας ἀναγούσης ἐς τὴν τοῦ Ἀντιπάτρου
ἰσχύν, ἣν εἶχε τότε, οὐκ ἄν ποτε ἔφη δουλεῦσαι
προικὶ μακρᾷ καὶ πενθεροῦ τύφῳ. ἐξωθούντων δὲ
811 αὐτὸν τῶν συγγενῶν ἐς τὸν γάμον καὶ Διὸς Κόριν-
θον ἡγουμένων τὸν Ἀντίπατρον οὐ πρότερον εἶξεν
ἢ Σεβῆρον αὐτοκράτορα μεταπέμψαντα αὐτὸν ἐς
τὴν ἑῴαν δοῦναι οἱ τὴν κόρην, ὅτε δὴ καὶ τῶν ἐπιτηδείων ἐρομένου τινὸς αὐτόν, πότε ἄγοι τὰ ἀνα-
καλυπτήρια, ἀστειότατα ὁ Ἑρμοκράτης "ἐγκαλυ-
πτήρια μὲν οὖν" ἔφη "τοιαύτην λαμβάνων." καὶ
διέλυσε μετ' οὐ πολὺ τὸν γάμον ὁρῶν οὔτε ἰδεῖν
ἡδεῖαν οὔτε ἐπιτηδείαν τὸ ἦθος.

Καὶ ἀκροατὴς δὲ τοῦ Ἑρμοκράτους ὁ αὐτοκράτωρ γενόμενος ἠγάσθη αὐτὸν ἴσα τῷ πάππῳ δω-
ρεάς τε αἰτεῖν ἀνῆκεν· καὶ ὁ Ἑρμοκράτης "στε-

----

[1] This probably refers to the *Flatterers* of Eupolis; *cf.*
Athenaeus 506 E; Callias was a rich patron of Sophists.

[2] This popular proverb was used in two ways: of empty
boasting, because the Corinthians boasted that their
eponymous hero was Corinthus, son of Zeus; and to express
aimless iteration as in Pindar, *Nemean* vii. 105; but here it
merely implies exaggerated respect for Antipater.

is not so easy to acquit him of another. For he had inherited from his father a very handsome property, but he squandered it, not on breeding horses, or on public services from which one may win a great reputation, but on strong drink and boon companions of the sort that furnish a theme for Comedy, such a theme, I mean, as was once furnished by the flatterers of Callias, the son of Hipponicus.[1] After Antipater had been promoted to be Imperial Secretary he desired to arrange a marriage between Hermocrates and his daughter who was very unattractive in appearance. But Hermocrates did not jump at the chance to share Antipater's prosperity, but when the woman who was arranging the affair called his attention to the great resources of which Antipater was then possessed, he replied that he could never become the slave of a large dowry and a father-in-law's swollen pride. And though his relatives tried to push him into this marriage, and regarded Antipater as "Corinthus, son of Zeus,"[2] he did not give way until the Emperor Severus summoned him to the East and gave him the girl in marriage. Then, when one of his friends asked him when he was going to celebrate the unveiling of the bride, Hermocrates replied with ready wit: "Say rather the veiling, when I am taking a wife like that." And it was not long before he dissolved the marriage, on finding that she had neither a pleasing appearance nor an agreeable disposition.

When the Emperor had heard Hermocrates declaim he admired him as much as his great-grandfather,[3] and gave him the privilege of asking for presents. Whereupon Hermocrates said: "Crowns

[3] Polemo; see p. 610.

φάνους μὲν " ἔφη " καὶ ἀτελείας καὶ σιτήσεις
καὶ πορφύραν καὶ τὸ ἱερᾶσθαι ὁ πάππος ἡμῖν
τοῖς ἀπ' αὐτοῦ παρέδωκεν, καὶ τί ἂν αἰτοίην
παρὰ σοῦ τήμερον, ἃ ἐκ τοσούτου ἔχω; ἐπεὶ δέ
ἐστί μοι προστεταγμένον ὑπὸ τοῦ κατὰ τὸ Πέργαμον Ἀσκληπιοῦ πέρδικα σιτεῖσθαι λιβανωτῷ θυμιώ-
μενον, τὸ δὲ ἄρωμα τοῦτο οὕτω τι σπανιστὸν καθ'
ἡμᾶς νῦν, ὡς ψαιστὸν καὶ δάφνης φύλλα τοῖς θεοῖς
θυμιᾶσθαι, δέομαι λιβανωτοῦ ταλάντων πεντήκοντα, ἵνα θεραπεύοιμι μὲν τοὺς θεούς, θερα-
πευοίμην δὲ αὐτός." ἔδωκε τὸν λιβανωτὸν ξὺν
ἐπαίνῳ ὁ αὐτοκράτωρ ἐρυθριᾶν εἰπών, ἐπειδὴ
μικρὰ ᾐτήθη.

Ξυνελάμβανε δὲ τῷ Ἑρμοκράτει τῶν ἐπιδείξεων
πρῶτον μὲν τὸ τοῦ πάππου κλέος, ἡ γὰρ φύσις ἡ
ἀνθρωπεία τὰς ἀρετὰς ἀσπάζεται μᾶλλον τὰς ἐκ
πατέρων ἐς παῖδας διαδοθείσας, ὅθεν εὐκλεέστερος
μὲν Ὀλυμπιονίκης ὁ ἐξ Ὀλυμπιονικῶν οἴκου, γεν-
ναιότερος δὲ στρατιώτης ὁ μὴ ἀστρατεύτων ἡδίους
τε τῶν ἐπιτηδεύσεων αἱ πατέρων τε καὶ προγόνων,
καί που καὶ¹ τέχναι βελτίους αἱ κληρονομού-
μεναι, ξυνελάμβανε δὲ αὐτῷ καὶ ἡ ὥρα ἡ περὶ τῷ
εἴδει, καὶ γὰρ ἐπίχαρις καὶ ἀγαλματίας, οἷα ἔφηβοι,
καὶ τὸ θάρσος δὲ τοῦ μειρακίου τὸ ἐν τοῖς πλήθε-
σιν ἔκπληξιν ἐς τοὺς πολλοὺς ἔφερεν, ἣν ἐκπλήτ-
τονται ἄνθρωποι τοὺς τὰ μεγάλα μὴ ξὺν ἀγωνίᾳ
πράττοντας. ἐδίδου τι καὶ ἡ εὔροια καὶ ὁ τῆς
γλώττης κρότος καὶ τὸ ἐν στιγμῇ τοῦ καιροῦ

¹ οἴκου Kayser; suggests καὶ που καί.

and immunities and meals at the public expense, and the consular purple and the high-priesthood our great-grandfather bequeathed to his descendants. Why then should I ask from you to-day what I have so long possessed? However, I have been ordered by Asclepius at Pergamon to eat partridge stuffed with frankincense, and this seasoning is now so scarce in our country that we have to use barley meal and laurel leaves for incense to the gods. I therefore ask for fifty talents' worth of frankincense, that I may treat the gods properly and get proper treatment myself." Then the Emperor gave him the frankincense with approving words, and said that he blushed for shame at having been asked for so trifling a gift.

In his public declamations Hermocrates was aided in the first place by his great-grandfather's renown, since it is human nature to set a higher value on abilities that have been handed down from father to son; and for this reason more glory is won by an Olympic victor who comes of a family of Olympic victors; more honourable is that soldier who comes from a fighting stock; there is a keener pleasure in pursuits that have been followed by one's fathers and forefathers; and in fact arts that have been inherited have an advantage over the rest. But he was also aided by the beauty of his personal appearance, and he was indeed possessed of great charm and looked like a statue with the bloom of early youth. Then, too, the courage of this stripling, when facing a crowded audience, produced in most of his hearers that thrill of admiration which human beings feel for those who achieve great things without intense effort. Moreover his easy flow of words and the striking effects of his voice contributed to his success, and

ξυνορᾶν τὰς ὑποθέσεις καὶ τὰ ἀναγιγνωσκόμενά τε
καὶ λεγόμενα πολιώτερα[1] ὄντα ἢ νέῳ γε ἐνθυμηθῆναι
καὶ ἑρμηνεῦσαι. αἱ μὲν δὴ μελέται τοῦ Ἑρμοκράτους ὀκτώ που ἴσως ἢ δέκα καί τις λόγος οὐ
μακρός, ὃν ἐν Φωκαίᾳ διῆλθεν ἐπὶ[2] τῷ Πανιωνίῳ
κρατῆρι. ἐμοὶ δὲ ἀποπεφάνθω μὴ ἄν τινα ὑπερ-
φωνῆσαι τὴν μειρακίου τούτου γλῶτταν, εἰ μὴ
ἀφῃρέθη τὸ παρελθεῖν ἐς ἄνδρας φθόνῳ ἁλούς.
ἐτελεύτα δὲ κατ᾽ ἐνίους μὲν ὀκτὼ καὶ εἴκοσι
γεγονώς, ὡς δὲ ἔνιοι, πέντε καὶ εἴκοσι, καὶ ἐδέξατο
αὐτὸν ἡ πατρῴα γῆ καὶ αἱ πατρῷαι θῆκαι.

κϛ΄. Ἀνὴρ ἐλλογιμώτατος καὶ Ἡρακλείδης ὁ
Λύκιος καὶ τὰ οἴκοι μέν, ἐπειδὴ πατέρων τε ἀγαθῶν ἔφυ καὶ ἀρχιερεὺς Λυκίων ἐγένετο, τὴν δὲ
613 λειτουργησίαν οὖσαν οὐ μεγάλου ἔθνους Ῥωμαῖοι[3]
μεγάλων ἀξιοῦσιν ὑπὲρ ξυμμαχίας, οἶμαι, παλαιᾶς,
ἐλλογιμώτερος δὲ ὁ Ἡρακλείδης τὰ σοφιστικά,
ἀποχρῶν μὲν γὰρ ξυνεῖναι, ἀποχρῶν δὲ ἑρμηνεῦσαι
καὶ τοὺς ἀγῶνας ἀπέριττος καὶ τὰς πανηγυρικὰς
ἐννοίας οὐχ ὑπερβακχεύων.

Ἐκπεσὼν δὲ τοῦ θρόνου τοῦ Ἀθήνησι ξυστάν-
των ἐπ᾽ αὐτὸν τῶν Ἀπολλωνίου τοῦ Ναυκρατίτου
ἑταίρων, ὧν πρῶτος καὶ μέσος καὶ τελευταῖος Μαρ-
κιανὸς ὁ ἐκ Δολίχης ἐγένετο, ἐπὶ τὴν Σμύρναν

---

[1] παλαιότερα Kayser; suggests πολιώτερα.
[2] ἐν Kayser; ἐπὶ Cobet.
[3] Ῥωμαίων MSS., Kayser; Ῥωμαῖοι Valckenaer and others.

---

[1] For this festival at Smyrna and for the ceremony of the
loving-cup from which the assembled Ionians drank as a
sign of their friendship, see *Life of Apollonius*, iv. 5–6.
[2] Nothing more is known of this sophist.
[3] This phrase, here meaninglessly applied, elsewhere
expresses extreme respect; *cf.* Theocritus xvii. 4; Euripides,
Iphigenia at Aulis 1125; and *Paradise Lost*, "Him first,
him last, him midst and without end."

the fact that he could review his themes in the twinkling of an eye, and that what he recited from a manuscript or declaimed was more what one expects from hoary old age than from a mere youth to invent and deliver.   There are extant perhaps eight or ten declamations by Hermocrates and a sort of short address which he delivered at Phocaea over the Pan-Ionian loving-cup.[1] But let me here record my judgement that the eloquence of this stripling would have been such that no one could surpass it, had he not been cut off by an envious deity and prevented from attaining to mature manhood.   He died, as some say, at the age of twenty-eight, though according to others he was only twenty-five, and the land of his fathers and the sepulchres of his fathers received him.

26. HERACLEIDES [2] THE LYCIAN was also a very notable person, in the first place as regards his family, since he was descended from distinguished ancestors and so became high-priest of Lycia, an office which, though it concerns a small nation, is highly considered by the Romans, I suppose on account of their long-standing alliance with Lycia.   But Heracleides was still more notable as a sophist, because of his great abilities both in invention and oratorical expression ; in judicial arguments also he was simple and direct, and in speeches composed for public gatherings he never revelled in a mere frenzy of rhetoric.

When he had been turned out of the chair of rhetoric at Athens in consequence of a conspiracy against him got up by the followers of Apollonius of Naucratis, in which Marcianus of Doliche was first, middle, and last,[3] he betook himself to Smyrna,[4] which

[4] For Smyrna as a centre of sophistic eloquence see p. 516.

ἐτράπετο θύουσαν μάλιστα δὴ πόλεων ταῖς τῶν σοφιστῶν Μούσαις. νεότητα μὲν οὖν Ἰωνικήν τε καὶ
Λύδιον καὶ τὴν ἐκ Φρυγῶν καὶ Καρίας ξυνδραμεῖν
ἐς Ἰωνίαν κατὰ ξυνουσίαν τοῦ ἀνδρὸς οὔπω μέγα,
ἐπειδὴ ἀγχίθυρος ἁπάσαις ἡ Σμύρνα, ὁ δὲ ἦγε μὲν
καὶ τὸ ἐκ τῆς Εὐρώπης Ἑλληνικόν, ἦγε δὲ τοὺς ἐκ
τῆς ἑῴας νέους, πολλοὺς δὲ ἦγεν Αἰγυπτίων οὐκ
ἀνηκόους αὐτοῦ ὄντας, ἐπειδὴ Πτολεμαίῳ τῷ Ναυ-
κρατίτῃ κατὰ Αἴγυπτον περὶ σοφίας ἤρισεν. ἐνέπλησε μὲν δὴ τὴν Σμύρναν ὁμίλου λαμπροῦ, ὤνησε
δὲ καὶ πλείω ἕτερα, ἃ ἐγὼ δηλώσω· πόλις ἐς
ξένους πολλοὺς ἐπεστραμμένη ἄλλως τε καὶ σοφίας
ἐρῶντας σωφρόνως μὲν βουλεύσει, σωφρόνως δὲ
ἐκκλησιάσει φυλαττομένη δήπου τὸ ἐν πολλοῖς τε
καὶ σπουδαίοις κακὴ ἁλίσκεσθαι, ἱερῶν τε ἐπιμε-
λήσεται καὶ γυμνασίων καὶ κρηνῶν καὶ στοῶν, ἵνα
ἀποχρῶσα τῷ ὁμίλῳ φαίνοιτο. εἰ δὲ καὶ ναύκληρος ἡ πόλις εἴη καθάπερ ἡ Σμύρνα, πολλὰ καὶ
ἄφθονα αὐτοῖς ἡ θάλασσα δώσει. ξυνήρατο δὲ τῇ
Σμύρνῃ καὶ τοῦ εἴδους ἐλαίου κρήνην ἐπισκευάσας
ἐν τῷ τοῦ Ἀσκληπιοῦ γυμνασίῳ χρυσῆν τοῦ ὀρόφου,
καὶ τὴν στεφανηφόρον ἀρχὴν παρ' αὐτοῖς ἦρξεν,
ἀφ' ὧν τοῖς ἐνιαυτοῖς τίθενται Σμυρναῖοι τὰ
ὀνόματα.

614 Ἐπὶ Σεβήρου δὲ αὐτοκράτορός φασιν αὐτὸν
σχεδίου λόγου ἐκπεσεῖν αὐλὴν καὶ δορυφόρους
δείσαντα. τουτὶ δὲ ἀγοραῖός μέν τις παθὼν κἂν
αἰτίαν λάβοι, τὸ γὰρ τῶν ἀγοραίων ἔθνος ἰταμοὶ

more than any other city sacrificed to the sophistic Muses. Now the fact that the youth of Ionia, Lydia, Phrygia, and Caria flocked to Ionia to study with him is not so wonderful, seeing that Smyrna is next door to all these countries, but he attracted thither the Hellenes from Europe, he attracted the youth of the Orient, and he attracted many from Egypt who had already heard him, because in Egypt he had contended for the prize of learning against Ptolemy of Naucratis. Thus, then, he filled Smyrna with a brilliant throng, and he benefited her in several other ways too, as I shall show. A city which is much frequented by foreigners, especially if they are lovers of learning, will be prudent and moderate in its councils, and prudent and moderate in its citizen assemblies, because it will be on its guard against being convicted of wrongdoing in the presence of so many eminent persons; and it will take good care of its temples, gymnasia, fountains and porticoes, so that it may appear to meet the needs of that multitude. And should the city have a sea trade, as Smyrna in fact has, the sea will supply them with many things in abundance. He also contributed to the beauty of Smyrna by constructing in the gymnasium of Asclepius a fountain for olive oil with a golden roof, and he held in that city the office of the priest who wears the crown; the people of Smyrna designate the years by the names of these priests.

They say that in the presence of the Emperor Severus he broke down in an extempore speech, because he was abashed by the court and the Imperial bodyguard. Now if this misfortune were to happen to a forensic orator, he might well be criticized; for forensic orators as a tribe are audacious

καὶ θρασεῖς, σοφιστὴς δὲ ξυσπουδάζων μειρακίοις
τὸ πολὺ τῆς ἡμέρας πῶς ἂν ἀντίσχοι ἐκπλήξει;
ἐκκρούει γὰρ σχεδίου λόγου καὶ ἀκροατὴς σεμνῷ
προσώπῳ καὶ βραδὺς ἔπαινος καὶ τὸ μὴ κροτεῖσθαι
συνήθως, εἰ δὲ καὶ φθόνου ὑποκαθημένου ἑαυτὸν
αἴσθοιτο, ὥσπερ ὁ Ἡρακλείδης τὸν τοῦ Ἀντιπάτρου τότε ὑφεωρᾶτο, ἧττον μὲν ἐνθυμηθήσεται,
ἧττον δὲ εὑροήσει, αἱ γὰρ τοιαίδε ὑποψίαι γνώμης
ἀχλὺς καὶ δεσμὰ γλώττης.

Ἱερὰς δὲ λέγεται κέδρους ἐκτεμὼν δημευθῆναι
τὸ πολὺ τῆς οὐσίας, ὅτε δὴ καὶ ἀπιόντι αὐτῷ τοῦ
δικαστηρίου ἐπηκολούθουν μὲν οἱ γνώριμοι παρα-
μυθούμενοί τε καὶ ἀνέχοντες τὸν ἄνδρα, ἑνὸς δὲ
αὐτῶν εἰπόντος '' ἀλλ' οὐ μελέτην ἀφαιρήσεταί τις,
ὦ Ἡρακλείδη, οὐδὲ τὸ ἐπ' αὐτῇ κλέος,'' καὶ ἐπιρ-
ραψῳδήσαντος αὐτῷ τὸ '' εἷς δή που λοιπὸς κατερύκεται εὐρέι '' — '' φίσκῳ '' ἔφη, ἀστειότατα δὴ ἐπι-
παίξας τοῖς ἑαυτοῦ κακοῖς.

Δοκεῖ δὲ μάλιστα σοφιστῶν οὗτος τὴν ἐπιστήμην πόνῳ κατακτήσασθαι μὴ ξυγχωρούσης αὐτῷ
τῆς φύσεως, καὶ ἔστιν αὐτῷ φρόντισμα οὐκ ἀηδές,
βιβλίον ξύμμετρον, ὃ ἐπιγέγραπται Πόνου ἐγκώ-
615 μιον, τὸ δὲ βιβλίον τοῦτο πρὸ χειρῶν ἔχων ἐνέτυχε
Πτολεμαίῳ τῷ σοφιστῇ κατὰ τὴν Ναύκρατιν, ὁ δὲ
ἤρετο αὐτόν, ὅ τι σπουδάζοι, τοῦ δὲ εἰπόντος, ὅτι
πόνου εἴη ἐγκώμιον, αἰτήσας ὁ Πτολεμαῖος τὸ βι-

---

[1] For this quotation, which was popular because it was
easily parodied, see p. 558; here the pupil means that
Heraclides and his fame survive, but the sophist by his
allusion to the confiscation of his property to the Emperor,
alters the sense of the verb to mean " is checked by," and
changes the last word from " sea " to " privy purse."

and self-confident; but a sophist spends the greater
part of his day in teaching mere boys, and how
should he resist being easily flustered? For an extempore speaker is disconcerted by a single hearer
whose features have a supercilious expression, or by
tardy applause, or by not being clapped in the way
to which he is accustomed; but if in addition he
is aware that malice is lying in wait for him, as
on that occasion Heracleides was subtly conscious
of the malice of Antipater, his ideas will not
come so readily, his words will not flow so easily,
for suspicions of that sort cloud the mind and tie
the tongue.

It is said that for cutting down sacred cedars he
was punished by the confiscation of a great part of
his estate. On that occasion, as he was leaving the
law-court, his pupils were in attendance to comfort
and sustain him, and one of them said: "But your
ability to declaim no one will ever take from you,
Heracleides, nor the fame you have won thereby."
And he went on to recite over him the verse: "One
methinks is still detained in a wide" — "privy
purse," [1] interrupted Heracleides, thus wittily jesting
at his own misfortunes.

This sophist, more than any of the others, seems
to have acquired his proficiency by means of hard
work, since it was denied to him by nature. And
there is extant a rather pleasing composition of his,
a book of moderate size, called *In Praise of Work*.
Once, when he was carrying this book in his hands,
he met Ptolemy the sophist in Naucratis, and the
latter asked him what he was studying. When
he replied that it was an encomium on work,
Ptolemy asked for the book, crossed out the letter

βλίον καὶ ἀπαλείψας τὸ πῖ " ὥρα σοι " ἔφη " ἀναγιγνώσκειν τὸ ὄνομα τοῦ ἐγκωμίου." καὶ αἱ διαλέξεις δέ, ἃς Ἀπολλώνιος ὁ Ναυκρατίτης κατ' αὐτοῦ
διελέγετο, ὡς νωθροῦ καθάπτονται καὶ μοχθοῦντος.

Ἡρακλείδου διδάσκαλοι Ἡρώδης μὲν τῶν οὐκ
ἀληθῶς πεπιστευμένων, Ἀδριανὸς δὲ καὶ Χρῆστος
ἐν γνησίοις, καὶ Ἀριστοκλέους δὲ ἠκροᾶσθαι αὐτὸν
μὴ ἀπιστῶμεν. λέγεται δὲ καὶ γαστρὶ κοίλῃ χρήσασθαι καὶ πλεῖστα ὀψοφαγῆσαι, καὶ ἡ πολυφαγία
αὕτη ἐς οὐδὲν αὐτῷ ἀποσκῆψαι. ἐτελεύτα γοῦν
ὑπὲρ τὰ ὀγδοήκοντα ἔτη ἄρτιος τὸ σῶμα καὶ τάφος
μὲν αὐτῷ Λυκία λέγεται, ἐτελεύτα δὲ ἐπὶ θυγατρὶ
καὶ ἀπελευθέροις οὐ σπουδαίοις, ὑφ' ὧν καὶ τὴν
Ῥητορικὴν ἐκληρονομήθη· ἡ δὲ Ῥητορικὴ γῄδιον
δεκατάλαντον ἦν αὐτῷ κατὰ τὴν Σμύρναν ἐωνη-
μένον ἐκ τῶν ἀκροάσεων.

κζ'. Μὴ δεύτερα τῶν προειρημένων σοφιστῶν
μηδὲ Ἱππόδρομόν τις ἡγείσθω τὸν Θετταλόν,
τῶν μὲν γὰρ βελτίων φαίνεται, τῶν δὲ οὐκ οἶδα ὅ
τι λείπεται. Ἱπποδρόμῳ τοίνυν πατρὶς μὲν ἦν Λά-
ρισσα πόλις εὖ πράττουσα ἐν Θετταλοῖς, πατὴρ δὲ
Ὀλυμπιόδωρος παρελθὼν ἱπποτροφίᾳ Θετταλοὺς
πάντας.

Μεγάλου δὲ ἐν Θετταλίᾳ δοκοῦντος τοῦ καὶ
ἅπαξ προστῆναι τῶν Πυθίων ὁ Ἱππόδρομος προέ-
616 στη δὶς τῶν Πυθικῶν ἄθλων, πλούτῳ τε ὑπερήνεγκε τοὺς ἄνω καὶ κόσμῳ τῷ περὶ τὸν ἀγῶνα καὶ
μεγέθει γνώμης καὶ δικαιότητι βραβευούσῃ τὸ

---

[1] By dropping the first letter πόνος, "work," is altered to
ὄνος, "ass."
[2] Nothing more is known of this sophist.

" p," [1] and said: " Now you must read the title of your encomium." Furthermore, the discourses which Apollonius of Naucratis delivered against Heracleides reproach him with being slow-witted and plodding.

As for the teachers of Heracleides, Herodes is one as to whom we have no sure evidence, whereas among those who were certainly his teachers are Hadrian and Chrestus ; and we may believe that he attended the school of Aristocles besides. It is said of him that he had an endless appetite, and gorged himself with rich food, but this gluttony had no ill effects on his health. At any rate he was over eighty and physically sound when he died. He is said to be buried in Lycia, and he left a daughter and some freedmen who were none too honest, to whom he bequeathed " Rhetoric " ; now " Rhetoric " was a small estate of his near Smyrna, worth ten talents, and he had bought it with the fees that he earned by his lectures.

27. Let none rate HIPPODROMUS [2] THE THESSALIAN lower than the sophists whom I have described above ; for to some of them he is evidently superior, while I am not aware that he falls short of the others in any respect. Now the birthplace of Hippodromus was Larissa, a flourishing city in Thessaly, and his father was Olympiodorus, who had a greater reputation as a breeder of horses than any other man in Thessaly.

Though in Thessaly it was thought a great thing to have been president at the Pythia even once, Hippodromus twice presided over the Pythian games, and he outdid his predecessors in wealth and in the elegance with which he ordered the games, and also in the magnanimity and justice which he showed as

285

εὐθύ. τὸ γοῦν περὶ τὸν τῆς τραγῳδίας ὑποκριτὴν
ὑπ' αὐτοῦ πραχθὲν οὐδὲ ὑπερβολὴν ἑτέρῳ καταλέ-
λοιπε δικαιότητός τε καὶ γνώμης· Κλήμης γὰρ ὁ
Βυζάντιος τραγῳδίας ὑποκριτὴς ἦν μὲν οἷος οὔπω
τις τὴν τέχνην, νικῶν δὲ κατὰ τοὺς χρόνους, οὓς
τὸ Βυζάντιον ἐπολιορκεῖτο, ἀπῄει ἁμαρτάνων τῆς
νίκης, ὡς μὴ δοκοίη δι' ἑνὸς ἀνδρὸς κηρύττεσθαι
πόλις ὅπλα ἐπὶ Ῥωμαίους ἠρμένη. ἄριστα δὲ
αὐτὸν ἀγωνισάμενον κἂν τοῖς Ἀμφικτυονικοῖς
ἄθλοις οἱ μὲν Ἀμφικτύονες ἀπεψηφίζοντο τῆς
νίκης δέει τῆς προειρημένης αἰτίας, ἀναπηδήσας δὲ
ξὺν ὁρμῇ ὁ Ἱππόδρομος " οὗτοι μὲν " εἶπεν " ἐρ-
ρώσθων ἐπιορκοῦντές τε καὶ παραγιγνώσκοντες τοῦ
δικαίου, ἐγὼ δὲ Κλήμεντι τὴν νικῶσαν δίδωμι."
ἐφέντος δὲ θατέρου τῶν ὑποκριτῶν ἐπὶ τὸν βασιλέα,
ηὐδοκίμησε πάλιν ἡ τοῦ Ἱπποδρόμου ψῆφος, καὶ
γὰρ δὴ καὶ ἐπὶ τῆς Ῥώμης ἐνίκα ὁ Βυζάντιος.

Τοιοῦτος δὲ ὢν ἐς τὰ πλήθη θαυμασίᾳ πρᾳό-
τητι ἐπὶ τὰς ἐπιδείξεις ἐχρῆτο· παραλαβὼν γὰρ τὴν
τέχνην φίλαυτόν τε καὶ ἀλαζόνα οὔτε ἐς ἔπαινον
ἑαυτοῦ κατέστη ποτὲ καὶ ἐπέκοπτε τὰς ὑπερβολὰς
τῶν ἐπαίνων· βοώντων γοῦν ἐπ' αὐτῷ ποτε τῶν
Ἑλλήνων πολλὰ καὶ εὔφημα καί που καὶ τῷ Πολέμωνι ὁμοιούντων αὐτὸν " τί μ' ἀθανάτοισιν
ἐΐσκεις;" ἔφη, οὔτε τὸν Πολέμωνα ἀφελόμενος
τὸ νομίζεσθαι θεῖον ἄνδρα, οὔτε ἑαυτῷ διδοὺς τὸ

---

[1] The siege of Byzantium lasted A.D. 193–196 when it was
taken by Severus. See Cassius Dio lxxv. 10 for the story
of its courageous defence by the Byzantines.

[2] *Odyssey* xvi. 187.

umpire. At any rate, his conduct in the affair of the tragic actor has left no one else a chance to surpass him in justice and good judgement. The facts are these. Clemens of Byzantium was a tragic actor whose like has never yet been seen for artistic skill. But since he was winning his victories at a time when Byzantium was being besieged,[1] he used to be sent away without the reward of victory, lest it should appear that a city that had taken up arms against the Romans was being proclaimed victor in the person of one of her citizens. Accordingly, after he had performed brilliantly in the Amphictyonic games, the Amphictyons were on the point of voting that he should not receive the prize, because for the reason that I have mentioned they were afraid. Whereupon Hippodromus sprang up with great energy and cried : "Let these others go on and prosper by breaking their oath and giving unjust decisions, but by my vote I award the victory to Clemens." And when another of the actors appealed to the Emperor against the award, the vote of Hippodromus was again approved ; for at Rome also the Byzantine actor carried off the prize.

But though he was so firm in the face of assembled crowds, in his public declamations he displayed an admirable mildness. For though he had adopted a profession that is prone to egotism and arrogance, he never resorted to self-praise, but used to check those who praised him to excess. At any rate, on one occasion when the Greeks were acclaiming him with flatteries, and even compared him with Polemo, " Why," said he, " do you liken me to immortals ?[2] " This answer, while it did not rob Polemo of his reputation for being divinely inspired, was also a

287

617 τοιούτῳ ὁμοιοῦσθαι. Πρόκλου δὲ τοῦ Ναυκρατίτου πομπείαν οὐ πρεσβυτικὴν¹ ξυνθέντος ἐπὶ
πάντας τοὺς παιδεύοντας Ἀθήνησι καὶ τὸν Ἱππόδρομον ἐγκαταλέξαντος τῷ λοιδορησμῷ τούτῳ
ἡμεῖς μὲν ᾠόμεθα λόγου ἀκροάσεσθαι² πρὸς τὴν
τῶν εἰρημένων ἠχὼ ξυγκειμένου, ὁ δὲ οὐδὲν εἰπὼν
φλαῦρον ἔπαινον εὐφημίας διεξῆλθεν, ἀρξάμενος
ἀπὸ τοῦ ταὼ³ ὡς ἀναπτεροῦντος αὐτὸν τοῦ ἐπαίνου. ὧδε μὲν δὴ διέκειτο πρὸς τοὺς ἑαυτοῦ πρε-
σβυτέρους καὶ χρόνῳ πολλῷ τε καὶ οὐ πολλῷ
προειληφότας, ὡς δὲ καὶ πρὸς τοὺς ἰσήλικας εἶχεν,
ὑπάρχει μαθεῖν ἐκ τῶνδε· νεανίας ἀπ' Ἰωνίας
ἥκων Ἀθήναζε διῄει ἐπαίνους τοῦ Ἡρακλείδου
πέρα ἀχθηδόνος· ἰδὼν οὖν αὐτὸν ὁ Ἱππόδρομος ἐν τῇ ἀκροάσει " ὁ νεανίας οὗτος " ἔφη " ἐρᾷ
τοῦ ἑαυτοῦ διδασκάλου. καλὸν οὖν ξυλλαβεῖν αὐτῷ
τῶν παιδικῶν· καὶ γὰρ ἂν καὶ ξὺν ἑρμαίῳ ἀπέλθοι
μαθὼν ἐγκωμιάζειν." καὶ εἰπὼν ταῦτα ἔπαινον
τοῦ Ἡρακλείδου διῆλθεν, οἷος ἐπ' αὐτῷ οὔπω
εἴρηται. τὰ δὲ ἐπὶ Διοδότῳ τῷ Καππαδόκῃ δάκρυα καὶ τὸ ἐσθῆτα μέλαιναν ἐπ' αὐτῷ ἐνδῦναι
φύσιν μὲν παρεσχημένῳ μελέτῃ ἐπιτηδείαν, ἐν⁴
ἐφήβῳ δὲ ἀποθανόντι πατέρα τοῦ Ἑλληνικοῦ
ἐκήρυξε τὸν Ἱππόδρομον καὶ περιωπὴν ἔχοντα τοῦ
καὶ μεθ' ἑαυτὸν γενέσθαι τινὰς ἀριπρεπεῖς ἄνδρας.
τουτὶ δὲ μάλιστα ἐν Ὀλυμπίᾳ ἐδήλωσεν· Φιλο-

---

¹ πρεσβευτικὴν Kayser; πρεσβυτικὴν Cobet.
² ἀκροάσασθαι Kayser; ἀκροάσεσθαι Cobet.
³ ταὼ τοῦ ὄρνιθος Kayser; Cobet omits τοῦ ὄρνιθος.
⁴ ἐν Cobet adds; cf. p. 610 ἐν μειρακίῳ ἀποθανόντι.

---

¹ i.e. a repetition of the other's abuse.

refusal to concede to himself any likeness to so great a genius. And when Proclus of Naucratis composed a coarse satire, unworthy of an old man, against all who were teaching at Athens, and included Hippodromus in this lampoon, we expected to hear from him a speech that would be a sort of echo[1] of what had been said about him. But he uttered nothing that was mean, but recited an encomium on fairspeaking, beginning with the peacock, and showing how admiration makes him spread his plumage aloft. Such then was his behaviour towards those who were older than himself and ranked as his seniors, whether by many years or few; but what was his bearing towards those of his own age the reader may learn from what follows. A young man from Ionia who had come to Athens used to recite the praises of Heracleides till he wearied his hearers out of all patience. So when Hippodromus saw him at his lecture, he said: "This young man is in love with his own teacher. Therefore we should do well to further his cause with his beloved. And certainly it will be a windfall for him if, when he leaves us, he has learned how to make an encomium." And forthwith he delivered a eulogy of Heracleides such as had never before been uttered on that theme. Again, the tears that he shed for Diodotus the Cappadocian and his wearing black in mourning for him, because he had displayed a great natural talent for declamation but had died on the threshold of manhood, proclaimed Hippodromus father of the Hellenic students, aud one who made it his concern that after his death there should continue to be a supply of really distinguished men. This he made very evident at Olympia. For when Philostratus of

στράτῳ γὰρ τῷ Λημνίῳ γνωρίμῳ μὲν ἑαυτοῦ ὄντι,
δύο δὲ καὶ εἴκοσιν ἔτη γεγονότι ἀναρριπτοῦντί τινα
αὐτοσχέδιον πλεῖστα μὲν ἐνέδωκε τῇ τέχνῃ τῶν
ἐπαίνων, ὧν τε εἰπεῖν ἔδει καὶ μή, ἀξιούσης δὲ
καὶ τὸν Ἱππόδρομον τῆς Ἑλλάδος αὐτίκα παριέναι,
" οὐκ ἐπαποδύσομαι " ἔφη " τοῖς ἐμαυτοῦ σπλάγ-
χνοις." καὶ εἰπὼν ταῦτα ἀνεβάλετο τὴν ἀκρόασιν
ἐπὶ τὴν τῆς θυσίας ἡμέραν. ταῦτα μὲν οὖν ἐχέτω
μοι δήλωσιν ἀνδρὸς πεπαιδευμένου φιλανθρώπου
τε καὶ πράου τὸ ἦθος.

618   Τὸν δὲ Ἀθήνησι τῶν σοφιστῶν θρόνον κατασχὼν ἐτῶν που τεττάρων ἀπηνέχθη αὐτοῦ ὑπὸ
τῆς γυναικὸς καὶ τοῦ πλούτου, ἐκείνη γὰρ ἐνεργο-
τάτη γυναικῶν ἐγένετο καὶ φύλαξ ἀγαθὴ χρημάτων, ἀμφοῖν τε ἀπόντων ἡ οὐσία ὑπεδίδου. τοῦ
γε μὴν φοιτᾶν ἐς τὰς τῶν Ἑλλήνων πανηγύρεις
οὐκ ἠμέλει, ἀλλ' ἐθάμιζεν ἐς αὐτὰς ἐπιδείξεων
ἕνεκα καὶ τοῦ μὴ ἀγνοεῖσθαι. βελτίων δὲ κἀκεῖνα ἐφαίνετο ὑπὸ τοῦ καὶ μετὰ τὸ πεπαῦσθαι
τοῦ παιδεύειν ἀεὶ σπουδάζειν. Ἱππόδρομος μὲν
γὰρ δὴ πλεῖστα μὲν ἐξέμαθεν Ἑλλήνων τῶν γε
μετὰ τὸν Καππαδόκην Ἀλέξανδρον μνήμην εὐ-
τυχησάντων, πλεῖστα δὲ ἀνέγνω μετά γε Ἀμ-
μώνιον τὸν ἀπὸ τοῦ Περιπάτου, ἐκείνου γὰρ
πολυγραμματώτερον ἄνδρα οὔπω ἔγνων. μελέτης δὲ ὁ Ἱππόδρομος οὔτε ἐν ἀγρῷ διαιτώμενος
ἠμέλει οὔτε ὁδοιπορῶν οὔτε ἐν θαλάττῃ,[1] ἀλλὰ
καὶ κρεῖττον ὄλβου κτῆμα ἐκάλει αὐτὴν ἐκ τῶν
Εὐριπίδου τε ὕμνων καὶ Ἀμφίονος.

---

[1] Θετταλίᾳ Kayser ; θαλάττῃ Jahn.

---

[1] The biographer's son-in-law, the author of the *Imagines*.
[2] The last day of the festival.

Lemnos,[1] his own pupil, aged twenty-two, was about to try his chances in an extempore oration, Hippodromus gave him many useful hints for the art of panegyric, namely what one ought and ought not to say. And when all Greece called on Hippodromus to come forward himself without delay, he replied: " I will not strip for a fight with my own entrails." Having said this, he put off the declamation till the day of the sacrifice.[2] I have said enough to show that he was a man truly well-educated, with a benevolent and humane disposition.

When he had held the chair of rhetoric at Athens for about four years, he resigned it at the instance of his wife, and also on account of his property; for she was a most energetic woman and an excellent guardian of his money, but in the absence of both the property was beginning to deteriorate. Nevertheless he did not fail to attend regularly the public festivals of Greece, but frequented them partly in order to declaim in public, partly that he might not be forgotten. And on these occasions also he showed himself superior by always keeping up his regular studies even after he had ceased to teach. For indeed Hippodromus, among those who ranked after Alexander the Cappadocian as blessed with a good memory, learned more by heart than any of the Greeks, and he was the most widely read, with the exception, that is, of Ammonius the Peripatetic; for a more erudite man than Ammonius I have never known. Moreover, Hippodromus never neglected his study of the art of declamation, either when he was living on his country estate or when travelling by road, or at sea, but he used to call it a possession even greater than wealth, quoting from the hymns of Euripides and Amphion.

Ἀγροικότερός τε ὢν τὸ εἶδος ὅμως ἀμήχανον
εὐγένειαν ἐπεδήλου τοῖς ὄμμασι γοργόν τε καὶ
φαιδρὸν βλέπων. τουτὶ δὲ καὶ Μεγιστίας ὁ Σμυρναῖος ἐν αὐτῷ καθεωρακέναι φησὶν οὐ τὰ δεύτερα
τῶν φυσιογνωμονούντων νομισθείς· ἀφίκετο μὲν
γὰρ ἐς τὴν Σμύρναν μετὰ τὸν Ἡρακλείδην ὁ
Ἱππόδρομος οὔπω πρὸ τούτου ἥκων, ἀποβὰς δὲ
τῆς νεὼς ἀπῄει ἐς ἀγοράν, εἴ τῳ ἐντύχοι πεπαιδευμένῳ τὰ ἐγχώρια. ἱερὸν δὲ κατιδὼν καὶ παιδ-
αγωγούς τε προσκαθημένους ἀκολούθους τε παῖδας ἄχθη βιβλίων ἐν πήραις ἀνημμένους, ξυνῆκεν
ὅτι παιδεύοι τις ἔνδον τῶν ἐπιφανῶν, καὶ ἔσω
παρῄει καὶ προσειπὼν τὸν Μεγιστίαν ἐκάθητο
ἐρωτῶν οὐδέν. ὁ μὲν δὴ Μεγιστίας ᾤετο ὑπὲρ
μαθητῶν αὐτὸν διαλέξεσθαί οἱ, πατέρα ἴσως ἢ
τροφέα παίδων ὄντα, καὶ ἤρετο, ὑπὲρ ὅτου ἥκοι,
619 ὁ δὲ " πεύσῃ " ἔφη " ἐπειδὰν αὐτοὶ γενώμεθα."
διακωδωνίσας οὖν ὁ Μεγιστίας τὰ μειράκια
" λέγε," ἔφη " ὅ τι βούλει." καὶ ὁ Ἱππόδρομος
" ἀντιδῶμεν ἀλλήλοις τὴν ἐσθῆτα " εἶπεν, ἦν δὲ
ἄρα τῷ μὲν Ἱπποδρόμῳ χλαμύς, τῷ δὲ αὖ δημη-
γορικὸν ἱμάτιον. " καὶ τίνα σοι νοῦν ἔχει τοῦτο;" ἦ δ' ὁ Μεγιστίας. " ἐπίδειξιν " ἔφη " σοι
μελέτης ποιήσασθαι βούλομαι." δαιμονᾶν μὲν
οὖν αὐτὸν ᾠήθη ταῦτα ἐπαγγείλαντα καὶ τὴν
γνώμην ἐλαύνεσθαι, τὰς βολὰς δὲ ἀνασκοπῶν τῶν
ὀμμάτων καὶ ὁρῶν αὐτὸν ἔννουν καὶ καθεστη-
κότα ἀντέδωκε τὴν ἐσθῆτα ὑπόθεσίν τε αἰτήσαντι
προὔβαλε τὸν μάγον τὸν ἀποθνήσκειν ἀξιοῦντα,

---

[1] The Ionian type.

Though he was somewhat rustic in appearance, yet an extraordinary nobility shone out of his eyes, and his glance was at once keen and good-natured. Megistias of Smyrna also says that he noticed this characteristic of his, and he was considered second to none as a physiognomist. For Hippodromus came to Smyrna after the death of Heracleides—he had never been there before—and on leaving the ship he went to the market-place in the hope of meeting someone who was proficient in the local style[1] of eloquence. And when he saw a temple with attendants sitting near it, and slaves in waiting carrying loads of books in satchels, he understood that someone of importance was holding his school inside. So he entered, and after greeting Megistias, sat down without making any inquiry. Now Megistias thought that he was going to talk to him about pupils, and that he was some father or guardian of boys, and asked him why he had come. "You shall learn that," he replied, "when we are alone." Accordingly when Megistias had finished examining his pupils, he said: "Tell me what you want." "Let us exchange garments," said Hippodromus. He was in fact wearing a travelling-cloak, while Megistias wore a gown suitable for public speaking. "And what do you mean by that?" asked Megistias. "I wish," he replied, "to give you a display of declamation." Now Megistias really thought that he was mad in making this announcement and that his wits were wandering. But when he observed the keenness of his glance and saw that he seemed sane and sober, he changed clothes with him. When he asked him to suggest a theme, Megistias proposed "The magician who wished to die because he was

293

ἐπειδὴ μὴ ἐδυνήθη ἀποκτεῖναι μάγον μοιχόν. ὡς
δὲ ἱζήσας ἐπὶ τοῦ θρόνου καὶ σμικρὸν ἐπισχὼν
ἀνεπήδησεν, μᾶλλον ἐσήει τὸν Μεγιστίαν ὁ τῆς
μανίας λόγος καὶ τὰ πλεονεκτήματα ἐμβροντη-
σίαν ᾤετο, ἀρξαμένου δὲ τῆς ὑποθέσεως καὶ
εἰπόντος " ἀλλ᾽ ἐμαυτόν γε δύναμαι" ἐξέπεσεν
ἑαυτοῦ ὑπὸ θαύματος καὶ προσδραμὼν αὐτῷ
ἱκέτευε μαθεῖν, ὅστις εἴη. " εἰμὶ μὲν " ἔφη
" Ἱππόδρομος ὁ Θετταλός, ἥκω δὲ σοι ἐγγυμνα-
σόμενος, ἵν᾽ ἐκμάθοιμι δι᾽ ἑνὸς ἀνδρὸς οὕτω πεπαιδευμένου τὸ ἦθος τῆς Ἰωνικῆς ἀκροάσεως.
ἀλλ᾽ ὅρα με δι᾽ ὅλης τῆς ὑποθέσεως."[1] περὶ
τέρμα δὲ τοῦ λόγου δρόμος ὑπὸ τῶν κατὰ τὴν
Σμύρναν πεπαιδευμένων ἐπὶ τὰς τοῦ Μεγιστίου
θύρας ἐγένετο, ταχείας τῆς φήμης διαδοθείσης ἐς
πάντας ἐπιχωριάζειν αὐτοῖς τὸν Ἱππόδρομον, ὁ
δὲ ἀναλαβὼν τὴν ὑπόθεσιν ἑτέρᾳ δυνάμει μετεχειρίσατο τὰς ἤδη εἰρημένας ἐννοίας, παρελθών
τε ἐς τὸ κοινὸν τῶν Σμυρναίων ἀνὴρ ἔδοξε θαυμάσιος καὶ οἷος ἐν τοῖς πρὸ αὐτοῦ γράφεσθαι.

820 Ἦν δὲ αὐτῷ τὰ μὲν τῆς διαλέξεως Πλάτωνος
ἀνημμένα καὶ Δίωνος, τὰ δὲ τῆς μελέτης κατὰ
τὸν Πολέμωνα ἐρρωμένα καί που καὶ ποτιμώτερα,
τὰ δὲ τῆς εὐροίας οἷα τοῖς ἀλύπως ἀναγιγνώ-
σκουσι τὰ σφόδρα αὐτοῖς καθωμιλημένα. Νικαγόρου δὲ τοῦ σοφιστοῦ μητέρα σοφιστῶν τὴν
τραγῳδίαν προσειπόντος διορθούμενος ὁ Ἱππόδρομος τὸν λόγον " ἐγὼ δὲ " ἔφη " πατέρα Ὅμηρον." ἐσπούδαζε δὲ καὶ ἀπὸ Ἀρχιλόχου καλῶν

---

[1] An echo of Plato, *Phaedrus* 228 E.
[2] *Cf.* above, *Life of Alexander*, p. 572.

unable to kill another magician, an adulterer." And
when he took his seat on the lecturer's chair, and
after a moment's pause sprang to his feet, the theory
that he was mad occurred still more forcibly to
Megistias, and he thought that these signs of proficiency were mere delirium. But when he had
begun to argue the theme and had come to the
words : " But myself at least I can kill," Megistias
could not contain himself for admiration, but ran to
him and implored to be told who he was. " I am,"
said he, " Hippodromus the Thessalian, and I have
come to practise my art on you [1] in order that I may
learn from one man so proficient as you are the
Ionian manner of declaiming. But observe me
through the whole of the argument." Towards the
end of the speech a rush was made by all lovers of
learning in Smyrna to the door of Megistias, for the
tidings had soon spread abroad that Hippodromus
was visiting their city. Thereupon he took up his
theme afresh, but gave a wholly different force to
the ideas that he had already expressed. [2] And when
later on he made his appearance before the public
of Smyrna, they thought him truly marvellous, and
worthy of being enrolled among men of former days.

His style in introductory discourse was wholly
dependent on Plato and Dio, while his declamations
had Polemo's vigour and an even greater suavity and
freshness ; and in his easy flow of words he resembled
one who reads aloud, without effort, a work with
which he is perfectly familiar. Once when Nicagoras
had called tragedy " the mother of sophists," Hippodromus improved on this remark, and said : " But I
should rather call Homer their father." He was,
moreover, a devoted student of Archilochus, and used

295

τὸν μὲν Ὅμηρον φωνὴν σοφιστῶν, τὸν δὲ Ἀρχίλοχον πνεῦμα. μελέται μὲν δὴ τοῦ ἀνδρὸς τούτου τριάκοντα ἴσως, ἄρισται δὲ αὐτῶν οἱ Καταναῖοι καὶ οἱ Σκύθαι καὶ ὁ Δημάδης ὁ μὴ ξυγχωρῶν ἀφίστασθαι Ἀλεξάνδρου ἐν Ἰνδοῖς ὄντος. ᾄδονται δὲ αὐτοῦ καὶ λυρικοὶ νόμοι, καὶ γὰρ δὴ καὶ τῆς νομικῆς λύρας ἥπτετο. ἐτελεύτα δὲ ἀμφὶ τὰ ἑβδομήκοντα καὶ οἴκοι καὶ ἐπὶ υἱῷ ἀγροῦ μὲν προστῆναι καὶ οἰκίας ἱκανῷ, παραπλῆγι δὲ καὶ ἔκφρονι, τὰ δὲ τῶν σοφιστῶν οὐ πεπαιδευμένῳ.

κη΄. Οἱ τὸν Λαοδικέα Οὔαρον λόγου ἀξιοῦντες αὐτοὶ μὴ ἀξιούσθων λόγου,[1] καὶ γὰρ εὐτελὴς καὶ διακεχηνὼς καὶ εὐήθης καὶ ἦν εἶχεν εὐφωνίαν αἰσχύνων καμπαῖς ᾀσμάτων, αἷς κἂν ὑπορχήσαιτό τις τῶν ἀσελγεστέρων· οὗ διδάσκαλον ἢ ἀκροατὴν τί ἂν γράφοιμι, τί δ᾽ ἂν φράζοιμι, εὖ γιγνώσκων, ὅτι μήτ᾽ ἂν τοιαῦτα διδάξειέ τις καὶ τοῖς μεμαθηκόσιν ὄνειδος τὸ τοιούτων ἠκροᾶσθαι;

κθ΄. Κυρίνῳ δὲ τῷ σοφιστῇ πατρὶς μὲν Νικομήδεια ἐγένετο, γένος δὲ οὔτε εὐδόκιμον οὔτε αὖ κατεγνωσμένον, ἀλλὰ φύσις ἀγαθὴ παραλαβεῖν 621 μαθήματα καὶ παραδοῦναι βελτίων, οὐ γὰρ μνήμην μόνον, ἀλλὰ καὶ σαφήνειαν ἤσκει. κομματίας ὁ σοφιστὴς οὗτος καὶ περὶ μὲν τὰ θετικὰ

---

[1] λόγων . . . λόγων Kayser; λόγου . . . λόγου Cobet; cf. p. 576 ἀξιούσθω λόγου.

---

[1] This theme was inspired by the eruption of Etna in 425 B.C., mentioned by Thucydides iii. 116. From other references to this theme in Hermogenes it seems that the citizens of Catana are supposed to debate whether they shall migrate.

[2] See p. 572.

to say that Homer was indeed the voice of the sophists, but Archilochus was their very breath. There are extant perhaps thirty declamations by this man, and of these the best are: "The citizens of Catana," [1] "The Scythians," [2] and "Demades argues against revolting from Alexander while he is in India." [3] His lyric nomes [4] are still sung, for he was skilful also in composing nomes for the lyre. He died at home aged about seventy, and left a son who, though he was well enough able to take charge of the country estate and the household, was crack-brained and foolish, and had not been educated for the sophistic profession.

28. Let those who think VARUS [5] OF LAODICEA worthy of mention receive no mention themselves. For he was trivial, vain, and fatuous, and such charm of voice as he had he degraded by uttering snatches of song which might serve as dance music for some shameless person. Why then should I record or describe any teacher or pupil of his, since I am well aware that one would not be likely to teach such arts, and that it would be disgraceful for his pupils to admit that they had listened to such teaching?

29. The birthplace of QUIRINUS [5] the sophist was Nicomedia. His family was neither distinguished nor altogether obscure, but he had a natural talent for receiving instruction and a still greater talent for handing it on, for he carefully trained not only his memory, but also his faculty for lucid expression. This sophist's sentences were very short, and when he was maintaining an abstract thesis he was

[3] Demades is supposed to oppose the advice of Demosthenes.
[4] These were hymns in honour of the gods.
[5] Nothing more is known of this sophist.

τῶν χωρίων οὐ πολύς, ἐρρωμένος μὴν καὶ σφοδρὸς
καὶ κατασεῖσαι δεινὸς ἀκροατοῦ ὦτα, καὶ γὰρ δὴ
καὶ ἀπεσχεδίαζεν, προσφυέστερος δὲ ταῖς κατηγορίαις δοκῶν ἐπιστεύθη ἐκ βασιλέως τὴν τοῦ
ταμιείου γλῶτταν, καὶ παρελθὼν ἐς τὸ δυνηθῆναί
τι οὔτε βαρὺς οὔτε ἀλαζὼν ἔδοξεν, ἀλλὰ πρᾷός
τε καὶ ἑαυτῷ ὅμοιος, οὔτε ἐρασιχρήματος, ἀλλ'
ὥσπερ τὸν Ἀριστείδην Ἀθηναῖοι ᾄδουσι μετὰ
τὴν ἐπίταξιν τῶν φόρων καὶ τὰς νήσους ἐπανελθεῖν σφισιν ἐν τῷ προτέρῳ τρίβωνι, οὕτω καὶ
ὁ Κυρῖνος ἀφίκετο ἐς τὰ ἑαυτοῦ ἤθη πενίᾳ σεμ-
νυνόμενος. αἰτιωμένων δὲ αὐτὸν τῶν κατὰ τὴν
Ἀσίαν ἐνδεικτῶν, ὡς πρᾳότερον περὶ τὰς κατηγορίας ἢ αὐτοὶ διδάσκουσιν " καὶ μὴν καὶ πολλῷ
βέλτιον " εἶπεν " ὑμᾶς λαβεῖν τὴν ἐμὴν πρᾳότητα
ἢ ἐμὲ τὴν ὑμετέραν ὠμότητα." ἐνδειξάντων δὲ
αὐτῶν καὶ πόλιν οὐ μεγάλην ἐπὶ πολλαῖς μυριάσιν
ἐκράτει μὲν ὁ Κυρῖνος τὴν δίκην ἄκων μάλα, προσ-
ιόντες δὲ αὐτῷ οἱ ἐνδεῖκται " αὕτη σε " ἔφασαν
" ἡ δίκη ἀρεῖ μέγαν παρελθοῦσα ἐς τὰ τοῦ βασιλέως ὦτα." καὶ ὁ Κυρῖνος " οὐκ ἐμοὶ πρέπον,"
ἔφη " ἀλλ' ὑμῖν ἐπὶ τῷ πόλιν ἀοίκητον εἰργάσθαι
τιμᾶσθαι." ἐπὶ δὲ υἱῷ τελευτήσαντι παραμυ-
θουμένων αὐτὸν τῶν προσηκόντων " πότε " εἶπεν
" ἀνὴρ ἢ νῦν δόξω ;" Ἀδριανοῦ δὲ ἀκροατὴς
γενόμενος οὐ πᾶσιν ὡμολόγει τοῖς ἐκείνου, ἀλλ'
ἔστιν ἃ καὶ διέγραφεν οὐκ ὀρθῶς εἰρημένα. τέρμα

not very successful. Nevertheless he was vigorous and energetic, and was skilled in startling into attention the ears of his audience. For indeed he used to speak extempore, but since he seemed better adapted by nature for making speeches for the prosecution in the courts, he was entrusted by the Emperor with the post of advocate for the treasury. Though he thereby attained to considerable power, he showed himself neither aggressive nor insolent but mild and unchanged in character, never greedy of gain but, like Aristeides in the story that the Athenians recite about him — how after he had arranged the amount of the tribute and the affairs of the islands, he came back to them wearing the same shabby cloak as before — so too Quirinus returned to his native place dignified by poverty. When the informers in Asia found fault with him for being more lenient in his prosecutions than accorded with the evidence furnished by them, he said : " Nay it were far better that you should adopt my clemency than I your ruthlessness." And when they cited a small town for the payment of many myriads of drachmae, Quirinus did indeed win the case, though much against his will, but when the informers came to him and said: " This case when it comes to the Emperor's ears will greatly enhance your reputation," he retorted: " It suits you but not me to win rewards for making a town desolate." When his relatives tried to console him for the death of his son, he said: " When, if not now, shall I prove myself a man ?" He had been a pupil of Hadrian, but he did not approve of all his writings, and even expunged some passages that had been incorrectly expressed. His life came to a close

δὲ αὐτῷ τοῦ βίου ἔτος ἑβδομηκοστὸν καὶ τὸ σῆμα
οἴκοι.

λ'. Φιλίσκος δὲ ὁ Θετταλὸς Ἱπποδρόμῳ μὲν
συνῆπται γένος, τοῦ δὲ Ἀθήνησι θρόνου προύστη
622 ἐτῶν ἑπτὰ τὴν ἀτέλειαν τὴν ἐπ' αὐτῷ ἀφαιρεθείς,
τουτὶ δὲ πῶς συνέβη, δηλῶσαι ἀνάγκη· Ἐορδαῖοι
Μακεδόνες ἀνειπόντες ἐς τὰς οἰκείας λειτουργίας
τὸν Φιλίσκον, ὡς δὴ ὑπάρχον αὐτοῖς ἐπὶ πάντας
τοὺς ἀπὸ μητέρων, ὡς δὲ οὐκ ὑπεδέξατο [1] ἐφίεσαν·
τῆς δίκης τοίνυν γενομένης ἐπὶ τὸν αὐτοκράτορα,
Ἀντωνῖνος δὲ ἦν ὁ τῆς φιλοσόφου παῖς Ἰουλίας,
ἐστάλη ἐς τὴν Ῥώμην ὡς τὰ ἑαυτοῦ θησόμενος,
καὶ προσρυεὶς τοῖς περὶ τὴν Ἰουλίαν γεωμέτραις
τε καὶ φιλοσόφοις εὕρετο παρ' αὐτῆς διὰ τοῦ
βασιλέως τὸν Ἀθήνησι θρόνον. ὁ δ', ὥσπερ οἱ
θεοὶ Ὁμήρῳ πεποίηνται οὐ πάντα ἑκόντες ἀλλήλοις [2] διδόντες, ἀλλ' ἔστιν ἃ καὶ ἄκοντες, οὕτω δὴ
ἠγρίαινε καὶ χαλεπὸς ἦν ὡς περιδραμόντι, ὡς δὲ
ἤκουσεν εἶναί τινα αὐτῷ καὶ δίκην, ἧς αὐτὸς
ἀκροατὴς ἔσοιτο, κελεύει τὸν ἐπιτεταγμένον ταῖς
δίκαις προειπεῖν οἱ τὸ μὴ δι' ἑτέρου, δι' ἑαυτοῦ δὲ
ἀγωνίσασθαι. ἐπεὶ δὲ παρῆλθεν ἐς τὸ δικαστήριον,
623 προσέκρουσε μὲν τὸ βάδισμα, προσέκρουσε δὲ ἡ
στάσις, καὶ τὴν στολὴν οὐκ εὐσχήμων ἔδοξε καὶ
τὴν φωνὴν μιξόθηλυς καὶ τὴν γλῶτταν ὕπτιος καὶ

---

[1] For the lacuna after μητέρων Kayser suggests ὡς δὲ οὐκ
ὑπεδέξατο.   [2] Valckenaer suggests ἀνθρώποις.

---

[1] For the family of this otherwise unknown sophist see
J. Pouilloux, " Une famille de sophistes thessaliens à Delphes
au IIe s. ap. J.-C.," *Revue des Études grecques*, 80 (1967), pp.
379 ff.

[2] This Macedonian clan, mentioned by Herodotus, vii. 185,
had the privilege of reckoning the *materna origo* ; *i.e.* they
reckoned their descent by the mother, not the father.

with his seventieth year; his tomb is in his native place.

30. PHILISCUS[1] THE THESSALIAN was a kinsman of Hippodromus and held the chair of rhetoric at Athens for seven years, but was deprived of the immunity that was attached to it. How this came about I must now relate. The Heordaean Macedonians[2] had summoned Philiscus to perform public services in their city, as was their right in the case of all who on the mother's side were Heordaeans, and since he did not undertake them they referred the matter to the courts. Accordingly the suit came before the Emperor (this was Antoninus[3] the son of the philosophic Julia); and Philiscus travelled to Rome to protect his own interests. There he attached himself closely to Julia's circle of mathematicians[4] and philosophers, and obtained from her with the Emperor's consent the chair of rhetoric at Athens. But the Emperor, like the gods in Homer who are portrayed as granting favours to one another, but sometimes against their will, nourished the same sort of resentment, and was ill-disposed to Philiscus because he thought that the latter had stolen a march on him. So when he heard that there was a suit brought against him and that he was to hear it tried, he ordered the official in charge of lawsuits to give notice to Philiscus that he must make his defence himself and not through another. And when Philiscus appeared in court he gave offence by his gait, he gave offence by the way in which he stood, his attire seemed far from suitable to the occasion, his voice effeminate, his language indolent

---

[3] Antoninus Caracalla.

[4] This is the regular word for astrologers.

βλέπων ἑτέρωσέ ποι μᾶλλον ἢ ἐς τὰ νοούμενα· ἐκ
τούτων ἀποστραφεὶς ὁ αὐτοκράτωρ ἐς τὸν Φιλίσκον
ἐπεστόμιζεν αὐτὸν καὶ παρὰ πάντα τὸν λόγον
διείρων ἑαυτὸν[1] τοῦ ὕδατος καὶ ἐρωτήσεις ἐν
αὐτῷ στενὰς ποιούμενος, ὡς δὲ οὐ πρὸς τὰ ἐρωτώ-
μενα αἱ ἀποκρίσεις ἐγένοντο Φιλίσκου " τὸν μὲν
ἄνδρα " ἔφη " δείκνυσιν ἡ κόμη, τὸν δὲ ῥήτορα ἡ
φωνή," καὶ μετὰ πολλὰς τοιαύτας ἐπικοπὰς ἐπήγαγεν ἑαυτὸν τοῖς Ἐορδαίοις. εἰπόντος δὲ τοῦ
Φιλίσκου " σύ μοι λειτουργιῶν ἀτέλειαν δέδωκας
δοὺς τὸν Ἀθήνησι θρόνον" ἀναβοήσας ὁ αὐτοκράτωρ " οὔτε σύ " εἶπεν " ἀτελὴς οὔτε ἄλλος
οὐδεὶς τῶν παιδευόντων· οὐ γὰρ ἄν ποτε διὰ
μικρὰ καὶ δύστηνα λογάρια τὰς πόλεις ἀφελοίμην
τῶν λειτουργησόντων." ἀλλ' ὅμως καὶ μετὰ ταῦτα
Φιλοστράτῳ τῷ Λημνίῳ λειτουργιῶν ἀτέλειαν ἐπὶ
μελέτῃ ἐψηφίσατο τέτταρα καὶ εἴκοσιν ἔτη γεγονότι.
αἱ μὲν δὴ προφάσεις, δι' ἃς ὁ Φιλίσκος ἀφῃρέθη
τὸ εἶναι ἀτελής, αἵδε ἐγένοντο, μὴ ἀφαιρείσθω δὲ
αὐτὸν τὰ περὶ τῷ βλέμματι καὶ τῷ φθέγματι καὶ
σχήματι ἐλαττώματα τὸ μὴ οὐ κράτιστα ῥητόρων
ἑλληνίσαι τε καὶ συνθεῖναι. ἡ δὲ ἰδέα τοῦ λόγου
λάλος μᾶλλον ἢ ἐναγώνιος, διεφαίνετο δὲ αὐτῆς καὶ
καθαρὰ ὀνόματα καὶ καινοπρεπὴς ἦχος. ἐτελεύτα
μὲν οὖν ἐπὶ θυγατρὶ καὶ υἱῷ οὐδενὸς ἀξίῳ, μέτρον
δὲ αὐτῷ τοῦ βίου ἔτη ἑπτὰ καὶ ἑξήκοντα. κεκτη-
μένος δὲ Ἀθήνησι χωρίον οὐκ ἀηδὲς οὐκ ἐν αὐτῷ
ἐτάφη, ἀλλ' ἐν τῇ Ἀκαδημίᾳ, οὗ τίθησι τὸν

---

[1] ἐς αὐτὸν Kayser ; ἑαυτὸν Jahn.

---

[1] i.e. it was curled and effeminate ; cf. p. 571.
[2] An echo of Demosthenes, On the False Embassy 421.

and directed to any subject rather than to the matter in hand. All this made the Emperor hostile to Philiscus, so that he kept pulling him up throughout the whole speech, both by interjecting his own remarks in the other's allotted time, and by interrupting with abrupt questions. And since the replies of Philiscus were beside the mark, the Emperor exclaimed : "His hair shows what sort of man he is,[1] his voice what sort of orator!" And after cutting him short like this many times, he ranged himself on the side of the Heordaeans. And when Philiscus said : "You have given me exemption from public services by giving me the chair at Athens," the Emperor cried at the top of his voice : "Neither you nor any other teacher is exempt! Never would I, for the sake of a few miserable speeches,[2] rob the cities of men who ought to perform public services." Nevertheless he did, even after this incident, decree for Philostratus of Lemnos, then aged twenty-four, exemption from public service as a reward for a declamation. These then were the reasons why Philiscus was deprived of the privilege of exemption. But we must not, on account of the shortcomings of his facial expression, his voice and his dress deprive him of that high place among rhetoricians which is due to his Hellenic culture and his ability to compose speeches. The style of his eloquence was colloquial rather than forensic, but it was illumined by a pure Attic vocabulary and had effects of sound that were original. He died leaving a daughter and a worthless son, and the measure of his life was sixty-seven years. Though he had acquired a charming little estate at Athens, he was not buried on it but in the Academy where the commander-in-chief

ἀγῶνα ἐπὶ τοῖς ἐκ τῶν πολέμων θαπτομένοις[1] ὁ
πολέμαρχος.

624 λαʹ. Αἰλιανὸς δὲ Ῥωμαῖος μὲν ἦν, ἠττίκιζε
δέ, ὥσπερ οἱ ἐν τῇ μεσογείᾳ Ἀθηναῖοι. ἐπαίνου
μοι δοκεῖ ἄξιος ὁ ἀνὴρ οὗτος, πρῶτον μέν, ἐπειδὴ
καθαρὰν φωνὴν ἐξεπόνησε πόλιν οἰκῶν ἑτέρᾳ
φωνῇ χρωμένῃ, ἔπειθ᾽, ὅτι προσρηθεὶς σοφιστὴς
ὑπὸ τῶν χαριζομένων τὰ τοιαῦτα οὐκ ἐπίστευσεν,
οὐδὲ ἐκολάκευσε τὴν ἑαυτοῦ γνώμην, οὐδὲ ἐπήρθη
ὑπὸ τοῦ ὀνόματος οὕτω μεγάλου ὄντος, ἀλλ᾽
ἑαυτὸν εὖ διασκεψάμενος ὡς μελέτῃ οὐκ ἐπιτήδειον
τῷ ξυγγράφειν ἐπέθετο καὶ ἐθαυμάσθη ἐκ τούτου.
ἡ μὲν ἐπίπαν ἰδέα τοῦ ἀνδρὸς ἀφέλεια προσβάλ-
λουσά τι τῆς Νικοστράτου ὥρας, ἡ δὲ ἐνίοτε πρὸς
Δίωνα ὁρᾷ καὶ τὸν ἐκείνου τόνον.

625 Ἐντυχὼν δέ ποτε αὐτῷ Φιλόστρατος ὁ Λήμνιος
βιβλίον ἔτι πρόχειρον ἔχοντι καὶ ἀναγιγνώσκοντι
αὐτὸ σὺν ὀργῇ καὶ ἐπιτάσει τοῦ φθέγματος ἤρετο
αὐτόν, ὅ τι σπουδάζοι, καὶ ὃς " ἐκπεπόνηταί μοι "
ἔφη " κατηγορία τοῦ Γύννιδος, καλῶ γὰρ οὕτω τὸν
ἄρτι καθῃρημένον τύραννον, ἐπειδὴ ἀσελγείᾳ πάσῃ
τὰ Ῥωμαίων ᾔσχυνε." καὶ ὁ Φιλόστρατος " ἐγώ
σε " εἶπεν " ἐθαύμαζον ἄν, εἰ ζῶντος κατηγόρη-
σας." εἶναι γὰρ δὴ τὸ μὲν ζῶντα τύραννον ἐπικόπτειν ἀνδρός, τὸ δὲ ἐπεμβαίνειν κειμένῳ παντός.

[1] Cobet would omit θαπτομένοις as too literal an echo of
Thucydides ii. 35 where the participle is appropriate.

---

[1] These were ceremonies in honour of the famous dead of
classical times and were held yearly. This type of speech
is called a polemarchic oration. Fictitious polemarchic
declamations were a favourite exercise of the sophists.
[2] For the purity of speech of the interior of Attica see
p. 553.

holds the funeral games in honour of those buried there who have fallen in war.[1]

31. AELIAN was a Roman, but he wrote Attic as correctly as the Athenians in the interior of Attica.[2] This man in my opinion is worthy of all praise, in the first place because by hard work he achieved purity of speech though he lived in a city which employed another language; secondly because, though he received the title of sophist at the hands of those who award that honour, he did not trust to their decision, but neither flattered his own intelligence nor was puffed up by this appellation, exalted though it was, but after taking careful stock of his own abilities, he saw that they were not suited to declamation, and so he applied himself to writing history and won admiration in this field. Simplicity was the prevailing note of his style, and it has something of the charm of Nicostratus, but at times he imitates the vigorous style of Dio.

Philostratus of Lemnos once met him when he was holding a book in his hands and reading it aloud in an indignant and emphatic voice, and he asked him what he was studying. He replied: " I have composed an indictment of Gynnis,[3] for by that name I call the tyrant who has just been put to death, because by every sort of wanton wickedness he disgraced the Roman Empire." On which Philostratus retorted: " I should admire you for it, if you had indicted him while he was alive." For he said that while it takes a real man to try to curb a living tyrant, anyone can trample on him when he is down.

[3] The " womanish man," applied to Heliogabalus, who was put to death in 222. This diatribe is lost.

Ἔφασκε δὲ ὁ ἀνὴρ οὗτος μηδ' ἀποδεδημηκέναι ποι τῆς γῆς ὑπὲρ τὴν Ἰταλῶν χώραν, μηδὲ ἐμβῆναι ναῦν, μηδὲ γνῶναι θάλατταν, ὅθεν καὶ λόγου πλείονος κατὰ τὴν Ῥώμην ἠξιοῦτο ὡς τιμῶν τὰ ἤθη. Παυσανίου μὲν οὖν ἀκροατὴς ἐγένετο, ἐθαύμαζε δὲ τὸν Ἡρώδην ὡς ποικιλώτατον ῥητόρων. ἐβίω δὲ ὑπὲρ τὰ ἑξήκοντα ἔτη καὶ ἐτελεύτα οὐκ ἐπὶ παισίν, παιδοποιίαν γὰρ παρῃτήσατο τῷ μὴ γῆμαί ποτε. τοῦτο δὲ εἴτε εὔδαιμον εἴτε ἄθλιον οὐ τοῦ παρόντος καιροῦ φιλοσοφῆσαι.

λβ΄. Ἐπεὶ δὲ ἡ τύχη κράτιστον ἐπὶ πάντα τὰ ἀνθρώπεια, μηδὲ Ἡλιόδωρος ἀπαξιούσθω σοφιστῶν κύκλου παράδοξον ἀγώνισμα τύχης γενόμενος· ἐχειροτονήθη μὲν γὰρ ὁ ἀνὴρ οὗτος πρόδικος τῆς ἑαυτοῦ πατρίδος ἐς τὰ Κελτικὰ ἔθνη ξὺν ἑτέρῳ, νοσοῦντος δὲ θατέρου καὶ λεγομένου τοῦ βασιλέως διαγράφειν πολλὰς τῶν δικῶν διέδραμεν ὁ Ἡλιόδωρος ἐς τὸ στρατόπεδον δείσας περὶ τῆ δίκη, ἐσκαλούμενος δὲ θᾶττον ἢ ᾤετο ἐς τὸν νοσοῦντα ἀνεβάλλετο, ὑβριστὴς δὲ ὢν ὁ τὰς δίκας ἐσκαλῶν οὐ
626 συνεχώρει ταῦτα, ἀλλὰ παρήγαγεν αὐτὸν ἐς τὰ δικαστήρια ἄκοντά τε καὶ τοῦ γενείου ἕλκων. ὡς δὲ ἔσω παρῆλθε καὶ θαρραλέον μὲν ἐς τὸν βασιλέα εἶδεν, καιρὸν δὲ ᾔτησεν ὕδατος, αὐτὴν δὲ τὴν παραίτησιν ἐντρεχῶς διέθετο εἰπὼν '' καινόν σοι δόξει, μέγιστε αὐτοκράτορ, ἑαυτόν τις παραγραφόμενος τῷ[1] μόνος ἀγωνίσασθαι τὴν δίκην ἐντολὰς

---

[1] τῷ Kayser suggests.

---

[1] A favourite sophistic theme for epideictic orations was " Should a man marry ? "
[2] Otherwise unknown.

This man used to say that he had never travelled to any part of the world beyond the confines of Italy, and had never set foot on a ship, or become acquainted with the sea; and on these grounds he was all the more highly esteemed in Rome as one who prized their mode of life. He was a pupil of Pausanias, but he admired Herodes as the most various of orators. He lived to be over sixty years of age and died leaving no children; for by never marrying he evaded begetting children. However this is not the right time to speculate as to whether this brings happiness or misery.[1]

32. Since Fortune plays the most important part in all human affairs, HELIODORUS[2] must not be deemed unworthy of the sophistic circle; for he was a marvellous instance of her triumphs. He was elected advocate of his own country among the Celtic tribes, with a colleague. And when his colleague was ill, and it was reported that the Emperor[3] was cancelling many of the suits, Heliodorus hastened to the military headquarters in anxiety about his own suit. On being summoned into court sooner than he expected, he tried to postpone the case till the sick man could be present; but the official who gave the notifications of the suits was an overbearing fellow and would not allow this, but haled him into court against his will, and even dragged him by the beard. But when he had entered he actually looked boldly at the Emperor, asked for time to be allotted to him in which to plead, and then with ready skill delivered his protest, saying: "It will seem strange to you, most mighty Emperor, that one should nullify his own suit by pleading it alone, without

[3] Caracalla.

οὐκ ἔχων," ἀναπηδήσας ὁ αὐτοκράτωρ ἄνδρα τε
" οἷον οὔπω ἔγνωκα, τῶν ἐμαυτοῦ καιρῶν εὕρημα "[1]
καὶ τὰ τοιαῦτα ἐκάλει τὸν Ἡλιόδωρον ἀνασείων
τὴν χεῖρα καὶ τὸν κόλπον τῆς χλαμύδος. κατ'
ἀρχὰς μὲν οὖν ἐνέπεσέ τις καὶ ἡμῖν ὁρμὴ γέλωτος
οἰομένοις ὅτι διαπτύοι αὐτόν, ἐπεὶ δὲ ἱππεύειν
αὐτῷ τε δημοσίᾳ ἔδωκε καὶ παισίν, ὁπόσους ἔχοι,
ἐθαυμάζετο ἡ τύχη ὡς τὴν ἑαυτῆς ἰσχὺν ἐνδεικνυ-
μένη διὰ τῶν οὕτω παραλόγων, καὶ πολλῷ πλέον
τοῦτο ἐκ τῶν ἐφεξῆς ἐδηλοῦτο· ὡς γὰρ ξυνῆκεν ὁ
Ἀράβιος, ὅτι κατὰ δαίμονα ἀγαθὸν τὰ πράγματα
αὐτῷ προὔβαινεν, ἀπεχρήσατο τῇ φορᾷ τοῦ βασιλέως, καθάπερ τῶν ναυκλήρων οἱ τὰ ἱστία πλήρη
ἀνασείοντες ἐν ταῖς εὐπλοίαις καὶ " ὦ βασιλεῦ,"
ἔφη " ἀνάθες μοι καιρὸν ἐς ἐπίδειξιν μελέτης,"
καὶ ὁ βασιλεὺς " ἀκροῶμαι," εἶπε " καὶ λέγε ἐς
τόδε· ὁ Δημοσθένης ἐπὶ τοῦ Φιλίππου ἐκπεσὼν
καὶ δειλίας φεύγων."[2] μελετῶντι δὲ οὐ μόνον
ἑαυτὸν εὔνουν παρεῖχεν, ἀλλ' ἡτοίμαζε καὶ τὸν ἐξ
ἄλλων ἔπαινον φοβερὸν βλέπων ἐς τοὺς μὴ ξὺν
ἐπαίνῳ ἀκούοντας. καὶ μὴν καὶ προὐστήσατο
αὐτὸν τῆς μεγίστης τῶν κατὰ τὴν Ῥώμην συνηγο-
ριῶν ὡς ἐπιτηδειότερον δικαστηρίοις καὶ δίκαις.[3]
ἀποθανόντος δὲ τοῦ βασιλέως προσετάχθη μέν τις
αὐτῷ νῆσος, λαβὼν δὲ ἐν τῇ νήσῳ φονικὴν αἰτίαν
ἀνεπέμφθη ἐς τὴν Ῥώμην ὡς ἀπολογησόμενος τοῖς
627 τῶν στρατοπέδων ἡγεμόσι, δόξαντι δὲ αὐτῷ καθαρῷ

---

[1] A sign of approval; cf. Eunapius, *Life of the Sophist Julian.*
[2] For this theme, based on Aeschines, *On the False Embassy*, 34, cf. Maximus Planudes v. 309 Walz.
[3] Like Quirinus, he was made an advocate of the Treasury, *advocatus fisci.*

having your commands to do so." At this the Emperor sprang from his seat and called Heliodorus "a man such as I have never yet known, a new phenomenon such as has appeared only in my own time," and other epithets of this sort, and raising his hand he shook back the fold of his cloak.[1] Now at first we felt an impulse to laugh, because we thought that the Emperor was really making fun of him. But when he bestowed on him the public honour of equestrian rank and also on all his children, men marvelled at the goddess Fortune who showed her power by events so incredible. And this power was illustrated still more clearly in what followed. For when the Arab comprehended that things were going well for him, he profited by the Emperor's impulsive mood, like a navigator who crowds on all sail when the wind is fair for sailing : " O Emperor," said he, " appoint a time for me to give a display of declamation." " I give you a hearing now, and speak on the following theme," said the Emperor : ' Demosthenes, after breaking down before Philip, defends himself from the charge of cowardice.' "[2] And while Heliodorus was declaiming he not only showed himself in a friendly mood, but also secured applause from the others present by looking sternly at those of the audience who failed to applaud. What is more, he placed him at the head of the most important body of public advocates[3] in Rome, as being peculiarly fitted for the courts and for conducting legal cases. But when the Emperor died he was deported to a certain island, and having incurred a charge of murder in the island he was sent to Rome to make his defence before the military prefects. And since he proved himself

εἶναι τῆς αἰτίας ἐπανείθη καὶ ἡ νῆσος. καὶ γηράσκει ἐν τῇ Ῥώμῃ μήτε σπουδαζόμενος μήτε ἀμελούμενος.

λγ΄. Ἀσπάσιον δὲ τὸν σοφιστὴν Ῥάβεννα μὲν ἤνεγκεν, ἡ δὲ Ῥάβεννα Ἰταλοί, Δημητριανὸς δὲ ὁ πατὴρ ἐπαίδευσεν εὖ γιγνώσκων τοὺς κριτικοὺς τῶν λόγων. πολυμαθὴς δὲ ὁ Ἀσπάσιος καὶ πολυήκοος καὶ τὸ μὲν καινοπρεπὲς ἐπαινῶν, ἐς ἀπειροκαλίαν δὲ οὐδαμοῦ ἐκπίπτων ὑπὸ τοῦ ἐν καιρῷ χρῆσθαι οἷς γιγνώσκει. τουτὶ δέ που καὶ ἐν μουσικῇ κράτιστον, οἱ γὰρ καιροὶ τῶν τόνων λύρᾳ τε φωνὴν ἔδωκαν καὶ αὐλῷ καὶ μελῳδίαν ἐπαίδευσαν. ἐπιμεληθεὶς δὲ τοῦ δοκίμως τε καὶ σὺν ἀφελείᾳ ἑρμηνεύειν πνεύματός τε καὶ περιβολῆς ἠμέλησε, τὸ σχεδιάζειν τε ἐκ φύσεως οὐκ ἔχων πόνῳ παρεστήσατο.

Ἦλθε δὲ καὶ ἐπὶ πολλὰ τῆς γῆς μέρη βασιλεῖ τε ξυνὼν καὶ καθ' ἑαυτὸν μεταβαίνων. προὔστη δὲ καὶ τοῦ κατὰ τὴν Ῥώμην θρόνου νεάζων μὲν εὐδοκιμώτατος, γηράσκων δὲ ξὺν αἰτίᾳ τοῦ μὴ ἑτέρῳ ἀποστῆναι βούλεσθαι. ἡ δὲ πρὸς τὸν Λήμνιον Φιλόστρατον τῷ Ἀσπασίῳ διαφορὰ ἤρξατο μὲν ἀπὸ τῆς Ῥώμης, ἐπέδωκε δὲ ἐν Ἰωνίᾳ ὑπὸ Κασσιανοῦ τε καὶ Αὐρηλίου τῶν σοφιστῶν αὐξηθεῖσα. ἦν δὲ αὐτοῖν ὁ μὲν Αὐρήλιος οἷος καὶ ἐν καπηλείοις μελετᾶν πρὸς τὸν ἐκεῖ οἶνον, ὁ δ' οἷος θρασύνεσθαι

---

[1] This sophist is occasionally cited by the scholiasts on Hermogenes.

[2] On oratory as a kind of musical science see Dionysius of Halicarnassus, On Literary Composition.

[3] Kayser thinks that Alexander Severus is meant, but there are good reasons for supposing that it was Caracalla.

innocent of the charge he was also released from
his exile on the island. He is spending his old
age in Rome, neither greatly admired nor altogether
neglected.

33. Ravenna was the birthplace of ASPASIUS[1] the
sophist—now Ravenna is an Italian city—and he
was educated by his father Demetrianus who was
skilled in the art of criticism. Aspasius was an
industrious student and was diligent in attending
the rhetorical schools. He used to praise novelty,
but he never lapsed into bad taste, because what
he invented he employed with a due sense of proportion. This is, of course, of the greatest importance in music also,[2] for it is the time measures
of the notes that have given a voice to the lyre
and the flute and taught us melody. But though
he took great pains to express himself appropriately
and with simplicity, he gave too little thought to
vigour and rhetorical amplification. Though he had
no natural ability for extempore speaking, he made
good the deficiency by hard work.

He visited many parts of the earth, both in the
train of the Emperor[3] and travelling independently.
He held the chair of rhetoric at Rome with great
credit to himself, so long as he was young, but as
he grew old he was criticized for not being willing
to resign it in another's favour. The quarrel between
Aspasius and Philostratus of Lemnos began in Rome,
but became more serious in Ionia, where it was
fomented by the sophists Cassianus and Aurelius.
Of these two men Aurelius was the sort of person
who would declaim even in low wine-shops while
the drinking was going on ; while Cassianus was a
man of such impudence of character that he aspired

μὲν ἐπὶ τὸν Ἀθήνησι θρόνον διὰ καιρούς, οἷς
ἀπεχρήσατο, παιδεῦσαι δὲ μηδένα, πλὴν Περίγητος[1]
τοῦ Λυδοῦ. περὶ μὲν οὖν τοῦ τρόπου τῆς διαφορᾶς
εἴρηταί μοι καὶ τί ἂν αὖθις ἑρμηνεύοιμι τὰ ἀπο-
χρώντως δεδηλωμένα; τὸ δὲ εἶναί τι χρηστὸν καὶ
628 παρ' ἐχθροῦ εὑρέσθαι ἐν πολλοῖς μὲν τῶν ἀνθρωπίνων διεφάνη, μάλιστα δὲ ἐπὶ τῶν ἀνδρῶν
τούτων· διενεχθέντε γὰρ ὁ μὲν Ἀσπάσιος προσε-
ποίησεν αὑτῷ τὸ σχεδιάζειν ξὺν εὐροίᾳ, ἐπειδὴ ὁ
Φιλόστρατος καὶ τούτου τοῦ μέρους ἐλλογίμως
εἶχεν, ὁ δ' αὖ τὸν ἑαυτοῦ λόγον τέως ὑλομανοῦντα
πρὸς τὴν ἀκρίβειαν τὴν ἐκείνου ἐκόλασεν.
Ἡ δὲ ξυγγεγραμμένη ἐπιστολὴ τῷ Φιλοστράτῳ
περὶ τοῦ πῶς χρὴ ἐπιστέλλειν πρὸς τὸν Ἀσπάσιον
τείνει, ἐπειδὴ παρελθὼν ἐς βασιλείους ἐπιστολὰς
τὰς μὲν ἀγωνιστικώτερον τοῦ δέοντος ἐπέστελλε,
τὰς δὲ οὐ σαφῶς, ὧν οὐδέτερον βασιλεῖ πρέπον·
αὐτοκράτωρ γὰρ δὴ ὁπότε ἐπιστέλλοι, οὐ δεῖ
ἐνθυμημάτων οὐδ' ἐπιχειρημάτων, ἀλλὰ δόξης,
οὐδ' αὖ ἀσαφείας, ἐπειδὴ νόμους φθέγγεται,
σαφήνεια δὲ ἑρμηνεὺς νόμου.
Παυσανίου μὲν οὖν μαθητὴς ὁ Ἀσπάσιος, Ἱπποδρόμου δὲ οὐκ ἀνήκοος, ἐπαίδευε δὲ κατὰ τὴν
Ῥώμην ἱκανῶς γηράσκων, ὁπότε μοι ταῦτα ἐγράφετο.
Τοσαῦτα περὶ Ἀσπασίου. περὶ δὲ Φιλοστράτου
Λημνίου καὶ τίς μὲν ἐν δικαστηρίοις ὁ ἀνὴρ οὗτος,

---

[1] Valckenaer would read Πίγρητος, because Pigres is a
name often occurring in Asia.

[1] Aristophanes, *Birds* 375.

to the chair at Athens, seizing on opportunities of which he made full use, and this though he had taught no one except Periges the Lydian. However since I have described the manner of their quarrel, why should I relate again what has been made sufficiently plain? The saying that even from an enemy one can learn something worth while [1] has often been illustrated in human affairs, but never more clearly than in the case of these men. For while their controversy lasted Aspasius achieved for himself the art of speaking extempore with ease and fluency, because Philostratus already had a great reputation in this branch of eloquence; while the latter in his turn pruned down his own style of oratory which was running to riot before, till it matched his opponent's accuracy and terseness.

The epistle composed by Philostratus called *How to Write Letters* is aimed at Aspasius, who on being appointed Imperial Secretary wrote certain letters in a style more controversial than is suitable; and others he wrote in obscure language, though neither of these qualities is becoming to an Emperor. For an Emperor when he writes a letter ought not to use rhetorical syllogisms or trains of reasoning, but ought to express only his own will; nor again should he be obscure, since he is the voice of the law, and lucidity is the interpreter of the law. Aspasius was a pupil of Pausanias, but he also attended the school of Hippodromus, and he was teaching in Rome, well advanced in years, when I was writing this narrative.

So much for Aspasius. But of Philostratus of Lemnos and his ability in the law courts, in political

τίς δὲ ἐν δημηγορίαις, τίς δὲ ἐν συγγράμμασι, τίς
δὲ ἐν μελέταις, ὅσος δὲ ἐν σχεδίῳ λόγῳ, καὶ περὶ
Νικαγόρου τοῦ Ἀθηναίου, ὃς καὶ τοῦ Ἐλευσινίου
ἱεροῦ κήρυξ ἐστέφθη, καὶ Ἀψίνης ὁ Φοῖνιξ ἐφ᾽ ὅσον
προὔβη μνήμης τε καὶ ἀκριβείας, οὐκ ἐμὲ δεῖ γράφειν, καὶ γὰρ ἂν καὶ ἀπιστηθείην ὡς χαρισάμενος,
ἐπειδὴ φιλία μοι πρὸς αὐτοὺς ἦν.

---

[1] From Suidas we learn that the father of Nicagoras was
Mnesaius, and his son Minucianus; the latter lived under
Gallienus, 253-268. Nicagoras taught at Athens during the
latter part of the life of our Philostratus.

harangues, in writing treatises, in declamation, and lastly of his talent for speaking extempore, it is not for me to write. Nay, nor must I write about Nicagoras[1] of Athens, who was appointed herald of the temple at Eleusis; nor of Apsines[2] the Phoenician and his great achievements of memory and precision. For I should be distrusted as favouring them unduly, since they were connected with me by the tie of friendship.

[2] Apsines of Gadara taught rhetoric at Athens about A.D. 235. We have two of his critical works, but his declamations have perished. He gives many examples of themes and was a devout student of Demosthenes.

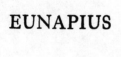

EUNAPIUS

INTRODUCTION

For the main facts of the life of Eunapius we depend on the allusions to himself in the following *Lives*. He was born in 346 at Sardis, and was related by marriage to Chrysanthius. In his sixteenth year he went to Athens and studied with a Christian sophist, the Armenian Prohaeresius. To him Eunapius gave a loyalty that was unaffected by his teacher's religion, though otherwise he is consistent in hating and fearing the steadily growing influence of Christianity. After five years in Athens, Eunapius was preparing to go to Egypt, but his parents recalled him to Lydia in 367, and for the rest of his life, for all we know to the contrary, he taught at Sardis. There, as he tells us, he devoted himself to the venerable Chrysanthius until the latter's death. His own death occurred about 414. He lived to see the decline of Greek studies so lamented by Libanius; the proscription of sacrifices to the gods, and the official abolition of paganism in 391; the invasion of Greece by Alaric, and the destruction of Eleusis in 395. His forebodings and his distress at all this colour the *Lives*.

His chief work was a *Universal History*, in which he continued the *Chronicle* of Dexippus, taking up the narrative at the year A.D. 270. In fourteen

319

INTRODUCTION

Books he brought it down to the reign of Arcadius at the opening of the fifth century, when it was probably cut short by his own death. Some fragments of this chronicle have been preserved in the *Lexicon* of Suidas, and from these and from his own frequent references to it we can see that it was written in considerable detail. It would be a valuable document for the times, for though Eunapius was a bitter partisan and the book was partly a polemic against Christianity, he knew personally the leading men of the Eastern Empire, and was an eyewitness of much that he related. The real hero of the work, however, seems to have been the Emperor Julian, and Photius says that it amounts as a whole to an encomium on that last hope of the pagan world. For his career Eunapius could derive much information from his friend the physician Oribasius, who had been with Julian in Gaul. In the fifth century Zosimus the pagan historian borrowed from Eunapius for his account of Julian's life.

In the *Lives* Eunapius refers to himself modestly in the third person, and never by name. Though he regarded the title of sophist as the most honourable possible, he actually devotes more space to those who were philosophers rather than sophists, such as Iamblichus and Maximus. The *Life* of Libanius, who was a typical sophist, is short and superficial, and he gives only a few lines to Himerius. At the beginning of the work there are strange omissions, for example of Diogenes Laertius, when he is speaking of the historians of philosophy and cites only Sotion and Porphyry. But no less capricious is his avoidance of any mention of the sophist and philosopher Themistius, his own con-

temporary and one of the most distinguished. In describing the intellectual life of the fourth Christian century he is naturally one-sided. His interests all centre in the East, and he has nothing to say about Rome or the men for whom Rome was still the capital of the world. Nor is it likely that in his *History* he wrote of certain fourth-century men, whose names are household words, where Libanius, Prohaeresius, and Himerius are unknown. Augustine, Jerome, Basil, and Gregory, the poets Prudentius and Ausonius are but a few of his celebrated contemporaries; but he ignores them, along with the historian Ammianus Marcellinus, to whom we must so often turn to supplement the *Lives*. Yet Ammianus went with the "divine Julian" to Persia, and we have no better guide for the history of that time.

Eunapius admires even absurd charlatans, such as Zeno and his successors the "iatrosophists," *healing sophists*,[1] partly because anything that could be called a sophist was sacred to him, partly because he was something of an iatrosophist himself, since he boasts of the knowledge of medicine that enabled him to treat Chrysanthius. Success in declamation is in his eyes the highest possible achievement, and in this he is akin to Philostratus. But intellectually he is greatly his inferior; he was not so well educated, and his Greek is less crowded with reminiscences of the classical authors. One author at least he knew well, and frequently echoes; this is Plutarch, but he does not always quote him correctly.

His style is difficult and often obscure, and he was

---

[1] For these sophists, who professed an art of healing, had sometimes studied medicine, and competed with regular physicians, see below, *Life of Magnus*, p. 498.

by no means an Atticist. He exaggerates on all
occasions, and uses poetical and grandiloquent words
for the simplest actions, such as eating and drinking.
At every step one has to discount his passion for
superlatives. He was, as far as we can judge, among
the least erudite of the fourth - century sophists.
During his lifetime Nicomedia, Antioch, Smyrna, and
Caesarea had almost superseded Athens, Alexandria,
and Constantinople as intellectual centres, and
Libanius of Antioch could boast that his school had
supplied with rhetoricians " three continents and all
the islands as far as the Pillars of Heracles." But,
on the whole, the fourth-century sophists lack the
distinction and brilliance of their predecessors in the
second century, probably because they were allowed
less brilliant opportunities under the Christian
Emperors. The renaissance of Hellenism under
Julian lasted less than two years, and his death in
363 blasted the hopes of the whole tribe of pagan
sophists, philosophers, and theurgists. It is true
that Christian Emperors such as Constantius had to
some extent patronized Sophistic, but they gave it a
divided attention, and under less cultured Emperors,
such as Theodosius, the study of Latin, and, still more,
of Roman law replaced Hellenic studies, so that
professors of law had a better standing than professors of rhetoric.

The following notices in the order of the *Lives* are
intended to supplement Eunapius with dates and
certain facts omitted by him. He takes more interest
in the historical background and gives more dates
than Philostratus, but is so discursive that, by con-
trast, Philostratus seems systematic.

INTRODUCTION

PLOTINUS OF LYCOPOLIS in Egypt (A.D. 204–270) may be called the founder of Neo-Platonism. For the facts of his life we depend on Porphyry's biography of him and the meagre notice by Eunapius. He studied at Alexandria with Ammonius, of whom little is known, and accompanied the Emperor Gordian on his disastrous expedition against Ctesiphon in 243. Then he came to Rome, where he spent the rest of his life in teaching; he died at his villa in Campania in 270. We have his *Enneads* (*Nines*), so called because each of the six sections contains nine discussions, fifty-four in all. They are the written monument of Neo-Platonism. He cared nothing for style and never revised, but left to his pupil Porphyry the arrangement of the work and even the correction of the spelling, which was a weak point in his acquired Greek. In the *Enneads* he expounded one by one, as they arose in his school, questions of ethics, psychology, metaphysics, cosmology, and aesthetics. In spite of Porphyry's editing there is no regular sequence in the work. The discipline of Plotinus is meant to detach the soul from material things and to enable it to attain to spiritual ecstasy, "the flight of the Alone to the Alone." [1] Plotinus himself is said to have achieved a vision of the Absolute four times in the five years of his association with Porphyry. Mystical asceticism has never been carried further, but it is usually more sombre and self-tormenting. Contemplation, rather than the worship of the gods, was the means by which Plotinus himself attained to union with the Absolute as he conceived it. But he accepted the theory of daemons and thus accounted for the existence of evil in the world. Thus he

[1] *Ennead* vi. 9.

opened the door to superstition and imposture, and his followers were frequently mere theurgists and charlatans, like the fourth-century Maximus. Perhaps Eunapius, when he says that in his time Plotinus was more read than Plato, exaggerates after his fashion, but the influence of the *Enneads* can be clearly traced in the religion and ethics of the fourth century, especially in the teaching of the popular "Syrian" school of Neo-Platonism. In fact, the terminology of mysticism and ascetism has always been derived from Plotinus. Porphyry received from a fellow-disciple, Amelius, and preserved in his *Life of Plotinus*, an oracle of Apollo which described the blessed state of the soul of Plotinus.[1]

PORPHYRY (233–301 ?), called "the Tyrian," was brought up at Tyre, though that was not certainly his birthplace. He studied at Athens with several professors, but especially with Longinus. Rome was still the centre of philosophic activity, and he left Athens in 263 to become the disciple of Plotinus at Rome, wrote his *Life*, and many years after his master's death, probably later than 298, edited and published the *Enneads*; but for him Plotinus might now be little more than a name. After he had spent six years in Rome he withdrew to Sicily, as Eunapius relates, but there is no evidence that Plotinus followed him thither. After the death of Plotinus he returned to Rome, married Marcella, the widow of a friend, and became the head of the Neo-Platonic school. He was a prolific writer on a great variety of subjects—grammar, chronology, history, mathematics, Homeric criticism, vegetarianism, psychology, and metaphysics; he is the savant

[1] Well translated by Myers in his *Classical Essays*.

among the Neo-Platonists. His treatise, *Against the Christians*, in fifteen Books, of which fragments survive, was the most serious and thorough document, as well as the fairest, in which Christianity has ever been attacked, and was free from the scorn and bitterness of Julian's work of the same name. It was burned in 448 by the edict of the Emperors Valentinian III. and Theodosius II. In his *Letter to Anebo*, the Egyptian priest, on divination, he speaks with astonishing frankness of the frauds of polytheism as it was practised in his day in the Mysteries, and appeals to all intellectuals to turn to philosophy; hence he has been called the Modernist of Paganism. As Plotinus had been the metaphysician, Porphyry was the moralist of the Neo-Platonic school. Several of his works, including the *Letter to Marcella* and the *Life of Plotinus*, survive. Of himself we have no such trustworthy biography as he wrote of Plotinus. Eunapius, however, though incorrect in minor details, is a fairly good authority, and he had access to reliable documents, such as the lost works of Porphyry himself.

The notice of Porphyry in Suidas is hardly more than a bibliography, and that not complete, of his writings.

IAMBLICHUS was the leading figure of the Syrian school of Neo-Platonism in the early fourth Christian century. He would have called himself a philosopher of all the schools, but his eclecticism was arbitrary and superficial. His metaphysics followed and developed the teaching of Plotinus. But his final appeal was to divination, and in his practice of theurgy he represents the decadence of Neo-Platonism. His disciples Maximus and Chrysanthius

were professed miracle-workers, and the Emperor Julian's fanatical admiration for him and constant reference to him as inspired is the most striking evidence of the Apostate's easy credulity. The writings of Iamblichus are full of allegorical interpretations and intermediary gods, and Julian's attempt to co-ordinate all the cults and to bring the Oriental deities into the Hellenic Pantheon is due to the influence of Iamblichus.

He died in the reign of Constantine, about 330, so that Julian cannot have known him personally, and the six *Letters* addressed to Iamblichus and once ascribed to Julian are now generally recognized as spurious. Iamblichus studied at Athens and returned to teach at his native Chalcis, where Eunapius describes him as surrounded by adoring and exacting disciples. The treatise *On the Mysteries*, an answer to Porphyry's *Letter to Anebo* and a defence of theurgy, is no longer ascribed by the majority of scholars to Iamblichus, but it reflects the teachings of his school. We have his works on Pythagoreanism and his mathematical treatises, but the treatise *On the Gods*, which Julian in his *Hymns* seems to have followed closely, is lost. For him, as for Julian, Mithras was the central deity. He was indifferent to style, and his writings, though useful to the historian of Neo-Platonism, have small literary merit.

AEDESIUS is badly treated by Eunapius, who in the so-called *Life* soon digresses from him to Sopater the pupil of Iamblichus. Sopater was put to death by Constantine, and must not be confused with the younger man of the same name, the correspondent of Libanius whom Julian met in Syria. Then comes an account of the corrupt official, Ablabius, of

Eustathius, and his more distinguished wife Sosipatra, and her career as a philosopher, theurgist, and clairvoyant, an amazing tale which illustrates the decadence of philosophy in the fourth century, and the strange things that were done in its name. Aedesius himself, to whom his biographer returns at the close of the *Life*, was about seventy and teaching at Pergamon, when, as Eunapius relates in his *Life of Maximus*, he kept at arm's length the future Emperor Julian, a dangerous and exacting pupil, and finally got rid of him by hints of more complete revelations to be had from his pupils and especially from Maximus the theurgist, at Ephesus. This must have occurred about 350. Perhaps Aedesius, who carried on the teachings of the Syrian school of his master Iamblichus, was more intelligent or more honest than his younger contemporaries. He died before the Hellenic reaction under Julian.

MAXIMUS OF EPHESUS, the most famous theurgist or miracle-working philosopher of the century, was said by Theodoret to look like a philosopher, though he was really a magician. From all sources we gather that he was unworthy to be called a Neo-Platonist, and that he was the most unscrupulous as well as the most successful of the followers of Iamblichus. His chief title to fame is the influence, plainly mischievous, that he gained over the Emperor Julian. When the latter became Emperor he summoned Maximus to Constantinople, and Ammianus describes how Julian interrupted a sitting of the Senate in order to greet and publicly embrace the newly arrived Maximus. According to Ammianus, Julian on his deathbed in Persia discussed the immortality of the soul with

Maximus and Priscus. The Romans, for political rather than religious reasons, feared the influence of the practice of magic, and, under Valens, Maximus was executed in 371. Libanius was no theurgist, but he congratulates Maximus in *Letter* 606 on his influence over Julian.

Priscus the Thesprotian or Molossian, was the last of a long line of professors who made the reputation of the school at Athens in the fourth century. He was the friend and adviser of the Emperor Julian whom he accompanied to Persia. We know very little about him apart from the *Life* of Eunapius, in which he appears as morose and aloof, sceptical and disdainful of popularity. In an extant letter Julian invites him to Gaul and calls him a genuine philosopher, but the Emperor would have said as much of Maximus the charlatan. After Julian's death Priscus returned to Antioch, and was there in the autumn of 363. Both he and Maximus were arrested by the Emperors Valens and Valentinian on a charge of magic which was supposed to have been employed to give them a fever from which they suffered. But Priscus was allowed to go to Greece, where he taught for many years. He survived as late as the invasion of Alaric, and died in 395, aged over ninety. He was a frequent correspondent of Libanius. Priscus was probably a Neo-Platonist, and less devoted to theurgy than was Maximus; hence he was regarded as less dangerous to the imperial government. His wife was named Hippia, and he had several children as we learn from a letter of the Emperor Julian.

Julian of Caesarea in Cappadocia was born about 275, and was a successful teacher of rhetoric at

Athens about 330. There he died about 340, and the succession to his chair was hotly contested by his pupils. Photius says that he wrote on the vocabulary of the Ten Attic Orators, but no work of his survives.[1] Eunapius does not make it clear why Julian and his contemporaries were obliged to teach in private, but probably this was due, not to the opposition of the Christians, since there were famous Christian sophists, notably Prohaeresius, but rather to the factions of the rival sophists, which had never been so violent as when Julian was at the height of his fame. We do not know how it happened that he had more than one official successor, but it is possible that the chair of philosophy was suppressed in favour of rhetoric, which was held to be less antagonistic to Christianity. In his later years the supremacy of Julian was challenged by the success of his pupils, Prohaeresius and Diophantus the Arab.

PROHAERESIUS the Christian sophist, when other Christian professors were hastening to enrol themselves as pagans and true Hellenes to win favour with the new Emperor Julian, seems to have said to himself, like the great bishop of Alexandria, Athanasius, " It is but a little cloud, and will pass." Eunapius says that in 362, when he went to Athens to study with Prohaeresius, the latter was eighty; but as this would make him about the same age as the sophist Julian whose chair he inherited, it seems

[1] Cumont believes that Julian of Caesarea wrote the six fulsome and foolish *Letters* to Iamblichus which the MS. tradition assigns to the Emperor Julian. They are certainly not the Emperor's, but there is no evidence that Julian the sophist had the slightest interest in Iamblichus and his doctrines; on the contrary he seems to have been wholly devoted to rhetoric.

likely that Eunapius exaggerated his age by about ten years. At any rate he was a well established rival of Julian when in 340 the latter died, and Prohaeresius succeeded to his position as leading sophist at Athens, though perhaps not to all the official emoluments, as Julian seems to have had no less than six nominal successors. In 345 Anatolius of Berytus came to Athens, and confirmed Prohaeresius in his office of "stratopedarch," which had been bestowed on him by Constans when he visited Gaul, so that he, like Lollianus in the second century, was a Food Controller.

After Julian's accession in 361 he enacted that the Christian sophists should no longer be allowed to teach Hellenic literature, a decree that shut them out of the field of education. He exempted Prohaeresius, but the sophist resigned his chair. Eunapius says only that Prohaeresius was barred from teaching because he was reputed to be a Christian, yet he was teaching at Athens when Eunapius came there as a student in 362, and it is unlikely that the decree was ever carried out with any thoroughness in the few months that elapsed before the Emperor's death. Prohaeresius died in 367 and his epitaph was written by Gregory Nazianzen. It is to be observed that all the rivals of Prohaeresius at Athens were foreigners, and that the city had ceased to produce great sophists. Prohaeresius himself was an Armenian, which perhaps accounts for his religion ; for Armenia was early converted to Christianity. There was a certain coolness between the Emperor Julian and Prohaeresius, apart from the incident of the exemption, for the sophist resented the Emperor's admiration of Libanius. However, in an extant letter

INTRODUCTION

Julian writes in a friendly tone to suggest that
Prohaeresius may intend to write an account of the
Emperor's return from Gaul, in which case he will provide him with documents. Prohaeresius was then,
according to Eunapius, eighty-seven! It is possible
that Julian in his student days at Athens had attended
the lectures of Prohaeresius. Anatolius of Berytus,
the Phoenician of whom Eunapius speaks in the *Life
of Prohaeresius,* was a frequent correspondent of
Libanius, and we have a number of letters addressed
to him by that sophist. Though Anatolius was a
devout pagan and Hellene, he held many offices
under the Christian Emperors, and was a distinguished
prefect of Egypt and also of Illyricum, entering on
the latter office in 356. His relations with Libanius
were somewhat strained by his refusal to give to
Libanius one of the many offices at his disposal.
Anatolius died in 360.[1]

EPIPHANIUS OF SYRIA, sometimes called the
Arab, was a poet as well as a sophist. He taught
rhetoric at Laodicea before he moved to Athens.
He is mentioned by Sozomenus, and was a correspondent of Libanius. Though he died young he left
several technical treatises on rhetoric, which are all
lost.

DIOPHANTUS the Arab was a pupil and one of
the successors of the sophist Julian, and was teaching
at Athens when Libanius came there as a student in
336. Libanius was forcibly enrolled as a pupil of
Diophantus by the sophist's pupils, but avoided his
lectures; he himself does not mention the name of
Diophantus though he relates the incident. Students
who came from Arabia were expected to study with

[1] Ammianus Marcellinus xxi. 6.

a sophist of their nationality, but the pupils of Diophantus had no right to kidnap Libanius of Antioch. Eunapius, in his *Life of Diophantus*, expresses the dislike that he would naturally feel for a successor to his admired Prohaeresius.

SOPOLIS was teaching at Athens when Eunapius lived there (362–367). In the *Life of Prohaeresius* he is referred to with scorn as only nominally a professor of rhetoric. He was one of the most insignificant successors of Julian the sophist, and secured his election by some manœuvre that Eunapius leaves obscure.

HIMERIUS in a speech delivered in 362 says that his hair is turning grey, so his birth may be dated about 315. Like other Bithynians he studied at Athens with Prohaeresius, and there he taught for about fifteen years, until the patronage of the Emperor Julian drew him into the main current of the life of the Empire in the East. He joined Julian at Antioch in 362, after delivering declamations at every important town on the way. Whether, like Maximus and Priscus, he went with Julian on the expedition against Persia we do not know, but after its disastrous ending he seems to have stayed at Antioch or in Bithynia until the death of Prohaeresius. He returned to Greece about 368, and for the rest of his life taught rhetoric at Athens. Probably he died before the Goths invaded Greece in 395. He had married an Athenian of noble family and acquired Athenian citizenship. In his *Oration* 23, a monody, he boasts of the ancestry, on the maternal side, of his only son Rufinus, who died, aged fourteen, at the time when his father was in temporary exile in Boeotia, driven away by the intrigues of rival sophists.

INTRODUCTION

Himerius was wounded in an encounter with the pupils of a rival sophist, and thereafter lectured in his own house. In *Oration* 22 he announces his recovery and the beginning of a new course of lectures.

Eunapius in his *Life* gives us no idea of the importance for our knowledge of the fourth century of this sophist, whose works have in great part survived. No doubt professional jealousy explains this neglect. In his *Orations*, of which thirty-four are extant, nine in a very imperfect and mutilated condition, are all the marks of Asianic oratory. He calls himself a swan, a cicada, a swallow, and his speeches hymns, odes, and songs. In fact it was only fashion that kept him from writing verse. We have the analyses by Photius of thirty-six other *Orations* which have survived as *Eclogues* or *Extracts*. Some of these are not only fictitious but falsely conceived; for example *Eclogue 5*, in which Themistocles spurns the peace terms offered by Xerxes. Himerius is all allegory, poetical allusion, and flowers of speech. In his work may be conveniently surveyed the characteristic weaknesses of fourth-century rhetoric, its lack of logical argument and of a literary or historical conscience, its dependence on commonplaces from the past, its shameless adulation of the great,[1] and even its occasional, surprising charm. With Priscus he represents the last days of the Athenian school of sophistic eloquence.

Libanius of Antioch was born in 314, so that

---

[1] Himerius seized on every chance, and they were many, to deliver a flattering address of welcome to a new proconsul.

he was nearly fifty when Julian became Emperor and raised high hopes in the breasts of all the Hellenic sophists. Though formally enrolled as a pupil of Diophantus when he arrived at Athens in 336, Libanius had already educated himself at Antioch, and so he continued to do at Athens for some years. Then, for about a decade, he taught, first at Constantinople, where his success aroused such enmity that he was driven to migrate to Nicaea, then at Nicomedia where he was contented and popular. Eunapius, who is inclined to disparage Libanius, omits to say that, as his fame increased, the citizens of Constantinople demanded his return, and he was recalled by an Imperial edict. But in 354 he was once more in Antioch, and on the plea of ill-health was allowed to remain in his native city. There for the next forty years his school was the most famous and the most frequented of the day. We are peculiarly well-informed as to this school, thanks to his autobiography and the numerous *Orations* in which he describes the conditions of teaching rhetoric in the fourth century. Though he openly mourned the Emperor, he weathered the storms that followed naturally on the death of Julian and the restoration of Christianity as the State religion. He was the official orator and mediator for Antioch on important occasions, such as the bakers' strike, or the revolt of the city under Theodosius. His last years were saddened by the fact that Greek studies were being neglected in favour of Latin, and that the Emperors had ceased to patronize Hellenism ; moreover he was constantly embroiled with oppressive officials and jealous rivals. He became partly blind, and lost his only son, and, one by one, his friends. It is possible

that he lived as late as 395, but the date of his death is uncertain.

Of all this Eunapius relates little, and he gives no account of the numerous works of Libanius with which he must have been familiar. His criticism of his style is not borne out by anything in the extant works, and this makes us hesitate to accept the judgements of Eunapius on sophists whose writings do not survive. Like Aristeides, Libanius repels the reader by the very mass of what remains of his eloquence. The new edition of his works by Foerster already amounts to eight Teubner volumes, and the *Letters*, of which we have more than 1600, are still to come. The 65 *Orations* are a valuable document for the life, manners, and education of the time; when Libanius narrates, his style is spirited and clear. He admired Aristeides the imitator of Demosthenes, but it would be unjust to Libanius to imply that his knowledge of Greek letters was at second hand. His pages are crowded with illustrations and echoes, rather than quotations, from Greek authors. He had a talent for declamation, and his formal sophistic compositions are strictly conventional, according to the types prescribed by the theorists. His *Monodies*, for instance that on Nicomedia when the city was destroyed by an earthquake, are in the most florid style. In *Oration* 25 he draws a gloomy picture of the slavery of a sophist to his pupils and their parents, a companion piece to Lucian's *Dependent Scholar* in the second century. It is interesting to see that in the later days of Libanius a sophist is no longer sure of his position and a tyrant in society, as Philostratus describes him. Eunapius is both spiteful and untrustworthy for

335

Libanius, but the latter has been more fortunate in his biographer Sievers [1] whose book is a valuable guide to the whole period; he has done more than any other writer to keep the name of Libanius alive.

ACACIUS OF CAESAREA was a frequent correspondent of Libanius, and from the *Letters* of that sophist we learn far more about him than Eunapius tells us in his *Life*. He was rather older than Libanius, and came of a family in which the sophistic profession was hereditary. He taught first in his native Phoenicia, then at Antioch, and finally settled in Palestine. At Antioch he was the rival of Libanius and not so friendly with him as the account of Eunapius makes him appear. Libanius triumphed, and Acacius left Antioch about 361 when the correspondence begins. There was a sort of reconciliation, and Libanius writes to Acacius sympathetically on the death of a son. It is hard to reconcile the statement of Eunapius that Acacius died young with the evidence that we can glean from Libanius as to the duration of the other's activities.

ZENO OF CYPRUS is identified by Boissonade with the physician and teacher of medicine at Alexandria to whom the Emperor Julian addressed an extant letter. If Eunapius is right in saying, in his *Life of Oribasius*, that Oribasius had been a pupil of Zeno, the latter must have been very old in 362, when Julian's letter *To Zeno* was written. It seems more likely that had Julian been addressing a talented orator, he would have mentioned this in his complimentary letter, whereas he only speaks of Zeno's teaching of medicine. At any rate the Zeno of Eunapius is an

---

[1] *Das Leben des Libanius*, Berlin, 1868.

"iatrosophist," a healing sophist. This seems to us a most unhappy combination of professions, and that the name inevitably became a synonym for charlatan we might assume, even if Eunapius had not, in his biography, shown us the absurd figure of Magnus talking down his fellow-practitioners and using his rhetorical talent for his own ends.

MAGNUS, the healing sophist, born at Nisibis, was a pupil of Zeno and taught medicine at Alexandria, that centre of the medical profession. Libanius mentions him in a letter written in 364. On his death Palladas wrote the well-known epigram in the *Palatine Anthology*:

"When Magnus went down to Hades, Aïdoneus trembled, and said: ' Here comes one who will raise up even the dead.' " [1]

This was not intended as a satire, nor did Eunapius think Magnus absurd, and it is clear that, though visibly declining, rhetoric could still charm the Graeco-Roman world. Magnus was alive in 388, when Libanius wrote to him *Letter* 763.[2]

ORIBASIUS according to Suidas was born at Sardis, but we may suppose that his friend Eunapius when he gave Pergamon as his birthplace was better informed. Julian evidently refers to Oribasius in his *Letter to the Athenians* 277 c where he speaks of a " certain physician" who had been allowed by Constantius to accompany him to Milan when he was summoned there to be made Caesar. Oribasius went with Julian to Gaul, and there is preserved by Photius a letter from him to Julian mentioning their sojourn

[1] xi. 281. Magnus is mentioned by Philostorgius viii. 10.
[2] So Seeck, *Die Briefe des Libanius*; but Sievers thinks that this is another Magnus.

337

there together; but we do not know whether he went on the expedition to Persia. When Eunapius says that Oribasius "made Julian Emperor," he probably means not so much that Oribasius was an accomplice in the plot to put Julian on the throne, though he does in fact, in his *Life* of Maximus, speak of Oribasius as the Caesar's "accomplice," but rather that the physician, by his virtuous teachings, had fitted Julian for the position. The historians at any rate are silent as to the connivance of Oribasius. It was probably in 358 that Julian wrote his extant letter to Oribasius, when the latter was editing an epitome of Galen. Oribasius was with him in Antioch on the way to Persia, and is no doubt one of the seven persons whom Julian mentions in *Misopogon* 354 c as newcomers to Antioch, and out of sympathy with its frivolous and ungodly citizens.

CHRYSANTHIUS, the pupil of Aedesius, whom he seems to have closely resembled in character, is the only rival of Prohaeresius in the affection and loyalty of Eunapius. But apart from this biography he is practically unknown. Julian, who must have been offended by his refusal of his pressing invitation to the court, never mentions him, and Libanius, who corresponded with nearly all the leading pagans of his day, ignores Chrysanthius. His refusal to join the Emperor Julian was perhaps due to a conviction, which must have been shared by many persons more cautious and better balanced than the headlong Maximus, that the pagan renaissance would be short-lived. His tolerant and tactful dealings with the Christians during Julian's brief reign may have preserved him from the harsh treatment that was suffered by Maximus.

INTRODUCTION

HELLESPONTIUS, the aged pupil of Chrysanthius in Sardis, whose sudden death is here described, was a native of Galatia, a sophist and philosopher. We have a letter [1] addressed to him by Libanius as early as 355, in which his son is mentioned.

[1] *Letter* 1259.

BIBLIOGRAPHY

Manuscripts.

THESE are few and very corrupt. All are derived from *Laurentianus* lxxxvi. 7, late 12th century, which was not collated by Boissonade or Wyttenbach, and was first recognized as the most reliable codex by Jordan in *De Eunapii codice Laurentiano*, Lemgo, 1888, followed by Lundström, *Prolegomena in Eunapii vitas*, Upsala, 1897; *Vaticanus* 140 (contains also Philostratus, *Lives*). There are inferior MSS. at Naples (*Borbonici*) and Paris. Cobet's emendations are in *Mnemosyne*, vols. vi. and viii. De Boor in *Rheinisches Museum*, xlvii. maintains that the new edition of the *Universal History* mentioned by Photius contained also the *Lives* and was made later than the time of Eunapius; whereas Lundström thinks that Eunapius himself revised his works and omitted many passages that were offensive to the Christians. This would account for the fact that we have two recensions of the *Life* of Libanius, the *Laurentianus* and the *Lacapenianus*; the latter, according to Lundström, is the modified version.

Editions.

Junius Hornanus, Antwerp, 1568 (with very incorrect Latin version). Commelinus, Heidelberg, 1596. Boissonade, Amsterdam, 1822 (Wyttenbach's notes are in vol. ii.). Boissonade, Didot, Paris, 1849, 1878[1] (a reprint of the edition of 1822, with Latin version of Junius, partly re-

[1] The text of the present edition is that of Boissonade, revised; the marginal numbers refer to his pages.

BIBLIOGRAPHY

vised; contains also the works of Philostratus and Himerius). G. Giangrande, *Eunapii Vitae Sophistarum.* Scriptores Gr. et Latini consilio Acad. Lync. editi, Rome, 1956, with relevant bibliography; cp. H. Gerstinger in *Gnomon*, 1958, pp. 105 ff.; R. Keydell, in *Byz. Zeitschr.*, 1960, pp. 119 ff. (reviews). IAMBLICHUS, *De Vita Pythagorica*, L. Deubner, Leipzig, 1937. *Protrepticus*, Pistelli, Leipzig, 1893. *De communi mathematica*, Festa, Leipzig, 1891. *Theologumena arithmeticae*, V. de Falco, Leipzig, 1922. *De mysteriis*, Partey, Berlin, 1857. LIBANIUS, *Opera*, Foerster, Leipzig, 1903–27. EUNAPIUS, *Eunapii historiarum quae supersunt*, Bekker and Niebuhr, Bonn, 1829. *Fragmenta historicorum Graecorum*, Müller, Paris, vol. iv, 1885. ORIBASIUS, *Opera*, Bussemaker-Daremberg, Paris, 1851. *Corpus Medicorum Graecorum*, vi. 1-3, J. Raeder, Leipzig, 1926–33. PLOTINUS, *Plotini Opera*, P. Henry and H.-R. Schwyzer, Paris and Brussels, 1951–, and ed. minor, Oxford, 1964–; *Plotinus*, text and trans. A. H. Armstrong, L.C.L., 1966–1967 (3 vols.) (*Enneads*).

Literature

Sievers, *Das Leben des Libanius*, Berlin, 1868. Petit de Julleville, *L'École d'Athènes au quatrième siècle*, Paris, 1868. Capes, *University Life in Ancient Athens*, London, 1877. France (Wright), *Julian's Relation to the New Sophistic*, London, 1896. Seeck, *Die Briefe des Libanius*, Leipzig, 1906; *Geschichte des Untergangs der antiken Welt*, Berlin, 1901–1910. Glover, *Life and Letters in the Fourth Century*, Cambridge, 1901. Bidez, *Vie de Porphyre*, Gand, 1913. Ammianus Marcellinus (A.D. 330–400) the Latin historian is the best authority for the period with which Eunapius deals.

ΕΥΝΑΠΙΟΥ

ΒΙΟΙ ΦΙΛΟΣΟΦΩΝ ΚΑΙ ΣΟΦΙΣΤΩΝ

ΠΡΟΟΙΜΙΟΝ

Ξενοφῶν ὁ φιλόσοφος, ἀνὴρ μόνος ἐξ ἁπάντων φιλοσόφων ἐν λόγοις τε καὶ ἔργοις φιλοσοφίαν

453 κοσμήσας (τὰ μὲν ἐς λόγους ἔστι τε ἐν γράμμασι καὶ τὴν ἠθικὴν ἀρετὴν γράφει, τὰ δὲ ἐν πράξεσί τε ἦν ἄριστος, ἀλλὰ καὶ ἐγέννα στρατηγοὺς τοῖς ὑποδείγμασιν· ὁ γοῦν μέγας Ἀλέξανδρος οὐκ ἂν ἐγένετο μέγας, εἰ μὴ Ξενοφῶν[1]), καὶ τὰ πάρεργά φησι δεῖν τῶν σπουδαίων ἀνδρῶν ἀναγράφειν. ἐμοὶ δὲ οὐκ εἰς τὰ πάρεργα τῶν σπουδαίων ὁ λόγος φέρει τὴν γραφήν, ἀλλ' εἰς τὰ ἔργα. εἰ γὰρ τὸ παίγνιον τῆς ἀρετῆς ἄξιον λόγου, ἀσεβοῖτο ἂν πάντως τὸ σπουδαζόμενον σιωπώμενον. διαλεχθήσεται δὲ ὁ λόγος τοῖς ἐντυγχάνειν βουλομένοις, οὔτε περὶ πάντων ἀσφαλῶς (οὐ γὰρ πάντα ἀκριβῶς ἦν ἀναλέγεσθαι), οὔτε ἀποκρίνων ἀλλήλων φιλοσόφους ἀρίστους καὶ ῥήτορας, ἀλλὰ παρα-

[1] Wyttenbach and Cobet think that after Ξενοφῶν a clause has been lost. In the translation ἐγένετο is understood.

EUNAPIUS

LIVES OF THE PHILOSOPHERS
AND SOPHISTS

INTRODUCTION

XENOPHON the philosopher, who is unique among all
philosophers in that he adorned philosophy not only
with words but with deeds as well (as regards words
he still lives in letters and writes of the moral virtues,
and as for deeds he excelled in them, and more,
by means of the examples that he gave, he begat
leaders of armies ; for instance great Alexander never
would have become great had Xenophon never been)
—he, I say, asserts that we ought to record even the
casual doings of distinguished men. But the aim
of my narrative is not to write of the casual doings
of distinguished men, but their main achievements.
For if even the playful moods of virtue are worth
recording, then it would be absolutely impious to be
silent about her serious aims. To those who desire
to read this narrative it will tell its tale, not
indeed with complete certainty as to all matters—
for it was impossible to collect all the evidence with
accuracy—nor shall I separate out from the rest the
most illustrious philosophers and orators, but I shall

τιθεὶς ἑκάστῳ τὸ ἐπιτήδευμα. ὅτι δὲ ἄριστος [1] ἦν
εἰς ἄκρον ὁ γραφόμενος ὑπὸ τοῦ λόγου, τῷ βουλομένῳ ταῦτα δικάζειν ἐκ τῶν ὑποκειμένων σημείων
καταλιμπάνει (βούλεται μὲν γάρ) ὁ ταῦτα γράφων.
καὶ ὑπομνήμασιν ἀκριβέσιν ἐντετύχηκε, δι᾽ ὧν, ἢ
διαμαρτάνων τῆς ἀληθείας, ἐφ᾽ ἑτέρους ἀναφέροι
τὸ ἁμάρτημα, ὥσπερ ἀγαθός τις μαθητὴς κακῶν
τετυχηκὼς διδασκάλων, ἢ κατηγοριῶν ἀλήθειαν
ἔχοι καὶ τοὺς ἡγουμένους ἀξίους θαύματος, καὶ
τό γε ἴδιον ἔργον αὐτοῦ καθαρὸν εἴη καὶ ἀμώμητον,
ἀκολουθήσαντος οἷς ἀκολουθεῖν προσῆκεν. ἐπεὶ
δὲ ὀλίγοι τε ἢ παντελῶς ἐλάχιστοί τινες ἦσαν οἱ
περὶ τούτων γράφοντες, ἵνα τοῦτο εἴπῃ τις μόνον,
οὔτε τὰ ὑπὸ τῶν πρότερον γραφέντα [2] λήσεται τοὺς
ἐντυγχάνοντας, οὔτε τὰ ἐξ ἀκοῆς ἐς τόνδε καθή-
κοντα τὸν χρόνον, ἀλλ᾽ ἀμφοτέροις ἀποδοθήσεται τὸ
πρέπον, τῶν μὲν γεγραμμένων τῷ [3] κινηθῆναι μηδέν,
τὰ δὲ ἐκ τῆς ἀκοῆς ὑπὸ τοῦ χρόνου κατασειόμενα
καὶ μεταβάλλοντα διαπῆξαι καὶ στηρίξαι τῇ γραφῇ
πρὸς τὸ στάσιμον καὶ μονιμώτερον.

ΟΙΤΙΝΕΣ ΤΗΝ ΦΙΛΟΣΟΦΟΝ ΙΣΤΟΡΙΑΝ ΑΝΕΛΕΞΑΝΤΟ

454 Τὴν φιλόσοφον ἱστορίαν καὶ τοὺς τῶν φιλοσόφων
ἀνδρῶν βίους Πορφύριος καὶ Σωτίων ἀνελέξαντο.
ἀλλ᾽ ὁ μὲν Πορφύριος (οὕτω συμβάν) εἰς Πλάτωνα

[1] τὸ δὲ ἄριστος ὅτι Boissonade ; ὅτι δὲ ἄριστος Cobet.
[2] ἀπό...γραφέντων Boissonade; ἀπό...γραφέντα Lundström.
ὑπό . . . γραφέντα Cobet.   [3] τῷ Wyttenbach adds.

[1] Eunapius ignores Diogenes Laertius. Sotion, the
Peripatetic philosopher at the close of the third century B.C.,
wrote an account of the successive heads of the schools of
philosophy ; he was used by Diogenes Laertius.

set down for each one his profession and mode of life. That in every case he whom this narrative describes attained to real distinction, the author—for that is what he aims at—leaves to the judgement of any who may please to decide from the proofs here presented. He has read precise and detailed commentaries, and therefore, if he misses the truth, he may refer his error to others, like a diligent pupil who has fallen into the hands of inferior teachers ; or, if he does go right, may have the truth on his side when he utters criticisms and be guided by those who are worthy of respect; that thus his own work may be perfectly blameless and secure from criticism, seeing that he followed those in whose steps it was his duty to follow. And inasmuch as there were few, or to say the truth, hardly any writers on this subject, nothing that has been composed by earlier authors will be concealed from my readers, nor what has come down by oral tradition to the present day, but the proper weight will be assigned to both sources; I mean that in written documents nothing has been altered, while what depends on hearsay, and hence is liable to become chaotic and confused by the lapse of time, has now been fixed and given stability by being written down, so that it is for the future a settled and abiding tradition.

THE WRITERS WHO HAVE COMPILED A HISTORY
OF THE PHILOSOPHERS

Porphyry and Sotion[1] compiled a history of philosophy and the *Lives* of the philosophers. But Porphyry, as it happened, ended with Plato and his

EUNAPIUS

ἐτελεύτα καὶ τοὺς ἐκείνου χρόνους· Σωτίων δὲ
καὶ καταβὰς φαίνεται, καίτοι γε ὁ Πορφύριος ἦν
νεώτερος. τῆς δὲ ἐν τῷ μέσῳ φορᾶς φιλοσόφων
τε ἀνδρῶν καὶ σοφιστῶν ἀδιηγήτου γενομένης
κατὰ τὸ μέγεθος καὶ τὸ ποικίλον τῆς ἀρετῆς,
Φιλόστρατος μὲν ὁ Λήμνιος τοὺς τῶν ἀρίστων
σοφιστῶν ἐξ ἐπιδρομῆς μετὰ χάριτος παρέπτυσε
βίους, φιλοσόφων δὲ οὐδεὶς ἀκριβῶς ἀνέγραψεν·
ἐν οἷς Ἀμμώνιός τε ἦν ὁ ἐξ Αἰγύπτου, Πλουτάρχου
τοῦ θειοτάτου γεγονὼς διδάσκαλος, Πλούταρχός
τε αὐτός, ἡ φιλοσοφίας ἁπάσης ἀφροδίτη καὶ
λύρα, Εὐφράτης τε ὁ ἐξ Αἰγύπτου, καὶ Δίων ὁ ἐκ
Βιθυνίας ὃν ἐπεκάλουν Χρυσόστομον, Ἀπολλώνιός
τε ὁ ἐκ Τυάνων, οὐκέτι φιλόσοφος· ἀλλ᾽ ἦν τι
θεῶν τε καὶ ἀνθρώπου μέσον. τὴν γὰρ Πυθαγόρειον
φιλοσοφίαν ζηλώσας, πολὺ τὸ θειότερον καὶ
ἐνεργὸν κατ᾽ αὐτὴν ἐπεδείξατο. ἀλλὰ τὸ μὲν ἐς
τοῦτον ὁ Λήμνιος ἐπετέλεσε Φιλόστρατος, βίον
ἐπιγράψας Ἀπολλωνίου τὰ βιβλία, δέον Ἐπιδημίαν ἐς ἀνθρώπους θεοῦ καλεῖν. Καρνεάδης δὲ
ἦν κατὰ τούτους τοὺς χρόνους, καὶ τῶν κατὰ
κυνισμὸν οὐκ ἀφανής, εἴ τινα καὶ κυνισμοῦ χρὴ
λόγον ποιεῖσθαι, παρ᾽ οἷς ἦν Μουσώνιος, καὶ
Δημήτριος καὶ Μένιππος, καὶ ἕτεροί γέ τινες
πλείους· οὗτοι δὲ ἦσαν ἐπιφανέστεροι. τούτων
δὲ σαφεῖς μὲν καὶ ἀκριβεῖς οὐκ ἦν ἀνευρεῖν τοὺς
βίους, ἅτε μηδενὸς συγγεγραφότος, ὅσα γε ἡμᾶς
εἰδέναι· ἱκανοὶ δὲ αὐτῶν ἦσάν τε καὶ εἰσὶ βίοι τὰ

---

[1] For this metaphor cf. Philostratus, *Aristeides*, p. 585.

[2] For Euphrates see Philostratus, *Lives of the Sophists*,
p. 488, note.

[3] The philosophers of other schools in the fourth century,

times, while Sotion, though he lived before Porphyry, carried on his narrative, as we see, to later times also. But the crop of philosophers and sophists who came between Sotion and Porphyry was not described as their importance and many-sidedness deserved ; and therefore Philostratus of Lemnos in a superficial and agreeable style spat forth [1] the *Lives* of the most distinguished sophists ; but the lives of the philosophers no one has recorded accurately. Among these latter were Ammonius of Egypt, who was the teacher of the divine Plutarch, and Plutarch himself, the charm and lyre of all philosophy ; Euphrates [2] of Egypt and Dio of Bithynia, whom men surnamed the " Golden-mouthed " ; and Apollonius of Tyana, who was not merely a philosopher but a demigod, half god, half man. For he was a follower of the Pythagorean doctrine, and he did much to publish to the world the divine and vivifying character of that philosophy. But Philostratus of Lemnos wrote a full account of Apollonius, and entitled his book *The Life of Apollonius,* though he ought to have called it *The Visit of God to Mankind.* Carneades also lived about this time, a celebrated figure among the Cynics, if indeed we ought to take any account of the Cynic school,[3] among whom were Musonius, Demetrius, and Menippus, and several others also ; but these were the more celebrated. Clear and accurate accounts of the lives of these men it was impossible to discover, since, so far as I know, no one has written them. But their own writings were and

especially the Neo-Platonists, despised and disliked the Cynics, partly because in some respects their mode of life resembled that of the Christians. This later Carneades is not otherwise known ; some identify him with Carneius (Cynulcus) in Athenaeus, *Deipnosophists.*

347

γράμματα, τοσαύτης ἀνάμεστα παιδείας καὶ
θεωρίας ἔς τε ἠθικὴν ἀρετὴν καὶ ὅση πρὸς τὴν
τῶν ὄντων διήρατο καὶ ἀνέβλεψε φύσιν, τὴν
ἄγνοιαν τῶν δυναμένων ἀκολουθεῖν, ὡς ἀχλύν τινα,
σκεδάσασα. αὐτίκα οὖν ὁ θεσπέσιος Πλούταρχος
τόν τε ἑαυτοῦ βίον ἀναγράφει τοῖς βιβλίοις ἐνδι-
εσπαρμένως καὶ τὸν τοῦ διδασκάλου, καὶ ὅτι γε
Ἀμμώνιος Ἀθήνησιν ἐτελεύτα, οὐ βίον προσειπών. καίτοι γε τὸ κάλλιστον αὐτοῦ τῶν συγγραμμάτων εἰσὶν οἱ καλούμενοι παράλληλοι βίοι τῶν
ἀρίστων κατὰ ἔργα καὶ πράξεις ἀνδρῶν· ἀλλὰ
τὸν ἴδιον καὶ τὸν τοῦ[1] διδασκάλου καθ᾽ ἕκαστον τῶν
βιβλίων ἐγκατέσπειρεν, ὥστε, εἴ τις ὀξυδορκοίη
περὶ ταῦτα, καὶ ἀνιχνεύοι κατὰ τὸ προσπῖπτον
καὶ φαινόμενον, καὶ σωφρόνως τὰ κατὰ μέρος
ἀναλέγοιτο, δύνασθαι τὰ πλεῖστα τῶν βεβιωμένων
αὐτοῖς εἰδέναι. Λουκιανὸς δὲ ὁ ἐκ Σαμοσάτων,
ἀνὴρ σπουδαῖος ἐς τὸ γελασθῆναι, Δημώνακτος
φιλοσόφου κατ᾽ ἐκείνους τοὺς χρόνους βίον ἀνέγραψεν, ἐν ἐκείνῳ τε τῷ βιβλίῳ καὶ ἄλλοις ἐλαχίστοις
δι᾽ ὅλου σπουδάσας.

Καὶ ταῦτά γε εἰς μνήμην ἐγὼ τίθεμαι, τοῦτο
συνορῶν, ὅτι τὰ μὲν ἔλαθεν ἴσως ἡμᾶς, τὰ δὲ οὐκ
ἔλαθεν. ἐκείνου δὲ καίπερ πολλὴν ποιούμενος
φροντίδα καὶ σπουδήν, τοῦ συνεχῆ καὶ περι-
γεγραμμένην εἰς ἀκρίβειαν ἱστορίαν τινὰ λαβεῖν
τοῦ φιλοσόφου καὶ ῥητορικοῦ βίου τῶν ἀρίστων
455 ἀνδρῶν, εἶτα οὐ τυγχάνων τῆς ἐπιθυμίας, ταὐτόν
τι τοῖς ἐρῶσιν ἐμμανῶς καὶ περιφλέκτως ἔπαθον.
καὶ γὰρ ἐκεῖνοι, τὴν μὲν ἐρωμένην αὐτὴν ὁρῶντες
καὶ τὸ περίψυκτον ἐν τῷ φαινομένῳ κάλλος, κάτω

---

[1] τὸ ἴδιον καὶ τοῦ Boissonade; τὸ ἴδιον καὶ τὸ τοῦ Cobet.

still are sufficient records of their lives, filled as they
are with such erudition and thorough research in the
field of ethics and also that research which aspires
to investigate the nature of things and disperses like
a mist the ignorance of such as are able to follow.
Thus, for example, the inspired Plutarch records
in statements scattered here and there in his books,
both his own life and that of his teacher ; and he
says that Ammonius died at Athens.   But he does
not entitle these records a *Life*, though he might
well have done so, since his most successful work
is that entitled *The Parallel Lives* of men most
celebrated for their deeds and achievements.   But
his own life and that of his teacher he scattered
piecemeal throughout every one of his books ;
so that if one should keep a sharp look-out for
these references and track them as they occur and
appear, and read them intelligently one after
another, one would know most of the events of
their lives.   Lucian of Samosata, who usually took
serious pains to raise a laugh, wrote a life of
Demonax, a philosopher of his own time, and in
that book and a very few others was wholly serious
throughout.

This much, then, I place on record, and am aware
that some things have perhaps escaped me, but other
things have not.   And in that, after expending
much thought and pains so that the result might
be a continuous and definite account of the lives
of the most celebrated philosophers and rhetoricians,
I fell short of my ambition, I have had the same
experience as those who are madly and feverishly
in love.   For they, when they behold the beloved and
the adored beauty of her visible countenance, bow

νεύουσιν, ὃ ζητοῦσιν ἰδεῖν ἐξασθενοῦντες, καὶ
περιλαμπόμενοι· ἐὰν δὲ πέδιλον αὐτῆς ἢ πλόκιον
ἢ ἐλλόβιον ἴδωσιν, ἐκείνοις καταθαρροῦντες, τὴν
ψυχήν τε τῇ ὄψει προσαφιᾶσι καὶ κατατήκονται
πρὸς τῷ θεάματι, τὰ σύμβολα τοῦ κάλλους μᾶλλον
ἢ τὸ κάλλος ὁρᾶν ἀνεχόμενοι καὶ στέργοντες. κἀγὼ
πρὸς ταύτην ἐξώρμησα τὴν γραφήν, ὅσα ἢ κατὰ
ἀκοήν, ἢ κατὰ ἀνάγνωσιν, ἢ κατὰ ἱστορίαν τῶν
κατ' ἐμαυτὸν ἀνθρώπων μὴ παρελθεῖν σιωπῇ καὶ
βασκάνως, ἀλλ', εἰς ὅσον οἷόν τε ἦν ἀληθείας
πρόθυρα καὶ πύλας προσκυνήσαντα, παραδοῦναι
τοῖς μετὰ ταῦτα ἢ βουλομένοις ἀκούειν ἢ δυνα-
μένοις ἀκολουθεῖν πρὸς τὸ κάλλιστον. ἔσχε μὲν
οὖν διακοπήν τινα καὶ ῥῆξιν ὁ χρόνος διὰ τὰς
κοινὰς συμφοράς· τρίτη δὲ ἀνδρῶν ἐγένετο φορὰ
(ἡ μὲν γὰρ δευτέρα μετὰ τὴν Πλάτωνος πᾶσιν
ἐμφανὴς ἀνακεκήρυκται) κατὰ τοὺς Κλαυδίου καὶ
Νέρωνος· τοὺς γὰρ ἀθλίους καὶ ἐνιαυσίους οὐ χρὴ
γράφειν (οὗτοι δ' ἦσαν οἱ περὶ Γάλβαν, Βιτέλλιον,
Ὄθωνα· Οὐεσπασιανὸς δὲ ὁ ἐπὶ τούτοις καὶ
Τίτος καὶ ὅσοι μετὰ τούτους ἦρξαν), ἵνα μὴ τοῦτο
σπουδάζειν δόξωμεν· πλὴν ἐπιτρέχοντί γε καὶ
συνελόντι εἰπεῖν, τὸ τῶν ἀρίστων φιλοσόφων
γένος καὶ εἰς Σεβῆρον διέτεινεν. ἀλλὰ εὐτυχές
γε ὑπάρχει τοῖς βασιλεῦσι κατὰ τὴν συγγραφήν,
ὅτι τὸ κατ' ἀρετὴν ὑπερέχον ἀριθμεῖται τῷ κατὰ
τὴν τύχην. νεμεσάτω δὲ μηδὲ εἷς, εἴ γε καὶ

---

[1] Eunapius seems to distinguish three groups of philo-
suphers, *i.e.* those up to Plato, those after Plato, and those
from Claudius A.D. 41 to Severus, died A.D. 211. He deals
with none of these, and begins his own narrative with a
brief mention of the Neoplatonist Plotinus who was born
not long before the death of Severus.

their heads, too weak to fix their gaze on that which
they desire, and dazzled by its rays. But if they
see her sandal or chain or ear-ring, they take heart
from these and pour their souls into the sight and melt
at the vision, since they can endure to see and love
the symbols of beauty more easily than the beauty
itself; thus too I have set out to write this narrative
in such a way as not to omit in silence and through
envy anything that I learned by hearsay, or by
reading, or by inquiry from men of my own time,
but, as far as in me lay, I reverenced the entrance
and gates of truth and have handed it down to
future generations who may either wish to hear
thereof or have power to follow with a view to the
fairest achievement. Now the period I describe
is somewhat interrupted and broken up by reason
of the calamities of the State. Still a third crop of
men began with the days of Claudius and Nero
(for the second which came next after Plato has
been commemorated and made clear to all). As
for those unlucky Emperors who lasted for a year
only, they are not worthy of record; I mean, for
example, Galba, Vitellius, Otho, and, following them,
Vespasian, Titus and those who ruled after these
men; and no one must suppose that I pay serious
attention to them. Anyhow, to speak cursorily and
in brief, the tribe of the best philosophers lasted on
even into the reign of Severus.[1] And surely this is
part of the felicity that belongs to emperors, that
in history the date which marks the superlative
virtue of a philosopher is that which dates the
superlative luck of an emperor.[2] Therefore let no

[2] *i.e.* the lives of philosophers are dated by the reigns of
emperors.

ἡμεῖς οὕτως ἀναγράφοντες τοὺς χρόνους, ἀφ' ὧν
γε ἦν δυνατὸν συντεκμηριώσασθαι ἢ παραλαβεῖν
τὴν προσήκουσαν ἀρχήν, ἀπὸ τούτων εἰς τὸν
λόγον ἐπιβησόμεθα.

Πλωτῖνος ἦν ἐξ Αἰγύπτου φιλόσοφος. τὸ ἐξ
Αἰγύπτου νῦν γράφων, καὶ τὴν πατρίδα προσθήσω.
Λυκὼ ταύτην ὀνομάζουσι· καίτοι γε ὁ θεσπέσιος
φιλόσοφος Πορφύριος τοῦτο οὐκ ἀνέγραψε, μαθητής
τε αὐτοῦ γεγενῆσθαι λέγων, καὶ συνεσχολακέναι
τὸν βίον ἅπαντα ἢ τὸν πλεῖστον τούτου. Πλωτίνου
θερμοὶ βωμοὶ νῦν, καὶ τὰ βιβλία οὐ μόνον τοῖς
πεπαιδευμένοις διὰ χειρὸς ὑπὲρ τοὺς Πλατωνικοὺς
λόγους, ἀλλὰ καὶ τὸ πολὺ πλῆθος, ἐάν τι παρα-
κούσῃ δογμάτων, ἐς αὐτὰ κάμπτεται. τὸν βίον
αὐτοῦ πάντα Πορφύριος ἐξήνεγκεν, ὡς οὐδένα
οἶόν τε ἦν πλέον εἰσφέρειν· ἀλλὰ καὶ πολλὰ τῶν
βιβλίων ἑρμηνεύσας αὐτοῦ φαίνεται. αὐτοῦ δὲ
Πορφυρίου βίον ἀνέγραψεν οὐδὲ εἷς, ὅσα γε καὶ
ἡμᾶς εἰδέναι· ἀναλεγομένῳ δὲ ἐκ τῶν δοθέντων[1]
κατὰ τὴν ἀνάγνωσιν σημείων τοιαῦτα ὑπῆρχε τὰ
περὶ αὐτόν.

Πορφυρίῳ Τύρος μὲν ἦν πατρίς, ἡ πρώτη τῶν
ἀρχαίων Φοινίκων πόλις, καὶ πατέρες δὲ οὐκ
ἄσημοι. τυχὼν δὲ τῆς προσηκούσης παιδείας,
ἀνά τε ἔδραμε τοσοῦτον καὶ ἐπέδωκεν, ὡς Λογγίνου
456 μὲν ἦν ἀκροατής, καὶ ἐκόσμει τὸν διδάσκαλον
ἐντὸς ὀλίγου χρόνου. Λογγῖνος δὲ κατὰ τὸν
χρόνον ἐκεῖνον βιβλιοθήκη τις ἦν ἔμψυχος καὶ
περιπατοῦν μουσεῖον, καὶ κρίνειν γε τοὺς παλαιοὺς

---

[1] τεθέντων Cobet suggests for δοθέντων.

one take it amiss if I, recording as I do the period for which it was possible for me to obtain evidence, or with which I could make an appropriate beginning, embark on my narrative at this point.

PLOTINUS was a philosopher of Egyptian birth. But though I just now called him an Egyptian, I will add his native place also; Lyco they call it. Yet the divine philosopher Porphyry did not record this, though he said that he was his pupil and studied with him during the whole of his life, or the greater part of it. Altars in honour of Plotinus are still warm, and his books are in the hands of educated men, more so than the dialogues of Plato. Nay, even great numbers of the vulgar herd, though they in part fail to understand his doctrines, nevertheless are swayed by them. Porphyry set forth his whole life so fully that no one could bring forward more evidence. Moreover, he is known to have interpreted many of his books. But a life of Porphyry himself no one has written, so far as I know. However, from what I have gathered in my reading of the evidence that has been handed down, I have learned the following facts concerning him.

Tyre was PORPHYRY's birthplace, the capital city of the ancient Phoenicians, and his ancestors were distinguished men. He was given a liberal education, and advanced so rapidly and made such progress that he became a pupil of Longinus, and in a short time was an ornament to his teacher. At that time Longinus was a living library and a walking museum; and moreover he had been entrusted with the function of critic of the ancient writers, like many

ἐπετέτραπτο,[1] καθάπερ πρὸ ἐκείνου πολλοί τινες
ἕτεροι, καὶ ὁ ἐκ Καρίας Διονύσιος πάντων ἀριδη-
λότερος. Μάλχος δὲ κατὰ τὴν Σύρων πόλιν ὁ
Πορφύριος ἐκαλεῖτο τὰ πρῶτα (τοῦτο δὲ δύναται
βασιλέα λέγειν)· Πορφύριον δὲ αὐτὸν ὠνόμασε
Λογγῖνος, ἐς τὸ βασιλικὸν τῆς ἐσθῆτος παράσημον
τὴν προσηγορίαν ἀποτρέψας. παρ' ἐκείνῳ δὴ
τὴν ἄκραν ἐπαιδεύετο παιδείαν, γραμματικῆς τε
εἰς ἄκρον ἁπάσης, ὥσπερ ἐκεῖνος, ἀφικόμενος καὶ
ῥητορικῆς· πλὴν ὅσον οὐκ ἐπ' ἐκείνην ἔνευσε,
φιλοσοφίας γε πᾶν εἶδος ἐκματτόμενος. ἦν γὰρ
ὁ Λογγῖνος μακρῷ τῶν τότε ἀνδρῶν τὰ πάντα
ἄριστος, καὶ τῶν βιβλίων τε αὐτοῦ πολὺ πλῆθος
φέρεται, καὶ τὸ φερόμενον θαυμάζεται. καὶ εἴ
τις κατέγνω τινὸς τῶν παλαιῶν, οὐ τὸ δοξασθὲν
ἐκράτει πρότερον, ἀλλ' ἡ Λογγίνου πάντως ἐκράτει
κρίσις. οὕτω δὲ ἀχθεὶς τὴν πρώτην παιδείαν καὶ
ὑπὸ πάντων ἀποβλεπόμενος, τὴν μεγίστην Ῥώμην
ἰδεῖν ἐπιθυμήσας, ἵνα κατάσχῃ διὰ σοφίας τὴν
πόλιν, ἐπειδὴ τάχιστα εἰς αὐτὴν ἀφίκετο καὶ τῷ
μεγίστῳ Πλωτίνῳ συνῆλθεν εἰς ὁμιλίαν, πάντων
ἐπελάθετο τῶν ἄλλων, καὶ προσέθετο φέρων
ἑαυτὸν ἐκείνῳ. ἀκορέστως δὲ τῆς παιδείας
ἐμφορούμενος καὶ τῶν πηγαίων ἐκείνων καὶ
τεθειασμένων λόγων, χρόνον μέν τινα εἰς τὴν
ἀκρόασιν ἤρκεσεν, ὡς αὐτός φησιν, εἶτα ὑπὸ τοῦ
μεγέθους τῶν λόγων νικώμενος, τό τε σῶμα καὶ
τὸ ἄνθρωπος εἶναι ἐμίσησε, καὶ διαπλεύσας εἰς
Σικελίαν τὸν πορθμὸν καὶ τὴν Χάρυβδιν, ᾗπερ
Ὀδυσσεὺς ἀναπλεῦσαι λέγεται, πόλιν μὲν οὔτε
ἰδεῖν ὑπέμεινεν, οὔτε ἀνθρώπων ἀκοῦσαι φωνῆς

---

[1] ἐπετέτακτο Boissonade ; ἐπετέτραπτο Cobet.

others before him, such as the most famous of them all, Dionysius of Caria. Porphyry's name in the Syrian town was originally Malchus (this word means "king"), but Longinus gave him the name of Porphyry, thus making it indicate the colour of imperial attire.[1] With Longinus he attained to the highest culture, and like him advanced to a perfect knowledge of grammar and rhetoric, though he did not incline to that study exclusively, since he took on the impress from every type of philosophy. For Longinus was in all branches of study by far the most distinguished of the men of his time, and a great number of his books are in circulation and are greatly admired. Whenever any critic condemned some ancient author, his opinion did not win approval until the verdict of Longinus wholly confirmed it. After Porphyry's early education had thus been carried on and he was looked up to by all, he longed to see Rome, the mistress of the world, so that he might enchain the city by his wisdom. But directly he arrived there and became intimate with that great man Plotinus, he forgot all else and devoted himself wholly to him. And since with an insatiable appetite he devoured his teaching and his original and inspired discourses, for some time he was content to be his pupil, as he himself says. Then overcome by the force of his teachings he conceived a hatred of his own body and of being human, and sailed to Sicily across the straits and Charybdis, along the route where Odysseus is said to have sailed;[2] and he would not endure either to see a city or to hear

---

[1] *i.e.* purple; for Porphyry's account of this *cf.* his *Life of Plotinus* xvii.
[2] An echo of Thucydides iv. 24.

(οὕτω τὸ λυπούμενον αὐτῷ[1] καὶ ἡδόμενον ἀπέθετο),
συντείνας δὲ ἐπὶ Λιλύβαιον ἑαυτὸν (τὸ δέ ἐστι τῶν
τριῶν ἀκρωτηρίων τῆς Σικελίας τὸ πρὸς Λιβύην
ἀνατεῖνον καὶ ὁρῶν), ἔκειτο καταστένων καὶ
ἀποκαρτερῶν, τροφήν τε οὐ προσιέμενος, καὶ
ἀνθρώπων ἀλεείνων πάτον. οὐδ' ἀλαοσκοπιὴν ὁ
μέγας εἶχε Πλωτῖνος ἐπὶ τούτοις, ἀλλὰ κατὰ
πόδας ἑπόμενος,[2] . . . . ἢ τὸν ἀπο-
πεφευγότα νεανίσκον ἀναζητῶν, ἐπιτυγχάνει κειμένῳ, καὶ λόγων τε πρὸς αὐτὸν ηὐπόρησε τὴν
ψυχὴν ἀνακαλουμένων ἄρτι ἐξίπτασθαι[3] τοῦ σώματος
μέλλουσαν, καὶ τὸ σῶμα ἔρρωσεν ἐς κατοχὴν τῆς
ψυχῆς. καὶ ὁ μὲν ἔμπνους τε ἦν καὶ διανίστατο,
ὁ δὲ τοὺς ῥηθέντας λόγους εἰς βιβλίον κατέθετο
τῶν γεγραμμένων. τῶν δὲ φιλοσόφων τὰ ἀπόρρητα
καλυπτόντων ἀσαφείᾳ, καθάπερ τῶν ποιητῶν τοῖς
μύθοις, ὁ Πορφύριος τὸ φάρμακον τῆς σαφηνείας
ἐπαινέσας καὶ διαπείρας γευσάμενος, ὑπόμνημα
γράψας εἰς φῶς ἤγαγεν. αὐτὸς μὲν οὖν ἐπὶ τὴν
Ῥώμην ἐπανῆλθε, καὶ τῆς περὶ λόγους εἴχετο
σπουδῆς, ὥστε παρῄει καὶ εἰς τὸ δημόσιον κατ'
ἐπίδειξιν· τὸ δὲ Πορφυρίου κλέος εἰς Πλωτῖνον
πᾶσα μὲν ἀγορά, πᾶσα δὲ πληθὺς ἀνέφερεν. ὁ μὲν

---

[1] αὐτῷ Laurentianus; αὐτῷ Wright; αὐτῶν Giangrande.
[2] After ἑπόμενος Laurentianus has a lacuna of about twelve
letters, not indicated by Boissonade. Before ἢ τὸν Lundström
would supply ἢ παραυτίκα αὐτῷ.
[3] διΐπτασθαι Boissonade; ἐξίπτασθαι Cobet.

---

[1] Iliad vi. 202.   [2] Iliad x. 515.
[3] Eunapius quotes incorrectly the account of this incident
given by Porphyry himself in his Life of Plotinus xi. 113.
When Plotinus found that he was contemplating suicide, he
persuaded him that his depression was due to ill-health, and

the voice of man, thus putting away from himself both pain and pleasure, but kept on to Lilybaeum; this is that one of Sicily's three promontories that stretches out and looks towards Libya. There he lay groaning and mortifying the flesh, and he would take no nourishment and "avoided the path of men." [1] But great Plotinus "kept no vain watch" [2] on these things, and either followed in his footsteps or inquired for the youth who had fled, and so found him lying there; then he found abundance of words that recalled to life his soul, as it was just about to speed forth from the body. Moreover he gave strength to his body so that it might contain his soul.[3]

So Porphyry breathed again and arose, but Plotinus in one of the books [4] that he wrote recorded the arguments then uttered by him. And while some philosophers hide their esoteric teachings in obscurity, as poets conceal theirs in myths,[5] Porphyry praised clear knowledge as a sovereign remedy, and since he had tasted it by experience he recorded this in writing and brought it to the light of day.

Now Porphyry returned to Rome and continued to study philosophical disputation, so that he even appeared in public to make a display of his powers; but every forum and every crowd attributed to Plotinus the credit of Porphyry's renown. For

sent him to Sicily to rest; Plotinus did not follow him, and later Porphyry returned to Rome, after the death of Plotinus.

[4] This is not extant. Eunapius may refer to the advice given by Plotinus, *Enneads* iii. 2, against succumbing to adversity, but possibly his source is a commentary on the *Enneads* by Porphyry himself, not now extant.

[5] *Cf.* Julian, *Orations*, v. 170, vii. 217 c.

γὰρ Πλωτῖνος τῷ τε τῆς ψυχῆς οὐρανίῳ καὶ τῷ
λοξῷ καὶ αἰνιγματώδει τῶν λόγων, βαρὺς ἐδόκει
457 καὶ δυσήκοος· ὁ δὲ Πορφύριος, ὥσπερ Ἑρμαϊκή
τις σειρὰ καὶ πρὸς ἀνθρώπους ἐπινεύουσα, διὰ
ποικίλης παιδείας πάντα εἰς τὸ εὔγνωστον καὶ
καθαρὸν ἐξήγγελλεν. αὐτὸς μὲν οὖν φησὶ (νέος
δὲ ὢν ἴσως ταῦτα ἔγραφεν, ὡς ἔοικεν), ἐπιτυχεῖν
χρηστηρίῳ μηδενὶ τῶν δημοσίων· ἐν δὲ αὐτῷ τῷ
βιβλίῳ καταγράφει, καὶ μετὰ ταῦτα ἄλλα πραγ-
ματεύεται πολλά, ὅπως χρὴ τούτων ποιεῖσθαι τὴν
ἐπιμέλειαν. φησὶ δὲ καὶ δαιμόνιόν τινα φύσιν ἀπὸ
λουτροῦ τινος ἐκδιῶξαι καὶ ἐκβαλεῖν· Καυσάθαν
τοῦτον ἔλεγον οἱ ἐπιχώριοι.

Συμφοιτηταὶ μὲν οὖν, ὡς αὐτὸς ἀναγράφει,
κράτιστοί τινες ὑπῆρχον, Ὠριγένης τε καὶ Ἀμέριος
καὶ Ἀκυλῖνος, καὶ συγγράμματά γε αὐτῶν περι-
σώζεται, λόγος δὲ αὐτῶν οὐδὲ εἷς· πολὺ γὰρ τὸ
ἀκύθηρον, εἰ καὶ τὰ δόγματα ἔχει καλῶς, καὶ
ἐπιτρέχει τοῖς λόγοις. ἀλλ᾽ ὅ γε Πορφύριος
ἐπαινεῖ τοὺς ἄνδρας τῆς δεινότητος, πᾶσαν μὲν
αὐτὸς ἀνατρέχων χάριν, μόνος δὲ ἀναδεικνὺς καὶ
ἀνακηρύττων τὸν διδάσκαλον, οὐδὲν παιδείας εἶδος
παραλελοιπώς. ἔστι γοῦν ἀπορῆσαι καθ᾽ ἑαυτὸν
καὶ θαυμάσαι, τί πλεῖόν ἐστι τῶν ἐσπουδασμένων·
πότερον τὰ εἰς ὕλην ῥητορικὴν τείνοντα, ἢ τὰ εἰς

---

[1] *Iliad* viii. 19. The golden chain there described sym-
bolized for the Neo - Platonists the succession of the
philosophers of their school as in Marinus, *Life of Proclus*
xxvi. 53, though here Eunapius strangely applies it to one
philosopher ; *cf.* Eunapius, *Fragments of History*, xxii. 71.
[2] Dr. G. A. Barton suggests that this word may be the
Syriac K^enesthā, which means both "cleansing" and
358

Plotinus, because of the celestial quality of his soul and the oblique and enigmatic character of his discourses, seemed austere and hard to listen to. But Porphyry, like a chain of Hermes let down to mortals,[1] by reason of his many - sided culture expounded all subjects so as to be clear and easy of comprehension. He himself says (but perhaps as seems likely he wrote this while he was still young), that he was granted an oracle different from the vulgar sort; and in the same book he wrote it down, and then went on to expound at considerable length how men ought to pay attention to these oracles. And he says too that he cast out and expelled some sort of daemon from a certain bath; the inhabitants called this daemon Kausatha.[2]

As he himself records, he had for fellow-disciples certain very famous men, Origen, Amerius, and Aquilinus,[3] whose writings are still preserved, though not one of their discourses; for though their doctrines are admirable, their style is wholly unpleasing, and it pervades their discourses. Nevertheless Porphyry praises these men for their oratorical talent, though he himself runs through the whole scale of charm, and alone advertises and celebrates his teacher, inasmuch as there was no branch of learning that he neglected. One may well be at a loss and wonder within oneself which branch he studied more than another; whether it was that which concerns the subject matter of rhetoric, or that which tends to

"filth"; in any case the incident probably occurred in Syria rather than at Rome.

[3] Porphyry, *Life of Plotinus*, xvi., does not call him a fellow-disciple, but says he was a Christian Gnostic who led others astray by his doctrines. The Origen here mentioned is not the famous Christian teacher.

γραμματικὴν ἀκρίβειαν φέροντα, ἢ ὅσα τῶν
ἀριθμῶν ἤρτηται, ἢ ὅσα νεύει πρὸς γεωμετρίαν,
ἢ ὅσα πρὸς μουσικὴν ῥέπει. τὰ δὲ εἰς φιλοσοφίαν,
οὐδὲ τὰ περὶ λόγους καταληπτόν,[1] οὔτε τὸ ἠθικὸν
ἐφικτὸν λόγῳ· τὸ δὲ φυσικὸν καὶ θεουργὸν τελεταῖς
ἀφείσθω καὶ μυστηρίοις· οὕτω παντομιγὲς πρὸς
ἅπασαν ἀρετὴν ὁ ἀνὴρ αὐτὸς χρῆμά τι γέγονεν.
καὶ τὸ κάλλος αὐτοῦ τῶν λόγων θαυμάσειεν ἄν
τις μᾶλλον ἢ τὰ δόγματα περὶ τοῦτο σπουδάζων,
καὶ πάλιν αὖ τὰ δόγματα ὁ πλέον εἰς αὐτὰ ἀπιδὼν
ἢ τὴν δύναμιν τοῦ λόγου.[2] γάμοις τε ὁμιλήσας
φαίνεται, καὶ πρὸς Μάρκελλάν γε αὐτοῦ γυναῖκα
γενομένην βιβλίον φέρεται, ἥν φησιν ἀγαγέσθαι
καὶ ταῦτα οὖσαν πέντε μητέρα τέκνων, οὐχ ἵνα
παῖδας ἐξ αὐτῆς ποιήσηται, ἀλλ' ἵνα οἱ γεγονότες
παιδείας τύχωσιν· ἐκ φίλου γὰρ ἦν αὐτοῦ τῇ
γυναικὶ τὰ τέκνα προϋπάρξαντα. φαίνεται δὲ ἀφικόμενος εἰς γῆρας βαθύ· πολλὰς γοῦν τοῖς ἤδη
προπεπραγματευμένοις βιβλίοις θεωρίας ἐναντίας
κατέλιπε, περὶ ὧν οὐκ ἔστιν ἕτερόν τι δοξάζειν,[3] ἢ
ὅτι προϊὼν ἕτερα ἐδόξασεν. ἐν Ῥώμῃ δὲ λέγεται
μετηλλαχέναι[4] τὸν βίον.

Κατὰ τούτους ἦσαν τοὺς χρόνους καὶ τῶν
ῥητορικῶν οἱ ἐν[5] Ἀθήνησι προεστῶτες Παῦλός τε
καὶ Ἀνδρόμαχος ἐκ Συρίας. τοὺς δὲ χρόνους ἐς
Γαλλίηνόν τε[6] καὶ Κλαύδιον ἀκμάζειν[7] συνέβαινεν,

---

[1] After καταληπτόν Bidez would read οὔτε τὸ ἠθικὸν ἐφικτὸν
λόγῳ; Boissonade τὸν οἰκεῖον . . . λόγον.
[2] I give Cobet's reconstruction. See Giangrande, p. 9.
Boissonade λόγων ἄν τις μᾶλλον ἢ τὰ δόγματα, πλέον.
[3] For δοξάζειν Cumont suggests εἰκάζειν.
[4] So Wyttenbach; μεταλαχεῖν.
[5] ἐπ' Boissonade; ἐν Wyttenbach.
[6] δὲ *Laurentianus*, Boissonade; τε Bidez.

precise accuracy in grammar, or that which depends on numbers, or inclines to geometry, or leans to music. As for philosophy, I cannot describe in words his genius for discourse, or for moral philosophy. As for natural philosophy and the art of divination, let that be left to sacred rites and mysteries. So true is it that the man was a being who combined in himself all the talents for every sort of excellence. One who cares most for this would naturally praise the beauty of the style of his discourse more than his doctrines, or again would prefer his doctrines, if one paid closer attention to these than to the force of his oratory. It seems that he entered the married state, and a book of his is extant addressed to his wife Marcella; he says that he married her, although she was already the mother of five[1] children, and this was not that he might have children by her, but that those she had might be educated; for the father of his wife's children had been a friend of his own. It seems that he attained to an advanced old age. At any rate he left behind him many speculations that conflict with the books that he had previously published; with regard to which we can only suppose that he changed his opinions as he grew older. He is said to have departed this life in Rome.

At this time those who were most distinguished for rhetoric at Athens were Paulus and the Syrian Andromachus. But Porphyry actually was at the height of his powers as late as the time of Gallienus,

---

[1] Marcella had five daughters and two sons.

---

[7] εἰκάζειν *Laurentianus*, Diels defends; βιβάζειν *Ottobonianus*, Boissonade; ἀκμάζειν Wyttenbach; προβιβάζειν Busse.

Τάκιτόν τε καὶ Αὐρηλιανὸν καὶ Πρόβον, καθ' οὓς
ἦν καὶ Δέξιππος ὁ τὴν χρονικὴν ἱστορίαν συγγράψας,
ἀνὴρ ἁπάσης παιδείας τε καὶ δυνάμεως λογικῆς
ἀνάπλεως.

Μετὰ τούτους ὀνομαστότατος ἐπιγίνεται φιλόσοφος Ἰάμβλιχος, ὃς ἦν καὶ κατὰ γένος μὲν
ἐπιφανὴς καὶ τῶν ἁβρῶν καὶ τῶν εὐδαιμόνων·
πατρὶς δὲ ἦν αὐτῷ Χαλκίς· κατὰ τὴν Κοίλην
Συρίαν¹ προσαγορευομένην ἐστὶν ἡ πόλις. οὗτος
Ἀνατολίῳ τῷ μετὰ Πορφύριον τὰ δεύτερα
φερομένῳ συγγενόμενος, πολύ γε ἐπέδωκε καὶ
458 εἰς ἄκρον φιλοσοφίας ἤλασεν.² εἶτα μετ' Ἀνατόλιον
Πορφυρίῳ προσθεὶς ἑαυτόν, οὐκ ἔστιν ὅ τι καὶ
Πορφυρίου διήνεγκεν, πλὴν ὅσον κατὰ τὴν συν-
θήκην καὶ δύναμιν τοῦ λόγου. οὔτε γὰρ εἰς
ἀφροδίτην αὐτοῦ καὶ χάριν τὰ λεγόμενα βέβαπται,
οὔτε ἔχει λευκότητά τινα καὶ τῷ καθαρῷ καλλω-
πίζεται· οὐ μὴν οὐδὲ ἀσαφῆ παντελῶς τυγχάνει,
οὐδὲ κατὰ τὴν λέξιν ἡμαρτημένα, ἀλλ' ὥσπερ
ἔλεγε περὶ Ξενοκράτους ὁ Πλάτων, ταῖς Ἑρμαϊκαῖς
οὐ τέθυται Χάρισιν. οὔκουν κατέχει τὸν ἀκροατὴν
καὶ γοητεύει πρὸς τὴν ἀνάγνωσιν, ἀλλ' ἀποστρέφειν
καὶ ἀποκναίειν τὴν ἀκοὴν ἔοικεν. δικαιοσύνην
δὲ ἀσκήσας, εὐηκοΐας ἔτυχε θεῶν τοσαύτης, ὥστε
πλῆθος μὲν ἦσαν οἱ ὁμιλοῦντες, πανταχόθεν δὲ
ἐφοίτων οἱ παιδείας ἐπιθυμοῦντες· ἦν δὲ ἐν αὐτοῖς

¹ Συρίαν Cobet adds.
² ἤκμασεν Boissonade; ἤλασεν Cobet.

---

¹ We have a few fragments of the *Universal History* of
Dexippus, which came down to Probus A.D. 269 and was
continued by Eunapius; he was a famous general who when

Claudius, Tacitus, Aurelian, and Probus. In those days there lived also Dexippus,[1] who composed historical annals, a man overflowing with erudition and logical power.

After these men comes a very celebrated philosopher, IAMBLICHUS, who was of illustrious ancestry and belonged to an opulent and prosperous family. His birthplace was Chalcis, a city in the region called Coele Syria.[2] As a pupil of Anatolius, who ranks next after Porphyry, he made great progress and attained to the highest distinction in philosophy. Then leaving Anatolius he attached himself to Porphyry, and in no respect was he inferior to Porphyry except in harmonious structure and force of style. For his utterances are not imbued with charm and grace, they are not lucid, and they lack the beauty of simplicity. Nevertheless they are not altogether obscure, nor have they faults of diction, but as Plato used to say of Xenocrates, "he has not sacrificed to the Graces" of Hermes.[3] Therefore he does not hold and enchant the reader into continuing to read, but is more likely to repel him and irritate his ears. But because he practised justice he gained an easy access to the ears of the gods; so much so that he had a multitude of disciples, and those who desired learning flocked to him from all parts. And it is hard to decide who among them

the Goths occupied Athens in 267 collected a small force and inflicted severe losses on the invaders.

[2] The district between Lebanon and Anti-Lebanon was called " Syria in the Hollow."

[3] Quoted from Diogenes Laertius iv. 6, or more probably from Plutarch, *Conjugal Precepts* 141 F. Eunapius adds the words "of Hermes" to the original passage; Hermes was the god of eloquence.

τὸ κάλλιστον δύσκριτον. Σώπατρος γὰρ ἦν ὁ ἐκ
Συρίας, ἀνὴρ εἰπεῖν τε καὶ γράψαι δεινότατος,
Αἰδέσιός τε καὶ Εὐστάθιος ἐκ Καππαδοκίας, ἐκ
δὲ τῆς Ἑλλάδος Θεόδωρός τε καὶ Εὐφράσιος, οἱ
κατ' ἀρετὴν ὑπερέχοντες, ἄλλοι τε πλῆθος, οὐ
πολὺ λειπόμενοι κατὰ τὴν ἐν λόγοις δύναμιν,
ὥστε θαυμαστὸν ἦν ὅτι πᾶσι ἐπήρκει· καὶ γὰρ
ἦν πρὸς ἅπαντας ἄφθονος. ὀλίγα μὲν οὖν χωρὶς
τῶν ἑταίρων καὶ ὁμιλητῶν ἔπραττεν ἐφ' ἑαυτοῦ,
τὸ θεῖον σεβαζόμενος· τὰ δὲ πλεῖστα τοῖς ἑταίροις
συνῆν, τὴν μὲν δίαιταν ὢν εὔκολος καὶ ἀρχαῖος,
τῇ δὲ παρὰ πότον ὁμιλίᾳ τοὺς παρόντας καθ-
ηδύνων καὶ διαπιμπλὰς ὥσπερ νέκταρος. οἱ δέ,
ἀλήκτως ἔχοντες καὶ ἀκορέστως τῆς ἀπολαύσεως,
ἠνώχλουν αὐτῷ συνεχῶς, καὶ προστησάμενοί γε
τοὺς ἀξίους λόγου, πρὸς αὐτὸν ἔφασκον· " τί
δῆτα μόνος, ὦ διδάσκαλε θειότατε, καθ' ἑαυτόν
τινα πράττεις, οὐ μεταδιδοὺς τῆς τελεωτέρας
σοφίας ἡμῖν; καίτοι γε ἐκφέρεται πρὸς ἡμᾶς
λόγος ὑπὸ τῶν σῶν ἀνδραπόδων, ὡς εὐχόμενος
τοῖς θεοῖς μετεωρίζῃ μὲν ἀπὸ τῆς γῆς πλέον ἢ
δέκα πήχεις εἰκάζεσθαι· τὸ σῶμα δέ σοι καὶ ἡ
ἐσθὴς εἰς χρυσοειδές τι κάλλος ἀμείβεται, παυο-
μένῳ δὲ τῆς εὐχῆς σῶμά τε γίνεται τῷ[1] πρὶν
εὔχεσθαι ὅμοιον, καὶ κατελθὼν ἐπὶ τῆς γῆς τὴν
πρὸς ἡμᾶς ποιῇ συνουσίαν." οὔ τι μάλα γελασείων,

[1] καὶ τῷ Boissonade ; καὶ Cobet deletes.

[1] This is the elder Sopater who was put to death by
Constantine ; his son and namesake was a correspondent of
Libanius and a friend of the Emperor Julian.
[2] Theodorus of Asine wrote a commentary on the *Timaeus*
of Plato ; it is possible that he is to be identified with the

was the most distinguished, for Sopater [1] the Syrian
was of their number, a man who was most eloquent
both in his speeches and writings; and Aedesius
and Eustathius from Cappadocia; while from Greece
came Theodorus [2] and Euphrasius, men of superlative
virtue, and a crowd of other men not inferior in
their powers of oratory, so that it seemed marvellous that he could satisfy them all; and indeed
in his devotion to them all he never spared himself.
Occasionally, however, he did perform certain rites
alone, apart from his friends and disciples, when
he worshipped the Divine Being. But for the most
part he conversed with his pupils and was unexact-
ing in his mode of life and of an ancient simplicity.
As they drank their wine he used to charm those
present by his conversation and filled them as with
nectar. And they never ceased to desire this
pleasure and never could have too much of it, so
that they never gave him any peace; and they appointed the most eloquent among them to represent
them, and asked: "O master, most inspired, why do
you thus occupy yourself in solitude, instead of
sharing with us your more perfect wisdom? Nevertheless a rumour has reached us through your slaves
that when you pray to the gods you soar aloft from
the earth more than ten cubits to all appearance; [3]
that your body and your garments change to a
beautiful golden hue; and presently when your
prayer is ended your body becomes as it was before
you prayed, and then you come down to earth and
associate with us." Iamblichus was not at all inclined

Theodorus who in a letter of Julian (Papadopulos 4*) is said
to have attacked the doctrines of Iamblichus.

[3] *Cf.* Philostratus, *Life of Apollonius* iii. 15, where the
same powers of levitation are ascribed to the Brahmans.

ἐγέλασεν ἐπὶ τούτοις τοῖς λόγοις Ἰάμβλιχος.
ἀλλ᾽ εἰπὼν πρὸς αὐτούς, ὡς "ὁ μὲν ἀπατήσας
ὑμᾶς οὐκ ἦν ἄχαρις, ταῦτα δὲ οὐχ οὕτως ἔχει·
τοῦ λοιποῦ δὲ οὐδὲν χωρὶς ὑμῶν πεπράξεται·"
τοιαῦτα ἐπεδείξατο· εἰς δὲ τὸν ταῦτα γράφοντα
ἦλθε παρὰ τοῦ διδασκάλου Χρυσανθίου τοῦ ἐκ
Σάρδεων. ἐκεῖνος δὲ ἦν Αἰδεσίου μαθητής, Αἰδέσιος δὲ ἀνὰ τοὺς πρώτους τοῦ Ἰαμβλίχου, καὶ
τῶν ταῦτα πρὸς αὐτὸν εἰρηκότων. ἔλεγεν οὖν
ἐπιδείξεις αὐτοῦ μεγάλας τῆς θειότητος γεγενῆσθαι
τάσδε. ἥλιος μὲν ἐφέρετο πρὸς τοῦ Λέοντος
ὅρια, ἡνίκα συνανατέλλει τῷ καλουμένῳ Κυνί,
καὶ θυσίας καιρὸς ἦν· ἡ δὲ εὐτρέπιστο ἔν τινι τῶν
ἐκείνου προαστείων. ὡς δὲ τὰ πάντα εἶχε καλῶς,
καὶ [1] ἐπὶ τὴν πόλιν ὑπέστρεφον, βάδην καὶ σχολαίως
προϊόντες· καὶ γὰρ διάλεξις ἦν αὐτοῖς περὶ θεῶν
τῇ θυσίᾳ πρέπουσα· τὸν νοῦν ἐπιστήσας ὁ Ἰάμβλιχος μεταξὺ διαλεγόμενος, ὥσπερ ἀποκοπεὶς
459 τὴν φωνήν, καὶ τὰ ὄμματα εἰς τὴν γῆν ἀτρεμίζοντα
χρόνον τινὰ ἐρείσας, ἀνά τε ἔβλεψεν εἰς τοὺς
ἑταίρους, καὶ πρὸς αὐτοὺς ἐξεβόησεν· "ἄλλην
ὁδὸν πορευώμεθα· νεκρὸς γὰρ ἐντεῦθεν ἔναγχος
παρακεκόμισται." ὁ μὲν οὖν ταῦτα εἰπών, ἄλλην
ἐβάδιζε καὶ ἥτις ἐφαίνετο καθαρωτέρα, καὶ σὺν
αὐτῷ τινὲς ὑπέστρεφον, ὅσοις τὸ καταλείπειν τὸν
διδάσκαλον αἰσχύνης ἄξιον ἔδοξεν· οἱ δὲ πλείους
καὶ φιλονεικότεροι τῶν ἑταίρων, ἐν οἷς καὶ ὁ

---

[1] καὶ Wyttenbach adds.

---

[1] An echo of Plato, *Phaedo* 64 B.
[2] This seems to imitate Plutarch, *On the Familiar Spirit of Socrates* 580.

366

to laughter, but he laughed at these remarks.[1]   And
he answered them thus: "He who thus deluded
you was a witty fellow; but the facts are otherwise.
For the future however you shall be present at all
that goes on."   This was the sort of display that he
made; and the report of it reached the author of
this work from his teacher Chrysanthius of Sardis.
He was a pupil of Aedesius, and Aedesius was one
of the leading disciples of Iamblichus, and one of
those who spoke to him as I have said.   He said
that there occurred the following sure manifesta-
tions of his divine nature.   The sun was travelling
towards the limits of the Lion at the time when it
rises along with the constellation called the Dog.
It was the hour for sacrifice, and this had been made
ready in one of the suburban villas belonging to
Iamblichus.   Presently when the rites had been
duly performed and they were returning to the city,
walking slowly and at their leisure,—for indeed their
conversation was about the gods as was in keeping
with the sacrifice—suddenly Iamblichus even while
conversing was lost in thought, as though his voice
were cut off, and for some moments he fixed his
eyes steadily on the ground[2] and then looked
up at his friends and called to them in a loud
voice: "Let us go by another road, for a dead
body has lately been carried along this way."
After saying this he turned into another road which
seemed to be less impure,[3] and some of them turned
aside with him, who thought it was a shame to
desert their teacher.   But the greater number
and the more obstinate of his disciples, among

[3] It was a Pythagorean doctrine that a funeral con-
taminates the bystander.

Αἰδέσιος ἦν, ἔμειναν αὐτοῦ, τὸ πρᾶγμα ἐπὶ τερατείαν
φέροντες, καὶ τὸν ἔλεγχον ὥσπερ κύνες ἀνιχνεύοντες.
καὶ μετὰ[1] μικρὸν ἐπανῄεσαν οἱ θάψαντες τὸν
τετελευτηκότα· οἱ δὲ οὐδὲ οὕτως ἀπέστησαν,
ἀλλ᾽ ἠρώτησαν εἰ ταύτην εἶεν παρεληλυθότες τὴν
ὁδόν· οἱ δέ, "ἀναγκαῖον ἦν." ἔφασαν· ἄλλην
γὰρ οὐκ ἔχειν.[2]

Ἔτι δὲ τούτου θειωδέστερον συνεμαρτύρουν, ὡς
ἐνοχλοῖεν αὐτῷ πολλάκις, μικρὸν τοῦτο εἶναι
φάσκοντες καὶ ὀσφρήσεως ἴσως που πλεονέκτημα,
βούλεσθαι δὲ διάπειραν λαβεῖν ἑτέρου μείζονος·
ὁ δὲ πρὸς αὐτούς "ἀλλ᾽ οὐκ ἐπ᾽ ἐμοί γε τοῦτο"
ἔλεγεν, "ἀλλ᾽ ὅταν καιρὸς ᾖ," μετὰ δὲ χρόνον
τινὰ δόξαν αὐτοῖς ἐπὶ τὰ Γάδαρα· θερμὰ δέ ἐστι
λουτρὰ τῆς Συρίας, τῶν γε κατὰ τὴν Ῥωμαϊκὴν
ἐν Βαΐαις δεύτερα, ἐκείνοις δὲ οὐκ ἔστιν ἕτερα
παραβάλλεσθαι· πορεύονται δὲ κατὰ τὴν ὥραν[3]
τοῦ ἔτους. ὁ μὲν ἐτύγχανε λούμενος, οἱ δὲ συν-
ελοῦντο, καὶ περὶ τῶν αὐτῶν ἐνέκειντο. μειδιάσας
δὲ ὁ Ἰάμβλιχος, "ἀλλ᾽ οὐκ εὐσεβὲς μέν," ἔφη
"ταῦτα ἐπιδείκνυσθαι, ὑμῶν δὲ ἕνεκα πεπράξεται."
τῶν θερμῶν κρηνῶν δύο, τὰς μὲν μικροτέρας, τῶν
δὲ ἄλλων χαριεστέρας, ἐκέλευσεν ἐκπυνθάνεσθαι
τοὺς ὁμιλητὰς παρὰ τῶν ἐπιχωρίων ὅπως ἐκ
παλαιοῦ προσωνομάζοντο. οἱ δὲ τὸ προσταχθὲν
ἐπιτελέσαντες, "ἀλλ᾽ οὐκ ἔστι γε πρόφασις"
εἶπον, "ἀλλ᾽ αὕτη μὲν Ἔρως καλεῖται, τῇ
παρακειμένῃ δὲ Ἀντέρως ὄνομα." ὁ δὲ εὐθὺς

---

[1] κατὰ Boissonade; μετὰ Cobet.
[2] ἔφασαν ἔχειν Boissonade; ἔφασαν· ἄλλην . . . ἔχειν Cobet.
[3] After ὥραν Cobet deletes εἰς τὰ Γάδαρα; εἰς τὰ Γάδαρα κατὰ
τὴν ὥραν τοῦ ἔτους Vollebregt.

whom was Aedesius, stayed where they were, ascribing the occurrence to a portent and scenting like hounds for the proof.[1]   And very soon those who had buried the dead man came back.   But even so the disciples did not desist but inquired whether they had passed along this road.   "We had to," they replied, for there was no other road.

But they testified also to a still more marvellous incident.   When they kept pestering Iamblichus and saying that this that I have just related was a trifle, and perhaps due to a superior sense of smell, and that they wished to test him in something more important, his reply to them was: "Nay, that does not rest with me, but wait for the appointed hour."   Some time after, they decided to go to Gadara, a place which has warm baths in Syria, inferior only to those at Baiae in Italy, with which no other baths can be compared.[2] So they set out in the summer season.   Now he happened to be bathing and the others were bathing with him, and they were using the same insistence, whereupon Iamblichus smiled and said: "It is irreverent to the gods to give you this demonstration, but for your sakes it shall be done."   There were two hot springs smaller than the others but prettier, and he bade his disciples ask the natives of the place by what names they used to be called in former times.   When they had done his bidding they said: "There is no pretence about it, this spring is called Eros, and the name of the one next to it is Anteros."   He at once touched the

---

[1] A favourite Platonic simile, frequently echoed by the sophists.

[2] Cf. Horace, Epistles i. 1. 85 "nullus in orbe locus Baiis praelucet amoenis."

ἐπιψαύσας τοῦ ὕδατος (ἐτύγχανε δὲ καὶ ἐπὶ τῆς
κρηπῖδος κατὰ τὴν ὑπέρκλυσιν καθήμενος), καὶ
βραχέα τινὰ προσειπών, ἐξεκάλεσεν ἀπὸ τῆς
κρήνης κάτωθεν παιδίον. λευκὸν ἦν τὸ παιδίον
καὶ μετρίως εὐμέγεθες, καὶ χρυσοειδεῖς αὐτῷ
κόμαι καὶ [1] τὰ μετάφρενα καὶ τὰ στέρνα περιέ-
στιλβον, καὶ ὅλον ἐῴκει λουομένῳ τε καὶ λελουμένῳ.
καταπλαγέντων δὲ τῶν ἑταίρων, "ἐπὶ τὴν ἐχο-
μένην" εἶπε "κρήνην ἴωμεν," καὶ ἡγεῖτο ἀπιών,
καὶ σύννους ἦν. εἶτα κἀκεῖ τὰ αὐτὰ δράσας,
ἐξεκάλεσεν ἕτερον Ἔρωτα τῷ προτέρῳ παραπλήσιον ἅπαντα, πλὴν ὅσον αἱ κόμαι μελάντεραί
τε καὶ ἡλιῶσαι κατεκέχυντο. καὶ περιεπλέκετό γε
ἀμφότερα αὐτῷ τὰ παιδία, καί, καθάπερ γνησίου
τινὸς πατρὸς ἐμφύντα,[2] περιείχετο. ὁ δὲ ἐκεῖνά
τε ταῖς οἰκείαις ἀπέδωκε λήξεσι, καί, σεβαζομένων τῶν ἑταίρων, ἐξῄει λουσάμενος. οὐδὲν
μετὰ τοῦτο ἐζήτησεν ἡ τῶν ὁμιλητῶν πληθύς,
ἀλλὰ ἀπὸ τῶν φανέντων δειγμάτων, ὥσπερ ὑπ'
ἀρρήκτου [3] ῥυτῆρος εἵλκοντο, καὶ πᾶσιν ἐπίστευον.
ἐλέγετο δὲ καὶ παραδοξότερα καὶ τερατωδέστερα,
ἐγὼ δὲ τούτων ἀνέγραφον οὐδέν, σφαλερόν τι καὶ
460 θεομισὲς πρᾶγμα ἡγούμενος εἰς συγγραφὴν στάσιμον καὶ πεπηγυῖαν ἐπεισάγειν ἀκοὴν διεφθαρ-
μένην καὶ ῥέουσαν. ἀλλὰ καὶ ταῦτα γράφω
δεδοικὼς ἀκοὴν οὖσαν, πλὴν ὅσαγε ἕπομαι ἀνδράσιν,
οἵ, τοῖς ἄλλοις ἀπιστοῦντες, πρὸς τὴν τοῦ φανέντος
αἴσθησιν συνεκάμφθησαν. οὐδεὶς δὲ αὐτοῦ τῶν
ἑταίρων ἀνέγραψεν, ὅσα γε ἡμᾶς εἰδέναι· τοῦτο

---

[1] After κόμαι Cobet adds καί.
[2] ἐμφύντα Laurentianus; Cobet and Wyttenbach rightly
retain; ἐκφύντα the other mss.
[3] ἀρρήτου Boissonade; ἀρρήκτου Cobet.

water with his hand—he happened to be sitting on
the ledge of the spring where the overflow runs
off—and uttering a brief summons [1] he called forth
a boy from the depth of the spring. He was white-
skinned and of medium height, his locks were
golden and his back and breast shone; and he
exactly resembled one who was bathing or had
just bathed. His disciples were overwhelmed with
amazement, but Iamblichus said, "Let us go to the
next spring," and he rose and led the way, with
a thoughtful air. Then he went through the same
performance there also, and summoned another Eros
like the first in all respects, except that his hair
was darker and fell loose in the sun. Both the boys
embraced Iamblichus and clung closely to him as
though he were a real father. He restored them
to their proper places and went away after his bath,
reverenced by his pupils. After this the crowd of
his disciples sought no further evidence, but believed
everything from the proofs that had been revealed
to them, and hung on to him as though by an un-
breakable chain. Even more astonishing and marvellous things were related of him, but I wrote
down none of these since I thought it a hazardous
and sacrilegious thing to introduce a spurious and
fluid tradition into a stable and well-founded narrative.
Nay even this I record not without hesitation, as
being mere hearsay, except that I follow the lead of
men who, though they distrusted other signs, were
converted by the experience of the actual revelation.
Yet no one of his followers recorded it, as far as I

---

[1] No doubt a magic formula. Note the use of δρᾶν below,
a verb regularly used for magic rites. For the fable of Eros
and Anteros *cf.* Themistius 304 D.

δὲ εἶπον μετρίως, Αἰδεσίου φήσαντος μήτε αὐτὸν γεγραφέναι, μήτε ἄλλον τινὰ τετολμηκέναι.

Κατὰ τοὺς Ἰαμβλίχου καιροὺς ἦν καὶ ὁ διαλεκτικώτατος Ἀλύπιος, ὃς ἔτυχε μὲν σώματος μικροτάτου, καὶ τὸ σῶμα πυγμαῖον παρέβαινεν ἐλάχιστον, ἐκινδύνευε δὲ καὶ τὸ φαινόμενον σῶμα ψυχὴ καὶ νοῦς εἶναι· οὕτω τὸ φθειρόμενον οὐκ ἐπέδωκεν εἰς μέγεθος, δαπανηθὲν εἰς τὸ θεοειδέστερον. ὥσπερ οὖν ὁ μέγας Πλάτων φησὶ τὰ θεῖα σώματα τὸ ἀνάπαλιν ἔχειν ἐγκείμενα ταῖς ψυχαῖς, οὕτως ἄν τις εἴποι κἀκεῖνον ἐμβεβηκέναι τῇ ψυχῇ καὶ συνέχεσθαι καὶ κρατεῖσθαι παρά[1] του κρείττονος. ζηλωτὰς μὲν οὖν εἶχε πολλοὺς ὁ Ἀλύπιος, ἀλλ᾽ ἡ παίδευσις ἦν μέχρι συνουσίας μόνης, βιβλίον δὲ προέφερεν οὐδὲ εἷς· ὥστε μάλα ἀσμένως πρὸς τὸν Ἰάμβλιχον ἀπέτρεχον, ὡς ἐκ πηγῆς ὑπερβλυζούσης, οὐ μενούσης καθ᾽ ἑαυτήν, ἐμφορησόμενοι. κατὰ δὲ τὸ κλέος ἀμφοῖν αὐξόμενον ἅμα,[2] καὶ συνέτυχόν ποτε ἀλλήλοις ἢ συνήντησαν ὥσπερ ἀστέρες, καὶ περιεκαθέσθη γε αὐτοὺς θέατρον οἷον εἰκάσαι μεγάλου μουσείου. Ἰαμβλίχου δὲ τὸ ἐπερωτηθῆναι μᾶλλον ὑπομείναντος ἢ τὸ ἐπερωτᾶν, ὁ Ἀλύπιος παρὰ πᾶσαν ὑπόνοιαν ἀφεὶς ἅπασαν φιλόσοφον ἐρώτησιν, τοῦ δὲ θεάτρου γενόμενος, " Εἰπέ μοι, φιλόσοφε," πρὸς αὐτὸν ἔφη " ὁ πλούσιος ἢ ἄδικος ἢ ἀδίκου κληρονόμος, ναὶ ἢ οὔ; τούτων γὰρ μέσον οὐδέν." ὁ δὲ τὴν

---

[1] ᾗ παρά Boissonade ; παρά Wyttenbach.
[2] ἄνω Boissonade ; ἅμα Wyttenbach.

---

[1] This seems to be a rather confused reference to *Timaeus* 36 where the world-soul is said to envelop the body of the universe.

know. And this I say with good reason, since Aedesius himself asserted that he had not written about it, nor had any other ventured to do so.

At the same time as Iamblichus, lived ALYPIUS, who was especially skilled in dialectic. He was of very small stature and his body was very little larger than a pigmy's, but even the body that he seemed to have was really all soul and intelligence; to such a degree did the corruptible element in him fail to increase, since it was absorbed into his diviner nature. Therefore, just as the great Plato says,[1] that in contradistinction to human bodies, divine bodies dwell within souls, thus also of him one might say that he had migrated into a soul, and that he was confined and dominated there by some supernatural power. Now Alypius had many followers, but his teaching was limited to conversation, and no one ever published a book by him. On this account they very eagerly betook themselves to Iamblichus, to fill themselves full as though from a spring that bubbles over and does not stay within its limits. Now as the renown of both men increased and kept pace they encountered one another by chance or met in their courses like planets, and round them in a circle sat an audience as though in some great seat of the Muses. Now Iamblichus was waiting to have questions put to him rather than to ask them, but Alypius, contrary to all expectation, postponed all questioning about philosophy and giving himself up to making an effect with his audience [2] said to Iamblichus: "Tell me, philosopher, is a rich man either unjust or the heir of the unjust, yes or no? For there is no middle course."

---

[2] Perhaps an echo of Plato, *Symposium* 194 B.

πληγὴν τοῦ λόγου μισήσας, "ἀλλ' οὐχ οὗτός γε,"
ἔφη "θαυμασιώτατε πάντων ἀνδρῶν, ὁ τρόπος
τῆς ἡμετέρας διαλέξεως, εἴ τῳ τι περιττόν ἐστι
κατὰ τὰ ἐκτός, ἀλλ' εἴ τι πλεονάζει κατὰ τὴν
οἰκείαν ἀρετὴν φιλοσόφῳ καὶ πρέπουσαν." ταῦτα
εἰπὼν ἀπεχώρησε, καί, διαναστάντος, οὐκ ἦν
σύλλογος. ἀπελθὼν δὲ καὶ γενόμενος ἐφ' ἑαυτοῦ,
καὶ τὴν ὀξύτητα θαυμάσας, πολλάκις τε ἰδίᾳ
συνέτυχεν αὐτῷ, καὶ οὕτως ὑπερηγάσθη τὸν
ἄνδρα τῆς ἀκριβείας καὶ συνέσεως, ὥστε καὶ
ἀπελθόντος βίον συνέγραψε. καὶ ἐνέτυχεν ὁ ταῦτα
γράφων τοῖς γεγραμμένοις· τὰ γεγραμμένα δὲ
ὑπὸ τῆς συνθήκης ἐμελαίνετο, καὶ νέφος αὐτοῖς
ἐπέτρεχε βαθύ, οὔ τι δι' ἀσάφειαν τῶν γενομένων,
ἀλλὰ διδασκαλικὸν εἶχε τὸν Ἀλυπίου λόγον
μακρόν τινα, καὶ διαλέξεων οὐ προσῆν μνήμη
λόγον ἐχουσῶν. ἀποδημίας τε εἰς τὴν Ῥώμην
ἔφραζε τὸ βιβλίον, αἷς οὔτε αἰτία προσῆν, οὔτε
τὸ τῆς ψυχῆς ἐνεφαίνετο[1] μέγεθος. ἀλλ' ὅτι μὲν
εἵποντο πολλοὶ τεθηπότες τὸν ἄνδρα παραδη-
λοῦται· ὅ τι δὲ εἶπεν ἢ ἔπραξεν ἀξιόλογον, οὐκ
ἐπιφαίνεται· ἀλλ' ἔοικεν ὁ θαυμάσιος Ἰάμβλιχος
ταὐτὸν πεπονθέναι τοῖς γραφικοῖς, οἳ τοὺς ἐν
ὥρᾳ γράφοντες, ὅταν χαρίσασθαί τι παρ' ἑαυτῶν
εἰς τὴν γραφὴν βουληθῶσι, τὸ πᾶν εἶδος τῆς
ὁμοιώσεως διαφθείρουσιν, ὥστε ἅμα τε τοῦ
461 παραδείγματος ἡμαρτηκέναι καὶ τοῦ κάλλους.
οὕτω κἀκεῖνος ἐπαινέσαι προελόμενος διὰ τὴν
ἀλήθειαν, τὸ μὲν μέγεθος ἐμφαίνει τῶν καθ'
ἑαυτὸν ἐν τοῖς δικαστηρίοις κολάσεων καὶ ἀτυ-
χημάτων, αἰτίας δὲ ἐπὶ τούτοις ἢ προφάσεις οὔτε

---

[1] συνεφαίνετο Boissonade; ἐνεφαίνετο Cobet.

Iamblichus disliked the catch in the question and replied, "Nay, most admired of men, this is not our method, to discuss anyone who more than other men possesses external things, but rather only one who excels in the virtue that is peculiar and appropriate to a philosopher." So saying he went away, and after he had risen the meeting broke up. But after he had left them and collected his thoughts, he admired the acuteness of the question, and often met Alypius privately; and he was so profoundly impressed by the subtlety and sagacity of the man, that when he died he wrote his biography. Indeed the author of this work once saw the book. The narrative was obscured by its style and it was hidden by a thick cloud, though not because of any lack of clearness in the subject matter, for his authority was a long discourse of Alypius; moreover, there was no mention of discourses that maintained an argument. The book told of journeys to Rome for which no reason was given, and it did not make manifest the greatness of his soul on those occasions, and though he insinuates that Alypius had many admiring followers it is not shown that he either did or said anything remarkable. No, the renowned Iamblichus seems to have made the same error as painters who are painting youths in their bloom and wish to add to the painting some charm of their own invention, whereby they destroy the whole character of the likeness, so that they fail to achieve either a resemblance or the beauty at which they aim. So it was with Iamblichus when he set out to praise by telling the exact truth; for though he clearly shows how severe were the punishments and sufferings in the law courts in his day, yet the causes of these things and their purposes he was

πεφυκὼς ἐξηγεῖσθαι πολιτικῶς, οὔτε προελόμενος, τὸν πάντα χαρακτῆρα συνέχεε τοῦ βίου, μόλις τοῦτο καταλιπὼν τοῖς ὀξυδορκοῦσι ξυλλαβεῖν, ὅτι τὸν ἄνδρα ἐθαύμαζε, καὶ διαφερόντως αὐτοῦ τήν τε παρὰ τὰ δεινὰ καρτερίαν καὶ τὸ ἀνέκπληκτον, τήν τε ἐν τοῖς λόγοις ὀξύτητα καὶ τόλμαν κατεσεβάζετο.[1] ἐξ Ἀλεξανδρείας δὲ οὗτος ἦν. καὶ τὰ μὲν εἰς Ἀλύπιον ταῦτα. καὶ ἐτελεύτα γε ἐν Ἀλεξανδρείᾳ γηραιός, Ἰάμβλιχός τε ἐπ᾽ αὐτῷ, πολλὰς ῥίζας τε καὶ πηγὰς φιλοσοφίας ἀφείς. ταύτης ὁ ταῦτα γράφων τῆς φορᾶς εὐτύχησεν. ἄλλοι μὲν γὰρ ἀλλαχοῦ τῶν εἰρημένων ὁμιλητῶν διεκρίθησαν εἰς ἅπασαν τὴν Ῥωμαϊκὴν ἐπικράτειαν· Αἰδέσιος δὲ κατέλαβε τὸ Μύσιον Πέργαμον.

Ἐκδέχεται δὲ τὴν Ἰαμβλίχου διατριβὴν καὶ ὁμιλίαν ἐς τοὺς ἑταίρους Αἰδέσιος ὁ ἐκ Καππαδοκίας. ἦν δὲ τῶν εὖ γεγονότων εἰς ἄκρον, πλοῦτος δὲ οὐχ ὑπῆν τῷ γένει πολύς, καὶ ὅ γε πατὴρ αὐτὸν ἐκπέμψας ἐπὶ παιδείαν χρηματιστικὴν ἐκ Καππαδοκίας ἐπὶ τὴν Ἑλλάδα, εἶτα ἐκδεχόμενος, ὡς θησαυρὸν ἐπὶ τῷ παιδὶ εὑρήσων, ἐπειδή ποτε, ἐπανελθόντος, φιλοσοφοῦντα ᾔσθετο, τῆς οἰκίας ὡς ἀχρεῖον ἀπήλαυνε. καὶ ἐκδιώκων "τί γάρ" ἔφη "φιλοσοφία ὠφελεῖ;" ὁ δὲ ὑποστραφεὶς "οὐ μικρά, πάτερ," ἔφη, "πατέρα καὶ διώκοντα προσκυνεῖν.[2]" καὶ τοῦτο ἀκούσας ὁ πατήρ, ἀνά τε ἐκαλέσατο τὸν παῖδα, καὶ τὸ ἦθος ἐθαύμασε. καὶ ὅλον ἐπιδοὺς ἑαυτὸν ἀνέθηκε φέρων ἐς τὴν ἔτι

---

[1] So Wyttenbach; τομὴν κατεσκευάζετο.
[2] προσκυνῶν Boissonade; προσκυνεῖν Wyttenbach.

---

[1] A similar story is told of an unnamed youth by Aelian, *Frag.* 1038, and it may be imitated here by Eunapius.

neither fitted by nature to expound like one versed
in politics, nor was that his purpose; hence he confused the whole outline and significance of the man's
life, and he hardly even left it open to the most keen-
sighted to grasp the fact that he admired Alypius,
and above all reverenced his fortitude and constancy
amid dangers, and the keenness and daring of his
style in his discourses. Alypius was by birth an
Alexandrian. This is all I have to say about him.
He died an old man, in Alexandria, and after him
died Iamblichus after putting forth many roots and
springs of philosophy. The author of this narrative
had the good fortune to benefit by the crop that
sprang therefrom. For others of his disciples who
have been mentioned were scattered in all directions
over the whole Roman Empire, but Aedesius chose
to settle at Pergamon in Mysia.

Aedesius the Cappadocian succeeded to the school
of Iamblichus and his circle of disciples. He was
extremely well born, but his family was not possessed
of great wealth, and therefore his father sent him
away from Cappadocia to Greece to educate himself
with a view to making money, thinking that he
would find a treasure in his son. But on his return,
when he discovered that he was inclined to philosophy
he drove him out of his house as useless.[1] And as
he drove him forth he asked: " Why, what good does
philosophy do you?" Whereupon his son turned
round and replied: " It is no small thing, father, to
have learned to revere one's father even when he is
driving one forth." When his father heard this, he
called his son back and expressed his approval of his
virtuous character. And for the future Aedesius
devoted himself entirely to finishing his interrupted

377

λειπομένην παιδείαν. καὶ ὁ μὲν τὸν παῖδα προπέμψας εὔθυμος ἦν, καὶ περιέχαιρεν, ὡς θεοῦ γεγονὼς μᾶλλον ἢ ἀνθρώπου πατήρ.

Ὁ δὲ τοὺς ἄλλους ἅπαντας παραδραμών, ὅσοι τῶν τότε ἦσαν εὐκλεέστεροι καὶ ὧν ἐτύγχανεν ἀκηκοώς, καὶ πείρᾳ τὴν σοφίαν συλλεξάμενος, ἐπὶ τὸν ἐρικυδέστατον Ἰάμβλιχον μακρὰν[1] ὁδὸν ἐκ Καππαδοκίας εἰς Συρίαν συνέτεινε καὶ διήνυεν. ὡς δὲ εἶδέ τε τὸν ἄνδρα καὶ ἤκουσε λέγοντος, ἐξεκρέματο τῶν λόγων, καὶ τῆς ἀκροάσεως οὐκ ἐνεπίμπλατο· ἐς ὃ τελευτῶν Αἰδέσιός τε ἐγένετο καὶ μικρὸν ἀποδέων Ἰαμβλίχου, πλὴν ὅσα γε εἰς θειασμὸν Ἰαμβλίχου φέρει. τούτων γὰρ οὐδὲν εἴχομεν ἀναγράφειν, ὅτι τὸ μὲν ἐπέκρυπτεν ἴσως Αἰδέσιος αὐτὸς διὰ τοὺς χρόνους (Κωνσταντῖνος γὰρ ἐβασίλευε, τά τε τῶν ἱερῶν ἐπιφανέστατα καταστρέφων καὶ τὰ τῶν χριστιανῶν ἀνεγείρων οἰκήματα), τὰ δὲ ἴσως καὶ τὸ τῶν ὁμιλητῶν ἄριστον πρὸς μυστηριώδη τινὰ σιωπὴν καὶ ἱεροφαντικὴν ἐχεμυθίαν ἐπιρρεπὲς ἦν καὶ συνεκέκλιτο. ὁ γοῦν ταῦτα γράφων ἐκ παιδὸς ἀκροατὴς Χρυσανθίου γενόμενος, μόλις εἰς εἰκοστὸν ἔτος ἠξιοῦτο τῶν ἀληθεστέρων, οὕτω μέγα τι χρῆμα εἰς ἡμᾶς τῆς Ἰαμβλίχου φιλοσοφίας διετάθη καὶ συμπαρέτεινε τῷ χρόνῳ.

Ἰαμβλίχου δὲ καταλιπόντος τὸ ἀνθρώπειον, 162 ἄλλοι μὲν ἀλλαχῇ διεσπάρησαν, καὶ οὐδεὶς ἦν ἔξω φήμης καὶ ἄγνωστος. Σώπατρος δὲ ὁ πάντων δεινότερος, διά τε φύσεως ὕψος καὶ ψυχῆς μέγεθος,

---

[1] Before μακρὰν Cobet deletes οὐ; Boissonade retains.

---

[1] Iamblichus died in the reign of Constantine the Great,

education. Moreover his father eagerly encouraged his son to go, and rejoiced exceedingly as though he were the father of a god rather than of a mere man.

When Aedesius had outstripped all the more notable men of his time, and all who had taught him, and by experience had gathered a store of wisdom, he made and completed a long journey from Cappadocia to Syria, to see the far-famed Iamblichus. And when he beheld the man and heard him discourse, he hung on his words and never could have enough of hearing him, till finally Aedesius himself became renowned and little inferior to Iamblichus, except as regards the latter's divine inspiration. On this head I had nothing to record, partly perhaps because Aedesius himself kept it secret owing to the times (for Constantine was emperor and was pulling down the most celebrated temples and building Christian churches); but perhaps it was partly because all his most distinguished disciples leaned towards and inclined to a silence appropriate to the mysteries, and a reserve worthy of a hierophant. At any rate, the present writer, though he became a pupil of Chrysanthius from boyhood, was scarcely in the twentieth year [of pupilage] deemed worthy of a share in the truer doctrines, so wondrous a thing was the philosophy of Iamblichus, extending and reaching down from that time even to our own day.[1]

When Iamblichus had departed from this world, his disciples were dispersed in different directions, and not one of them failed to win fame and reputation.

SOPATER,[2] more eloquent than the rest because of his lofty nature and greatness of soul, would not

and probably before A.D. 333; Eunapius is writing about fifty years later.   [2] See above, p. 458.

οὐκ ἐνεγκὼν τοῖς ἄλλοις ἀνθρώποις ὁμιλεῖν, ἐπὶ
τὰς βασιλικὰς αὐλὰς ἔδραμεν ὀξύς, ὡς τὴν Κωνσταντίνου πρόφασίν τε καὶ φορὰν τυραννήσων καὶ
μεταστήσων τῷ λόγῳ. καὶ ἐς τοσοῦτόν γε ἐξίκετο
σοφίας καὶ δυνάμεως, ὡς ὁ μὲν βασιλεὺς ἑαλώκει
τε ὑπ᾽ αὐτῷ, καὶ δημοσίᾳ σύνεδρον εἶχεν, εἰς τὸν
δεξιὸν καθίζων τόπον, ὃ καὶ ἀκοῦσαι καὶ ἰδεῖν
ἄπιστον. οἱ δὲ παραδυναστεύοντες ῥηγνύμενοι τῷ
φθόνῳ πρὸς βασιλείαν ἄρτι φιλοσοφεῖν μεταμαν-
θάνουσαν, τὸν Κερκώπων ἐπετήρουν καιρόν, οὐ
τὸν Ἡρακλέα καθεύδοντα μόνον, ἀλλὰ καὶ τὴν
ἄλογον ἐγρηγορυῖαν Τύχην, καὶ συλλόγους τε
λαθραίους ἐποιοῦντο, καὶ οὐκ ἔστι καθ᾽ ὅ τι μέρος
τῆς κακοδαίμονος ἐπιβουλῆς ἠμέλουν. ὥσπερ οὖν
ἐπὶ τοῦ παλαιοῦ καὶ μεγάλου Σωκράτους, ἁπάντων
Ἀθηναίων (εἰ καὶ δῆμος ἦσαν) οὐκ ἄν τις ἐτόλμησε
κατηγορίαν καὶ γραφήν, ὅν γε ᾤοντο πάντες
Ἀθηναῖοι περιπατοῦν ἄγαλμα σοφίας τυγχάνειν,
εἰ μὴ μέθῃ καὶ παραφροσύνῃ καὶ τῷ τῶν Διονυσίων
τῆς ἑορτῆς καὶ παννυχίδος ἀνειμένῳ, ὑπὸ γέλωτος
καὶ ὀλιγωρίας καὶ τῶν εὐκόλων καὶ σφαλερῶν
παθῶν ἐπὶ τοῖς ἀνθρώποις ἐξευρημένων, πρῶτος
Ἀριστοφάνης ἐπὶ διεφθαρμέναις ψυχαῖς τὸν γέλωτα
ἐπεισαγαγὼν καὶ τὰ ἐπὶ τῆς σκηνῆς κινήσας
ὑπορχήματα, τότε θέατρον ἀνέπεισεν, ἐπὶ τοσαύτῃ
σοφίᾳ ψυλλῶν πηδήματα καταμωκώμενος, καὶ
νεφελῶν διαγράφων εἴδη καὶ σχήματα καὶ τἆλλα
ὅσα κωμῳδία ληρεῖν εἴωθεν εἰς γέλωτος κίνησιν.
ὡς δὲ εἶδον ἐγκεκλικὸς πρὸς τὴν ἡδονὴν τὸ θέατρον,
κατηγορίας ἥψαντό τινες, καὶ τὴν ἀσεβῆ γραφὴν

---

¹ A fabulous, monkey-like race who caught Heracles
asleep.

condescend to associate with ordinary men and went
in haste to the imperial court, hoping to dominate
and convert by his arguments the purpose and headlong policy of Constantine. And he attained to such
wisdom and power that the emperor was captivated
by him and publicly made him his assessor, giving
him a seat at his right hand, a thing incredible to
hear and see. The courtiers, bursting with jealous
malice against a court so lately converted to the
study of philosophy, lay in wait for their opportunity,
like the Cercopes,[1] to catch not only Heracles asleep
but also irrational unsleeping Fortune, and they held
secret meetings and neglected no detail of their
unhallowed plot. So it was just as in the time of the
renowned Socrates, when no one of all the Athenians,
even though they were a democracy, would have
ventured on that accusation and indictment of one
whom all the Athenians regarded as a walking image
of wisdom, had it not been that in the drunken-
ness, insanity, and licence of the Dionysia and the
night festival, when light laughter and careless and
dangerous emotions are discovered among men,
Aristophanes first introduced ridicule into their
corrupted minds, and by setting dances upon the
stage won over the audience to his views; for he
made mock of that profound wisdom by describing
the jumps of fleas,[2] and depicting the shapes and
forms of clouds, and all those other absurd devices to
which comedy resorts in order to raise a laugh.
When they saw that the audience in the theatre was
inclined to such indulgence, certain men set up an
accusation and ventured on that impious indictment

---

[2] An allusion to Aristophanes, *Clouds* 144.

EUNAPIUS

εἰς ἐκεῖνον ἐτόλμησαν, καὶ δῆμος ὅλος ἐπ᾿ ἀνδρὸς
ἠτύχει φόνῳ. ἔστι γὰρ ἐκ τῶν χρόνων λογιζομένῳ
συλλαβεῖν ὅτι, Σωκράτους ἀπελθόντος βιαίως,
οὐδὲν ἔτι λαμπρὸν Ἀθηναίοις ἐπράχθη, ἀλλ᾿ ἥ τε
πόλις ὑπέδωκε, καὶ διὰ τὴν πόλιν τὰ τῆς Ἑλλάδος
ἅπαντα συνδιεφθάρη.[1] οὕτω καὶ τότε συνορᾶν
ἐξῆν τὸ κατὰ Σώπατρον ἐπιβούλευμα. ἡ μὲν γὰρ
Κωνσταντινούπολις, τὸ ἀρχαῖον Βυζάντιον, κατὰ
μὲν τοὺς παλαιοὺς χρόνους Ἀθηναίοις παρεῖχε
τὴν σιτοπομπείαν, καὶ περιττὸν ἦν τὸ ἐκεῖθεν
ἀγώγιμον· ἐν δὲ τοῖς καθ᾿ ἡμᾶς καιροῖς, οὐδὲ τὸ
ἀπ᾿ Αἰγύπτου πλῆθος τῶν ὁλκάδων, οὐδὲ τὸ ἐξ
Ἀσίας ἁπάσης, Συρίας τε καὶ Φοινίκης καὶ τῶν
ἄλλων ἐθνῶν συμφερόμενον πλῆθος σίτου, κατὰ
ἐπαγωγὴν φόρου, ἐμπλῆσαι καὶ κορέσαι τὸν
μεθύοντα δύναται δῆμον, ὃν Κωνσταντῖνος, τὰς
ἄλλας χηρώσας πόλεις ἀνθρώπων, εἰς τὸ Βυζάντιον
μετέστησε, καὶ πρὸς τοὺς ἐν τοῖς θεάτροις κρότους
παραβλυζόντων κραιπάλης ἀνθρώπων ἑαυτῷ συνε-
στήσατο, σφαλλομένων ἀνθρώπων ἀγαπήσας ἐγκώμια καὶ μνήμην ὀνόματος, τῶν μόλις ὑπὸ εὐηθείας
φθεγγομένων τοὔνομα· συμβέβηκε δὲ καὶ τῇ
θέσει τοῦ Βυζαντίου μηδὲ εἰς πλοῦν ἁρμόζειν τῶν
καταφερομένων πλοίων, ἂν μὴ καταπνεύσῃ νότος
ἀκραὴς καὶ ἄμικτος.[2] καὶ τότε δὴ τοῦ πολλάκις
463 συμβαίνοντος κατὰ τὴν ὡρῶν φύσιν συμβάντος, ὅ
τε δῆμος ὑπὸ λιμοῦ παρεθέντες συνῄεσαν ἐς τὸ

[1] συνδιεφθάρη Cobet.
[2] καὶ ἄμικτος Cobet would omit as a gloss on the Homeric word ἀκραής.

382

against him ; and so the death of one man brought
misfortune on the whole state. For if one reckons
from the date of Socrates' violent death, we may
conclude that after it nothing brilliant was ever
again achieved by the Athenians, but the city
gradually decayed and because of her decay the
whole of Greece was ruined along with her. So, too,
in the time I speak of one could observe what
happened in the affair of the plot against Sopater.
For Constantinople, originally called Byzantium, in
distant times used to furnish the Athenians with a
regular supply of corn,[1] and an enormous quantity
was imported thence. But in our times neither the
great fleet of merchant vessels from Egypt and from
all Asia, nor the abundance of corn that is contributed
from Syria and Phoenicia and the other nations as
the payment of tribute, can suffice to satisfy the intoxicated multitude which Constantine transported
to Byzantium by emptying other cities, and established near him because he loved to be applauded in
the theatres by men so drunk that they could not
hold their liquor. For he desired to be praised by
the unstable populace and that his name should
be in their mouths, though so stupid were they
that they could hardly pronounce the word. It
happens, moreover, that the site of Byzantium is
not adapted for the approach of ships that touch
there, except when a strong wind is blowing due
from the south. At that time, then, there happened
what often used to happen according to the nature
of the seasons ; and the citizens were assembled in
the theatre, worn out by hunger. The applause from

---

[1] *Cf.* Demosthenes, *On the Crown* 87, for the dependence of Athens on corn from Byzantium.

EUNAPIUS

θέατρον, καὶ σπάνις ἦν τοῦ μεθύοντος ἐπαίνου,
καὶ τὸν βασιλέα κατεῖχεν ἀθυμία. καὶ οἱ πάλαι
βασκαίνοντες, εὑρηκέναι καιρὸν ἡγούμενοι κάλλιστον, "ἀλλὰ Σώπατρός γε," ἔφασαν "ὁ παρὰ
σοῦ τιμώμενος κατέδησε τοὺς ἀνέμους δι᾽ ὑπερβολὴν σοφίας, ἣν καὶ αὐτὸς ἐπαινεῖς, καὶ δι᾽ ἣν
ἔτι τοῖς βασιλείοις ἐγκάθηται θρόνοις." καὶ ὁ
Κωνσταντῖνος ταῦτα ἀκούσας καὶ συμπεισθείς,
κατακοπῆναι κελεύει τὸν ἄνδρα, καὶ ἐγίνετο διὰ
τοὺς βασκαίνοντας ταῦτα θᾶττον ἢ ἐλέγετο. ὁ δὲ
τῶν κακῶν ἁπάντων αἴτιος ἦν Ἀβλάβιος, ἔπαρχος
μὲν τῆς βασιλικῆς αὐλῆς, ὑπὸ Σωπάτρου δὲ
παρευδοκιμούμενος ἀπήγχετο. ἐμοὶ δέ, ὥσπερ
προείρηται, πεπαιδευμένων ἀνδρῶν εἰς πᾶσαν
παιδείαν ἀναγράφοντι βίους, τὰ εἰς τὴν ἐμὴν
ἀκοὴν σωζόμενα, δύσφορον οὐδὲν εἰ καὶ τῶν εἰς
αὐτοὺς ἐξημαρτηκότων βραχέα τινὰ ἐπιδράμοιμι.

Ἀβλαβίῳ τῷ τὸν φόνον ἐργασαμένῳ γένος ἦν
ἀδοξότατον, καὶ τὰ ἐκ πατέρων τοῦ μετρίου καὶ
φαύλου ταπεινότερα. καὶ λόγος τε ὑπὲρ αὐτοῦ
τοιοῦτος διασώζεται, καὶ οὐδεὶς τοῖς λεγομένοις
ἀντέλεγεν. τῶν ἐξ Αἰγύπτου τις περὶ τὸ καλούμενον μάθημα συντεταμένων, παρελθὼν εἰς τὴν
πόλιν (ἱκανοὶ δέ εἰσιν Αἰγύπτιοι καὶ δημοσίᾳ μετ᾽
ὀλιγωρίας ἐν ταῖς ἀποδημίαις ἀσχημονεῖν· εἰκὸς
δὲ αὐτοὺς καὶ οἴκοθεν οὕτω παιδεύεσθαι), παρελθὼν
δὲ ὅμως, εἰς τὸ πολυτελέστερον ὠθεῖται τῶν
καπηλείων, καὶ ξηρός τε εἶναι, πολλὴν ἀνύσας
ὁδόν, ἔφασκεν καὶ ὑπὸ δίψους αὐτίκα μάλα ἀπο-

---

[1] An echo of *Odyssey* x. 20.

[2] Μάθημα is often used technically of the science of
drawing horoscopes.

the drunken populace was scanty, and the Emperor was greatly discouraged. Then those who had long been envious thought that they had found an excellent occasion, and said: "It is Sopater, he whom you honour, who has fettered the winds [1] by that excessive cleverness which you yourself praise, and through which he even sits on the Imperial throne." When Constantine heard this he was won over, and ordered Sopater's head to be cut off; and those envious persons took care that this was no sooner said than done. Ablabius was responsible for all these evils, for, though he was pretorian prefect, he felt stifled with envy of Sopater, who received more consideration than himself. And since I am, as I have already said, recording the lives of men who were trained in every kind of learning, so much, that is, as is preserved and has come to my ears, it will not be amiss if I also touch briefly on those who wrongfully injured them.

Ablabius who brought about the murder came of a very obscure family, and on his father's side did not even attain to the humble middle class. The following anecdote about him survives, and no one contradicted the facts alleged. A certain Egyptian of the class devoted to the study called astrology,[2] who was visiting the city [3] (and when they are on their travels Egyptians are capable of behaving even in public with a lack of decorum, so that they are probably trained at home to manners of that sort); as I say, he came on a visit, pushed his way into one of the more expensive wineshops, and called out that he was parched after finishing a long journey, and that he would choke in a moment with thirst,

[3] Rome.

πεπνίξεσθαι, καὶ γλυκὺν ἠρτυμένον ἐγχεῖν ἐκέλευσε
τὸν οἶνον, καὶ προέκειτο τὸ ἀργύριον. ἡ δὲ
προεστῶσα τοῦ καπηλείου τὸ κέρδος ὁρῶσα, πρὸς
τὴν ὑπηρεσίαν παρεσκευάζετο, καὶ διετρόχαζεν.
ἡ δὲ ἐτύγχανε μὲν ἱκανὴ καὶ μαιώσασθαι γυναῖκας
ἐπὶ τῷ λοχεύεσθαι. προθεμένης αὐτῆς κύλικα τῷ
Αἰγυπτίῳ καὶ τὸν ἠρτυμένον οἶνον καταχεομένης,
προσδραμοῦσά τις ἐκ γειτόνων "ἀλλὰ κινδυνεύει
σοι" εἶπε λέγουσα πρὸς τὸ οὖς "ἐπὶ ταῖς ὠδῖσιν
ἡ φίλη καὶ συγγενής," καὶ γὰρ οὕτως εἶχεν, "εἰ
μὴ θᾶττον ἀφίκοιο." καὶ ἡ μὲν ταῦτα ἀκούσασα,
καὶ καταλιποῦσα τὸν Αἰγύπτιον, πρὶν τὸ θερμὸν
ὕδωρ ἐπιβαλεῖν,[1] κεχηνότα, κἀκείνην ἀπολύσασα
τῶν ὠδίνων, καὶ συντελέσασά γε ὅσα ἐπὶ ταῖς
λοχείαις γίνεται, παρῆν αὐτίκα, διακαθήρασα τὰς
χεῖρας, πρὸς τὸν ξένον. ὡς δὲ ἀγανακτοῦντα κατέλαβε καὶ τῷ θυμῷ περιζέοντα, τὴν αἰτίαν ἀπήγ-
γειλεν ἡ γυνὴ τῆς βραδυτῆτος. ὡς δὲ ἤκουσεν ὁ
βέλτιστος Αἰγύπτιος καὶ πρὸς τὴν ὥραν εἶδεν,
ὀξέως μᾶλλον ἐδίψησεν ἐξειπεῖν τὸ παρὰ τῶν θεῶν
ἐπελθὸν ἢ τὸ τοῦ σώματος θεραπεῦσαι πάθος, καὶ
μέγα φθεγξάμενος· "ἀλλ' ἄπιθί γε, ὦ γύναι·
φράζε τῇ τεκούσῃ ὅτι μικροῦ βασιλέα τέτοκε."
καὶ τοῦτο δηλώσας, ἑαυτόν τε ἐπλήρωσεν ἀφθόνως
τῆς κύλικος, καὶ τὸ ὄνομα ὅστις εἴη κατέλιπε τῇ
γυναικὶ εἰδέναι. καὶ ὁ τεχθεὶς ἦν Ἀβλάβιος, καὶ
τοσοῦτον ἐγένετο παίγνιον τῆς εἰς ἅπαντα νεωτερι-
ζούσης Τύχης, ὥστε οὕτω πλείονα ἐδύνατο τοῦ
464 βασιλεύοντος, ὥστε καὶ Σώπατρον ἀπέκτεινεν,
αἰτίαν ἐπενεγκὼν τῆς Σωκρατικῆς εὐηθεστέραν,

---

[1] ἐπιχεῖν Cobet.

and ordered them to prepare and pour for him some
sweet spiced wine, and the money for it was produced.
The hostess of the wineshop, seeing her profits
actually under her eyes, made ready to serve him
and began bustling about. But she happened to be
skilled in midwifery also. And when she had just
set the goblet before the Egyptian and was in the
act of pouring out the wine that she had prepared,
one of her neighbours ran in and whispered in her
ear: "Your friend and kinswoman," as indeed she
actually was, "is in mortal danger in child-birth,
unless you come quickly." When she heard this
she then and there left the Egyptian open-mouthed,
and did not stay to pour in the hot water. When
she had relieved the woman in her travail and done
all that is usual in case of child-birth, she washed
her hands and came back at once to her customer.
When she found him in deep chagrin and boiling
over with rage, the woman explained the reason for
her tardiness. On hearing it, the excellent Egyptian
noted the time and season, and straightway felt
more thirst to utter the message that had come to
him from the gods than to cure his own thirst; and
he cried out in a loud voice: "Go, woman, tell
the mother that she has given birth to one only
second to an emperor." After this revelation he
drank his fill of the cup and spared not; and he
left his name for the information of the woman.
The infant's name was Ablabius, and he proved to be
so much the darling of Fortune who delights in
novelties, that he became even more powerful than
the emperor. So much more powerful was he that
he even put Sopater to death, after bringing against
him a charge more foolish even than that against

ὥσπερ ἀτάκτῳ δήμῳ τῷ τότε βασιλεύοντι χρώμενος.[1] Κωνσταντῖνος μὲν οὖν καὶ Ἀβλάβιον
τιμῶν ἐκολάζετο, καὶ ὅπως γε ἐτελεύτα ἐν τοῖς
περὶ ἐκείνου γέγραπται. Ἀβλαβίῳ δὲ τὸν παῖδα
κατέλιπε Κωνστάντιον, συμβασιλεύσαντα μὲν αὐτῷ,
διαδεξάμενον δὲ τὴν ἀρχὴν τοῦ πατρὸς σὺν Κων-
σταντίνῳ καὶ Κώνσταντι τοῖς ἀδελφοῖς. ἐν δὲ
τοῖς κατὰ τὸν θειότατον Ἰουλιανὸν ἀκριβέστερον
ταῦτα εἴρηται. διαδεξάμενος δὲ ὁ Κωνστάντιος
τὴν βασιλείαν καὶ κληρωθεὶς ὅσα γε ἐκληρώθη,
ταῦτα δὲ ἦν τὰ ἐξ Ἰλλυριῶν εἰς τὴν ἑῴαν καθή-
κοντα, τὸν μὲν Ἀβλάβιον αὐτίκα παραλύει τῆς
ἀρχῆς, ἄλλο δὲ περὶ αὐτὸν ἑταιρικὸν συνέστησε.
καὶ ὁ μὲν Ἀβλάβιος τὰ περὶ Βιθυνίαν χωρία πάλαι
παρεσκευασμένος,[2] βασιλικάς τε καταφυγὰς καὶ
ῥᾳθυμίας ἔχοντα, διέτριβεν ἐν ἀφθόνοις, πάντων
ἀνθρώπων θαυμαζόντων ὅτι βασιλεύειν οὐ βούλεται.
ὁ δὲ Κωνστάντιος ἐγγύθεν ἐκ τῆς τοῦ πατρὸς
πόλεως ξιφηφόρους τινὰς ἐπ᾽ αὐτὸν ἐκπέμψας οὐκ
ὀλίγους, τοῖς μὲν πρώτοις ἐκέλευσεν ἀποδιδόναι
γράμματα. καὶ προσεκύνησάν γε αὐτόν, ὥσπερ
νομίζουσι Ῥωμαῖοι βασιλέα προσκυνεῖν, οἱ τὰ
γράμματα ἐγχειρίζοντες· καὶ ὃς μάλα σοβαρῶς
δεξάμενος τὰ γράμματα καὶ παντὸς ἀπολυθεὶς
φόβου, τήν τε ἁλουργίδα τοὺς ἐλθόντας ἀπῄτει,
βαρύτερος ἤδη γινόμενος, καὶ φοβερὸς ἦν τοῖς
ὁρωμένοις. οἱ δὲ ἔφασαν πρὸς αὐτόν, αὐτοὶ μὲν
τὰ γράμματα κομίζειν, πρὸ θυρῶν δὲ εἶναι τοὺς

---

[1] χρώμενος Wyttenbach adds.
[2] παρεσκευασμένα Boissonade ; -μένος Cobet.

Socrates, and in those days he influenced the
emperor as though the latter were an undisciplined
mob. Constantine, however, was punished for the
honour that he paid to Ablabius, and the manner of
his death I have described in my account of his
life. He bequeathed to Ablabius his son Constantius
who had been his consort in the Empire and succeeded to the throne of his father together with his
brothers Constantine and Constans. But in my
account of the sainted Julian I have related these
matters more fully. When Constantius had succeeded
to the throne and had been allotted his proper
portion of the Empire, that is to say the countries
that extend from Illyricum to the East, he at once
relieved Ablabius of his authority, and gathered
about himself a different set of favourites. Ablabius
spent his time in luxury on an estate that he had
long before made ready in Bithynia, which provided
him a safe retreat of regal splendour and complete
idleness; meanwhile all men marvelled that he did
not aspire to be emperor. Then Constantius, from
his father's city hard by, dispatched certain swords-
men to him in considerable numbers, and to the
leaders he gave orders that they should hand him a
letter. Those who delivered the letter into his
hands prostrated themselves before him, as Romans
are accustomed to prostrate themselves before the
emperor. He received the document with great
arrogance, and, freed from all apprehension, he
demanded the imperial purple from those who had
come, while his expression became more stern, and
he inspired terror in the spectators. They replied
that their task had only been to bring the letter, but
that those who had been entrusted with this other

ταῦτα πεπιστευμένους. καὶ ὁ μὲν ἐκείνους ἐκάλει
μέγα φρονῶν καὶ τῇ γνώμῃ διῃρμένος· οἱ δὲ
συγχωρηθέντες εἰσελθεῖν πλῆθός τε ἦσαν καὶ
ξιφηφόροι πάντες, καὶ ἀντὶ τῆς ἀλουργίδος ἐπῆγον
αὐτῷ "τὸν πορφύρεον θάνατον," κρεουργηδόν,
ὥσπερ τι τῶν ἐν ταῖς εὐωχίαις ζῷον, κατακόψαν-
τες. καὶ ταύτην[1] ἔτισε Σωπάτρῳ δίκην ὁ πάντα
εὐδαίμων Ἀβλάβιος.

Τούτων δὴ οὕτω κεχωρηκότων καὶ τῆς Προνοίας
οὐκ ἀφιείσῃ τὸ ἀνθρώπινον, ὁ τῶν περιλειφθέντων
ἐνδοξότατος Αἰδέσιος κατελίπετο. καταφυγὼν δὲ
ἐπί τινα μαντείαν δι᾽ εὐχῆς ᾗπερ ἐπίστευε μάλιστα
(αὕτη δὲ ἦν δι᾽ ὀνείρατος), ὁ μὲν θεὸς ἐφίστατο
πρὸς τὴν εὐχήν, καὶ ἔχρησεν ἐν ἑξαμέτρῳ τόνῳ
τάδε· ὁ δ᾽ ἀνακαλύψας ἄρτι[2] τὰ βλέφαρα καὶ
περίφοβος ὢν ἔτι, τὸν μὲν νοῦν ἐμέμνητο τῶν
εἰρημένων, τὸ δὲ ὑπερφυὲς καὶ οὐρανόμηκες τῶν
ἐπῶν περιέφευγεν αὐτὸν καὶ διωλίσθαινε. τόν τε
οὖν παῖδα καλεῖ, τὴν ὄψιν καὶ τὸ πρόσωπον ἀπο-
σμῆσαι τῷ ὕδατι βουλόμενος, καὶ ὁ θεράπων πρὸς
αὐτὸν ἔλεγεν, "ἀλλ᾽ ἡ ἀριστερά γε χεὶρ ἔξωθεν
κατάπλεως ἐστὶ γραμμάτων." καὶ ὃς εἶδε καὶ
τὸ πρᾶγμα θεῖον εἶναι συνεφρόνησε, καὶ προσκυνή-
σας τὴν ἑαυτοῦ χεῖρα καὶ τὰ γεγραμμένα, εὗρε τὸν
χρησμὸν ἐπὶ τῆς χειρὸς γεγραμμένον. ἔστι δὲ
οὗτος·

δοιῶν Μοιράων ἐπὶ νήμασι νήματα κεῖται
εἵνεκα σῆς βιοτῆς. εἰ μὲν πτολίεθρ᾽ ἀγαπάζοις
ἄστεά τ᾽ αὖ φωτῶν, καί σοι κλέος ἄφθιτον ἔσται,

---

[1] ταῦτα Boissonade ; ταύτην Cobet.
[2] ἔτι Boissonade ; ἄρτι Wyttenbach.

mission were at the door. Thereupon he insolently
summoned them within, and was inflated with pride.
But those who were then admitted were more in
number and all carried swords, and instead of the
purple robe they brought him " purple death," [1] and
hacked him to pieces like some animal cut up at a
public feast. Thus did the shade of Sopater avenge
itself on Ablabius " the fortunate."

When these events had happened and Providence
had shown that she had not deserted mankind, there
remained AEDESIUS, the most renowned of those
that survived. Once when he resorted with prayer
to a form of oracle in which he placed most trust
(it came in a dream), the god appeared in answer to
his prayer and made in hexameter verse the response
which I give below. And just after he had opened his
eyelids, while he was still spellbound with awe, he
remembered the verbal sense of what had been said,
though the supernatural and prodigious element in
the verses escaped him and was slipping from his
mind. So he called a slave, since he wished to
cleanse his eyes and face with water,[2] and the servant
said to him : " Look, the back of your left hand is
covered with writing." He looked, and concluded
that the thing was a divine portent, and after reverently saluting his hand and the letters, he found that
the following oracle was written on his hand : " On
the warp of the two Fates' spinning lie the threads of
thy life's web. If thy choice is the cities and towns
of men, thy renown shall be deathless, shepherding

[1] *Iliad* v. 83 ; this is the verse that Julian quoted when
he was invested with the purple as Caesar, and distrusted
the intentions of Constantius ; Ammianus Marcellinus xv. 8.
[2] The regular procedure after such a vision ; *cf.* Aristophanes, *Frogs* 137 f. ; Aeschylus, *Persae* 201.

ἀνδρῶν ποιμαίνοντι νέων θεοείκελον ὁρμήν.
165 ἢν δ' αὖ ποιμαίνῃς μήλων νομὸν ἠδ' ἔτι ταύρων,
δὴ πότε σαυτὸν ἔελπε συνήμονα[1] καὶ μακάρεσσιν
ἔμμεναι ἀθανάτοισι. λίνον δέ τοι ὧδε νένευκεν.

Καὶ ὁ μὲν χρησμὸς ταῦτα εἶχεν· ὁ δὲ ἑπόμενος,
ὥσπερ ἕπεσθαι χρή, πρὸς τὸν κρείττονα ὁδὸν συνηπείγετο, καὶ χωρίδιον τέ τι περιεσκόπει καὶ πρὸς
αἰπόλου[2] τινὸς ἢ βοτῆρος ἑαυτὸν ἐνέτεινε βίον· τοὺς
δὲ λόγων δεομένους ἢ παιδείας διὰ τὸ προκατα-
κεχυμένον κλέος οὐκ ἐλάνθανεν, ἀλλ' ἀνιχνεύοντες αὐτὸν περιεστήκεσαν, ὥσπερ κύνες ὠρυόμενοι
περὶ τὰ πρόθυρα, καὶ διασπάσασθαι ἀπειλοῦντες,
εἰ τοσαύτην καὶ τηλικαύτην σοφίαν ἐπὶ τὰ ὄρη
καὶ τοὺς κρημνοὺς καὶ τὰ δένδρα τρέποι, καθάπερ
οὐδὲ ἄνθρωπος γεγονὼς οὐδὲ εἰδὼς τὸ ἀνθρώπινον.
τοιούτοις δὲ λόγοις τε καὶ ἔργοις ἐκβιασθεὶς εἰς
τὴν κοινὴν ὁμιλίαν, ἐπέδωκεν ἑαυτὸν φέρων τῇ
χείρονι τῶν ὁδῶν, καὶ τὴν μὲν Καππαδοκίαν ἐξ-
έλιπεν, Εὐσταθίῳ παραδοὺς ἐπιμελεῖσθαι τῶν ἐκείνῃ
(καὶ κατὰ γένος οὐκ ἀφεστήκεσαν). αὐτὸς δὲ εἰς
τὴν Ἀσίαν διαβάς, ὅλης Ἀσίας προτεινούσης
αὐτῷ χεῖρας, ἐν τῷ παλαιῷ Περγάμῳ καθιδρύθη,
καὶ παρ' ἐκεῖνον μὲν Ἕλληνές τε ἐφοίτων καὶ οἱ
πρόσχωροι, καὶ ἡ δόξα τῶν ἄστρων ἔψαυεν.

Περὶ δὲ Εὐσταθίου καὶ ἀσεβές ἐστι παραλιπεῖν
τὰ ἐς ἀλήθειαν φέροντα· παρὰ πάντων γὰρ συνωμολογεῖτο τὸν ἄνδρα τοῦτον καὶ ὀφθῆναι[3] εἶναι
κάλλιστον, καὶ εἰς πεῖραν λόγων ἐλθεῖν δεινότατον,
τό τε ἐπὶ τῇ γλώσσῃ καὶ τοῖς χείλεσιν αἱμύλιον

[1] συνήορα Boissonade; συνήμονα Cobet; συνήονα Vollebregt.
[2] αἰπολίου Giangrande.
[3] ὀφθῆναι καὶ Boissonade; καὶ ὀφθῆναι Cobet.

the god-given impulse of youth. But if thou shalt
be a shepherd of sheep and bulls, then hope that
thou thyself shalt one day be the associate of the
blessed immortals. Thus has thy woven thread or-
dained."

Thus ran the oracle. In obedience to it, as it was
his duty to obey, he set out with all speed in pursuit
of the better way, and looked about for a small estate
and devoted his energies to the life of a goat-herd or
neat-herd. But so great was his previous renown
and so widespread that this purpose could not be
hidden from those who longed for training in
eloquence, or for learning. They tracked him down
and beset him like hounds baying before his doors,
and threatened to tear him in pieces if he should
devote wisdom so great and so rare to hills and rocks
and trees, as though he were not born a man or with
knowledge of human life. He was forced by speeches
and actions of this sort to return to the life and
converse of ordinary men; and now he applied his
talents to the inferior of the two ways. He left
Cappadocia, and handed over to Eustathius the charge
of his property there—they were indeed kinsmen—
while he himself passed into the province of Asia;
for all Asia was holding out her arms in welcome.
He settled in ancient Pergamon, and his school was
attended by Greeks and by the neighbouring people,
so that his fame touched the stars.

With regard to Eustathius, it would be sacrilegious
to leave out what would convey the truth. All men
were agreed that he was not only observed to be a
most noble character, but also most gifted with
eloquence when put to the test, while the charm
that sat on his tongue and lips seemed to be nothing

οὐκ ἔξω γοητείας ἐδόκει. καὶ τὸ μείλιχον καὶ
ἥμερον ἐπὶ τοῖς λεγομένοις ἐπήνθει καὶ συνεξ-
εχεῖτο τοσοῦτον, ὥστε οἱ τῆς φωνῆς ἀκούσαντες
καὶ τῶν λόγων, παραδόντες αὑτούς, καθάπερ οἱ
τοῦ λωτοῦ γευσάμενοι, τῆς φωνῆς ἐξεκρέμαντο
καὶ τῶν λόγων. οὕτω δὴ πολύ τι τῶν μουσικῶν
οὐκ ἀπεῖχε Σειρήνων, ὥστε ὁ βασιλεὺς αὐτὸν
μετεκάλεσε, καί τοί γε τοῖς τῶν χριστιανῶν
ἐνεχόμενος βιβλίοις, ἐπειδὴ θόρυβος αὐτὸν κατεῖχε,
καὶ παρὰ τοῦ Περσῶν βασιλέως ἀνάγκη τις ἐπ-
έκειτο, καὶ τὴν Ἀντιόχειαν ἤδη περιειργασμένου
καὶ συντοξεύοντος, ὅς γε τὴν ἄκραν τὴν ὑπερκειμένην τοῦ θεάτρου καταλαβὼν ἀδοκήτως καὶ
ἐξαπιναίως, τὸ πολὺ πλῆθος τῶν θεωμένων συν-
ετόξευσε καὶ διέφθειρε. τούτων δὲ ὅμως[1] κατ-
εχόντων, οὕτως πάντες ἦσαν ᾑρημένοι καὶ κατα-
κεκηλημένοι, ὥστε μὴ κατοκνῆσαί τινα Ἕλληνα
ἄνθρωπον ἐς τὰ ὦτα τοῦ βασιλέως παραβαλεῖν·
καί τοί γε εἰώθεσαν πρότερον οἱ βασιλεύοντες
τοὺς κατὰ στρατιὰν ἐπαινουμένους ἐπὶ τὰς πρεσβείας χειροτονεῖν, ἤτοι γε στρατοπεδάρχας ἢ
ὅσοι γε μετ' ἐκείνους ἐς τὸ ἄρχειν ἐξῃρημένοι·
τότε καὶ ἀνάγκης τυραννούσης, ὁ φρονιμώτατος
ἁπάντων περιεσκοπεῖτο καὶ συνωμολογεῖτο Εὐστάθιος. μετεκλήθη τε οὖν ἐκ τοῦ βασιλέως, καὶ
αὐτίκα παρῆν, καὶ τοσαύτη τις ἐπῆν ἀφροδίτη
τοῖς χείλεσιν, ὥστε οἱ συμβουλεύσαντες τὴν
πρεσβείαν δι' Εὐσταθίου πεμφθῆναι, ἀξιωμάτων

---

[1] ὅμως Boissonade ; ὁμῶς Wright.

---

[1] Constantius sent Eustathius on this embassy, but the
incident at Antioch here described occurred much earlier,

less than witchcraft. His mildness and amiability so blossomed out in what he said and gushed forth with his words, that those who heard his voice and speeches surrendered themselves like men who had tasted the lotus, and they hung on that voice and those speeches. So closely did he resemble the musical Sirens, that the emperor,[1] for all that he was wrapped up in the books of the Christians, sent for him at the time when he was alarmed by the state of affairs, and was hard pressed by impending danger from the king of the Persians, who had once already laid siege to Antioch and raided it with his bowmen. For unexpectedly and on a sudden he seized the height that commanded the theatre, and with his arrows shot and massacred that great crowd of spectators. In this similar crisis all men were so held captive and enchanted by Eustathius, that they did not hesitate to commend a man of the Hellenic faith to the ears of the emperor; although the earlier emperors had been accustomed to elect for embassies men who had won distinction in the army, or military prefects, or men who were next in rank to these and had been selected for office. But at that time, at the imperious call of necessity, Eustathius was sought out and admitted by general consent to be the most prudent of all men. Accordingly he was summoned by the emperor, and came forthwith, and so potent was the charm on his lips[2] that those who had advised that the embassy should be dispatched in charge of Eustathius won greater consideration than

in the reign of Gallienus, about A.D. 258; cf. Ammianus Marcellinus xxiii. 5.

[2] A sophistic commonplace derived from the famous saying of Eupolis about the oratory of Pericles; cf. Julian 33 A, 426 B.

τε ἔτυχον παρὰ τῷ βασιλεῖ μειζόνων, καὶ πρὸς
τὴν εὔνοιαν αὐτῶν ὁ βασιλεὺς ἐπεκλίνετο. τούτων
μὲν οὖν τινὲς αὐτῷ καὶ ἐθελονταὶ συνεξώρμησαν
466 ἐπὶ τὴν πρεσβείαν, μείζονα διάπειραν θέλοντες
λαβεῖν, εἰ καὶ πρὸς τοὺς βαρβάρους ἔχοι τὸ αὐτὸ
θελκτήριον ὁ ἄνθρωπος. ὡς δὲ εἰς τὴν τῶν
Περσῶν ἀφίκοντο χώραν, καί τοί γε τυραννικὸς
καὶ ἄγριός τις Σαπώρης εἶναι πρὸς τοὺς ἐσιόντας,
ἦν τε ἀληθῶς, καὶ ἐξηγγέλλετο, ἀλλ' ὅμως ἐπεὶ
πρόσοδος Εὐσταθίῳ κατὰ τὴν κοινὴν πρεσβείαν
ἐγένετο πρὸς τὸν βασιλέα, τήν τε ὑπεροψίαν τὴν
ἐν τοῖς ὄμμασι καὶ τὸ μείλιχον ἐθαύμασε, καί τοί
γε πολλὰ ἐς κατάπληξιν τοῦ ἀνδρὸς μηχανησά-
μενος. καὶ ὡς ἡμέρως καὶ ἀλύπως διαλεγομένου
τῆς φωνῆς ἤκουσε, καὶ τῶν ἐπιτρεχουσῶν κοσμίως
καὶ εὐκόλως ἀποδείξεων, ἐξελθεῖν μὲν αὐτὸν
κελεύει, καὶ ὃς ἐξῄει λόγῳ συνῃρηκὼς τύραννον·
ὁ δὲ ἐπὶ τράπεζάν τε εὐθὺς διὰ τῶν θαλαμηπόλων
εἰσεκάλει, καί, πρὸς τοῦτο ὑπακούσαντος (ἐῴκει
γὰρ εὖ πεφυκέναι πρὸς ἀρετῆς ῥοπήν), ἀπήντησεν
ἐπὶ τὴν θοίνην. καὶ ὁμοτράπεζος ἐγένετο, καὶ
κατεκράτει τῷ λόγῳ τοσοῦτον, ὥστε μικροῦ τινὸς
ἐδέησε τὸν Περσῶν βασιλέα τήν τε ὀρθὴν μεταβαλεῖν τιάραν καὶ τοὺς περιπορφύρους καὶ λιθο-
κολλήτους ἀποδῦσαι κόσμους, καὶ τὸ τριβώνιον
Εὐσταθίου μεταμφιάσασθαι· τοσαύτην τῆς τρυφῆς [1]
ἐποιήσατο καταδρομὴν καὶ τῶν περὶ σῶμα κόσμων,
καὶ εἰς τοσοῦτο κακοδαιμονίας τοὺς φιλοσω-
μάτους ἀνήγαγεν. ἀλλὰ τοῦτο μὲν ἐκώλυσαν οἱ

---

[1] τύχης Boissonade: τρυφῆς Cobet.

before from the emperor, and he inclined more
favourably towards them. Moreover, some of these
men set out of their own accord to accompany the
embassy, because they wished to employ a still greater
test, whether in his encounter with the barbarians
Eustathius should prove to possess the same power
to enchant and persuade. When they arrived in
Persia, Sapor was reported to be and actually was
tyrannical and savage towards those who approached
him ; nevertheless, when Eustathius, for the embassy
in general, was allowed access to the king, the
latter could not but admire the expression of his
eyes which was at once amiable and proudly indifferent, in spite of the many preparations that the
king had devised in order to dazzle and overawe
the man. And when he heard his voice conversing
so equably and with no effort, when he heard him
run over his arguments so modestly and good-
naturedly, he bade him withdraw ; and Eustathius
went out, leaving the tyrant a captive to his eloquence.
Presently he sent a message by his household officials
to invite him to his table, and when he obeyed the
summons, since the king seemed to him to have a
natural bent for virtue, Sapor joined him at the
banquet. Thus Eustathius became his companion at
table, and by his eloquence won such influence over
him that the king of Persia came within an ace of
renouncing his upright tiara, laying aside his purple
and bejewelled attire, and putting on instead the
philosopher's cloak of Eustathius ; so successfully did
the latter run down the life of luxury and the pomps
and vanities of the flesh, to such depths of misery
did he seem to bring down those who loved their
bodies. But this was prevented by certain magi who

παρατυχόντες τῶν μάγων, γόητα εἶναι τελείως τὸν
ἄνδρα φάσκοντες, καὶ τὸν βασιλέα συμπείσαντες
ἀποκρίνασθαι τῷ βασιλεῖ Ῥωμαίων· τί δήποτε
ἄνδρας εὐτυχοῦντες τοσούτους,[1] εἶτα πέμπουσιν
ἀνδραπόδων πλουτούντων οὐδὲν διαφέροντας; τὰ
δὲ κατὰ τὴν πρεσβείαν ἅπαντα ἦν παρ᾽[2] ἐλπίδας.

Περὶ τούτου γε τοῦ ἀνδρὸς καὶ τοιοῦτόν τι ἐς τὴν
ἐμὴν ἱστορίαν συνέπεσεν, ὡς ἅπασα μὲν ἡ Ἑλλὰς
ἰδεῖν αὐτὸν ηὔχοντο καὶ ᾔτουν τοὺς θεοὺς τὴν
ἐπιδημίαν· καὶ αἵγε μαντεῖαι τοῖς περὶ ταῦτα
δεινοῖς ἐς τοῦτο συνέβαινον. ὡς δὲ διημάρτανον,
οὐ γὰρ ἐπεδήμει, πρεσβείαν παρ᾽ αὐτὸν στέλ-
λουσιν οἱ Ἕλληνες, τοὺς ἄκρους ἐπὶ σοφίᾳ κατὰ
τὴν πρεσβείαν προελόμενοι. νοῦς δὲ ἦν αὐτοῖς
διαλέγεσθαι πρὸς τὸν μέγαν Εὐστάθιον· τί δήποτε
ἐπὶ τοῖσδε τοῖς σημείοις τὸ ἔργον οὐκ ἀπήντησεν;
ὁ δὲ ἀκούσας, καὶ τοὺς ὀνομαστοὺς ἐπ᾽ ἐκείνοις
καὶ πολυυμνήτους ἀναθεωρῶν καὶ διακρίνων
ἐβασάνιζε, καὶ συνηρώτα τό τε μέγεθος καὶ τὴν
χροιὰν καὶ τὸ σχῆμα τῶν σημείων, εἶτα μειδιάσας
συνήθως πρὸς αὐτούς, ὡς ἤκουσε τὰ ὄντα (ψεῦδος
γὰρ οὐ μόνον ἔξω θείου χοροῦ, ἀλλὰ καὶ λόγου
ἵσταται), " ἀλλὰ ταῦτά γε " εἶπε " τὴν ἐμὴν τήνδε
ἐπιδημίαν οὐκ ἐμαντεύετο." καί πού τι καὶ
παρὰ τὸ ἀνθρώπειον κατά γε ἐμὴν ἐφθέγξατο
κρίσιν· ἀπεκρίνατο γὰρ ὡς " μικρότερα ἦν καὶ
βραδύτερα τῶν ἐμῶν καλῶν τὰ φανθέντα σημεῖα."

Οὕτως Εὐστάθιος ὁ τοσοῦτος Σωσιπάτρᾳ συνῴκη-

---

[1] τοιούτους Boissonade ; τοσούτους Cobet.
[2] ὑπὲρ Boissonade ; παρ᾽ Cobet.

---

[1] Ammianus Marcellinus xvii. 5 mentions this embassy,
which was sent to Ctesiphon in 358.

happened to be at the court, and kept asserting that the man was nothing but a mere conjuror; and they persuaded the king to reply to the Roman emperor by asking him why, when Fortune had bestowed on them so many distinguished men, they sent persons no better than slaves who had enriched themselves. And the whole result of the embassy was contrary to men's expectations.[1]

In my researches concerning this man, I have come upon evidence of the following, namely that the whole of Greece prayed to see him and implored the gods that he might visit them. Moreover, the omens and those who were skilled to interpret them agreed that this would come to pass. But when they proved to be mistaken, for he did not visit Greece, the Greeks sent an embassy to him and chose for this embassy their most famous wise men. The purpose of their mission was to discuss with the renowned Eustathius this question: "Why did not the facts accord with these omens?" He listened to them, and then investigated and sifted the evidence of men who were famed in this science and had a wide renown, and cross-examined them, asking what was the size, colour, and shape of the omens. Then, as his manner was, he smiled at them, on hearing the true facts (for as falsehood has no place in the choir of the gods,[2] so too it has none in their utterance), and said: "Nay, these omens did not foretell this visit from me." Then he said something that in my judgement was too high for a mere mortal, for this was his reply: "The omens revealed were too trivial and too tardy for such dignity as mine."

After this the renowned Eustathius married

[2] An echo of Plato, *Phaedrus* 247 A; a rhetorical commonplace.

σεν, ἢ τὸν ἄνδρα τὸν ἑαυτῆς δι' ὑπεροχὴν σοφίας
εὐτελῆ τινὰ καὶ μικρὸν ἀπέδειξε. περὶ ταύτης
δὲ ἐν ἀνδρῶν σοφῶν καταλόγοις καὶ διὰ μακροτέρων εἰπεῖν ἁρμόζει, τοσοῦτον κλέος τῆς γυναικὸς
ἐξεφοίτησεν. ἦν γὰρ ἐκ τῆς περὶ Ἔφεσον Ἀσίας,
ὅσην Κάϋστρος ποταμὸς ἐπιὼν καὶ διαρρέων[1]
467 τὴν ἐπωνυμίαν ἀφ' ἑαυτοῦ τῷ πεδίῳ δίδωσι.
πατέρων δὲ ἦν καὶ γένους εὐδαίμονός τε καὶ
ὀλβίου· παιδίον δὲ ἔτι νήπιον οὖσα, ἅπαντα ἐποίει
ὀλβιώτερα, τοσοῦτόν τι κάλλους καὶ αἰδοῦς τὴν
ἡλικίαν κατέλαμπε. καὶ ἡ μὲν εἰς πενταετῆ
συνετέλει χρόνον· ἐν δὲ τούτῳ πρεσβῦται δύο
τινές (ἄμφω μὲν τὴν ἀκμὴν παρήλλαττον, ὁ δὲ
ἕτερος ἦν ἀφηλικέστερος) πήρας βαθείας ἔχοντες,
καὶ δέρματα ἐπὶ τῶν νώτων ἐνημμένοι, πρός τι
χωρίον συνωθοῦνται τῶν γονέων τῆς Σωσιπάτρας,
καὶ τὸν ἐπιτροπεύοντα συμπείθουσι (ῥᾴδιον δὲ
ἦν αὐτοῖς τοῦτο ποιεῖν) ἀμπελίων ἐπιμέλειαν
αὐτοῖς πιστεῦσαι. ὡς δὲ ὁ καρπὸς ἀπήντησε
ὑπὲρ[2] τὴν ἐλπίδα (καὶ ὁ δεσπότης παρῆν καὶ τὸ
παιδίον ἡ Σωσιπάτρα συμπαρῆν), τὸ μὲν θαῦμα
ἄπειρον ἦν καὶ πρὸς ὑπόνοιαν ἔφερε θειασμοῦ
τινός· ὁ δὲ τοῦ χωρίου δεσπότης ὁμοτραπέζους
αὐτοὺς ἐποιήσατο καὶ πολλῆς ἐπιμελείας ἠξίου,
τοῖς συγγεωργοῦσι τὸ χωρίον καταμεμφόμενος,
ὅτι μὴ τὰ αὐτὰ πράττοιεν. οἱ δὲ πρεσβῦται ξενίας
τε Ἑλληνικῆς καὶ τραπέζης τυχόντες, τοῦ δὲ
παιδίου τῆς Σωσιπάτρας τῷ τε περιττῶς καλῷ
καὶ λαμπρῷ δηχθέντες καὶ ἁλόντες, " ἀλλ' ἡμεῖς
γε " ἔφασαν " τὰ μὲν ἄλλα κρύφια καὶ ἀπόρρητα

---

[1] After διαρρέων Cobet deletes γῆν.
[2] παρὰ Boissonade ; ὑπὲρ Cobet.

Sosipatra, who by her surpassing wisdom made her own husband seem inferior and insignificant. So far did the fame of this woman travel that it is fitting for me to speak of her at greater length, even in this catalogue of wise men. She was born in Asia, near Ephesus, in that district which the river Cayster traverses and flows through, and hence gives its name to the plain. She came of a prosperous family, blessed with wealth, and while she was still a small child she seemed to bring a blessing on everything, such beauty and decorum illumined her infant years. Now she had just reached the age of five, when two old men (both were past the prime of life, but one was rather older than the other), carrying ample wallets and dressed in garments of skins, made their way to a country estate belonging to Sosipatra's parents, and persuaded the steward, as they were easily able to do, to entrust to them the care of the vines. When a harvest beyond all expectation was the result—the owner himself was there, and with him was the little girl Sosipatra—men's amazement was boundless, and they went so far as to suspect the intervention of the gods. The owner of the estate invited them to his table, and treated them with the highest consideration; and he reproached the other labourers on the estate with not obtaining the same results. The old men, on receiving Greek hospitality and a place at a Greek table, were smitten and captivated by the exceeding beauty and charm of the little girl Sosipatra, and they said: " Our other powers we keep to ourselves hidden and

πρὸς ἑαυτοὺς ἔχομεν, καὶ ταυτησὶ τῆς ἐπαινου-
μένης εὐοινίας [1] ἐστὶ γέλως, καὶ παίγνιόν τι μετ᾽
ὀλιγωρίας τῶν παρ᾽ ἡμῖν πλεονεκτημάτων. εἰ
δέ τι βούλει σοι τῆς τραπέζης ταύτης καὶ τῶν
ξενίων ἄξιον [2] δοθῆναι παρ᾽ ἡμῶν οὐκ ἐν χρήμασιν
οὐδὲ ἐν ἐπικήροις καὶ διεφθαρμέναις χάρισιν, ἀλλ᾽
ὅσον ὑπὲρ σέ τέ ἐστι καὶ τὸν σὸν βίον, δῶρον
οὐρανόμηκες καὶ τῶν ἀστέρων ἐφικνούμενον, ἄφες
παρ᾽ ἡμῖν τὴν Σωσιπάτραν ταύτην τροφεῦσι καὶ
πατράσιν ἀληθεστέροις, καὶ εἴς γε πέμπτον ἔτος
μὴ νόσον [3] περὶ τῇ παιδίσκῃ φοβηθῇς, μὴ θάνατον,
ἀλλ᾽ ἥσυχος ἔσο καὶ ἔμπεδος. μελέτω δέ σοι μὴ
πατῆσαι τὸ χωρίον μέχρις ἂν τὸ πέμπτον ἔτος,
περιτελλομένων τῶν ἡλιακῶν κύκλων, ἐξίκηται.
καὶ πλοῦτός τέ σοι αὐτόματος ἀπὸ τοῦ χωρίου
φύσεται καὶ ἀναθηλήσει, καὶ ἡ θυγάτηρ οὐ κατὰ
γυναῖκα καὶ ἄνθρωπον ἔσται μόνον, ἀλλὰ καὶ
αὐτὸς ὑπολήψῃ τι περὶ τῆς παιδίσκης πλέον. εἰ
μὲν οὖν ἀγαθὸν ἔχεις θυμόν, ὑπτίαις χερσὶ δέξαι
τὰ λεγόμενα· εἰ δέ τινας ὑπονοίας ἀνακινεῖς,
οὐδὲν ἡμῖν εἴρηται.᾽᾽ πρὸς ταῦτα τὴν γλῶτταν
ἐνδακὼν καὶ πτήξας ὁ πατήρ, τὸ παιδίον ἐγχειρίζει
καὶ παραδίδωσι, καί, τὸν οἰκονόμον μετακαλέσας,
᾽᾽χορήγει᾽᾽ πρὸς αὐτὸν εἶπεν ᾽᾽ὅσα οἱ πρεσβύται
βούλονται, καὶ πολυπραγμόνει μηδέν.᾽᾽ ταῦτα
εἶπεν· οὔπω δὲ ἕως ὑπέφαινεν, ἐξῄει καθάπερ
φεύγων καὶ τὴν θυγατέρα καὶ τὸ χωρίον.

Οἱ δὲ παραλαβόντες τὸ παιδίον (εἴτε ἥρωες,
εἴτε δαίμονες, εἴτε τι θειότερον ἦσαν γένος), τίσι

---

[1] εὐοινίας Boissonade; εὐνοίας.   [2] ἄξιον Cobet adds.
[3] μηδενὸς *Laurentianus*; μηδὲν Boissonade; μὴ νόσον Cobet; μηδὲ νόσον Giangrande.

unrevealed, and this abundant vintage that you so highly approve is laughable and mere child's-play which takes no account of our superhuman abilities. But if you desire from us a fitting return for this maintenance and hospitality, not in money or perishable and corruptible benefits, but one far above you and your way of life, a gift whereof the fame shall reach the skies and touch the stars, hand over this child Sosipatra to us who are more truly her parents and guardians, and until the fifth year from now fear no disease for the little girl, nor death, but remain calm and steadfast. But take care not to set your feet on this soil till the fifth year come with the annual revolutions of the sun. And of its own accord wealth shall spring up for you and shall blossom forth from the soil. Moreover, your daughter shall have a mind not like a woman's or a mere human being's. Nay, you yourself also shall have higher than mortal thoughts concerning the child. Now if you have good courage accept our words with outspread hands, but if any suspicions awake in your mind consider that we have said nothing." Hearing this the father bit his tongue, and humble and awestruck put the child into their hands and gave her over to them. Then he summoned his steward and said to him: "Supply the old men with all that they need, and ask no questions." Thus he spoke, and before the light of dawn began to appear he departed as though fleeing from his daughter and his estate.

Then those others—whether they were heroes or demons or of some race still more divine—took

403

μὲν συνετέλουν αὐτὴν μυστηρίοις ἐγίνωσκεν οὐδὲ
εἷς, καὶ πρὸς τί τὴν παῖδα ἐξεθείαζον ἀφανὲς ἦν
καὶ τοῖς πάνυ βουλομένοις εἰδέναι. ὁ δὲ χρόνος
ἤδη προσῄει, καὶ τά τε ἄλλα πάντα συνέτρεχε
προσόδων πέρι[1] τοῦ χωρίου, καὶ ὁ πατὴρ τῆς
468 παιδὸς παρῆν εἰς τὸν ἀγρόν, καὶ οὔτε τὸ μέγεθος
ἐπέγνω τῆς παιδός, τό τε κάλλος ἑτεροῖον αὐτῷ
κατεφαίνετο· τὸν δὲ πατέρα σχεδόν τι καὶ ἠγνόει.
ὁ δὲ καὶ προσεκύνησεν αὐτήν, οὕτως ἄλλην τινὰ
ὁρᾶν ἔδοξεν. ὡς δὲ οἵ τε διδάσκαλοι παρῆσαν καὶ
ἡ τράπεζα προὔκειτο, οἱ μὲν ἔφασαν· "ἐρώτα ὅ
τι βούλει τὴν παρθένον." ἡ δὲ ὑπέλαβεν· "ἀλλὰ
ἐρώτησόν γε, πάτερ, τί σοι πέπρακται κατὰ τὴν
ὁδόν." τοῦ δὲ εἰπεῖν ἐπιτρέψαντος (διὰ δὲ εὐδαιμονίαν ἐπὶ τετρακύκλου ὀχήματος ἐφέρετο·
συμβαίνει δὲ πολλὰ ἐπὶ τοῖς τοιούτοις ὀχήμασι
πάθη), πάντα οὕτως ἐξήγγειλε φωνάς τε καὶ
ἀπειλὰς καὶ φόβους, ὥσπερ αὐτὴ συνηνιοχοῦσα·
καὶ εἰς τοσόνδε προῄει θαύματος ὁ πατήρ, ὥστε
οὐκ ἐθαύμαζεν, ἀλλὰ κατεπλήττετο, καὶ θεὸν
εἶναι τὴν παῖδα ἐπέπειστο. προσπεσὼν δὲ τοῖς
ἀνδράσιν, ἱκέτευεν εἰπεῖν οἵτινες εἶεν· οἱ δὲ
μόλις καὶ βραδέως (δόξαν δὲ ἴσως οὕτω καὶ θεῷ)
παρέφηναν εἶναι τῆς Χαλδαϊκῆς καλουμένης σοφίας οὐκ ἀμύητοι, καὶ τοῦτο δι' αἰνίγματος καὶ
κάτω νεύοντες. ὡς δὲ ὁ τῆς Σωσιπάτρας πατὴρ
προσπεσὼν τοῖς γόνασιν ἱκέτευε, δεσπότας εἶναι
τοῦ χωρίου παρακαλῶν, καὶ τὴν παῖδα ἔχειν ὑφ'

[1] περὶ Boissonade; πέρι Cobet.

404

charge of the child, and into what mysteries they
initiated her no one knew, and with what religious
rite they consecrated the girl was not revealed
even to those who were most eager to learn. And
now approached the appointed time when all the
accounts of the revenue of the estate were due.
The girl's father came to the farm and hardly
recognized his daughter, so tall was she and her
beauty seemed to him to have changed its character;
and she too hardly knew her father. He even
saluted her reverently, so different did she appear
to his eyes. When her teachers were there and the
table was spread, they said: "Ask the maiden whatever you please." But she interposed: "Nay, father,
ask me what happened to you on your journey."
He agreed that she should tell him. Now since he
was so wealthy he travelled in a four-wheeled
carriage, and with this sort of carriage many
accidents are liable to happen. But she related
every event, not only what had been said, but his
very threats and fears, as though she had been driving
with him. Her father was roused to such a pitch of
admiration that he did not merely admire her but
was dumb with amazement, and was convinced that
his daughter was a goddess. Then he fell on his
knees before those men and implored them to tell
him who they were. Slowly and reluctantly, for
such was perhaps the will of heaven, they revealed
to him that they were initiates in the lore called
Chaldean, and even this they told enigmatically and
with bent heads. And when Sosipatra's father clung
to their knees and supplicated them, adjuring them
to become masters of the estate and to keep his
daughter under their influence and initiate her into

ἑαυτοῖς καὶ μυεῖν εἰς τὸ τελεώτερον, οἱ μὲν ἐπινεύ-
σαντες ὅτι οὕτω ποιήσουσιν, οὐκέτι ἐφθέγξαντο·
ὁ δὲ ὥσπερ ἔχων ὑπόσχεσίν τινα ἢ χρησμόν,
ἐθάρσει καθ' ἑαυτόν, καὶ πρὸς τὸ χρῆμα ἠπόρει·
καὶ ὑπερεπήνει γε τὸν Ὅμηρον κατὰ ψυχήν, ὡς
ὑπερφυές τι χρῆμα καὶ δαιμόνιον τοῦτο ἀνυμνή-
σαντα·

   καί τε θεοὶ ξείνοισιν ἐοικότες ἀλλοδαποῖσι,
   παντοῖοι τελέθοντες, ἐπιστρωφῶσι πόληας.

καὶ γὰρ αὐτὸς ᾤετο ξένοις μὲν ἀνδράσι, θεοῖς δὲ
συντετυχηκέναι. καὶ ὁ μὲν τοῦ πράγματος ἐμ-
πιμπλάμενος ὕπνῳ κατείχετο, οἱ δὲ ἀποχωρήσαντες
τοῦ δείπνου καὶ τὴν παῖδα παραλαβόντες, τήν τε
στολὴν τῆς ἐσθῆτος ἐν ᾗ τετέλεστο μάλα φιλοφρόνως
αὐτῇ καὶ συνεσπουδασμένως παρέδοσαν, καὶ ἄλλα
τινὰ προσθέντες ὄργανα, καὶ τὴν κοιτίδα τῇ
Σωσιπάτρᾳ κατασημάνασθαι κελεύσαντες, προ-
εμβαλόντες¹ τινα βιβλίδια. καὶ ἡ μὲν ὑπερ-
εγάννυτο τοὺς ἄνδρας τοῦ πατρὸς οὐκ ἔλαττον.
ὡς δὲ ἕως ὑπέφαινε καὶ ἀνεῴγνυντο θύραι, καὶ
πρὸς ἔργα ἐχώρουν ἄνθρωποι, κἀκεῖνοι τοῖς ἄλλοις
συνεξέβησαν κατὰ τὸ εἰωθός. ἡ μὲν παῖς παρὰ
τὸν πατέρα ἔδραμεν εὐαγγέλια φέρουσα, καὶ τὴν
κοιτίδα τῶν τις θεραπευτήρων ἐκόμιζεν· ὁ δὲ
πλοῦτόν τε ὃν εἶχε ἐς τὸ παρατυχόν, καὶ παρὰ
τῶν οἰκονόμων ὅσον ἦν ἀναγκαῖον αὐτοῖς αἰτήσας,
μετεκάλει τοὺς ἄνδρας· οἱ δὲ ἐφάνησαν οὐδαμοῦ.
καὶ πρὸς τὴν Σωσιπάτραν εἶπε· "τί δὴ τοῦτό
ἐστιν, ὦ τέκνον;" ἡ δὲ ἐπισχοῦσα μικρόν, "ἀλλὰ

___
¹ καὶ προσεμβάλλοντές Boissonade ; προεμβαλόντες Cobet.

still more sacred things, they nodded their assent
to this, but spoke no word more. Then he took
courage as though he had received some sacred
promise or oracle, but could not grasp its meaning.
In his heart he applauded Homer above all poets for
having sung of such a manifestation as this, so
marvellous and divine :

> Yea, and the gods in the likeness of strangers from far
> countries put on all manner of shapes and wander
> through the cities.[1]

He did indeed believe that he had fallen in with
gods in the likeness of strangers. While his mind
was full of this he was overcome by sleep, and the
others left the table, and taking the girl with them
they very tenderly and scrupulously handed over to
her the whole array of garments in which she had
been initiated, and added certain mystic symbols
thereto ; and they also put some books into Sosipatra's chest, and gave orders that she should have
it sealed. And she, no less than her father, took
the greatest delight in those men. When the day
began to break and the doors were opened, and
people began to go to their work, the men also,
according to their custom, went forth with the rest.
Then the girl ran to her father bearing the good
news, and one of the servants went with her to carry
the chest. Her father asked for all the money
belonging to him that happened to be available, and
from his stewards all that they had for their necessary expenses, and sent to call those men, but they
were nowhere to be seen. Then he said to Sosipatra :
" What is the meaning of this, my child ? " After a
brief pause she replied : " Now at last I understand

[1] *Odyssey* xvii. 485.

νῦν γε " ἔφη " συνορῶ τὸ λεχθέν. ὡς γὰρ ταῦτα
ἐμοὶ δακρύοντες ἐνεχείριζον, σκόπει, ἔφασαν, ὦ
τέκνον· ἡμεῖς γὰρ ἐπὶ τὸν ἑσπέριον ὠκεανὸν
ἐνεχθέντες, αὐτίκα ἐπανήξομεν." τοῦτο συμ-
φανέστατα δαίμονας εἶναι τοὺς φανέντας ἀπήλεγξε.
καὶ οἱ μὲν ἀπιόντες ᾤχοντο ὁποιδήποτε καὶ
ἀπῆεσαν· ὁ δὲ πατὴρ τὴν παῖδα παραλαβὼν
469   τεθειασμένην καὶ σωφρόνως ἐνθουσιῶσαν, συνεχώρει τε ζῆν ὅπως βούλεται, καὶ περιειργάζετο
τῶν κατ' ἐκείνην οὐδέν, πλὴν ὅσα γε πρὸς τὴν
σιωπὴν αὐτῆς ἐδυσχέραινεν. ἡ δὲ προϊοῦσα εἰς
μέτρον ἀκμῆς, διδασκάλων τε ἄλλων οὐ τυχοῦσα,
τά τε τῶν ποιητῶν βιβλία διὰ στόματος εἶχε καὶ
φιλοσόφων καὶ ῥητόρων, καὶ ὅσα γε τοῖς πεπο-
νηκόσι καὶ τεταλαιπωρημένοις μόλις ὑπῆρχε καὶ
ἀμυδρῶς εἰδέναι, ταῦτα ἐκείνη μετ' ὀλιγωρίας
ἔφραζεν, εὐκόλως καὶ ἀλύπως εἰς τὸ σαφὲς ἐπιτρέ-
χουσα. ἔδοξε γοῦν αὐτῇ καὶ ἀνδρὶ συνελθεῖν.
καὶ ἀναμφίλεκτον ἦν ὅτι ἐξ ἁπάντων ἀνδρῶν
μόνος Εὐστάθιος ἄξιος ἦν τοῦ γάμου. ἡ δὲ πρὸς
Εὐστάθιον καὶ τοὺς παρόντας εἰποῦσα· "ἀλλ'
ἄκουε μὲν σύ,[1] Εὐστάθιε, συμμαρτυρούντων δὲ οἱ
παρόντες. παῖδας μὲν ὑπὸ σοὶ τέξομαι τρεῖς,
πάντες δὲ τὸ ἀνθρώπινον δοκοῦν ἀγαθὸν ἀτυχήσουσι,
πρὸς τὸ θεῖον δὲ οὐδὲ[2] εἷς. καὶ σὺ δὲ προαπο-
λείψεις ἐμέ, καλὴν μεταλαχὼν λῆξιν καὶ πρέπουσαν,
ἐγὼ δὲ ἴσως κρείσσονα. σοὶ μὲν γὰρ περὶ σελήνην
ἡ χορεία, καὶ οὐκέτι λατρεύσεις καὶ φιλοσοφήσεις

---

[1] σύ Cobet adds.
[2] Giangrande deletes, putting οὐδὲν after ἀγαθόν.

[1] Homer's ζόφος, "darkness of the West," has always
been regarded as consecrated to the heroic dead and to
supernatural powers.

what they said. For when they wept and put these things into my hands, they said: ' Child, take care of them; for we are travelling to the Western Ocean,[1] but presently we shall return.' " This proved very clearly that they who had appeared were blessed spirits. They then departed and went whithersoever it was; but her father took charge of the girl, now fully initiated, and though without pride, filled with divine breath, and he permitted her to live as she pleased and did not interfere in any of her affairs, except that sometimes he was ill pleased with her silence. And as she grew to the full measure of her youthful vigour, she had no other teachers, but ever on her lips were the works of the poets, philosophers, and orators; and those works that others comprehend but incompletely and dimly, and then only by hard work and painful drudgery, she could expound with careless ease, serenely and painlessly, and with her light swift touch would make their meaning clear. Then she decided to marry. Now beyond dispute Eustathius of all living men was alone worthy to wed her. So she said to him and to those who were present: " Do you listen to me, Eustathius, and let those who are here bear me witness: I shall bear you three children, and all of them will fail to win what is considered to be human happiness, but as to the happiness that the gods bestow, not one of them will fail therein. But you will go hence before me, and be allotted a fair and fitting place of abode, though I perhaps shall attain to one even higher. For your station will be in the orbit of the moon,[2] and only five years longer will you devote your

[2] The moon was the home of good daemons, heroes, and so on. But Sosipatra will attain as high as the sun.

τὸ πέμπτον, οὕτω γάρ μοί φησι τὸ σὸν εἴδωλον,
ἀλλὰ καὶ τὸν ὑπὸ σελήνην παρελεύσῃ τόπον σὺν
ἀγαθῇ καὶ εὐηνίῳ φορᾷ· ἐγὼ δὲ καὶ ἐβουλόμην
μὲν εἰπεῖν τὰ κατ' ἐμαυτήν," εἶτα ἐπισιωπήσασα [1]
τῷ λόγῳ βραχύν τινα χρόνον, "ἀλλ' ὁ ἐμός,"
ἀνεφθέγξατο, "θεός με κωλύει." ταῦτα εἰποῦσα,
Μοῖραι γὰρ οὕτως ἔνευον, τῷ τε Εὐσταθίῳ
συνῆλθε, καὶ τὰ λεχθέντα οὐδὲν διέφερε τῶν
ἀκινήτων μαντειῶν, οὕτω πανταχόσε ἐγένετο καὶ
ἀπέβη καθάπερ ἦν εἰρημένα.[2]

Προσιστορῆσαι δὲ τοῖς γεγενημένοις τάδε ἀναγκαίως εἴη· Σωσιπάτρα, μετὰ τὴν ἀποχώρησιν
Εὐσταθίου, πρὸς τὰ αὑτῆς ἐπανελθοῦσα κτήματα,
περὶ τὴν Ἀσίαν καὶ τὸ παλαιὸν Πέργαμον διέτριβε·
καὶ ὁ μέγας Αἰδέσιος θεραπεύων αὐτὴν ἠγάπα,
καὶ τοὺς παῖδας ἐξεπαίδευε. καὶ ἀντεκάθητό
γε αὐτῷ φιλοσοφοῦσα κατὰ τὴν ἑαυτῆς οἰκίαν ἡ
Σωσιπάτρα, καί, μετὰ τὴν Αἰδεσίου συνουσίαν,
παρ' ἐκείνην φοιτῶντες, οὐκ ἔστιν ὅστις τὴν μὲν
ἐν λόγοις ἀκρίβειαν Αἰδεσίου οὐ ὑπερηγάπα [3] καὶ
συνεθαύμαζε, τὸν δὲ τῆς γυναικὸς ἐνθουσιασμὸν
προσεκύνει καὶ ἐσεβάζετο.

Φιλομήτωρ γοῦν τις αὐτῆς ἀνεψιὸς ὤν, τοῦ
τε κάλλους ἡττηθεὶς καὶ τῶν λόγων, εἰς ἔρωτα
ἀφίκετο, καὶ τὴν γυναῖκα εἰδὼς θειοτέραν· ἔρως
δὲ καὶ συνηνάγκαζε καὶ κατεβιάζετο. καὶ ὁ
μὲν ἀμφὶ ταῦτα ἦν πολύς, καὶ ἡ γυνὴ συν-
ησθάνετο τῆς πείρας· καὶ πρὸς τὸν Μάξιμον,
οὗτος δὲ ἀνὰ τὰ πρῶτα τῆς ὁμιλίας ἐφέρετο
τοῦ Αἰδεσίου, καὶ οὐδὲ συγγενείας κεχώριστο·
"ἀλλὰ κατάμαθέ γε, ὦ Μάξιμε, ἵνα μὴ πράγ-

---

[1] ἐπισκοπήσασα Boissonade; ἐπισιωπήσασα Cobet.

services to philosophy—for so your phantom tells me—but you shall traverse the region below the moon with a blessed and easily guided motion. Fain would I tell you my own fate also." Then after keeping silence for a short time, she cried aloud: "No, my god prevents me!" Immediately after this prophecy—for such was the will of the Fates—she married Eustathius, and her words had the same force as an immutable oracle, so absolutely did it come to pass and transpire as had been foretold by her.

I must relate also what happened after these events. After the passing of Eustathius, Sosipatra returned to her own estate, and dwelt in Asia in the ancient city of Pergamon, and the famous Aedesius loved and cared for her and educated her sons. In her own home Sosipatra held a chair of philosophy that rivalled his, and after attending the lectures of Aedesius, the students would go to hear hers; and though there was none that did not greatly appreciate and admire the accurate learning of Aedesius, they positively adored and revered the woman's inspired teaching.

Now there was one Philometor, a kinsman of hers, who, overcome by her beauty and eloquence, and recognizing the divinity of her nature, fell in love with her; and his passion possessed him and completely overmastered him. Not only was he completely conquered by it but he also felt its onslaught. So she said to Maximus, who was one of the most distinguished pupils of Aedesius and was moreover his kinsman: "Maximus, pray find out

---

² γεγενημένα Boissonade; ἦν εἰρημένα Cobet.
³ περιηγάπα Boissonade; ὑπερηγάπα Cobet.

ματα ἐγὼ ἔχω, τί τὸ περὶ ἐμὲ πάθος ἐστί."
τοῦ δὲ ὑπολαβόντος· "τί γάρ ἐστι τὸ πάθος;"
"ἂν μὲν παρῇ Φιλομήτωρ," ἔφη πρὸς αὐτόν
"Φιλομήτωρ γέ ἐστι, καὶ διαφέρει τῶν πολλῶν
οὐδὲ ἕν· ἂν δὲ ἀποχωροῦντα θεάσωμαι, δά-
κνεταί μου καὶ στρέφεταί πως πρὸς τὴν ἔξοδον
ἔνδον ἡ καρδία. ἀλλ' ὅπως ἀθλήσῃς περὶ ἐμοὶ
καὶ θεοφιλὲς ἐπιδείξῃ τι," προσέθηκεν. καὶ ὁ
470 μὲν Μάξιμος ἐξῄει τοιαῦτα ἀκηκοώς, ὑπέρογκος
ὤν, ὡς ἂν ἤδη τοῖς θεοῖς ὁμιλῶν, ὅτι ὑπὸ[1] τοσαύτης
γυναικὸς τοιαῦτα ἐπεπίστευτο. Φιλομήτωρ δὲ
τοῖς προτεθεῖσιν ἐνέκειτο. Μάξιμος δὲ ἀντεν-
έκειτο, διὰ σοφίας μὲν θυτικῆς καταμαθὼν ᾧτινι
κέχρηται, βιαιοτέρῳ τε καὶ δυνατωτέρῳ καταλῦσαι
τὸ ἔλαττον. καὶ ὁ μὲν ταῦτα συντελέσας ὁ Μάξιμος ἔδραμε παρὰ τὴν Σωσιπάτραν, καὶ παρα-
φυλάττειν ἠξίου μάλα ἀκριβῶς, εἰ τὸ αὐτὸ τοῦ
λοιποῦ πείσεται· ἡ δὲ οὐκέτι πάσχειν ἔφη, καὶ
τήν γε εὐχὴν ἀπήγγειλε τῷ Μαξίμῳ καὶ τὴν
ἅπασαν πρᾶξιν, καὶ τήν γε ὥραν προσέθηκεν,
ὥσπερ συμπαροῦσα, καθ' ἣν ταῦτα ἔπραττεν,
καὶ τὰ φανέντα ἀνεκάλυψε σημεῖα. τοῦ δὲ πεσόν-
τος ἐπὶ τὴν γῆν ἀχανοῦς, καὶ θεὰν ἄντικρυς εἶναι
τὴν Σωσιπάτραν ὁμολογοῦντος, "ἀνίστω" φησίν
"ὦ τέκνον· θεοί σε φιλοῦσιν, ἐὰν σὺ πρὸς ἐκείνους
βλέπῃς καὶ μὴ ῥέπῃς ἐπὶ τὰ γήϊνα καὶ ἐπίκηρα
χρήματα." καὶ ὁ μὲν ταῦτα ἀκούσας, ἐξῄει
μεγαλαυχότερος γεγονώς, ὡς[2] καὶ τῆς κατὰ τὴν
γυναῖκα θειότητός γε ἀσφαλῶς πεπειραμένος.
ὁ δὲ Φιλομήτωρ φαιδρὸς ἀπήντα περὶ θύρας αὐτῷ

---

[1] Before ὑπὸ Cobet deletes καί.
[2] ὡς Wyttenbach adds.

what ailment I have, that I may not be troubled by it." When he inquired: "Why what ails you?" she replied: "When Philometor is with me he is simply Philometor, and in no way different from the crowd. But when I see that he is going away my heart within me is wounded and tortured till it tries to escape from my breast. Do you exert yourself on my behalf," she added, "and so display your piety." When he had heard this, Maximus went away puffed up with pride as though he were now associating with the gods, because so wonderful a woman had put such faith in him. Meanwhile Philometor pursued his purpose, but Maximus having discovered by his sacrificial lore what was the power that Philometor possessed, strove to counteract and nullify the weaker spell by one more potent and efficacious. When Maximus had completed this rite he hastened to Sosipatra, and bade her observe carefully whether she had the same sensations in future. But she replied that she no longer felt them, and described to Maximus his own prayer and the whole ceremony; she also told him the hour at which it took place, as though she had been present, and revealed to him the omens that had appeared. And when he fell to the earth in amazement and proclaimed Sosipatra visibly a goddess, she said: "Rise, my son. The gods love you if you raise your eyes to them and do not lean towards earthly and perishable riches." On hearing this he went away more uplifted than before with pride, seeing that he now had clear and certain proof of the woman's divine nature. Near the door he was met by Philometor who was coming in in

μετὰ πολλῶν ἑταίρων εἰσιών· ὁ δὲ πόρρωθεν
μέγα φθεγξάμενος εἶπεν ὁ Μάξιμος· "τοὺς θεούς
σοι, Φιλομήτωρ" εἶπεν "ἑταῖρε, παῦσαι μάτην
κατακαίων τὰ ξύλα." ἐνεωρακώς[1] τι τοιοῦτον
ἴσως αὐτῷ περὶ ἃ κακουργῶν ἔπραττε. καὶ ὁ
μὲν τὸν Μάξιμον ὑπερευλαβηθεὶς θεὸν ᾠήθη,
καὶ τῆς γε ἐπιβουλῆς ἐπαύσατο, καταγελάσας
τῆς προθέσεως ὅ τι καὶ ἐνεχείρησεν· ἡ δὲ Σωσιπάτρα γνησίως καὶ διαφερόντως ἑώρα τοῦ λοιποῦ
τὸν Φιλομήτορα, θαυμάζουσα αὐτὸν ὅτι αὐτὴν
ἐθαύμασε. ποτὲ γοῦν συνεληλυθότων ἁπάντων παρ'
αὐτῇ Φιλομήτωρ δὲ οὐ παρῆν, ἀλλ' ἐν ἀγρῷ
διέτριβεν, ἡ μὲν πρόθεσις ἦν καὶ τὸ ζήτημα περὶ
ψυχῆς· πολλῶν δὲ κινουμένων λόγων, ὡς ἤρξατο
Σωσιπάτρα λέγειν, κατὰ μικρὸν ταῖς ἀποδείξεσι
διαλύουσα τὰ προβαλλόμενα, εἶτα εἰς τὸν περὶ
καθόδου ψυχῆς καὶ τί τὸ κολαζόμενον καὶ τί τὸ
ἀθάνατον αὐτῆς ἐμπίπτουσα λόγον, μεταξὺ τοῦ
κορυβαντιασμοῦ καὶ τῆς ἐκβακχεύσεως, ὥσπερ
ἀποκοπεῖσα τὴν φωνήν, ἐσιώπησε, καὶ βραχὺν
ἐλλιποῦσα χρόνον, "τί τοῦτο;" ἀνεβόησεν εἰς
μέσους· "ὁ συγγενὴς Φιλομήτωρ φερόμενος ἐπ'
ὀχήματος, τό τε ὄχημα κατά τινα δυσχωρίαν
περιτέτραπται, κἀκεῖνος κινδυνεύει περὶ τὼ σκέλη·
ἀλλ' ἐξῃρήκασί γε αὐτὸν οἱ θεράποντες ὑγιαίνοντα,
πλὴν ὅσα περὶ τοῖς ἀγκῶσι καὶ χερσὶ τραύματα
εἴληφε, καὶ ταῦτά γε ἀκίνδυνα· ἐπὶ φορείου δὲ
φέρεται ποτνιώμενος." ταῦτα ἔλεγε καὶ εἶχεν
οὕτως, καὶ πάντες ᾔδεσαν ὅτι πανταχοῦ εἴη

ἐνεωρακώς Vollebregt: συνεωρακώς

high spirits with many of his friends, and with a loud
voice Maximus called out to him from some distance ·
" Friend Philometor, I adjure you in Heaven's name,
cease to burn wood to no purpose." Perhaps he
said this with some inner knowledge of the mal-
practices in which the other was engaged. Thereupon Philometor was overawed by Maximus, believed
him to be divine, and ceased his plotting, even
ridiculing the course of action that he had entered
on before. And for the future Sosipatra beheld
Philometor with pure and changed eyes, though
she admired him for so greatly admiring herself.
Once, for example, when they were all met at her
house—Philometor however was not present but was
staying in the country—the theme under discussion
and their inquiry was concerning the soul. Several
theories were propounded, and then Sosipatra began
to speak, and gradually by her proofs disposed of their
arguments; then she fell to discoursing on the
descent of the soul, and what part of it is subject to
punishment, what part immortal, when in the midst
of her bacchic and frenzied flow of speech she
became silent, as though her voice had been cut off,
and after letting a short interval pass she cried aloud
in their midst : " What is this ? Behold my kinsman
Philometor riding in a carriage ! The carriage has
been overturned in a rough place in the road and both
his legs are in danger ! However, his servants have
dragged him out unharmed, except that he has
received wounds on his elbows and hands, though
even these are not dangerous. He is being carried
home on a stretcher, groaning loudly." These were
her words, and they were the truth, for so it actually
was. By this all were convinced that Sosipatra was

Σωσιπάτρα, καὶ πᾶσι πάρεστι τοῖς γινομένοις,
ὥσπερ οἱ φιλόσοφοι περὶ τῶν θεῶν λέγουσι. καὶ
ἐτελεύτα δὲ ἐπὶ τοῖς τρισὶ παισί. καὶ τῶν μὲν
δύο τὰ ὀνόματα οὐδὲν δέομαι γράφειν. 'Αντωνῖνος
δὲ ἦν ἄξιος τῶν πατέρων, ὅς γε τὸ Κανωβικὸν τοῦ
Νείλου καταλαβὼν στόμα, καὶ τοῖς ἐκεῖ τελου-
μένοις προσθεὶς ὅλον ἑαυτόν, τήν τε ἀπὸ τῆς
μητρὸς πρόρρησιν ἐξεβιάζετο. καὶ ἡ νεότης τῶν
ὑγιαινόντων τὰς ψυχὰς καὶ φιλοσοφίας ἐπιθυμούν-
471 των ἐφοίτων πρὸς αὐτόν, καὶ τὸ ἱερὸν νεανίσκων
ἱερέων μεστὸν ἦν. αὐτὸς μὲν οὖν ἔτι ἄνθρωπος
εἶναι δοκῶν καὶ ἀνθρώποις ὁμιλῶν, πᾶσι τοῖς
ὁμιληταῖς προύλεγεν, ὡς μετ' ἐκεῖνον οὐκ ἔτι τὸ
ἱερὸν ἔσοιτο, ἀλλὰ καὶ τὰ μεγάλα καὶ ἅγια τοῦ
Σαράπιδος ἱερὰ πρὸς τὸ σκοτοειδὲς καὶ ἄμορφον
χωρήσει καὶ μεταβληθήσεται, καί τι μυθῶδες καὶ
ἀειδὲς σκότος τυραννήσει τὰ ἐπὶ γῆς κάλλιστα.
ὁ δὲ χρόνος ἀπήλεγξεν ἅπαντα, καὶ τὸ πρᾶγμά γε
εἰς χρησμοῦ συνετελέσθη βίαν.

Τούτου δὲ τοῦ γένους, οὐ γὰρ τὰς 'Ησιόδου
καλουμένας 'Ηοίας ἔσπευδον γράφειν, ἀπόρροιαί
τινες, ὥσπερ ἀστέρων περιελείφθησαν, καὶ εἰς
φιλοσοφούντων ἕτερα ἄττα γένη διεσπάρησαν καὶ
κατενεμήθησαν, οἷς τοῦ φιλοσοφεῖν ἡ συγγένεια
κέρδος ἦν. τὰ πλεῖστα δὲ ἐν δικαστηρίοις, ὥσπερ
ὁ Σωκράτης περὶ τὴν τοῦ βασιλέως στοάν, ἐκιν-
δύνευον· οὕτω περιεφρόνησαν χρήματα καὶ κατε-
στύγησαν χρυσίον. ἦν γοῦν αὐτοῖς φιλοσοφία, τὸ

---

[1] Antoninus died about 390; the Serapeum was destroyed
in 391.

[2] A lost poem in which each theme began with ἢ οἵη " Or
ike such a woman as. " In the plural ἢ οἵη becomes ἢ οἷαι.

[3] Plato, *Euthyphro init.* Socrates, charged with impiety.

omnipresent, and that, even as the philosophers assert concerning the gods, nothing happened without her being there to see. She died leaving the three sons of whom she had spoken. The names of two of them I need not record. But Antoninus was worthy of his parents, for he settled at the Canobic mouth of the Nile and devoted himself wholly to the religious rites of that place, and strove with all his powers to fulfil his mother's prophecy. To him resorted all the youth whose souls were sane and sound, and who hungered for philosophy, and the temple was filled with young men acting as priests. Though he himself still appeared to be human and he associated with human beings, he foretold to all his followers that after his death [1] the temple would cease to be, and even the great and holy temples of Serapis would pass into formless darkness and be transformed, and that a fabulous and unseemly gloom would hold sway over the fairest things on earth. To all these prophecies time bore witness, and in the end his prediction gained the force of an oracle.

From this family—for it is not my purpose to write an *Eoiae*,[2] as Hesiod's poem is called—there survived certain effluences as though from the stars, and these were dispersed and distributed among various classes of professed philosophers who made a profit out of their affinity with genuine philosophy, and they spent most of their time running risks in the law courts, like Socrates in the porch of the King Archon.[3] Such was their contempt for money and their detestation of gold! In fact their philosophy consisted in wearing the philosopher's cloak

is found in the porch of the archon who investigated such charges ; these sham philosophers frequented the courts whereas Socrates, as a rule, avoided them.

τριβώνιον καὶ τὸ μεμνῆσθαι τῆς Σωσιπάτρας,
καὶ τὸν Εὐστάθιον διὰ στόματος φέρειν, τὰ δὲ ἐν
τοῖς ὁρωμένοις σακκία τε ἁδρὰ καὶ ὑπόμεστα
βιβλιδίων, καὶ ταῦτα ὡς ἂν ἄχθος εἶναι καμήλων
πολλῶν. καὶ ἐξηπίσταντό γε πάνυ ἀκριβῶς τὰ
βιβλία· καὶ ταῦτά γε ἦν εἰς οὐδένα φέροντα τῶν
παλαιῶν φιλοσόφων, ἀλλὰ διαθῆκαί τε καὶ ἀντί-
γραφα τούτων, καὶ συμβόλαια περὶ¹ πράσεων,
καὶ ὅσα ὁ κακοδαίμων καὶ ὁ πρὸς τὴν πλανωμένην
καὶ ἄτακτον ἄτην ἐπικλίνων βίος ἐπαινεῖν εἴωθεν.
οὕτως οὐδὲ ἐν τοῖς μετὰ ταῦτα Σωσιπάτρα ἐς
τὸν χρησμὸν ἀπετύγχανε, καὶ τούτων γε τὰ
ὀνόματα οὐδὲν δέομαι γράφειν· ὁ γὰρ λόγος οὐκ
ἐπὶ τοὺς φαύλους ἀλλ' ἐπὶ τοὺς ἀγαθοὺς φέρειν
συνεπείγεται. πλὴν ὅσα εἰς αὐτῆς τῶν παίδων
('Αντωνῖνος ὄνομα ἦν αὐτῷ, οὗ καὶ πρὸ βραχέος
ἐπεμνήσθην, ὁ διαβαλὼν ἐς τὴν 'Αλεξάνδρειαν,
εἶτα τὸ Κανωβικὸν θαυμάσας τε καὶ ὑπεραγα-
σθεὶς τοῦ Νείλου στόμα, καὶ τοῖς ἐκείνῃ θεοῖς τε
καὶ ἀρρήτοις ἱεροῖς ἀναθεὶς καὶ προσαρμόσας
ἑαυτόν) ταχὺ μάλα πρὸς τὴν τοῦ θείου συγγένειαν
ἐπέδωκε, σώματός τε περιφρονήσας καὶ τῶν
περὶ τοῦτο ἡδονῶν ἀπολυθείς, σοφίαν τε ἄγνωστον
τοῖς πολλοῖς ἐπιτηδεύσας· περὶ οὗ προσῆκε καὶ
διὰ μακροτέρων εἰπεῖν. ἐπεδείκνυτο μὲν γὰρ
οὐδὲν θεουργὸν καὶ παράλογον ἐς τὴν φαινομένην
αἴσθησιν, τὰς βασιλικὰς ἴσως ὁρμὰς ὑφορώμενος
ἑτέρωσε φερούσας· τοῦ δὲ τὴν καρτερίαν καὶ τὸ
ἄκαμπτον καὶ ἀμετάστατον ἐθαύμαζον ἅπαντες.
καὶ κατῄεσάν γε παρ' αὐτὸν ἐπὶ θάλασσαν οἱ

___

¹ Before περὶ Wyttenbach deletes , καὶ.

and constantly alluding to Sosipatra, while Eustathius was ever on their lips; moreover they carried other obvious and external signs, big wallets so crammed with books that they would have laden several camels. They had learned these very carefully by heart. And these books of theirs anyhow bore upon none of the ancient philosophers, but were wills and copies of wills, contracts of sales and suchlike documents, which are highly esteemed in that life which is prone to dissolute folly and licence. Thus it proved that Sosipatra could also divine correctly what should happen after these events. But I need not write down even the names of these men, for my narrative is eager to lead on to those that are not unworthy but worthy. An exception must be made of one of her sons; his name was Antoninus, and I mentioned him just now; he crossed to Alexandria, and then so greatly admired and preferred the mouth of the Nile at Canobus, that he wholly dedicated and applied himself to the worship of the gods there, and to their secret rites. He made rapid progress towards affinity with the divine, despised his body, freed himself from its pleasures, and embraced a wisdom that was hidden from the crowd. On this matter I may well speak at greater length. He displayed no tendency to theurgy and that which is at variance with sensible appearances, perhaps because he kept a wary eye on the imperial views and policy which were opposed to these practices.[1] But all admired his fortitude and his unswerving and inflexible character, and those who were then pursuing their studies at

[1] For the wholesale persecution of those suspected of sorcery see Ammianus xxviii. 1.

κατὰ τὴν Ἀλεξάνδρειαν τότε σχολάζοντες, ἡ δὲ
Ἀλεξάνδρεια διά γε τὸ τοῦ Σαράπιδος ἱερὸν ἱερά
τις ἦν οἰκουμένη· οἱ γοῦν πανταχόθεν φοιτῶντες
ἐς αὐτὴν πλῆθός τε ἦσαν τῷ δήμῳ παρισούμενοι,
καί, μετὰ τὰς θεραπείας τοῦ θείου, παρὰ τὸν
Ἀντωνῖνον ἔτρεχον, οἱ μὲν διὰ γῆς, ὅσοι γε
ἔτρεχον, τοῖς δὲ ἐξῆρκει τὰ ποτάμια πλοῖα, μετὰ
ῥᾳστώνης ἐπὶ τὴν σπουδὴν ὑποφέροντες. συνουσίας δὲ ἀξιωθέντες, οἱ μὲν λογικὸν πρόβλημα
προθέμενοι, ἀφθόνως καὶ αὐθωρὸν τῆς Πλατωνικῆς
472 ἐνεφοροῦντο σοφίας, οἱ δὲ τῶν θειοτέρων τι
προβάλλοντες, ἀνδριάντι συνετύγχανον· οὐκοῦν
ἐφθέγγετο πρὸς αὐτῶν οὐδένα, ἀλλὰ τὰ ὄμματα
στήσας καὶ διαθρήσας εἰς τὸν οὐρανόν, ἄναυδος
ἔκειτο καὶ ἄτεγκτος, οὐδέ τις εἶδεν αὐτὸν περὶ τῶν
τοιούτων ῥᾳδίως εἰς ὁμιλίαν ἐλθόντα ἀνθρώπων.

Ὅτι δὲ ἦν τι θειότερον τὸ κατ' αὐτόν, οὐκ εἰς
μακρὰν ἀπεσημάνθη· οὐ γὰρ ἔφθανεν ἐκεῖνος ἐξ
ἀνθρώπων ἀπιών, καὶ ἥ τε θεραπεία τῶν κατὰ
τὴν Ἀλεξάνδρειαν καὶ τὸ Σαραπεῖον ἱερῶν[1] δι-
εσκεδάννυτο· οὐχ ἡ θεραπεία μόνον, ἀλλὰ καὶ τὰ
οἰκοδομήματα, καὶ πάντα ἐγίνετο καθάπερ ἐν
ποιητικοῖς μύθοις, τῶν Γιγάντων κεκρατηκότων.
καὶ τὰ περὶ τὸν Κάνωβον ἱερὰ ταὐτὸ τοῦτο ἔπασχον,
Θεοδοσίου μὲν τότε βασιλεύοντος, Θεοφίλου δὲ
προστατοῦντος τῶν ἐναγῶν, ἀνθρώπου τινὸς
Εὐρυμέδοντος

ὅς ποθ' ὑπερθύμοισι Γιγάντεσσιν βασίλευεν,

---

[1] ἱερὸν Boissonade; ἱερῶν Wyttenbach.

---

[1] Theophilus was the Christian bishop of Alexandria; cf.
Zosimus v. 28; Theodoret v. 22.

Alexandria used to go down to him to the seashore. For, on account of its temple of Serapis, Alexandria was a world in itself, a world consecrated by religion : at any rate those who resorted to it from all parts were a multitude equal in number to its own citizens, and these, after they had worshipped the god, used to hasten to Antoninus, some, who were in haste, by land, while others were content with boats that plied on the river, gliding in a leisurely way to their studies. On being granted an interview with him, some would propound a logical problem, and were forthwith abundantly fed with the philosophy of Plato ; but others, who raised questions as to things divine, encountered a statue. For he would utter not a word to any one of them, but fixing his eyes and gazing up at the sky he would lie there speechless and unrelenting, nor did anyone ever see him lightly enter into converse with any man on such themes as these.

Now, not long after, an unmistakable sign was given that there was in him some diviner element. For no sooner had he left the world of men than the cult of the temples in Alexandria and at the shrine of Serapis was scattered to the winds, and not only the ceremonies of the cult but the buildings as well, and everything happened as in the myths of the poets when the Giants gained the upper hand. The temples at Canobus also suffered the same fate in the reign of Theodosius, when Theophilus[1] presided over the abominable ones like a sort of Eurymedon

Who ruled over the proud Giants,[2]

[2] *Odyssey* vii. 59.

421

Εὐαγρίου[1] δὲ τὴν πολιτικὴν ἀρχὴν ἄρχοντος, Ῥωμανοῦ δὲ τοὺς κατ' Αἴγυπτον στρατιώτας πεπιστευμένου· οἵτινες, ἅμα φραξάμενοι κατὰ τῶν ἱερῶν καθάπερ κατὰ λίθων καὶ λιθοξόων θυμόν, ἐπὶ ταῦτα ἀλλόμενοι, πολέμου δὲ μήτε ἀκοὴν ὑφιστάμενοι, τῷ τε Σαραπείῳ κατελυμήναντο καὶ τοῖς ἀναθήμασιν ἐπολέμησαν, ἀνανταγώνιστον καὶ ἄμαχον νίκην νικήσαντες. τοῖς γοῦν ἀνδριάσι καὶ ἀναθήμασιν ἐς τοσόνδε γενναίως ἐμαχέσαντο, ὥστε οὐ μόνον ἐνίκων αὐτά, ἀλλὰ καὶ ἔκλεπτον, καὶ τάξις ἦν αὐτοῖς πολεμικὴ τὸν ὑφελόμενον λαθεῖν. τοῦ δὲ Σαραπείου μόνον τὸ ἔδαφος οὐχ ὑφείλοντο διὰ βάρος τῶν λίθων, οὐ γὰρ ἦσαν εὐμετακίνητοι· συγχέαντες δὲ ἅπαντα καὶ ταράξαντες, οἱ πολεμικώτατοι καὶ γενναῖοι, καὶ τὰς χεῖρας ἀναιμάκτους μέν, οὐκ ἀφιλοχρημάτους δὲ προτείναντες, τούς τε θεοὺς ἔφασαν νενικηκέναι, καὶ τὴν ἱεροσυλίαν καὶ τὴν ἀσέβειαν εἰς ἔπαινον σφῶν αὐτῶν κατελογίζοντο.

Εἶτα ἐπεισῆγον τοῖς ἱεροῖς τόποις τοὺς καλουμένους μοναχούς, ἀνθρώπους μὲν κατὰ τὸ εἶδος, ὁ δὲ βίος αὐτοῖς συώδης, καὶ ἐς τὸ ἐμφανὲς ἔπασχόν τε καὶ ἐποίουν μυρία κακὰ καὶ ἄφραστα. ἀλλ' ὅμως τοῦτο μὲν εὐσεβὲς ἐδόκει, τὸ καταφρονεῖν τοῦ θείου· τυραννικὴν γὰρ εἶχεν ἐξουσίαν τότε πᾶς ἄνθρωπος μέλαιναν φορῶν ἐσθῆτα, καὶ δημοσίᾳ βουλόμενος ἀσχημονεῖν· ἐς τοσόνδε ἀρετῆς ἤλασε τὸ ἀνθρώπινον. ἀλλὰ περὶ τούτων μὲν καὶ ἐν τοῖς καθολικοῖς τῆς ἱστορίας συγγράμ-

---

[1] Εὐετίου *Laurentianus*, Boissonade ; Εὐαγρίου restored by Seeck, *Die Briefe des Libanius*, p. 130.

and Evagrius was prefect of the city, and Romanus in command of the legions in Egypt.[1] For these men, girding themselves in their wrath against our sacred places as though against stones and stone-masons, made a raid on the temples, and though they could not allege even a rumour of war to justify them, they demolished the temple of Serapis and made war against the temple offerings, whereby they won a victory without meeting a foe or fighting a battle. In this fashion they fought so honourably against the statues and votive offerings that they not only conquered but stole them as well, and their only military tactics were to ensure that the thief should escape detection. Only the floor of the temple of Serapis they did not take, simply because of the weight of the stones which were not easy to move from their place. Then these warlike and honourable men, after they had thrown everything into confusion and disorder and had thrust out hands, unstained indeed by blood but not pure from greed, boasted that they had overcome the gods, and reckoned their sacrilege and impiety a thing to glory in.

Next, into the sacred places they imported monks, as they called them, who were men in appearance but led the lives of swine, and openly did and allowed countless unspeakable crimes. But this they accounted piety, to show contempt for things divine. For in those days every man who wore a black robe and consented to behave in unseemly fashion in public,[2] possessed the power of a tyrant, to such a pitch of virtue had the human race advanced! All this however I have described in my *Universal*

---

[1] Sozomenus vii. 15 gives the Christian account of the conversion of the Serapeum into a church.

[2] *Cf.* Libanius, *On the Temples*, 474.

μασιν εἴρηται. τοὺς δὲ μοναχοὺς τούτους καὶ
εἰς τὸν Κάνωβον καθίδρυσαν, ἀντὶ τῶν ὄντων[1]
θεῶν εἰς ἀνδραπόδων θεραπείας, καὶ οὐδὲ χρηστῶν,
καταδήσαντες τὸ ἀνθρώπινον. ὀστέα γὰρ καὶ
κεφαλὰς τῶν ἐπὶ πολλοῖς ἁμαρτήμασιν ἑαλω-
κότων συναλίζοντες, οὓς τὸ πολιτικὸν ἐκόλαζε
δικαστήριον, θεούς τε ἀπεδείκνυσαν, καὶ προσ-
εκαλινδοῦντο τοῖς μνήμασι,[2] καὶ κρείττους ὑπελάμ-
βανον εἶναι μολυνόμενοι πρὸς τοῖς τάφοις. μάρ-
τυρες γοῦν ἐκαλοῦντο καὶ διάκονοί τινες καὶ πρέ-
σβεις τῶν αἰτήσεων παρὰ τῶν θεῶν, ἀνδράποδα
δεδουλευκότα κακῶς, καὶ μάστιξι καταδεδαπανη-
μένα, καὶ τὰς τῆς μοχθηρίας ὠτειλὰς ἐν τοῖς
εἰδώλοις φέροντα· ἀλλ' ὅμως ἡ γῆ φέρει τούτους
τοὺς θεούς. τοῦτο γοῦν εἰς μεγάλην πρόνοιαν καὶ
473 Ἀντωνίνου συνετέλεσεν, ὅτι πρὸς ἅπαντας ἔφασκεν
τὰ ἱερὰ τάφους γενήσεσθαι· ὥσπερ που καὶ
Ἰάμβλιχος ὁ μέγας (ὅπερ ἐν τοῖς κατ' ἐκεῖνον
παραλελοίπαμεν), ἀνδρός τινος Αἰγυπτίου τὸν
Ἀπόλλω καλέσαντος, τοῦ δὲ ἐλθόντος, καὶ καταπλαγέντων τὴν ὄψιν τῶν παρόντων, "παύσασθε,"
ἔφη " ἑταῖροι, θαυμάζοντες· μονομαχήσαντος γὰρ
ἀνδρός ἐστιν εἴδωλον·" οὕτως ἕτερόν τί ἐστι τῷ
νῷ θεωρεῖν καὶ τοῖς τοῦ σώματος ἀπατηλοῖς
ὄμμασιν. ἀλλ' Ἰάμβλιχος μὲν τὰ παρόντα δεινὰ
εἶδεν,[3] Ἀντωνῖνος δὲ τὰ μέλλοντα προεῖδε· καὶ
τοῦτό γε αὐτοῦ μόνον εὐσθένειαν φέρει. ἄλυπον
δὲ αὐτῷ τὸ τέλος εἰς γῆρας ἄνοσον ἀφικομένῳ[4]

[1] νοητῶν Boissonade ; ὄντων Cobet.
[2] For a lacuna of about six letters Boissonade supplies
μνήμασι ; Lundström approves Jordan's ὀστεοῖς.
[3] εἶδεν Cobet adds.
[4] ἀφικόμενον Boissonade ; ἀφικομένῳ Wyttenbach.

History. They settled these monks at Canobus also, and thus they fettered the human race to the worship of slaves, and those not even honest slaves, instead of the true gods. For they collected the bones and skulls of criminals who had been put to death for numerous crimes, men whom the law courts of the city had condemned to punishment, made them out to be gods, haunted their sepulchres,[1] and thought that they became better by defiling themselves at their graves. "Martyrs" the dead men were called, and "ministers" of a sort, and "ambassadors" from the gods to carry men's prayers,—these slaves in vilest servitude, who had been consumed by stripes and carried on their phantom forms the scars of their villainy.[2] However these are the gods that earth produces! This, then, greatly increased the reputation of Antoninus also for foresight, in that he had foretold to all that the temples would become tombs.[3] Likewise the famous Iamblichus, as I have handed down in my account of his life, when a certain Egyptian invoked Apollo, and to the great amazement of those who saw the vision, Apollo came: "My friends," said he, "cease to wonder; this is only the ghost of a gladiator." So great a difference does it make whether one beholds a thing with the intelligence or with the deceitful eyes of the flesh. But Iamblichus saw through marvels that were present, whereas Antoninus foresaw future events. This fact of itself argues his superior powers. His end came painlessly, when he had attained to a ripe old

---

[1] An echo of *Phaedo* 81 D; *cf.* Julian, *Misopogon* 344 A; *Against the Galilaeans* 335 C. Christian churches were built over the graves of martyrs.

[2] An echo of *Gorgias* 524 E.   [3] *Cf.* Julian, *Or.* vii. 228c.

καὶ βαθύ. καὶ λυπηρὸν τοῖς νοῦν ἔχουσι τὸ προεγνωσμένον ἐκείνῳ τῶν ἱερῶν τέλος.

Μαξίμου καὶ πρότερον ἐμνήσθημεν, καὶ ὁ ταῦτα γράφων οὐκ ἦν ἀθέατος τοῦ ἀνδρός, ἀλλὰ νέος ἔτι γηραιῷ συνετύγχανε καὶ φωνῆς τε ἤκουσεν, οἵας ἄν τις ἤκουσε τῆς Ὁμηρικῆς Ἀθηνᾶς ἢ τοῦ Ἀπόλλωνος. τῷ δὲ καὶ πτηνοὶ μέν τινες ἦσαν αἱ τῶν ὀμμάτων κόραι, πολιὸν δὲ καθεῖτο γένειον, τὰς δὲ ὁρμὰς τῆς ψυχῆς διεδήλου τὰ ὄμματα. καὶ ἁρμονία γέ τις ἐπῆν καὶ ἀκούοντι καὶ ὁρῶντι, καὶ δι᾽ ἀμφοῖν τῶν αἰσθήσεων ὁ συνὼν ἐπλήττετο, οὔτε τὴν ὀξυκινησίαν φέρων τῶν ὀμμάτων, οὔτε τὸν δρόμον τῶν λόγων. ἀλλ᾽ οὐδὲ εἴ τις τῶν ἐμπειροτάτων πάνυ καὶ δεινῶν διελέγετο πρὸς αὐτόν, ἀντιλέγειν ἐτόλμα, ἀλλ᾽ ἡσυχῇ παραδόντες αὐτούς, τοῖς λεγομένοις ὥσπερ ἐκ τριπόδων εἴποντο· τοσαύτη τις ἀφροδίτη τοῖς χείλεσιν ἐπεκάθητο. ἦν μὲν οὖν τῶν εὖ γεγονότων, καὶ πλοῦτος ἁδρότερος ὑπῆν αὐτῷ, ἀδελφοὺς δὲ εἶχε γνησίους, οὓς ἐκώλυεν εἶναι πρώτους αὐτὸς ὤν, Κλαυδιανόν τε τὸν καταλαβόντα τὴν Ἀλεξάνδρειαν κἀκεῖ παιδεύσαντα, καὶ Νυμφιδιανὸν τὸν ἐν Σμύρνῃ περιφανῶς σοφιστεύσαντα.

Ἦν δὲ ὁ ἀνὴρ οὗτος τῶν διαπλησθέντων τῆς Αἰδεσίου σοφίας. Ἰουλιανοῦ δὲ τοῦ βασιλεύσαντος ἠξιώθη γενέσθαι διδάσκαλος. οὗτος, πάντων ἀνῃρημένων ὑπὸ τοῦ Κωνσταντίου (ταῦτα δὲ ἐν τοῖς κατὰ Ἰουλιανὸν ἀκριβέστερον γέγραπται),

---

[1] See note, p. 395.
[2] Some scholars think that Claudianus was the father of the Latin poet Claudianus (*floruit* 400 A.D.), but there is no sure evidence for this.

age free from sickness. And to all intelligent men
the end of the temples which he had prognosticated
was painful indeed.

Of MAXIMUS I have spoken earlier, and indeed the
author of this narrative did not fail to see the man
with his own eyes, but while still a youth met him in
his old age and heard his voice, which was such as one
might have heard from Homer's Athene or Apollo.
The very pupils of his eyes were, so to speak,
winged; he had a long grey beard, and his glance
revealed the agile impulses of his soul. There was
a wonderful harmony in his person, both to the eye
and ear, and all who conversed with him were
amazed as to both these faculties, since one could
hardly endure the swift movements of his eyes or his
rapid flow of words. In discussion with him no one
ventured to contradict him, not even the most
experienced and most eloquent, but they yielded to
him in silence and acquiesced in what he said as
though it came from the tripod of an oracle ; such a
charm sat on his lips.[1] He came of an honourable
family and possessed ample means ; and he had two
lawful brothers whom he kept from holding the very
highest rank because he held it himself. They
were Claudianus [2] who settled in Alexandria and
taught there, and Nymphidianus who became very
distinguished as a sophist at Smyrna.

Maximus was one of those who had been saturated
with the wisdom of Aedesius ; moreover he received
the honour of being the teacher of the Emperor
Julian. After all his relatives had been put to
death by Constantius, as I have recorded with more
details in my account of Julian, and the whole

καὶ ψιλωθέντος τοῦ γένους, περιελείφθη[1] μόνος,
δι' ἡλικίαν περιφρονηθεὶς καὶ πραότητα. εὐ-
νοῦχοι δὲ ὅμως αὐτὸν ἀμφεπόλευον βασιλικοὶ καὶ
παραφυλακαί τινες ἦσαν, ὅπως εἴη χριστιανὸς
βέβαιος· ὁ δὲ καὶ πρὸς ταῦτα τὸ μέγεθος τῆς
φύσεως ἐπεδείκνυτο. πάντα γοῦν οὕτω διὰ στόματος εἶχε τὰ βιβλία, ὥστε ἠγανάκτουν ἐκεῖνοι
πρὸς τὴν βραχύτητα τῆς παιδείας, ὡς οὐκ ἔχοντες
ὅ τι διδάξουσι τὸ παιδίον. ὡς δὲ οὔτε ἐκεῖνοι
παιδεύειν εἶχον, οὔτε Ἰουλιανὸς μανθάνειν, ἐξ-
ῄτησεν τὸν ἀνεψιὸν ἐπιτραπῆναί οἱ καὶ ῥητορικῶν
ἀκροάσασθαι καὶ φιλοσόφων λόγων. ὁ δέ, θεοῦ
νεύσαντος, ἐπέτρεψε, περὶ τὰ βιβλία πλανᾶσθαι
βουλόμενος αὐτὸν καὶ ἀργεῖν μᾶλλον ἢ τοῦ γένους
καὶ τῆς βασιλείας ὑπομιμνήσκεσθαι. τοῦτο δὲ
ἐπιτραπὲν αὐτῷ, πανταχοῦ βαθέων καὶ βαρυτάτων
474 ὑποκειμένων κτημάτων, μετὰ βασιλικῆς ὑπονοίας
καὶ δορυφορίας περιεφοίτα, καὶ διέστειχεν ὅπῃ
βούλοιτο. καὶ δὴ καὶ εἰς Πέργαμον ἀφικνεῖται
κατὰ κλέος τῆς Αἰδεσίου σοφίας. ὁ δὲ ἤδη μὲν
εἰς μακρόν τι γῆρας ἀφῖκτο,[2] καὶ τὸ σῶμα ἔκαμνε·
τῆς δὲ ὁμιλίας αὐτοῦ προεστήκεσαν καὶ ἀνὰ τοὺς
πρώτους ἐφέροντο Μάξιμός τε, ὑπὲρ οὗ τάδε
γράφεται, καὶ Χρυσάνθιος ὁ ἐκ Σάρδεων, Πρίσκος
τε ὁ Θεσπρωτὸς ἢ Μολοσσός, Εὐσέβιός τε ὁ ἐκ
Καρίας Μύνδου πόλεως. καὶ συνουσίας ἀξιωθεὶς
τῆς Αἰδεσίου, ὁ καὶ ἐν μειρακίῳ πρεσβύτης Ἰουλιανός, τὴν μὲν ἀκμὴν καὶ τὸ θεοειδὲς τῆς ψυχῆς
καταπλαγείς, οὐκ ἐβούλετο χωρίζεσθαι, ἀλλ',

---

[1] Before περιελείφθη Cobet deletes Ἰουλιανὸς ; retained by
Boissonade; Giangrande reads Ἰουλιανοῦ.
[2] ἀφίκετο Boissonade: ἀφῖκτο Cobet.

---

[1] Cf., however, Julian, *Letter to the Athenians* 273 B.

family had been stripped bare, Julian alone was
left alive, being despised on the score of his
tender years and his mild disposition.   Nevertheless, eunuchs from the palace took charge of
him, and were assigned to keep watch so that he
might not waver from the Christian faith.   But even
in the face of these difficulties he displayed the
greatness of his genius.   For he had their books
so thoroughly by heart that they fretted at the
scantiness of their erudition, since there was nothing
that they could teach the boy.   Now since they had
nothing to teach him and Julian had nothing to
learn from them, he begged his cousin's permission
to attend the schools of the sophists and lectures on
philosophy.   He, as the gods so willed, permitted
this, because he wished Julian to browse among
books and to have leisure for them, rather than
leave him to reflect on his own family and his claim
to empire.   After he had obtained this permission,
since ample and abundant wealth from many sources
was at his disposal,[1] he used to travel about accompanied by the emperor's suspicions and a bodyguard,
and went where he pleased.   Thus it was that he
came to Pergamon, following on the report of the
wisdom of Aedesius.   But the latter was by this time
far on in years, and his bodily strength was failing.
First and foremost of all his students were Maximus,
about whom I am now writing, Chrysanthius of
Sardis, Priscus the Thesprotian or Molossian, and
Eusebius who came from Myndus, a city of Caria.
On being allowed to study under Aedesius, Julian,
who was old for his boyish years, in amazement and
admiration of his vigour and the divine qualities of
his soul, refused to leave him, but like those who had

ὥσπερ οἱ κατὰ τὸν μῦθον ὑπὸ τῆς διψάδος δηχθέντες, χανδὸν καὶ ἀμυστὶ τῶν μαθημάτων ἕλκειν ἐβούλετο, καὶ δῶρά γε ἐπὶ τούτοις βασιλικὰ διέπεμπεν· ὁ δὲ οὐδὲ ταῦτα προσίετο, καὶ μετακαλέσας τὸν νεανίσκον, εἶπεν· " ἀλλὰ σὺ μὲν καὶ τὴν ψυχὴν τὴν ἐμὴν οὐκ ἀγνοεῖς, τηλικαύταις ἀκοαῖς ἀκροώμενος, τὸ δὲ ὄργανον αὐτῆς συνορᾷς ὅπως διάκειται, τῆς γομφώσεως καὶ πήξεως διαλυομένης εἰς τὸ συντιθέν[1]· σὺ δέ, εἴ τι καὶ δρᾶν βούλει, τέκνον σοφίας ἐπήρατον (τοιαῦτα γάρ σου τὰ τῆς ψυχῆς ἰνδάλματα καταμανθάνω), πρὸς τοὺς ἐμοὺς παῖδας πορευθεὶς ὄντας γνησίους, ἐκεῖθεν ῥύδην ἐμφοροῦ σοφίας ἁπάσης καὶ μαθημάτων· κἂν τύχῃς τῶν μυστηρίων, αἰσχυνθήσῃ πάντως ὅτι ἐγένου καὶ ἐκλήθης ἄνθρωπος. ἐβουλόμην μὲν ἂν[2] παρεῖναι καὶ Μάξιμον, ἀλλ' ἐπὶ τὴν Ἔφεσον ἔσταλται. καὶ περὶ Πρίσκου τὰ ὅμοια διελέχθην ἄν, ἀλλὰ κἀκεῖνος ἐπὶ τῆς Ἑλλάδος πέπλευκε· λοιποὶ δὲ τῶν ἐμῶν ἑταίρων Εὐσέβιός τε καὶ Χρυσάνθιος, ὧν ἀκροώμενος ἐλάχιστα τὸ ἐμὸν ἐνοχλήσεις γῆρας."

Ὡς δὲ ταῦτα ἤκουσεν Ἰουλιανός, τοῦ φιλοσόφου μὲν οὐδ' ὡς ἀφίστατο, προσέκειτο δὲ κατὰ τὸν πολὺν χρόνον Εὐσεβίῳ τε καὶ Χρυσανθίῳ. ἦν δὲ ὁ Χρυσάνθιος ὁμοψύχως Μαξίμῳ τὰ περὶ θειασμὸν συνενθουσιῶν, καὶ ὑφείλκεν ἑαυτὸν ἐν τοῖς μαθήμασι, καὶ τὸ ἄλλο ἦθος τοιοῦτον ἔχων.

[1] συντεθέν Boissonade ; συντιθέν Cobet.
[2] οὖν Boissonade ; ἂν Cobet.

[1] The bite of this snake, as its Greek name implies, caused insatiable thirst.
[2] This is an echo of Porphyry's famous saying about Plotinus : ἐῴκει μὲν αἰσχυνομένῳ ὅτι ἐν σώματι εἴη.

been bitten by the snake [1] in the story he longed to drink down learning open-mouthed and at a gulp, and to win his end used to send Aedesius gifts worthy of an emperor. But Aedesius would not accept these, and having summoned the youth he said : " Well, thou also knowest my soul, for thou hast listened many a time to my teachings ; but thou seest how its instrument is affected now that that whereby it is connected and held together is dissolving into that from which it was composed. But if thou dost desire to accomplish aught, beloved child of wisdom as thou art, such signs and tokens of thy soul do I discern, go to those who are true sons of mine. From their store fill thyself to overflowing with every kind of wisdom and learning. Once admitted to their mysteries thou shalt be utterly ashamed to have been born and to be called a man.[2] I could have wished that Maximus also were here, but he has been dispatched to Ephesus. Of Priscus [3] too I should have said the same, but he also has sailed to Greece. But there remain of my disciples Eusebius and Chrysanthius, and if thou wilt study with them thou wilt cease to harass my old age."

On hearing this, Julian did not even then leave the philosopher, but for the greater part of his time he devoted his attention to Eusebius and Chrysanthius. Now Chrysanthius had a soul akin to that of Maximus, and like him was passionately absorbed in working marvels, and he withdrew himself in the study of the science of divination, and in other respects also had a very similar

---

[3] For Priscus see below, p. 481, Ammianus Marcellinus xxv. 3, and Julian, vol. iii. *Letters.*

Εὐσέβιος δέ, παρόντος μὲν Μαξίμου, τὴν ἀκρίβειαν τὴν ἐν τοῖς μέρεσι τοῦ λόγου καὶ τὰς δια-
λεκτικὰς μηχανὰς καὶ πλοκὰς ὑπέφευγε, ἀπόντος
δὲ ὥσπερ ἡλιακοῦ φέγγους ἀστὴρ ἀπέλαμπε·
τοσαύτη τις εὐκολία καὶ χάρις ἐπήνθει τοῖς λόγοις.
καὶ ὁ Χρυσάνθιος παρὼν ἐπήνει καὶ συνεπένευεν,
ὅ τε Ἰουλιανὸς τὸν ἄνδρα ἐσεβάζετο. προσετίθη
δὲ μετὰ τὴν ἐξήγησιν ὁ Εὐσέβιος, ὡς ταῦτα εἴη
τὰ ὄντως ὄντα, αἱ δὲ τὴν αἴσθησιν ἀπατῶσαι μαγ-
γανεῖαι καὶ γοητεύουσαι, θαυματοποιῶν ἔργα,
καὶ πρὸς ὑλικάς τινας δυνάμεις παραπαιόντων
καὶ μεμηνότων. τοῦτο ἀκούων τὸ ἐπιφώνημα
πολλάκις ὁ θειότατος Ἰουλιανός, ἰδίᾳ τὸν Χρυσάνθιον
ἀπολαβών, " εἴ τί σοι μέτεστιν ἀληθείας, ὦ φίλε
Χρυσάνθιε," πρὸς αὐτὸν ἔφη " φράσον μοι σαφῶς
τίς ὁ ἐπίλογος οὗτος τῆς ἐξηγήσεως." ὁ δὲ
βαθέως μάλα καὶ σωφρόνως ἀνενεγκὼν " ἀλλὰ
πρᾶγμα ποιήσεις " ἔφη " σοφόν, μὴ παρ' ἐμοῦ
ταῦτα, ἀλλὰ παρ' ἐκείνου πυθόμενος." καὶ μαθὼν
475 τοῦτο ἤκουσε καὶ ἐποίησε, θεόν τινα νομίσας τὸν
Χρυσάνθιον ἐπὶ τῷ λόγῳ. γενομένης δὲ τῆς
συνουσίας, ὁ μὲν τὰ αὐτὰ προσεπέραινεν,[1] ὁ δὲ
Ἰουλιανὸς θαρσαλέως ἤρετο, τί τοῦτο αὐτῷ βούλεται συνεχῶς ἐπιλεγόμενον. ἐνταῦθα ὁ Εὐσέβιος τὴν
ἑαυτοῦ πετάσας εὐγλωττίαν, καὶ τὸ εὔστομον ἐπὶ
τὸ φράζειν ἀκώλυτον ἀφεὶς φέρεσθαι, " Μάξιμος "
εἶπε " τίς ἐστι τῶν πρεσβυτέρων ἀκροατῶν καὶ
πολλὰ ἐκπεπαιδευμένων· οὗτος διὰ μέγεθος φύσεως καὶ λόγων ὑπεροχὴν καταφρονήσας τῶν ἐν

---

[1] προσεπέρραινεν Boissonade ; προσεπέραινεν Cobet.

---

[1] *i.e.* dialectical discussions. Eusebius was devoted to
philosophical rhetoric, whereas Chrysanthius and Maximus

character. But Eusebius, at least when Maximus was present, used to avoid precise and exact divisions of a disputation and dialectical devices and subtleties; though when Maximus was not there he would shine out like a bright star, with a light like the sun's; such was the facility and charm that flowered in his discourses. Chrysanthius too was there to applaud and assent, while Julian actually reverenced Eusebius. At the close of his exposition Eusebius would add that these[1] are the only true realities, whereas the impostures of witchcraft and magic that cheat the senses are the works of conjurors who are insane men led astray into the exercise of earthly and material powers. The sainted Julian frequently heard the closing words, and at last took Chrysanthius aside, and said: " If the truth is in you, dear Chrysanthius, tell me plainly what is the meaning of this epilogue that follows his exposition?" Having reflected deeply and with prudence, he said: "The wise thing for you to do will be to inquire this not of me but of himself." Julian listened, took the hint and acted on it, and regarded Chrysanthius as little short of divine on account of what he had said. Then when the next lecture took place, Eusebius ended with the same words as before, and Julian boldly asked him what was the meaning of the epilogue that he perpetually recited. Thereupon Eusebius spread the sails of the eloquence that was his by nature, and giving free rein to his powers of speech said: " Maximus is one of the older and more learned students, who, because of his lofty genius and superabundant eloquence scorned all logical proof in these subjects and

were thaumaturgists, or miracle-workers. Julian from this time fell under the baleful influence of Maximus.

EUNAPIUS

τούτοις ἀποδείξεων, ἐπὶ μανίας τινὰς ὁρμήσας καὶ
δραμών, συνεκάλεσεν ἡμᾶς πρώην τοὺς παρόντας
εἰς τὸ Ἑκατήσιον, καὶ πολλοὺς ἐδείκνυ τοὺς
καθ᾽ ἑαυτοῦ μάρτυρας. ὡς δὲ ἀπηντήσαμεν, καὶ
τὴν θεὸν προσεκυνήσαμεν, "καθῆσθε μὲν," εἶπε
πρὸς ἡμᾶς, "ὦ φίλτατοι ἑταῖροι, καὶ τὸ μέλλον
ὁρᾶτε, καὶ εἴ τι διαφέρω τῶν πολλῶν ἐγώ." τοῦτο
δὲ εἰπών, καὶ καθεσθέντων ἡμῶν ἁπάντων, χόν-
δρον καθαγίσας λιβανωτοῦ, καὶ πρὸς ἑαυτὸν
ὅντινα δήποτε ὕμνον περαίνων, εἰς τοσόνδε παρῆλθεν ἐπιδείξεως, ὥστε τὸ μὲν πρῶτον ἐμειδία
τὸ ἄγαλμα, εἶτα καὶ γέλως ἦν τὸ φαινόμενον.
θορυβουμένων δὲ ἡμῶν ὑπὸ τῆς ὄψεως, "ἀλλὰ
ταραχθήτω γε ὑμῶν ὑπὸ τούτων μηδὲ εἷς, αὐτίκα
γὰρ καὶ αἱ λαμπάδες ἀνάψουσιν, ἃς ἐν ταῖν χεροῖν
ἡ θεὸς φέρει·" καὶ τοὺς λόγους ἔφθανε τὸ φῶς
ταῖς λαμπάσι περιφλεγόμενον. ἡμεῖς μὲν οὖν
τὸν θεατρικὸν ἐκεῖνον θαυματοποιὸν πρὸς τὸ
παρὸν καταπλαγέντες, ἀνεχωρήσαμεν· σὺ δὲ τούτων μηδὲν θαυμάσῃς, ὥσπερ οὐδὲ ἐγώ, τὴν διὰ
τοῦ λόγου κάθαρσιν μέγα τι χρῆμα ὑπολαμβάνων."
ὁ δὲ θειότατος Ἰουλιανὸς τοῦτο ἀκούσας, "ἀλλ᾽
ἔρρωσο" εἶπε "καὶ πρόσεχε τοῖς βιβλίοις, ἐμοὶ
δὲ ἐμήνυσας ὃν ἐζήτουν." καὶ ταῦτα εἰπών, καὶ
Χρυσανθίου καταφιλήσας τὴν κεφαλήν, ἐπὶ τὴν
Ἔφεσον ἐξώρμησε. συντυχὼν δὲ ἐκεῖ Μαξίμῳ,
ἐξεκρέματό τε τοῦ ἀνδρός, καὶ ἀπρὶξ τῆς ὅλης
σοφίας εἴχετο. ὁ δὲ Μάξιμος ὑφηγεῖται αὐτῷ
καὶ τὸν θειότατον μετακαλέσαι Χρυσάνθιον, καί,
γενόμενον οὕτως, μόλις ἤρκουν ἄμφω τῇ τοῦ
παιδὸς ἐς τὰς μαθήσεις εὐρυχωρίᾳ.

impetuously resorted to the acts of a madman. Not long since, he invited us to the temple of Hecate and produced many witnesses of his folly. When we had arrived there and had saluted the goddess: 'Be seated,' said he, 'my well-beloved friends, and observe what shall come to pass, and how greatly I surpass the common herd.' When he had said this, and we had all sat down, he burned a grain of incense and recited to himself the whole of some hymn or other, and was so highly successful in his demonstration that the image of the goddess first began to smile, then even seemed to laugh aloud. We were all much disturbed by this sight, but he said: 'Let none of you be terrified by these things, for presently even the torches which the goddess holds in her hands shall kindle into flame.' And before he could finish speaking the torches burst into a blaze of light. Now for the moment we came away amazed by that theatrical miracle-worker. But you must not marvel at any of these things, even as I marvel not, but rather believe that the thing of the highest importance is that purification of the soul which is attained by reason." However, when the sainted Julian heard this, he said: "Nay, farewell and devote yourself to your books. You have shown me the man I was in search of." After saying this he kissed the head of Chrysanthius and started for Ephesus. There he had converse with Maximus, and hung on to him and laid fast hold on all that he had to teach. Maximus persuaded him to summon thither the divine Chrysanthius also, and when this had been done the two of them barely sufficed to satisfy the boy's great capacity for acquiring this kind of lore.

'Ως δὲ καὶ ταῦτα εἶχε καλῶς, ἀκούσας τι πλέον εἶναι κατὰ τὴν Ἑλλάδα παρὰ τῷ ταῖν Θεαῖν ἱεροφάντῃ, καὶ πρὸς ἐκεῖνον ὀξὺς ἔδραμε. τοῦ δὲ ἱεροφάντου, κατ' ἐκεῖνον τὸν χρόνον ὅστις ἦν, τοὔνομα οὔ μοι θέμις λέγειν· ἐτέλει γὰρ τὸν ταῦτα γράφοντα. καὶ εἰς Εὐμολπίδας ἦγε· καὶ οὗτός γε ἦν ὁ καὶ τὴν τῶν ἱερῶν καταστροφὴν καὶ τῆς Ἑλλάδος ἀπώλειαν ἁπάσης προγνούς, τοῦ συγγραφέως παρόντος, καὶ φανερῶς δια-μαρτυρόμενος ὡς μεθ' αὐτὸν ἱεροφάντης γενή-σοιτο, ᾧ μὴ θέμις ἱεροφαντικῶν ἅψασθαι θρόνων, ἐπειδὴ θεοῖς ἑτέροις καθιέρωται, καὶ ὀμώμοκεν ἀρρήτους ὅρκους ἑτέρων ἱερῶν μὴ προστήσεσθαι· προστήσεσθαι δὲ ἔλεγεν ὅμως αὐτὸν μηδὲ Ἀθηναῖον ὄντα. καὶ (εἰς τοσόνδε προνοίας ἐξικνεῖτο) ἐφ' ἑαυτοῦ τὰ ἱερὰ κατασκαφήσεσθαι καὶ δῃωθή-σεσθαι ἔφασκε, κἀκεῖνον ζῶντα ταῦτα ἐπόψεσθαι, διὰ φιλοτιμίαν περιττὴν ἀτιμαζόμενον, καὶ προ-
476 τελευτήσειν γε αὐτοῦ τὴν θεραπείαν ταῖν Θεαῖν, τὸν δὲ τῆς τιμῆς ἀποστερηθέντα, μήτε τὸν ἱερο-φάντην μήτε τὸν γηραιὸν βίον ἕξειν. καὶ ταῦτά γε οὕτως· ἅμα τε γὰρ ὁ ἐκ Θεσπιῶν ἐγένετο, πατὴρ ὢν τῆς Μιθριακῆς τελετῆς, καὶ οὐκ εἰς μακρὰν πολλῶν καὶ ἀδιηγήτων ἐπικλυσθέντων κακῶν,[1] ὧν τὰ μὲν ἐν τοῖς διεξοδικοῖς τῆς ἱστορίας εἴρηται, τὰ δέ, ἐὰν ἐπιτρέπῃ τὸ Θεῖον, λελέξεται,

---

[1] Here there is either an anacoluthon or some words have fallen out of the ms.

---

[1] *i.e.* Demeter and Persephone worshipped at Eleusis.
[2] Lucian, *Lexiphanes* 10, alludes to the crime of naming the hierophant and torch-bearers of the Mysteries.
[3] The hereditary priests of Demeter at Eleusis.

Now when his studies with them were prospering, he heard that there was a higher wisdom in Greece, possessed by the hierophant of the goddesses,[1] and hastened to him with all speed. The name of him who was at that time hierophant it is not lawful for me to tell[2]; for he initiated the author of this narrative. By birth he was descended from the Eumolpidae.[3] He it was who in the presence of the author of this book foretold the overthrow of the temples and the ruin of the whole of Greece, and he clearly testified that after his death there would be a hierophant who would have no right to touch the hierophant's high seat, because he had been consecrated to the service of other gods and had sworn oaths of the uttermost sanctity that he would not preside over temples other than theirs. Nevertheless he foretold that this man would so preside, though he was not even an Athenian. To such prophetic power did he attain that he prophesied that in his own lifetime the sacred temples would be razed to the ground and laid waste, and that that other would live to see their ruin and would be despised for his overweening ambition; that the worship of the Goddesses would come to an end before his own death, and that deprived of his honour his life would no longer be that of a hierophant, and that he would not reach old age. Thus indeed it came to pass. For no sooner was the citizen of Thespiae made hierophant, he who fathered the ritual of Mithras,[4] than without delay many inexplicable disasters came on in a flood. Some of these have been described in the more detailed narrative of my *History*, others, if it be permitted by the powers above, I shall

---

[4] *i.e.* he had been the priest of Mithras.

ὅτε Ἀλλάριχος ἔχων τοὺς βαρβάρους διὰ τῶν
Πυλῶν παρῆλθεν, ὥσπερ διὰ σταδίου καὶ ἱππο-
κρότου πεδίου τρέχων· τοιαύτας αὐτῷ τὰς πύλας
ἀπέδειξε τῆς Ἑλλάδος ἥ τε τῶν τὰ φαιὰ ἱμάτια
ἐχόντων ἀκωλύτως προσπαρεισελθόντων ἀσέβεια,
καὶ ὁ τῶν ἱεροφαντικῶν θεσμῶν παρραγεὶς
νόμος καὶ σύνδεσμος. ἀλλὰ ταῦτα μὲν ἐς ὕστερον
ἐπράχθη, καὶ ὁ λόγος διὰ τὴν πρόγνωσιν παρ-
ήνεγκε.

Τότε δὲ ὁ μὲν Ἰουλιανὸς τῷ θειοτάτῳ ἱεροφαντῶν συγγενόμενος καὶ τῆς ἐκεῖθεν σοφίας
ἀρυσάμενος χανδόν, ὁ μὲν ὑπὸ τοῦ Κωνσταντίου
ἀπήγετο σφοδρῶς, ὡς παραβασιλεύσων εἰς τὸν
Καίσαρα, Μάξιμος δὲ ἦν κατὰ τὴν Ἀσίαν, Αἰδεσίου
δὲ μεταλλάξαντος, πήχεσί γε ἐπὶ πᾶσαν σοφίαν
αὐξόμενος· ὥστε ὁ μὲν Ἰουλιανὸς ἔτυχεν ὢν
οὐκ ἐβούλετο μέν, ἀλλ’ ἠναγκάζετο. πεμφθεὶς
δὲ Καῖσαρ ἐπὶ Γαλατίας οὐχ ἵνα βασιλεύῃ τῶν
ἐκείνῃ μόνον, ἀλλ’ ἵνα ἐν τῇ βασιλείᾳ διαφθαρῇ,
παρὰ δόξαν ἅπασαν ἐκ τῆς τῶν θεῶν προνοίας
ἀνήνεγκεν, πάντας μὲν λανθάνων ὅτι θεραπεύει
θεούς, πάντας δὲ νικῶν ὅτι ἐθεράπευε θεούς, καὶ
τόν τε Ῥῆνον ἐπεραιώθη, καὶ πάντα ὅσα ὑπὲρ
ἐκεῖνον ἔθνη βάρβαρα συνελὼν καὶ δουλωσάμενος,
πολλῶν ἐπιβουλῶν καὶ μηχανημάτων πλεκομένων
αὐτῷ (ὡς ἐν τοῖς περὶ ἐκεῖνον ἀναγέγραπται),
τὸν ἱεροφάντην μετακαλέσας ἐκ τῆς Ἑλλάδος
καὶ σὺν ἐκείνῳ τινὰ μόνοις ἐκείνοις γνώριμα

---

[1] *i.e.* the Christian monks. This invasion of the Goths
in 395 is mentioned again in the *Life* of Priscus.

[2] These incidents are related by Julian himself in his
Letter to the Athenians and by Ammianus Marcellinus.

relate   It was the time when Alaric with his
barbarians invaded Greece by the pass of Thermopylae, as easily as though he were traversing an open
stadium or a plain suitable for cavalry.   For this
gateway of Greece was thrown open to him by the
impiety of the men clad in black raiment,[1] who
entered Greece unhindered along with him, and by
the fact that the laws and restrictions of the hiero-
phantic ordinances had been rescinded.   But all this
happened in later days, and my narrative digressed
because I mentioned the prophecy.

At the time I now speak of, Julian had no sooner
become intimate with that most holy of hierophants
and greedily absorbed his wisdom, than he was
forcibly removed by Constantius to be his consort in
the Empire and elevated to the rank of Caesar,[2]
while Maximus remained in Asia (Aedesius had
now passed away), and progressed by leaps and
bounds in every kind of wisdom.   Thus did Julian
obtain what he did not desire, but had thrust upon
him.   As Caesar he was dispatched to Gaul, not so
much to rule there as with the intention that he
should perish by violent means, while holding his
imperial office ; but contrary to all expectation, by
the providence of the gods he emerged alive, con-
cealing from all men his pious devotion to the gods,
but overcoming all men by reason of that very
devotion.   He crossed the Rhine and defeated and
subjugated all the barbarian tribes beyond that
river, and this in spite of numerous plots and
schemes that were woven against him, as I have
related in full in his *Life*.   Then he summoned the
hierophant from Greece, and having with his aid

διαπραξάμενος, ἐπὶ τὴν καθαίρεσιν ἠγέρθη τῆς
Κωνσταντίου τυραννίδος. ταῦτα δὲ συνῄδεσαν
Ὀρειβάσιος ἐκ τοῦ Περγάμου, καί τις τῶν ἐκ
Λιβύης, ἣν Ἀφρικὴν καλοῦσι Ῥωμαῖοι κατὰ τὸ
πάτριον τῆς γλώττης, Εὐήμερος. ταῦτα δὲ πάλιν
ἐν τοῖς κατὰ Ἰουλιανὸν βιβλίοις ἀκριβέστερον
εἴρηται. ὡς δ' οὖν καθεῖλε τὴν τυραννίδα Κωνσταντίου, καὶ τὸν ἱεροφάντην ἀπέπεμψεν ἐπὶ τὴν
Ἑλλάδα, καθάπερ θεόν τινα ἀποπέμπων φανέντα,
καὶ παρασχόντα ἃ ἐβούλετο, καὶ βασιλικά γε
αὐτῷ δῶρα καὶ θεραπείαν συνέπεμψε πρὸς τὴν
ἐπιμέλειαν τῆς Ἑλλάδος ἱερῶν, τὸν Μάξιμον
εὐθὺς μετεπέμψατο καὶ τὸν Χρυσάνθιον. καὶ μία
γε ἦν ἐπ' ἀμφοῖν ἡ κλῆσις. τοῖς δὲ ἐπὶ τοὺς
θεοὺς καταφεύγειν ἐδόκει, καὶ ἄνδρες οὕτω δρα-
στήριοι καὶ πεῖραν ἔχοντες, καὶ συνενεγκόντες
εἰς ταὐτὸ τὴν πεῖραν, καὶ τὴν περὶ ταῦτα ὀξυδορ-
κίαν καὶ διάθρησιν τῆς ψυχῆς ἀνεγείραντες καὶ
συστησάμενοι, σημείοις ἐγχρίπτουσιν ἀπηνέσι καὶ
ἀγρίοις. ἐκεῖνοι ᾔδεσαν τὰ φανθέντα σημεῖα. ὁ
μὲν οὖν Χρυσάνθιος εὐθὺς καταπλαγεὶς καὶ πρὸς
τὴν ὄψιν ὑποπτήξας, τὴν γλῶσσαν ἐνδακών,
" οὐ μενετέον " εἶπεν " ἐμοὶ μόνον ἐνταῦθα, ὦ
Μάξιμε φίλτατε, ἀλλὰ καὶ φωλευτέον." ὁ δὲ
ἀναστήσας ἑαυτόν " ἀλλ' ἐπιλελῆσθαί μοι δοκεῖς,"
477 εἶπεν " ὦ Χρυσάνθιε, τῆς παιδείας ἣν ἐπαιδεύθημεν,
ὡς τῶν ἄκρων γέ ἐστιν Ἑλλήνων καὶ ταῦτα
πεπαιδευμένων μὴ πάντως εἴκειν τοῖς πρώτως
ἀπαντήσασιν, ἀλλ' ἐκβιάζεσθαι τὴν τοῦ θείου
φύσιν ἄχρις ἂν ἐπικλίνοις πρὸς τὸν θεραπεύοντα."

---

[1] For Oribasius see his *Life*, pp. 498-499.
[2] Constantius died in November 361 and Julian entered
Constantinople in triumph in December.

performed certain rites known to them alone, he mustered up courage to abolish the tyranny of Constantius. His accomplices were Oribasius[1] of Pergamon and a certain Euhemerus, a native of Libya, which the Romans in their native tongue call Africa. But all this has been described in fuller detail in my work on Julian. When he had abolished the tyranny of Constantius,[2] and had sent back the hierophant to Greece as though he were sending back some god who had revealed himself and bestowed on him what he desired, and had sent with him also gifts worthy of an emperor, and attendants to take care of the temples of Greece, he at once sent for Maximus and Chrysanthius. One summons came for them both. They decided to have recourse to the aid of the gods, and energetic and experienced as they both were, they combined their experience for this common purpose, and summoned and brought to bear all their keen sight in such matters and all their mental perspicacity; but they encountered forbidding and hostile omens. Well did they know the meaning of the omens then revealed. Now Chrysanthius was overwhelmed and awestruck by what he saw, and biting his tongue he said: "Not only must I stay here, beloved Maximus, I must also hide myself from all men." But Maximus asserted the force of his will, and replied: "Nay, Chrysanthius, I think that you have forgotten that we have been educated to believe that it is the duty of genuine Hellenes, especially if they are learned men, not to yield absolutely to the first obstacles they meet; but rather to wrestle with the heavenly powers till you make them incline to their servant." But Chrysanthius

EUNAPIUS

Χρυσανθίου δὲ ὑπολαβόντος, "ἴσως σὺ ταῦτα
πράττειν εἶ δεινὸς καὶ τολμηρός, ἐγὼ δὲ τούτοις
οὐκ ἂν μαχεσαίμην τοῖς σημείοις·" καὶ μετὰ
τοὺς λόγους ἀποχωρήσαντος, ὁ μὲν Μάξιμος
ἐπέμεινεν ἅπαντα πράττων, ἔστε ἔτυχεν ὧν ἐβούλετο καὶ κατεπεθύμει· ὁ δὲ Χρυσάνθιος ἀκινη-
τότερος ἐπέμενεν ἀνδριάντος, τοὺς ἐξ ἀρχῆς
πεπηγότας παρ' ἑαυτῷ λογισμοὺς μηδὲ κινῆσαι
διανοούμενος. πάντες οὖν ἄνθρωποι παρὰ τὸν
Μάξιμον ἤδη συνετρόχαζον κατὰ τὴν Ἀσίαν,
ὅσοι τε ἦσαν ἐν ἀρχαῖς καὶ ὅσοι τούτων ἀπελέλυντο,
τό τε κρεῖττον τῶν βουλευτηρίων. καὶ δῆμος
ἐστενοχώρει τὰς προόδους τῷ Μαξίμῳ μετὰ
βοῆς πηδῶντες, ἣν δῆμος, ὅταν τινὰ θεραπεύῃ,
ἐκ πολλοῦ μεμελέτηκεν· αἵ τε γυναῖκες παρὰ
τὴν γυναῖκα τῇ πλαγίᾳ θύρᾳ παρεισεχέοντο, τὴν
εὐδαιμονίαν θαυμάζουσαι καὶ μεμνῆσθαι σφῶν
ἀξιοῦσαι· ἡ δὲ φιλοσοφίας ἕνεκεν Μάξιμον οὔτε
νεῖν[1] οὔτε γράμματα εἰδότα ἀπέφαινεν. ὁ μὲν
οὖν Μάξιμος ὑπὸ τῆς Ἀσίας πάσης προσκυνού-
μενος, ἐπὶ τὴν συντυχίαν ἀνῄει τοῦ βασιλέως,
Χρυσάνθιος δὲ ἔμεινε κατὰ χώραν, ἐκεῖνο θεοῦ
κατ' ὄναρ, ὡς πρὸς τὸν ταῦτα γράφοντα ἔλεγεν ἐς
ὕστερον, εἰπόντος·

ὅς κε θεοῖς ἐπιπείθηται, μάλα τ' ἔκλυον αὐτοῦ.

Ὡς δὲ καὶ ὁ Μάξιμος μετὰ τοσαύτης πομπείας
ἐπὶ τὴν Κωνσταντινούπολιν ὥρμησέ τε καὶ διὰ
ταχέων εἰς αὐτὴν παρελθὼν ἐξέλαμψεν, ὅ τε γὰρ
βασιλεὺς καὶ οἱ βασιλευόμενοι πάντα ἦσαν ἐπὶ
Μαξίμῳ, νὺξ καὶ ἡμέρα διέφερεν αὐτοῖς οὐδέν,

[1] οὔτε νεῖν Cobet adds from Plato, Laws 689 D.

442

retorted : " Perhaps you have the skill and the
daring to do this, but I refuse to contend against
these omens." With these words he went away,
but Maximus remained and tried every method till
he obtained the results that he wished and desired.
Chrysanthius, however, remained more immovable
than a statue, resolved not to alter in the least the
conclusions that had originally been firmly fixed in
his mind. Thereupon all the people of Asia flocked
in haste to Maximus, not only those who at the time
held office or had been relieved of their offices,
but also the leading men in the various senates.
The common people too blocked the streets
before the house of Maximus, leaping and uttering
shouts, as is from of old the custom of the mob
whenever it would win someone's favour. Meanwhile the women poured in by the side-door to see
his wife, marvelled at her felicity, and begged her not
to forget them : and so profound was her knowledge
of philosophy that she made Maximus seem not to
know how to swim or even know his alphabet.
Thus, then, Maximus, adored by all Asia, went his
way to meet the emperor, but Chrysanthius stayed
where he was, since a god had appeared to him in
a dream, and, as he later on told the author of this
narrative, recited the following verse :

If a man obeys the gods, they in turn hearken to his
    prayer.[1]

Maximus with a numerous escort set out for
Constantinople, and on arriving there he very soon
shone out in all his glory. For both ruler and
ruled were entirely devoted to Maximus. Whether
it were day or night made no difference to them,

[1] *Iliad* i. 218.

οὕτως ὑπὲρ τῶν παρόντων ἐπὶ τοὺς θεοὺς ἅπαντα
ἀνέφερον· ἐνταῦθα ὁ μὲν Μάξιμος βαρὺς ἦν ἤδη
περὶ τὰ βασίλεια, στολήν τε ἁβροτέραν ἢ κατὰ
φιλόσοφον περιχεόμενος, καὶ πρὸς τὰς ἐντεύξεις
ὢν χαλεπώτερος καὶ δυσχερέστερος· ὁ δὲ βασιλεὺς
ἠγνόει τὰ πραττόμενα. μεταπέμψασθαι γοῦν
αὐτοῖς, ἐκβιασαμένου τοῦ βασιλέως, ἔδοξε καὶ τὸν
Πρίσκον· ὁ δὲ Μάξιμος ἐπῄτει προσαναγκάζων
καὶ τὸν Χρυσάνθιον. καὶ ἄμφω γε ἦσαν μετά-
πεμπτοι, ὁ μὲν Πρίσκος ἐκ τῆς Ἑλλάδος, Χρυσάνθιος δὲ ἀπὸ Λυδίας καὶ Σάρδεων. καὶ οὕτω γε
ἐξεκρέματο τῆς τοῦ ἀνδρὸς συνουσίας ὁ θεσπέσιος
Ἰουλιανός, ὥστε τοῖς μὲν ὡς φίλοις ἐπέστειλε,
καθάπερ θεοὺς ἱκετεύων ἐλθεῖν καὶ συνεῖναι· τῷ
δὲ Χρυσανθίῳ καὶ γυναῖκα εἶναι πυθόμενος,
Μελίτην ὄνομα ἔχουσαν καὶ ὑπ' αὐτοῦ θαυμαζο-
μένην διαφερόντως (τοῦ δὲ ταῦτα γράφοντος
ἀνεψιὰ ἦν[1]), ἰδίᾳ που καθίσας ἑαυτόν, καὶ πρὸς
τὴν γυναῖκα ἐπέστειλεν αὐτὸς γράφων, οὐδενὸς
εἰδότος, καὶ παντοίας ἀφιεὶς φωνάς, τὸν ἄνδρα
πείθειν μηδαμῶς ἀπαγορεῦσαι τὴν ἔξοδον· καὶ
τὴν πρὸς Χρυσάνθιον αἰτήσας ἐπιστολήν, εἶτα
ἐσβαλὼν ἐκείνην καὶ σφραγῖδα ἀμφοτέραις ἐπιθείς,
ὡς ἂν τὴν μίαν τοὺς ἄξοντας ἔστειλεν, πολλὰ καὶ
ἀπὸ στόματος φράσας ἃ χρήσιμα ἐνόμιζε πρὸς τὸ

ῥηϊδίως πεπιθεῖν μεγάλας φρένας Αἰακίδαο.

ὁ μὲν οὖν Πρίσκος ἦλθε, καὶ ἐλθὼν ἐσωφρόνει· καί

---

[1] ἀνεψιάν Boissonade; ἀνεψιὰ ἦν Wyttenbach.

---

[1] None of these letters by the emperor is extant.
[2] *Iliad* ix. 184.

so incessantly did they refer to the gods all questions that arose in their daily life. The result was that at the imperial court Maximus began to grow insolent, wore flowing raiment of a stuff too luxurious for a philosopher, and became more and more difficult of access and unapproachable; but the emperor knew nothing of what was going on. Then they decided, according to the urgent wishes of the emperor, to send for Priscus also; and Maximus persisted in his demand that Chrysanthius should come as well. Both men were accordingly summoned, Priscus from Greece, and Chrysanthius from Sardis in Lydia. The divine Julian was so dependent on the latter's society that he wrote to both men as though they were his intimate friends, and implored them as though they were gods to come and live with him. But in the case of Chrysanthius, on hearing that he had a wife named Melite to whom he was devotedly attached (she was a cousin of the present author), Julian retired in private and, unknown to all, he wrote with his own hand to this woman and expended every possible argument to induce her to persuade her husband not to refuse to make the journey. Then he asked for the letter that had been written to Chrysanthius, enclosed his own, set his seal on both, and dispatched messengers to take what seemed to be only one letter.[1] Moreover, he sent many verbal messages which he thought would be useful

To persuade with ease the mighty soul of the grandson of
    Aeacus.[2]

Priscus accordingly came,[3] and when there he

[3] *Cf.* Julian, *Letter to Libanius* (55 Wright), written at Antioch early in 363, in which he complains that Priscus delays his coming.

478 τοί γε οὐκ ἐλάττους ἦσαν αὐτὸν οἱ θεραπεύοντες,
ἀλλ᾽ ἔμενεν ὅμως ἀκίνητος, οὐχ ὑπὸ τῆς βασιλείας
ἐπαιρόμενος, ἀλλὰ τὴν βασιλείαν καταφέρων καὶ
ὁμαλίζων ἐς τὸ φιλοσοφώτερον.

Ὁ δὲ Χρυσάνθιος οὐδὲ ταύταις ἑάλω ταῖς
ἄρκυσι καὶ μηχαναῖς, ἀλλὰ τοῖς θεοῖς ἐντυχών,
ὡς τὰ παρὰ τῶν θεῶν ἦν ἀμετάβλητα, καὶ αὐτὸς
εἵπετο τοῖς θεοῖς, καὶ πρὸς τὸν βασιλέα ἐπέστειλεν,
ὡς ἡ κατὰ Λυδίαν ὑπὲρ αὐτοῦ γίνοιτο μονή, καὶ οἱ
θεοὶ ταῦτα ἔφραζον. ὁ δὲ ὑπώπτευσε μὲν τὴν
ἀποτυχίαν τῆς κλήσεως, ἀρχιερέα δὲ ἀποδείξας
τόν τε ἄνδρα καὶ τὴν γυναῖκα τῆς Λυδίας, καὶ
ὑπ᾽ ἐκείνοις ἐπιτρέψας εἶναι τῶν ἄλλων τὴν
αἵρεσιν, αὐτὸς ἐπὶ τὸν Περσικὸν συνηπείγετο [1]
πόλεμον. Μαξίμου δὲ καὶ Πρίσκου συνεπομένων,
καὶ ἄλλοι δέ τινες συμπαρωμάρτουν εἰς πλῆθος
συντελοῦντες, ἑαυτοὺς ἐγκωμιαζόντων ἀνθρώπων
ὄχλος, καὶ σφόδρα γε διογκουμένων, ὅτι ὁ βασιλεὺς
ἔφησεν αὐτοῖς συντετυχηκέναι. ὡς δὲ τὰ πράγματα συντόνως ἀπὸ τῶν μεγάλων ἐκείνων καὶ
λαμπρῶν ἐλπίδων ἐς τὸ ἀφανὲς καὶ ἄμορφον
κατερρύη [2] καὶ διωλίσθησεν, ὡς ἐν τοῖς διεξοδικοῖς
τοῖς κατὰ Ἰουλιανὸν εἴρηται, ὅ τε Ἰοβιανὸς
ἐβασίλευσε καὶ τιμῶν τοὺς ἄνδρας διετέλεσεν·
εἶτα μάλα ταχέως καὶ σφοδρῶς συναπῆλθε τῷ
προβασιλεύσαντι (εἴ γε δὴ παρὰ τοὺς πλείονας

---

[1] συνήγετο Boissonade ; συνηπείγετο Cobet.
[2] κατερράγη Boissonade ; κατερρύη Cobet.

---

[1] They were both present at Julian's death (Ammianus
Marcellinus xxv. 3).
[2] On Julian's death in Persia in June 363, the general
Jovian was elected emperor by the army.

behaved with great modesty. And though there were just as many who sought his favour, he nevertheless remained unmoved, and was not puffed up by the emperor's court, but rather endeavoured to lower the pride of the court and to bring it to a more philosophic level.

Chrysanthius, however, could not be caught even by such snares and devices as these, but he consulted the gods, and since the will of heaven was unchanged, he for his part obeyed the gods, and wrote to the emperor that it was in the latter's interest that he should stay in Lydia, and that the gods had informed him of this. The emperor was suspicious about the refusal of his invitation, but he appointed Chrysanthius high priest of Lydia, along with his wife, and entrusted to them the selection of other priests. Meanwhile he himself was setting out in haste for the war against Persia. Both Maximus and Priscus accompanied him,[1] and certain other sophists joined the expedition, so that they amounted to a considerable number; they were, in fact, a mob of men who sang their own praises and were inflated with pride because the emperor said that he had associated with them. But when the enterprise which began with such great and splendid hopes had fallen with a crash to a vague and shapeless ruin and had slipped through his fingers, as I have described more fully in my *Life* of Julian, Jovian[2] was made emperor, and he continued to award honours to these men. Then too swiftly and violently he passed away to join his predecessor in Empire (if, indeed, we can say of that predecessor that he merely joined the majority[3]!), and then

---

[3] Eunapius means that Julian became a god.

EUNAPIUS

οὕτως ἀπῆλθε), Βαλεντινιανός τε καὶ Βάλης ἐπέστησαν τοῖς πράγμασιν. ἐνταῦθα συναρπάζονται μὲν Μάξιμος καὶ Πρίσκος, πολὺ τῆς κλήσεως διαφερούσης ἢ ὅτε Ἰουλιανὸς ἐκάλει. ἐκείνη μὲν γάρ τις ἦν πανηγυρικὴ καὶ πρὸς τιμὴν περιττῶς διαλάμπουσα, ταύτης δὲ τῆς δευτέρας πρὸ τῶν ἐλπιζομένων καὶ τὸ φαινόμενον κίνδυνος ἦν, οὕτως ἀτιμία τις ἁδρὰ καὶ περιφανὴς κατεκέχυτο τῶν ὁρωμένων. ἀλλ' ὁ μὲν Πρίσκος οὐδὲν ὑποστὰς δεινόν, ἀλλὰ καὶ προσμαρτυρηθεὶς ἀγαθὸς εἶναι καὶ γεγενῆσθαι κατὰ τὸν καιρὸν ἐκεῖνον, ἐπανῆλθεν εἰς τὴν Ἑλλάδα· καὶ ὁ ταῦτα γράφων ἐπαιδεύετο κατ' ἐκείνους τοὺς χρόνους παῖς ὢν καὶ εἰς ἐφήβους ἄρτι τελῶν. ὁ δὲ Μάξιμος, πολλοὶ μὲν γὰρ αὐτοῦ κατεβόων δημοσίᾳ τε ἐν τοῖς θεάτροις καὶ ἰδίᾳ πρὸς τὸν βασιλέα, θαυμαστὸς δὲ ἦν καὶ οὕτως, ὅτι πρὸς τοσαύτας ἀνέφερε συμφοράς· πλὴν ἐς τὸ βαθύτατον αὐτὸν τῆς τιμωρίας περιάγουσι, τοσούτων τιμήσαντες χρημάτων, ὅσα μήτε ἀνὴρ ἀκούειν ἐδύνατο φιλοσοφῶν (ὑπώπτευον γὰρ αὐτὸν τὰ πάντων ἔχειν), καὶ μετεγίνωσκον, ὡς[1] ὀλίγου τιμήσαντες αὐτῷ. καὶ ἀνεπέμφθη γε εἰς τὴν Ἀσίαν ἐπὶ καταβολῇ τῶν χρημάτων, καὶ ὅσα μὲν ἔπασχεν ὑπὲρ πᾶσάν ἐστι τραγῳδίαν, καὶ οὐδεὶς ἂν εἴη μεγαλόφωνος, οὐδὲ ἡδόμενος κακοῖς, ὥστε ἐξαγγέλλειν ἀνδρὸς τοσούτου τηλικαύτας συμφοράς. μικρὰ γὰρ καὶ ἡ Περσῶν λεγομένη σκάφευσις, καὶ οἱ γυναικεῖοι

[1] καὶ Boissonade ; ὡς Wyttenbach.

[1] Or "The Trough"; for this torture see Plutarch, *Artaxerxes* 16, where it is fully described.

448

Valentinian and Valens succeeded to the Imperial
throne. Thereupon Maximus and Priscus were
carried off in custody, and this time their summons
was very different from the time when Julian
invited them. For then the summons was, as it
were, to some public festival and it lit up the path
to ample honours; but in that second summons,
instead of bright hopes, danger was clearly visible,
for the fear of public and overwhelming disgrace
veiled for them the whole prospect. Priscus, however, suffered no harm, and since evidence was
produced that he was a righteous man and had
behaved virtuously at the time I speak of, he
returned to Greece. It was at the time when the
author of this narrative was being educated, and
was still a boy just arrived at adolescence.
But Maximus, though many clamoured against
him, both in public in the theatres and privately
to the emperor, in spite of this won admiration
because he bore up against such great misfortunes.
Nevertheless they inflicted on him the severest
possible punishment; for they fined him a sum of
money so large that a philosopher could hardly even
have heard of such an amount (this was because
they suspected that he possessed the property of all
the others); and then they regretted it on the
ground that they had made his fine too small. He
was sent into Asia to make payment of the money,
and what he suffered there was beyond any tragedy,
and none could have the power of utterance or take
such pleasure in the misfortunes of others as to
report fully the terrible sufferings of this great man.
For even the Persian torture called "The Boat," [1] or
the painful toil of the women with the hoe among

449

τῶν Ἀρτάβρων σκαλισμοί, πρὸς τὰς ἐπιφερομένας
479 ὀδύνας τῷ σώματι. καὶ ἡ θαυμασία γυνὴ παρῆν
καὶ ὑπερήλγει. ὡς δὲ ἦν ἄπειρον, καὶ ἐπετείνετο,
" πριαμένη," φησίν " ὦ γύναι, φάρμακον, ἐπίδος,
καὶ ἐλευθέρωσον." ἡ δὲ καὶ ἐπρίατο καὶ παρῆν
ἔχουσα. ἐνταῦθα ὁ μὲν ᾔτει πιεῖν, ἡ δὲ ἠξίωσε
προπιεῖν, καὶ αὐτίκα γε ἀπολομένης, τὴν μὲν οἱ
προσήκοντες ἔθαπτον· ὁ δὲ Μάξιμος ἔπιεν οὐκέτι.

Ἐνταῦθα δὴ πᾶς λόγος ἐλάττων, καὶ πᾶν ὅσον
ἂν τὸ ποιητικὸν ὑμνήσειε γένος, πρὸς τὰς Κλεάρχου
πράξεις. ἦν μὲν γὰρ ὁ Κλέαρχος ἐκ Θεσπρωτῶν
τῶν εὐδαιμόνων, καὶ διαφερόντως περὶ δόξαν
καλὴν γενόμενος, τῶν πραγμάτων ἤδη μετα-
βεβλημένων, καὶ Βαλεντινιανοῦ μὲν εἰς τὴν ἑσπέραν
ἀποκεχωρηκότος, τοῦ δὲ βασιλέως Βάλεντος
κινδύνοις τοῖς ἐσχάτοις ἐμβεβηκότος, καὶ οὐ τὸν
περὶ βασιλείας, ἀλλὰ τὸν περὶ σωτηρίας ἀγῶνα
τρέχοντος· ὁ γὰρ Προκόπιος ἀνταναστὰς πολλαῖς
καὶ ἀπείροις δυνάμεσι, πανταχόθεν αὐτὸν περιέ-
κοπτεν εἰς τὸ συλληφθῆναι,[1] τῆς οὖν Ἀσίας ἁπάσης κατ' ἐκεῖνον τὸν καιρὸν ὁ Κλέαρχος ἐπεστάτει,
ὅση κατὰ τὴν ἐξουσίαν ἀφ' Ἑλλησπόντου διὰ
Λυδίας καὶ Πισιδίας ἐπὶ Παμφυλίαν ἀφορίζεται.
καὶ[2] πολλὴν εἰς τὰ πράγματα συνέφερεν εὔνοιαν,
τῷ τε σώματι παραβαλλόμενος ἐς τοὺς πρώτους
κινδύνους, καὶ πρὸς τὸν τῆς αὐλῆς ἔπαρχον ἄντικρυς
διαφερόμενος, ὥστε οὐδὲ ὁ βασιλεὺς τὴν διαφορὰν

---

[1] συνήμεναι MSS.; συλληφθῆναι Wyttenbach, to improve the
sense. Giangrande suggests συνημμένον.
[2] καὶ before πολλὴν Wyttenbach adds.

[1] Strabo iii. 220 describes the toilsome gold-digging of the
women of this tribe in Lusitania. Tzetzes, *Chiliad* x. 885.
echoes Eunapius.

the Artabri[1] is not to be compared with the agonies inflicted on the body of Maximus. His wonderful wife was ever by his side and grieved over his sufferings. But when there seemed to be no limit to them and they even grew more intense, he said to her: " My wife, buy poison, give it to me and set me free." Accordingly she bought it and came with it in her hand. Thereupon he asked for it to drink but she insisted on drinking first, and when she had straightway died her relatives buried her: but after that Maximus did not drink.

And now all my eloquence and all the praises that the tribe of poets might sing would prove unequal to describe the conduct of Clearchus.[2] Clearchus came of a rich family in Thesprotis and had himself won a distinguished reputation when the whole course of events was changed. For Valentinian withdrew to the empire of the West,[3] while the Emperor Valens became involved in the utmost dangers, and had to enter a contest not only for empire but for his very life. For Procopius had revolted against him with unlimited forces and was harassing him from all sides to bring about his capture. Now Clearchus was at that time governor of all Asia, that is to say of the domain that extends from the Hellespont through Lydia and Pisidia as far as the boundaries of Pamphylia. And he displayed great kindness in his government and exposed his own person to the greatest risks, and openly carried on a quarrel with the pretorian prefect, so that not even the emperor could ignore

[2] Clearchus was a frequent correspondent of Libanius. He was prefect of Constantinople 398–402.
[3] In 363. The revolt of Procopius was in 365.

ἠγνόει. καί τοί γε ἦν ἔπαρχος Σαλούτιος, ἀνήρ
καὶ ἐπὶ τῆς Ἰουλιανοῦ βασιλείας κοσμήσας τὴν
ἑαυτοῦ ψυχήν,[1] ἀλλ᾽ ὅμως τήν τε βλακείαν αὐτοῦ
διὰ τὸ γῆρας ἀπήλεγξε καὶ Νικίαν ἀπεκάλει· καὶ
γὰρ ἔμελεν αὐτῷ κατὰ τὸν καιρὸν ἐκεῖνον μοσ-
χεύειν καὶ ῥωννύναι τὴν ψυχὴν ὑπ᾽ ἀναγνώσεώς
τε καὶ τῆς ἱστορικῆς ἐμπειρίας.

Χωρησάντων δὲ καλῶς τῶν πραγμάτων, ὁ
Βάλης ὑπερηγάσθη Κλέαρχον, καὶ οὐκ ἀπέλυσε
τῆς ἀρχῆς, ἀλλ᾽ εἰς ἀρχὴν μετέστησε μείζονα,
ἀνθύπατον αὐτὸν ἐπιστήσας τῆς νῦν ἰδίως Ἀσίας
καλουμένης. αὕτη δὲ ἀπὸ Περγάμου τὸ ἀλιτενὲς
ἐπέχουσα τὴν[2] ὑπερκειμένην ἤπειρον ἄχρι Καρίας
ἀποτέμνεται, καὶ ὁ Τμῶλος αὐτῆς περιγράφει τὸ
πρὸς Λυδίαν. ἔστι δὲ ἀρχῶν ἐνδοξοτάτη, καὶ οὐ
κατήκοος τοῦ τῆς αὐλῆς ἐπάρχου, πλὴν ὅσα γε
νῦν πάλιν ἐς τὸν νεώτερον τουτονὶ θόρυβον ἅπαντα
συμπέφυρται[3] καὶ ἀνατετάρακται. τότε δὲ τὴν
ὑγιαίνουσαν Ἀσίαν ἀπολαβὼν ὁ Κλέαρχος, εὗρεν
ἐκεῖ τὸν Μάξιμον κατατεινόμενον ταῖς βασάνοις,
καὶ μόλις ἀνέχοντα. θεῖον δὴ τὸ μετὰ ταῦτά ἐστιν
εἰπεῖν ἔργον, οὐ γὰρ ἄν τις τὸ οὕτω παράλογον ἐς
ἄλλον τινὰ ἀναφέροι δικαίως ἢ θεόν· τούς τε
γὰρ στρατιώτας ἅπαντας, οἳ ταύταις ἐφεστήκεσαν

---

[1] τύχην Boissonade ; ψυχήν Cobet.
[2] Before τὴν Wyttenbach deletes πρός.
[3] συμπεφύρκται Boissonade ; συμπέφυρται Cobet.

---

[1] This is the prefect of Gaul to whom Julian addressed
his *Orations* iv. and viii. The spelling in the Greek text,
"Salutius," is often used instead of Sallustius. I give
the more usual form. His official name, *e.g.* in inscriptions,
was Secundus. After Julian's death he was offered and
refused the throne, and again on the death of Jovian, in 364,

their quarrel. The prefect's name was Sallust,[1] and
in the reign of the Emperor Julian he had perfected
and adorned his own mind. Nevertheless Clearchus
exposed his slothfulness due to old age, and nicknamed him Nicias.[2] And in fact in those days he
thought only of nurturing and strengthening his
mind by reading and by inquiry into the facts of
history.

Now when he saw that things went so well,
Valens felt unbounded admiration for Clearchus, and
far from removing him from his office he transferred
him to a post of greater importance and appointed
him proconsul of all that is to-day properly called
Asia. This province embraces the sea coast from
Pergamon and includes the hinterland of that coast
as far as Caria, while Mount Tmolos circumscribes
its limits in the direction of Lydia. It is the most
illustrious of all the provinces and is outside the
jurisdiction of the pretorian prefect, save in so far as
everything has been thrown into confusion and disorder in these later troubles.[3] But, at the time I
speak of, Asia was still free from sedition when
Clearchus took over the government; and there he
discovered Maximus racked by tortures and barely
able to endure them. I must now relate a supernatural occurrence; for none could justly ascribe to
any other than a god a thing so amazing. For all the
soldiers who had been assigned to punish Maximus

refused it for himself and his son. He seems to have been
prefect of the East in 365, but resigned because of the
hostility of the proconsul of Asia, Clearchus.

[2] Nicias, the Athenian general, pursued a policy of
" watchful waiting " in the Peloponnesian War.

[3] Perhaps he refers to the supremacy of the Goths about
398, or the sedition of Antioch in 387.

ἀλήκτως ταῖς κολάσεσι, μείζονι βίᾳ φυγεῖν ἐπηνάγκασε,[1] καὶ τὸν Μάξιμον ἀνῆκε τῶν δεσμῶν, ἐπιμέλειάν τε ἐποιήσατο τοῦ σώματος, καὶ ὁμοτράπεζον ἔθετο, καὶ πρὸς τὸν βασιλέα τοσαύτῃ κατεχρήσατο παρρησίᾳ, ὥστε ὁ βασιλεὺς ἤδη καὶ μεθῆκε τὴν ψυχήν, καὶ πάντα γε συνεχώρησεν ὅσα Κλέαρχος ἔπειθε. τῷ γοῦν Σαλουτίῳ τὴν ἀρχὴν παραλύσας, Αὐξόνιον ἐπέστησε[2] τοῖς τῆς αὐλῆς ἔργοις. ὁ δὲ Κλέαρχος τούς τε κολαστῆρας ἐκείνους στρατιώτας, καὶ ὅσοι[3] κατὰ τὸν ἀτυχῆ χρόνον ἐκεῖνον ἦσαν ὑφελόμενοί τι καὶ ὑβρίσαντες, τοὺς μὲν ἠμύνετο, τοὺς δὲ εἰσεπράττετο· καὶ πάντες τοῦτο διὰ στόματος εἶχον ὡς εἴη δεύτερος Ἰουλιανὸς τῷ Μαξίμῳ. ἐνταῦθα δὴ καὶ δημοσίας τινὰς ἐπιδείξεις ὁ Μάξιμος ἐποιήσατο, ἀλλ' (οὐ γὰρ ἐπεφύκει πρὸς θέατρον) τὴν δόξαν εἰς ἐλάχιστον ἤνεγκεν, ἕως ἀνέφερεν ἑαυτόν, διαλεγόμενος πάλιν. πολλὰ γοῦν τῶν τε κτημάτων ἀνεκομίζετο,[4] καὶ τῶν ἑτέρως πως διακεκλεμμένων, καὶ ἦν ταχὺ μάλα ὄλβιος, καὶ ὥσπερ ἄρτι παριὼν εἰς τὴν Ἰουλιανοῦ βασιλείαν. ὁ δὲ καὶ εἰς τὴν Κωνσταντινούπολιν περιφανὴς ὢν ἐπεδήμησε, καὶ πάντες αὐτὸν ἐδεδοίκεσαν, τήν τε τύχην ἀνισταμένην ὁρῶντες· † καὶ τῆς ἀσινότητος τῆς περὶ θεουργίας ἐστὶ μὲν πεπειραμένος, τὴν δὲ ἐς τόνδε ἐπὶ πλέον ἐδόξαζεν.†[5] ἐνταῦθα δὲ αὐτῷ πάλιν διὰ τὸ πολὺ κλέος τραχύτερον ἀνέφυ πάθος. οἱ

---

[1] ἀπηνάγκασε Boissonade; ἐπηνάγκασε Cobet.
[2] ἐπενόησε Boissonade; ἐπέστησε Wyttenbach.
[3] ὅσον Boissonade; ὅσοι Wyttenbach.
[4] κατεκομίζετο Boissonade: ἀνεκομίζετο Cobet.

without respite, by superior force he compelled to flee,
released him from his fetters, charged himself with
the cure of his body, and made him sit at his own
table. Moreover he spoke so boldly and frankly to the
emperor that the latter not only relaxed his wrath
but conceded everything that Clearchus advised.
Thus he relieved Sallust of his office and appointed
Auxonius[1] to the duties of pretorian prefect. Then
Clearchus proceeded to punish the soldiers who had
tortured Maximus, from all who in that unhappy
time had stolen anything from him he exacted re-
payment, and punished those who had insulted him ;
so that this saying was in the mouths of all that
he was a second Julian to Maximus. Thereupon
Maximus even delivered public declamations, but since
he was not naturally fitted to speak to a sophistic
audience he increased his reputation little thereby,
until at last he began to lift up his head again and
resumed his lectures on philosophy. Thus he recovered much of his wealth and of what had been
stolen from him in various ways, and very speedily
he became prosperous and as well off as when he
first arrived at Julian's court. Next he actually
visited Constantinople as a distinguished personage,
and all men regarded him with awe when they found
that his fortunes were restored. He even risked a
test of his innocence in the matter of theurgy, and
still further increased his reputation.[2] Thereupon
once more his widespread renown gave birth to
harsh feelings against him. For the courtiers framed

[1] Zosimus iv. 10.
[2] The text is mutilated and the meaning obscure.

[5] καὶ . . . ἐδόξαζεν is corrupt. Mayor reads δεινότητος
for ἀσινότητος, Giangrande τὸν λόγον for τόνδε.

γὰρ περὶ τὰ βασίλεια τοῖς βασιλεῦσιν ἐπιβουλὴν [1]
τινὰ συστησάμενοι καὶ προστησάμενοι μαντεῖον
ἰδιωτικὸν (οὐ παντός ἐστι καταμαθεῖν ὃ λέγω),
χρησμοῦ τινος ἐκπεσόντος ἀσαφεστέρου, τὸν χρησμὸν ἐπὶ τὸν Μάξιμον ἀνήνεγκαν, τὸ μὲν πρᾶγμα
οὐχ ὁμολογήσαντες, ὡς δ᾽ ἂν αὐτοῦ χρήσαντος
καὶ ἀνελόντος τι σαφέστερον βουλόμενοι μαθεῖν·
δέδεικτο γὰρ τότε τὰ τῶν θεῶν Μάξιμον μόνον
εἰδέναι, κἂν ἐπικεκαλυμμένα πρὸς τοὺς ἄλλους
φέρηται. ὁ δὲ τὸν νοῦν ἐπιστήσας καὶ διαθρῶν
τὰ λεγόμενα, τὸ κεκρυμμένον μὲν ἐν τοῖς λόγοις,
ὃν δὲ ἀληθῶς, εἶδεν ὀξέως, καὶ μαντείαν ἀλη-
θέστερον ἐξήνεγκεν, ὡς τόν τε ἀναγνόντα (λέγων
ἑαυτόν) ἀπώλεσαν, καὶ πάντας, οὐ τοὺς εἰδότας
τὴν τάξιν [2] μόνον, προσέθηκεν, ἀλλὰ καὶ τὸ κολα-
σθησόμενον ἀδίκως πλέον ἀπέφηνεν, ἐξ ἀδύτων δὲ
ἐπέθηκεν ὅτι " μετὰ τὴν ἁπάντων κοινὴν καὶ
πολύτροπον φθοράν, ἐν ᾗ τοῦ φόνου ἔργον ἐσό-
μεθα, ὁ βασιλεὺς ξένον τινὰ διαφθαρήσεται [3] τρόπον
οὐδὲ ταφῆς ἀξιωθείς, οὐδὲ ἐνδόξου τάφου." καὶ
ταῦτα ἔσχεν οὕτως, καὶ ἐν τοῖς διεξοδικοῖς ἀκριβέστερον γέγραπται. ἑαλώκεσαν μὲν γὰρ αὐτίκα
οἵ τε συστησάμενοι καὶ ἀρθμήσαντες· πάντων δὲ
πανταχόθεν ἁρπαζομένων καὶ κατακοπτομένων,
ὥσπερ ἀλεκτορίδων ἐν ἑορτῇ καὶ συμποσίῳ κοινὴν
εὐωχίαν ἐχόντι, καὶ ὁ Μάξιμος συνηρπάσθη μέν,
καὶ εἰς τὴν Ἀντιόχειαν ἦλθεν, ἔνθα ὁ βασιλεὺς
διέτριβεν· αἰσχυνθέντες δὲ αὐτοῦ τὸν φόνον, ὡς

---

[1] βαστα . . . twelve letters missing. Wyttenbach suggests βασιλεῦσιν ἀχθόμενοι συνωμοσίαν; Lundström βασιλεῦσι
ἐπιβουλήν. [2] παράταξιν Giangrande.
[3] ἅμα φθαρήσεται Boissonade: ἀναφθαρήσεται Giangrande

a conspiracy against the emperors and put forward some private oracle of their own (it is not everyone who can understand what I mean), and when some obscure oracular utterance was given they referred it to Maximus, without admitting to him their real aim, but as though he himself had given forth and reported the oracle, and they desired to learn its meaning more clearly. For it had been made manifest at that time that Maximus alone knew the purposes of the gods, however obscurely they might be conveyed to other men. Accordingly, by putting his mind on the oracle and closely observing what it said, he quickly saw the hidden sense of the words, that is, the truth itself, and he revealed it more truly than an oracle, namely that they had ruined both him who published it, meaning himself, and all men besides, added he, not only those who knew of their plot; but he declared that many more would be unjustly chastised. Moreover from the inmost shrine, as it were, he announced: "After the general and multiform slaughter of all men, in which we shall be the victims of the massacre, the emperor will die a strange death, and will not be given burial or the honour of a tomb." Thus indeed it came to pass, as I have described more fully in my *Universal History*. For presently the conspirators who had banded together were arrested, and while they were being dragged to prison from all directions and beheaded, like hens at some festival or banquet to entertain the whole populace, Maximus too was dragged away with them, and so came to Antioch where the emperor[1] was staying at the time. But they were ashamed to put him to

[1] Valens. For the execution of Maximus at Ephesus in 371 *cf.* Ammianus Marcellinus xxix. 1; Zosimus iv. 15.

πάντα ἐπὶ τῆς κρίσεως ἠλέγχθη, καὶ ὅτι κατέγνω
τῶν ἐγχειρησάντων, καὶ ὅτι προεῖπεν ἀκριβῶς
ἅπαντα, καθάπερ ἐν τῷ Μαξίμου σώματι θεόν
τινα κολάζοντες, φονικήν τινα καὶ μαγειρώδη
ψυχὴν τὸν Φῆστον ἐπὶ τὴν Ἀσίαν αὐτῷ συνεξ-
έπεμψαν, τὴν Ἀσίαν τοιούτου τινὸς ἀξιώσαντες.
ὁ δὲ παραγενόμενος τὸ προσταχθὲν ἔπραξε καὶ
παρ' ἑαυτοῦ προσέθηκεν, ἄφθονόν τινα χορηγίαν
τῷ συώδει καὶ λελυσσηκότι τῆς ψυχῆς νέμων·
πολλοὺς γὰρ προκατακόψας αἰτίους τε καὶ ἀναιτίους,
καὶ τὸν μέγαν Μάξιμον αὐτοῖς ἐπέσφαξε. κἀκεῖνο
μὲν εἶχεν ἡ μαντεία τέλος, ἀπέβαινε δὲ καὶ τὰ
λειπόμενα. ὅ τε γὰρ βασιλεὺς ἐν μεγάλῃ τῶν
Σκυθῶν μάχῃ ξένον τινὰ ἠφανίσθη τρόπον, ὥστε
οὐδὲ ὀστέον εἰς ἀναίρεσιν εὑρέθη· προσεπέθηκε
481 δὲ ὁ δαίμων καὶ ἕτερόν τι μεῖζον· ὁ γὰρ Φῆστος
ἐκεῖνος (καὶ ταῦτα δὲ ἀκριβῶς ὁ γράφων παρὼν
συνηπίστατο) παραλυθεὶς τῆς ἀρχῆς, καὶ ἀποδη-
μήσας πρὸς τὸν νεωστὶ βασιλεύοντα Θεοδόσιον,
εἶτα ἐπανελθὼν (ἐγεγαμήκει γὰρ ἐκ τῆς Ἀσίας
γάμον τυραννίδι πρέποντα), καὶ τὴν τρυφὴν
ἐπιδεικνύμενος καὶ τὸ διαπεφευγέναι τὰ ἐγκλήματα,
ἑορτήν τε ἐπήγγελλε πολυτελῆ τοῖς ἐν ἀξιώματι
καὶ κατὰ εὐγένειαν προβεβηκόσιν. ἡ τρίτη δὲ
ἦν ἡμέρα τῶν καλανδῶν ἃς οὕτως Ἰανουαρίας
ἡμέρας Ῥωμαῖοι προσονομάζουσι, καὶ προσκυνήσαντες πάντες αὐτῷ ὑπέσχοντο τὴν εὐωχίαν. ὁ δὲ

---

[1] For Festus cf. Ammianus xxix. 2.

[2] Ammianus xxxi. 13 "nec postea repertus est usquam."
The battle was at Adrianople in 378, against the Goths ; late
writers often confuse them with the Scythians.

death, both because he had refuted every charge
at the trial and convicted of falsehood those who
had laid hands on him, and because he had so
precisely foretold all that was happening; therefore just as though in the person of Maximus they
were punishing some god, they sent away with
him into Asia a certain Festus,[1] a man of a
murderous disposition with the soul of a butcher,
judging Asia to be a worthy abode for such a
man. When he arrived he carried out his orders,
and of his own accord even went beyond them
and indulged to the top of his bent his beast-
like and rabid temperament. For first he cut off
the heads of many, guilty and innocent alike,
and next he slaughtered Maximus, that great man.
So the oracle was fulfilled, and the rest of it
also came to pass. For the emperor in a fierce
battle with the Scythians was done away with in
a strange fashion,[2] so that not even a bone was
found to bury. The will of Heaven added to all
this a still more wonderful occurrence. For that
same Festus (and this the author learned accurately
as an eyewitness), was deprived of his office, and
first he went to visit Theodosius who had lately
been made emperor; then he returned to Asia
(for he had there contracted a marriage splendid
enough for a tyrant), and to make a display of his
luxurious living and his escape from all the charges
against him, he announced that he would give a
magnificent banquet to those who held the most
distinguished offices or were of the highest nobility.
Now it was the third day after the January Calends,
as the Romans call them, and they all saluted him
and promised to come to the banquet. Then Festus

παρῆλθε μὲν εἰς τὸ τῶν Νεμέσεων ἱερόν (καὶ τοί γε οὐδέποτε φήσας θεραπεύειν θεούς, ἀλλ᾽ οὓς ἐκόλασεν ἅπαντας διὰ τοῦτο ἀνῃρηκώς), παρελθὼν δὲ ὅμως, αὐτοῖς ὄναρ ἀπήγγειλε καὶ κατεδάκρυε τὴν ὄψιν διηγούμενος. τὸ δὲ ὄνειρον ἦν· τὸν Μάξιμον ἔφασκε τραχηλάγχην ἐπιλαβόμενον ἕλκειν αὐτὸν εἰς τὸν ᾅδην, ὡς δικασόμενον ἐπὶ τοῦ Πλουτέως. οἱ δὲ παρόντες, καίπερ δεδιότες καὶ πρὸς τὸν ὅλον τοῦ ἀνδρὸς ἀναφέροντες βίον, τά τε δάκρυα ἀπέψηχεν ἕκαστος, καὶ ταῖν Θεαῖν ἐκέλευον εὔχεσθαι· ὁ δὲ ἐπείθετο καὶ ηὔχετο. ἐξιόντι δὲ αὐτῷ, τοῖν ποδοῖν ἀμφοῖν ὑπενεχθέντων, ἐπὶ τὰ νῶτα ἐξολισθαίνει τὸ σῶμα, καὶ ἄναυδος ἔκειτο· καὶ ἀπενεχθεὶς αὐτίκα ἐτελεύτησε, καὶ τοῦτο ἔδοξεν εἶναι τῆς Προνοίας ἔργον ἄριστον.

Περὶ δὲ Πρίσκου τὰ μὲν πολλὰ κατὰ τὴν περιπεσοῦσαν ἀνάγκην καὶ πρότερον εἴρηται, ὅθεν τε ἦν· ἴδιον δὲ κατὰ τὸ ἦθος αὐτοῦ τοιοῦτον ἀπομνημονεύεται· κρυψίνους τε ἦν ἄγαν καὶ βαθυγνώμων, μνήμης τε εἰς ἄκρον ἀφιγμένος, καὶ τὰς δόξας ἁπάσας τῶν παλαιῶν συνῃρηκὼς καὶ ἐπὶ στόματος ἔχων· κάλλιστος δὲ ὢν καὶ μέγας ὀφθῆναι, καὶ ἀπαίδευτος ἂν ἔδοξεν εἶναι διὰ τὸ μόλις χωρεῖν ἐς διάλεξιν, ἀλλ᾽ ὡς θησαυρόν γέ τινα ἐφύλαττε τὰ δόγματα, καὶ τοὺς εὐκόλως περὶ αὐτῶν προϊεμένους φωνὴν ἀσώτους ἔφασκεν. οὐ γὰρ τὸν νικώμενον ἐν ταῖς διαλέξεσιν ἐξημεροῦσθαι μᾶλλον

---

[1] Two deities called Nemesis were worshipped in Asia, and especially at Smyrna.

entered the temple of the Goddesses Nemesis,[1] though he had never professed any reverence for the gods, nay it was for their worship of the gods that he punished all his victims with death; still he did enter, and related to those present a vision he had had, and as he told the tale his face was bathed in tears. Now the dream was as follows: he said that Maximus threw a noose round his neck, seized him, and dragged him down to Hades to have his case tried before Pluto. All present were terrified when they recalled the whole life of the man, but they each of them dried their tears, and bade him pray to the Goddesses. He obeyed them and offered up his prayers. But as he came forth from the temple both his feet slipped from under him, and he fell on his back and lay there speechless. He was carried home and at once expired, an event that was considered to be a most admirable dispensation of Providence.

Concerning PRISCUS I have already related many facts, for I had to do so now and then, as it fell out, and so I have spoken of his birthplace. But of his character the following account is separately recorded. He was of a too secretive disposition, and his learning was recondite and abstruse; moreover, his memory was extraordinarily good, and he had collected all the teachings of the ancients and had them ever on his tongue. In appearance he was very handsome and tall, and he might have been thought uneducated, because it was so hard to induce him to engage in disputation, and he kept his own convictions hidden as though he were guarding a treasure, and used to term prodigals those who too lightly gave out their views on these matters. For he used to say that one who is beaten in philosophical

461

ἔφασκεν, ἀλλὰ πρὸς τὴν δύναμιν τῆς ἀληθειας
ἀντιβαίνοντα, ταῖς τε ὀδύναις καὶ τῷ φιλοτίμῳ
κατακλώμενον ἀγριοῦσθαι, καὶ μισόλογόν τε ἅμα
καὶ μισοφιλόσοφον ἀποτελεῖσθαι καὶ διαταράτ-
τεσθαι. διὰ ταύτην οὖν τὴν αἰτίαν ἐπεῖχε τὰ
πολλά. καὶ βραδὺς ἦν καὶ ὀγκώδης κατὰ τὸ ἦθος,
καὶ τὸ ἦθος ἐφύλαττεν οὐ μόνον ὅτε ἑταίροις καὶ
ὁμιληταῖς συνῆν, ἀλλ᾽ ἐκ νεότητος αὐτῷ τὸ ἀξίωμα
συνεγήρασεν. ὁ γοῦν Χρυσάνθιος πρὸς τὸν ταῦτα
γράφοντα ἔλεγεν, ὡς ὁ μὲν Αἰδεσίου τρόπος κοινὸς
ἦν καὶ δημοτικός, καὶ μετά γε τοὺς ἄθλους ὅσοι
περὶ λόγους ἦσαν, πρὸς περίπατον ἐξῄει κατὰ τὸ
Πέργαμον, καὶ τῶν ἑταίρων παρῆσαν οἱ τιμιώ-
τεροι· ὁ δὲ διδάσκαλος ἁρμονίαν τινὰ καὶ ἐπιμέλειαν
πρὸς τὸ ἀνθρώπειον ἐμφυτεύων τοῖς μαθηταῖς,
ὡς ἀσυφήλους αὐτοὺς ἑώρα, καὶ δι᾽ ἀγερωχίαν
τῶν δογμάτων ὑπέρφρονας, καὶ τὰ πτερὰ μακρό-
482 τερα καὶ ἁπαλώτερα τοῦ Ἰκαρίου, καταβιβάζων
αὐτοὺς οὐκ ἐπὶ τὸν πόντον, ἀλλ᾽ ἐπὶ τὴν γῆν καὶ
τὸ ἀνθρώπινον. αὐτὸς ὁ ταῦτα διδάσκων λαχανό-
πωλίν τε ἀπαντήσας ἡδέως ἂν εἶδε, καὶ τὴν
πορείαν ἐπιστήσας προσεφθέγξατο, καὶ περὶ τιμῆς
ἂν διελέχθη πρὸς αὐτήν, ὅτι πολὺ τὸ καπηλεῖον
ἐργάζεται, καὶ ἅμα διῄει τὴν γεωργίαν τοῦ λαχάνου
πρὸς αὐτήν. καὶ πρὸς ὑφάντην τοιοῦτον ἄν τι
ἐποίησεν ἕτερον, καὶ πρὸς χαλκέα καὶ τέκτονα.
οἱ μὲν οὖν σωφρονέστεροι τῶν ἑταίρων ἐξεπαι-
δεύοντο ταῦτα, καὶ μάλιστα Χρυσάνθιος, καὶ εἴ τις
ἦν ἐκείνης τῆς διατριβῆς Χρυσανθίῳ παραπλήσιος.

argument does not thereby become milder, but rather, as he fights against the might of the truth and suffers the pains of thwarted ambition, he becomes more savage, and ends by hating both letters and philosophy equally, and by being thoroughly confused in his mind. For this reason, therefore, he usually maintained his reserve. His bearing was deliberate and lofty, and he preserved this bearing not only when he was with his friends and disciples, but the authority of his manner remained with him from youth to old age. Hence Chrysanthius used to say to the author of this work that the manners of Aedesius were sociable and democratic, and after their competitions in literature and disputations, he would go for a walk in Pergamon accompanied by the more distinguished of his pupils. And their teacher used to implant in his pupils a feeling of harmony, and of responsibility towards mankind when he observed that they were intolerant and overbearing because of their pride in their own opinions; and when they spread their wings further than those of Icarus, though they were even more fragile, he would lead them gently down, not into the sea, but to the land and to human life. While he thus instructed them, he himself, if he met a woman selling vegetables, was pleased to see her and would stop in his walk to speak to her and discuss the price she charged, and say that her shop was making a good profit; and at the same time he used to talk with her about the cultivation of vegetables. He would behave in the same fashion to a weaver, or a smith, or a carpenter. Thus the more diligent of his pupils were trained in this affability, especially Chrysanthius and all who in that school resembled Chrysanthius.

463

Μόνος δὲ ὁ Πρίσκος οὐδὲ παρόντος ἐφείδετο
τοῦ διδασκάλου, ἀλλὰ προδότην τε αὐτὸν ἐκάλει
τοῦ τῆς φιλοσοφίας ἀξιώματος, καὶ ἄνθρωπον
λογάρια εἰδότα, κρείττονα μὲν πρὸς ψυχῆς ἀνα-
γωγήν, οὐ φυλαττόμενα δὲ ἐπὶ τῶν ἔργων. ἀλλ'
ὅμως τοιοῦτος ὤν, καὶ μετὰ[1] τὴν Ἰουλιανοῦ βασιλείαν ἀμώμητος ἔμεινε, καὶ πολλούς τε νεω-
τερισμοὺς ἐνεγκὼν κορυβαντιώντων ἐπὶ σοφίᾳ
μειρακίων, καὶ ἐπὶ πᾶσι τὸ βαθὺ διαφυλάττων
ἦθος, καὶ γελῶν τὴν ἀνθρωπίνην ἀσθένειαν, τοῖς
τῆς Ἑλλάδος ἱεροῖς, εἰς μακρόν τι γῆρας ἀνύσας,
ὅς γε ἦν ὑπὲρ τὰ ἐνενήκοντα, συναπώλετο· πολλῶν
καὶ ἄλλων ἐν τῷδε τῷ χρόνῳ τῶν μὲν διὰ λύπην
προϊεμένων τὸν βίον, οἱ δὲ ὑπὸ τῶν βαρβάρων
κατεκόπτοντο· ἐν οἷς Προτέριός τε ἦν τις ἐκ
Κεφαληνίας τῆς νήσου, καὶ ἐμαρτυρεῖτο καλὸς
καὶ ἀγαθὸς εἶναι. Ἱλάριον δὲ καὶ ὁ ταῦτα γράφων
ἠπίστατο, ἄνδρα Βιθυνὸν μὲν τὸ γένος, Ἀθήνησι
δὲ καταγηράσαντα, πρὸς δὲ τῷ καθαρῷ τῆς ἄλλης
παιδείας, κατὰ γραφικὴν οὕτω φιλοσοφήσαντα,
ὥστε οὐκ ἐτεθνήκει ἐν ταῖς ἐκείνου χερσὶν ὁ
Εὐφράνωρ. καὶ ὁ ταῦτα γράφων διὰ τοῦτο τὸ
ἐν εἴδεσι καλὸν ἐθαύμαζε καὶ ὑπερηγάπα. ἀλλ'
ὅμως καὶ Ἱλάριος τῶν ἀπολαυσάντων ἦν τῆς
κοινῆς συμφορᾶς, ἔξω μὲν εὑρεθεὶς τῶν Ἀθηνῶν
(πλησίον γάρ που Κορίνθου διέτριβε), κατακοπεὶς
δὲ παρὰ τῶν βαρβάρων ἅμα τοῖς οἰκέταις. καὶ

---

[1] For μετὰ Cobet prefers κατὰ in the sense that Priscus was
popular *in spite of* Julian's patronage. The change is unnecessary.

[1] For this phrase see Demosthenes, *On the False Embassy*
421, echoed by Philostratus, *Lives of the Sophists*, p. 623.

But Priscus alone did not spare the feelings of their teacher, but to his face would call him a traitor to the dignity of philosophy, a man versed in petty maxims,[1] which, while they might be useful for elevating the soul, were never observed in practical life. Nevertheless, in spite of his disposition, even after the reign of Julian, Priscus remained exempt from criticism; and after introducing many innovations among his disciples, who, like Corybants, were intoxicated with the desire for wisdom, and while still maintaining on all occasions his secretive manners and sneering at human weakness, he at last died, having reached a great age (for he was over ninety), at the time of the destruction of the temples of Greece. And, in those days, there were many who in their grief threw away their lives, while others were slaughtered by the barbarians, among whom was Proterius, a native of the island Cephallenia, as to whose worth and probity there is good evidence. Hilarius too was known to the author; he was by birth a Bithynian, but he grew old at Athens, and, besides the whole range of learning, he had so mastered the art of painting that it seemed as though in his hands Euphranor was still alive. The author of this narrative used to admire and love him beyond other men, because of the beauty of his portraits. Nevertheless, even Hilarius could not escape his share in the general disasters, for he was captured outside Athens (he was staying somewhere near Corinth), and together with his slaves was beheaded by the barbarians.[2] These events, if it be the will of heaven,

---

[2] *i.e.* by the Goths in 395.

ταῦτα μὲν ἐν τοῖς διεξοδικοῖς, ἐὰν τῷ δαίμονι δόξῃ, γραφήσεται, οὐ τὸ καθ᾽ ἕκαστον ἔχοντα, ἀλλὰ τὸ κοινὸν ἐκεῖ σαφέστερον λελέξεται· νυνὶ δὲ ὅσον ἐπέβαλε τὸ καθ᾽ ἕκαστον ἱκανῶς εἰς ἀφήγησιν εἴρηται.

Ἰουλιανὸς δὲ ὁ ἐκ Καππαδοκίας σοφιστὴς εἰς τοὺς Αἰδεσίου χρόνους ἤκμαζε, καὶ ἐτυράννει γε τῶν Ἀθηνῶν, καὶ παρὰ τοῦτον ἡ πᾶσα νεότης πανταχόθεν ἐχώρει, ῥητορικῆς ἕνεκεν τὸν ἄνδρα καὶ μεγέθους φύσεως σεβαζόμενοι. ἦσαν μὲν γὰρ καὶ κατὰ ταὐτὸν ἕτεροί τινες παραψαύοντες τοῦ καλοῦ, καὶ πρὸς τὴν ἐκείνου δόξαν διαιρόμενοι, Ἀψίνης τε ὁ ἐκ Λακεδαίμονος, δόξαν ἔχων τεχνικοῦ τινος, καὶ Ἐπάγαθος, καὶ τοιαύτη τις ὀνομάτων χορηγία· ὁ δὲ τῷ μεγέθει τῆς φύσεως ἁπάντων κατεκράτει, καὶ τὸ ἔλαττον μακρῷ τινι ἦν ἔλαττον. ὁμιληταὶ δὲ αὐτοῦ πολλοὶ μὲν καὶ πανταχόθεν, ὡς εἰπεῖν, καὶ πανταχῇ διασπαρέντες, καὶ θαυμασθέντες ὅπου ποτὲ[1] ἱδρύθησαν· ἀπόλεκτοι 483 δὲ τῶν ἄλλων ἁπάντων ὅ τε θειότατος Προαιρέσιος, καὶ Ἡφαιστίων, Ἐπιφάνιός τε ὁ ἐκ Συρίας, καὶ Διόφαντος ὁ Ἀράβιος. Τουσκιανοῦ δὲ μνησθῆναι καλόν, καὶ γὰρ οὗτος ἐκείνου μετέσχε τῆς ὁμιλίας, ἀλλὰ τούτου μὲν καὶ ἐν τοῖς κατὰ Ἰουλιανὸν ἐμνήσθημεν διεξοδικοῖς. Ἰουλιανοῦ δὲ καὶ τὴν οἰκίαν ὁ συγγραφεὺς Ἀθήνησιν ἑώρα, μικρὰν μὲν καὶ εὐτελῆ τινα, Ἑρμοῦ δὲ ὅμως καὶ Μουσῶν ἀποπνέουσαν,[2] οὕτως ἱεροῦ τινος ἁγίου διέφερεν οὐδέν· Προαιρεσίῳ δὲ αὐτὴν καταλελοίπει. καὶ

---

[1] τε Boissonade; ποτὲ Cobet.
[2] περιπνέουσαν Boissonade; ἀποπνέουσαν Cobet.

I shall relate more fully in my *Universal History*, since there they will be told more clearly, not with reference to the individual, but as they concerned the interests of all. For the present, however, their bearing on individuals has been set forth as far as is suitable to my narrative.

JULIAN of Cappadocia, the sophist, flourished in the time of Aedesius, and was a sort of tyrant at Athens. For all the youths from all parts flocked to him, and revered the man for his eloquence and his noble disposition. For there were indeed certain other men, his contemporaries, who in some degree attained to the comprehension of true beauty and reached the heights of his renown, namely Apsines of Lacedaemon who won fame as a writer on rhetoric, and Epagathus, and a whole host of names of that sort. But Julian surpassed them all by his great genius, and he who was second to him was a bad second. He had numerous pupils who came, so to speak, from all parts of the world, and when dispersed in every country were admired wherever and whenever they established themselves. But most distinguished of them all were the inspired Prohaeresius, Hephaestion, Epiphanius of Syria, and Diophantus the Arab. It is fitting that I should also mention Tuscianus, since he too was one of Julian's pupils, but I have already spoken of him in my account of the reign of the Emperor Julian.[1] The author himself saw Julian's house at Athens; poor and humble as it was, nevertheless from it breathed the fragrance of Hermes and the Muses, so closely did it resemble a holy temple. This house he had bequeathed to Prohaeresius. There, too,

[1] *i.e.* in his *Universal History*.

εἰκόνες τῶν ὑπ᾽ αὐτοῦ θαυμασθέντων ἑταίρων
ἀνέκειντο, καὶ τὸ θέατρον ἦν ξεστοῦ λίθου, τῶν
δημοσίων θεάτρων εἰς μίμησιν, ἀλλὰ ἔλαττον καὶ
ὅσον πρέπειν οἰκίᾳ. τοσαύτη γὰρ ἦν Ἀθήνησιν
ἡ στάσις τῶν τότε ἀνθρώπων καὶ νέων, καθάπερ
τῆς πόλεως, ἐκ τῶν παλαιῶν ἐκείνων πολέμων,
τὸν ἐντὸς τείχους ἀσκούσης κίνδυνον, ὥστε οὐδεὶς
ἐτόλμα τῶν σοφιστῶν δημοσίᾳ καταβὰς διαλέγεσθαι, ἀλλ᾽ ἐν τοῖς ἰδιωτικοῖς θεάτροις ἀπο-
λαβόντες τὰς φωνὰς αὐτῶν μειρακίοις διελέγοντο,
οὐ τὸν περὶ ψυχῆς θέοντες, ἀλλὰ τὸν περὶ κρότου
καὶ φωνῆς ἀγωνιζόμενοι.

Πολλῶν δὲ σιωπωμένων, τοῦτο ἀνάγκη περὶ
αὐτοῦ καταβαλεῖν καὶ συνεισενεγκεῖν ἐς τὸν
λόγον, δεῖγμα τῆς ὅλης τοῦ ἀνδρὸς παιδείας καὶ
συνέσεως. ἔτυχον μὲν γὰρ οἱ θρασύτατοι τῶν
Ἀψίνου μαθητῶν ταῖς χερσὶ κρατήσαντες τῶν
Ἰουλιανοῦ κατὰ τὸν ἐμφύλιον ἐκεῖνον πόλεμον·
χερσὶ δὲ βαρείαις καὶ Λακωνικαῖς χρησάμενοι, τῶν
πεπονθότων περὶ τοῦ σώματος κινδυνευόντων,
ὥσπερ ἀδικηθέντες, κατηγόρουν. ἀνεφέρετο δὲ
ἐπὶ τὸν ἀνθύπατον ἡ δίκη, καὶ ὃς βαρύς τις εἶναι
καὶ φοβερὸς ἐνδεικνύμενος, καὶ τὸν διδάσκαλον
συναρπασθῆναι κελεύει καὶ τοὺς κατηγορηθέντας
ἅπαντας δεσμώτας, ὥσπερ τοὺς ἐπὶ φόνῳ κατα-
κεκλεισμένους. ἐῴκει δὲ ὡς[1] Ῥωμαῖός τις οὐκ

───────

[1] ὥσπερ Boissonade ; ὡς Cobet.

───────

[1] The undying antagonism of " Town " and " Gown " was
probably intensified by religious differences, since most of
the students were opposed to Christianity.

[2] The faction fights of the sophists and their pupils are
often mentioned by Libanius ; cf. Himerius, *Oration* iv. 9,
and his *Oration* xix., which is addressed to those pupils who

were erected statues of the pupils whom he had most admired; and he had a theatre of polished marble made after the model of a public theatre, but smaller and of a size suitable to a house. For in those days, so bitter was the feud at Athens between the citizens and the young students,[1] as though the city after those ancient wars of hers was fostering within her walls the peril of discord, that not one of the sophists ventured to go down into the city and discourse in public, but they confined their utterances to their private lecture theatres and there discoursed to their students. Thus they ran no risk of their lives, but there competed for applause and fame for eloquence.

Though I leave much unsaid, I must set down and introduce into this narrative the following sample of all Julian's learning and prudence. It so happened that the boldest of the pupils of Apsines had, in a fierce encounter, got the upper hand of Julian's pupils in the course of the war of factions[2] that they kept up. After laying violent hands on them in Spartan fashion,[3] though the victims of their ill-treatment had been in danger of their lives, they prosecuted them as though they themselves were the injured parties. The case was referred to the proconsul, who, showing himself stern and implacable, ordered that their teacher also be arrested, and that all the accused be thrown into chains, like men imprisoned on a charge of murder. It seems, however, that, for

are so occupied with these encounters that they neglect their lectures. The incident here described with lively interest by Eunapius had occurred seventy years before he wrote the *Lives.*

[3] Spartan violence, *Laconica manus,* was apparently a proverb, but here there is a further allusion to the nationality of Apsines.

εἶναι τῶν ἀπαιδεύτων, οὐδὲ τῶν ὑπ' ἀγροίκῳ καὶ
ἀμούσῳ τύχῃ τεθραμμένων. ὅ τε γοῦν Ἰουλιανὸς
παρῆν, οὕτως ἐπιταχθέν, καὶ ὁ Ἀψίνης συμπαρῆν,
οὐκ ἐπιταχθέν, ἀλλ' ὡς συνηγορήσων τοῖς κατη-
γορηκόσι. καὶ ἡ μὲν ἐξέτασις προὔκειτο, καὶ τοῖς
διώκουσιν εἴσοδος ἐδόθη. προειστήκει δὲ τῆς
ἀτάκτου Σπάρτης Θεμιστοκλῆς τις Ἀθηναῖος, ὃς
ἦν καὶ τῶν κακῶν αἴτιος· προπετέστερος δὲ ὢν
καὶ θρασύτερος, ἐς τὴν ἐπωνυμίαν ὕβριζεν. εὐθὺς
μὲν οὖν ὁ ἀνθύπατος ταυρηδὸν ὑπιδὼν τὸν Ἀψίνην,
" σὲ δὲ τίς " εἶπεν " ἐλθεῖν ἐκέλευσεν; " ὁ δὲ ἀπεκρίνατο περὶ τοῖς ἑαυτοῦ τέκνοις ἀγωνιῶν ἐληλυθέναι.[1]
καὶ τῇ σιωπῇ κρύψαντος τὴν ἔννοιαν τοῦ ἄρχοντος,
εἰσῄεσαν πάλιν οἱ δεσμῶται καὶ ἠδικημένοι, καὶ
ὁ διδάσκαλος μετ' αὐτῶν, κόμας ἔχοντες καὶ τὰ
σώματα κεκακωμένοι λίαν, ὥστε οἰκτροὺς αὐτοὺς
φανῆναι καὶ τῷ κρίνοντι. δοθέντος δὲ τοῦ λόγου
τοῖς κατηγοροῦσιν, ἤρξατο μὲν ὁ Ἀψίνης τοῦ
λόγου, ἀλλ' ὁ ἀνθύπατος ὑπολαβών, " ἀλλ' οὐ
τοῦτό γε " εἶπε " Ῥωμαῖοι δοκιμάζουσιν· ἀλλ' ὁ
τὴν πρώτην εἰπὼν κατηγορίαν, κινδυνευέτω περὶ
τῆς δευτέρας." ἐνταῦθα παρασκευὴ μὲν οὐκ ἦν
πρὸς τὴν τῆς κρίσεως ὀξύτητα· ἦν δὲ Θεμιστοκλῆς
484 ὁ[2] κατηγορηκώς, καὶ λέγειν ἀναγκαζόμενος, χροιάν
τε ἤλλαξε καὶ τὰ χείλη διέδακεν ἀπορούμενος,
καὶ πρὸς τοὺς ἑταίρους ὑπέβλεπε καὶ παρεφθέγξατο
τί πρακτέον· εἰσεληλύθεσαν γὰρ ὡς ἐπὶ τῇ συν-
ηγορίᾳ τοῦ διδασκάλου μόνον κεκραξόμενοι καὶ
βοησόμενοι. πολλῆς οὖν σιωπῆς καὶ ταραχῆς

---

[1] ἐληλύθειν Boissonade ; ἐληλυθέναι Cobet.
[2] ὁ Θεμιστοκλῆς Boissonade ; Cobet transposes.

a Roman, he was not uneducated or bred in a boorish
and illiberal fashion. Accordingly Julian was in
court, as he had been ordered, and Apsines was there
also, not in obedience to orders but to help the case
of the plaintiffs. Now all was ready for the hearing
of the case, and the plaintiffs were permitted to
enter. The leader of the disorderly Spartan faction
was one Themistocles, an Athenian, who was in fact
responsible for all the trouble, for he was a rash and
headstrong youth and a disgrace to his famous name.
The proconsul at once glared fiercely at Apsines,
and said : " Who ordered you to come here ? " He
replied that he had come because he was anxious
about his children. The magistrate concealed his
real opinion and said no more ; and then the prisoners
who had been so unfairly treated again came before
the court, and with them their teacher. Their hair
was uncut and they were in great physical affliction,
so that even to the judge they were a pitiful sight.
Then the plaintiffs were permitted to speak, and
Apsines began to make a speech, but the proconsul
interrupted him and said : " This procedure is not
approved by the Romans. He who delivered the
speech for the prosecution at the first hearing must
try his luck at the second also." There was then no
time for preparation because of the suddenness of
the decision. Now Themistocles had made the
speech for the prosecution before, but now on being
compelled to speak he changed colour, bit his lips
in great embarrassment, looked furtively towards his
comrades, and consulted them in whispers as to
what they had better do. For they had come into
court prepared only to shout and applaud vociferously
their teacher's speech in their behalf. Therefore

οὔσης, σιωπῆς μὲν καθ᾽ ὅλον τὸ δικαστήριον, ταραχῆς δὲ περὶ τὸ τῶν διωκόντων μέρος, ἐλεεινόν τι παραφθεγξάμενος ὁ Ἰουλιανός, "ἀλλ᾽ ἐμέ γε εἰπεῖν" ἔφη "κέλευσον·" ὁ δὲ ἀνθύπατος ἀναβοήσας· "ἀλλ᾽ οὐδεὶς ὑμῶν γ᾽ ἐρεῖ τῶν ἐσκεμμένων διδασκάλων, οὐδὲ κροτήσει τις τῶν μαθητῶν τὸν λέγοντα, ἀλλ᾽ εἴσεσθέ γε αὐτίκα ἡλίκον ἐστὶ καὶ οἷον τὸ παρὰ Ῥωμαίοις δίκαιον. ἀλλὰ Θεμιστοκλῆς μὲν περαινέτω τὴν κατηγορίαν, ἀπολογείσθω δὲ ὃν ἂν σὺ ἀποκρίνοις ἄριστον." ἐνταῦθα κατηγόρει μὲν οὐδείς, ἀλλὰ Θεμιστοκλῆς ὀνόματος ἦν ὕβρις. ἀπολογεῖσθαι δὲ πρὸς τὴν προτέραν κατηγορίαν ὡς ἐκέλευσε τὸν δυνάμενον, ὁ σοφιστὴς Ἰουλιανός "σὺ μέν," εἶπεν "ἀνθύπατε, διὰ τὴν ὑπεροχὴν τοῦ δικαίου πεποίηκας Πυθαγόραν Ἀψίνην, βραδέως τὸ σιωπᾶν, ἀλλ᾽ ὅμως δικαίως, μαθόντα· ὁ δὲ πάλαι (τοῦτο γὰρ αὐτὸς καταμανθάνεις) καὶ τοὺς ἑταίρους πυθαγορίζειν[1] ἐδίδαξεν. εἰ δὲ ἀπολογεῖσθαι κελεύεις τῶν ἐμῶν ἑταίρων τινά, κέλευσον ἀπολυθῆναι τῶν δεσμῶν Προαιρέσιον, καὶ δοκιμάσεις αὐτὸς πότερον ἀττικίζειν ἢ πυθαγορίζειν πεπαίδευται." ὡς δὲ ταῦτα ἐπέτρεψε καὶ μάλ᾽[2] εὐκόλως (ταῦτα δὲ πρὸς τὸν συγγραφέα Τουσκιανὸς ἐξήγγελλε παρὼν τῇ κρίσει), καὶ ἐκ τῶν κατηγορουμένων παρελθὼν εἰς μέσους Προαιρέσιος ἄδεσμος, ἐμβοήσαντος αὐτῷ τοῦ διδασκάλου οὐ σφοδρόν[3] τε καὶ διάτορον[4]

---

[1] After πυθαγορίζειν Cobet omits καὶ σιωπᾶν.
[2] ἅμα Boissonade; μάλ᾽ Cobet.
[3] Before σφοδρόν Cobet would read οὐ.
[4] διάτονον Boissonade; διάτορον Cobet.

---

[1] Tuscianus, who must have been very old when Eunapius

472

profound silence and confusion reigned, a general
silence in the court and confusion in the ranks of the
accusers. Then Julian, in a low and pitiful voice
said: "Nay, then, give me leave to speak." Whereupon, the proconsul exclaimed: "No, not one of you
shall plead, you teachers who have come with your
speeches prepared, nor shall anyone of your pupils
applaud the speaker; but you shall learn forthwith
how perfect and how pure is the justice that the
Romans dispense. First let Themistocles finish his
speech for the prosecution, and then he whom you
think best fitted shall speak in defence." But no
one spoke up for the plaintiffs, and Themistocles was
a scandal and a disgrace to his great name. When,
thereupon, the proconsul ordered that anyone who
could should reply to the earlier speech of the prosecution, Julian the sophist said: "Proconsul, in
your superlative justice you have transformed
Apsines into a Pythagoras, who tardily but very
properly has learned how to maintain silence; for
Pythagoras long ago (as you are well aware) taught
his *pupils* the Pythagorean manner. But, if you
allow one of my pupils to make our defence, give
orders for Prohaeresius to be released from his bonds,
and you shall judge for yourself whether I have
taught him the Attic manner or the Pythagorean."
The proconsul granted this request very graciously,
as Tuscianus,[1] who was present at the trial, reported
to the author, and Prohaeresius came forward from
the ranks of the defendants without his fetters
before them all, after his master had called out
to him not in a loud and piercing voice, such as

knew him, was a correspondent of Libanius; he held various
offices in the East and was for a time a colleague of Anatolius
in the government of Illyricum.

ὥσπερ ἐπὶ τῶν στεφανιτῶν οἱ παρακελευόμενοι
καὶ προτρέποντες, ἐμβοήσαντος δὲ ὀξέως τό
" λέγε, Προαιρέσιε, νῦν καιρὸς τοῦ λέγειν" ὁ μὲν
προοίμιόν τι ἔφη (οὐ γὰρ ἠπίστατό γε αὐτὸ
Τουσκιανός, τὸν δὲ νοῦν ἔφραζεν)· ἐξήνεγκεν
εἴς τε οἶκτον ὧν ἐπεπόνθεσαν ῥέπον, καὶ μεμιγ-
μένον τινὰ εἶχε τὸ προοίμιον ἔπαινον τοῦ διδα-
σκάλου· καί που καὶ διὰ λέξεως μιᾶς διαβολή τις
ἐγκατεσπείρετο τῷ προοιμίῳ, προπέτειαν ἐμφαί-
νουσα τῆς ἀνθυπατικῆς ἀρχῆς, ὡς οὐ προσῆκον
αὐτοῖς οὐδὲ μετὰ τοὺς ἐλέγχους τοιαῦτα ὑποστῆναι
καὶ παθεῖν. κάτω δὲ τοῦ ἀνθυπάτου νεύοντος,
καὶ τόν τε νοῦν τῶν λεγομένων καταπεπληγμένου
καὶ τὸ βάθος τῶν λέξεων καὶ τὴν εὐκολίαν καὶ
τὸν κρότον, καὶ πάντων μὲν βουλομένων ἐπαινεῖν,
καταπτηξάντων δὲ ὥσπερ διοσημίαν, καὶ σιωπῆς
κατακεχυμένης μυστηριώδους, εἰς δεύτερον προοίμιον ὁ Προαιρέσιος ἐντείνων τὸν λόγον (τοῦτο γὰρ ἐμέμνητο Τουσκιανός), ἐνθένδε ἤρξατο·
" εἰ μὲν οὖν ἔξεστι καὶ ἀδικεῖν ἅπαντα καὶ κατηγορεῖν καὶ λέγοντα πιστεύεσθαι πρὸ τῆς ἀπολογίας,
ἔστω, γινέσθω Θεμιστοκλέους ἡ πόλις." ἐνταῦθα
ἀνά τε ἐπήδησεν ὁ ἀνθύπατος ἐκ τοῦ θρόνου, καὶ
τὴν περιπόρφυρον ἀνασείων ἐσθῆτα (τήβεννον
αὐτὴν Ῥωμαῖοι καλοῦσιν), ὥσπερ μειράκιον ὁ
βαρὺς ἐκεῖνος καὶ ἀμείλικτος ἐκρότει τὸν Προαι-
485 ρέσιον· συνεκρότει δὲ ὁ Ἀψίνης οὔτι ἑκών, ἀλλὰ
ἀνάγκης βιαιότερον οὐδέν· ὁ διδάσκαλος Ἰουλιανὸς
ἐδάκρυε μόνον. ὁ δὲ ἀνθύπατος τὸ μὲν διωκόμενον

---

[1] Eunapius gives the Greek word used by the Romans
for the *toga* or *trabea*. For the gesture as a sign of

is used by those who exhort and incite athletes contending for a garland, but still in penetrating accents: "Speak, Prohaeresius! Now is the time to make a speech!" He then first delivered a prooemium of some sort. Tuscianus could not exactly recall it, though he told me its purport. It launched out and soon slid into a pitiable account of their sufferings and he inserted an encomium of their teacher. In this prooemium he let fall only one allusion to a grievance, when he pointed out how headlong the proconsular authority had been, since not even after sufficient proof of their guilt was it proper for them to undergo and suffer such treatment. At this the proconsul bowed his head and was overcome with admiration of the force of his arguments, his weighty style, his facility and sonorous eloquence. Meanwhile they all longed to applaud, but sat cowering as though forbidden to do so by a sign from heaven, and a mystic silence pervaded the place. Then he lengthened his speech into a second prooemium as follows (for this part Tuscianus remembered): "If, then, men may with impunity commit any injustice and bring accusations and win belief for what they say, before the defence is heard, so be it! Let our city be enslaved to Themistocles!" Then up jumped the proconsul, and shaking his purple-edged cloak (the Romans call it a "tebennos[1]"), that austere and inexorable judge applauded Prohaeresius like a schoolboy. Even Apsines joined in the applause, not of his own free will, but because there is no fighting against necessity. Julian his teacher could only weep. The proconsul ordered all

approval *cf.* Philostratus, *Lives of the Sophists* (Heliodorus) 626.

μέρος ἐξελθεῖν κελεύσας, τοῦ δὲ διώκοντος τὸν διδάσκαλον μόνον, εἶτα ἀπολαβὼν τὸν Θεμιστοκλέα καὶ τοὺς Λάκωνας, τῶν ἐν Λακεδαίμονι[1] μαστίγων ὑπέμνησε, προσθεὶς αὐτοῖς καὶ τῶν Ἀθήνησι. εὐδοκιμῶν δὲ καὶ αὐτὸς ἄγαν καὶ διὰ τῶν ὁμιλητῶν, Ἀθήνησιν[2] ἐτελεύτα, μέγαν ἐπιτάφιον ἀγῶνα τοῖς ἑαυτοῦ παραδεδωκὼς ἑταίροις.

Περὶ Προαιρεσίου καὶ προλαβοῦσιν ἱκανῶς εἴρηται, καὶ ἐν τοῖς ἱστορικοῖς κατὰ τὴν ἐξήγησιν ὑπομνήμασι. καὶ νῦν δὲ ἐπελθεῖν καιρὸς εἰς τὸ ἀκριβέστερον εἰδότι τε ἀσφαλῶς καὶ ἀξιωθέντι τῆς ἐκείνου γλώττης καὶ ὁμιλίας· καὶ ταῦτά γε, εἰ καὶ πάνυ μεγάλα καὶ οὐρανομήκη πρὸς χάριν, εἴ τις διδάσκαλος, ἀλλ' ὅμως πολλῷ τινι καὶ μακρῷ τῆς εἰς τὸν συγγραφέα φιλίας ἀφεστήκεσαν αἱ τοσαῦται καὶ ἀδιήγητοι χάριτες. διέβαλε μὲν γὰρ ὁ ταῦτα συντιθεὶς ἐξ Ἀσίας εἰς τὴν Εὐρώπην καὶ Ἀθήνας, τελῶν εἰς ἕκτον καὶ δέκατον ἔτος. ὁ δὲ Προαιρέσιος προεληλύθει μὲν ἐπὶ τὸ ἕβδομον ἐπὶ τοῖς ὀγδοήκοντα ἔτεσιν, ὡς αὐτὸς ἔλεγεν· καὶ περὶ τὴν ἡλικίαν ταύτην οὔλη τε ἦν αὐτῷ καὶ ἄγαν συνεχὴς ἡ κόμη, καὶ διὰ πλῆθος πολιῶν τριχῶν ἀφριζούσῃ θαλάσσῃ προσεμφερὴς καὶ ὑπαργυρίζουσα. ἤκμαζε δὲ οὕτω τὰ εἰς λόγους, τῇ νεότητί τε τῆς ψυχῆς τὸ σῶμα κεκμηκὸς συνηγείρετο, ὥστε ὁ ταῦτα συγγράφων ἀγήρων τινὰ καὶ ἀθάνατον αὐτὸν ἐνόμιζε, καὶ προσεῖχεν ὥσπερ αὐτοκλήτῳ καὶ ἄνευ τινὸς πραγματείας φανέντι

[1] Λακεδαιμονίᾳ Boissonade ; Λακεδαίμονι Wyttenbach.
[2] Ἀθηναίων Boissonade ; Ἀθήνησιν Cobet.

---

[1] Perhaps an echo of Alexander's dying speech, which became a proverb; Diodorus Siculus xvii. 117; Arrian vii. 26;

the accused, but of the accusers their teacher only,
to withdraw, and then, taking aside Themistocles
and his Spartans, he reminded them forcibly
of the floggings of Lacedaemon, and added besides
the kind of flogging in vogue at Athens. Julian
himself won a great reputation by his own eloquence, and also through the fame of his disciples,
and when he died at Athens he left to his
pupils a great occasion for competing over his
funeral oration.[1]

Of PROHAERESIUS I have said enough in the above
narrative, and have set forth his life still more fully
in my historical commentaries. Yet it is convenient
here and now to go over the facts in more precise
detail, seeing that I had unerring knowledge of him
and was admitted to his conversation and teaching.
And that is a very great privilege, and has immense
power to excite the gratitude due to a teacher; but
even this great and inexpressible gratitude falls very
far short of what the author owes to Prohaeresius for
his intimate friendship. The compiler of this book
had crossed over from Asia to Europe and to Athens
in the sixteenth year of his age. Now Prohaeresius
had reached his eighty-seventh year, as he himself
stated. At this advanced age his hair was curly and
very thick, and because of the number of grey hairs
it was silvered over and resembled sea foam. His
powers of oratory were so vigorous, and he so sustained his worn body by the youthfulness of his soul,
that the present writer regarded him as an ageless
and immortal being, and heeded him as he might
some god who had revealed himself unsummoned

Plutarch, *Apophthegmata* 181 ε μέγαν ὁρῶ μου τὸν ἐπιτάφιον
ἐσόμενον.

θεῷ. καίτοι γε ἦν ἥκων εἰς τὸν Πειραιᾶ περὶ
πρώτην φυλακήν, ἐπὶ πυρετῷ λάβρῳ κατὰ πλοῦν
γενομένῳ, καὶ πολλοί τινες ἄλλοι κατὰ γένος γε
αὐτῷ προσήκοντες συνεισπεπλεύκεσαν, καὶ περὶ
τὴν ὥραν ἐκείνην, πρίν τι γενέσθαι τῶν εἰωθότων
(τὸ γὰρ πλοῖον ἦν τῶν Ἀθήνηθεν, καὶ περὶ τὰς
κατάρσεις οὐκ ὀλίγοι τινὲς ἐναυλόχουν ἀεὶ τῶν
εἰς ἕκαστον διδασκαλεῖον μεμηνότων), ὁ ναύκληρος
εἰς Ἀθήνας συνέτεινε, τῶν μὲν ἄλλων βαδιζόντων,
ὁ δὲ βαδίζειν ἀδυνάτως ἔχων, ὅμως ἐκ διαδοχῆς
ἀνεχόμενος, ἀνεκομίσθη πρὸς τὴν πόλιν. ἦν τε
νυκτὸς τὸ σταθερώτατον, ἡνίκα ἥλιος μακροτέραν
ποιεῖ τὴν νύκτα γινόμενος νοτιώτερος· ἐνεβεβήκει
γὰρ τῷ Ζυγῷ, καὶ τὰ νυκτερεῖα ἔμελλε· καὶ ὁ
ναύκληρος ὤν που καὶ ξένος Προαιρεσίου παλαιός,
τοσοῦτον ὄχλον ὁμιλητῶν, ἀράξας τὴν θύραν,
εἰσήγαγεν εἰς τὴν οἰκίαν, ὥστε, ἡνίκα πόλεμοί
τινες ἐγίνοντο περὶ ἑνὸς μειρακίου καὶ δυοῖν,
πλήρωμα διατριβῆς ὅλους σοφιστικῆς τοὺς ἐληλυ-
θότας φαίνεσθαι. τούτων οἱ μὲν εἰς σώματος
ἀλκὴν ἐτέλουν, οἱ δὲ εἰς πλοῦτον ἦσαν ἁδρότεροι,[1]
τὸ δὲ εἶχεν ἀνὰ μέσον· ὁ δὲ συγγραφεὺς ἐλεεινῶς
διακείμενος τὰ πλεῖστα τῶν ἀρχαίων ἐπὶ στόματος
εἶχε μόνον βιβλία. εὐθὺς μὲν οὖν χαρμονή τε ἦν
περὶ τὴν οἰκίαν καὶ διαδρομαί τινες ἀνδρῶν τε
καὶ γυναικῶν, καὶ οἱ μὲν ἐγέλων, οἱ δὲ ἐχλεύαζον.

---

[1] ἁκρότεροι Boissonade ; ἁδρότεροι Wyttenbach.

[1] A reference to the competition of the pupils who lay in
wait for new arrivals and kidnapped them for their own
sophists. Here the captain kidnaps them all for Prohaeresius.

[2] i.e. it was the autumnal equinox.

[3] νυκτερεῖα = νυκτερεία (Plato, Laws 824), it seems. But
it may mean " a lodging for the night." Then the sentence

and without ceremony. Now it happened that the
writer arrived at the Piraeus about the first watch,
and on the voyage had been attacked by a raging
fever; and several other persons, his relatives, had
sailed over with him. At that time of night, before
any of the usual proceedings could take place [1] (for
the ship belonged to Athens and many used to lie
in wait for her arrival at the dock, mad enthusiasts
each for his own particular school), the captain went
straight on to Athens. The rest of the passengers
walked, and the writer, too feeble to walk, was nevertheless supported by them in relays, and so was conveyed to the city. It was by then deepest midnight,
at the season when the sun makes the nights longer
by retiring farther to the South; for he had entered
the sign of Libra,[2] and night-hunting[3] was on the way
The captain, who was an old-time friend and gues:
of Prohaeresius, knocked at his door and ushered in
all this crowd of disciples, so many in fact that, at a
time when battles were being fought to win only one
or two pupils, the newcomers seemed enough in
themselves to man all the schools of the sophists.
Some of these youths were distinguished for physical
strength, some had more bulky purses, while the
rest were only moderately endowed. The author,
who was in a pitiable state, had most of the works
of the ancient writers by heart, his sole possession.[4]
Forthwith there was great rejoicing in the house,
and men and women alike ran to and fro, some

would mean that to stay at an inn at the Piraeus would cause
delay. Giangrande suggests διανυκτερεύειν.
  [4] Others understand μόνον to be self-depreciatory, *i.e.*
Eunapius could recite, but did not understand them. But
nearly always when he uses the phrase ἐπὶ στόματος it implies
praise.

ὁ δὲ Προαιρέσιος συγγενεῖς ἰδίους κατὰ τὴν ὥραν
486 ἐκείνην μεταπεμψάμενος, παραλαβεῖν τοὺς ἐλθόντας κελεύει. ἦν δὲ αὐτός τε ἐξ Ἀρμενίας (ὅσον
ἐστὶν Ἀρμενίας Πέρσαις εἰς τὰ βαθύτατα συνημμένον), καὶ Ἀνατόλιος οὗτοι καὶ Μάξιμος ἐκαλοῦντο. καὶ οἱ μὲν ἀπεδέξαντο τοὺς ἐλθόντας,
καὶ ἦξαν εἰς γειτόνων καὶ περὶ τὰ λουτρὰ μετὰ
πάσης ἐπιδείξεως, ἥ τε νεότης ἐς αὐτοὺς ἐπεδείκνυτο καὶ χλευασίαν καὶ γέλωτα. καὶ οἱ μὲν
τούτων ποτὲ ἀπηλλάγησαν ἅπαξ λουσάμενοι, ὁ
δὲ συγγραφεύς, ἐντείναντος αὐτῷ τοῦ νοσήματος,
διεφθείρετο, μήτε Προαιρέσιον μήτε τὰς Ἀθήνας
ἰδών, ἀλλὰ ὀνειρῶξαι δοκῶν ἐκεῖνα ὧν ἐπεθύμησεν,
οἱ δὲ ὁμοεθνεῖς καὶ ἐκ Λυδίας βαρέως ἔφερον.
καὶ ὥσπερ τοῖς κατὰ τήνδε τὴν ἡλικίαν ἀπιοῦσιν ἐπὶ
τὸ πλέον ἅπαντες εἰώθασι χαρίζεσθαι, πολλά τινα
καὶ μεγάλα περὶ αὐτοῦ καταψευσάμενοι καὶ
συμφορήσαντες ἐτερατεύσαντο, καὶ πένθος κατεῖχε
τὴν πόλιν παράλογον, ὡσὰν ἐπὶ μεγάλῃ συμφορᾷ.
Αἰσχίνης δέ τις, οὐκ Ἀθηναῖος (ἀλλὰ ἡ Χίος ἦν
αὐτῷ πατρίς), πολλοὺς ἀνηρηκὼς οὐχ ὅσους
ἐπηγγείλατο θεραπεύειν, ἀλλὰ καὶ ὅσους εἶδε
μόνον, εἰς μέσους ἀναβοήσας τοὺς πενθοῦντας, ὡς
μετὰ ταῦτα ἐγένετο φανερόν " ἀλλὰ συγχωρήσατέ
γε," εἶπε " τῷ νεκρῷ με δοῦναι φάρμακον." οἱ
δὲ συνεχώρησαν Αἰσχίνῃ διαφθεῖραι καὶ τοὺς
ἀπολωλότας. ὁ δὲ ὅ τι μὲν ἐνέχεεν, ὀργάνοις τισὶ
τὸ στόμα διαστήσας, μετὰ ταῦτα ἐξεῖπε, καὶ ὁ

---

[1] This was part of the regular " hazing " or " ragging " of
the novices by the older pupils, described by Libanius and
others; cf. Gregory Nazianzen, *Oration* xix. 328 B.

laughing, others bandying jests. Prohaeresius at that time of night sent for some of his own relatives and directed them to take in the newcomers. He was himself a native of Armenia, that is to say he came from that part of Armenia which borders most closely on Persia, and these kinsmen of his were named Anatolius and Maximus. They welcomed the new arrivals, and led them to the houses of neighbours and to the baths, and showed them off in every way; and the other students made the usual demonstrations with jokes and laughter at their expense.[1] The rest, once they had been to the baths, were let off and went their way, but the writer, as his sickness grew more severe, was wasting away without seeing Prohaeresius or Athens, and all that he so desired seemed to have been only a dream. Meanwhile his own relatives and those who had come from Lydia were greatly concerned; and as all men are prone to attribute greater talent to those who are leaving us in the flower of their youth, they told many surprising falsehoods about him, and conspired to invent prodigious fictions, so that the whole city was overwhelmed by extraordinary grief, as though for some great calamity. But a certain Aeschines, not an Athenian, for Chios was his birthplace, who had slain many, not only those whom he had undertaken to cure but also those whom he had merely looked at, called out in the midst of my sorrowing friends, as became known later: "Come, allow me to give medicine to the corpse." And so they gave Aeschines permission to murder those too who were already dead. Then he held my lips apart with certain instruments and poured in a drug; what it was he revealed afterwards, and the god

θεὸς πολλοῖς ὕστερον ἐμαρτύρησε χρόνοις, ἐμβαλὼν
δὲ ὅμως, τοῦ μὲν ἡ γαστὴρ ἀθρόως ἀπελυμάνθη,
καὶ τὸν ἀέρα εἶδε καὶ ἐπέγνω τοὺς οἰκείους. ὁ
δὲ Αἰσχίνης ἑνὶ τούτῳ γε ἔργῳ θάψας τὰ προ-
γεγενημένα τῶν ἁμαρτημάτων, ὑπό τε τοῦ σω-
θέντος προσεκυνεῖτο, καὶ τῶν ἡδομένων ὅτι
σέσωσται. καὶ ὁ μέν, ἐπὶ τῇ τοιαύτῃ πράξει
πάντων σεβαζομένων αὐτόν, εἰς τὴν Χίον ἀπῆρε,
πλὴν ὅσα γε παραμείνας εἰς ῥῶσιν τοῦ σώματος
προσέδωκε πάλιν τῆς δυνάμεως τοῦ φαρμάκου,
καὶ τότε συνῆλθεν ἀκριβῶς ὁ σωθεὶς τῷ σώσαντι.

Ὁ δὲ θειότατος Προαιρέσιος οὔπω τὸν συγγραφέα τεθεαμένος, ἀλλὰ καὶ αὐτὸν ὅσον οὐκ ἤδη
κατοδυρόμενος, ὡς ἐπύθετο τὴν ἄλογον ταύτην
καὶ ἀνεκλάλητον σωτηρίαν, μετακαλέσας τοὺς
κρατίστους καὶ γενναιοτάτους τῶν ὁμιλητῶν καὶ
παρ' οἷς ἐπῃνεῖτο χειρῶν ἀλκῆς ἔργον, " πέπονθά
τι " πρὸς αὐτοὺς εἶπεν " ἐπὶ τῷ σωθέντι παιδίῳ,
καί τοί γε οὔπω τεθεαμένος, ἀλλ' ὅμως ἔπασχον
ἡνίκα ἀπώλλυτο. εἴ τι δὴ βούλεσθε χαρίσασθαί
μοι, τῷ δημοσίῳ λουτρῷ τοῦτον καθήρατε, πάσης
χλευασίας φεισάμενοι καὶ παιδιᾶς, ὥσπερ ἐμόν
τινα παῖδα ψαίροντες." καὶ ταῦτα μὲν ἔσχεν
οὕτως, καὶ ἀκριβέστερον ἐν τοῖς κατ' ἐκεῖνον
χρόνοις λελέξεται· ὅμως δὲ ὁ συγγραφεύς, ὁμολογῶν τὰ ἐς αὐτὸν θεοῦ τινος προνοίας τετυχηκέναι,
ἐκ τῆς Προαιρεσίου σπουδῆς οὐδὲν εἰς τὸ καθόλου
περὶ τοῦ ἀνδρὸς ἀποστήσεται τῆς ἀληθείας, εἴ
γε πεπηγὼς ὁ Πλάτωνος λόγος, ὡς ἀλήθεια

---

[1] Eunapius uses a grandiloquent word from *Iliad* i. 313.

many years later bore witness thereto; at any rate he poured it in, and the patient's stomach was at once expurged,[1] he opened his eyes to the light and recognized his own people. Thus Aeschines by this single act buried his past errors and won reverence both from him who had been delivered from death and from those who rejoiced at his deliverance. For so great an achievement he was worshipped by all, and he then crossed over to Chios, only waiting long enough to give the patient more of that strong medicine, that he might recover his strength; and thus he who had been preserved became the intimate friend of his preserver.

Now the divine Prohaeresius had not yet beheld the author, but he too had mourned for him almost as though he were dead, and when he was told of this unexpected and unheard-of recovery he sent for the best and most distinguished of his pupils and those who had proved the strength of their muscles, and said to them: " I was anxious for this boy who has recovered, though I have not yet seen him; nevertheless I grieved when he was on the point of death. Now if you wish to do me a favour, initiate him in the public bath, but refrain from all teasing and joking, and scrub him gently as though he were my own son." Thus then it came about, and a fuller account will be given when the author describes the times in which Prohaeresius lived. Yet though the author asserts that all that happened to Prohaeresius was under the direction of some divine providence, he will not in his zeal for the man depart in any way whatsoever from the truth about him, seeing that Plato's saying

483

πάντων μὲν ἀγαθῶν θεοῖς, πάντων δὲ ἀνθρώποις
ἡγεῖται.

Προαιρεσίῳ δὲ (φερέσθω γὰρ ἐπ' αὐτὸν ὁ λόγος)
τὸ μὲν κάλλος ἦν τοῦ σώματος τοιοῦτον, καί τοι
γηραιὸς ὢν ἦν, ὥστε ἀπορεῖν τε εἴ τις ἐφ' ἡλικίας
487 οὕτω γέγονε καλός, καὶ θαυμάζειν τὴν τοῦ κάλλους
δύναμιν ὅτι πρὸς τοσοῦτον σῶμα διὰ πάντων εἰς
τὴν ἀρίστην πλάσιν ἐξήρκεσε· τὸ δὲ μέγεθος ἦν
ἡλίκον ἄν τις οὐ πιστεύσειεν, ἀλλὰ εἰκάσειε μόλις.
ἀνεστηκέναι γὰρ εἰς ἔνατον[1] πόδα κατεφαίνετο,
ὥστε κολοσσὸς ἐδόκει, παρὰ τοὺς μεγίστους
ὁρώμενος τῶν καθ' ἑαυτὸν ἀνθρώπων. νέον δὲ
αὐτὸν ἐξ Ἀρμενίας ἀναστήσαντος τοῦ δαίμονος,
καὶ πρὸς τὴν Ἀντιόχειαν διαβάλλοντος (οὐ γὰρ
ἐπεθύμησεν εὐθὺς τῶν Ἀθηνῶν, ἥ τε ἔνδεια παρε-
λύπει τῶν χρημάτων· γεγονὼς γὰρ ἄνωθεν καλῶς,
τοῦτο ἠτύχει), καὶ πρὸς τὸν Οὐλπιανὸν κρατοῦντα
τῆς Ἀντιοχείας ἐπὶ λόγοις ὠσθείς, καὶ παρελθών,
εὐθὺς ἀνὰ τοὺς πρώτους ἦν. καὶ χρόνον οὐκ
ὀλίγον ὁμιλήσας ἐκείνῳ, συνέτεινεν ἐπὶ τὰς Ἀθήνας
καὶ τὸν Ἰουλιανὸν σφοδρῶς, καὶ πάλιν Ἀθήνησι
πρῶτος ἦν. Ἡφαιστίων δὲ αὐτῷ συνείπετο,
φιλοῦντες μὲν ἀλλήλους ἄμφω καὶ πάνυ, φιλο-
νεικοῦντες δὲ ἀλλήλοις εἰς πενίαν καὶ περὶ τῶν ἐν
λόγοις πρωτείων. ἐν γοῦν αὐτοῖς ὑπῆν ἱμάτιον
καὶ τριβώνιον, καὶ πλέον οὐδέν, καὶ στρώματα
τρία που ἢ τέτταρα, τὴν οἴκοθεν βαφὴν μετὰ τῆς
παχύτητος διὰ χρόνον ἀπαγορεύοντα. περιῆν οὖν

---

[1] ἔνναται Boissonade ; ἔνατον Cobet.

---

[1] Plato, *Laws* 730 B, quoted by Julian, *Oration* vi. 188 B.
[2] Not the famous jurist, but a sophist who lived under
Constantine.

is fixed and sure, that truth for gods and men alike is the guide to all good.[1]

The physical beauty of Prohaeresius (for my narrative must now return to him) was so striking, even though he was then an old man, that one may well doubt whether anyone had ever been so handsome, even in the flower of youth, and one may marvel also that in a body so tall as his the power of beauty sufficed to model a shape so admirable in all respects. His height was greater than anyone would be inclined to believe, in fact one would hardly guess it correctly. For he seemed to stand nine feet high, so that he looked like a colossus when one saw him near the tallest men of his own time. When he was a young man, fate forced him to leave Armenia and transferred him to Antioch. He did not desire to visit Athens immediately, since he was embarrassed by lack of means; for he was unlucky in this respect, though he was well born. At Antioch he hastened to Ulpian,[2] who was the principal teacher of rhetoric there, and on his arrival he at once ranked with the foremost pupils. When he had studied with Ulpian for a long time, he held on his way to Athens and to Julian with the greatest determination, and again at Athens he gained the first place. Hephaestion accompanied him, and these two were devoted friends and rivalled one another in their poverty, just as they were rivals for the highest honours in rhetoric. For instance they had between them only one cloak and one threadbare mantle and nothing more, and, say, three or four rugs which in the course of time had lost their original dye and their thickness as well. Their only resource therefore was

αὐτοῖς ἑνί τε ἀνθρώπῳ καὶ δυεῖν εἶναι, ὥσπερ τὸν
Γηρυόνην οἱ μῦθοί φασιν ἐκ τριῶν συντεθῆναι·
κἀκεῖνοι δύο τε ἦσαν καὶ εἷς. Προαιρεσίου μὲν
γὰρ δημοσίᾳ φανέντος, Ἡφαιστίων ἦν ἀφανὴς ἐν
τοῖς στρώμασι κατακείμενος, καὶ συνασκῶν ἑαυτὸν
περὶ τοὺς λόγους· ταὐτὰ δὲ καὶ Προαιρεσίῳ συνέβαινεν Ἡφαιστίωνος φανέντος· τοσαύτη τις εἶχεν
αὐτοὺς ἔνδεια.

Ἀλλ' ὅμως Ἰουλιανὸς ἐπὶ τὸν Προαιρέσιον
ἐπέκλινε τὴν ψυχήν, καὶ πρὸς ἐκεῖνον αὐτῷ τὰ
ὦτα ἀνειστήκει, καὶ τὸ μέγεθος κατεδείμαινε
τῆς φύσεως. ὡς δέ, ἀπελθόντος Ἰουλιανοῦ,
τὰς Ἀθήνας εἶχεν ἔρως τῆς διαδοχῆς τῶν ἐπὶ
τοῖς λόγοις πλεονεκτημάτων, παραγγέλλουσι μὲν
ἐπὶ τῷ κράτει τῆς σοφιστικῆς πολλοὶ καὶ ἄλλοι,
ὥστε ὄχλος ἦν καὶ ταῦτα γράφειν. χειροτονοῦνται
δὲ δοκιμασθέντες ἁπάσαις κρίσεσι, Προαιρέσιός
τε καὶ Ἡφαιστίων καὶ Ἐπιφάνιος καὶ Διόφαντος,
καὶ Σώπολις ἐκ τῆς παραβύστου καὶ παρημελημένης
ἐς τὸν ἀριθμὸν ἐνδείας, καὶ Παρνάσιός τις ἐκ τῆς
εὐτελεστέρας. ἔδει γὰρ πολλοὺς εἶναι, κατὰ τὸν
νόμον τὸν Ῥωμαϊκόν, Ἀθήνησι τοὺς μὲν λέγον-
τας, τοὺς δὲ ἀκούοντας. χειροτονηθέντων δὲ τούτων, οἱ μὲν εὐτελέστεροι τὸ ὄνομα εἶχον, καὶ
μέχρι τῶν σανίδων ἦν τὸ κράτος καὶ τοῦ βήματος
ἐφ' ὃ παρῆεσαν, εἰς δὲ τοὺς δυνατωτέρους ἡ πόλις
εὐθὺς διῄρητο, καὶ οὐχ ἡ πόλις μόνη, ἀλλὰ τὰ
ὑπὸ Ῥωμαίοις ἔθνη, καὶ περὶ λόγων οὐκ ἦν αὐτοῖς
ἡ στάσις, ἀλλ' ὑπὲρ ἐθνῶν ὅλων ἐπὶ τοῖς λόγοις.
ἡ μὲν γὰρ ἑῴα καθάπερ τι γέρας Ἐπιφανίῳ σαφῶς

---

[1] i.e. Mesopotamia and Syria.

to be two men in one, just as the myths say that Geryon was made up of three bodies; so these students were two men in one. For when Prohaeresius appeared in public Hephaestion remained invisible and lay under the rugs in bed while he studied the art of rhetoric. Prohaeresius did the same when Hephaestion appeared abroad; in such poverty did they both live.

Nevertheless Julian's soul leaned towards Prohaeresius, his ears were on the alert to listen to him, and he was awed by the nobility of his genius. And when Julian had departed this life, and Athens desired to choose a successor of equal ability to teach rhetoric, many others gave in their names for this influential sophistic chair, so many that it would be tedious even to write them down. But by the votes of all there were approved and selected Prohaeresius, Hephaestion, Epiphanius, and Diophantus. Sopolis also was added, from a class of men that was of no account but was merely supplementary and despised; and also a certain Parnasius who was of still humbler rank. For in accordance with the Roman law there had to be at Athens many to lecture and many to hear them. Now when these had been elected, the humbler men were sophists only in name, and their power was limited to the walls of their lecture rooms and the platform on which they appeared. But the city at once took sides with the more influential, and not only the city but all the nations under the rule of Rome, and their quarrels did not concern oratory alone, for they strove to maintain the credit of whole nations for oratorical talent. Thus the East[1] manifestly fell to the lot of Epiphanius, Diophantus was

487

ἐξῄρητο, τὴν δὲ Ἀραβίαν εἰλήχει Διόφαντος,
Ἡφαιστίων δὲ καταδείσας Προαιρέσιον ἀπῆλθεν
ἐξ Ἀθηνῶν τε καὶ ἀνθρώπων, Προαιρεσίῳ δὲ ὁ
Πόντος ὅλος καὶ τὰ ἐκείνῃ πρόσοικα τοὺς ὁμιλητὰς
ἀνέπεμπεν, ὥσπερ οἰκεῖον ἀγαθὸν τὸν ἄνδρα
θαυμάζοντες· προσετέθη δὲ καὶ Βιθυνία πᾶσα
καὶ Ἑλλήσποντος, ὅσα τε ὑπὲρ Λυδίας, διὰ τῆς
488 καλουμένης νῦν Ἀσίας ἐπὶ Καρίαν καὶ Λυκίαν
τείνοντα, πρὸς Παμφυλίαν καὶ τὸν Ταῦρον ἀφορίζεται, Αἴγυπτός τε πᾶσα τῆς ἐπὶ τοῖς λόγοις
ἀρχῆς κλῆρος ἦν οἰκεῖος αὐτῷ, καὶ ὅσα, ὑπὲρ
Αἰγύπτου πρὸς Λιβύην συρόμενα, τό τε γνωστὸν[1]
τέλος ἔχει καὶ τὸ οἰκήσιμον. ταῦτα δὲ ὡς ἐπὶ
πλέον εἴρηται, ἐπεί, τό γε ἀκριβῶς, καὶ διαφορὰς
ἔσχε τὰ ἔθνη ἐν ὀλίγοις τισὶ μειρακίοις ἢ μεταναστᾶσιν παρ' ἑτέρους ἢ εἴ[2] πού τις καὶ κατ' ἀρχὰς
ἀπατηθεὶς ἑτέρῳ προσῆλθε. πρὸς δὲ τὸ μέγεθος
τῆς Προαιρεσίου φύσεως, συστάσεως νεανικῆς
καὶ μάλα σφοδρᾶς γενομένης, τῶν ἄλλων ἁπάντων ἐς τοσόνδε ἴσχυσεν ἡ σύστασις, ὥστε τὸν
ἄνδρα ἐξόριστον τῶν Ἀθηνῶν εἰργάσαντο[3] δεκά-
σαντες τὸν ἀνθύπατον, καὶ τὴν ἐπὶ λόγοις βασιλείαν
εἶχον αὐτοί. ὁ δὲ καὶ πρὸς τὴν φυγὴν μετὰ
πενίας ἰσχυρᾶς ὥσπερ ὁ Πεισίστρατος ἐκπεσὼν
κατῆλθε τὸ δεύτερον· ἀλλ' ὁ[4] μὲν διὰ πλοῦτον,
Προαιρεσίῳ δὲ ὁ λόγος ἤρκει μόνος, ὥσπερ ὁ
Ὁμηρικὸς Ἑρμῆς ἐπὶ τὴν σκηνὴν τὴν Ἀχιλλέως
κἂν τοῖς πολεμίοις παρέπεμπεν τὸν Πρίαμον.
συνέβη[5] δέ τις αὐτῷ καὶ ἀγαθὴ τύχη νεώτερον

---

[1] ἄγνωστον Boissonade; γνωστὸν Cobet.
[2] μετανάστασιν . . . εἴ Boissonade: μεταναστᾶσιν . . . ἢ ε
Cobet.   [3] εἰργάσατο Boissonade: εἰργάσαντο Cobet.
[4] ἄλλοι Boissonade; ἀλλ' ὁ Cobet.
[5] συνῆν Boissonade; συνέβη Cobet.

awarded Arabia, while Hephaestion, overawed by Prohaeresius, forsook Athens and the society of men; but the whole Pontus and its neighbouring peoples sent pupils to Prohaeresius, admiring the man as a marvel that their own country had produced. So, too, did all Bithynia and the Hellespont, and all the region that extends beyond Lydia through what is now called Asia as far as Caria and Lycia, and is bounded by Pamphylia and the Taurus. Nay the whole of Egypt also came into his exclusive possession and under his sway as a teacher of rhetoric, and also the country that stretches beyond Egypt towards Libya and is the limit to known and inhabited parts. All this, however, I have stated in the most general terms, for, to speak precisely, there were a few students who were exceptions in these national divisions, because they had either migrated from one teacher to another, or sometimes one had originally been deceived and gone to a teacher other than he had intended. Now a great and violent quarrel arose on account of the extraordinary genius of Prohaeresius, and the faction of all the other sophists so gained the upper hand that they drove him from Athens into exile by bribing the proconsul; and so they themselves held sway over the domain of oratory. But after being driven into exile, and that in the utmost poverty, like Peisistratus[1] he came back again. But the latter had wealth to aid him while for Prohaeresius his eloquence sufficed, even as Hermes in Homer escorted Priam to the hut of Achilles, though it was in the midst of his foes. Good luck also came to his aid by placing at the

----

[1] Tyrant at Athens, lived c. 605–527 B.C.: exiled twice.

489

ἀνθύπατον κατὰ φήμην ἀγανακτοῦντα ἐπὶ τοῖς
γινομένοις ἐπιστήσασα τοῖς πράγμασι. καὶ ὁ
μέν, οὕτω βασιλέως ἐπιτρέψαντος, καὶ μεταπεσόν-
τος ὀστράκου, κατῄει τὸ δεύτερον εἰς τὰς Ἀθήνας,
οἱ δὲ ἐχθροί, τὸ δεύτερον αὖθις ἑλιχθέντες καὶ
συσπειρασάμενοι καθ' ἑαυτούς, ἀνίσταντο καὶ
πρὸς τὸ μέλλον ἑτέρας ἐξηρτύοντο μηχανάς. καὶ
οἱ μὲν ἐν τούτοις ἦσαν· προηγουμένων δὲ τῶν
εὐτρεπιζόντων τὴν κάθοδον, κατελθὼν ὁ Προαιρέσιος (ταῦτα δὲ ἀκριβῶς ὁ Λυδὸς παρὼν Τουσκιανὸς
ἐξήγγελλεν, ὃς Προαιρέσιος ἂν ἦν, εἰ μὴ Προαιρέσιος ἦν), κατελθὼν δέ, ὅμως, εὑρίσκει μέν, ὥσπερ
τις Ὀδυσσεὺς διὰ μακροῦ παραγενόμενος, ὀλίγους
τῶν ἑταίρων, ἐν οἷς καὶ ὁ Τουσκιανὸς ἦν, ὑγιαί-
νοντας, καί, ἐπὶ τῷ ἀπίστῳ τοῦ θαύματος, τοὺς
πρὸς ἐκεῖνον βλέποντας· εὑρὼν δέ, καὶ πληρωθεὶς
ἀγαθῶν ἐλπίδων "περιμένετε," φησί, "τὸν ἀνθύπατον"· ὁ δὲ θᾶττον ἦλθεν ἐλπίδος. ἀφικόμενος δὲ Ἀθήναζε, συνεκάλει τε τοὺς σοφιστάς,
καὶ διετάραττεν ἅπαντα. οἱ δὲ μόλις μὲν καὶ
βάδην συνῄεσαν. ἀνάγκης δὲ καλούσης, προ-
βλήματά τε αὐτοῖς προεβλήθη, καὶ κατὰ δύναμιν
αὐτῶν ἕκαστος ἐνεχθέντες, ἐκ παρακλήσεως καὶ
παρασκευῆς τῶν κρότων συντελουμένων, ἀπηλλάγησαν, καὶ τοὺς Προαιρεσίου φίλους εἶχεν
ἀθυμία. ὁ δὲ ἀνθύπατος αὐτοὺς τὸ δεύτερον ὡς
ἐπὶ τιμαῖς συγκαλέσας, ἅπαντας κατασχεθῆναι

---

[1] A proverb derived from the game ὀστρακίνδα. There is
an allusion here to " ostracism " in ancient Athens.

490

head of affairs a younger proconsul who was indignant at the report of what had taken place. So,
as the proverb says, "heads became tails," [1] and with
the emperor's permission he returned to Athens
from exile; whereupon his enemies for the second
time coiled and twisted themselves and reared their
heads to attack him, framing other devices against
him to suit any future emergencies. They busied
themselves with these plots, but meanwhile his
friends were beforehand and were smoothing the
path of his return, and when Prohaeresius came back
(a precise account of all this was given me by
an eyewitness, Tuscianus of Lydia, who would have
been a Prohaeresius, had not Prohaeresius existed);
when, I say, he did return, like some Odysseus
arriving home after a long absence, he found a few
of his friends safe and sound (among whom was
Tuscianus), and these looked to him for aid after
this incredible miracle. Filled with good hopes
on finding them there, he said: "Wait for the
proconsul to come." The latter came sooner than
could have been believed possible. On his arrival
at Athens he called a meeting of the sophists, and
by this means threw all their plans into confusion.
They assembled slowly and reluctantly, and since
they had to obey the voice of necessity they discussed, each according to his ability, certain questions that were proposed to them, while they were
provided with applause by persons who had received
their instructions and had been invited for the
purpose. Then the meeting broke up, and the
friends of Prohaeresius felt discouraged. But the
proconsul summoned them a second time, as though
to award them honours, ordered them all to be

κελεύει, καὶ τὸν Προαιρέσιον ἐξαπιναίως εἰσκαλεῖ.
οἱ δὲ παρῆσαν ἀγνοοῦντες τὰ μέλλοντα. ὁ δὲ
ἀνθύπατος " βούλομαι " ἀνέκραγε, "πᾶσιν ὑμῖν ἓν
ζήτημα προβαλών, πάντων ὑμῶν ἀκροάσασθαι
σήμερον· ἐρεῖ δὲ μεθ' ὑμᾶς, ἢ ὅπως ἂν βούλησθε,
καὶ Προαιρέσιος." τῶν δὲ τὸ πρᾶγμα φανερῶς
παραιτησαμένων, καὶ τὰ Ἀριστείδου μετὰ πολλῆς
σκέψεως καὶ πόνου (ἔδει γὰρ μηδὲν ἴδιον αὐτοὺς
λέγειν), προενεγκόντων δὲ ὅμως ὡς οὐκ εἰσὶ τῶν
ἐμούντων ἀλλὰ τῶν ἀκριβούντων, τὸ δεύτερον
ἐμβοήσας ὁ ἀνθύπατος " λέγε," φησίν " ὦ Προ-
489 αιρέσιε." ὁ δὲ ἀπὸ τῆς καθέδρας εἰς προάγωνά
τινα διαλεχθεὶς οὐκ ἀχαρίτως,[1] καὶ τὸν σχέδιον
ὅσος ἐστὶν ἐξάρας λόγον, ἀνέστη θαρραλέως ἐπὶ
τὸν ἀγῶνα. ἐνταῦθα ὁ μὲν ἀνθύπατος ὅρον τινὰ
προβαλεῖν ἕτοιμος ἦν, ὁ δὲ ἀνενεγκὼν τὸ πρόσωπον, περιέβλεπε κύκλῳ τὸ θέατρον. ὡς δὲ
πολὺ μὲν ἑώρα τὸ πολέμιον, τὸ δὲ φίλιον μικρὸν
καὶ διαλανθάνον, ἐγένετο μὲν κατὰ λόγον ἀθυμό-
τερος· ζέοντος δὲ καὶ συγχορεύοντος αὐτῷ δαίμονος, περισκοπῶν ἅπαντα, συγκεκαλυμμένους
ὁρᾷ περὶ τὴν ἐσχάτην ἄντυγα τοῦ θεάτρου δύο
τινὰς ἄνδρας τῶν περὶ ῥητορικὴν τετριμμένων
καὶ ὑφ' ὧν ἐπεπόνθει τὰ πλεῖστα τῶν κακῶν, καὶ
ἀναβοήσας " ὦ θεοί," φησίν " ἐνταῦθα οἱ βέλτιστοι
καὶ σοφοί. τούτους ἐμοὶ κέλευσον, ἀνθύπατε,
προβαλεῖν· ἴσως γὰρ ὅτι ἠσέβησαν πεισθήσονται."
οἱ μὲν οὖν ταῦτα ἀκούσαντες, εἰς τὸν ὄχλον τε

---

[1] ἀχαρίστως Boissonade ; ἀχαρίτως Cobet.

---

[1] This saying of Aristeides is quoted by Philostratus,
Lives of the Sophists 583 ; it became a proverb.

detained, and suddenly he called in Prohaeresius. So they arrived, not knowing what was going to happen. But the proconsul called out : " I wish to propose a theme for you all, and to hear you all declaim on it this very day. Prohaeresius also will speak, either after you or in what order you please." When they openly demurred and, after much consideration and effort, quoted the saying of Aristeides (for it would never do for them to utter anything original); when after all they did produce it, saying that their custom was "not to vomit but to elaborate every theme," [1] the proconsul exclaimed again with a loud voice : " Speak, Prohaeresius ! " Then from his chair the sophist first delivered a graceful prelude by way of preliminary speech, in which he extolled the greatness of extempore eloquence, then with the fullest confidence he rose for his formal discussion. The proconsul was ready to propose a definition for the theme, but Prohaeresius threw back his head and gazed all round the theatre. And when he saw that his enemies were many while his friends were few, and were trying to escape notice, he was naturally somewhat discouraged. But as his guardian deity began to warm to the work and to aid him by playing its part, he again surveyed the scene, and beheld in the farthest row of the audience, hiding themselves in their cloaks, two men, veterans in the service of rhetoric, at whose hands he had received the worst treatment of all, and he cried out : " Ye gods ! There are those honourable and wise men ! Proconsul, order them to propose a theme for me. Then perhaps they will be convinced that they have behaved impiously." Now the men, on hearing this, slunk away into the crowd that was

τῶν καθημένων κατεδύοντο, καὶ διαλανθάνειν
ἔσπευδον. ὁ δὲ ἀνθύπατος, διαπέμψας τινὰς τῶν
στρατιωτῶν, εἰς μέσον αὐτοὺς περιήγαγε· καὶ
καταστήσας ἔκ τινος προτροπῆς τὸ προβαλεῖν τὸν
καλούμενον ὅρον, ὡς ἐκεῖνοι, βραχύν τινα χρόνον
σκεψάμενοι καὶ πρὸς ἀλλήλους διαλεχθέντες, τὸν
τραχύτατον ὧν ᾔδεσαν καὶ φαυλότατον ἐξήνεγκαν,
ἰδιωτικὸν καὶ τοῦτον, καὶ οὐ βάσιμον ῥητορικῇ
πομπείᾳ, ταυρηδὸν μὲν αὐτοὺς ὑπέβλεψε, πρὸς
δὲ τὸν ἀνθύπατον· "ἃ πρὸ τοῦ ἀγῶνος αἰτῶ δί-
καια, ταῦτά σε ἱκετεύω δοῦναι." τοῦ δὲ εἰπόντος
ὡς οὐδενὸς ἀτυχήσει δικαίου, "ἀξιῶ" φησί "δο-
θῆναί μοι τοὺς ταχέως γράφοντας, καὶ στῆναι κατὰ
τὸ μέσον οἳ καθ᾽ ἡμέραν μὲν τῆς Θέμιδος γλῶτταν
ἀποσημαίνονται, σήμερον δὲ τοῖς ἡμετέροις ὑπη-
ρετήσονται λόγοις." τοῦ δὲ παρελθεῖν τοὺς ἄκρους
τῶν γραφέων ἐπιτρέψαντος, οἱ μὲν ἑκατέρωθεν
ἔστησαν ἐς τὴν γραφὴν ἕτοιμοι, καὶ τὸ μέλλον
οὐδεὶς ἠπίστατο· τοῦ δὲ εἰπόντος ὡς "καὶ ἕτερον
αἰτήσω βαρύτερον," εἶτα κελευσθέντος εἰπεῖν,
"κροτείτω με" φησί "μηδὲ εἷς." ὡς δὲ καὶ
τοῦτο μετὰ πολλοῦ πᾶσιν ἐπέτειλε φόβον, ἄρχεται
μὲν ὁ Προαιρέσιος λέγειν ῥύδην, κατὰ τὸν κρότον ἀναπαύων ἑκάστην περίοδον, τὸ δὲ ἀναγκαίως
Πυθαγορικὸν θέατρον ὑπὸ τοῦ θαύματος καταρ-
ρηγνύμενον, μυκηθμοῦ καὶ στόνου διάμεστον ἦν.

---

[1] Hermogenes, *On Invention* iii. 13, gives five kinds of
ὅρος, "definition"; the kind of argumentation required for
each kind was elaborate and technical; it was part of the
exposition of the case, the *constitutio definitiva*; *cf.*
Quintilian vii. 3.
[2] Literally "rapid scribes," sometimes called ταχυγράφοι.

seated there and did their best to avoid detection.
But the proconsul sent some of his soldiers and
brought them into full view. After a brief sort of
exhortation he appointed them to propose a theme
involving the precise definition of terms.[1] Whereupon, after considering for a short time and consulting together, they produced the hardest and most
disagreeable theme that they knew of, a vulgar one,
moreover, that gave no opening for the display of
fine rhetoric. Prohaeresius glared at them fiercely,
and said to the proconsul: "I implore you to grant
me the just demands that I make before this contest."
On his replying that Prohaeresius should not fail to
have what was just and fair, the latter said: "I ask
to have shorthand writers[2] assigned to me, and that
they take their place in the centre of the theatre;
I mean men who every day take down the words of
Themis,[3] but who to-day shall devote themselves to
what I have to say." The proconsul gave his permission for the most expert of the scribes to come
forward, and they stood on either side of Prohaeresius
ready to write, but no one knew what he meant to
do. Then he said: "I shall ask for something even
more difficult to grant." He was told to name it,
and said: "There must be no applause whatever."
When the proconsul had given all present an order
to this effect under pain of the severest penalties,
Prohaeresius began his speech with a flood of
eloquence, rounding every period with a sonorous
phrase, while the audience, which perforce kept a
Pythagorean silence, in their amazed admiration
broke through their restraint, and overflowed into
murmurs and sighs. As the speech grew more

[3] The goddess of the law courts.

ὡς δὲ ὁ λόγος ἐπεδίδου, καὶ ὁ ἀνὴρ ὑπὲρ πάντα
ἐφέρετο λόγον καὶ πᾶσαν δόξαν ἀνθρωπίνην,
πρόεισι μὲν εἰς θάτερον μέρος καὶ συμπληροῖ τὴν
κατάστασιν· ἐνθουσιῶν δὲ καὶ πηδῶν, ὥσπερ
ἀναπολόγητον τὸ λειπόμενον ἀφιεὶς μέρος, εἰς
τὴν ἐναντίαν ὑπόθεσιν ἐπαφῆκε τὸν λόγον. καὶ
οἱ γράφοντες μόλις εἴποντο, καὶ τὸ θέατρον μόλις
σιωπᾶν ἠνείχετο, καὶ πλῆθος ἦν τῶν εἰρημένων.
ἐπιστρέψας εἰς τοὺς γράφοντας τὸ πρόσωπον,
" ὁρᾶτε ἀκριβῶς " ἔφη " εἰ πάντα ταῦτα ἃ προ-
λαβὼν εἶπον μέμνημαι·" καὶ μηδὲ περὶ μίαν λέξιν
σφαλείς, τὰ αὐτὰ δεύτερον ἀπήγγελλεν. οὔτε ὁ
ἀνθύπατος ἐνταῦθα τοὺς ἑαυτοῦ νόμους ἐφύλαττεν,
οὔτε τὸ θέατρον τὰς ἀπειλὰς τοῦ ἄρχοντος· καὶ τὰ
στέρνα τοῦ σοφιστοῦ περιλιχμησάμενοι καθάπερ
ἀγάλματος ἐνθέου πάντες οἱ παρόντες, οἱ μὲν
πόδας, οἱ δὲ χεῖρας προσεκύνουν, οἱ δὲ θεὸν ἔφασαν,
490 οἱ δὲ Ἑρμοῦ Λογίου τύπον· οἱ δὲ ἀντίτεχνοι διὰ
φθόνον παρεθέντες ἔκειντο, τινὲς δὲ αὐτῶν οὐδὲ
κείμενοι τῶν ἐπαίνων ἠμέλουν. ὁ δὲ ἀνθύπατος
καὶ δορυφόρων μετὰ πάντων καὶ τῶν δυνατῶν[1] ἐκ
τοῦ θεάτρου παρέπεμψε. μετὰ ταῦτα οὐδεὶς ἀντέλεγεν, ἀλλ' ὥσπερ ὑπὸ σκηπτοῦ πληγέντες,
ἅπαντες συνεχώρησαν αὐτῷ εἶναι κρείττονι.
χρόνῳ δὲ ὕστερον ἀναφέροντες, ὥσπερ αἱ τῆς Ὕδρας
κεφαλαί, πρὸς τὸ οἰκεῖον ἀνωρθοῦντο καὶ διηγεί-

[1] τῶν δυνάμεων Boissonade ; τῶν δυνατῶν Kayser.

---

[1] This phrase, first used by Aristeides to describe
Demosthenes, became a sophistic commonplace ; cf. Julian.
Oration vii. 237 c.

vehement and the orator soared to heights which the mind of man could not describe or conceive of, he passed on to the second part of the speech and completed the exposition of the theme. But then, suddenly leaping in the air like one inspired, he abandoned the remaining part, left it undefended, and turned the flood of his eloquence to defend the contrary hypothesis. The scribes could hardly keep pace with him, the audience could hardly endure to remain silent, while the mighty stream of words flowed on. Then, turning his face towards the scribes, he said: "Observe carefully whether I remember all the arguments that I used earlier." And, without faltering over a single word, he began to declaim the same speech for the second time. At this the proconsul did not observe his own rules, nor did the audience observe the threats of the magistrate. For all who were present licked the sophist's breast as though it were the statue of some god; some kissed his feet, some his hands, others declared him to be a god or the very model of Hermes, the god of eloquence.[1] His adversaries, on the other hand, lay in the dust eaten up with envy, though some of them even from where they lay could not refrain from applauding; but the proconsul with his whole bodyguard and the notables escorted him from the theatre. After this no one dared to speak against him, but as though they had been stricken by a thunderbolt they all admitted that he was their superior. However, some time after, they recovered themselves, like the heads of the Hydra, and were restored to their natural dispositions and reared up their heads; so they tempted certain of the most powerful men

ροντο, καὶ τραπέζαις τε πολυτελέσι καὶ θεραπαι-
νιδίοις κομψοῖς τινὰς τῶν ἀκμαζόντων δελεά-
ζοντες, ὥσπερ οἱ τῶν βασιλέων ἔννομον καὶ ὀρθὴν
μάχην νενικημένοι, καὶ ἐν τοῖς ἀπόροις εἰς τὸ
ἔσχατον συνελαθέντες, ἐπὶ ψιλοὺς καὶ σφενδονήτας
καὶ γυμνήτας καὶ τὸ εὐτελὲς ἐπικουρικὸν κατα-
φεύγουσιν, οὐ ταῦτα τιμῶντες ἐξ ἀρχῆς, ὅμως
δὲ δι᾽ ἀνάγκην ταῦτα τιμῶντες[1]· οὕτω κἀκεῖνοι
πρὸς ἀναγκαῖον συμμαχικὸν ἐπτοημένοι, τοιαύτας
ἐπιβουλὰς ἤρτυον, αἰσχρὰς μέν, ἀνεπίφθονοι δὲ
ἦσαν, εἴ τις ἑαυτὸν καὶ κακῶς φιλεῖ. εἶχον γοῦν
ἑταίρων πλῆθος, καὶ ἀπήντα τὸ σόφισμα κατὰ
λόγον αὐτοῖς. τὸ δὲ Προαιρεσίου τυραννὶς ἐδόκει
τις εἶναι, καὶ εὐτυχεῖν ἡ ἀρετὴ τῶν λόγων ἐδόκει
καλῶς· ἢ γὰρ οἱ νοῦν ἔχοντες ἅπαντες αὐτὸν
ἡροῦντο, ἢ οἱ προσελθόντες εὐθὺς νοῦν εἶχον ὅτι
Προαιρέσιον ᾕρηντο.

Κατὰ δὲ τούτους τοὺς χρόνους ἤνεγκεν ὁ βασιλικὸς τῆς αὐλῆς ὅμιλος ἄνδρα καὶ δόξης ἐραστὴν
καὶ λόγων. ἦν μὲν γὰρ ἐκ Βηρυτοῦ πόλεως, καὶ
Ἀνατόλιος ἐκαλεῖτο· οἱ δὲ βασκαίνοντες αὐτῷ
καὶ Ἀζουτρίωνα ἐπίκλησιν ἔθεντο, καὶ ὅ τι μὲν
τὸ ὄνομα σημαίνειν βούλεται ὁ κακοδαίμων ἴστω
τῶν θυμελῶν χορός. δόξης δὲ ἐραστὴς ὁ Ἀνατόλιος
καὶ λόγων γενόμενος, ἀμφοτέρων ἔτυχε· καὶ τῆς
τε νομικῆς καλουμένης παιδείας εἰς ἄκρον ἀφ-

---

[1] ταῦτα τιμῶντες is probably either a gloss or repeated by
a copyist's error.

---

[1] Himerius addresses a speech, *Eclogue* 32, to this
Anatolius, the prefect of Illyricum ; he visited Athens
about 345.

[2] No explanation of this word is to be found.   Such nick-

in the city by means of costly banquets and smart
maidservants, just as kings do when they have been
defeated in a regular pitched battle, and in their
difficulties are driven to extreme measures, so that
they have recourse to light-armed forces and slingers,
troops without heavy armour and their inferior re-
serves; for if they valued these not at all before
they are forced to do so now. Just so those sophists,
fleeing in their panic to such allies as they could
muster, framed their plots, which were base indeed
but the men were not to be envied, nor are any
who love themselves fatuously. At any rate they
had a crowd of adherents, and the plot proceeded so
that they could reckon on success. However, the
genius of Prohaeresius seemed to possess a sort of
tyranny over men's minds, and the power of his
eloquence to have extraordinary good fortune. For
either all intelligent men chose him as their teacher,
or those who had attended his school forthwith
became intelligent, because they had chosen Prohaeresius.

Now in these days the throng at the imperial
court produced a man who passionately desired both
fame and eloquence. He came from the city of
Berytus and was called Anatolius.[1] Those who
envied him nicknamed him Azutrion,[2] and what
that name means I leave to that miserable band of
mummers to decide! But Anatolius who desired
fame and eloquence achieved both these things.
For first he won the highest distinction in what is
called the science of law, as was natural since his

names were common in the fourth century, and the fashion
flourished till by the sixth century they are almost surnames
and in regular use.

ικόμενος, ὡσὰν πατρίδα ἔχων τὴν Βηρυτὸν ἢ τοῖς
τοιούτοις μήτηρ ὑποκάθηται παιδεύμασι, καὶ διαπλεύσας εἰς Ῥώμην, καὶ φρονήματος ἐμπλησθεὶς
καὶ λόγων ὕψος ἐχόντων καὶ βάρος, εἰσφρήσας τε
εἰς τὰ βασίλεια, ταχὺ μάλα πρῶτος ἦν, καὶ διὰ
πάσης ἐλθὼν ἀρχῆς, ἐν πολλαῖς τε ἀρχαῖς εὐδο-
κιμήσας (καὶ γὰρ οἱ μισοῦντες αὐτὸν ἐθαύμαζον),
προϊὼν καὶ εἰς τὸν ἔπαρχον τῆς αὐλῆς ἤλασεν·
ἡ δὲ ἀρχὴ βασιλεία ἐστὶν ἀπόρφυρος. τυχὼν
δὲ κατὰ τὴν ἑαυτοῦ φιλοτιμίαν τύχης ἀξίας (τὸ
γὰρ καλούμενον Ἰλλυρικὸν ἐπετέτραπτο), καὶ φιλο-
θύτης ὢν καὶ διαφερόντως Ἕλλην (καί τοί γε
ἡ κοινὴ κίνησις πρὸς ἄλλας ἔφερε ῥοπάς), ἐξὸν
αὐτῷ πρὸς τὰ καίρια τῆς ἀρχῆς ἐλθεῖν, καὶ διοικεῖν
ἕκαστα πρὸς ὃ βούλοιτο, ὁ δέ, χρυσῆς τινὸς αὐτὸν
μανίας ὑπολαβούσης ἰδεῖν τὴν Ἑλλάδα, καὶ τὰ
τῶν λόγων εἴδωλα διὰ τῆς παιδεύσεως ἐπὶ τὴν
αἴσθησιν, μεθ' οὕτως ἀριπρεποῦς ἀξιώματος φερόμενος, συλλαβεῖν, καὶ τὸ νοούμενον ἐκ τῶν
ἀρχαίων ἰνδαλμάτων φάντασμα ἐπὶ τὴν ὄψιν
σπάσαι, πρὸς τὴν Ἑλλάδα ἔσπευσε. καὶ πρό-
βλημά γέ τι τοῖς σοφισταῖς προπέμψας (ἐτεθήπεσαν δὲ αὐτὸν ἡ Ἑλλάς, τό τε φρόνημα ἀκούοντες
491 καὶ τὴν παιδείαν, καὶ ὅτι ἀκλινὴς ἦν καὶ ἀδωρο-
δόκητος), ἐκέλευεν ἅπαντας τὸ αὐτὸ μελετᾶν
πρόβλημα. οἱ δὲ τοῦτο αὐτὸ ἐπιτηδεύοντες καὶ
κατὰ τὴν ἑκάστην ἡμέραν ἀλλήλοις ἐπιβουλεύοντες,

---

[1] Berytus (Beirut) was, as Libanius describes, famous for
its school of Roman law. When the youths began to flock
thither instead of to the Greek sophists the decay of
Greek letters was inevitable.

[2] Or "proposition," Latin *quaestio.*

birthplace was Berytus, the foster-mother of all such studies.[1] Then he sailed to Rome where, since his wisdom and eloquence were elevated and weighty, he made his way to court. There he soon obtained the highest rank, and after holding every high office and winning a great reputation in many official positions (and indeed even his enemies admired him), he finally attained to the rank of pretorian prefect, a magistracy which, though it lacks the imperial purple, exercises imperial power. He had now attained to a fortune in accord with his lofty ambition (for the district called Illyricum had been assigned to him), and since he was devout in offering sacrifices to the gods and peculiarly fond of Greek studies, in spite of the fact that the main current was setting in other directions, instead of choosing as he might have done to visit the most important places in his dominion and administer everything according to his pleasure, he was overcome by a sort of golden madness of desire to behold Greece, and, supported by his distinguished reputation, to turn into realities the mere images of eloquence derived from his learning, and to see for himself what had been an intellectual concept received from such presentation of eloquence as ancient writings could give. He therefore hastened to Greece. Moreover, he sent to the sophists beforehand a certain problem[2] for them to consider, and bade them all practise declaiming on this same problem. All the Greeks marvelled at him when they heard of his wisdom and learning and that he was unswervingly upright and incorruptible. Then they set themselves to consider his problem and plotted every day to outwit one another. Neverthe-

EUNAPIUS

ὅμως (ἀνάγκη γὰρ ἐκέλευε) συνεκρίθησαν, καὶ
περὶ τῆς καλουμένης στάσεως τοῦ προβλήματος
πολλοὺς ἐν ἀλλήλοις λόγους ἀντεπιχειρήσαντες
(οὐκ ἔγνω τούτου τοῦ πράγματος γελοιότερον ὁ
συγγραφεύς), διεκρίθησαν ἀπ' ἀλλήλων ἕκαστος,
διὰ φιλοτιμίαν ἕκαστος ἐπαινῶν τὴν ἰδίαν δόξαν
καὶ πρὸς τὰ μειράκια φιλοτιμούμενος. ὡς δὲ
βαρύτερος ἦν τῆς Περσικῆς ἐκείνης καὶ πολυυμνήτου
στρατιᾶς ἐπὶ τὴν Ἑλλάδα κατιὼν ὁ Ἀνατόλιος,
καὶ ὁ κίνδυνος ἦν παρὰ πόδας οὐ τοῖς Ἕλλησιν
ἀλλὰ τοῖς σοφιστεύουσιν, ἐνταῦθα οἱ μὲν ἄλλοι
πάντες (προσεγεγένητο γὰρ αὐτοῖς καὶ Ἱμέριός
τις σοφιστὴς ἐκ Βιθυνίας· οὐκ ἔγνω τοῦτον ὁ
συγγραφεύς, πλὴν ὅσα γε διὰ συγγραμμάτων),
ἐταλαιπωροῦντο δὲ ὅμως ἅπαντες, καὶ πολλῷ
καμάτῳ παρετείνοντο, τὴν δόξασαν ἕκαστος μελε-
τῶντες στάσιν. ἐνταῦθα ὁ Προαιρέσιος θαρσῶν τῇ
φύσει, βαρὺς ἦν οὔτε φιλοτιμούμενος οὔτε ἐκ-
φέρων τὸ ἀπόρρητον. ὁ δὲ Ἀνατόλιος ἐγγύθεν,
καὶ εἰσεδήμησεν Ἀθήναζε. θύσας δὲ θαρσαλέως
καὶ περιελθὼν τὰ ἱερὰ πάντα, ᾗ θεσμὸς ἱερὸς
ἐκέλευεν, ἐξεκάλει τοὺς σοφιστὰς ἐπὶ τὸν ἀγῶνα.
καὶ οἱ παρόντες ἕκαστος πρῶτος ἐς τὴν ἐπίδειξιν
ἠπείγετο· οὕτω φίλαυτόν τι χρῆμα ἄνθρωπος· ὁ
δὲ Ἀνατόλιος καὶ τοὺς κροτοῦντας, τὰ μειράκια,
ἐγέλα, καὶ τοὺς πατέρας ἠλέει τῆς τῶν παίδων
παιδείας ὑπὸ τίσι παιδεύονται. ἐκάλει δὲ τὸν
Προαιρέσιον· μόνος γὰρ ἀπολέλειπτο· ὁ δὲ
θεραπεύσας τινὰ τῶν οἰκείων αὐτοῦ καὶ πάντα
ἐξειδότων, μαθὼν τὴν στάσιν ἣν ἐπαινεῖ (τοῦτο

¹ This was a courageous act because Christian emperors,
Constantius and Constans, were on the throne.
502

less, since necessity constrained them, they did meet together, and after bringing forward many opposing theories among themselves as to what is called the constitution of the problem (the author never knew of anything so ridiculous as this problem), they were in complete disagreement one with another, since each man in his vanity lauded his own theory and jealously maintained it in the presence of the students. But since Anatolius descending on Greece was more formidable than the famous Persian expedition, that oft - told tale, and the danger stared not indeed all the Greeks but the sophists in the face, all the others (among whom was included a certain Himerius, a sophist from Bithynia; the author knew him only from his writings) toiled and spared no pains or effort, as each one studied the constitution of the theme that he approved. In this crisis Prohaeresius, who trusted in his genius, offended them deeply because he neither showed ambition nor published his secret theory. But now Anatolius was at hand and had made his entry into Athens. When he had with great courage offered sacrifices [1] and formally visited all the temples, as the divine ordinance commanded, he summoned the sophists to the competition. When they were in his presence they one and all strove to be the first to declaim; so prone to self-love is man! But Anatolius laughed at the boy pupils who were applauding them, and commiserated the fathers whose sons were being educated by such men. Then he called on Prohaeresius who alone was left. Now he had cultivated the acquaintance of one of the friends of Anatolius who knew all the circumstances, and had learned from him the constitution of the

γὰρ ὁ συγγραφεὺς ἔφη γελοῖον ἐν τοῖς ἄνω λόγοις),
καί τοί γε οὐδενὸς ἦν ἄξιον λόγου, οὐδὲ Ἀνατόλιον
ἔδει ταῦτα νικᾶν, ὅμως πρός τε τὴν κλῆσιν ὑπ-
ήκουσεν ἀθρόως, καὶ πρὸς ἐκείνην τὴν στάσιν
διαθέμενος τὸν ἀγῶνα, πρὸς τοσόνδε ἤρκεσε πρὸς
τὸ κάλλος τοῦ λόγου, ὥστε ἐπήδα τε ὁ Ἀνατόλιος,
καὶ τὸ θέατρον βοῶν τε ἐρρήγνυτο, καὶ οὐδεὶς ἦν
ὃς οὐχὶ θεὸν ὑπελάμβανε. τιμήσας οὖν ἐκεῖνον
διαφερόντως φαίνεται, καί τοί γε τοὺς ἄλλους
μόλις ἀξιώσας τῆς ἑαυτοῦ τραπέζης. ὁ δὲ Ἀνατόλιος σοφιστὴς ἦν ἐν τοῖς κατ' εὐωχίαν καὶ πρὸς
συμπόσιον· οὐδὲ τὸ συμπόσιον ἦν ἄλογον καὶ
ἀπαίδευτον. ἀλλὰ ταῦτα μὲν ἐγένετο πρὸ πολλῶν
χρόνων, καὶ οὕτως ἐξηκρίβου τὴν ἀκοὴν ὁ συγγραφεύς. ὁ δὲ Ἀνατόλιος καὶ τὸν Μιλήσιον
ὑπερεθαύμαζεν, ὃς ἦν μὲν ἐκ Σμύρνης τῆς Ἰωνικῆς,
φύσεως δὲ ἀρίστης τυχών, ἐς ἀφιλότιμόν τινα καὶ
σχολαστὴν ἑαυτὸν ἐμβαλὼν βίον, πρός τε ἱεροῖς
ἦν καὶ γάμων ἠμέλησε, ποίησίν τε ἅπασαν καὶ
μέλος ἐξήσκησε, καὶ ποιήσεως ὅσον ἐπαινοῦσι
Χάριτες. οὕτω γοῦν εἷλε τὸν Ἀνατόλιον, ὥστε
καὶ Μοῦσαν ἐκάλει τὸν ἄνθρωπον. Ἐπιφανίου
δὲ τοῦ σοφιστεύοντος τὰ ζητήματα διαιρέσεις[1]
ἔφασκεν, εἰς μικρολογίαν καὶ περιττὴν ἀκρίβειαν
κωμῳδῶν τὸν παιδεύοντα. περὶ δὲ τῆς διαφωνίας[2]
αὐτῶν τῆς κατὰ τὴν στάσιν, διασιλλαίνων ἅπαντας,

---

[1] Or "Subdivisions," *partitiones*, arrangement of the
speech under headings.
[2] For the rhetorical term see Glossary.

theme that Anatolius approved. (This is what the author called ridiculous in what he said above.) And even though the theme was unworthy of consideration, and it was not right that the view of Anatolius should prevail, nevertheless Prohaeresius, when his name was called, obeyed the summons promptly, and modelled his disputation on the constitution of the theme that I have mentioned, and his argument was so able and so elegant that Anatolius jumped up from his seat, the audience shouted applause till they burst, and every man there regarded him as a divine being. Accordingly Anatolius openly showed him peculiar honour, though he would hardly admit the others to his table. He himself was an accomplished sophist in table-talk and themes suited to a symposium; hence his symposium was a feast of reason and of learned conversation. But all this happened many years ago, and therefore the author has been very careful in his report of what he learned from hearsay. Now Anatolius felt great admiration for Milesius also, a man who came from Smyrna in Ionia. Though fortune had endowed him with the greatest talents, he abandoned himself to an unambitious and leisurely life, frequented the temples, neglected to marry, and cultivated every sort of poetry and lyric and every kind of composition that is favoured by the Graces. By this means, then, he won the favour of Anatolius so that he actually called the man a "Muse." But he used to call the problems raised by Epiphanius the sophist "Analyses,"[1] making fun in this way of that teacher's triviality and pedantic accuracy. He satirized all the sophists for their disagreements over the constitution[2] of a theme, and said : "If there had been

505

" εἰ πλείους " ἔφη " τῶν δεκατριῶν ἐτύγχανον οἱ
σοφιστεύοντες, τάχ' ἂν ἑτέρας προσεξεῦρον στά-
492 σεις, ἵνα διαφόρως ἓν πρόβλημα μελετήσωσι."
Προαιρέσιον δὲ πάντων ἕνα καὶ μόνον ὑπερεθαύμαζεν. ἐτύγχανε δὲ ὁ Προαιρέσιος οὐ πρὸ πολλοῦ
χρόνου μετάπεμπτος ὑπὸ τοῦ βασιλεύοντος γεγονὼς
Κώνσταντος ἐς τὰς Γαλλίας, καὶ κρατήσας τοῦ
βασιλεύοντος ἐς τοσοῦτον, ὥστε ὁμοτράπεζος ἅμα
τοῖς τιμιωτάτοις ἦν αὐτῷ, καὶ ὅσον γε τῶν ἐκείνῃ
τότε ἀνθρώπων οὐκ ἐξικνοῦντο τούς τε λόγους
ἀναθεωρεῖν καὶ τὰ ἀπόρρητα τῆς ψυχῆς θαυμάζειν,
πρὸς τὴν ὄψιν καὶ τὰ φαινόμενα μεταφέροντες
τὴν ἔκπληξιν, τοῦ τε σώματος αὐτοῦ τὸ κάλλος
καὶ τὸ ὕψος ἐτεθήπεσαν, ὥσπερ ἐς ἀνδριάντα τινὰ
καὶ κολοσσὸν μόλις ἀναβλέποντες·[1] οὕτω τὰ
πάντα ἦν ὑπὲρ ἄνθρωπον. τήν γε μὴν καρτερίαν
ὁρῶντες, ὄντως ἀπαθῆ τινα καὶ σιδήρεον ὑπελάμ-
βανον, ὅτι λεπτὸν ἔχων τριβώνιον, ἀνυπόδητος,
τρυφῆς περιουσίαν ἐτίθετο τοὺς Γαλατικοὺς χει-
μῶνας καὶ πεπηγότα σχεδόν τι τὸν 'Ρῆνον ἔπινε·
καὶ τόν γε ὅλον οὕτω διετέλεσε βίον, ἀπείρατος
θερμοῦ γενόμενος ποτοῦ. ἀπέστειλε γοῦν αὐτὸν
ὁ βασιλεὺς εἰς τὴν μεγάλην 'Ρώμην, φιλοτιμούμενος οἵων βασιλεύειν ἔλαχεν· οἱ δὲ οὐκ εἶχον ὅ
τι θαυμάσουσιν, οὕτω πάντα ἦν παρὰ τὴν ἀνθρωπίνην φύσιν. πολλὰ δὲ ἐπὶ πολλοῖς ἀγασθέντες,
καὶ τυχόντες ἐπαίνων, ἀνδριάντα κατασκευασά-
μενοι χαλκοῦν ἰσομέτρητον, ἀνέθηκαν ἐπιγράψαν-

---

[1] Here Eunapius seems to imitate Philostratus, *Life of
Adrian* 589, where that sophist makes a similar effect on
audiences that knew no Greek.

[2] This may echo Plato's description of Socrates in
Symposium 220 A, B.

more than thirteen of these professional sophists,
they would no doubt have invented still more ' con-
stitutions' in order to declaim on a single problem
from every different angle possible." Prohaeresius
was the one and only sophist of them all whom he
genuinely admired. Now it happened that Prohaeresius had not long before been summoned to the
Gallic provinces by Constans, who then held imperial
sway, and he had so won over Constans that he sat at
his table along with those whom he most honoured.
And all the inhabitants of that country who
could not attain to a thorough understanding of his
lectures and thus admire the inmost secrets of his
soul, transferred their wonder and admiration to
what they could see plainly before their eyes, and
marvelled at his physical beauty and great stature,
while they gazed up at him with an effort as
though to behold some statue or colossus, so much
beyond the measure of man was he in all respects.[1]
Moreover, when they observed his abstinence and
self-denial they believed him to be passionless and
made of iron; for clad in a threadbare cloak and
barefooted [2] he regarded the winters of Gaul as the
height of luxury, and he would drink the water of
the Rhine when it was nearly freezing. Indeed
he passed his whole life in this fashion, and was
never known to touch a hot drink. Accordingly
Constans dispatched him to mighty Rome, because
he was ambitious to show them there what great
men he ruled over. But so entirely did he surpass
the ordinary human type that they could select no
one peculiarity to admire. So they admired his
many great qualities one after another, and were
in turn approved by him, and they made and set

τες· Η ΒΑΣΙΛΕΥΟΥΣΑ ΡΩΜΗ ΤΟΝ ΒΑΣΙΛΕΥΟΝΤΑ ΤΩΝ
ΛΟΓΩΝ.

Ὁ δὲ βασιλεὺς ἀπιόντι[1] πάλιν Ἀθήναζε δωρεὰν[2]
αἰτεῖν ἔδωκεν. ὁ δὲ τῆς ἑαυτοῦ φύσεως ἄξιον
ᾔτησε, νήσους οὐκ ὀλίγας οὐδὲ μικρὰς εἰς ἀπαγωγὴν
φόρου κατὰ σιτηρέσιον ταῖς Ἀθήναις. ὁ δὲ καὶ
ταῦτα ἔδωκεν, καὶ προσέθηκε τὸ μέγιστον τῶν
ἀξιωμάτων, στρατοπεδάρχην ἐπιτρέψας καλεῖσθαι,
ὅπως νεμεσῴη μηδεὶς εἰ τοσαῦτα ἐκ τοῦ δημοσίου
κομίζοιτο. ταύτην τὴν δωρεὰν ἔδει βεβαιοῦν
τὸν τῆς αὐλῆς ἔπαρχον (νεωστὶ γὰρ παρῆν ἐκ
Γαλατίας ὁ ἔπαρχος)· καὶ μετὰ τοὺς ἐπὶ τοῖς
λόγοις ἐκείνους ἀγῶνας, παρὰ τὸν Ἀνατόλιον
ἐλθών, ἠξίου βεβαιοῦν τὴν χάριν, καὶ συνηγόρους
οὐκ ἐκάλεσε μόνους, ἀλλὰ σχεδόν τι πάντας τοὺς
πεπαιδευμένους ἐκ τῆς Ἑλλάδος· πάντες γὰρ
ἦσαν Ἀθήνησι διὰ τὴν ἐπιδημίαν. ὡς δὲ ἐπλη-
ρώθη τὸ θέατρον, καὶ ὁ Προαιρέσιος ἠξίου τοὺς
συνηγόρους λέγειν, παραδραμὼν τὴν ἁπάντων
δόξαν ὁ ἔπαρχος, καὶ βασανίζων τὸν Προαιρέσιον
ἐς τὸ σχέδιον "λέγε," φησίν, "ὦ Προαιρέσιε·
αἰσχρὸν γάρ ἐστι καὶ λέγειν καὶ βασιλέα ἐπαινεῖν
σοῦ παρόντος ἕτερον." ἐνταῦθα ὁ Προαιρέσιος,
ὥσπερ ἵππος εἰς πεδίον κληθείς, τοὺς ἐπὶ τῇ
δωρεᾷ λόγους, τόν τε Κελεὸν καὶ Τριπτόλεμον
καὶ τὴν Δήμητρος ἐπιδημίαν ἐπὶ τῇ τοῦ σίτου

---

[1] ἀπιόντα Boissonade ; ἀπιόντι Cobet.
[2] Before δωρεὰν Cobet deletes καὶ.

---

[1] Libanius, *Letter* 278, mentions this statue at Rome and
another at Athens.
[2] This office, originally military, had become that of a

up in his honour a bronze statue life size with this inscription : " Rome the Queen of cities to the King of Eloquence." [1]

When he was about to return to Athens, Constans permitted him to ask for a present. Thereupon he asked for something worthy of his character, namely several considerable islands that should pay tribute to Athens to provide it with a corn supply. Constans not only gave him these, but added the highest possible distinction by bestowing on him the title of " stratopedarch," [2] lest any should resent his acquisition of so great a fortune from the public funds. It was necessary for the pretorian prefect to confirm this gift ; for the prefect had lately arrived from Gaul. Accordingly, after the competitions in eloquence that I have described, Prohaeresius approached Anatolius and begged him to confirm the favour, and summoned not only professional advocates for his cause but almost all the educated men of Greece ; for on account of the prefect's visit they were all at Athens. When the theatre was crowded, and Prohaeresius called on his advocates to speak, the prefect ran counter to the expectation of all present, because he wished to test the extempore eloquence of Prohaeresius, and he said : " Speak, Prohaeresius ! For it is unbecoming for any other man to speak and to praise the emperor when you are present." Then Prohaeresius, like a war-horse summoned to the plain,[3] made a speech about the imperial gift, and cited Celeus and Triptolemus and how Demeter sojourned among men that she might

Food Controller, *cf.* Julian, *Oration* i. 8 c, where he says that Constantine did not disdain it for himself.

[3] A proverb ; *cf.* Plato, *Theaetetus* 183 D. It is used by Lucian and Julian.

δωρεᾷ παρήγαγε, καὶ τὴν τοῦ βασιλέως χάριν ἐκείνοις προσάπτων τοῖς διηγήμασι, ταχὺ μάλα μετέστησεν εἰς τὸν ἀρχαῖον ὄγκον τὰ γινόμενα, καὶ τοῖς λεγομένοις ἐπεχόρευεν, ἐπιδεικνύμενος εἰς τὴν ὑπόθεσιν· καὶ ὁ τῶν λόγων ἔλεγχος ἦν αὐτῷ φιλοτιμία.

Γάμος δὲ αὐτῷ συνέπεσεν ἐξ Ἀσίας τῆς Τραλλιανῶν πόλεως, καὶ Ἀμφίκλεια μὲν ὄνομα τῇ
493 γυναικί· θυγάτρια δὲ αὐτοῖς ἐγενέσθην τοσοῦτον παραλλάττοντα κατὰ τὴν ἡλικίαν χρόνον, ὅσος ἐς τὸ κύειν καὶ γίνεσθαι καταναλίσκεται. προελθόντα δὲ εἰς ὥραν ἐν ᾗ πάγκαλόν τι χρῆμα καὶ μακάριον παιδίον, καὶ τὴν τοῦ πατρὸς ψυχὴν ὑφ' ἡδονῆς ἀνασείσαντα, ἐν ὀλίγαις ἡμέραις ἄμφω τοὺς πατέρας ἀπέλιπεν, ὥστε μικροῦ τὸ πάθος καὶ τῶν προσηκόντων ἐκβαλεῖν λογισμῶν τὸν Προαιρέσιον. ἀλλὰ πρὸς τοῦτο μὲν ἤρκεσεν ἡ Μιλησίου μοῦσα, τὰς ἁρμονικὰς ἀναψαμένη χάριτας, καὶ πολλὰ παίζουσα μετ' ἀφροδίτης, καὶ τὸν λογισμὸν ἀνακαλουμένη. τοῖς δὲ Ῥωμαίοις ἀξιοῦσιν ὁμιλητὴν ἴδιον ἀποπέμπειν, ὁ Προαιρέσιος τὸν Εὐσέβιον ἐξέπεμψεν, ὃς ἦν μὲν ἐξ Ἀλεξανδρείας, ἐναρμόσειν δὲ ἄλλως ἐδόκει τῇ πόλει, κολακεύειν τε εἰδὼς καὶ σαίνειν τὸ ὑπερέχον· στασιώδης δὲ κατὰ τὰς Ἀθήνας ἐφαίνετο. καὶ ἅμα ἐβούλετο μεῖζον τὸ καθ' ἑαυτὸν ποιεῖν, ἄνδρα πέμπων πολιτικῆς κακοτεχνίας οὐκ ἀμύητον· ἐπεὶ τά γε κατὰ ῥητορικὴν ἐξαρκεῖ τοσοῦτον εἰπεῖν ὅτι ἦν Αἰγύπτιος. τὸ δὲ ἔθνος ἐπὶ ποιητικῇ μὲν

bestow on them the gift of corn. With that famous
narrative he combined the tale of the generosity
of Constans, and very speedily he invested the
occurrence with the splendour and dignity of ancient
legend. Then, as he declaimed, his gestures became
more lively, and he displayed all his sophistic art
in handling the theme. The fact that he obtained
the honour that he asked for shows what his
eloquence must have been.

His wife came from Asia, from the city of Tralles,
and her name was Amphiclea. They had two little
girls, between whose ages there was only so much
difference as the time necessary for their conception
and birth. But no sooner had they reached that
time of life when a child is a wholly lovely and
charming thing, and made their father's heart
tremble with joy, than they left their parents
desolate, both within a few days; so that his grief
almost shook Prohaeresius from the reflections that
become a philosopher. However, the Muse of
Milesius [1] proved able to meet this crisis, and by composing lovely harmonies and expending all his gifts of
charm and gaiety he recalled him to reason. When
the Romans asked him to send them one of his own
pupils, Prohaeresius sent forth Eusebius who was a
native of Alexandria. He seemed to be peculiarly
suited to Rome, because he knew how to flatter and
fawn on the great; while in Athens he was regarded
as a seditious person. At the same time Prohaeresius
wished to increase his own reputation by sending a
man who had been initiated into the sharp practices
of political oratory. As for his talent for rhetoric, it
is enough to say that he was an Egyptian; for this

[1] For Milesius see above, p. 491.

σφόδρα μαίνονται, ὁ δὲ σπουδαῖος Ἑρμῆς αὐτῶν
ἀποκεχώρηκεν. ἐπανέστη δὲ αὐτῷ ὁ Μουσώνιος,
εἰς σοφιστικὴν ὁμιλητὴς ὢν αὐτοῦ (περὶ οὗ πολλὰ
διὰ τὰς ἄλλας αἰτίας[1] ἐν τοῖς διεξοδικοῖς γέγραπται),
καὶ ὅτε γε ἀντῆρε, καταμαθὼν πρὸς τίνα ἔχει τὸν
ἀγῶνα, ταχὺ μάλα ἐπὶ τὴν πολιτικὴν κατεπήδησεν.[2]

Ἰουλιανοῦ δὲ βασιλεύοντος, τόπου τοῦ παιδεύειν
ἐξειργόμενος (ἐδόκει γὰρ εἶναι χριστιανός) συνορῶν τὸν ἱεροφάντην ὥσπερ Δελφικόν τινα τρί-
ποδα πρὸς τὴν τοῦ μέλλοντος πρόνοιαν πᾶσι τοῖς
δεομένοις ἀνακείμενον, σοφίᾳ τινὶ περιῆλθε ξένῃ
τὴν πρόγνωσιν. ἐμέτρει μὲν γὰρ ὁ βασιλεὺς τὴν
γῆν τοῖς Ἕλλησιν εἰς τὸν φόρον, ὅπως μὴ βαρύ-
νοιντο· ὁ δὲ Προαιρέσιος ἠξίωσεν αὐτὸν ἐκμαθεῖν
παρὰ τῶν θεῶν, εἰ βέβαια μενεῖ τὰ τῆς φιλαν-
θρωπίας. ὡς δὲ ἀπέφησεν, ὁ μὲν ἔγνω τὸ πραχ-
θησόμενον, καὶ ἦν εὐθυμότερος. ὁ δὲ συγγραφεὺς
κατὰ τουτονὶ τὸν χρόνον εἰς ἕκτον που καὶ δέκατον
ἔτος τελῶν, παρῆλθέ τε εἰς τὰς Ἀθήνας καὶ τοῖς
ὁμιληταῖς ἐγκατεμίγη· καὶ ἀγαπηθεὶς ὑπ' αὐτοῦ
καθάπερ παῖς γνήσιος, ἠπείγετο μὲν μετὰ πέμπτον
ἔτος εἰς τὴν Αἴγυπτον, οἱ δὲ πατέρες καλοῦντες
ἐπὶ Λυδίας ἐξεβιάσαντο· κἀκείνῳ μὲν σοφιστικὴ
προὔκειτο, καὶ πρὸς τοῦτο ἐξεκάλουν ἅπαντες.
Προαιρέσιος δὲ ἐξ ἀνθρώπων ἀνεχώρει μετ' οὐ
πολλὰς ἡμέρας· τοσοῦτος καὶ τοιοῦτος γενόμενος

---

[1] αἰτίας Junius adds.
[2] μετεπήδησεν Cobet suggests.

---

[1] Probably "those of the Hellenic faith."

race passionately loves the poetic arts, whereas the Hermes who inspires serious study has departed from them. He had for an adversary Musonius, who had been his pupil in the sophistic art. (I have for other reasons written about him at length in my *Universal History*.) When Musonius reared his head to oppose him, Eusebius knew well against what sort of man he had to contend, so he very speedily deserted to take up political oratory.

In the reign of the Emperor Julian, Prohaeresius was shut out of the field of education because he was reputed to be a Christian; and since he observed that the hierophant, like a sort of Delphic tripod, was open to all who had need of him to foretell future events, by strange and wonderful arts he fraudulently intercepted that foreknowledge. For the emperor was having the land measured for the benefit of the Hellenes,[1] to relieve them from oppression in respect of taxes. Thereupon Prohaeresius requested the hierophant[2] to find out from the god whether this benevolence would be permanent. And when he declared that it would not, Prohaeresius learned in this way what the future would bring, and took courage. The author, who had attained at this time to about his sixteenth year, arrived at Athens and was enrolled among his pupils, and Prohaeresius loved him like his own son.[3] Five years later the author was preparing to go to Egypt, but his parents summoned him and compelled him to return to Lydia. To become a sophist was the obvious course to which all urged him. Now a few days later Prohaeresius departed this life. He was a great and gifted man, even as I have described, and

[2] *i.e.* of Eleusis; *cf.* pp. 475, 476.   [3] See above, p. 486.

καὶ διαπλήσας τῶν ἑαυτοῦ λόγων τε καὶ ὁμιλητῶν
τὴν οἰκουμένην.

Ἐπιφάνιος· οὗτος ἦν μὲν ἐκ Συρίας, δεινότατος
δὲ εἶναι περὶ τὰς διακρίσεις δόξας τῶν ζητημάτων,
τὸν δὲ λόγον ἀτονώτερος, ὅμως ἀνισοφιστεύσας
τῷ[1] Προαιρεσίῳ καὶ εἰς πολὺ δόξης ἐχώρησεν· οὐ
γὰρ φέρει τὸ ἀνθρώπινον ἕνα θαυμάζειν, ἀλλ' ἐγκεκλικὸς καὶ ἡττώμενον ὑπὸ φθόνου, τοῖς πολυκρα-
τοῦσι καὶ ὑπερέχουσιν ἕτερον ἀντικαθίστησιν, ὥσπερ
ἐν φυσικῇ τὰς ἀρχὰς ἐκ τῶν ἐναντίων λαμβάνοντες.
494 ἐτελεύτα δὲ οὐκ εἰς βαθὺ γῆρας ἀφικόμενος, τὸ
αἷμα νοσήσας· καὶ ἡ γυνὴ ταὐτὸ τοῦτο ἔπαθε,
καλλίστη πασῶν γενομένη. καὶ παιδίον οὐκ ἦν
αὐτοῖς. τοῦτον ὁ ταῦτα γράφων οὐκ ἔγνω, πολὺ
προαπελθόντα τῆς ἐπιδημίας.

Καὶ Διόφαντος ἦν μὲν ἐξ Ἀραβίας, καὶ εἰς τοὺς
τεχνικοὺς ἐβιάζετο· ἡ δὲ αὐτὴ δόξα τῶν ἀνθρώπων
Προαιρεσίῳ κἀκεῖνον ἀντήγειρεν, ὡσεὶ Καλλί-
μαχον Ὁμήρῳ τις ἀναστήσειεν. ἀλλ' ἐγέλα ταῦτα
ὁ Προαιρέσιος, καὶ τοὺς ἀνθρώπους ὅ τι εἰσὶν ἐν
διατριβῆς εἶχεν μέρει. τοῦτον ἐγίγνωσκεν ὁ συγγραφεύς, καὶ ἠκροάσατό γε πολλάκις δημοσίᾳ
λέγοντος. παραθεῖναι δὲ τῇ γραφῇ τῶν λεχθέντων
καὶ μνημονευθέντων οὐδὲν ἐδόκει καλῶς ἔχειν·
μνήμη γάρ ἐστιν ἀξιολόγων ἀνδρῶν, οὐ χλευασμός,
ἡ γραφή. ἀλλ' ὅμως ἐπιτάφιόν γε εἰπεῖν τινα

---

[1] ὅμως τε σοφιστεύσας τῷ Boissonade ; ὅμως ἀντισοφιστεύσας
τῷ Wyttenbach ; ὅμως ἀντεσοφίστευσέ τε Cobet.

he filled the whole known world with the fame of his discourses, and with those who had been his pupils.

EPIPHANIUS was a native of Syria, and he was reputed to be very skilful in distinguishing and defining controversial themes, but as an orator he was slack and nerveless. Nevertheless, as the rival of Prohaeresius in the sophistic profession he actually attained to great fame. For human beings are not content to admire one man only, but so prone are they to envy, so completely its slave, that when a man excels and towers above the rest they set up another as his rival; and thus derive their controlling principles from opposites just as in the science of physics. Epiphanius did not live to be old, but died of blood-poisoning, and his wife also, who was an exceedingly handsome woman, met the same fate. They left no children. Epiphanius was not personally known to the author, for he died long before the latter's sojourn in Athens.

DIOPHANTUS was a native of Arabia who forced his way into the ranks of the professors of rhetoric. That same envious opinion of mankind of which I have just spoken set him up as another rival of Prohaeresius, as though one should oppose Callimachus to Homer. But Prohaeresius laughed all this to scorn, and he refused to give serious thought to human beings and their foibles. The writer knew Diophantus and often heard him declaim in public. But he has not thought fit to quote in this work any of his speeches or what he remembers of them. For this document is a record of noteworthy men; it is not a satire. However it is said that he delivered a funeral oration in honour

EUNAPIUS

τοῦ Προαιρεσίου λέγεται (προαπῆλθε γὰρ ὁ Προαιρέσιος), καί τι τοιοῦτον ἐπιφθέγξασθαι διαμνη-
μονεύουσιν ἐπὶ τῇ Σαλαμῖνι καὶ τοῖς Μηδικοῖς·
" ὦ Μαραθὼν καὶ Σαλαμίν, νῦν σεσίγησθε. οἵαν
σάλπιγγα τῶν ὑμετέρων τροπαίων ἀπολωλέκατε."
οὗτος ἀπέλιπε δύο παῖδας ἐπὶ τρυφὴν καὶ πλοῦτον
ὁρμήσαντας.

Καὶ Σωπόλιδος ἠκροάσατο πολλάκις ὁ ταῦτα
γράφων. καὶ ἦν ἀνὴρ εἰς τὸν ἀρχαῖον χαρακτῆρα
τὸν λόγον ἀναφέρειν βιαζόμενος, καὶ τῆς ὑγιαι-
νούσης Μούσης ψαύειν ὀριγνώμενος. ἀλλ᾽ ἔκρουε
μὲν τὴν θύραν ἱκανῶς, ἠνοίγετο δὲ οὐ πολλάκις·
ἀλλ᾽ εἴ πού τι καὶ ψοφήσειεν ἐκεῖθεν, λεπτόν τι
καὶ ἀσθενὲς παρωλίσθαινεν ἔσωθεν τοῦ θείου
πνεύματος· τὸ δὲ θέατρον ἐμεμήνεσαν, οὐδὲ τὴν
πεπιεσμένην ῥανίδα τὴν Κασταλίαν φέροντες.
τούτῳ παῖς ἐγένετο· καὶ ἐπιβεβηκέναι τοῦ θρόνου
τὸν παῖδα φάσκουσιν.

Ἱμέριος· τὸν ἄνδρα τοῦτον ἤνεγκε μὲν Βιθυνία,
οὐκ ἔγνω δὲ αὐτὸν ὁ ταῦτα γράφων· καί τοί γε ἦν
κατ᾽ ἐκείνους τοὺς χρόνους. ἀλλὰ πρὸς τὸν αὐτοκράτορα διαβὰς Ἰουλιανὸν κατ᾽ ἐπίδειξιν, ὡς, διὰ
τὴν ἐς Προαιρέσιον ἀχθηδόνα τοῦ βασιλέως,
ἀσμένως ὀφθησόμενος, Ἰουλιανοῦ καταλείποντος
τὸ ἀνθρώπινον, ἐνδιέτριψε τῇ ἀποδημίᾳ, καί,
Προαιρεσίου τελευτήσαντος, Ἀθήναζε ἠπείγετο.
εὔκολος δὲ ἀνὴρ εἰπεῖν καὶ συνηρμοσμένος· κρότον
δὲ ἔχει καὶ ἦχον ἡ συνθήκη πολιτικόν· καί που
σπάνιος καὶ παρὰ τὸν θεῖον Ἀριστείδην ἵσταται.

of Prohaeresius (for the latter died before he did), and they relate that he concluded with these words about Salamis and the war against the Medes: "O Marathon and Salamis, now are ye buried in silence! What a trumpet of your glorious victories have ye lost!"[1] He left two sons who devoted themselves to a luxurious life and money-making.

The author of this work often heard SOPOLIS lecture. He was a man who tried with all his might to reproduce the style of the ancients in his oratory, and did his utmost to reach the level of a saner Muse. But though he knocked diligently at her door, it was seldom opened. Nay, if ever it did creak open a little, it was but a thin and feeble spark of the divine afflatus that slipped forth from within. But at this his audience would grow frenzied with enthusiasm, unable as they were to receive calmly even a single drop squeezed from the fount of Castalia. Sopolis had a son, and they say that he too ascended the professorial chair.

HIMERIUS was a native of Bithynia, yet the author never knew him, though he lived in the same period. He travelled to the court of the Emperor Julian to declaim before him, in the hope that he would be regarded with favour on account of the emperor's dislike of Prohaeresius; and when Julian left this world, Himerius spent his time abroad. Then, on the death of Prohaeresius, he hastened to Athens. He was an agreeable and harmonious speaker. His style of composition has the ring and assonance of political oratory. Sometimes, though rarely, he rises as high as the godlike Aristeides. He left a daughter,

---

[1] *i.e.* Prohaeresius had used these commonplaces effectively.

ἐπὶ θυγατρὶ δὲ τελευτᾷ, τῆς ἱερᾶς νόσου πρὸς γήρᾳ μακρῷ καταλαβούσης αὐτόν.

Ἐν τούτοις ἦν τοῖς χρόνοις καὶ Παρνάσιος ἐπὶ τοῦ παιδευτικοῦ θρόνου, ὁμιλητὰς εὐαριθμήτους ἔχων· καί τοί γε ὀνόματος οὐκ ἀπεστερημένος.

495 Λιβάνιον δὲ Ἀντιόχεια μὲν ἤνεγκεν ἡ τῆς Κοίλης καλουμένης Συρίας πρώτη πόλεων, Σελεύκου τοῦ Νικάτορος ἐπικληθέντος ἔργον. ἦν δὲ τῶν εὖ γεγονότων καὶ εἰς τοὺς ἄκρους ἐτέλει. νέος δὲ ὢν ἔτι καὶ κύριος ἑαυτοῦ, πατέρων ἀπολελοιπότων, ἀφικόμενος Ἀθήναζε, οὔτε ὡς ἐκ Συρίας Ἐπιφανίῳ προσῆλθε μεγίστην ἔχοντι δόξαν, οὔτε παρὰ Προαιρέσιον ἐφοίτησεν, ὡς ἐν τῷ πλήθει τῶν ὁμιλητῶν καὶ τῷ μεγέθει τῆς δόξης τῶν διδασκάλων καλυφθησόμενος. ἐνεδρευθεὶς δὲ ὑπὸ τῶν Διοφαντείων, Διοφάντῳ προσένειμεν ἑαυτόν· καί, ὡς οἱ πάνυ τὸν ἄνδρα καταμεμαθηκότες ἔφασκον, ταῖς μὲν ὁμιλίαις καὶ συνουσίαις, τὸ γεγονὸς συμμαθών, ἐλάχιστα παρεγίνετο, καὶ τῷ διδασκάλῳ τις ὀχληρὸς οὐκ ἦν· αὐτὸς δὲ ἑαυτὸν ἐπὶ ταῖς μελέταις συνεῖχε, καὶ πρὸς τὸν ἀρχαῖον ἐξεβιάζετο τύπον, τὴν ψυχὴν διαπλάττων καὶ τὸν λόγον. ὥσπερ οὖν οἱ πολλάκις πέμποντες, ἔστιν ὅτε καὶ τυγχάνουσι[1] τοῦ σκοποῦ, καὶ τὸ συνεχὲς τῆς μελέτης αὐτοῖς διὰ τῆς γυμνασίας τῶν ὀργάνων ὡς ἐπὶ τὸ πλεῖστον εὐστοχίας οὐκ ἐπιστήμην ἔφυσεν, ἀλλὰ τὴν τέχνην· οὕτω καὶ Λιβάνιος, ἐκ τοῦ ζήλου καὶ τῆς παραθέσεως τῆς

[1] τυγχάνουσι Foerster; τυγχάνοντες Boissonade.

―――――――――――――

[1] For Parnasius see *Life* of Prohaeresius, p. 487· he is otherwise unknown.
[2] In A.D. 336.

when he died of epilepsy, a disease which attacked him in extreme old age.

PARNASIUS[1] also lived in those days and filled a teacher's chair. His pupils were soon counted, but for all that he did not fail to win a certain reputation.

LIBANIUS was born at Antioch, the capital of Coele Syria as it is called. This city was founded by Seleucus surnamed Nicator. Libanius came of a noble family and ranked among the first citizens. While he was still a youth and his own master, since his parents were dead, he came to Athens,[2] and there, though he too came from Syria, he did not attach himself to Epiphanius, who enjoyed the very highest reputation, nor did he attend the school of Prohaeresius. This would have been to run the risk of being obscured, partly by so great a crowd of fellow-pupils, partly by the celebrity of his teachers. But he fell into a trap that was set for him by the pupils of Diophantus, and therefore attached himself to that sophist. It is asserted by those who knew the man intimately that, when he learned what had happened to him, he very seldom attended the lectures and meetings of the school, and gave his master very little trouble. But by himself he devoted his time to the study of rhetoric, and worked very hard to acquire the style of the ancient writers, moulding to that end both his mind and his speech. And even as those who aim at a mark sometimes succeed in hitting it, and their constant practice and regular exercise with their weapons usually begets dexterity in shooting straight rather than scientific knowledge; even so Libanius in his zeal to compare and imitate them was inseparable from the ancient

519

κατὰ μίμησιν, προσαρτῶν ἑαυτὸν καὶ παραξέων
ἡγεμόσιν ἀρίστοις τοῖς ἀρχαίοις,[1] καὶ οἷς ἐχρῆν
ἑπόμενος, ἐς ἴχνος τε ἄριστον ἐνέβαινε καὶ ἀπ-
ήλαυσε τῆς ὁδοῦ τὰ εἰκότα. θαρσήσας δὲ ἐπὶ τῷ
λέγειν καὶ πείσας ἑαυτὸν ὡς ἐνάμιλλος εἴη τοῖς
ἐπὶ τούτῳ μεγαλοφρονοῦσιν,[2] οὐχ εἵλετο περὶ
μικρὰν πόλιν κρύπτεσθαι, καὶ συγκαταπίπτειν
τῷ τῆς πόλεως ἀξιώματι, ἀλλ' ἐπὶ τὴν Κωνσταντίνου πόλιν διαβαλὼν ἄρτι παριοῦσαν εἰς μέγεθος
καὶ ἀκμάζουσαν, καὶ δεομένην ἔργων τε ὁμοῦ καὶ
λόγων οἳ κατακοσμήσουσι, ταχὺ μάλα καὶ κατ'
αὐτὴν ἐξέλαμψεν, εἰς συνουσίαν τε ἄριστος καὶ
χαριέστατος φανείς, καὶ εἰς ἐπίδειξιν λόγων
ἐπαφρόδιτος. διαβολῆς δέ τινος αὐτῷ γενομένης
περὶ τὰ μειράκια, ἣν θεμιτὸν οὐκ ἦν ἐμοὶ γράφειν,
ἐς μνήμην ἀξιολόγων ἀνέντι τὴν γραφήν, ἐκπεσὼν
τῆς Κωνσταντίνου πόλεως, κατέσχε τὴν Νικο-
μήδειαν. κἀκεῖθεν, τῆς φήμης ἐπισπομένης καὶ
παραθεούσης αὐτῷ διὰ ταχέων ἀποκρουσθείς,
μετὰ χρόνον τινὰ ἐπὶ τὴν ἑαυτοῦ πατρίδα καὶ
πόλιν ἐπανέρχεται, κἀκεῖ τὸν πάντα ἐβίω χρόνον,
μακρὸν καὶ παρατείνοντα γενόμενον.

Μνήμην μὲν οὖν αὐτοῦ[3] τὴν πρέπουσαν κἂν
τοῖς βιβλίοις τοῖς κατὰ τὸν Ἰουλιανὸν ἡ γραφὴ
πεποίηται, τὰ δὲ καθ' ἕκαστον νῦν ἐπεξελεύσεται.
οὐδεὶς τῶν συλλεγέντων Λιβανίῳ καὶ συνουσίας

---

[1] τοῖς ἀρχαίοις Sievers would omit.
[2] μεγαλοφρονοῦσιν Boissonade ; μέγα φρονοῦσιν Foerster.
[3] αὐτοῦ Foerster ; αὐτῷ Boissonade.

---

[1] In 340; he left Constantinople in 343. There is no
other evidence for the scandalous charge mentioned later.

authors, and so to speak rubbed shoulders with those
most excellent guides; and by following the right
leaders he trod in the footsteps of the best and
reaped the fruits of that course. As he gained
confidence in his eloquence and convinced himself
that he could rival any that prided themselves on
theirs, he resolved not to bury himself in a small
town and sink in the esteem of the world to that city's
level. Therefore he crossed over to Constantinople,[1]
a city which had recently attained to greatness, and,
being at the height of her prosperity, needed both
deeds and words to adorn her as she deserved.
There he very soon became a shining light, since he
proved to be an admirable and delightful teacher
and his public declamations were full of charm. But
a scandalous charge was brought against him in
connexion with his pupils. I cannot allow myself
to write about it, because I am determined to
record in this document only what is worthy to be
recorded. For this reason, then, he was expelled
from Constantinople, and settled at Nicomedia.
When the scandalous tale followed him there and
obstinately pursued him, he was soon[2] thrust out
of that city also, and after a time[3] he returned to
his native land and the city of his birth, and there
he spent his whole life, which proved to be long and
long drawn out.

Though I have composed in my annals of the
reign of Julian a fitting account of the career of
Libanius, I will now run over it in detail. Not one
of all those who associated with him and were

[2] Libanius himself says that he was in Nicomedia five
years, the happiest of his life.

[3] Eunapius ignores the second sojourn of Libanius at
Constantinople; see Introduction, p. 334.

ἀξιωθέντων ἀπῆλθεν ἄδηκτος· ἀλλὰ τό τε ἦθος
εὐθὺς οἷός τις ἦν ἔγνωστο, καὶ συνεῖδεν [1] αὐτοῦ
τά τε τῆς ψυχῆς ἐπί τε τὸ χεῖρον καὶ τὸ κρεῖττον
ῥέποντα, καὶ τοσοῦτος ἦν ἐς τὴν πλάσιν καὶ τὴν
πρὸς ἅπαντας ἐξομοίωσιν, ὥστε ὁ μὲν πολύπους
λῆρος ἠλέγχετο, τῶν δὲ συγγιγνομένων ἕκαστος
ἄλλον ἑαυτὸν ὁρᾶν ὑπελάμβανεν. ἔφασκον γοῦν
αὐτὸν οἱ πεπειραμένοι, πίνακά τινα καὶ ἐκμαγεῖον
εἶναι παντοδαπῶν ἠθῶν καὶ ποικίλων· οὐδ' ἂν
496 ἥλω ποτὲ πολλῶν καὶ διαφόρων συνεληλυθότων
ὅτῳ μᾶλλον τέρπεται, ἀλλὰ καὶ ἐπὶ τοῖς ἐναντίοις
ἐπῃνεῖτο παρὰ τῶν τὸν ἐναντίον ἐλαυνόντων βίον,
καὶ πᾶς τις αὐτὸν τὰ σφέτερα θαυμάζειν ᾤετο·
οὕτω πολύμορφόν τι χρῆμα καὶ ἀλλοπρόσαλλον ἦν.
γάμου δὲ καὶ οὗτος ἠμέλησε, πλὴν ὅσα γε αὐτῷ
γυνή τις ξυνῆν, οὐκ ἀπὸ ὁμοίας τῆς ἀξιώσεως.

Ὁ δὲ λόγος αὐτῷ, περὶ μὲν τὰς μελέτας, παντελῶς ἀσθενὴς καὶ τεθνηκὼς καὶ ἄπνους, καὶ
διαφαίνεταί γε οὗτος μὴ τετυχηκὼς διδασκάλου·
καὶ γὰρ τὰ πλεῖστα τῶν κοινῶν καὶ παιδὶ γνωρίμων
περὶ τὰς μελέτας ἠγνόει· περὶ δὲ ἐπιστολὰς καὶ
συνουσίας ἑτέρας, ἱκανῶς ἐπὶ τὸν ἀρχαῖον ἀναφέρει
καὶ διεγείρεται τύπον, καὶ χάριτός γε αὐτῷ καὶ
κωμικῆς βωμολοχίας καταπέπλησται τὰ συγ-
γράμματα, καὶ ἡ κομψότης περιτρέχει πανταχοῦ
διακονουμένη τοῖς λόγοις, καὶ ὃ πάντες οἱ Συρο-

---

[1] συνεῖχεν Boissonade ; συνεῖδεν Wyttenbach, Foerster.

---

[1] The adaptability of the polypus is a favourite commonplace ; cf. Lucian, Dialogues of the Sea-Gods 4 ; Philostratus,
Lives of the Sophists 487, note.
[2] This criticism is inconsistent with the reputation of
Libanius as a declaimer ; cf. Introduction, p. 335.

admitted to his teaching left him without being smitten by his charm. For he knew at first sight every man's character for what it was, and understood the propensities of his soul, whether to vice or virtue. And indeed he was so clever in adapting and assimilating himself to all sorts of men that he made the very polypus look foolish [1]; and everyone who talked with him thought to behold in him a second self. At any rate those who had had this experience used to declare that he was a sort of picture or wax impression of all the manifold and various characters of mankind. In a gathering of many men of various sorts one could never have detected who it was that he preferred. Hence those who pursued modes of life directly opposed to one another would applaud in him qualities that were directly opposed, and everyone without exception was convinced that it was his views that Libanius admired; so multiform was he, so completely all things to all men. He too avoided marriage, though in fact a woman lived with him, a person of a social position inferior to his own.

His style of eloquence in his declamations was altogether feeble, lifeless, and uninspired, and it is very evident that he had not had the advantage of a teacher; indeed he was ignorant of most of the ordinary rules of declamation, things that even a schoolboy knows.[2] But in his *Letters* and other familiar addresses he succeeds in rousing himself and rises to the level of the ancient models. His writings are full of charm and facetious wit, while a refined elegance pervades the whole and is at the service of his eloquence. Moreover the peculiar

φοίνικες ἔχουσι κατὰ τὴν κοινὴν ἔντευξιν ἡδὺ καὶ
κεχαρισμένον, τοῦτο παρ' ἐκείνου λαβεῖν μετὰ
παιδείας ἔξεστιν· οἱ μὲν οὖν Ἀττικοὶ μυκτῆρα
καὶ ἀστεϊσμὸν αὐτὸ καλοῦσιν· ὁ δὲ ὥσπερ κο-
ρυφὴν παιδείας τοῦτο ἐπετήδευσεν, ἐκ τῆς ἀρχαίας
κωμῳδίας ὅλος εἰς τὸ ἀπαγγέλλειν εἰλκυσμένος,
καὶ τοῦ κατὰ θύραν τερπνοῦ καὶ γοητεύοντος τὴν
ἀκοὴν γενόμενος. παιδείας δὲ ὑπερβολὴν καὶ
ἀναγνώσεώς ἐστιν εὑρεῖν ἐν τοῖς λόγοις, λέξεσι
κατεγλωττισμέναις ἐντυγχάνοντα. τὰ γοῦν Εὐ-
πόλιδος δένδρα Λαισποδίαν καὶ Δαμασίαν οὐκ
ἂν παρῆκεν, εἰ τὰ ὀνόματα ἔγνω τῶν δένδρων, οἷς
νῦν αὐτὰ καλοῦσιν οἱ ἄνθρωποι. οὗτος λέξιν
εὑρών τινα περιττὴν καὶ ὑπ' ἀρχαιότητος διαλαν-
θάνουσαν, ὡς ἀνάθημά τι παλαιὸν καθαίρων,[1] εἰς
μέσον τε ἦγε καὶ διακαθήρας ἐκαλλώπιζεν, ὑπόθεσίν τε αὐτῇ περιπλάττων ὅλην καὶ διανοίας
ἀκολουθούσας, ὥσπερ ἄβρας τινὰς καὶ θερα-
παίνας δεσποίνῃ νεοπλούτῳ καὶ τὸ γῆρας ἀπεξε-
σμένη. ἐθαύμασε μὲν οὖν αὐτὸν ἐπὶ τούτοις καὶ
ὁ θειότατος Ἰουλιανός, ἐθαύμασε δὲ καὶ ὅσον
ἀνθρώπινον τὴν ἐν τοῖς λόγοις χάριν. καὶ πλεῖστά
γε αὐτοῦ περιφέρουσι βιβλία, καὶ ὁ νοῦν ἔχων
ἀναλεγόμενος ἕκαστον αὐτῶν εἴσεται. ἱκανὸς δὲ
ἦν καὶ πολιτικοῖς ὁμιλῆσαι πράγμασι, καὶ παρὰ
τοὺς λόγους ἕτερά τινα συντομῆσαι καὶ ῥᾳδιουρ-

[1] αἴρων? Foerster.

---

[1] Eunapius unjustly accuses Libanius of the "precious"
Atticism derided by Lucian, *Lexiphanes*.

[2] Quoted from the *Demoi* by the scholiast on Aristophanes,
Birds 1569, ταδὶ δὲ τὰ δένδρα Λ. καὶ Δ. αὐταῖσι ταῖς κνήμαισιν
ἀκολουθοῦσί μοι, "they go with me knots and all." κνήμη
used of a tree is the part between two knots. In Thucydides

charm and sweetness that all Syro-Phoenicians display
in general intercourse one may safely look for in
him, over and above his erudition. I mean that
quality which the people of Attica call a keen scent,
or urbane wit. This he cultivated as the very
flower and crown of true culture; indeed he drew
wholly on ancient comedy for his style of expression,
and was master of all that shows a pleasing surface
and enchants the ear. In his orations you will find
the most profound erudition and the widest possible
reading. You will meet also with unusual Attic
forms and phrases.[1] For example he would not
have omitted those "trees" of Eupolis,[2] Laispodias,
and Damasias, if he had known the names by which
men call the trees nowadays. Whenever he discovered
some strange expression which because of its great
antiquity had fallen into disuse, he cleansed it as
though it were a sacred relic of the past, and when
he had brushed off the dust and adorned it afresh he
would bring it forth to the light, draped with a whole
new theme and appropriate sentiments, like the
dainty slaves and handmaids of a mistress who has just
come into a fortune and has smoothed and polished
away the signs of old age. For these reasons the
sainted Julian[3] also admired him, and indeed every
man alive admired the charm of his oratory. Very
many of his works are in circulation, and any
intelligent man who reads them one by one will
appreciate that charm. He had also a talent for
administering public affairs, and in addition to his
formal orations he would confidently undertake and

viii. 86 Laispodias is an Athenian general. Both men were
ridiculed by the comic poets because of their thin legs.
Plutarch, *Quaestiones* 712 A, says the passage in Eupolis is a
crux for commentators.   [3] *i.e.* the emperor.

γῆσαι πρὸς τέρψιν θεατρικωτέραν. τῶν δὲ μετὰ
ταῦτα βασιλέων καὶ τῶν ἀξιωμάτων τὸ μέγιστον
αὐτῷ προσθέντων (τὸν γὰρ τῆς αὐλῆς ἔπαρχον
μέχρι προσηγορίας ἔχειν ἐκέλευον), οὐκ ἀπέ-
δέξατο[1] φήσας τὸν σοφιστὴν εἶναι μείζονα. καὶ
τοῦτό γέ ἐστιν οὐκ ὀλίγος ἔπαινος, ὅτι δόξης
ἐλάττων ἀνήρ, μόνης ἥττητο τῆς περὶ τοὺς λόγους,
τὴν δὲ ἄλλην δημώδη καὶ βάναυσον ὑπελάμβανεν.
ἀλλ᾽ ἐτελεύτησε καὶ οὗτος εἰς γῆρας ἀφικόμενος
μακρότατον, καὶ θαῦμα οὐκ ὀλίγον ἀπολιπὼν
ἅπασιν. τούτῳ δὲ ὁ ταῦτα γράφων οὐ συνεγένετο,
ἄλλοτε ἄλλων ἐμποδισμάτων ἐπηρείᾳ τύχης συμ-
βάντων.

Παλαιστίνης Καισάρεια τὸν Ἀκάκιον ἤνεγκε,
497 καὶ ἦν συνανασχὼν τῷ Λιβανίῳ κατὰ τοὺς αὐτοὺς
χρόνους· τόνου δὲ σοφιστικοῦ καὶ πνεύματος,
εἴπερ τις ἄλλος, γέμων, καὶ ἡ λέξις μετὰ κρότου
πρὸς τὸν ἀρχαῖον ἐπέστρεφε τύπον[2]· συνανασχὼν
δὲ Λιβανίῳ, κατέσεισε τὰ πρῶτα, καὶ περιῆν
ἰσχυρῶς. βιβλίδιον γοῦν τῷ Λιβανίῳ περὶ εὐφυΐας
τι γέγραπται, πρὸς τὸν Ἀκάκιον ἅπαν ἐκτεθει-
μένον, ἐν ᾧ δῆλός ἐστιν ἐπὶ τῷ κρατεῖσθαι τὸ
μέγεθος τῆς ἐκείνου φύσεως αἰτιώμενος, αὐτὸς
δὲ ἑαυτῷ μαρτυρῶν τὴν περὶ τὰ λεξείδια στάσιν
καὶ ἀκρίβειαν· ὥσπερ ἀγνοῶν ὅτι μήτε Ὁμήρῳ
παντὸς ἔμελε μέτρου, ἀλλ᾽ εὐφωνίας τινὸς καὶ
μέλους, μήτε Φειδίᾳ τοῦ τὸν δάκτυλον παραλαβεῖν

---

[1] ἐδέξατο Boissonade; ἀπεδέξατο Foerster.
[2] τρόπον Boissonade; τύπον Wyttenbach.

---

[1] This essay is lost; see Introduction, p. 336.

easily compose certain other works more suited to please an audience in the theatre. When the later emperors offered him the very highest of all honours —for they bade him use the honorary title of pretorian prefect—he refused, saving that the title of sophist was more distinguished. And this is indeed not a little to his credit, that though he was a man who longed most ardently for renown, he enslaved himself only to that renown which an orator can win, and held that any other sort is vulgar and sordid. He, too, when he died, had attained to a very great age, and he left in the minds of all men the profoundest admiration for his talents. The present author was not personally acquainted with him, inasmuch as an unkind fate on every occasion put one obstacle or another in the way.

Acacius was born at Caesarea in Palestine and he dawned on the world about the same time as Libanius. No man was more abundantly endowed with sophistic force and inspiration, and his diction was sonorous and tended to the imitation of the ancient classical models. Having risen to eminence at the same time as Libanius, he overthrew his rival's supremacy, and maintained his superiority by sheer strength. Libanius accordingly wrote an essay *On Genius*,[1] entirely devoted and dedicated to Acacius, in which he clearly ascribes his defeat by him to the man's great natural talents, while at the same time he gives evidence of his own position and exactitude in the use of erudite words; as though he did not know that Homer did not take pains about every single foot of his verses, but tried rather to secure beauty of expression and melody throughout; that Pheidias never thought of dis-

527

καὶ τὸν πόδα πρὸς ἔπαινον τῆς θεᾶς, ἀλλὰ τυ-
ραννεῖν τὸ μὲν κατὰ τὴν ἀκοήν, τὸ δὲ κατὰ τοὺς
ὀφθαλμούς,[1] καὶ τὸ αἴτιον ὑπάρχειν ἀνεύρετον ἢ
δύσκριτον, ὥσπερ ἐν τοῖς καλοῖς καὶ ἐρασμίοις
σώμασιν, οὐ πάντες τὸ αὐτὸ θαυμάζουσιν, ὁ δὲ
ἁλοὺς οὐκ οἶδεν ὅθεν εἴληπται. ὁ μὲν οὖν Ἀκάκιος
ἐς τὸ ἄριστον ἀναδραμών, καὶ πολλὴν ἑαυτῷ
παρασχὼν δόξαν ὡς τοῦ Λιβανίου κρατήσων,
ἀπῄει νέος ὢν ἔτι· οἱ δὲ ἄνθρωποι, ὅσον σπου-
δαῖον ἐν αὐτοῖς, ἐθαύμαζον αὐτὸν ὥσπερ εἰς
γῆρας ἀφιγμένον.

Νυμφιδιανὸς δὲ ἦν μὲν ἐκ Σμύρνης, Μάξιμος δὲ
ἦν ὁ φιλόσοφος ἀδελφὸς αὐτῷ, καὶ Κλαυδιανὸς
ἕτερος, φιλοσοφῶν καὶ αὐτὸς ἄριστα. ἀνὴρ δὲ
τῆς μὲν Ἀθήνησι παιδείας καὶ ἀγωγῆς οὐ μετε-
σχηκώς, γεγονὼς δὲ εἰς ῥητορικὴν καὶ τοῦ τῶν
σοφιστῶν ὀνόματος ἄξιος. ὁ δὲ αὐτοκράτωρ Ἰουλιανὸς αὐτῷ καὶ τὴν βασιλικὴν γλῶτταν ἐπέτρεψε,
ταῖς ἐπιστολαῖς ἐπιστήσας, ὅσαι διὰ τῶν ἑλληνικῶν ἑρμηνεύονται λόγων. κρείττων δὲ κατὰ τὰς
καλουμένας μελέτας καὶ τὰ ζητήματα, τὰ δὲ ἐν
προάγωσι[2] καὶ τῷ διαλεχθῆναι οὐκ ἔθ᾽ ὅμοιος.
τελευτὴ δὲ αὐτῷ συνέβη γενομένῳ πρεσβύτῃ, καὶ
μετὰ τὸν ἀδελφὸν Μάξιμον.

Ἰατροὶ δὲ κατὰ τούτους ἤκμαζον τοὺς χρόνους,
Ζήνων τε ὁ Κύπριος, διδασκαλίαν τε πολυύμνητον
συστησάμενος, ἀλλ᾽ ἐπέβαλε τοῖς χρόνοις Ἰουλιανῷ
τῷ σοφιστῇ, καὶ μετ᾽ ἐκεῖνον, κατὰ τοὺς Προαι-

———
[1] τὸ δὲ κατὰ τοὺς ὀφθαλμοὺς Wright adds.

———
[1] We know nothing more about this sophist; cf. p. 427.
[2] See Philostratus, *Life of Antipater*, 607 note.
[3] The proagon is the preliminary statement of proofs in a rhetorical argument; for μελέτη see Glossary.

528

playing a finger or a foot to win praise for his goddess; that they exercised their tyranny the one over the ears of men, the other over their eyes; and that the cause of their success is undiscoverable or hard to define, just as in fair and lovely bodies not all admire the same points, and the captive of that beauty knows not what it was that took him captive. Thus, then, Acacius quickly rose to the first rank in his profession, and after winning a great reputation as one who would prove to have excelled Libanius, he passed away while still a young man. Yet all men, at least all who truly loved learning, revered him no less than if he had attained to old age.

NYMPHIDIANUS[1] was a native of Smyrna, whose own brother was Maximus the philosopher, while Claudianus, himself a very distinguished philosopher, was another brother. He was a man who, though he never shared in the education and training enjoyed at Athens, nevertheless in the art of rhetoric proved himself worthy of the reputation of the sophists. The Emperor Julian entrusted him with the task of expressing the imperial utterances, and made him Imperial Secretary for such letters as were composed in the Greek tongue.[2] He had the greatest skill in the composition of "Meletai," as they are called, and in handling problems; but he was not so skilful with "Proagones"[3] and philosophical disputations. When he died he was an old man, and he outlived his brother Maximus.

In those days many famous physicians flourished, among whom was ZENO of Cyprus, who established a celebrated school of medicine. Nay, he survived down to the time of Julian the sophist, and after him there were contemporaries of Prohaeresius who

EUNAPIUS

ρεσίου χρόνους, οἱ διάδοχοι Ζήνωνος. ἄμφω δὲ
ὁ Ζήνων ἐξήσκητο λέγειν τε καὶ ποιεῖν ἰατρικήν.
τῶν δὲ ὀνομαστῶν ὁμιλητῶν αὐτοῦ διαλαχόντες,
οἱ μὲν τὸ ἕτερον, οἱ δὲ ἀμφότερα, κατελείφθησαν·
ἐκράτουν δὲ ὅμως καὶ καθώς τις ἐκληρονόμησεν
ἔργου τε[1] καὶ λόγου.

Μάγνος· οὗτος ἐκ μὲν Ἀντιοχείας ἦν γεγονώς,
τῆς ὑπὲρ τὸν Εὐφράτην, ἣν νῦν Νίσιβιν ὀνομά-
ζουσιν· ἀκροατὴς δὲ γενόμενος Ζήνωνος καὶ τῇ
περὶ τῶν σωμάτων τῶν προαιρετικῶν φύσει[2] τὸν
Ἀριστοτέλην ἐς τὸ δύνασθαι λέγειν συνεφελ-
498 κυσάμενος[3] σιωπᾶν μὲν ἐν τῷ λέγειν τοὺς ἰατροὺς
ἠνάγκαζε, θεραπεύειν δὲ οὐκ ἐδόκει δυνατὸς εἶναι
καθάπερ λέγειν. ὥσπερ οὖν οἱ παλαιοί φασιν
Ἀρχίδαμον, εἰ Περικλέους εἴη δυνατώτερος ἐρω-
τώμενον " ἀλλὰ κἂν καταβάλλω Περικλέα," φάναι
" λέγων ἐκεῖνος ὅτι μὴ καταβέβληται, νενίκηκεν,"
οὕτω καὶ τοὺς θεραπευθέντας ὑφ' ἑτέρων ἀπεδείκνυ
Μάγνος ἔτι νοσοῦντας. οἱ δὲ ὑγιαίνοντες καὶ
ἐρρωμένοι χάριν ὡμολόγουν τοῖς θεραπεύσασιν·
ἀλλ' ἐκράτει τῶν ἰατρῶν μέχρι τοῦ στόματος καὶ

---

[1] γε Boissonade; τε Wright.

[2] πεύσει = "his investigation of" Wright suggests; for
πεῦσις cf. below, p. 503.

[3] Boissonade fails to translate the curious phrase προαι-
ρετικὰ σώματα. If the text is sound there is a reference to
Aristotle's discussion of προαίρεσις; but Galen, the medical
writer, uses κατὰ προαίρεσιν = "voluntarily," of certain bodily
functions, and Eunapius may have alluded to this medical
term. A possible translation is "to aid his natural talent
for dealing with bodies (or "parts of bodies"?) endowed
with volition," but this is an awkward construction of φύσει.

---

[1] Or "enlisted Aristotle to aid nature"? Magnus seems
to have been a sort of Christian Scientist who borrowed from

530

were the successors of Zeno. He had trained himself in oratory as well as in the practice of medicine. Of his famous pupils some took up one or other of these professions, thus dividing among them what they had learned from him; others again took up both; but whether they inherited his medical practice or his oratory, every one of them prospered mightily.

MAGNUS was a native of that Antioch which lies beyond the Euphrates and is now called Nisibis. He had been a pupil of Zeno, and, in order to give force to his rhetoric, he dragged in Aristotle in connexion with the nature of bodies endowed with volition,[1] and so compelled the doctors to keep silence in the matter of rhetoric, but he was thought to be less able as a healer than as an orator. The ancient writers relate that when Archidamus was asked whether he was stronger than Pericles, he replied: " Nay, even when I throw Pericles a fall, he still carries off the victory by declaring that he has not been thrown at all." [2] In the same way Magnus used to demonstrate that those whom other doctors had cured were still ill. And when those who had been restored to health were endeavouring to express their gratitude to those who had healed them, Magnus still got the better of the doctors in the matter of talking and putting

---

[1] Aristotle, *Ethics* iii. 2, on the exercise of deliberate purpose (προαίρεσις), to persuade patients that they could decide as to whether to be well or ill.

[2] An echo of Plutarch, *Pericles* 8. Eunapius, though so well read in Plutarch, misquotes this familiar anecdote, which is told of Pericles and Thucydides (not the historian). Archidamus asked the question of Thucydides who made the answer quoted here.

τῶν ἐρωτήσεων. καὶ διδασκαλεῖον μὲν ἐξῄρητο κοινὸν αὐτῷ κατὰ τὴν Ἀλεξάνδρειαν, καὶ πάντες ἔπλεον καὶ παρ' αὐτὸν ἐφοίτων, ὡς θαυμάσαντές τι μόνον ἢ ληψόμενοι τῶν παρ' ἐκείνου καλῶν. καὶ ἀποτυγχάνειν οὐ συνέβαινεν αὐτοῖς· ἢ γὰρ τὸ λαλεῖν ἐκέρδαινον, ἢ τὸ δύνασθαι ποιεῖν τι καὶ ἐνεργεῖν διὰ τῆς σφετέρας ἐπιμελείας προσελάμβανον.

Ὀρειβάσιον δὲ Πέργαμος ἤνεγκε, καὶ τοῦτο εὐθὺς οὕτω συνετέλει πρὸς δόξαν, ὥσπερ τοῖς Ἀθήνῃσι γεγονόσιν, ὅταν εὐδοκιμῶσι κατὰ τοὺς λόγους, πολὺς ἄνω χωρεῖ λόγος ὅτι Ἀττικὴ Μοῦσα καὶ τὸ ἀγαθὸν οἰκεῖον. ἑκατέρων δὲ εὖ πεφυκώς, ἐκ παιδὸς ἦν ἐπιφανής, πάσης παιδείας μετεσχηκὼς ἢ πρὸς ἀρετὴν συμφέρει τε καὶ τελεῖ. προϊὼν δὲ ἐς ἡλικίαν, ἀκροατής τε ἐγένετο τοῦ μεγάλου Ζήνωνος, καὶ Μάγνου συμφοιτητής. ἀλλὰ τὸν Μάγνον ἀπολιπὼν παλαίοντα τοῖς νοήμασιν, αὐτὸς καὶ ἐν τούτοις δὲ ἄριστος ὤν, καὶ πρὸς τὸ ἄκρον ἐκδραμὼν τῆς ἰατρικῆς, τὸν πάτριον ἐμιμεῖτο θεόν, ὅσον ἀνθρώπῳ δυνατὸν ἐς τὴν μίμησιν ὑπελθεῖν τοῦ θείου. ἐκ μειρακίου δὲ ἐπιφανὴς γενόμενος, Ἰουλιανὸς μὲν αὐτὸν εἰς τὸν Καίσαρα προϊὼν συνήρπασεν ἐπὶ τῇ τέχνῃ, ὁ δὲ τοσοῦτον ἐπλεονέκτει ταῖς ἄλλαις ἀρεταῖς, ὥστε καὶ βασιλέα τὸν Ἰουλιανὸν ἀπέδειξε· καὶ ταῦτά γε ἐν τοῖς κατ' ἐκεῖνον ἀκριβέστερον εἴρηται. ἀλλ' οὐδὲ κορυδαλλίς, ἡ παροιμία φησίν, ἄνευ

---

[1] Asclepius; cf. Lucian, Icaromenippus 24.
[2] See, however, Introduction, p. 338.

questions. At Alexandria a public school was especially assigned for him to teach in, and everyone sailed thither and attended his lectures, either merely in order to see and admire him or to enjoy the advantages of his teaching. This they never failed to do, for they either acquired the power of facile and fluent speech, or the ability to do and achieve some practical work by their own industry.

Pergamon was the birthplace of ORIBASIUS, and in fact this contributed to his renown, just as is the case with those who are born at Athens; for whenever such men win a name for eloquence, the report spreads far and wide that their Muse is Attic and that this paragon is a home product. Oribasius came of a good family on both sides, and from his boyhood he was distinguished because he acquired every kind of learning that conduces to virtue and perfects it. When he reached early manhood he became a pupil of the great Zeno and a fellow-disciple of Magnus. But he outstripped Magnus, and left him wrestling with the task of expressing his ideas, an art in which he himself excelled; and he lost no time in attaining to the first rank in medicine, thereby imitating the patron god [1] of his country, so far as it is possible for a mortal to progress towards the imitation of the divine. Since he won fame even from his earliest youth, Julian, when he was promoted to the rank of Caesar, carried him away with him to practise his art; but he so excelled in every other excellence that he actually made Julian emperor.[2] However, these matters have been more fully described in my account of Julian's reign. Nevertheless, as the proverb says, " No lark is with-

λόφου, οὐδὲ 'Ορειβάσιος ἦν ἄνευ φθόνου. ἀλλὰ
διὰ τὴν ὑπεροχὴν τῆς δόξης, οἱ μετὰ 'Ιουλιανὸν
βασιλεύοντες τῆς τε οὐσίας ἀφείλοντο, καὶ διαφθεῖραι τὸ σῶμα βουληθέντες, τὸ μὲν ἔργον ὤκνησαν,
ἑτεροίως δὲ ἔπραξαν ὅπερ ᾐσχύνθησαν· ἐξέθηκαν
γὰρ αὐτὸν εἰς τοὺς βαρβάρους, ὥσπερ 'Αθηναῖοι
τοὺς κατ' ἀρετὴν ὑπερέχοντας ἐξωστράκιζον.
ἀλλ' ἐκείνοις μὲν τὸ τῆς πόλεως ἐκβαλεῖν ὁ νόμος
ἔλεγε, καὶ προσῆν οὐδέν· οἱ δὲ βασιλεύοντες καὶ
τὸ παραδοῦναι τοῖς ὠμοτάτοις βαρβάροις ἐπέ-
θεσαν, ἐκείνους ποιοῦντες κυρίους τοῦ σφετέρου
βουλεύματος. 'Ορειβάσιος δὲ ἐκτεθεὶς εἰς τὴν
πολεμίαν, ἔδειξε τῆς ἀρετῆς τὸ μέγεθος, οὐ τόποις
ὁριζομένης, οὐδὲ γραφομένης ἤθεσιν, ἀλλὰ τὸ
στάσιμον καὶ μόνιμον ἐπιδεικνυμένης κατὰ τὴν
ἑαυτῆς ἐνέργειαν, κἂν ἀλλαχόθι κἂν παρ' ἄλλοις
φαίνηται, ὥσπερ τοὺς ἀριθμούς φασι καὶ τὰ μαθήματα. εὐδοκίμει τε γὰρ εὐθὺς παρὰ τοῖς
βασιλεῦσι τῶν βαρβάρων, καὶ ἀνὰ τοὺς πρώτους
ἦν, καὶ κατὰ τὴν 'Ρωμαίων ἀρχὴν ἀποβλεπό-
499 μενος παρὰ τοῖς βαρβάροις προσεκυνεῖτο καθάπερ
τις θεός, τοὺς μὲν ἐκ νοσημάτων χρονίων ἀνασώζων,
τοὺς δὲ ἀπὸ τῆς τοῦ θανάτου πύλης διακλέπτων.
καὶ ἦν αὐτῷ τὸ τῆς λεγομένης συμφορᾶς εὐδαι-
μονίας ἁπάσης πρόφασις, ὥστε καὶ οἱ βασιλεύοντες
ἀπαγορεύσαντες μάχεσθαι πρὸς τὴν διὰ πάντων
τοῦ ἀνδρὸς δύναμιν, ἐπανιέναι συνεχώρησαν. ὁ

---

[1] Πάσαισιν κορυδαλλίσιν χρὴ λόφον ἐγγενέσθαι Simonides,
frag. 68.

out a crest," [1] and so too Oribasius was not without
envious enemies. For it was because of his extraordinary celebrity that the emperors who followed
Julian deprived him of his property, and they desired to take his life also but shrank from the deed.
However, by other means they carried out the crime
which they were ashamed to commit openly. For
they exposed his person to the barbarians, just as
the Athenians ostracized from Athens men whose
virtue was above the average. However, in their
case the law allowed them to exile men from the
state, and there was no further penalty; whereas
the emperors added to his exile this abandonment
to the most savage barbarians, thus giving them
absolute power to carry out their imperial purpose. But Oribasius, after being thrust out into
the enemy's country, showed the greatness of his
virtue, which could not be limited to this place or
that, or circumscribed by the manners of the people
about him, but ever displayed its stability and
constancy in independent activity whenever and
wherever it showed itself; just as we are told is the
case with numbers and mathematical truths. For
he forthwith rose to great renown at the courts of
the rulers of the barbarians, and held the first rank
there; and while throughout the Roman empire he
was highly regarded, among the barbarians he was
worshipped like a god; since some he restored from
chronic diseases and snatched others from death's
door. Indeed that which men had reckoned his
misfortune proved to be the occasion of nothing
but good fortune; so that even the emperors gave
up fighting against the man's power so universally
displayed, and permitted him to return from exile.

δέ, ὡς ἔτυχε τῆς ἐπανόδου, μόνον ἑαυτὸν ἔχων
ἀντὶ πάσης οὐσίας, καὶ τὸν ἀπὸ τῶν ἀρετῶν
πλοῦτον ἐπιδεικνύμενος, γυναῖκά τε ἠγάγετο τῶν
κατὰ πλοῦτον ἐπιφανῶν καὶ γένος, καὶ παῖδας
ἔσχε τέτταρας, οἵτινές εἰσί τε καὶ εἴησαν· αὐτὸς
δὲ κατὰ τὸν καιρὸν τοῦτον τῆς γραφῆς ἐν ἀνθρώποις
ἔστι τε καὶ εἴη· ἀλλὰ τὸν ἀρχαῖον πλοῦτον ἐκ
τῶν δημοσίων ἀνακομισάμενος, τῶν μετὰ ταῦτα
βασιλέων συγκεχωρηκότων, ὡς ἐπ' ἀδίκῳ τῇ
προτέρᾳ κρίσει. ταῦτα μὲν οὖν ἐστι καὶ οὕτως
ἔχει. Ὀρειβασίῳ τε συντυχεῖν ἀνδρὸς ἐστι φιλο-
σοφοῦντος γενναίως, ὥστε εἰδέναι τί πρὸ τῶν
ἄλλων θαυμάσει· τοσαύτη τις ἡ διὰ πάντων ἐστὶ
προΐουσα καὶ παρατρέχουσα ταῖς συνουσίαις ἁρμονία καὶ χάρις.

Ἰωνικὸς δὲ ἦν μὲν ἐκ Σάρδεων, καὶ πατρὸς
ἰατρεύσαντος ἐπιφανῶς· Ζήνωνος δὲ ἀκροατὴς
γενόμενος, εἰς ἄκρον τε ἐπιμελείας ἐξίκετο, καὶ
Ὀρειβάσιός γε αὐτοῦ θαυμαστὴς ἐτύγχανεν. ὀνομάτων δὲ πάντων ἰατρικῆς ἐμπειρότατος γενόμενος καὶ πραγμάτων, κρείττων ἦν ἐν τῇ καθ'
ἕκαστον πείρᾳ, τῶν τε τοῦ σώματος μορίων ἄκρως
δαημονέστερος γενόμενος, καὶ τῆς ἀνθρωπίνης
φύσεως ἐξεταστικός. οὐκοῦν οὔτε φαρμάκου τινὸς
ἔλαθε κατασκευὴ αὐτὸν καὶ κρᾶσις,[1] οὐδ' ὅσα
ἐμπλάττουσιν οἱ τεχνικώτατοι τοῖς ἕλκεσι, τὰ
μὲν τὴν ἐπιρροὴν ἐπέχοντες, τὰ δὲ τὴν ἐμπεσοῦσαν
διασκιδνάντες, ἐκεῖνον ἐλάνθανεν. ἀλλὰ καὶ δῆσαι
τὸ πεπονθὸς μόριον, καὶ σχίσαι τοῖς μέρεσιν
εὑρετικώτατός τε ἦν καὶ διεξητασμένος. ἔργα τε
οὖν καὶ ὀνόματα τούτων ἠπίστατο, ὥστε τοὺς

---

[1] κρίσις Boissonade ; κρᾶσις Wyttenbach.

After he had gained permission to return, lord of himself though not of wealth, for the only riches that he had to show were the virtues, he married a wife who came of a family illustrious both for wealth and noble blood. By her he had four children who are still alive; long life to them! He himself, at this time of writing, is alive; long life to him! Nay more, he recovered his original fortune from the public treasury with the consent of the later emperors, on the ground of the injustice of the earlier verdict. Thus and in this wise it stands with him. And any man who is a genuine philosopher can meet and converse with Oribasius, that so he may learn what above all else he ought to admire. Such harmony, such charm radiates from Oribasius and attends on all intercourse with him.

Ionicus was a native of Sardis, and his father was a celebrated physician. As a pupil of Zeno he attained to the highest degree of industry and diligence and won the admiration of Oribasius. While he acquired the greatest skill in the theory and practice of medicine in all its branches, he showed peculiar ability in every kind of experiment, was thoroughly acquainted with the anatomy of the body, and also made researches into the nature of man. Thus he understood the composition and mixture of every kind of drug that exists; he knew every sort of plaster and dressing that the most skilful healers apply to wounds, whether to stop a haemorrhage or to disperse what has gathered there. Also he was most inventive and expert in bandaging an injured limb, and in amputating or dissecting. He was so thoroughly versed in the theory and practice of all these arts that even those who prided them-

537

μεγαλοφρονοῦντας ἐπὶ τῷ θεραπεύειν ἐξίστασθαι
πρὸς τὴν ἀκρίβειαν, καὶ φανερῶς ὁμολογεῖν ὅτι
συντυγχάνοντες Ἰωνικῷ, τὰ παρὰ τοῖς παλαιοῖς
εἰρημένα μανθάνουσιν ἔργῳ, καὶ πρὸς τὴν χρείαν
ἐξάγουσιν, ὥσπερ ὀνόματα κρυπτόμενα μέχρι
τῆς γραφῆς.

Τοιοῦτός τε ὢν κατὰ τὴν ἐπιστήμην, καὶ πρὸς
φιλοσοφίαν ἅπασαν ἔρρωτο, καὶ πρὸς θειασμόν,
ὅσος τε ἐξ ἰατρικῆς ἐς ἀνθρώπους ἥκει τῶν καμ-
νόντων ἐς πρόγνωσιν, καὶ ὅσος, ἐκ φιλοσοφίας
παράβακχος ὤν, ἐς τοὺς δυναμένους ὑποδέχεσθαι
καὶ σώζειν ἀπολήγει καὶ διασπείρεται. ἔμελε
δὲ αὐτῷ καὶ ῥητορικῆς ἀκριβείας, καὶ λόγων
ἁπάντων τέχνης· οὐκοῦν οὐδὲ ποιήσεως ἀμύητος
ἦν. ἀλλ' ἐτελεύτα μικρόν τι πρὸ τῆς γραφῆς
ἐπὶ δύο παισὶν ἀξίοις λόγου τε καὶ μνήμης.

Καὶ Θέων δέ τις ἐν Γαλατίᾳ κατὰ τούτους τοὺς
καιροὺς πολλῆς δόξης ἐτύγχανεν.

Ἐπανιτέον δὲ ἐπὶ τοὺς φιλοσόφους πάλιν ὅθεν
ἐξέβημεν.

500   Ταυτησὶ τῆς γραφῆς αἴτιος ἐγένετο Χρυσάνθιος,
τόν τε γράφοντα ταῦτα πεπαιδευκὼς ἐκ παιδός,
καὶ διασεσωκὼς εἰς τέλος, ὥσπερ νόμον τινά,
τὴν περὶ αὐτὸν εὔνοιαν. ἀλλ' οὐδέν γε διὰ τοῦτο
ῥηθήσεται πρὸς χάριν· ἐκεῖνός τε γὰρ ἀλήθειαν
ἐτίμα διαφερόντως καὶ τοῦτο πρῶτον ἐπαίδευεν,
ἡμεῖς τε οὐ διαφθεροῦμεν τὴν δοθεῖσαν δωρεάν,

---

[1] *i.e.* as a physician.

selves on their ability as healers were amazed at his accurate knowledge, and openly admitted that by conversing with Ionicus they really understood the precepts that had been uttered by the physicians of earlier times and could now apply them to their use, though before they had been like words whose meaning is completely obscured, save only that they had been written down.

Such were his attainments in the science of his profession, but he was also well equipped in every branch of philosophy and both kinds of divination; for there is one kind that has been bestowed on man for the benefit of the science of medicine, so that doctors may diagnose cases of sickness; and another that derives its inspiration from philosophy and is limited to and disseminated among those who have the power to receive and preserve it. He also studied the art of rhetoric with exact thoroughness, and the complete art of oratory; and was an initiate in the art of poetry. But he died not long before this work was written, and left two sons who deserve all honourable mention and remembrance.

There was also one THEON who about this time acquired a great reputation [1] in Gaul.

But I must return once more to the philosophers from whom I have digressed.

It was CHRYSANTHIUS who caused this commentary to be written, for he educated the author of this work from boyhood, and to the last maintained his kindness towards him as though it were some legal obligation. Nevertheless, I shall not on that account say anything merely to show my gratitude. For above all else he honoured the truth, and taught me this first of all, so that I shall not corrupt that gift

πλὴν εἴ πού τι καὶ ὑφήσομεν ἐπὶ τὸ καταδεέστερον
ἄγοντες, ἐπειδὴ ταῦτα συνωμολογήσαμεν.

Τῶν μὲν οὖν εἰς βουλὴν τελούντων ἦν ὁ Χρυσάνθιος, καὶ τῶν ἀνὰ τοὺς πρώτους ἐπ᾽ εὐγενείᾳ
φερομένων· ἐγεγόνει δὲ αὐτῷ πάππος, Ἰνοκέντιός
τις, εἴς τε πλοῦτον ἐλθὼν οὐκ ὀλίγον, καὶ δόξαν ὑπὲρ
ἰδιώτην τινὰ λαχών, ὅς γε νομοθετικὴν εἶχε
δύναμιν παρὰ τῶν τότε βασιλευόντων ἐπιτε-
τραμμένος. καὶ βιβλία γε αὐτοῦ διασώζεται,
τὰ μὲν εἰς τὴν Ῥωμαίων γλῶσσαν, τὰ δὲ εἰς
τὴν Ἑλλάδα φέροντα, τό τε ἐξεταστικὸν καὶ
βαθὺ τῆς γνώμης ἑρμηνεύοντα, καὶ τὴν περὶ ταῦτα
κατάληψιν τοῖς ταῦτα βουλομένοις θαυμάζειν συν-
ειληφότα. Χρυσάνθιος δὲ αὐτός, νέος ἀπὸ τοῦ
πατρὸς ἀπολειφθείς, καὶ φιλοσοφίας ἐρασθεὶς διὰ
φύσεως θειότητα, πρός τε τὸ Πέργαμον καὶ τὸν
μέγαν Αἰδέσιον συνέτεινεν· ἀκμάζοντι δὲ πρὸς
μετάδοσιν σοφίας διψῶν περιτυχών, χανδόν, ἑαυτὸν ὑποθείς, ἐνεφορεῖτο τῆς τοιαύτης σοφίας οὐ
τυχούσης,[1] οὔτε πρὸς ἀκρόασιν ἀπαγορεύων τινά,
οὔτε εἰς μελέτην ἐλάττων τινὸς φαινόμενος· καὶ
γὰρ ἔτυχεν ἀτρύτου καὶ ἀδαμαντίνου σώματος,
ἐς πᾶσαν ἄσκησιν ὑπουργεῖν εἰωθότος. ὁ δὲ
τῶν τε Πλάτωνος καὶ τῶν Ἀριστοτέλους λόγων
μετασχὼν ἱκανῶς, καὶ πρὸς πᾶν εἶδος φιλοσοφίας

---

[1] σοφίας . . . τυχούσης Laurentianus; οὐ τυχούσης Boissonade; οὐ τῆς συντυχούσης Lundström.

which I received at his hands, save as perhaps I may somewhat moderate my statements and say less than the truth, since this was the agreement that we made.

Chrysanthius was of senatorial rank and was rated among the most nobly born in his city. His grandfather was one Innocentius, who had made a considerable fortune and had acquired greater celebrity than is the lot of the average private citizen, inasmuch as the emperors who reigned at that time entrusted to him the task of compiling the legal statutes. Indeed certain of his works still survive, and they deal partly with the language of the Romans, partly with Greece, and bear witness to the judicial and profound character of his mind; they contain a comprehensive treatment of these subjects for the benefit of those who are disposed to be interested in them. Chrysanthius himself, having been bereaved of his father while he was still a youth, was inflamed with the love of philosophy because of the divine qualities of his nature, and therefore betook himself to Pergamon and to the famous Aedesius. The latter was at the very height of his teaching powers when Chrysanthius encountered him thirsty for knowledge, submitted himself open-mouthed to his influence, feasted on his great and singular wisdom, was untiring in his attendance at lectures, and in his devotion to study showed himself second to none. Indeed he possessed an untiring and even adamantine frame, inured to undergo every kind of severe exercise. When he had been sufficiently imbued with the doctrines of Plato and Aristotle, he turned his attention to every other school of philosophy and read

541

τρέψας τὴν ψυχήν, καὶ πᾶν εἶδος ἀναλεγόμενος,
ὡς περὶ τὴν γνῶσιν τῶν ἐν τοῖς λόγοις ὑγίαινε
καὶ ἔρρωτο, καὶ τῇ συνεχεῖ χρήσει πρὸς τὴν κρίσιν
αὐτῶν ἕτοιμος ὑπῆρχε, καὶ πρὸς ἐπίδειξιν ἐθάρσει
τοῦ κατωρθωμένου, τὰ μὲν εἰπεῖν, τὰ δὲ σιωπῆ-
σαι δυνάμενος, καὶ πρὸς τὸ δύνασθαι κρατεῖν, εἴ
που βιασθείη, τυγχάνων πομπικώτερος, ἐντεῦθεν
ἀφῆκεν αὐτὸν ἐπὶ θεῶν γνῶσιν, καὶ σοφίαν ἧς
Πυθαγόρας τε ἐφρόντιζε καὶ ὅσοι Πυθαγόραν
ἐζήλωσαν, Ἀρχύτας τε ὁ παλαιός, καὶ ὁ ἐκ Τυάνων
Ἀπολλώνιος, καὶ οἱ προσκυνήσαντες Ἀπολλώνιον,
οἵτινες σῶμά τε ἔδοξαν ἔχειν καὶ εἶναι ἄνθρωποι.
καὶ πρὸς ταῦτά γε Χρυσάνθιος ἀναδραμὼν καὶ
πρώτης τινὸς λαβῆς ἐπιδραξάμενος, ταῖς ἀρχαῖς
αὐταῖς ἡγεμόσι χρώμενος, εἰς τοσοῦτον ἐκουφίσθη
τε καὶ ἀνηγέρθη παρὰ τοῦ τῆς ψυχῆς πτερώματος,[1]
ᾗ φησιν ὁ Πλάτω:, ὥστε πᾶν μὲν εἶδος αὐτῷ
παντοίας παιδείας εἰς ἄκρον ὑπάρχειν, καὶ πᾶσαν
κατορθοῦσθαι πρόγνωσιν. ὁρᾶν γοῦν ἄν τις αὐτὸν
ἔφησε τὰ ἐσόμενα μᾶλλον ἢ προλέγειν τὰ μέλλοντα,
οὕτως ἅπαντα διήθρει καὶ συνελάμβανεν, ὡσανεὶ
παρών τε καὶ συνὼν τοῖς θεοῖς.

Χρόνον δὲ ἱκανόν τινα περὶ ταῦτα διατρίψας,
καὶ συναθλήσας[2] τῷ Μαξίμῳ πολύ τι, τὸν κοινωνὸν
ἀπέλιπεν. ὁ μὲν γὰρ ἔχων τι φιλόνεικον ἐν τῇ
φύσει καὶ δυσεκβίαστον, τοῖς φανθεῖσι σημείοις
501 παρὰ τῶν θεῶν ἀντιβαίνων, ἕτερα ᾔτει καὶ προσ-
ηνάγκαζεν· ὁ δὲ Χρυσάνθιος, τοῖς πρώτοις θεω-

---

[1] τελειώματος Boissonade; πτερώματος Wyttenbach, cf.
Plato, *Phaedrus* 246 E.
[2] συναναθλήσας Boissonade; συναθλήσας Cobet.

deeply in every branch. Then when he had a sure
and firm hold on the science of oratory, and by
constant practice was fully equipped to exercise
instant judgement in this field, he confidently displayed in public his well-trained talents, since he
knew what to say and what to leave unsaid, while
he was endowed with splendid and impressive rhetoric
which helped him to win when he was hard pressed.
Next he applied himself wholly to comprehending
the nature of the gods and that wisdom to which
Pythagoras devoted his mind, as did the disciples of
Pythagoras such as Archytas of old, and Apollonius
of Tyana, and those who worshipped Apollonius as a
god, all of them beings who only seemed to possess a
body and to be mortal men. Chrysanthius lost no
time in devoting himself to these studies also, and
seized hold of the first handle that offered itself in
every case, taking first principles as his guide. Thus
he was so marvellously enlightened and uplifted by the
plumage of his soul, as Plato says, that he arrived
at equal perfection in every branch of every type of
wisdom, and was an adept in every branch of divination. Hence one might have said of him that he
rather saw than foretold future events, so accurately
did he discern and comprehend everything, as
though he dwelt with and were in the presence
of the gods.

After spending a considerable time in these studies
and collaborating with Maximus in the most arduous
tasks, he left this partner of his. For Maximus had
in his nature a tendency to be jealous and obstinate,
and in direct opposition to the omens revealed by
the gods he would keep demanding further omens
and trying to extort them. Chrysanthius, on the

EUNAPIUS

μένοις, κατὰ μικρὸν ἐκ παραγωγῆς ἐπὶ τὴν κίνησιν
τῶν δοθέντων ἐβάδιζε· εἶτα τυχὼν μὲν ἐνίκα,
διαμαρτὼν δέ, τῷ φαινομένῳ τὸ παρὰ τῆς ἀνθρωπίνης βουλῆς ἐφήρμοζεν. οὕτω γοῦν καὶ ἡνίκα
ὁ βασιλεὺς Ἰουλιανὸς ἄμφω μετεκάλει διὰ μιᾶς
κλήσεως, καὶ οἱ πεμφθέντες στρατιῶται μετὰ
τιμῆς τὴν Θετταλικὴν ἐπῆγον πειθανάγκην, ὡς
ἔδοξε κοινῶσαι[1] τοῖς θεοῖς τὸ ἔργον, καὶ περιφανῶς,
ὡς κἂν ἰδιώτην καὶ βάναυσον διακρῖναι τὰ σημεῖα,
τοῦ θεοῦ τὴν ὁδὸν ἀπαγορεύσαντος, ὁ μὲν Μάξιμος
ἐνεφύετο τοῖς ἱεροῖς, καὶ ποτνιώμενος ἐπὶ τοῖς
δρωμένοις μετ᾽ ὀλοφυρμῶν ἐνέκειτο, τυχεῖν ἑτέρων
σημείων ἱκετεύων τοὺς θεοὺς καὶ μετατεθῆναι
τὰ εἱμαρμένα· καὶ πολλά γε ἐπὶ πολλοῖς αὐτῷ
διατεινομένῳ καὶ παρακλίνοντι ὡς ἐξηγεῖτο Χρυσάνθιος, ἡ βούλησις τελευτῶντι τὰ φαινόμενα ἔκρινε,
καὶ τὸ δοκοῦν ἐν τοῖς ἱεροῖς ἐφαίνετο, οὐ τὸ φαν-
θὲν ἐδοξάζετο. οὕτως οὖν ὁ μὲν ὥρμησε τὴν
ἀρχέκακον ὁδὸν ἐκείνην καὶ ἀποδημίαν, ὁ δὲ
Χρυσάνθιος ἔμεινε κατὰ χώραν. καὶ τὰ πρῶτα
μὲν ὁ βασιλεὺς ἤλγησεν ἐπὶ τῇ μονῇ, καί πού τι
καὶ τῶν ἀληθῶν προσυπενόησεν, ὡς οὐκ ἂν ἠρνή-
σατο Χρυσάνθιος τὴν κλῆσιν, εἰ μή τι δυσχερὲς
ἐνεῖδε τοῖς μέλλουσιν. ἔγραφεν οὖν καὶ πάλιν

---

[1] κοινώσας Mediceus; κοινωνῆσαι Boissonade; κοινῶσαι
Cobet.

---

[1] For the tyrannical manners of the Thessalians *cf.*
Philostratus, *Life* of Critias above, p. 501. Ἡ Θετταλικὴ πειθ-
ανάγκη was a proverb; *cf.* Julian 31 D, 274 c.
[2] For these incidents see the *Life* of Aedesius, pp. 476, 477.

contrary, would use the first omens that appeared, then, by gradual divergence from these, would proceed to alter the signs that had been vouchsafed; then, if he got the omens he wanted, he had the best of it, but if he failed he adapted his human counsel to fit whatever came to light. For instance, on the occasion when the Emperor Julian by a single summons invited them both together to his court, and the soldiers who had been sent to escort them were applying with all due respect the Thessalian way of " forcible persuasion," [1] they resolved to communicate with the gods on this matter; and when the god warned them against the journey so plainly that any private person, even a tradesman, could have judged the omens, Maximus could not tear himself away from the sacrificial victims, and after the rites had been duly completed he persisted in wailing and lamentations, beseeching the gods to vouchsafe him different omens and to alter the course of destiny. And since he stubbornly persisted in many attempts, one after another, and always perverted the explanation that Chrysanthius gave, in the end his own will and pleasure interpreted the divine revelation, and the victims gave only the signs that he would accept, since he would not accept the signs they gave. [2] So he set out on that ill-fated journey and the travels that were the cause of all his troubles; whereas Chrysanthius stayed at home. And at first the emperor was vexed at his tardiness, and moreover, I think he even guessed something of the truth, that Chrysanthius would not have refused the invitation if he had not observed something ill-omened in events to come. Accordingly, he wrote and summoned him

μετακαλῶν, καὶ οὐ πρὸς αὐτὸν μόνον αἱ παρακλή-
σεις ἦσαν· ὁ δὲ τὴν γυναῖκα συμπείθειν τὸν ἄνδρα
διὰ τῶν γραμμάτων ἐνῆγε. καὶ πάλιν ἦν πρὸς
τὸ θεῖον ἀναφορὰ παρὰ τοῦ Χρυσανθίου, καὶ τὰ
παρὰ τῶν θεῶν οὐκ ἔληγεν εἰς ταὐτὸ συμφερόμενα.
ὡς δὲ πολλάκις τοῦτο ἦν καὶ ὁ μὲν βασιλεὺς ἐπείσθη,[1]
ὁ δὲ Χρυσάνθιος τὴν ἀρχιερωσύνην τοῦ παντὸς
ἔθνους λαβών, καὶ τὸ μέλλον ἐξεπιστάμενος
σαφῶς, οὐ βαρὺς ἦν κατὰ τὴν ἐξουσίαν, οὔτε τοὺς
νεὼς ἐγείρων, ὥσπερ ἅπαντες θερμῶς καὶ περι-
καῶς ἐς ταῦτα συνέθεον, οὔτε λυπῶν τινας τῶν
χριστιανῶν περιττῶς· ἀλλὰ τοσαύτη τις ἦν ἁπλό-
της τοῦ ἤθους, ὡς κατὰ Λυδίαν μικροῦ καὶ ἔλαθεν
ἡ τῶν ἱερῶν ἐπανόρθωσις. ὡς γοῦν ἑτέρωσε τὰ
πρῶτα ἐχώρησεν, οὐδὲν ἐδόκει πεπρᾶχθαι νεώτερον,
οὐδὲ πολύ τι καὶ ἀθρόον κατὰ μεταβολὴν ἐφαίνετο,
ἀλλ᾽ ἐπιεικῶς ἐς ὁμαλότητά τινα καὶ ἀκινησίαν
ἅπαντα συνέστρωντο, καὶ μόνος ἐθαυμάζετο, τῶν
ἄλλων ἁπάντων ὥσπερ ἐν κλύδωνι κινουμένων,
καὶ τῶν μὲν ἐξαπιναίως κατεπτηχότων, τῶν δὲ
πρότερον ταπεινῶν ἀνεστηκότων· ἐθαυμάσθη γοῦν
ἐπὶ τούτοις, ὡς οὐ μόνον δεινὸς τὰ μέλλοντα
προνοεῖν, ἀλλὰ καὶ τοῖς γνωσθεῖσι χρήσασθαι.

Ἦν δὲ τὸ πᾶν ἦθος τοιοῦτος, ἢ πρὸς τὸν Πλα-
τωνικὸν Σωκράτην ἀναπεφυκώς, ἢ κατά τινα
ζῆλον καὶ μίμησιν ἐκ παιδὸς αὐτῷ γενομένην ἐς
ἐκεῖνον συνεσχηματισμένος. τό τε γὰρ ἐπιφαινό-

---

[1] After τοῦτο ἦν lacuna in mss. ; ἐπαίτης mss. Boissonade;
ἐπείσθη Wyttenbach ; ἐπ᾽ Ἀσίης sc. ἠπείγετο Boissonade
suggests ; Lundström, to fill lacuna, καὶ ἔληγεν ὢν ὁ μὲν
βασιλεὺς ἐπαίτης (ἐπαίτης ὤν = ἐπαιτῶν).

a second time, and his invitations were not addressed
to Chrysanthius only. For in a special letter he
urged his wife to help him to persuade her husband.
Once more, then, Chrysanthius referred the matter
to the divine will, and the gods continued to give a
response to the same effect. When this had happened several times, even the emperor was convinced; but Chrysanthius having been appointed
high priest of the whole country, since he knew
clearly what was about to happen, was not oppressive
in the exercise of his office. He built no temples,
as all other men in their hot haste and perfervid
zeal hastened to do, nor was he excessively harsh
to any of the Christians. But such was the mildness of his character that throughout Lydia the
restoration of the temples almost escaped notice.
At any rate, when the powers that be pursued
a different policy, there proved to have been no
serious innovation, nor did there seem to be any
great and universal change, but everything calmed
down in a friendly spirit and became smooth and tran-
quil; by which means he alone won admiration when
all the rest were tossed to and fro as though by
tempest; since on a sudden some cowered in con-
sternation, while they that were humbled before
were once more exalted. For all this, then, he won
admiration as one who was not only skilled in fore-
casting the future, but also in rightly using his
foreknowledge.

Such was the man's whole disposition, whether it
was that in him the Platonic Socrates had come to
life again, or in his ambition to imitate him he
carefully formed himself from boyhood on his
pattern. For an unaffected and indescribable

EUNAPIUS

μενον ἁπλοῦν καὶ ἀφελὲς καὶ ἀδιήγητον ἐπεκάθητο
τοῖς λόγοις, ἥ τε ἐπὶ τούτοις ἀφροδίτη τῶν ῥημάτων
κατέθελγε τὸν ἀκροώμενον. πᾶσί τε εὔνους ἦν
κατὰ τὴν συνουσίαν, καὶ τῶν ἀπιόντων ἕκαστος,
ὅτι φιλοτιμοῖτο μᾶλλον, ἀπῄει πεπεισμένος. ὥσπερ
οὖν τὰ κάλλιστα καὶ γλυκύτερα τῶν μελῶν πρὸς
πᾶσαν ἀκοὴν ἡμέρως καὶ πράως καταρρεῖ καὶ
502 διολισθαίνει καὶ μέχρι τῶν ἀλόγων διϊκνούμενα,
καθάπερ φασὶ τὸν Ὀρφέα, οὕτω καὶ Χρυσανθίου
λόγος πᾶσιν ἦν ἐναρμόνιος, καὶ τοσαύταις δια-
φοραῖς ἠθῶν ἐνέπρεπε καὶ καθηρμόζετο. δυσ-
κίνητος δὲ ἦν περὶ τὰς διαλέξεις καὶ φιλονεικίας,
ἐν τούτοις μάλιστα τοὺς ἀνθρώπους ὑπολαμβάνων
ἐκτραχύνεσθαι· οὐδ' ἂν ῥᾳδίως ἤκουσέ τις αὐτοῦ
τὴν παιδείαν ἣν εἶχεν ἐπιδεικνυμένου, καὶ διὰ
τοῦτο πρὸς τοὺς ἄλλους οἰδοῦντος καὶ διογκυλ-
λομένου, ἀλλὰ τά τε λεγόμενα ὑπ' αὐτῶν ἐθαύμαζεν, εἰ καὶ φαύλως ἐλέγετο, καὶ τὰ δοξαζόμενα
κακῶς ἐπήνει, καθάπερ οὐδὲ τὴν ἀρχὴν ἀκούων,
ἀλλὰ ἐς τὸ συμφατικὸν διὰ τὸ μὴ λυπεῖν γεγονώς.
εἰ δέ πού τις, τῶν ἐπὶ σοφίᾳ πρώτων παρόντων,
ἐγένετο κίνησις, καὶ συμβαλέσθαι τι τοῖς λεγομένοις ἔδοξεν αὐτῷ, πάντα ἦν ἡσυχίας μεστά,
καθάπερ οὐ παρόντων ἀνθρώπων· οὕτως οὔτε
τὰς ἐρωτήσεις, οὔτε τοὺς διορισμούς, οὔτε τὰς
μνήμας ὑπέμενον τοῦ ἀνδρός, ἀλλ' ἀνέχαζον,
ἔξω λόγου καὶ ἀντιρρήσεως ἑαυτοὺς φυλάττοντες,
ὅπως μὴ καταφανεῖς ἁμαρτάνοντες γίνωνται. καὶ
πολλοὶ τῶν μετρίως ἐγνωκότων αὐτόν, διὰ τοῦ
βάθους τῆς ψυχῆς οὐκ ἀφιγμένων, κατηγορούντων

simplicity was manifest in him and dwelt in his speech, and moreover there was about every word of his a charm that enchanted the hearer. In intercourse he was amiable to all men, so that everyone went away from him with the conviction that he was especially beloved. And just as the most charming and sweetest songs flow gently and smoothly, as they insinuate themselves into all men's ears and reach even irrational animals, as they tell of Orpheus, even so the eloquence of Chrysanthius was modulated to suit all ears and was in harmony with and adapted to all those diverse temperaments. But it was not easy to rouse him to philosophical discussions or competitions, because he perceived that it is especially in such contests that men become embittered. Nor would anyone readily have heard him showing off his own erudition or inflated because of it, or insolent and arrogant towards others; rather he used to admire whatever they said, even though their remarks were worthless, and he would applaud even incorrect conclusions, just as though he had not even heard the premises, but was naturally inclined to assent, lest he should inflict pain on anyone. And if in an assembly of those most distinguished for learning any dissension arose, and he thought fit to take part in the discussion, the place became hushed in silence as though no one were there. So unwilling were they to face his questions and definitions and power of quoting from memory, but they would retire into the background and carefully refrain from discussion or contradiction, lest their failure should be too evident. Many of those who knew him only slightly, and therefore had not sounded the depths of his soul, accused him of

EUNAPIUS

τε ἀλογίαν, καὶ τὴν πραότητα μόνον ἐπαινούντων,
ὡς ᾔσθοντο διαλεγομένου καὶ ἀνελίττοντος ἑαυτὸν
εἰς δόγματα καὶ λόγους, ἕτερόν τινα τοῦτον ἐνό-
μισαν παρ' ὃν ᾔδεισαν· οὕτως ἀλλοιότερός τις
ἐν ταῖς λογικαῖς κινήσεσιν ἐφαίνετο, τῆς τε τριχὸς
ὑποφριττούσης αὐτῷ, καὶ τῶν ὀφθαλμῶν ἑρμη-
νευόντων χορεύουσαν ἔνδον τὴν ψυχὴν περὶ τὰ
δόγματα. εἰς μακρὸν δὲ γῆρας ἀφικόμενος, τὸν
πάντα διετέλεσε βίον, οὐδενὸς τῶν κατ' ἀνθρώπους
ἑτέρου φροντίσας ἢ οἰκονομίας τινός, ἢ γεωργίας,
ἢ χρημάτων ὅσα δικαίως παραγίνεται. ἀλλὰ
πενίαν μὲν ἔφερε ῥᾷον ἢ πλοῦτον ἕτεροι, διαίτῃ δὲ
τῇ παραπεσούσῃ προσεκέχρητο, τῶν μὲν ὑείων
οὐδέποτε, τῶν ἄλλων χρεῶν ἐλάχιστα γευόμενος,
τὸ δὲ θεῖον θεραπεύων συντονώτατα. τῆς τῶν
ἀρχαίων ἀναγνώσεως ἀπρὶξ εἴχετο, καὶ διέφερεν
οὐδὲν νεότης τε καὶ γῆρας, ἀλλ' ὑπὲρ ὀγδοήκοντα
γεγονὼς ἔτη, τοσαῦτα ἔγραφεν αὐτοχειρίᾳ, ὅσα
μόλις ἀναγινώσκουσι νεάζοντες ἕτεροι. τῶν γοῦν
γραφόντων τὰ ἄκρα δακτύλων ὑπὸ τῆς ἀλήκτου
μελέτης καὶ χρήσεως συνεκέκαμπτο.[1] ἀναστὰς δὲ
ἀπὸ τῆς ἀσκήσεως, ταῖς τε δημοσίαις προόδοις
ἐτέρπετο, καὶ τόν τε ταῦτα γράφοντα παραλαβών,
μακροὺς μὲν τοὺς περιπάτους, σχολαίους δὲ
ἀπέτεινεν· ἔλαθέ τε ἄν τις περιαλγὴς τοὺς πόδας
γενόμενος, οὕτως ὑπὸ τῶν διηγημάτων κατεθέλ-
γετο. λουτροῖς δὲ ἐλάχιστα ἐκέχρητο, καὶ ὅμως
ἐῴκει διὰ παντὸς ἄρτι λελουμένῳ. πρὸς δὲ τὰς

---

[1] ἐνεκέκαπτο Boissonade ; συνεκέκαμπτο Cobet, *cf.* Diogenes
Laertius vi. 29 συγκεκαμμένων τῶν δακτύλων.

lack of intelligence and would praise only his mild disposition; but when they heard him maintaining a philosophical theme and unfolding his opinions and arguments, they decided that this was a very different person from the man they thought they knew. So transformed did he seem by the excitement of dialectical debate, with his hair standing on end, and his eyes testifying that the soul within him was leaping and dancing around the opinions that he expressed. He survived to an advanced old age, and during the whole of his long life he took thought for none of the ordinary affairs of human life, except the care of his own household and agriculture and just so much money as may be honestly acquired. Poverty he bore more easily than other men wealth, and moreover his diet was plain and whatever came to hand. He never ate pork, and other kinds of meat but seldom. He worshipped the gods with the utmost devotion and assiduity, and never slackened in his reading of the ancient authors. In old age he was still the same as he had been in youth, and when he was over eighty he wrote more books with his own hand than others, even in youth, find time to read. Hence the ends of the fingers with which he wrote became curved and crooked with constant work and use. When his work was done he would rise and amuse himself by walking in the public streets with the author of this narrative to keep him company; and he would take very long but leisurely walks. Meanwhile he would tell such charming and agreeable stories that one might have been terribly footsore without being aware of it. He very seldom went to the baths, and yet he always seemed fresh from a bath. In his intercourse with those in

τῶν ἀρχόντων συντυχίας τὸ ὑπερφυὲς οὐκ ἦν δι'
ἀλαζονείαν συνιδεῖν ἢ τύφον γινόμενον, ἀλλ'
ἁπλότητα ἄν τις ὑπέλαβεν ἀγνοοῦντος ἀνδρὸς ὅ
τι ἐστὶν ἐξουσία· οὕτω διελέγετο κοινῶς αὐτοῖς
καὶ ἐπιδεξίως. τὸν δὲ ταῦτα γράφοντα ἐκπαιδεύσας νέον ἔτι ὄντα, ἡνίκα ἐπανῆλθεν Ἀθήνηθεν,
οὐκ ἔλαττον ἠγάπα, ἀλλὰ καὶ προσετίθει καθ'
ἡμέραν τῷ διαφέροντι τῆς εὐνοίας, ἐς τοῦτο
ἐκνικήσας, ὥστε τὰ ἑωθινὰ μὲν ὁ συγγραφεὺς ἐπὶ
503 ῥητορικοῖς λόγοις ἑτέροις συνῆν, καὶ τοὺς δεομένους ἐπαίδευεν, μικρὸν δὲ ὑπὲρ μεσημβρίας
ἐπαιδεύετο, παρὰ τὸν ἐξ ἀρχῆς ἰὼν διδάσκαλον,
τοὺς θειοτέρους καὶ φιλοσόφους τῶν λόγων·
ἡνίκα οὔτε ὁ παιδεύων ἔκαμνεν ἐρῶντι συνών,
τῷ τε ἐκδεχομένῳ τὰ μαθήματα τὸ ἔργον ἦν
πανήγυρις.

Τοῦ δὲ τῶν χριστιανῶν ἐκνικῶντος ἔργου καὶ
κατέχοντος ἅπαντα, διὰ μακροῦ τις ἀπὸ τῆς
Ῥώμης εἰσεφοίτησεν ἄρχων τῆς Ἀσίας (Ἰοῦστος
ὠνομάζετο), πρεσβύτης μὲν ἤδη κατὰ τὴν ἡλικίαν,
γενναῖος καὶ καλὸς[1] τὸ ἦθος, καὶ τῆς ἀρχαίας καὶ
πατρίου πολιτείας οὐκ ἀπηλλαγμένος, ἀλλὰ τὸν
εὐδαίμονα κὶ μακάριον ἐκεῖνον ἐζηλωκὼς τρόπον,
πρός τε ἱεροῖς ἦν ἀεί, καὶ μαντείας ἐξεκρέματο
πάσης, μέγα φρονῶν ὅτι τούτων ἐπεθύμησέ τε
καὶ κατώρθωσεν. οὗτος εἰς τὴν Ἀσίαν διαβὰς
ἐκ τῆς Κωνσταντινουπόλεως, καὶ τὸν ἡγεμόνα
τοῦ ἔθνους καταλαβὼν (Ἱλάριος ἐκεῖνος ἐκαλεῖτο)
συγκορυβαντιῶντα πρὸς τὴν ἐπιθυμίαν, βωμοὺς

---

[1] ἄλλως Boissonade ; καλὸς Wyttenbach.

authority, if he seemed to use excessive freedom
of manner this was not due to arrogance or pride,
but must rather be regarded as the perfect simplicity
of one who was wholly ignorant of the nature of
power and authority; so familiar and so witty was his
language when he talked with such persons. He
had taught the author of this work, then still a
youth, and when the latter returned from Athens
Chrysanthius showed him no less kindness, but day
by day he even multiplied the signs of his peculiar
goodwill; and he gained such influence over him
that the author in the early morning used to give
his time to his own pupils and instruct any who so
desired in the art of rhetoric, but soon after midday
he betook himself to his old master and was by him
instructed in the teachings of religion and philosophy.
And in this period the teacher never grew weary of
instructing his devoted admirer, while the task was
like a holiday festival for him who received his
teaching.

Now when the practice of Christianity was gaining
ground and usurping all men's minds, there arrived
from Rome after a long interval a prefect of Asia
named Justus, already well on in years, a man of
noble and beautiful character, who had not cast aside
the time-honoured ritual of his ancestors, for he was
an ardent disciple of that happy and blessed form
of worship. He was constant in his attendance at
the temples, wholly under the sway of every kind
of divination, and took great pride in his zeal for
these things and his success in restoring them. He
crossed from Asia to Constantinople, and when he
found that the chief man of the country (his name
was Hilarius) was as enthusiastic as himself in

τε ἀνέστησεν αὐτοσχεδίους ἐν Σάρδεσιν (οὐ γὰρ
ἦσαν αὐτόθι), καὶ τοῖς ἴχνεσι τῶν ἱερῶν, εἴπου
τι ἴχνος εὑρέθη, χεῖρα ἐπέβαλεν, ἀνορθῶσαι
βουλόμενος. δημοσίᾳ τε θύσας, ἔπεμπε καὶ συνεκάλει τοὺς πανταχόθεν ἐπὶ παιδείᾳ δόξαν ἔχοντας.
οἱ δὲ παρῆσαν θᾶττον ἢ κληθῆναι, τόν τε ἄνδρα
θαυμάζοντες, καὶ καιρὸν τῆς σφῶν αὐτῶν ἐπιδείξεως ἡγούμενοι, τινὲς δὲ αὐτῶν ἐπὶ τῇ κολακείᾳ
θαρροῦντες ὥσπερ παιδείᾳ, καὶ διὰ ταύτης ἐλπί-
ζοντες ἢ τιμὴν ἢ δοξάριον ἢ ἀργύριον ἀποκερδανεῖν.[1]
ἱερουργίας οὖν δημοσίᾳ προτεθείσης, παρῆσαν
μὲν ἅπαντες, καὶ ὁ ταῦτα γράφων παρῆν· ὁ δὲ
Ἰοῦστος ἐπιστήσας, καὶ τὴν τῶν ὀφθαλμῶν
στάσιν ἐπερείσας (ἔκειτο δὲ τὸ ἱερεῖον ἐν ᾧ δήποτε
τῷ σχήματι), καὶ τοὺς παρόντας ἀνηρώτα· "τί
βούλεται τὸ σχῆμα τοῦ πτώματος;" ἔνθα οἱ μὲν
κόλακες παρεφρύγοντο θαυμάζοντες, ὅτι καὶ ἀπὸ
σχημάτων ἐστὶ μαντικός, καὶ μόνῳ παρεχώρουν
ἐκείνῳ ταῦτα εἰδέναι· οἱ δὲ σεμνότεροι τὰς ὑπήνας
καταψήσαντες ἄκροις τοῖς δακτύλοις, καὶ τὰ
πρόσωπα διαστυγνάσαντες, τάς τε κεφαλὰς βαρύ
τι καὶ ἠρεμαῖον ἐπισείοντες, παρεθεώρουν ἐς τὸ
προκείμενον, ἄλλος ἄλλο λέγοντες. ὁ δὲ Ἰοῦστος,
ὡς μόλις τὸν γέλωτα ἐνεῖχεν, ἐπιστρέψας εἰς τὸν
Χρυσάνθιον "σὺ δὲ τί φής," ἐβόησεν, "ὦ πρεσ-
βύτατε;" καὶ ὁ Χρυσάνθιος οὐδὲν διαταραχθείς,
πάντων ἔφησε καταγινώσκειν· "ἀλλ' εἴ τι βούλει
κἀμέ," ἔφη "περὶ τούτων εἰπεῖν, τίς μὲν ὁ τρόπος
τῆς μαντείας, εἴ γε τοὺς μαντικοὺς τρόπους ἐπί-

[1] ἀποκερδαίνειν Boissonade ; ἀποκερδανεῖν Cobet.

his zeal, he built altars offhand at Sardis where there were none, and wherever a vestige was to be found he set his hand to the remains of the temples with the ambition of rebuilding them. After offering sacrifices in public, he sent to summon from all sides the men who had a reputation for learning. They were no sooner summoned than they came, partly because they admired the man himself, partly because they thought this was an opportunity to show off their own abilities, while some of them put their trust in their power to flatter quite as much as in their erudition, and hoped by this means to gain honour or glory or wealth. Therefore when a public sacrifice was announced they were all present, and the author of this work was present also. Then Justus set himself to the task, and fixing the steady gaze of his eyes on the victim, which lay in any sort of posture, he asked the bystanders: "What is portended by the posture in which the victim has fallen?" Thereupon the flatterers were warm in their admiration, because he was able to divine even from postures, and they deferred to him as alone possessed of this knowledge. But the more dignified stroked their beards with the tips of their fingers, and put on a serious expression of face, and shook their heads solemnly and slowly while they gazed at the victim lying there, and each one offered a different solution. But Justus, who could hardly contain his laughter, turned to Chrysanthius and cried: "And what do you say about this, reverend sir?" Chrysanthius replied with equanimity that he rejected the whole proceeding. "But," said he "if you wish me also to give an opinion about this, first, if you really understand the modes of

στασαι, εἰπὲ πρότερον, καὶ ποίου τινὸς εἴδους,
τίς δὲ ἡ πεῦσις, καὶ κατὰ τίνα μέθοδον ἐπηρώτηται.
καὶ εἰ ταῦτα λέγοις, εἴποιμ᾽ ἂν ὅπη τὸ φαινόμενον
εἰς τὸ μέλλον φέρει. πρὶν δὲ ταῦτα λέγειν,
βάναυσόν ἐστι πρὸς τὴν σὴν ἐρώτησιν, σημαινόν-
των τὸ μέλλον τῶν θεῶν, ἐμὲ καὶ περὶ τῆς ἐρωτή-
σεως καὶ τοῦ μέλλοντος λέγειν, συνάπτοντα τῷ
γεγονότι τὸ ἐσόμενον· δύο γὰρ οὕτως ἂν γίνεσθαι
τὰς ἐρωτήσεις. περὶ δύο δὲ ἢ πλειόνων οὐδεὶς
ἐρωτᾷ κατὰ ταὐτόν· τὸ γὰρ ἐν τοῖς ὡρισμένοις
διάφορον ἕνα λόγον οὐκ ἔχει." ἐνταῦθα Ἰοῦστος
ἀνέκραγεν ὡς μανθάνων ὅσα μὴ πρότερον ἠπίστατο,
504 καὶ τοῦ λοιποῦ γε οὐκ ἐπαύσατο συνὼν ἰδίᾳ καὶ
τῆς πηγῆς ἀρυόμενος. καὶ εἴ τινες ἕτεροι κατ᾽
ἐκείνους τοὺς χρόνους τῶν ἐπὶ σοφίᾳ περιβοήτων
Χρυσανθίῳ κατὰ κλέος ἦλθον εἰς λόγους, πει-
σθέντες ὅτι πόρρω τῆς δεινότητος ἐκείνης εἰσίν,
ἀπιόντες ᾤχοντο. τοῦτο δὲ καὶ Ἑλλησπόντιος
ὁ ἐκ Γαλατίας ἔπαθεν, ἀνὴρ διὰ πάντα ἄριστος,
καὶ εἰ μὴ Χρυσάνθιος ἦν, πρῶτος ἁπάντων ἂν[1]
φανείς. σοφίας μὲν γὰρ ἐραστὴς οὗτος ὁ ἀνὴρ
ἐς τοσόνδε ἐγένετο, ὥστε ἐπῆλθε μικροῦ καὶ τὴν
ἀοίκητον, μαστεύων εἴ που τινι περιτύχοι πλέον
εἰδότι· καλῶν δὲ ἔργων καὶ λόγων ἀνάπλεως
γενόμενος, καὶ εἰς τὰς παλαιὰς Σάρδεις ἀφίκετο
διὰ τὴν Χρυσανθίου συνουσίαν. ἀλλὰ ταῦτα μὲν
ὕστερον.

Ἐγένετο δὲ Χρυσανθίῳ καὶ παῖς ἐπώνυμος τῷ

---

[1] ἂν Cobet adds.

divination, tell me what mode of divination this is, to what type it belongs, what you seek to learn, and what method you followed in your inquiry. If you will tell me all this, I will tell you what is the bearing on the future of this thing that we see. But until you tell me these things, since the gods themselves reveal the future, it would be unworthy on my part, in answer to your question, at the same time to answer your inquiry and to speak of the future, thus connecting the future with what has just happened. For thus would arise two different questions at once; but no one asks two or more questions at the same time. For when things have two separate definitions, one explanation does not suit both." Then Justus exclaimed that he had learned something that he never knew before, and for the future he consulted him constantly in private and drank deep from that fount of knowledge. There were others also in those days, renowned for wisdom, who were attracted by the fame of Chrysanthius and entered into discussions with him, but whenever this happened they went away convinced that they could not approach his oratorical genius. This is what happened to Hellespontius of Galatia, an unusually gifted man in every way, who, if Chrysanthius had not existed, would have shown himself worthy of the first place. For he was so ardent a lover of learning that he travelled almost to the uninhabited parts of the world in the desire of finding out whether he could meet anyone who knew more than himself. Thus, then, crowned with noble words and deeds he came to ancient Sardis to enjoy the society of Chrysanthius. But all this happened later.

Chrysanthius had a son whom he named after

κατὰ τὸ Πέργαμον αὐτῷ γενομένῳ διδασκάλῳ
(μεμνήμεθα δὲ πρότερον) Αἰδεσίῳ, καὶ ἦν ὁ παῖς
ἐκ παιδὸς ἐπτερωμένον τι χρῆμα πρὸς ἅπασαν
ἀρετήν, καὶ τῶν ἵππων οὐκ εἶχε θάτερον, ᾗ φησιν
ὁ Πλάτων, οὐδὲ ἐβρίθετο κάτω νοῦς αὐτῷ, ἀλλὰ
πρός τε μαθήματα σφοδρὸς καὶ ἄγαν ὀξὺς γενόμενος, καὶ πρὸς θεῶν θεραπείαν διαρκέστατος, ἐς
τοσόνδε διέφευγε τὸ ἀνθρώπινον, ὥστε ἄνθρωπος
ὢν ἐκινδύνευεν ὅλος εἶναι ψυχή. τὸ γοῦν σῶμα
ἐν ταῖς κινήσεσιν οὕτως αὐτοῦ κοῦφον ἦν, ὥστε
ἦν ἀπίθανον γράφειν, καὶ μάλα ποιητικῶς, εἰς
ὅσον ὕψος ἐφέρετο μετάρσιος. ἡ δὲ πρὸς τὸ θεῖον
οἰκειότης οὕτως ἦν ἀπραγμάτευτος καὶ εὔκολος,
ὥστε ἐξήρκει τὸν στέφανον ἐπιθεῖναι τῇ κεφαλῇ,
καὶ πρὸς τὸν ἥλιον ἀναβλέποντα χρησμοὺς ἐκφέρειν, καὶ τούτους ἀψευδεῖς, καὶ πρὸς τὸ κάλλιστον
εἶδος ἐνθέου πνεύματος γεγραμμένους· καί τοί
γε οὔτε μέτρον ἠπίστατο, οὔτε εἰς γραμματικὴν
ἐπιστήμην ἔρρωτο, ἀλλὰ θεὸς ἅπαντα ἦν αὐτῷ.
νοσήσας δὲ οὐδαμῶς κατὰ τὸν ὡρισμένον βίον,
ἀμφὶ τὰ εἴκοσιν ἔτη μετήλλαξεν. ὁ δὲ πατὴρ καὶ
τότε διέδειξε φιλόσοφος ὤν· ἢ γὰρ τὸ μέγεθος
τῆς συμφορᾶς εἰς ἀπάθειαν αὐτὸν μετέστησεν,
ἢ τῷ παιδὶ συγχαίρων τῆς λήξεως, ἔμεινεν ἄ-
τρεπτος· καὶ ἡ μήτηρ δέ, πρὸς τὸν ἄνδρα ὁρῶσα,

Aedesius of whom I have written above, formerly his teacher at Pergamon. From his childhood this boy was a creature winged for every excellence, and of the two horses as Plato [1] describes them, his soul possessed only the good steed, nor did his intellect ever sink; but he was a devoted student, keen-witted, and assiduous in the worship of the gods; and so completely was he emancipated from human weaknesses, that though a mortal man he was all soul. At any rate his body was so light in its movements that it would seem incredible and would take a genuine poet to describe to what a height it rose aloft. His kinship and affinity with the gods was so unceremonious and familiar that he had only to place the garland on this head and turn his gaze upwards to the sun, and immediately deliver oracles which, moreover, were always infallible and were composed after the fairest models of divine inspiration. Yet he neither knew the art of writing verse nor was trained in the science of grammar; but for him the god took the place of all else. Though he had never been ill during his allotted span of life, he died when he was about twenty years of age. On this occasion also his father showed himself a true philosopher. For whether it was that the greatness of the calamity reduced him to a state of apathy, or whether he rejoiced with his son in the latter's blessed portion, the fact is that he remained unshaken. The youth's mother also, observing her husband, rose above the

---

[1] Plato, *Phaedrus* 246 B. The human soul is represented as borne along by two horses, of which one represents the appetites, the other, reason and sobriety.

τὴν γυναικείαν ὑπερήνεγκε φύσιν, πρὸς τὴν ἀξίαν
τοῦ πάθους ὀλοφύρσεις ἐκδύσασα.

Τούτων δὲ οὕτω κεχωρηκότων, ὁ Χρυσάνθιος
ἦν ἐν τοῖς συνήθεσι· καὶ πολλῶν καὶ μεγάλων
ἐμπιπτόντων δημοσίων καὶ κοινῶν πραγμάτων,
ἃ τὰς ἁπάντων ψυχὰς κατέσεισεν εἰς φόβον, μόνος
ἔμεινεν ἀσάλευτος, ὥστε εἰκασέ τις ἂν[1] οὐδὲ ἐπὶ
γῆς εἶναι τὸν ἄνδρα. κατ' ἐκείνους δὴ τοὺς
χρόνους καὶ Ἑλλησπόντιος παρ' αὐτὸν ἀφικνεῖται,
καὶ βραδέως μὲν συνῆλθον εἰς λόγους· ἐπεὶ δὲ
εἰς ταὐτὸν συνήντησαν, τοσοῦτον Ἑλλησπόντιος
ἑαλώκει, ὥστε, πάντα μεθέμενος, ἕτοιμος ἦν
σκηνοῦσθαι παρὰ Χρυσανθίῳ, καὶ νεάζειν ἐν τῷ
μανθάνειν· μετεμέλετο δὲ[2] τοσοῦτον πεπλανη-
μένος χρόνον, καὶ εἰς γῆρας ἀφικόμενος, πρίν τι
τῶν χρησίμων ἐκμαθεῖν. καὶ ὁ μὲν ἐπὶ τούτῳ
τὴν γνώμην ἔτεινε· τῷ δὲ Χρυσανθίῳ συμβὰν ἔκ
τινος συνηθείας τὴν φλέβα διελεῖν, ὅ τε συγγραφεὺς παρῆν, οὕτω προστάξαντος, καὶ τῶν
ἰατρῶν κενῶσαι βουλομένων τὸ φερόμενον, αὐτὸς
505 ἐπὶ τὸ συμφέρον σπευσάμενος, παράλογον εἶναι
τὸ κενωθὲν ἔφη, καὶ οὕτως ἐπισχεῖν ἐκέλευσεν·
οὐδὲ γὰρ ἄπειρος ἦν ἰατρικῆς ὁ ταῦτα γράφων.
Ἑλλησπόντιος δὲ ἀκούσας παρῆν, ἀγανακτῶν καὶ
ποτνιώμενος, ὡς μεγάλου κακοῦ γεγονότος, εἰ
πρεσβύτης οὕτως ἀνὴρ τοσούτου διὰ τῆς χειρὸς
αἵματος ἀφῄρηται. ὡς δὲ ἤκουσε τῆς φωνῆς,
καὶ ὑγιαίνοντα εἶδεν, πρὸς τὸν συγγραφέα τὸν

---

[1] εἰκάσειεν ἄν τις Cobet suggests.
[2] μετέμελε δὲ αὐτῷ Boissonade ; μετεμέλετο δὲ Cobet.

ordinary feminine nature and put away from her
all loud lamentation, that her grief might have
its due dignity.

After these events had taken place, Chrysanthius
pursued his accustomed studies. And when many
great public and universal calamities and disturb-
ances befell, which shook all men's souls with terror,
he alone remained unshaken by the storm; so
much so that one would have thought that he was
really elsewhere than on earth. About this time
Hellespontius came to see him, and they met and
conversed, though only after some delay. When,
however, they did actually meet, Hellespontius was
so captivated that he abandoned all else and was
ready to live under the same roof as Chrysanthius
and to renew his youth by studying with him. For
he regretted that he had so long wandered in error,
and had arrived at old age before learning anything
useful. Accordingly he bent his whole mind to this
task. But it chanced that Chrysanthius had to have
a vein cut open as was his custom, and the author
was present in obedience to his orders; and when
the doctors prescribed that the blood should be
allowed to flow freely, the author in his anxiety to
apply the right treatment declared that the blood-
letting was beyond all reason, and gave orders that
it should be stopped then and there; for the
author of this work had considerable knowledge of
medicine. Hellespontius hearing what had happened
came at once, indignant and loudly lamenting that
it was a great calamity that a man of so great
an age should lose so much blood from his arm.
But when he heard Chrysanthius talking and saw
that he was unharmed, he directed his remarks to

561

EUNAPIUS

λόγον ἐπιστρέψας " ἀλλά σέ γε " φησίν " ἡ πόλις
αἰτιῶνται δεινόν τι δεδρακέναι· νῦν δὲ ἅ-
παντες σιωπήσουσιν, ὁρῶντες ὑγιαίνοντα." τοῦ δὲ
εἰπόντος, ὡς οὐκ ἠγνόει τὸ συμφέρον, ὁ μὲν
Ἑλλησπόντιος ὡς συσκευασόμενος[1] τὰ βιβλία,
καὶ παρὰ τὸν Χρυσάνθιον ἥξων ἐπὶ μαθήσει, τῆς
πόλεως ἐξῄει. καὶ ἡ γαστὴρ αὐτοῦ νοσεῖν ἤρχετο,
καὶ παρελθὼν εἰς Ἀπάμειαν τῆς Βιθυνίας μετ-
ήλλαξε τὸ ζῆν, τῷ παρόντι τῶν ἑταίρων Προκοπίῳ
πολλὰ ἐπισκήψας μόνον θαυμάζειν Χρυσάνθιον.
καὶ ὁ Προκόπιος παραγενόμενος εἰς τὰς Σάρδεις,
ταῦτα ἐποίει τε καὶ ἀπήγγελλεν.

Ὁ δὲ Χρυσάνθιος, εἰς τὴν ἐπιοῦσαν ὥραν τοῦ
ἔτους, κατὰ θέρος ἱστάμενον, ἐπὶ τὴν αὐτὴν
θεραπείαν ἐλθών, καί τοι τοῦ συγγραφέως προειπόντος τοῖς ἰατροῖς περιμένειν αὐτὸν κατὰ τὸ σύν-
ηθες, οἱ μὲν ἔφθασαν ἐλθόντες, ὁ δὲ ὑπέσχε τὴν
χεῖρα, καὶ παρὰ μέτρον γενομένης τῆς κενώσεως,
παρέσεις τε τῶν μερῶν ἠκολούθησαν καὶ τὰ ἄρθρα
συνέκαμνε, καὶ κλινοπετὴς ἦν. καὶ Ὀρειβάσιος
ἐνταῦθα παραγίνεται, δι᾽ ἐκεῖνον καθ᾽ ὑπερβολὴν
μὲν ἐπιστήμης μικροῦ καὶ βιασάμενος τὴν φύσιν
καὶ χρίσμασι θερμοτέροις καὶ μαλάττουσι τὰ
κατεψυγμένα μικροῦ πρὸς τὸ νεάζειν ἐπήγαγεν.
ἀλλ᾽ ἐνίκα τὸ γῆρας· ὀγδοηκοστὸν γὰρ ὑπελθὸν[2]
ἔτος ἐτύγχανε, καὶ τῇ τοῦ θερμοῦ κατὰ τὸ πλεονάζον
ἀλλοτριώσει τὸ γῆρας ἐδιπλασιάσθη· καὶ τε-

---

[1] Cobet: συσκευασάμενος Boissonade.
[2] Cobet: ὑπελθὼν Boissonade.

the author and said: "The whole city is accusing you of having done a terrible thing; but now they will all be silenced, when they see that he is unharmed." The author replied that he knew what was the proper treatment, whereupon Hellespontius made as though he would collect his books and go to Chrysanthius for a lesson; but he really left the city. Presently he began to suffer from a pain in his stomach, and he turned aside to Apamea in Bithynia and there departed this life, after laying the strictest injunctions on his comrade Procopius, who was present, to admire none but Chrysanthius. Procopius went to Sardis and did as he said, and reported these facts.

Now Chrysanthius, at the same season in the following year, that is at the beginning of summer, had recourse to the same remedy, and though the author of this work had given instructions to the doctors beforehand that they must wait for him as usual, they arrived without his knowledge. Chrysanthius offered his arm to them, and there was an excessive flux of blood, the result of which was that his limbs relaxed and he suffered acute pain in his joints, so that he had to stay in bed. Oribasius was immediately called in, and for the sake of Chrysanthius he almost succeeded, so extraordinary was his professional skill, in doing violence to the laws of nature, and by means of hot and soothing fomentations he almost restored the vigour of youth to those rigid limbs. Nevertheless old age gained the victory; for his eightieth year was now approaching, and the influence of his age was doubly felt when his temperature was so greatly changed by the excessive application of heat. After an illness

ταρταῖος νοσηλευθείς, εἰς τὴν πρέπουσαν λῆξιν ἀνεχώρησεν.

Εἰσὶ δὲ μετ' αὐτὸν διάδοχοι φιλοσοφίας Ἐπίγονός τε ὁ ἐκ Λακεδαίμονος, καὶ Βερονικιανὸς ὁ ἐκ Σάρδεων, ἄνδρες ἄξιοι τοῦ τῆς φιλοσοφίας ὀνόματος· πλὴν ὅσα γε ὁ Βερονικιανὸς ταῖς Χάρισιν ἔθυσε, καὶ ἱκανὸς ἀνθρώποις ὁμιλεῖν ἐστι· καὶ εἴη.

of four days he departed to a destiny that was worthy of him.

The successors of Chrysanthius in the profession of philosophy are Epigonus of Lacedaemon and Beronicianus of Sardis, men well worthy of the title of philosopher. But Beronicianus has sacrificed more generously to the Graces and has a peculiar talent for associating with his fellows. Long may he live to do so!

GLOSSARY OF RHETORICAL TERMS

The references are to the pages of this edition.

ἀγωνίζεσθαι, p. 104, *to deliver an oration.* But also in the sense of making a speech in the character of some definite person, *cf.* p. 202 τὸν δὲ Ἀρτάβαζον ἀγωνιζόμενος.

ἀκμή, p. 218, *virility* and *brilliance.* Pathos, energy, and splendour of diction combined produce the crowning moment of eloquence. But the word also means, less technically, the highest point touched either in eloquence of thought or diction, p. 120. The adjective ἀκμαῖος is applied, p. 84, to themes that call for intensity and pathos of expression.

ἀκρόασις *passim, lesson in rhetoric, course in rhetoric.* Cf. συνουσία and σπουδή used in Philostratus as synonyms.

ἀμφιβολία, p. 272, *ambiguity, double entendre.* Hermocrates is praised for his ingenuity in the use of such ambiguities in "simulated" speeches, ἐσχηματισμέναι ὑποθέσεις, *cf.* Hermogenes, Περὶ δεινότητος 72.

ἀπαγγελία *passim, style of delivery, mode of expression.* A late word for style in general. So ἀπαγγέλλειν, *deliver a speech.* But it is technical also in the sense of announcing that a declamation is to be given.

ἀπέριττος, pp. 100, 278, *simple, unaffected.* The opposite of περιττός which, in later rhetoric, means both "affected" and "redundant," though it can be a term of praise, "elaborate," "highly-wrought." The negative form is rare and is not in Ernesti.

ἀπόστασις, p. 30 and *Letter* 73. *Separation of clauses.* This is a difficult word to define briefly. It is a form of asyndeton which produces greater liveliness and swing. The new sentence is independent in structure and

GLOSSARY OF RHETORICAL TERMS

sometimes in thought. It is certainly a break with a fresh start for emphasis, but critics differ as to the precise kind of asyndeton that is meant. *Cf.* P. C. Robertson, *Gorgianic Figures*, Baltimore, 1893 ; Frei, *Beiträge* in *Rh. Museum* vii. ; Hermogenes, *On the Forms of Oratory*, iii. 247 Walz ; Aristeides, *Art of Rhetoric*, ix. 346. Walz gives instances from Demosthenes.

ἀρχαῖος, p. 64, *ancient, antique, classical.* ἀρχαΐζειν and ἀττικίζειν are practically synonyms. See Norden, *Antike Kunst-Prosa*, p. 357. *Cf.* Eunapius on Sopolis, p. 516, and on Libanius, p. 518. The true archaist (*antiquarius*) will follow the rule of Aristeides, *Rhetoric* ii. 6, and use no word or phrase that cannot be found in a classical author. The νεώτεροι, Asianists, ignore this rule.

ἀφέλεια, pp. 178, 304, *straightforward simplicity, naïveté of style.* This style was admired and sought after by the sophists, but it was beyond their reach, and nowhere do they seem more affected and "precious" than where they strive to be simple and graceful in the manner of Xenophon. Aelian and Philostratus (in the *Imagines*) both aim at ἀφέλεια and fail. *Cf.* Norden, p. 432.

γνώριμοι, p. 232, *disciples, pupils.* A synonym for the more usual ἀκροαταί or ἑταῖροι.

γοργιάζειν, p. 30, *to write like Gorgias, cf.* p. 178 κριτιάζειν, *to write like Critias*, said of Herodes Atticus.

δεινότης *passim, oratorical skill, mastery.* This word as a rhetorical term has no invidious sense, but sums up the highest qualities of eloquence. It is especially ascribed to Demosthenes by the technical writers, and always implies vigour. δεινός, however, when used of Antiphon (p. 42), retains, as the context shows, the classical sense of "over ingenious," and therefore distrusted by the crowd. Hermogenes, *On the Forms of Oratory*, 304. On p. 10 Philostratus seems to use δεινότης in this earlier sense of "too great cleverness."

διάλεξις *passim.* In late writers on rhetoric this word has two distinct meanings : (1) *philosophical discourse, dissertation.* This was a popular discourse on an abstract theme and was not extemporaneous. Philostratus says (p. 4) that this διάλεξις was characteristic of the earlier

568

sophists. διαλέγεσθαι is used in this sense, and is opposed to the forensic style, pp. 184, 186. Philostratus uses the phrase θετικὴ ὑπόθεσις as a synonym for διάλεξις. (2) But it is the regular term also for the prooemium which the sophist delivered before the formal declamation ; it was often an encomium of the city to which he came as a visitor or a newly-appointed professor, cf. p. 194. Philostratus wrote a volume of such introductory " talks " which has perished. Evidently the formal μελέτη, the declamation itself, ranked much higher as a form of composition.

διατίθεσθαι, pp. 124, 272, 306, to deliver a speech, like ἀπαγγέλλειν or ἑρμηνεύειν. So often in Dionysius of Halicarnassus ; not in Ernesti.

ἔκφυλον, p. 208, alien, outlandish, cf. ἐκφύλως ἀττικίζειν, p. 50, and Lucian, Lexiphanes xxiv. Used of a word or phrase such as a latinism foreign to classical Attic usage and so avoided by a purist.

Ἕλληνες, οἱ or τὸ Ἑλληνικόν, pp. 192, 228, 280, 288, students of rhetoric. This is often used by Philostratus ; cf. Eunapius, p. 500.

ἐπεστραμμένη, pp. 16, 52, vehement ; cf. ἐπιστροφή and ἐπιστρεφής. A classical usage revived by Philostratus, cf. Longinus, On the Sublime, xii. 3 ἐπέστραπται. Not in Ernesti.

ἐπιβολή, abundant use of synonyms. Dio Chrysostom, Oration xviii. 14, praises Xenophon for this characteristic. The participle ἐπιβεβλημένος is used in this sense to express copiousness, Philostratus, p. 70. This is quite separate from and seems opposed to its more frequent rhetorical meaning, " a direct and simple approach " to one's subject, as opposed to περιβολή. Cf. Hermogenes, On the Forms of Oratory, i. 28.

ἐπίδειξις p. 208, display of rhetoric, Vortrag. The regular term for a public declamation by a sophist ; ἀκρόασις is also used in this sense.

ἐπὶ πᾶσιν or τὸ ἐπὶ πᾶσιν passim, epilogue, peroration, concluding clause or argument. A favourite expression in Philostratus. Not in Ernesti.

ἐπιστροφή, pp. 54, 82, vehemence or emphasis ; cf. ἐπεστραμμένη above.

GLOSSARY OF RHETORICAL TERMS

ἐπιχειρηματικόν, p. 98, *dialectical, argumentative.* The ἐπιχείρημα is the rhetorical syllogism used or " essayed " as a form of proof. The adjective is rare.

ἐσχηματισμένη (ὑπόθεσις) *passim, sermo coloratus. Veiled argument, covert allusion.* So σχηματίζειν λόγον, " to compose a speech with veiled meaning." ἐσχ. ὑπόθεσις κατ᾽ ἔμφασιν is the full expression in Hermogenes, *On Invention,* p. 259 Spengel (the wider meaning "figured speech," *i.e.* in which figures of speech and thought are used, is ignored by Philostratus). In such a speech the true intent should show or " shimmer " through. The device may be used throughout a speech or only in certain passages : for safety, when one aims at tyrants ; for piquancy, or as a test, *e.g.* Agamemnon's exhortation to flight in the *Iliad,* the first instance in literature of a speech ἐν σχήματι ; for covert criticism (*cf.* Demetrius, *On Style,* 288, 294). It was useful for the βασιλικὸς λόγος, and perhaps the Emperor Julian in his fulsome panegyrics of Constantius was playing this dangerous game. Herodes presumed on the clemency of Marcus Aurelius, and scorned to " schematize " when he scolded the emperor. Synonyms in Philostratus are ἐπαμφοτέρως εἰπεῖν, ὑποθέσεις κατὰ σχῆμα προηγμέναι or συγκείμεναι. It is skating on thin ice, and to fail to keep one's footing is ἐκφέρεσθαι τῆς ὑποθέσεως, p. 132. It is distinct from εἰρωνεία and offers more of a riddle to the audience. It was considered a very difficult type of speech. A great orator like Demosthenes employed it as a matter of course, but in the sophistic speech it becomes mere frigid ostentation.

εὔροια, p. 26, *fluency, volubility, fine flow of words.* Every declaimer must have this talent ; so that the term becomes a synonym for the ready eloquence of the successful sophist, and is always used as praise.

ἠχώ, pp. 178, 234 (where it is opposed to κρότος), 184, *sonorousness, assonance.* This is always used of effects of sound or rhythm, whether of pronunciation or diction ; *cf.* ἡ κριτιάζουσα ἠχώ. On p. 198 τὴν ἠχὼ τῆς διαλέξεως προσῆρεν means that Herodes raised the pitch of his eloquence so as to intensify the effects of sound

and rhythm. ἠχή is used, more rarely, in the same sense.

θετικός *passim*, αἱ θετικαὶ ὑποθέσεις, described as characteristic of ancient sophistic on p. 6, *cf.* p. 296 τὰ θετικὰ τῶν χωρίων. *Themes* that maintain a general philosophical thesis, as opposed to αἱ ἐς ὄνομα ὑποθέσεις, *quaestiones definitae*, p. 6. The former were more generally called θέσεις. Philostratus in general uses ὑπόθεσις for any sort of theme, but occasionally distinguishes the special from the general.

κομματίας, p. 296, *one who uses brief, incisive phrases*; *cf.* κομματικῶς, Dionys. of Hal. *Demosthenes*, 39; Cicero, *Orator*, lxii. *incise membratimque dicere*; Demetrius, *On Style*, 9. The adjective is used only by Philostratus. This is the glaring fault of the style of Hegesias who used it to excess. Philostratus is fond of words ending in *-ias*, *e.g.* δογματίας, ἀγαλματίας.

κριτικός, pp. 94, 122, 178, *an expert in grammar and criticism*. Julius Pollux, rhetorician and grammarian, might be thus described. This is the more scholarly type of grammarian who examined questions of authenticity of authorship. Such a scholar was evidently highly respected, and on friendly terms with the sophists. A λόγος κριτικός is a treatise on some question of criticism and is not sophistic.

κρότος, pp. 120, 178, 234, *the grandiose manner*. In the last passage it is opposed to ἠχώ. The other meaning of κρότος is *applause*, and the verb retains this sense in Philostratus, *cf.* Eunapius, pp. 472, 474. Usually κρότος and ἠχώ are synonyms; *cf.* the adjective ἐπίκροτος "sonorous," p. 124. Eunapius, *Prohaeresius*, p. 494 κατὰ τὸν κρότον ἀναπαύων ἑκάστην περίοδον, means that he closed his periods with harmonious effects of sound.

μελέτη, p. 262, *a declamation*; also *a lesson in declamation*, or a practice speech on a fictitious theme; *cf.* μελετηραὶ συνουσίαι, p. 100, lessons in declamation, at which the teacher himself declaimed.

ὁμοιοτέλευτα, p. 38, *similar endings*. Used especially in

precisely balanced clauses of equal length, which give almost the effect of rhyme. This assonance is part of the attempt to supersede poetry by poetical prose. It was an excessive use of this figure, combined with antithesis in balanced clauses, that in Gorgias offended the taste of the Atticists, and finally became a mark of Asianism; cf. πάρισα below.

πανηγυρικὴ ἰδέα λόγου, p. 16, *the type of speech suited to a religious festival.* This is not necessarily a panegyric in the later sense, but it praised the god in whose honour the festival was held, the city and so on, hence a festival speech is likely to be an encomium. The style is not argumentative but highly rhetorical, and has its own appropriate commonplaces and mannerisms. Heracleides, p. 278, is praised for avoiding excessive sensationalism in the ideas (ἔννοιαι) that he used in this type of speech. The *Panathenaicus* of Aristeides is a good example.

πάρισα, p. 38, *clauses of equal length.* In symmetrical clauses, assonance of the endings (ὁμοιοτέλευτα) and antithesis were often combined; *e.g.* Aristotle, *Rhetoric* iii. 9. 9 τί ἂν ἔπαθες δεινόν, εἰ ἄνδρ' εἶδες ἀργόν; A good example of carefully measured clauses used to excess is the passage quoted from Isaeus the Syrian by Philostratus, p. 70. This is what Aulus Gellius, xviii. 8, says the rhetoricians *faciunt immodice et rancide.*

περιβολή, pp. 50, 64 and *passim, fulness of expression, expansion, amplification, circumducta* or *circumiecta oratio.* There is no one word or phrase that exactly defines this method of amplifying a statement, and one can only describe here one of the many ways in which περιβολή is effected. When the main statement is held up while the speaker swings round the circle, collecting every possible illustration or circumstance, positive and negative, and then resumes the thread, that is technically "peribletic." "Amplification," which is merely αὔξησις, is quite inadequate to translate περιβολή as described and illustrated by Aristeides and Hermogenes. But in the *Lives* Philostratus uses the term rather vaguely for rhetorical ornament and fulness of statement in general.

GLOSSARY OF RHETORICAL TERMS

So, too, the verb, *e.g.* p. 234 τὴν παρασκευὴν τῆς λέξεως
. . . περιεβάλλετο, where the metaphor is of an " ample
garment " of style. The style that eschews περιβολή is
" pure " (καθαρός), and is naturally rarely found in the
sophists. The excess of περιβολή is a vice, *plethora*,
redundancy.

πνεῦμα and πνεῖν, pp. 50, 244, *inspiration, energy, vis et
spiritus.* This word has lost in late rhetoric its earlier
specialized meaning, and is a synonym of ἀκμή or ἰσχύς,
the quality of energy in a speech.

πότιμος, pp. 248, 294, ποτίμως, p. 26, *sweet* and *fresh style* of
speech. This is a favourite usage with the late sophists
and the Christian fathers, and is always a more or
less conscious echo of Plato, *Phaedrus*, 243 D; *cf.*
Libanius, *Or. parent.* § 9 ἀπεκλύσατο τῷ ποτίμῳ λόγῳ.
The adjective is constantly used with λόγος or with νᾶμα
metaphorically.

προβάλλειν, pp. 104, 292, *to propose a theme* for declamation.
Any member of a sophist's audience could suggest a
theme. The choice was naturally left to any distinguished visitor; otherwise a vote was taken, and the
theme thus chosen was ἡ νενικηκυῖα or σπουδασθεῖσα
ὑπόθεσις, *the theme that won most votes.* *Cf.* διδόναι
ὑπόθεσιν in the same sense. The sophist αἰτεῖ, " invites,"
the audience to name a theme.

προσβολή, p. 30. This figure is not defined by the
rhetoricians or Ernesti. But it is evidently a kind of
asyndeton, and twice Philostratus brackets it with
ἀπόστασις (*cf. Letters*, p. 287) as characteristic of the
style of Gorgias; *cf.* προσβάλλειν in the same sense;
ἀσυνδέτως χωρίῳ προσβάλλειν evidently means an abrupt
attachment of clauses or words, a heaping up without
regular connectives. The natural order was abandoned,
and unexpected things were put together. προσβολή
and ἀπόστασις are mentioned together by Apsines i.
359. No author except Philostratus ascribes these
figures to Gorgias.

ῥοῖζος, p. 244, *rush, impetus.* This is a very rare rhetorical
term and in the single instance here cited has lost its
onomatopoeic force when it represented the use of the
letter *r* (" Grate on their scrannel pipes of wretched

573

GLOSSARY OF RHETORICAL TERMS

straw "). In Philostratus it is a synonym for πνεῦμα or δεινότης in the sense of "vigour."

σκηνή, pp. 120, 244, *outfit* or *get-up* of a sophist who declaims. The term includes all the "theatrical properties" of the sophist; his voice, expression, smile, dress, and any mannerism of diction or delivery. It is twice used of Polemo, who was the model, the mirror of fashion for the sophists ; they imitated his effects as though he had been a popular actor.

σοφιστικός, pp. 22, 198 and *passim, suitable for a declaimer.* As applied to a speech (λόγος), a theme (ὑπόθεσις), a rhetorical image (εἰκών), or the temperament (φύσις) of an orator, in Philostratus this epithet is the most flattering possible, since for him the declamation is the highest and most difficult type of oratory. He uses it to distinguish the declamation from the forensic speech and the dialectical discourse. Ernesti ignores this late specialized meaning. *Cf.* Philostratus, p. 182 οἱ ὑπερσοφιστεύοντες λόγοι = "purely declamatory speeches."

στάσις *passim, status, constitutio.* The precise meaning of στάσις as a rhetorical term is discussed by the rhetoricians, especially Hermogenes. *Cf.* Quintilian iii. 6, where he says it is the equivalent of the Latin *quaestio* or *constitutio* or *status.* Roughly speaking, it is the "stand" taken by a speaker when he defines his case. In Eunapius, *Life of Prohaeresius*, p. 506, Anatolius implies that there are thirteen possible στάσεις of the "case" or problem that he had proposed ; *cf.* Eunapius, *Prohaeresius*, p. 496 for κατάστασις in the same sense.

τόνος, p. 198, *intensity, high pitch of eloquence.* A synonym of κρότος and πνεῦμα, *cf.* Longinus, *On the Sublime*, ix. 13.

τυμπανίζειν, p. 84, *to beat the drum* of eloquence. An allusion to the loud instruments used in the worship of Cybele and Dionysus. The style of Scopelian was criticized for its frenzied and Bacchic violence ; *cf.* κορυβαντιᾶν often used of emotional eloquence.

φιλοτιμία, pp. 28, 223, *affectation, artificiality,* excessive care

574

for effects of style. Philostratus, *Letter* i., says that
φιλοτιμία is out of place in a letter, *i.e.* its style should
not be artificial. Used as a synonym of κακοζηλία, for
bad taste in rhetorical style. In Julian, *Letters* (Papa-
dopoulos iv.), *To Priscus*, φιλοτιμία was charged against
Iamblichus by Theodorus (of Asine?) his pupil. It is
a form of misdirected ambition to shine by effects of
style rather than by treatment of the subject matter.

ᾠδή, pp. 28, 68, 232, *sing-song*. The Asianists from the first
(Cicero, *Orator* xxvii.) indulged in a sort of chant which
suited their metrical rhythms; this seems to have been
especially the case in the epilogue, where all the rhetorical
effects, especially of pathos, reached the highest pitch.
Cf. Lucian, *Demonax* 12; *Guide to Rhetoric* 19. This
was sometimes too much even for Philostratus; see
p. 296, *Life of Varus*, where the ᾠδή is called καμπαί
ᾀσμάτων, "turns or twists of song."

INDEX TO PHILOSTRATUS

INDEX TO PHILOSTRATUS

577

INDEX TO PHILOSTRATUS

INDEX TO PHILOSTRATUS

INDEX TO PHILOSTRATUS

INDEX TO PHILOSTRATUS

586

INDEX TO PHILOSTRATUS

INDEX TO EUNAPIUS

591

595

INDEX TO EUNAPIUS